PAYMENTS AND BANKING IN AUSTRALIA

FROM COINS TO CRYPTOCURRENCY:

HOW IT STARTED, HOW IT WORKS AND HOW IT MAY BE DISRUPTED

Nikesh Lalchandani

First Edition, First Printing

Published by:

Innovations Accelerated Pty Ltd, ABN 22 629 141 466

www.iaccelerated.com

info@iaccelerated.com

PO Box 304, Miranda NSW 1490, Australia

ISBN:

Paperback:	**978-0-6488824-0-4**
Hardcover:	**978-0-6488824-1-1**
eBook Kindle:	**978-0-6488824-2-8**
eBook Google:	**978-0-6488824-3-5**

A catalogue record for this work is available from the National Library of Australia

Songlines tell of an ancient connection with the land, and of trade across a vast continent. This book acknowledges the traditional custodians of Australia, and pays respect to elders past, present and emerging.

About the Author

Nikesh Lalchandani's parents migrated from India in the late 1960s to Australia, where Nikesh was born. His first home, located next door to a bank, was in Strathfield, Sydney, the land of the Wangai people of the Eora nation. Nikesh was educated at Sydney Grammar School, and later studied engineering, computer science, and finance. He has travelled broadly and has been an early member or founder of startups, some of which now are or have been acquired by multinationals. He has been a professional services consultant and worked directly on large and small transformation initiatives for traditional organisations, neo banks, fintechs and government. Nikesh has extensive experience in all the Australian Big Four banks, including the Commonwealth Bank of Australia, where he held executive and head-of positions in emerging technology, innovation and payments. Nikesh has had the good fortune of being in the middle of many innovations of our time, from mainstream payments to blockchain and artificial intelligence. He has held board positions with startups and is the Chair of the NSW branch executive of the Australian Computer Society where he is a certified professional member. Nikesh is also a member of the Australian Institute of Company Directors, and has taken the Banking and Finance oath. He now lives in the Sutherland Shire of Sydney with his wife, two daughters and their pet dog.

Table of Contents

ACKNOWLEDGEMENTS I

1. INTRODUCTION 1

2. EARLY DEVELOPMENT 7

History of Money 9
Foreign Currency in the Colony 12
Commissariat 14
Promissory Notes 14
Early Monetary Policy 14
First Coins 16
Early Banking in Australia 17
The Gold Rush 19
The Banking Crisis of 1893 20
Federation and Centralisation of Currency 21
Central Banking 21
Australian Currency Pegging 24
Technology and Early Payment Systems 24
Inflation and Hyperinflation 25
The Great Depression 26
Clearing and Settlement 26
Computerisation 28

3. REGULATION IN BANKING AND PAYMENTS 29

Early Banking Regulation 31
The Reserve Bank of Australia 34
Monetary Policy 35
International Banks 41
Royal Australian Mint 41
Entering the Global Market 42
Gold Currency Reserves 44
Fiat Currency 44
Government Inquiries 44
Crises 50
United Nations Security Council 52
Financial Action Task Force 53
AUSTRAC 53
Payment Systems Board 56
Australian Prudential Regulation Authority (APRA) 57
Flaws in the Risk-based Approach 66
Australian Securities and Investments Commission 66
Australian Competition and Consumer Commission 68
Australian Financial Complaints Authority 69
Productivity Commission 69

Office of the Australian Information Commissioner 71
Australian Taxation Office 71
Administrative Appeals Tribunal 76
Courts 76

4. BANKS 79
The Big Four 81
The Tier 2 Banks 84
Neo Banks 85
Mutual Banks 85
Building Societies 89
Credit Unions 90
Banks Owned by Foreign Banks 92
Branches of Foreign Banks 92
ADI-licensed Payment Organisations 94
Specialist Credit Card Institutions 96
Agency Banking 96
Different Types of Banks 97
Australian Banks Overseas 98
Business Units in Banks 98
Staff 99
Hours and Holidays 101
Indigenous Australians 101
Innovation Culture 103
Account Types 103
Associations and Spin-offs 124
Monetary and Fiscal Policy 126
Liquidity Management 130

5. INFORMATION TECHNOLOGY 131
Mainframes 133
Data Centres 134
Personal Computers 134
x86-based Servers 134
Cloud Computing 135
Software Development Life Cycle 135
Conway's Law 139
Enterprise Architecture 139
Core Banking 146
Online Banking 147
Payment Systems 147
Outsourcing 153
Offshoring 155
Big Data 156
Artificial Intelligence 158
Consumer Data Right: Open Banking 159
Encryption 163
Transport Layer Security 166
Authentication 166
Risk Readiness 167

6. CASH 169
Features 171
Plastic Notes 157
Spin-off 173
Circulation 174
Australian Cash Distribution and Exchange System 175
Logistics 175
Notes and Coin Issuers 175
Bank Participants 176
Approved Cash Centre Operators 177
Seigniorage 177
Cash Regulation 177

7. PAPER INSTRUMENTS 179
Stamp Duty 181
Credit Transfer 182
Personal or Business Cheques 182
Bank Cheques 185
Letters of Credit 186
Postal Money Orders 186
Travellers Cheques 186
Bank Guarantees 186
Processing Cheques 187
Australian Paper Clearing System 188
Decline of Cheques 189
The Fiserv Cheque Processing Centre 189
Cheque Settlement 190

Cheque Payment System Operation 190

8. CARDS 193

Store Credit and the Credit Card 195

Automatic Teller Machines 197

The Card Schemes 198

BIN Sponsorship 214

Card Messaging: AS 2805 and ISO 8583 214

Consumer Electronic Clearing System 216

Cards and the Internet 217

Card-not-present Transactions 218

Rewards 219

Card Security Measures 220

Merchant Solutions 228

The Mobile Generation 231

The Resurrection of eftpos? 238

Basic Card Operation 238

Cards: Impact on the Economy 241

Card Economics 241

ATM Direct Charging 253

9. DIRECT ENTRY 255

Tape Swaps 257

Bulk Electronic Clearing System 259

Corporate BECS Users 259

Direct Debit 260

BECS Data Exchanged 261

Government Direct Entry System 262

The Penny Test 262

ABA File 263

Sub Accounting 263

Settlement in Direct Entry 263

Float on BECS 263

Costs of BECS 263

10. BPAY BILL PAYMENTS 265

Check Digits 267

BPAY Credit Card Payments 267

Costs 267

Reconciliation 268

BPAY Operation 268

BPAY View 269

MAMBO 269

Competitive Bill Payments Solutions 270

Later Innovations 271

11. INTERNATIONAL PAYMENTS 273

Telegraphic Transfers and the Telex 275

SWIFT 275

Foreign Exchange 291

International Trade and Payment Risks 293

SWIFT Costs 296

Alternative International Transfers 297

Real-time Gross Settlements 300

CLS Bank 300

High Value Clearing System 302

12. NEW PAYMENTS PLATFORMS 303

Emerging P2P Payments 306

Resistance 307

NPP Australia Limited 308

NPP Payments Access Gateway 309

Settlement in NPP 309

Core Operation 310

Early Security Flaws 311

Overlay Services and Extensions 312

Rich Information 315

NPP Costs 316

NPP: An Unloved Payment System 316

13. OTHER REGULATED PAYMENT SYSTEMS 319

Delivery versus Payment 321

Austraclear 321

CHESS/ASX Settlement 322

PEXA 323

14. EXTERNAL INNOVATIONS IN PAYMENTS 327
The Investment Ecosystem 329
Big Techs 330
Accounting Systems 332
Alternative Payment Methods 332
The Adoption and Hype Cycles 333
Startup Fintechs 336
Barcodes 338
Loyalty Cards and Offers 338
Gaming and Casinos 339
Vending Machines 340
Account Aggregation 340
P2P Lending and Crowdfunding 341
Buy Now, Pay Later 341
Payments on Behalf of 342
Embedded Payments 343
Hospitality 343
Travel Payments 344
Shared Economy 348
Electronic Money 348
Bitcoin 349
Cryptocurrency 355
Blockchain 359
Smart Contracts 362
Digital Identity 362

15. THE JOURNEY SO FAR 367
What is Money, Really? 369
And What is a Payment? 369
Differential Value 370
Trust 372
Regulation 373
Regulatory Homogenisation 373
Competition 374
Shifting Paradigm 377
Australia's Impact 377

16. DISRUPTION 379
Innovation as a Science 381
Decentralised Settlement 383
Power to the People 385
Organisational Size and Structure 386
Credit Crunch 388
Payment Unification 389
Securing Unsecured Assets 390
Account Unification 391
Payments and Banking as a Service 392
Open APIs 392
Open Ratings 393
Shared Ledger 394
Future of Cryptocurrencies 395
Security and Encryption 395
Regulation and Regtech 397
Global and Local Marketplaces 399
B2B Payments 402
National and Global Biometric Online Identity 403
Bank Corporate Profitability 403
Banking Centralisation 404
Consumer Innovation in Payments 406
Future of the Schemes 410
Alternative Investments 411
Investment Product Distribution 412
The Rise of the Expert 413
Workforce of the Future 414
Culture Shift 416
The Enigma of Central Banking 419
The End of Money? 419

Appendix 1. BANKS 425
Appendix 2. TIMELINE 427
GLOSSARY 435
BIBLIOGRAPHY 459
INDEX 473

Acknowledgements

Oh mindless fool!
Give up this thirst for acquiring money.
Use your mind to find what is real.

Shankaracharya, circa 8th century

Like all endeavours of substance, this book is not the work of one person. I would like to give thanks and apologise to my wife Jagrati, who put up with my neglect and supported me all these years, particularly while I was researching and writing the book. Thanks to my daughters Jeevika and Shivani, and my brother Sunay, for their help, my father Dr Anand Lalchandani and late mother Pushpa Lalchandani, who would take me along to the Maroubra Junction bank branches every day after school to complete the complex banking for the medical practice — which got me interested in the industry, as well as technology, from 1970s carbon paper transfer forms, printers and ultraviolet lights for passbooks, to computer modelling: how they could automate their banking and pay off the mortgage earlier during the phenomenal interest rates of the 1980s. My mother was an English teacher in Australia, and patiently encouraged my literary abilities, however poor they were, for, at school, my handwriting was terrible and, if you could read it, my spelling was worse, two deficits which technology has kindly covered up. I thank my uncle Professor Nanik Lahori, who inspired me both in technology and to publish (he was an early pioneer in the field of computer science), and my uncle Harish Lahori, a writer himself and a bank manager, who gave me an inside look at the operations of the banking system at an early age, and my cousins the late Prakash and the late Sushil Balani, both with monetary/banking experience, who also encouraged my interest in the area. I did not know it at the time, but there is a certain insight one gets in knowing how the system works from every angle, over a long period of time. Knowledge and learning is an osmotic experience and, for me, there are so many sources of this knowledge and too many to name.

This work would not have happened if not for the support and encouragement of so many: Sybil Crasto, Graham Mackenzie, Nick Woodruff, and Prem Naraindas for their help, contribution and inspiration; Rana Peries, Michael Harte, Hans Gyllstrom, Dilan Rajasingham, Paul Franklin, Oswin Martin, Paul Rickard, Tim Whiteley, Peter Koller, David Whiteing, Dave Curran, Adam Bennett, Kelly Bayer Rosmarin and Nick Giles for providing the opportunity for this story to be told; Andrew Cheesman, Phillip Finnegan, Dr Andrew Blair, Dr Michael Eidel, Mac Walker, Joy Mcguire, Andrew Stabbard, Dr Shann Turnbull, Stuart Johnston, Sharona Torrens, Lucy Brereton, Mark Nagy, Aaron French, Mundanara Bayle and Aunty Lila of Blackcard for their valuable input, and countless others who provided input and were interviewed for this book. I have to call out the organisations large and small that contributed to the knowledge contained in these pages — and the silent workers who make the world of payments and banking operate so smoothly — I have learnt from them and express my gratitude to them.

In the book, I talk about accessible means of production being an underlying disruptive force and, in order to put into practice the future that is envisioned, I have avoided the establishment and turned to my family and friends, and to the shared economy, to give you this publication — platforms Reedsy, Freelancer, Fiverr and Airtasker have contributed to this work, and behind them are the priceless and undervalued works of a number of individuals.

For the final product, my thanks to: Belinda Downie and Paul Ratcliffe from Coinworks for their help with sourcing some images used in this work. Thanks also for the hard work of editors Audrey van Ryn (and team), Kym Dunbar, layout designer Petya Tsankova, and illustrators Nicholas Coyle (hand drawings), Marc Sorio and Rebecca De Roxas (both digital artists), cover designer S M Shamim-Ur-Rashid, cover photographer Thilo Hirscheider, printer Karen Seage and Snap Underwood. Acknowledgement is due also for the support of the publishing team at Innovations Accelerated: Eddy Ku, Eryk Korfel, Mari Alkhamesi, Peter Harper-Bilreiro, Georgia Park and the whole team — demonstrating that startups can accomplish great things.

1.

INTRODUCTION

COMMERCE, MONEY AND PAYMENTS are integral to our economies and systems and, for the vast majority of us, they shape and influence the very way we think and behave, yet most of us have very little idea about how they really operate.

We have been inextricably involved with these systems since humans understood how to use bartering and simple forms of money to trade and exchange between one another, and it has now permeated almost every corner of our lives, facilitating the majority of what we do, where we go and the very lives we choose to live — all needing payments of some kind.

So, are we slaves to the payment processes and systems that have evolved over the past 4 000 years or are we their masters? The answer, and our future opportunities, might surprise you.

It might also surprise you to learn that very little about how payments actually work is written down, and you would discover, as I have, through sheer hard work, application of payment models, and an unwavering curiosity about how things operate, that much of the information is not available through any publicly accessible means, which is why this book has been written.

Part of the reason is because today's highly interconnected financial markets and payment systems are underpinned by complex, sophisticated technology and processes, understood by the expert few who design these systems. This has added to the manual and technology payment systems that have incrementally evolved over centuries, and we now stand on the verge of a brave new payments universe: a universe seeking to adopt distributed ledgers and disruptive technology to massively transform the very ways things can and will be paid for, and, in doing so, moving us further away from our elementary concepts of what cash is and how to use it.

Most of society is not even aware, nor, frankly, wants or needs to be aware about how systems run, until, of course, they don't, because we now regard it as a utility, baked into our lives, always there and necessary to run an advanced, well-functioning society.

However, there is real value in understanding how it all works, and those who do that best will understand the supposedly immutable laws of these systems and recognise how to apply the lessons learnt over time on the evolution of payments. Those armed with this insight and knowledge will be at a distinct advantage when it comes to identifying and maximising the potential on offer, and particularly, to avoiding repeating the mistakes of the past.

This book, therefore, is intended for those of you who have a little, but not in-depth familiarity with common methods of payments and would like to learn more about why things are as they are, or perhaps for bankers and those in the financial technology ecosystem looking for an inside track on what may be possible.

For the expert, this book will build upon your substantial knowledge and allow you to focus on other dimensions of the payment landscape, its systems and their history — critical for understanding how best to maximise your influence and effect in this rapidly evolving arena.

In this book, you will find a privileged insight into the workings of this space and a unique body of knowledge that explores the breadth of this subject in a manner you can understand, so that you can properly evaluate your opportunities, be it in education, law or commerce.

For that definitive text, or detailed technical specification or deep financial know-how on some given topic, this book will point you in the right direction.

A little bit about me

I am not an academic, but a practitioner who has cut his teeth architecting payment systems in Australia's leading and emerging banks and has had the fortune to have worked directly on many of the facets covered in this book. Putting this together has afforded me a fascinating opportunity to approach this subject much like you might any anthology, researching and uncovering facts and topics and finding the best way to connect all the dots. And then I felt it needed a little splash of colour to brighten up a subject one might otherwise consider rather dry. My experience writing this book has helped dispel any such thoughts of this being dry, and I hope you too see this in a different light once you read it.

A great deal of the work is based on my own study, experience and interviews so much of the text, references and footnotes have been replaced with opinions and ideas.

I hope you find this story as interesting, informative and as inspiring as I found it when researching and writing it.

Definitions

Clear definitions are always useful, and a glossary in this book expands acronyms and provides basic meanings of many terms not explained in the body of the work. During my research, I was reminded of a parliamentary report of recent vintage begging for a proper definition of a bank, despite 700 years of banking and volumes upon volumes of legislation on the topic. (There is literally a Banking Act in Australia.)

The truth is that what constitutes a bank today differs massively from the past, and further differs depending on the context of the questioner. So, rather than provide a pedantic treatment of the words *bank, money, currency, payment* and *transaction*, and many other terms you will come across in this book, which even experts have seen as an exercise in futility, perhaps as my first insight: do not tie yourself up in knots trying to define them and be prepared to be liberal in your interpretations.

The Journey to Understanding Payments

This book will take you on a journey through the Australian world of payments and banking, from the earliest forms of money through to the potential transformation and disruption standing at our gates.

Starting with early trade and payments, you will travel through the evolution of our regulatory environment and the banks. There is a timeline in the appendix that can help guide you through the sequence of events.

You will then move on to and examine deeply the major payment methods: cash, paper instruments, cards, Direct Entry, international and high-value payments, the New Payments Platform in Australia, other regulated payments like CHESS and PEXA. You will not find a more comprehensive treatment of this breadth.

On the next stage of the journey, you will take a look at the many innovations in payments, especially recently, that have notably taken place outside the walls of the banks — we look at these, such as the big tech companies, startups, fintech and the cryptocurrency industry. I provide an insight into this world of innovation based on an insider's view from Barangaroo to Mountain View.

We then take a philosophical view and summarise the developments and reflect on the journey so far.

Finally, this book invites you to complete the journey of disruption, and examine and really understand both the small and large steps that will change payments, banking and money as we know it.

2.

EARLY DEVELOPMENT

FOR YEARS, BUILDING DEVELOPERS attempted to redevelop the dilapidated buildings of Paddy's Markets in Sydney. It was a large plot on prime real estate, close to the Central Business District. In 1990, they got their way, with approval from the government. However, there was one more stumbling block. An archaeological survey of the demolished site was demanded, as the area was as old as the colony itself. The home of some of Australia's first industries, the site had been partly occupied by Indigenous Australians as late as the 1840s,[1] and was the location of the colony's early trade with the world, so there were plenty of reasons for the survey.

A $10 cheque to volunteers to cover expenses was the reward for a day's work in the sun, with a brush and a tray to painstakingly unearth a part of Australia's history. This was no typical dig. The clock was ticking. The builders were waiting to pour concrete over what many thought was another delay tactic.

Sweeping through the rubble and sediment, one millimetre at a time, was frustrating. For many volunteers, the day would pass with little more than a bucket of dirt to show for their labour. Eventually, the archaeological work bore fruit:[2] 34 203 bags of artefacts revealed evidence of early Aboriginal use of the land, collectable or tradable cowry shells, copper and bronze store tokens used as payment for one or half a penny, our dealings with pandemics (the cleansing of Sydney during the bubonic plague that spread around the world even then), and evidence of early trade with China and Arabia. Australia's history and connection with the world through trade was deep, and all this was revealed under just a few metres of rubble.

From the shell to cheques to cryptocurrency — how Australia developed its money and payment systems — is an untold story central to the nation's history, and a significant part of the story of global payments and banking systems.

History of Money

Anatomically, modern humans are probably as old as 200 000 years.[3] The use of tools predates this, and to enable the exchange of tools that has been observed, some trade must have taken place. Though it is not clear when such exchanges began, scientists agree that by 2000 BCE, people had engaged in long-distance trade.[4]

Australia's Indigenous people used songlines to describe trade routes that go back to ancient times, and the movement of ochre used in ceremonial paint across vast distances confirms the view that trade in Australia was well established and prehistoric,[5] with evidence of trade in shells and blades clearly evident in the archaeological records.[6]

---

[1] Fitzgerald

[2] Crook

[3] Relethford

[4] Nelson

[5] Kerwin

[6] Hook

While many would say that before money there was barter,[7] a study of human behaviour and anthropology indicates that perhaps there was an informal debt system[8] in which a favour granted would be paid back. So an *exchange of value*, the precursor to money, was probably more loosely understood and possibly occurred over an extended period of time.

This informal debt system became more formal with the earliest ledgers dating back to at least 4 000 years ago.[9] These ledgers were used to record both sides of these debts.

With the utilisation of domesticated animals, the cart and the boat, regular travel was possible, and a commercial counterparty could be a stranger from a distant land. Trade had to be transactional, that is, both sides had to complete as the parties may not meet for some time, perhaps not ever. Barter would have been the mode of commerce.[10] Exchange of value in barter was the precursor to money. For millennia, it would have served its purpose. Barter had its drawback: direct exchanges limited the possibilities in commerce to occasions where supply and demand could be mutually fulfilled between two traders.

At some point, people must have noticed that certain goods could be standardised. A bag of wheat was a bag of wheat. Ten fresh coconuts were consistent from one sample to the next. These items were *fungible commodities*, meaning they could be exchanged for similar items from someone else, or at another time. They could be used more efficiently in trade than unique items.

The earliest currency, that is, the use of a valuable commodity to exchange value, may have begun by at least 2000 BCE.[11] By that time, Australia's first peoples were a thriving civilisation, and there is evidence of interaction and trade, especially towards the north. Barter-based trade with the Makassar people (in what is now Indonesia) happened well before European settlement. Metal tools were exchanged for trepang (a kind of sea-cucumber) valued by the Chinese.[12] Trade between Aboriginal nations would have been largely by barter; however, there is evidence that shell money may have been used.[13]

The *unit of account* would have developed within established trade routes. Five trepangs could buy one tool (say), while 10 could buy two tools or one large blade. Between Aboriginal Australians and the Indonesians, a fair system of accounting would likely have developed. Between visits, the unit of account was established, and the value of goods and services would have been generally static, though perhaps subject to relative inflation and supply and demand dynamics or, to put it simply, bargaining.

---

[7] Smith

[8] Graeber

[9] Keister

[10] Smith

[11] Balmuth

[12] Marks

[13] Balme; Connell

» NOTE

The absence of metal coins in Indigenous Australia should by no means be taken as any indication of lack of advancement. Modern monetary policy regards employment, prosperity and welfare as cornerstones to success. There is no reason to suggest they did.[14] As we will see, money and coins were not widely available among the early colonial arrivals either so, fundamentally, at least from a monetary policy point of view, Australian Aboriginal society was arguably ahead. An interesting note, though, is that 1 000-year-old coins from Africa were discovered on Northern Territory beaches during World War II.[15]

Some of the first objectified man-made currency was made between 2500 BCE and 1750 BCE and represented a tangible asset, such as a quantity of grain, rice or livestock.16 These proto-coins are not classified as money as they may have been established only for the duration of trade in a marketplace. Technically, these would have been used to represent units of account, but had one advantage: rather than carrying heavy bags of grain, objects that were representatives of the bag could be exchanged and then redeemed through the market authority (the local chief) at the end of the market period.

The discovery of metals and metal technology introduced a new commodity. Useful metals (copper and silver) were relatively rare. Unlike shells, which had limited utility, and bags of grain that were perishable, they were a better store of value.

In three separate parts of the globe, around 700 BCE to 500 BCE, the first coins appeared.17 Coins were difficult to make and, therefore, difficult to counterfeit. Only a lord or seignior-like authority had the means of production to strike a coin and, to this day, the equipment required to produce money remains with the government of the day. Rather than being used in just one trading session, coins had no expiry. As they were metal, they had their own intrinsic value. We generally say that this is when money was invented: with the confluence of a unit of account, the exchange of value and store of value.18

The foundation of the early European colonisation of Australia came at a turning point in trade and payments. By the middle of the 18th century, the importance of trade was well established.19 However, David Hume's vision of free trade was corrupted by his countrymen's desire to make a quid. The taxation of transactions, introduced by the Stamp Act in 1765, initiated the American Revolution. The British East India Company became less about trade

---

[14] Webb

[15] Owen

[16] Pal

[17] Dhavalikar; Kagan; Scheidel

[18] Jevons's original definition of money has been refined over the years. The RBA (Doherty) uses a modern definition: unit of account, exchange of value and store of value.

[19] Hume

and more about occupation, and when the Tea Act was passed in 1773, ostensibly to enable trade by the East India Company directly to the colonies, the disruption of merchant trade triggered the Boston Tea Party, and the eventual demand for United States independence.

In 1788, the British colonised Australia as a penal settlement. London supposed that this military-ruled colony had little need for money, and so the early fleets were under-supplied with currency, perhaps only £300 in the hands of the governor in order to trade and to pay staff.

›› NOTE

The United States War of Independence ended in 1783, and stopped the transportation of convicts from early industrialising England to the US. Another location was required. The settlement in New South Wales in 1788 brought over 750 convicts to the country, along with 550 crew, soldiers and their families. Most of these convicts were transported by a zero-tolerance legal system for trivial crimes, such as theft of a loaf of bread or minor personal theft (larceny). A retrospective analysis may suggest that economic challenges in England were the root cause (salaries were not keeping up with the price of food), so Australia was born in tough economic times and, as we will see, many challenges of the British Empire brushed off on the new colony, such as a shortage of money and resources. Indeed, despite the distance, the economy of Australia was greatly impacted and shaped by the British economy for many years.

In addition to the few coins, the first governor, Governor Arthur Phillip, was authorised to fund modest expenses on bills drawn on the British Treasury. These were simply letters with the governor's seal that could be redeemed in London. While they allowed government expenditure, they did not create currency for general use in the colony.

By the late 1790s, a community of free settlers had emerged from freed convicts, retired marines and free immigrant settlers from Great Britain. Most trade was with the Spanish and the other nearest British colony, India. An amount of coins, but supplies and a significant amount of rum, arrived with these ships, and both these items — coins and rum — became the new currencies.

Foreign Currency in the Colony

As a British colony, New South Wales should have adopted British money and coinage. At the time, the currency was pounds (£), shillings (s) and pence (d), with one pound equal to 20 shillings, and one shilling equal to twelve pence.

By the late 1790s, there was a serious shortage of British coins in the colony. There was no recourse to the Bank of England as, due to a shortage of bullion, the banks there had stopped gold and silver payments on bank accounts. Paper notes under £5 (over one troy ounce of gold) were not legal even in England until 1797.[20] Even then, there were no banks in New South Wales to issue banknotes.

Currency was central to the problems of the new colony. In the final days of Governor John Hunter's tenure, Philip Gidley King, the incoming governor, requested copper coins (pennies) be sent to the colony. The problem of accumulation of money was an issue — with Governor King declaring that £5 of payment in coins would not be regarded as legal tender, and the import or export of this amount would result in a penalty of four times the amount.[21] Unfortunately, there were not enough Spanish dollars and copper coins to go around so, in 1800, a table of conversion of popular coins, from the Indian rupee to the Dutch guilder, was decreed.

This proclamation (*Table 1*) can be regarded as the first foreign exchange sign, something that now frequents the streets of Sydney and other cities of Australia. It declared Sydney as a truly international city, recognising the coins of any passing trader and ready to do commerce. Every shop was a dealer in foreign currency.

It is interesting to note that, in the proclamation, the values of the three British coins were inflated. A guinea (then a gold standard) was not £1. 1s. as in England, but inflated to be £1. 2s. Likewise, an English shilling was 1s.1d in New South Wales. The purpose of this was likely to encourage the retention of British currency in the colony, where it was officially worth more than the rest of the Empire, rather than take the limited currency abroad. This simultaneously created Australia's own currency and started a centralised pegged foreign exchange that would last 183 years.

Table 1

Proclamation of coins.

Coin	Origin	Pounds	Shillings	Pence
Guinea	Great Britain	1	2	0
Johanna	Portugal	4	0	0
Half-Johanna	Portugal	2	0	0
Ducat	Netherlands	0	9	6
Gold Mohur	India	1	17	6
Pagoda	India	0	8	0
Dollar	Spain	0	5	0
Rupee	India	0	2	6
Guilder	Netherlands	0	2	0
English shilling	Great Britain	0	1	1
Copper coin of one ounce	various (including Great Britain)	0	0	2

[20]Cobbett

[21]Butlin

Commissariat

In order to distribute food and provisions to people, a commissariat (a kind of general store), was established by Governor Hunter around 1796. Goods produced could be taken there and, due to a shortage of money, a receipt would be given. This was the first official publicly usable currency issued by the colony.[22] The receipt could be passed around as a payment in the colony. The foundation stone of the second commissariat (now demolished) is still visible in First Fleet Park, The Rocks, Sydney, on the west side of Circular Quay near the Museum of Contemporary Art.

Promissory Notes

Between "gentlemen", promissory notes were a common way of making or receiving payments. The promissory note was quite simply a piece of paper with the amount owed, and the name and signature of the debtor. If the payer was not specified, that note could be passed around, and the ultimate holder could call on the original debt. However, just how effective an instrument these were came into question early on.

Promissory notes could be circulated indefinitely. They could be written on any scrap of paper, and the ingenuity of the early convict settlement in using these features for fraudulent payments was remarkable. The bottom of letters would be torn off, and the signature would be prepended by a promissory declaration. Fading ink would be used to render the note unusable after some time. Several notes from the same payer could be cut up and pasted together to be worth more than the original.[23]

Early Monetary Policy

By the time of Governor William Bligh's arrival in the colony, the monetary system was out of control. Bligh was a character. Earlier, as a naval officer, his ship, the HMS Bounty, was subject to a mutiny. This should have been a warning sign for London.

His problem was not that he lacked empathy but that he took sides. On a ship literally in the middle of the Pacific Ocean, and in a colony, again literally at the other end of the world, one needed to take the more powerful side.

In the black market, the real currency was the bottle of rum. Bligh saw the widespread use of rum and quite logically banned it as a payment.

---

[22] Booker

[23] Butlin

» NOTE

So desperate was the need for rum that when one ship from Calcutta was shipwrecked off the coast of Tasmania, the crew travelled hundreds of kilometres to Sydney. On arrival, a party was sent back to the wreckage to rescue the remaining crew and, of course, the cargo.

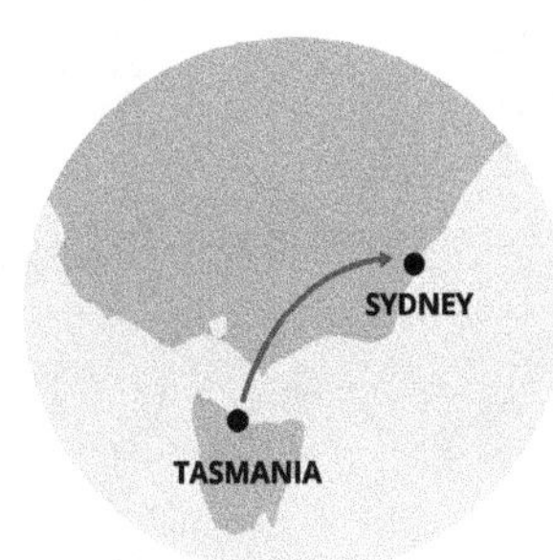

In addition to the use of rum, some promissory notes were written (with Bligh's predecessor, Governor King's blessing) in wheat, wool or other farm produce. After the floods of 1806, the price of wheat went from a level of 7s. 6d. per bushel to 30s.[24] This meant that a promissory note would be subject to an exorbitant interest rate as the note needed to be paid back in produce. Bligh sought to ban the practice.

Former NSW Corps officer, and later self-appointed leader of the free settlers, John Macarthur was disappointed with the way the colony was being administered. Macarthur, incidentally, is credited with playing a part in developing another of Australia's pseudo-currencies through his involvement in the wool industry. A showdown between the belligerent Macarthur and the authoritarian Bligh was not going to go down well.

In 1806, the order was made to outlaw the use of rum as a currency and ban other produce in promissory notes. These, along with other issues, prompted Macarthur and associates in the NSW Corps to stage the only successful coup in Australia, the Rum Rebellion.

Eventually, Macarthur's day in court arrived. He objected to the judges. The Chief Judge, Richard Atkins, Macarthur claimed, was his debtor and, as such, biased against Macarthur and not fit to try him. John Macarthur had acquired a promissory note signed by the judge, and it was unclear about interest so Macarthur was able to avoid trial.

The need for a monetary system in the colony became increasingly important. Australia was growing fast in both economy and population. Melbourne, Brisbane and Hobart were established in 1797, 1799 and 1804 respectively.

» NOTE

In 1890, wool accounted for 54% of Australia's exports, so the adage was born that "Australia rides on the sheep's back". The value of a bale (120 kg or more) of wool was a key economic indicator. Today, wool accounts for just 1.4% of exports, while the price has seen a resurgence in recent years. Neither wool nor rum took off as a lasting currency, and, in a posthumous sign of victory, John Macarthur's portrait appeared on early federal Australian £20 notes and was later printed again, along with his Merino sheep, on the newly decimalised $2 note (*Figure 1*).

[24] Ibid.

Figure 1. **Australian $2 note.**

First Coins

Governor Lachlan Macquarie restored some stability to the colony after the rebellion, and took important steps in the evolution of currency and of the financial system in Australia.

First, he took less of a high-handed approach to rum. He had the exchange of rum limited to licensed dealers, banned on Sundays (supported by the church) and, in a move that indicated a talent in monetary policy, he increased the supply of rum, thereby reducing its value, through legitimate contracts in the import of rum to the colony (which he bartered for construction contracts such as the construction of Sydney Hospital). His request for permission from England to complete the transaction was denied, but by the time word returned from London, it was too late — the deal was done.

The shortage of coins was not unique to Australia. Between 1797 and 1804, in the middle of the Anglo-Spanish war, the British Treasury was re-stamping acquired Spanish dollars with the head of King George III on the neck of the Spanish King Charles IV.[25]

In the quest for a new coin for the colony, in 1812, Macquarie ordered £10 000 worth of Spanish dollars (40 000 coins) from Madras (now Chennai), India. He hired a forger to create new coins: a hole was punched through and both parts became legal currency, the *holey dollar* worth 5s. and the *dump* worth 15d. (*Figure 2*). The colony's attempts at recycling its enemy's coins was far more elegant and productive than London's — an innovation edge that would continue for centuries.

[25] Manville

Figure 2. **1813 Holey dollar and dump stamped on and through an 1809 Spanish dollar**
Images courtesy of Coinworks.

By 1822, after the British Great Recoinage of 1816, and after commercial exports were maturing, Australia could receive coinage from Great Britain and the holey dollar was removed from circulation.

›› NOTE

There are believed to be about 300 holey dollars remaining. The value of these coins could be as much as $300 000 each these days. However, in the 1820s, turning the coins in for sterling currency was better value than keeping them for their silver content

Early Banking in Australia

Banks, or a practice facilitating the safe storage of valuables and providing loans, and later, promissory notes, originated in the Middle East, India and China,[26] and later appeared in Greece and Rome.[27] European banking that can be related to modern practices emerged in Rome in the 13th and 14th centuries.

In 1816, the first bank in Australia, the Bank of New South Wales (now called Westpac), was inaugurated by Governor Lachlan Macquarie. It was a central bank of sorts as it had the power to print notes. However, it did not hold that position exclusively for long.

The denominations of notes issued were five shillings, 10 shillings, one pound and five pounds. Paper tokens for one shilling, one shilling sixpence, two shillings and two shillings sixpence were also issued. Later, curiously, the bank also issued Spanish dollar notes (*Figure 3*) as late as 1824.

---

[26] Eidem; Roy; Liu & Chai

[27] Barnish

Figure 3. **Bank of NSW Spanish dollar note.**

Image courtesy of Coinworks.

» NOTE

The Bank of NSW could hold deposits and issue notes without oversight — this gave the bank great power. However, with that unchecked power came corruption, for in 1821, the chief cashier of the bank was accused of embezzling £12 000. This was, at the time, a significant portion of the subscribed capital of the bank. The discovery was made when the sealed bags of notes did not tally and deposits were found to have been faked by Williams.

A rival bank was soon set up. The Bank of Australia, known as the Pure Merino Bank, representing honest settlers and excluding (as they put it) ex-convicts accepted by the Bank of New South Wales, was set up in 1826. The convicts had the last laugh, for in a daring robbery, tunnelling through a sewer and into the vault, £14 000 was stolen. This remains, in relative terms, the largest bank theft in Australia's history.

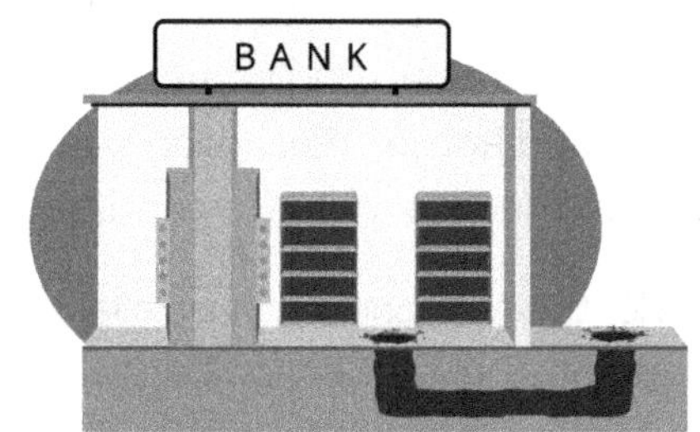

Since this time, Australian banks have been regarded with a certain amount of mistrust by both the public and the government.

Following the Bank of New South Wales, early banks were established rapidly, sometimes by the governor's proclamation (and later parliamentary acts), and sometimes directly from the United Kingdom.

Over time, two distinct kinds of banks were formed: *trading banks* (dealing with international trade, or cross-bank payments, supporting institutions and companies) and *savings banks* (whose primary purpose was the holding of funds and issuing notes).

The Gold Rush

California had just been annexed by the US. During the next year, 1848, almost the entire population of San Francisco's 1 000 people headed to the American River in search of gold, starting a period of movement known as the Gold Rush. Many supplies and prospectors came from New South Wales,[28] one of the closest settlements to the then relatively unknown frontier state of California (sea travel was faster than land travel). The population of San Francisco had increased to about 25 000 by 1849. Many of the Forty-Niners, as the new migrants were called, were Australian and stayed on to develop what would become the largest state of the US.

Some fossickers returned. With their new-found skills, they turned their attention to Macquarie River near Bathurst. The Gold Rush in New South Wales started in 1851. The impact on the economy was significant. Moderate amounts of alluvial gold were enough to keep people interested, and not too much to lead to mass wealth. Whatever was dug up was invested back into the economy. New towns were created in the middle of seemingly nowhere. Just like California, immigration and commerce increased in New South Wales, and helped establish a vibrant economy. Some of the wealth found its way back to the big cities, and regional and city banks formed and multiplied.

With an abundance of gold in Australia, it was possible to produce bullion coins.

The gold rush quickly spread throughout the country. In Adelaide, locals sought to withdraw their money from bank accounts and headed to the Adelaide Hills. In order to stave off a run on the banks, the South Australian Government passed a Gold Bullion Act in 1852 that allowed the governor to temporarily construct "a smelting, assay, and bullion establishment for the purpose of making ingots". The ingots could be accepted as deposits, and any call on the bank could be met through the issue of these ingots (*Figure 4*). The fear was that the Queen (i.e., London) would reject it, for the establishment was not a Royal Mint. The move was successful, with two to three times the expected volume of gold returning to the banks, saving the Bank of Australasia from an early extinction. The Bank of Australasia was formed in England and established in Sydney, Melbourne, Tasmania and South Australia in the late 1830s. Its survival ensured the eventual creation of the ANZ Bank.

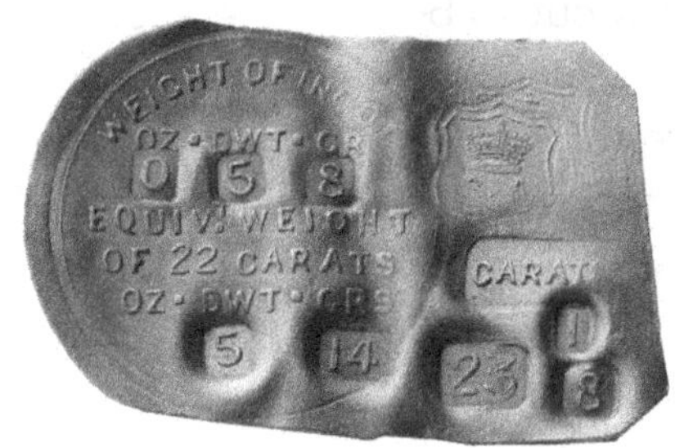

***Figure 4.* Australia's early minted coins (South Australia): ingot, left, and pound, right**

Images courtesy of Coinworks.

[28] Monaghan

In 1855, a branch of the Royal Mint was established in Sydney, largely to produce gold sovereigns (*Figure 5*). During the Great Recoinage of 1816, the 22-carat gold sovereigns were designed to weigh approximately the value of £1 sterling. Slightly smaller than the £1. 1d. guinea, but more precise, they remain a popular bullion coin today. These coins, and the half sovereign, were minted post-haste at the Sydney Royal Mint.

***Figure* 5. Royal Sydney Mint gold sovereign, 1855.**
Images courtesy of Coinworks.

» NOTE

Somewhat curiously, the oddly shaped ingots of Adelaide's Government Assay Office recently sold for $1.35 million — 3 000 times the gold value. By 1853, the office was minting high-quality £1 coins (*Figure 4*), also highly valued at $475 000. On the other hand, the more official Sydney and Melbourne Royal Mint coins are generally barely worth more than their gold content.

As the Gold Rush moved to Victoria, the Royal Mint established a branch in Melbourne in 1872.

Melbourne, with its booming economy, turned out to be far more appealing to European settlers than the less temperate Sydney and, by 1888, it was becoming bigger and just as financially active as Sydney, if not more so. New banks were forming and loans for property were sought. Very soon there was a housing boom in Melbourne.

The Banking Crisis of 1893

In the 19th century, Australia was a frontier country with lots of rewards, but also lots of risks. Droughts, crop infestations or floods could break an investment, and if the impact was portfolio-wide, it could be disastrous for a financial institution. London financiers complained of the risk as, back home in the old country, a new building or a new factory was a standard and well-documented investment. However, an investment in the colonies was exposed to other significant variables.

Sure enough, in 1890, loans began defaulting[29] as a significant drought had impacted the economy and demand for wool, the majority export, had dropped. Assets were worth nothing. A number of banks with their capital in London had cut the colony branches loose, causing a major banking failure in 1893 with at least 11 banks permanently closing and others temporarily shutting their doors.

Federation and Centralisation of Currency

In 1901, the separate states of Australia were federated to form the Commonwealth of Australia. Section 51(vii) of the new constitution gave the power to the government to legislate on matters concerning currency, coinage and legal tender. Section 115 prevented states from coining legal tender. There was one exception. The states could (and did) continue to mint silver and gold coins.

Curiously, perhaps foreseeing the loss of sovereignty, or perhaps coinciding with their own gold rush starting in 1893, the Perth Mint was established as a branch of the Royal Mint in 1899, while the federation was being negotiated. In fact, there was talk of Western Australia seceding or, rather, failing to join the union. Self-sufficiency gave them a strong footing either way.

To this day, the Perth Mint continues to make gold and silver coins supplied by the resource-rich state miners. These coins are largely used for bullion and collections, though they do have legal tender value. Interestingly, a one troy ounce gold coin with a metal value of over $2 500 is worth $100 as legal tender. The Sydney Royal Mint closed in 1926 and the Melbourne Royal Mint in 1969.

For the first 10 years of the federation, with banks issuing private notes and the royal mints producing coins, the currency needs of the new country were met.

Central Banking

In the Australian Notes Act of 1910, the Federal Treasury made it an offence for banks to print notes and it took over this function. For the following three years, existing notes were endorsed by the treasury with it eventually printing its own notes. The treasury was required to publish information on notes issued and on gold reserves (*Figure 6*) in the government gazette on the last Wednesday of every month.

---

[29] Merrett

AUSTRALIAN NOTES.

STATEMENT ISSUED IN PURSUANCE OF SECTION 11 OF THE "AUSTRALIAN NOTES ACT 1910."

THE number and amount of Australian Notes issued and not redeemed at this date are as follow :—

Denomination.	Number.	Amount.
£1	1,243,599	£1,243,599
£5	207,509	1,037,545
£10	80,500	805,000
£20	10,875	217,500
£50	6,725	336,250
£100	1,168	116,800
Totals ...	1,550,376	£3,756,694

The amount of gold coin held by the Treasurer for the purposes of the Act at this date is £1,232,358.

Notes to the value of £188,000 have been issued and included above, in respect of which one-third in gold will be received within the next few days.

ANDREW FISHER,
Treasurer.

GEO. T. ALLEN,
Secretary to the Treasury.

JAS. R. COLLINS,
Accountant to the Treasury.

Treasury, Melbourne,
25th January, 1911.
C.18882.

Figure 6. **Australian notes on issue, 1911. Commonwealth of Australia Gazette, NLA.**

In 1911, the federal government, under Labor Prime Minister Andrew Fisher, established the first federal bank, the Commonwealth Bank of Australia (CBA) and, later, the closely associated Commonwealth Savings Bank of Australia.[30]

The CBA had two purposes: first, to act as the central bank, a bank to the other banks and their regulator and, second, to act as a secure savings bank in its own right, offering services directly to retail customers.

In 1920, the CBA took over note printing from the treasury.[31]

» NOTE

The governor of the CBA was treated with pomp and ceremony. Bearing robes and a chain, similar to a mayor, his portrait would be commissioned and, until recently, adorned the hallways to the offices of the board and CEO. No longer fashionable, these portraits have been relegated to the archives as modern executives prefer a more down-to-earth look, while their salaries have reversed the trend

[30] Commonwealth Bank Act 1911

[31] Commonwealth Bank Act 1920

A note or payment greater than £2 was really nothing other than a promissory note backed by gold. In fact, that is what the notes actually said. A £50 note around 1918, as shown in *Figure 7*, stated "THE TREASURER OF THE COMMONWEALTH OF AUSTRALIA Promises to pay the Bearer FIFTY POUNDS in gold coin on DEMAND at the Commonwealth Treasury at the Seat of Government." It was signed by the assistant secretary and secretary to the treasurer. This contract implied that Australian paper currency was *hard currency*.

***Figure 7*. Fifty-pound note, hard currency, 1918.**
Image courtesy of Coinworks.

The minimum gold required to be held by the central bank was eventually set as 25% in the Commonwealth Bank Act of 1920.

Known as a specie payment, exactly how many people took up the offer to walk into the treasury and walk out with gold coins is unknown. To keep their promise, the treasury and, later, the Commonwealth Bank would keep the reserves in a high security vault in the basement, first at 120 Pitt Street, Sydney and later up the road at 48 Martin Place.

The Government Savings Bank of NSW became a significant state bank; however, the state government used the money to fund payments during the Great Depression. With six times the deposit holdings of the emerging CBA, the Government Savings Bank closed its doors at 48 Martin Place at this critical economic time. Eight months later, it reopened its doors as a part of the Commonwealth Bank.[32] The building at 48 Martin Place was magnificent, built during the boom times. It had a classical bank facade, elegant ceilings and a grand vault. The safe of 48 Martin Place is still in use today by customers of the CBA to keep their personal valuables. The building became the offices of a newer bank: Macquarie Bank.

The physical buildings were very secure with metal bars and iron doors. In the event of an emergency (like a run on the bank), the governor and his aides could escape through an iron stairwell that would come crashing through the windows onto Elizabeth Street.

[32] Sykes

Painted-over gun cabinets are still embedded in the sandstone walls of the upper floors. Even up to the late 1990s, senior bank staff were trained and licensed in the use of firearms. The era saw its fair share of robberies, armed and otherwise.

Australian Currency Pegging

With some slight deviations, such as the Proclamation Coins of 1800, efforts were made to align the Australian pound to its British equivalent.

The Coinage Act of 1909 specified the production of Australian coins that imitated their British counterparts. These consisted of two bronze coins: the penny (famous even today from the ANZAC game of Two-Up) and the half penny. There were also five 92.5% silver coins: a small threepence, a sixpence (that would later be used as a 5 cent coin), the shilling itself, the bigger florin (face value 2 shillings), and a larger coin, the crown, worth 5 shillings (only produced in two runs, in 1937 and 1938). The other coins continued to be produced until around 1963, with production ceasing in anticipation of the new currency.

The value of the Australian pound was effectively pegged to the British pound one-to-one. This changed in 1930 after the Great Depression and a currency devaluation. Specie payments could not be honoured. Australia's high debt and its financial profile meant that an Australian pound was not worth much gold.

To prevent a run on the banks (remember the promise on the note above), in 1930, the government took the Australian pound off the gold standard. A move that devalued the dollar against the sterling by perhaps 30%. Around this time, the promise had disappeared from the notes as well. Fortunately, old habits die hard and the notes held their value.

From this point in Australia's history, the government set the official currency value against the pound sterling. From 1930, the value was 80% for many years and, in 1949, when the British pound was devalued against the United States dollar, Australian Prime Minister Robert Menzies followed suit, declaring that the Australian economy was tied to that of the United Kingdom.

Technology and Early Payment Systems

The sheer size of Australia meant communication needed to become more efficient. By 1858, the first Australian telegraph lines were established. Originally along the east coast, and later across the country, with the Australian Overland Telegraph Line from Adelaide to Darwin completed in 1872, and with the British-Australia Telegraph Company connecting an undersea cable to Indonesia — connecting Australia to the world.

The telegraph, or cablewire as it was then known, was used to communicate transfers between banks and accounts, to request notes and so forth.

A typical visit to a bank in Australia consisted of filling in a form and taking it to a cashier or clerk. The teller, as they came to be known, had a collection of ink stamps, uniquely issued to the staff member with their serial number. The appropriate ink stamp would be impressed on the form. There was little talking, and the sound of stamps rhythmically indicated the business of the branch and provided a satisfying feeling that the work was complete. If a customer was making a withdrawal, they were then given a number and asked to wait. While they waited, a clerk would check the ledger and approve the withdrawal.

A branch tended to have a large office, with clerks running around entering items in one ledger and taking them off another. The branch controlled the ledger, and often was a bank in itself. In some banks, this continued until 2000, the customer's signature file was still stored in their home branch, meaning that going to another branch was like visiting another bank where they did not have the customer's records.

Account numbers adopted a numbering system: first the state, then the branch, then the branch ledger record number. Each branch could create an account number. To ward against the bank losing the ledger, they gave the customer a copy: a savings passbook — their own personal ledger. The use of a branch number today, and a branch address when addressing payments, is a legacy of the past, when the payment could only be processed in the home branch of the account.

The original form of payment was the direct exchange of coins and notes. Legally, this was the statutory way to pay for goods and services (*legal tender*).

In the Bills of Exchange Act of 1909, the government stipulated the format of paper agreements, including cheques to pay between parties. They also introduced a revenue stream (stamp duty) to give the bills *legal recognition*.

Treasury bills were also introduced in the Australian Notes Act of 1910. These could be issued for various periods and had an associated interest rate.

Payments typically consisted of cash and cheques.

Inflation and Hyperinflation

Inflation is the tendency of a currency to lose value over time.

Many economists believed that modest inflation is a good thing. The logic was that some inflation encourages spending and growth in an economy, and that fulfilling the need for increased wages is more achievable in an environment that has some inflation.

In the transition to a fiat currency (a currency without recourse to gold), many countries discovered they could print money freely. This was a necessary measure in times of recession. However, if done too quickly, people could lose confidence in the value of the currency and, together with oversupply, this leads to very high inflation and hyperinflation.

Fortunately, Australia avoided hyperinflation; however, images of the German hyperinflation at a staggering 300 times during 1923, and the even larger Greek and Hungarian inflation rates at the end of World War II (when it was better value to burn notes for heat than to buy the little firewood the same currency could buy) created fear in the hearts of treasuries and governments. Strong monetary policy was necessary.

The Great Depression

A stock market crash on Wall Street triggered a global depression that impacted Australia heavily in 1930 and 1931, and overshadowed the economy for years to come.

Demand for Australia's limited exports (such as wool) slumped. The unpegging of the pound to gold further eroded confidence in the economy.

›› NOTE

The human toll of a failing economy is significant. The Great Depression affected all sectors of the economy. A successful investor with stocks, property, perhaps an investment in agriculture, and plenty of money in the bank found all their assets were devalued, perhaps by as much as 80%, including the pounds that were meant to be as good as gold. Someone else, living to make ends meet, found themselves out of work. The once rich, and the poor, the young and the old all found themselves on the same queue a mile long, hoping to get the one or two jobs that were on offer. Similar sights have been visible with the COVID-19 pandemic

There were two schools of thought at the time on how to deal with a recession or depression. Australia, still under the wing of Great Britain, sought the official position of London. Labor Prime Minister John Scullin invited Otto Niemeyer of the Bank of England to Australia to advise. The advice was to pay back debt (in hindsight, which debtor would not give that advice?) and balance the budget (effectively reducing spending). The alternative would be to see hyperinflation, the government believed.

This ran counter to the emerging Keynesian economic philosophy that progressives were suggesting (and would be the dominant approach to this day): to increase spending to buffer the economy during difficult times, always tolerating modest inflation.

Clearing and Settlement

Moving currency instantly is not always possible. At the time of the deal, the coins and notes may not be readily available or transferable. A transaction may take place via mail, telex, phone, and, more recently, through the Internet.

Due to the constraints of moving currency, there has been a separation of concerns between the payment instruction and the actual movement of money.

Banks tended to operate on an honour system. A commitment by a bank was as good as the currency itself, whether by an order on telegram, a letter of credit, or a verbal cry in a money market. Eventually, though, with every commitment, came the request to close the deal or "Show me the money".

 NOTE

There have been numerous cases where banks have had to honour mistakes by their staff, either through mistaken data entry or fraud. A staff member making a commitment on behalf of a bank needs to be honoured under the "My word is my bond" principle. In 2012, a JP Morgan trader caused a $6 billion loss for his company.

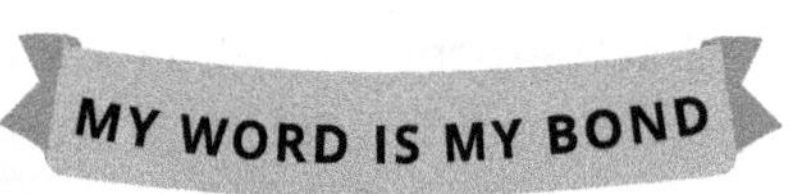

Clearing is the initial commitment and the transfer of instruction from the payer to the payee (and often back again), while settlement is the actual movement of money to back it up.

In the case of a cheque, the cheque may take time to make its way through the system — it may be written on day one, given to the payee on day two, deposited in the account on day three, and cleared for withdrawal (settled) on day four. The payer and payee banks may not settle until day five when they exchange institutional checks drawn on the central bank (interbank settlement) and receive value on their ledger account on day six (central bank settlement).

The flows for clearing and settlement can be quite different from each other, and can vary between payment types.

Differences in clearing and settlement also introduce risk. What if one of the banks in the chain fails after clearing but before settlement? What if the clearing files don't reconcile with the settlement files; for example, if a paper slip is lost? These risks are compounded when dealing with overseas payments and, in addition, there is currency fluctuation risk between clearing and settlement.

There are different kinds of settlement:

- Batch settlement: transactions are totalled up and only the grand total is settled in one go.
- Real-time settlement: the settlement happens at the same time as the clearing message.
- Bilateral settlement: each bank settles with each counterparty, separately.
- Net settlement: a trusted party like a card scheme or the central bank calculates the total amount owing or receivable by each bank so each bank only makes one payment.
- Deferred settlement or, commonly, deferred net settlement: settlement takes place on a net basis after the day of transaction, with the net off of each payment normally first thing in the morning.
- Merchant settlement or scheme settlement: generally for cards, a stage before financial settlement when the day's totals are tallied to calculate total amounts due. This is then reconciled with transactions to ensure nothing was missed. The merchant sends this settlement to the scheme, which splits (or switches it) to the issuer.

- Financial settlement: the final movement of money to settle clearing debts.
- T+2 settlement (or T+1, T+3, etc.): a protocol where settlement takes place after the specified number of days from the transaction date (e.g., FX spot and ASX share settlements are T+2, cheques and cards are T+1 though, in the case of cheques, clearing is not complete until T+2).

Computerisation

The earliest computers installed in Australia were in the CSIRO, universities and banks. By the mid-1960s, major banks were starting on their transformation journey.

The cost of these machines was substantial, but the pay-offs made them worthwhile.

Gradually, central computerised ledgers were updated with branch records. Branches were still king, but the head office could keep a watchful eye on operations throughout its empire.

From 1972, starting with the St George Building Society and then through to the 1980s, mainframe-based terminals were installed in branches. Most were connected through X.25 landlines, others through satellite connections. The computer itself was still in the head office, but it could be accessed remotely. Telling functions could now access a central ledger.

3.

REGULATION IN BANKING AND PAYMENTS

CENTRAL TO AN UNDERSTANDING OF PAYMENTS is a deeper understanding of the regulations that govern them. In this section, we present a listing of regulators, their purpose in payments and banking, and their key impacts.

Early Banking Regulation

Initial steps at centralisation of note and coin issuing, while initially effective, failed to regulate the diversifying banks. The federal government had little control over the economy, as demonstrated by the Great Depression.

Royal Commission Appointed to Inquire Into the Monetary and Banking Systems at Present in Operation in Australia (1935–1937)

In the aftermath of the Great Depression, there was concern over the conduct of both the private banks and the CBA.

The government of Joseph Lyons initiated a royal commission in 1935.[33] In those days, royal commissions were not entirely independent and the government would choose representatives to sit on them. One of the representatives, who would eventually become prime minister, was Labor politician Ben Chifley.

The commission, despite being conservative, recommended stronger regulation:

- A considerable increase in central banking functions and the powers of the Commonwealth Bank.
- That private trading banks should be licensed so that a decisive sanction would lie with the Commonwealth Bank and with government to enforce observance of statutory and central bank requirements.
- That trading bank credit should be controlled by requiring trading banks to deposit a portion of customers' deposits in the central bank.

›› NOTE

The commission did not address nationalisation, but Ben Chifley dissented and put forth an eloquent case for how banking affected most elements of the community and that it was wrong to put profits first. His views ended up becoming a central platform of a future government he was to lead. Chifley Square and Chifley Tower, in Sydney, ironically became the centre of up-town institutional banking, where all the money was made, especially in the 1990s. A giant statue casts his shadow on the square ... a ghost or a warning?

[33] Napier

Aftermath of the Royal Commission

World War II prevented the full implementation of the review; however, in 1941, as an emergency measure, banks were required to deposit funds earned from 1939 in the Commonwealth Bank in a *Special Account*. The purpose, as the Prime Minister, John Curtin put it, was to ensure investment of funds was in line with war-time policy (i.e., that the government would get the money) and that profit was not higher than the profit incurred in the three years preceding the control through the Special Account receiving a fixed fee.

In 1941, National Security (War-time Banking Control) Regulations were issued. This regulation recognised 14 banks (not counting the Commonwealth Bank or the state banks):

- Ballarat Banking Company
- Bank of Adelaide
- Bank of Australasia
- Bank of New South Wales
- Bank of New Zealand
- Brisbane Permanent Building and Banking Company
- Commercial Bank of Australia
- Commercial Banking Company of Sydney
- Comptoir National d'Escompte de Paris (later a part of BNP)
- English, Scottish and Australian Bank
- National Bank of Australasia
- Queensland National Bank
- Union Bank of Australia
- Yokohama Specie Bank (established in Sydney in 1915 until the Japanese attack on Pearl Harbour in 1941 when, soon after, staff were interned and the bank closed. Later it merged into the Bank of Tokyo.)

Missing from the list were the state banks of the day — the constitution prevented federal control of these banks:

- Rural Bank of New South Wales
- State Savings Bank of Victoria
- Rural and Industries Bank of Western Australia
- State Bank of South Australia
- Savings Bank of South Australia.

Banking Act 1945, and the Proposed Nationalisation of Banks

The newly recognised banks were required to hold a Special Account with the Commonwealth Bank as a central deposit of funds in excess of the balances held by the bank in August 1939, report profit and loss, and file a balance sheet with the treasurer.

The Special Accounts initiated in the middle of the war were formalised in 1945, along with the other recommendations of the royal commission, by the Labor Government of Ben Chifley in a Banking Act.

This was to set in motion the biggest political war over banking in Australia's history, and that brought down two governments: one state and one federal.

Australians had just returned from the war victorious. They returned to a country that had not advanced industrially since the depression. In fact, it would take 30 years (until 1967) before Australian shares recovered. Fingers pointed to the banks.

The Special Account regulations were formalised in the Banking Act of 1945 with the addition of the Bank of China, Hobart Savings Bank and Launceston Bank for Savings. In addition, payments between banks were to be made through cheques drawn on the Commonwealth Bank, a precursor to the Exchange Settlement Accounts. Reporting requirements were extended and made more onerous.

The distinction between savings banks and trading banks was not always clear, though trading banks tended to support complex investments and payment methods including cheques, while savings banks would only allow deposits and withdrawals.

》 NOTE

There has been recent criticism that bank executives are highly paid, but take no personal responsibility if there are issues or faults. With that in mind, it is interesting to note that the Banking Act of 1945, section 57 held the CEO directly liable for penalties not the bank. This was dropped from the Banking Act of 1959.

Two parts of the new act came into immediate question: first, section 48, which required states and local councils to effectively bank with the Commonwealth Bank or their state bank, rather than with a private bank. Melbourne City Council, supported by the Melbourne-based National Bank of Australasia, instigated a challenge. They also challenged sections 18-22 which dealt with the Special Accounts and were quite central to the act. Prime Minister Ben Chifley told the banks, it seems, to provide assurances that they would not object to sections 18-22. Section 48, he could understand and would accept the court's opinion, but the removal of the Special Accounts would defeat the purpose of the act and he would propose stricter laws on private banking (nationalisation), which the federal parliament had the right to do. Section 48 was put into hibernation until 1947. At this point, the High Court was invoked (notably with objections to sections 18-22 dropped by the lawsuit, possibly with some deference to Chifley), and in Melbourne Corporation v Commonwealth 1947, the judges found section 48 unconstitutional and explicitly did not make any judgement on the rest of the act. Sections 18-22 were a time bomb; no assurance was given that they would not be challenged again in the future.[34] Why they dropped objects, no one really knows. As Chifley himself said, "You can never know what really happened. Each side tells its own story."[35]

Banking Act 1947: Nationalisation of the Banks

Later in 1947, Ben Chifley made good his promise and proposed a replacement Banking Act 1947 that would nationalise the private banks. This act was vigorously and passionately debated by Ben Chifley and Robert Menzies, the opposition leader.

While it was being debated, the newly forming Liberal Party used the nationalisation of the banks proposed by Labor as an election issue. In Victoria, the 1947 state election was lost on this issue, despite it being a federal concern. Private bank officers and the Australian Bank Officers' Association had helped in the canvassing of voter support against the Labor Government.

The legislation passed both houses and was assented to. The private banks were to be controlled by the Commonwealth Bank.

The High Court case Bank of New South Wales v Commonwealth overturned much of the legislation. It was then appealed to the British Privy Council. London backed the High Court. Nationalisation had failed. This may have been a contributing factor to the Chifley government's eventual loss in 1949.

The Reserve Bank of Australia

Private banks remained concerned about the CBA's position as both a central bank and a savings and trading bank. There was concern that this gave it an unfair market advantage, and also a conflict of interest in administering its own compliance. An initial attempt to set out controls in the Banking Act 1953 amendment was insufficient and, in 1959, the Reserve Bank Act was passed along with a replacement banking act, and all central bank functions moved to the new body, the Reserve Bank of Australia (RBA).

Along with more stringent reporting requirements, the Reserve Bank had almost complete discretion over the regulation of banks. The Special Accounts became the Statutory Reserve Deposit Accounts and the bank moved up the road to Martin Place, Sydney.

---

[34] Lenihan

[35] Hasluck, 40

» NOTE

One criticism of the Reserve Bank is that it still provided banking services to government agencies and responded to tenders issued to the private bank sector. Institutional bankers complained that the regulator competes with them in this segment, something that could be a conflict of interest and was reminiscent of the CBA central bank days.

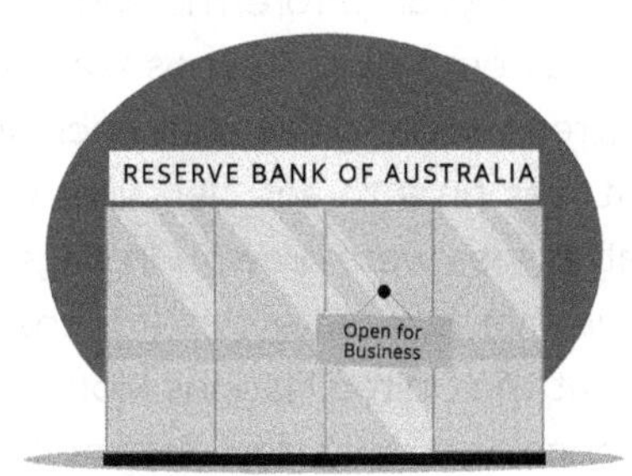

Monetary Policy

John Maynard Keynes was a macroeconomist who influenced much of the world's economic policy and directly guided policy in various countries, including Australia, corresponding with and being quoted by economists and politicians on all sides of politics. He challenged treasuries to consider the dilemma of inflation and employment. Keynes took an unconventional, softer approach to both the German reparations after World War I (unsuccessfully arguing for less compensation at Versailles), and recommended more employment during the Great Depression rather than wage reduction.[36]

» NOTE

Australia was quick off the mark during the COVID-19 pandemic with JobKeeper payments that paid employers to cover wages rather than unemployment benefits, and assistance for businesses from the outset, together with general easing of monetary and fiscal policies, perhaps the opposite of what happened in the depression. John Keynes would have been proud.

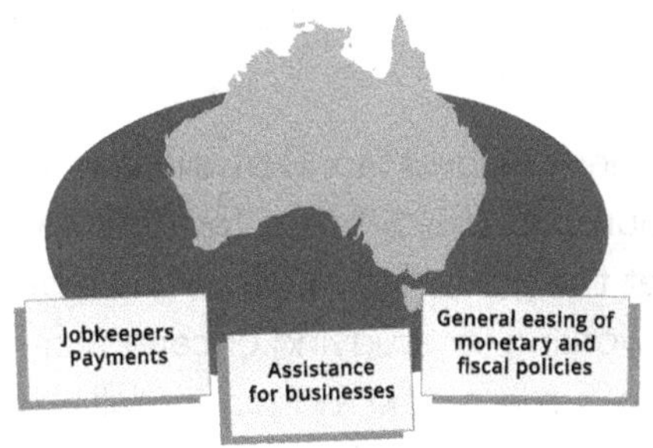

Arguably, the cost of ignoring Keynes was one depression and one world war. By the end of World War II, everyone was paying attention to the economist. Modern monetary policy is traced back to this time.

The Bretton Woods System

Bretton Woods is an area in New Hampshire, USA, near Mount Washington. Even today, it is an idyllic retreat amid expansive natural views, away from the busy city life and, in 1944, away from a horrific war.

---

[36] Keynes 1936

Just one month after a successful D-Day landing, with battles still raging in Normandy and more than a year before the surrender of Japan, the light at the end of the World War II tunnel was emerging. Keynes was now, for many, the father of macroeconomics. The 44 nations representing the allies (including the Soviet Union and Australia) and their delegates knew it was time to act. Versailles was not to be repeated. In the Sydney Morning Herald, the battle lines were drawn. On page one, it was the allies versus Germany on the war front. On page five, it was Keynes (for the United Kingdom) up against Harry Dexter White (for the US) at the United Nations Monetary and Financial Conference. It was just day one of the conference and early days for the liberation of Europe. By the end of the war, half of the world's industrial production would come from one country,[37] so both pages had the same messages. The Americans would win.

A few things came out of the conference. Keynes's vision was for an international clearing union to settle payments between central banks, as well as an international settlement currency known as the Bancor that would be transferred within the international clearing union. Each member state could overdraw based on the importance of its foreign trade.

Instead of a clearing union, the International Monetary Fund (IMF) was established to ensure monetary stability. A cut-down version of the clearing union, it had less money and relied heavily on member countries. The fund can lend to member countries in times of need (balance of payments deficits). Instead of the Bancor, the US dollar was the reserve currency. The new world power had spoken. Keynes compromised, as did most other nations.

The conference also created the World Bank's International Bank for Reconstruction and Development aimed at uplifting the poorest nations, especially those ravaged by wartime occupation. Economic development was the key to lasting peace. IMF member currencies were to be pegged to gold, and could be varied by plus or minus 10% to achieve a balance of payments.

Keynes's biggest fan, Australia, pushed back on the IMF in favour of the clearing union. Fearing a slump in the demand for their national exports, the Australian delegation took the view that the goal of any policy should be full employment: that every person who was capable of working (or studying or caring for family) would be able to earn a decent living from their employment. The motion for full employment was raised by Australia and defeated by the US. Keynes himself accepted the US position; however, Australia was recalcitrant, failing to join the IMF and World Bank until 1947. (The delay was partly to get other concessions such as an increased quota and more flexibility on exchange rates.) As Keynes said, Australia was the last black sheep. By the time Australia did join, Keynes had passed away at the age of 62.

Australia was "More Keynesian than Keynes"[38] in its uncompromising approach to Keynes economics. While fighting World War II, the nation took up another fight, the fight for full employment.

[37] Burns

[38] Markwell

» NOTE

Australia not signing the Bretton Woods Treaty is a curious story in the history of monetary policy. Australia has signed almost every international treaty by its own hand (and, prior to World War II, as part of the British Commonwealth). Australia had a strong involvement at Bretton Woods and had sent its best experts. However, by the time it came to signing the agreements, Australia's Prime Minister John Curtin was pushing back. He wanted full employment for all nations as well as other concessions. The delegates tried their best to convince Canberra to sign the final act. Meanwhile, news of the Soviet Union signing the agreement for the full $1.2 billion resulted in (in Keynes's own words) "loud and continued applause, and embraces all round." Curtin conceded, but they were to sign the agreement with the words "for purpose of certification." What those words meant, no one knows to this day, as every treaty must be ratified by parliament regardless. The final act was simply a thank-you note. Although technically Australia signed, the Americans reported it as a slap in the face. Curtin spun it as the Australian delegation to Bretton Woods not having authority to agree. In fact, authority was, obscurely, withheld. It was our last stand. Like Keynes, Curtin died soon after also from a heart attack.[39]

Full Employment

By the time of the institutionalisation of the Reserve Bank of Australia, a clear directive was given. The bank was to be independent. It had the goals of ensuring:[40]

- The stability of the currency of Australia.
- The maintenance of full employment in Australia.
- The economic prosperity and welfare of the people of Australia.

Eventually, the Bretton Woods gold-based pegging (plus or minus 10%) broke down with frequent unpunished breaches (as the IMF was toothless). The Australian dollar was pegged against the United States dollar and, later, a trade-weighted index. The currency was eventually floated.

The ideal of full employment was one thing, realising it was quite another. In Australia, employment is defined as being employed for one hour a week or more. People not counted as part of the workforce are those under 15 years of age, students, carers of children or family members, retirees, and those who are physically unable to work for at least an hour

---

[39] Ibid.

[40] Reserve Bank Act, 1959

a week.[41] The one hour a week definition was controversial but consistent with the OECD definition. Also, the employment figures included those who were underemployed, that is, in jobs earning significantly less than other jobs that the worker would be reasonably qualified for. So the inability of the economy to actually provide full employment is worse than the official unemployment rate.

Today, the Reserve Bank has achieved its goals for full employment, currency stability and prosperity by setting an inflation target of 2-3% achieved through controlling interest rates in the wholesale money markets.

A decision is made on the first Tuesday of every month on the direction of interest rates. It is a big event in the calendar of many homeowners — as a rise or drop could correspond to changes in their mortgage rates. The decision also gives an indication of where the economy is heading in the minds of the RBA Board.

» NOTE

As in most economies, the unemployment rate is an important measure of the success of a government in its handling of the economy. In Australia, it was a cornerstone for monetary policy. In 1975, Gough Whitlam's federal Labor Government was removed from power by the governor general in what was regarded as the biggest constitutional crisis in Australia's history, dubbed The Dismissal. The opposition had prevented the money supply to the government. They had a majority in the senate, resulting in the governor general sacking the prime minister. Malcolm Fraser's Liberal Government came into power in an election under the idea that it was better able to handle government finances and the economy. Three years into its term, in 1978, Australia was experiencing unemployment rates at levels not seen since the Great Depression (though in hindsight, the worst was yet to come). As unemployment became worse, the government began publishing two numbers. The first was from the Commonwealth Employment Services (CES) and was based on the number of people actually applying for unemployment benefits, while the second number was the Australian Bureau of Statistics (ABS), based on survey results.[42] Perhaps due to the fact that ABS respondents were less likely to state they were unemployed due to embarrassment (*dole bludgers*, as they were unaffectionately known), or perhaps due to inaccuracies of CES in obtaining a total labour force baseline, the CES unemployment numbers were higher than the ABS numbers. From 1978 to 1979, the less appealing CES numbers were discredited by the government and finally dropped. To this day, the ABS number is used, implemented by a Labour Force Survey asking 50 000 people about their participation in the labour market. This also explains why most Australian employment statistics only go back to 1978.

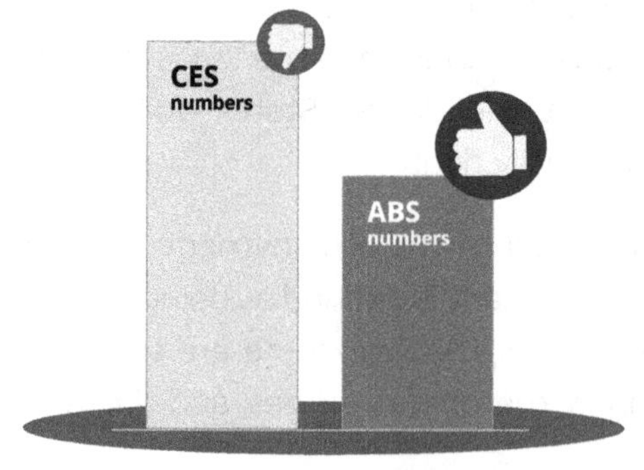

Unemployed Statistics

[41] Reserve Bank of Australia c. 2020

[42] ABS

Interest Rates: The Dance of the Banks

Since World War II, the government and the central bank have attempted to restrict the excess profit a bank makes by managing interest rates and applying various forms of pressure to ensure margins are adequate but minimal. Whenever a new RBA rate comes out, banks attempt to establish a profit margin, especially on home loans. This means quickly increasing the rates as they go up and slowly (or avoiding) implementing full downward revisions.

Frequently, politicians, usually the prime minister or treasurer, make a public remark about the banks being too quick or too slow to pass on a change, especially if the change is out of line with the rate change.

Banks, on the other hand, are torn in their decision to either succumb to pressure or attempt a move to strengthen profit. The decision on rates is made at the highest levels of the bank; however, it is rare for a CEO to be the bearer of bad news; that privilege is left to a lower senior executive, avoiding media attention.

A rate change is followed by a game of chicken: which big bank will be the first to move. It is unlikely that there is any collusion, as this is against Australian competition law, though the ACCC has noted accommodative and synchronised pricing behaviour as we will see. Generally, when one moves, the others follow, and follow relatively quickly to avoid either a loss of profit opportunity or a negative market perception.

On occasion, banks have unsuccessfully tried to explain a contrary motion with regards to their approach on interest rates, like the worst case: increasing them out of cycle. In one famous case, in 2009, Westpac produced a banana smoothie cartoon to explain (during the GFC) how costs had gone up and they couldn't bring down the cost of a smoothie (retail rates). The ad was promptly removed after a public backlash, but is still accessible on the Internet. In another case, in 2011, ANZ attempted to change their policy to say they would not change interest rates in line with the RBA cycle (to avoid perhaps the corresponding media hype cycle and give them space to deviate). ANZ would, instead, follow their own calendar. The policy lasted 2½ years and was dropped in 2014.

Money Markets

Money markets are trading markets for short-term debt instruments such as::

- Treasury notes issued by the Australian Government. These are issued for a period of less than a year, and are discounted by the pro-rata interest rate so that, on maturity, the face value is paid.
- Bank bills. These are issued by various institutions, purchased at a discount and payable at face value.
- Promissory notes. These are not in general contemporary use in Australia.
- Bonds. These are issued by governments and various institutions — a wholesale loan.
- Repurchase agreements (repos). These are double-sided transactions that start and end on fixed dates, to inject or remove liquidity from the market. They are generally defined for a shorter term than bonds.

- Foreign exchange swap (FX swap). These are similar to a repo, but the exchange is made in foreign currency. During the period of the swap the currency rate is fixed, meaning that if there is an anticipated change in the relative value of a currency pair, it is priced in at the outset along with interest.

The quality of the instrument is generally measured by its rating (Standard & Poors, Moodys, etc.). An instrument can be issued by different types of organisations in accordance with ASIC guidelines, and the value of that instrument is shaped by its rating. Low ratings (e.g., BBB- and below) bonds are referred to as *junk bonds*. Banking deregulation has meant that, these days, most bonds are issued by banks.[43]

The Reserve Bank acts in the money market to bring the interest rate to the target cash rate. This means that to raise interest rates, it will sell or issue debt instruments and to lower interest rates, it will buy them. Buying debt instruments means putting money into the economy. This is referred to as *quantitative easing*.

Quantitative easing, while not necessarily literally involving printing money, is often referred to as such as it has the same effect and does increase the volume of money (known as *money base*) that is in the economy, which we will cover later.

Increasingly, it seems that, in the developed world with a high reliance on borrowings, low interest rates are here to stay. Any immediate rise in rates would have a significant tightening impact on the economy, without a long-term weaning off of credit and, in particular, borrowings for residential property.

In Australia, like in many other developed countries, house prices are high relative to income, even at low interest rates, so an increase in interest rates is likely to have a strong negative effect on spending. Immediate regulatory measures to reduce the cost of homes will have a negative impact on existing homeowners and would be politically unpopular. Take, for example, the recent attempt in 2019 to end negative gearing, which itself was a proposal for future investors, not a policy that would affect existing owners, but was nevertheless received poorly. Moderate growth in property prices is important for maintaining the potency of monetary policy in helping achieve full employment and economic prosperity. This is one reason that tougher credit policies and other measures have been instituted by the government and regulators. Weaning Australians off credit will be an important exercise for governments and regulators in the future.

Capital Markets

While most of the central bank action and bank liquidity function sits in the money markets, capital markets have a role to play. Money markets are for instruments less than a year. For instruments greater than a year, there are the capital markets made up of mainly the stock market and bond market. An increasing number of non-resident institutions issue bonds in Australian dollars onshore (Kangaroo Bonds) or offshore (Australian dollar Eurobonds). Since the deregulation of the 1980s, Australian banks can tap into bond markets overseas to get cheaper funding. Instruments can be bought and sold on the primary (original issuer) or secondary markets (resale). The stock market includes shares and preference shares (both of which are paid back to holders before ordinary shareholders receive their money).

[43] Black

In order to increase shareholder capital, many of the banks went to the capital markets. Rights issues allowed existing shareholders to buy shares at a discount relative to the market. Capital notes were issued as a hybrid investment — essentially like a bond (subordinate debt — i.e., it would not get paid out until other debtors had been paid), it paid interest and in some cases, at the end of the period, it would convert to a share. This technique allowed banks to obtain capital at current stock valuations without creating immediate supply (that would lower the share price).

International Banks

There are a number of international banks; however, some of these are not really banks per se, but are designed to enable international cooperation, development project funding for poorer nations, and financial stability and security.

The International Monetary Fund, founded as a critical part of the Bretton Woods agreement, is designed to assist with the financial stability of most countries in the world through coordination, and especially to assist with balance of payments through funding via a quota system or loans.

The World Bank includes the International Bank for Reconstruction and Development. Among other functions, the World Bank funds developing countries through money from richer nations by means of long-term loans.

The Bank for International Settlements, founded in 1930, is a cooperative international organisation for bank regulation and is famous for the Basel accords. Australia's RBA and APRA send representatives to the Bank for International Settlements and implement their standards.

The Asia Development Bank, initiated by Japan in 1966, is similar to but separate from the World Bank, and focuses on loans to aid the development of the Asia region. Australia, the US, Canada and the European Union are also members.

The Asian Infrastructure Investment Bank was initiated by China in 2015. It is similar to the World Bank and the Asia Development Bank. By 2015, China was a major economy and wanted to have a greater say in the development of Asia. Australia was probably keen to be part of an emerging economic giant but (it is speculated), under pressure from the US, did not participate in the original formation[44] joining one year later. The Asian Infrastructure Investment Bank's initial capital was much larger than that of the World Bank or the Asia Development Bank.

Royal Australian Mint

In 1909, was the development of specifications of coins. As Australian coins were similar to their British counterparts, for a number of years, they were pressed in London and imported.

[44] Heydarian

By 1916, the Melbourne Royal Mint was producing Australian silver-alloy coins and, in 1923, began producing all Australian coins, including the lower-denomination bronze coins. This continued until decimalisation in 1966.

In 1965, The Royal Australian Mint opened in Deakin, a suburb of Canberra, where it continues to this day. It immediately started producing decimal coins (supplemented by the Melbourne Royal Mint, which produced the copper one cent and two cent coins). These coins were produced and distributed in readiness for the 1966 decimalisation. .

Entering the Global Market

After the Robert Menzies era and World War II, Australia started to drift away from the United Kingdom's shadow. The country was now signing treaties in its own right. Australia had made new friends in the world and was diversifying its trading partners.

Decimalisation

The exact reason for changing currency was unclear, but at some point, perhaps due to global interaction, the appeal of a decimal currency inspired a change in our £1:20s:240d currency system. It was getting hard to calculate totals and divide money using the old system and decimalisation had an appeal.

⟫ NOTE

Throughout this period, Australia remained a firm member of the British Empire, or the Commonwealth, with the monarch of England being head of state and their head appearing on the obverse side of all coins, and on at least one paper note (generally the smallest denomination). There was no firmer lover of the monarch than Prime Minister Robert Menzies, who said of the newly crowned Queen Elizabeth II (quoting a poem by Thomas Ford):

> ***I did but see her passing by,***
> ***And yet I love her till I die.***

So it was curious that Menzies would go against tradition and go decimal. A television commercial of the time explained it well: most of the world had moved to decimal, and it was difficult to calculate in pounds, shillings and pence. The new computers must have struggled to deal with the old non-decimal currency with most of the hardware and software designed in and for decimal currency countries. (To demonstrate the issue, try to confirm this with a calculator:

£17 13 s. 5½ d. + £15 7s. 7½ d. = £33 11s. 1 d.)

A song to the tune of *Click Go the Shears* explained it:

In come the dollars and in come the cents,
to replace the pounds and the shillings and the pence.
Be prepared folks when the coins begin to mix,
on the 14th of February 1966.
Clink go the cents folks,
clink, clink, clink. Changeover day is closer than you think.
Learn the value of the coins and the way that they appear,
and things will be much smoother when the decimal point is here.
In come the dollars and in come the cents,
to replace the pounds and the shillings and the pence.
Be prepared folks when the coins begin to mix,
on the 14th of February 1966.[45]

In 1966, the Australian dollar, with 1 dollar being 100 cents, was issued with a value of half an Australian pound, then worth £0.4 sterling. There were $20, $10, $2 and $1 notes circulated along with 50, 20, 10, 5, 2, and 1 cent coins. As inflation impacted the currency, these would later be supplemented with the $50 note in 1973 and the $100 note in 1984. Then $1 and $2 coins replaced their respective notes, due to wear, and the copper 1 cent and 2 cent coins were removed from circulation.

Foreign Currency Markets

The late 1960s saw a boom time. Australian exports started to move positively and, for the first time, the currency saw a gain against the British pound. Eventually, with the breakdown of the Bretton Woods system, most currencies moved to a free market exchange. Australia (at that time still a small global player) maintained a peg and, from 1971 to 1974, the Australian currency was shifted to be pegged against the US dollar.

Setting the value of the currency above or below its current value relative to other currencies has the effect of either increasing the attractiveness of exports (if the currency value is low) or increasing the attractiveness of imports (if it is high).

Where trading partners vary, a more complex value needs to be ascertained and, from 1974 to 1985, Australian currency was pegged to a trade-weighted index based on the country's trading relationships. Countries with whom we did more trade had a bigger impact on our currency value than others.

In 1985, Australian currency was floated on the foreign currency market. The free market would decide the currency's value, for better or worse.

[45] Taylor

Gold Currency Reserves

The reduction in gold reserves from 100% to 25% in the 1930s continued with the institutionalisation of the Reserve Bank. Essentially, the Reserve Bank could choose how to back currency on issue.

In 1969, the Reserve Bank held the equivalent of $230 million in gold (17% of its assets). This gradually increased to $4.8 billion in 1980 (76% of its assets, largely due to the gold price surge of 1980). On 3 July 1997, the Reserve Bank took the strategic step of selling gold assets. The bank reduced its reserves by over two thirds to $1.2 billion the next year (5% of its assets). The popular view was that gold had lost its lustre. Officially, as per Reserve Bank guidance, Australia was already gold-heavy (counting in the ground) so it did not make sense to hold as much in reserves. By 2020, with increases in the price of gold, gold assets were worth $5.5 billion (a similar 6% of assets). As with the trend of other central banks, gold was replaced with currency investments in other top tier currencies.

» NOTE

Modern human's fascination with gold and its consequential value is often cause for intellectual debate. Shiny is one thing, but so is plastic. Rarity is another. Rhenium, rhodium, iridium, ruthenium, tellurium and osmium are about four times rarer than gold, but not four times the price. As for utility, platinum and the others are at least as useful, if not more so. Gold's use as an investment, and its attraction even against the competitors platinum and silver, is less about logic than it is about convention.

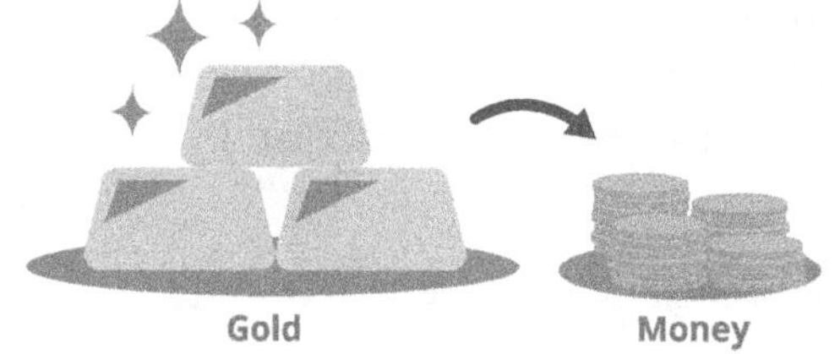

Fiat Currency

If there was any doubt, by 1997, the Australian dollar, like many of the world's currencies today, had transformed into a fiat currency. The value was the value. There was no fundamental underlying commodity, no recourse to precious metals or any other asset. Supply and demand economics gave it its value, and it was controlled by the government or the central bank.

Government Inquiries

The government of the day, as the representative of the people, was the source of The government of the day, as the representative of the people, was the source of much of the regulation, and rightly so as is expected in a democracy.

Through policy, legislation, inquiries or pressure on regulators, politicians pulled the strings on the system. In many cases, they recognised that the system generally worked and, especially after Ben Chifley's foray mentioned earlier, with few exceptions, tried to not rock the boat, at least not too much.

Inquiries into banking and payments were often set up by the government, generally as a result of public concern, to address key issues and to provide a justifiable and powerful policy foundation. While the inquiries are intended to be independent, they are often at least partially influenced by the political forces and sentiments of the time. That said, many inquiries received bipartisan support and, due to the short political lifecycle in Australia (with elections every three years or sooner), inquiries were set up by one government, but implemented by the then opposition.

The workings of the committees and inquiries are at two levels: first, an often impenetrable volume of submissions and writings (that may or may not be proportionally representative of the issues) and second, lobbying and back room discussions (that need to be backed up by front room submissions) — which are a necessary part of the inquirers obtaining a deeper understanding of the subject area for, without this understanding, it is impossible to know what is politically and publicly important, and what recommendations could be practically implemented. The inquirer's job is to juggle the public interest with the conflicting interests of those who present their case. Unfortunately, the process makes the findings less of a science and more of an art. For the most part, the inquiries have done a good job in trying to improve a most complex human industry.

The following inquiries were initiated by the federal government.

Inquiry into the Australian Financial System (1979-1981)

In 1979, John Howard, then Treasurer in the Malcolm Fraser government, set up an inquiry into the Australian financial system. This was the first such inquiry since the 1935-1937 royal commission.

A committee led by Keith Campbell was set up and became known as the Campbell Committee. Its goal was to inquire into the operations and efficiency of the Australian financial system against the background of the government's free-enterprise objectives and broad goals for economic prosperity.

The inquiry spawned an examination of credit cards (then Bankcard) by the Trade Practices Commission.

The Campbell Committee ushered a move to bank deregulation, away from direct intervention, and towards a more supervisory function. It also suggested the Reserve Bank take an interest in payment systems and technology.

The Australian Financial System Review Group (1983-1984)

The Bob Hawke government announced an Australian Financial System Review Group, chaired by Vic Martin, also chair of MLC (a wealth management company) and former CEO of the Commercial Banking Company of Sydney (which later merged with NAB). The inquiry was known as the Martin Review. It noted that there were four major banks that created an oligopoly and that more competition was required. The report proposed banking deregulation and the qualified entry of foreign banks. It also noted the restrictive access to EFTPOS, and recommended an Australian Payments Systems Council (chaired by the Reserve Bank of Australia) which the then treasurer, Paul Keating, did set up. (The Australian

Payments Systems Council is distinct from the Payments System Board and the Australian Payments Council.)

The inquiry was limited, taking no submissions, but politically it had the effect of moving the agenda from the Campbell Inquiry of the previous Malcolm Fraser/John Howard government (for this was the era of treasury-led government) to Bob Hawke and his Treasurer Paul Keating. The Martin Review triggered the 1980s bank regulation period.

Inquiry into Banking and Deregulation (1990-1991)

The House of Representatives Standing Committee on Finance and Public Administration tabled its report on the inquiry into banking and deregulation entitled *A Pocket Full of Change.* Chaired by Stephen Martin, and known as the Martin Committee (often confused with the earlier, separate Martin Review), the committee looked at financial deregulation and the effectiveness and benefits of competition in the banking sector. This was one of the most effective reviews of banking in modern Australian history with over 100 impactful recommendations.

The committee noted the obscurity of the definition of a bank and requested that the RBA come up with one. It also wanted to understand and publish the profitability of banks relative to other OECD nations. They entrenched the Four Pillars policy by recommending mergers or acquisitions that would lessen competition. It recommended that non-bank financial intermediaries have access to RBA regulated payments, and that foreign bank restrictions be removed (provided those foreign nations had reciprocal arrangements).

» NOTE

Bank of China has been a foreign bank in Australia, with a full authorised deposit-taking institution (ADI) license since World War II, yet China has failed to substantially open its bank market to overseas-owned banks. Despite this, Australian banks have attempted to establish retail banking presences in China and many other countries, especially in Asia. As time progresses, barriers are being lowered; however, the ability of foreign banks to compete in established markets is diminished without considerable investment. On the other side of this challenge, we have seen the failure of Citibank and HSBC to substantially compete against the Big Four, despite three decades of growth, though the GFC and the COVID-19 crisis did not help these two banks in their international plans.

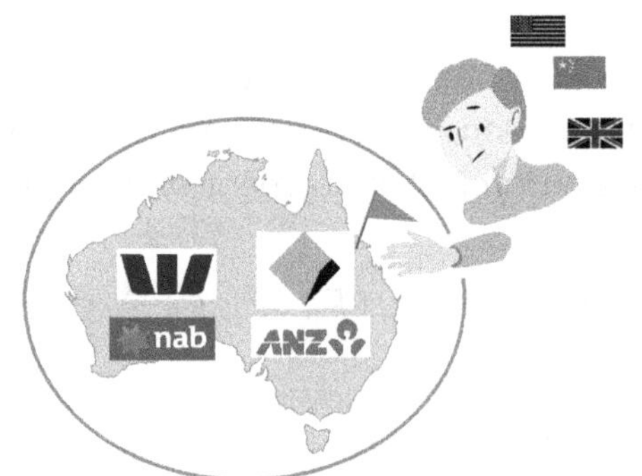

The report recommended that:

- High Value Clearing Systems (HVCS) modelled on the Swiss system (RTGS) be established.
- Banks should be regulated by the federal government.
- There should be equal supervision of private and publicly-owned banks.
- Cooperative building societies and credit unions should be supervised by banks.
- A bank's subsidiaries should be wound into the parent company from a guaranty and regulatory point of view.
- Credit assessments for small businesses should be improved.
- A right to access personal information held by private organisations (compared with the Consumer Data Right almost 30 years later).

Financial System Inquiry (1996-1997)

Not to be outdone by its predecessor, the Treasurer of the new coalition government, Peter Costello, appointed the Chairman of the Business Council of Australia and CEO of Amcor, Stan Wallis, to head an inquiry. The Wallis Report recommended the unification of the Australian Securities Commission, the Insurance and Superannuation Commission, and the Australian Payments Systems Council into one organisation, which became ASIC (see below).[46] It also recommended the establishment of what was to be APRA by combining state and federal prudential regulation into one organisation. The report also recommended removing Paul Keating's Six Pillar policy (to be described later). The report recognised inefficiency in the payment systems, especially EFTPOS, and recommended setting up, within the RBA, a Payment System Board.

Inquiry into Home Loan Lending Practices and the Processes Used to Deal with People in Financial Difficulty (2007)

The House of Representatives Standing Committee on Economics, Finance and Public Administration, chaired by Bruce Baid, undertook a home loan inquiry in 2007. It recommended regulation of lending advice, especially for mortgage brokers. It also recommended reporting of the volume of repossessions. Due to a change of government, these recommendations were not immediately implemented.

Inquiry into Competition in Banking and Non-Banking Sectors (2008)

The House of Representatives Standing Committee on Economics was convened by the treasurer during the GFC to look at competition. The committee's recommendations[47] included what would become the National Credit Code, instigated by the Law Society. It recommended account portability to make account provider switching easy (compare with phone number portability — during telecommunications deregulation). The industry

[46] Wallis

[47] Thomson

payment modernisation initiative at the time was MAMBO (covered in detail later) and the inquiry supported and encouraged it. The report also recommended banning unsolicited credit limit increases for credit cards.

Parliamentary Joint Committee on Corporations and Financial Services (2009)

After a number of failures in the financial advice industry, a joint parliamentary committee provided recommendations to better regulate it. This became the Future of Financial Advice reforms (2012) and the Streamlining Future of Financial Advice reforms (2014).[48]

Report on Bank Mergers (2009)

After the acquisition of St George Bank by Westpac and, during the GFC, the acquisition of Bankwest by CBA, further concentrating banking in the Big Four, the Senate Economics Reference Committee published a report in 2009 on the topic.[49] The committee recommended the retention of the Four Pillars policy.

Inquiry into Competition within the Australian Banking Sector (2011)

The Senate Economics Reference Committee established an Inquiry into Competition within the Australian Banking Sector in 2011.[50] The report was written after the GFC and recommended a broad-ranging inquiry into the Australian financial system. It identified the problem of concentration in the banking sector (the Big Four banks) and suggested that competition would help more than regulation. It also recommended that the Financial Claims Scheme introduced during the GFC be made permanent.

Financial System Inquiry (2014)

The Government Treasurer, Joe Hockey, formed an inquiry headed by David Murray, former CEO of CBA, into the financial system, known as the Murray Report. Forty-four recommendations were provided, including increasing capital adequacy ratios to guard against bank failure, increasing major bank risk weightings for mortgages to facilitate greater competition by smaller banks, innovation collaboration initiated by regulators, implementation of a federated digital ID, payments to cap card fees paid by consumers, banning of merchant surcharges on debit cards and other surcharge limits on credit cards, and that tax inconsistencies should be managed. Capital gains tax with a discount incurred on the sale of an investment was taxed at half the tax rate (or less) than was claimed by negative gearing the costs of the same investment, franking credits on dividends were taxed at 30%, yet withholding tax on interest rate income was taxed at close to 50%..

---

[48] Ripoll

[49] Eggleston

[50] Ibid

Digital Currency — Game Changer or Bit Player (2014-2015)

The senate asked its Economics Reference Committee to look into digital currencies. The following recommendations were made: that cryptocurrency be treated as money for the purpose of GST, that a task force look at digital currency regulation and that AML/CTF regulations be applied.[51]

Annual Review into the Four Major Banks (2016 onwards)

In 2016, the government treasurer requested the House Standing Committee on Economics to review the four major banks every year.[52] The following recommendations were made:

- A one-stop Banking and Financial Services Tribunal.
- Open data for consumers and small businesses.
- A review of regulatory requirements for starting a new bank.
- Least cost routing at merchants for debit cards.
- A request for the ACCC to examine the interest-only rate increase of 2017.
- Comprehensive credit reporting (CCR), including positive aspects.

Royal Commission into Misconduct in the Banking, Superannuation and Financial Services Industry (2017-2019)

After an AUSTRAC statement of claim on the CBA's failure to report threshold transactions on Intelligent Deposit Machines, insurance claim controversies, risky investments being recommended by financial planners, and many other issues, calls for a royal commission were made with the banks ultimately conceding. The prime minister requested Australia's second royal commission into the banking industry.

The royal commission resulted in a number of revelations, and in the departure of the CEOs of Westpac, CBA, NAB and AMP.

While the report made a large number of recommendations, many of these would not be overtly perceptible to consumers. Time will be the best judge of whether behaviour changes.

Select Committee on Financial Technology and Regulatory Technology (2019-2021)

Financial technology (fintech) and regulatory technology (regtech) are areas of potential innovation. In 2019, a senate inquiry was established, chaired by Andrew Bragg, to look into the fintech and regtech industries, what is impeding them and how they can be supported. Due to the COVID-19 pandemic, the report was delayed to 2021.

---

[51] Dastyari

[52] Coleman 2016, 2017a, 2017b; Wilson 2019, 2020

State Government Inquiries

After federation, and through the centralisation of banking and finance controls, states had less of a say in these affairs and few inquiries were conducted. Two notable exceptions were the 1991 Royal Commission into the Collapse of the State Bank of South Australia, which resulted in the resignation of the premier of the time. The following year, a Victorian Royal Commission into the Tricontinental Group of Companies that saw the near-collapse of the State Bank of Victoria covering a similar topic. The conclusion of both inquiries was that the state governments did not have the resources to manage ADIs.

Crises

After the banking failures of the 1890s, Great Depression and world wars, a number of relatively small yet significant crises have impacted both the world and Australia.

Oil Shocks of the 1970s and 1980s

A long post-war boom ended abruptly in 1973 with an oil crisis in the Middle East. Bank failures in Europe resulted in the formation of the Bank for International Settlement's Basel Committee for international standardisation on bank supervision. The Australian economy stalled for many years. Inflation went from 3.5% in 1970 to a staggering 17.6% in 1975, resulting in a change of government in Australia. In 1983, unemployment was at 10%, and the view was that the banking sector was over-regulated and, therefore, deregulation was initiated.[53]

Deregulation took place in a number of areas following inquiries begun in 1979 and 1983. The float of the Australian dollar resulted in a purist approach to monetary policy by the RBA. Term deposit restrictions were removed and banks could compete for access to overnight funds. Foreign bank restrictions were reduced, which created a threat to local banks who, therefore, had to increase their innovation and product capability. Up until today, penetration of large overseas banks into the Australian retail market has been low, due in part to a threat and, more directly, the response to that threat, a textbook example of how free trade improves the competition capability of local providers.[54]

Recession of the Early 1990s

A short boom was followed by a deep recession in the early 1990s. To quote the Australian Government Treasurer Paul Keating, "This is a recession Australia had to have,"[55] with unemployment rising again to about 10%. Banks that failed included the Pyramid Building Society, State Bank of Victoria and State Bank of South Australia. These incidents spawned two state royal commissions and saw the resignation of the premier of South Australia. An inquiry (the Martin Committee) was made into deregulation and the eventual centralisation of banking regulation for state institutions, building societies and credit unions.

---

[53] Phillips

[54] Sturm

[55] November 1990

11 September 2001

On 11 September, 2001, or 9/11, four passenger aircraft were hijacked and, unlike traditional hijackings where the hijackers made demands, the planes were flown directly into buildings in the US: two into the World Trade Centre, demolishing the largest buildings in the world in the heart of the financial capital New York, and one into the Pentagon (the US military headquarters). The fourth aircraft crashed before it could hit the United States Capitol Building, the centre of democratic government in the US. Around 3 000 people died.

There were many ancillary causes that facilitated this calamity, from airport and aircraft security to rogue nation-states encouraging terrorists. One enabling factor was the ability to transfer money anonymously around the world to fund terrorism.

In the payments industry, 9/11 brought added urgency and attention to worldwide efforts to control financial crime (FATF and AML/CTF).

In addition, in the immediate aftermath of 9/11, there was a decline in the stock market and a loss of banking services, with some major financial institutions losing some operational capability, causing a liquidity bottleneck in the US.[56]

9/11 had a major impact on many aspects of society, including on payments and banking.

The Global Financial Crisis 2008

The Global Financial Crisis (GFC) came as the result of banks incorrectly declaring the underlying risk of assets such as, in the US, subprime mortgages which were worth not as much as was claimed.

Australia experienced a loss of confidence, however, due to monetary policy and the actions of the Rudd government at that time a potential disaster was averted. One thing the government did was to establish the Financial Claims Scheme. To be administered by APRA, this scheme entitled any depositor to a guarantee of their funds up to $1 000 000 (later reduced to $250 000) per financial institution they bank with. The move was designed to avoid a speculative run on the banks, and also gave reason for the government to put greater regulatory controls on the banks.

Though there was a popular understanding that banks had some backing from the RBA, and that the government would not let them collapse, this was not really codified. One criticism of the measures was that this now formally put a wedge between non-bank financial institutions (such as fund managers) and banks, in providing government balance guarantees. It also further entrenched money as a potentially more reliable store of wealth than other wealth investments.

[56] Ferguson

» NOTE

One of the requirements introduced for compliance as part of the Financial Claims Scheme was that banks test-run a failure. The test-run scenario was to see what would happen if a bank were liquidated. APRA and the RBA wanted to see whether the banks could support final payments from accounts, and whether they could report on the balances and account names of each account, including recent payments. The idea was that the balances would be given to another ADI, along with the funding guarantee, to allow those balances to be paid out or appropriately transferred. While the practice runs worked, they have never been put to a real test and open questions remain: will employees still show up to work after a bank fails? Will vendors keep the lights on if they have not been paid?

Coronavirus 2019-2021

After an apparent outbreak in China in late 2019, by April 2020, most of the world was in lockdown. The coronavirus (COVID-19) caused a significant number of deaths around the world. In addition, there was an economic effect with businesses shutting down.

Faced with a recession, the Australian Government, having learnt from the Great Depression, was quick to act. Money was put into the economy to increase production: small business relief, loans, and JobKeeper government-funded payments to enable companies to pay staff salaries. Banks postponed repayments and courts were asked to ignore rent defaulters. However, many workers were stood down, and a number of businesses, including large corporations, were pushed over the edge with Virgin Australia and countless smaller operations appointing administrators.

United Nations Security Council

The United Nations body with the most clout is probably its Security Council (UNSC). As a small group of 15 nations, with the US, the United Kingdom, France, Russia and China as permanent members, the council can pass a resolution to sanction a country (or an individual). This sanction must be observed by all UN members, including Australia, lest they be sanctioned as well.

A sanction is an enforcement action under the United Nations Charter that generally does not involve the use of force. Restrictions include prevention of trade and, particularly, disallowing payments.

Sanctions are currently in place against people, organisations and states including Somalia, North Korea, the Democratic Republic of the Congo, Iraq, Iran, Sudan, South Sudan, Libya, Guinea-Bissau, the Central African Republic, Yemen, and Mali, as well as the alleged perpetrators of the Lebanon Bombing, the Taliban, ISIL, Al-Qaeda and other terrorist organisations.

The Australian Department of Foreign Affairs and Trade publishes a list of over 6 000 UNSC sanctioned entities.

Financial Action Task Force

At the end of the G7 meeting in Paris in 1989, in order to combat international financial crime (specifically money laundering), the Financial Action Task Force (FATF), a group involving several nations, was established. Australia was an early member.

Forty recommendations were proposed in 1990. After 9/11, an additional nine special recommendations were proposed to include combating terrorism financing and, in 2012, these were integrated into the original so today a new set of 40 recommendations is provided.[57]

The recommendations set forth a common legislative standard across countries for taking a risk-based approach to preventing money laundering. They require the proper identification of bank customers, and include key originator and beneficiary information on wire transfers. Countries should also consistently apply financial sanctions as directed by the UN Security Council.

The recommendations also advise the signing of key international conventions including:

- The United Nations Convention against Illicit Traffic in Narcotic Drugs and Psychotropic Substances, 1988
- The Terrorist Financing Convention, 1999
- The United Nations Convention against Transnational Organised Crime, 2000
- The United Nations Convention against Corruption, 2003.

Today, there are 39 core members of the FATF and, together with affiliated bodies, this covers most of the world.

The FATF publishes sanction lists from the UNSC and member countries as blacklists (banned entities) and greylists (high-risk countries). These lists are used by banks to screen payments.

Preventing financial crime, and specifically anti-money laundering and counter-terrorism financing (AML/CTF) as it has come to be known, is today a micro-industry of its own.

AUSTRAC

As a result of emerging national and international regulation against money laundering, a new regulatory authority was required.

The Cash Transaction Reports Agency had been set up as a result of the Cash Transaction Reports Act 1988. The agency and the act were renamed in 1991 to the Australian Transaction Reports and Analysis Centre (AUSTRAC) and the Financial Transaction Reports Act 1988

---

[57] FATF 2012

(FTR Act) respectively. AUSTRAC later took on the responsibility of ensuring compliance with the Anti-Money Laundering and Counter-Terrorism Financing Act 2006 (AML/CTF Act).

AUSTRAC has imposed the largest fines in Australian history, including $700 million in 2018 against the CBA for a breach of the AML/CTF Act. Even before this fine, banks feared AML/CTF fines and globally these are the largest fines, often being as much as a bank's annual profit.

Risk-Based Approach

Adherence to AML/CTF regulations (with most FATF countries having equivalent laws) is one of the major compliance issues for banks worldwide. Due to the risk-based approach, many things are not written down, especially in relation to new technologies (FATF Recommendations Nos. 1 & 15). For this reason, a company taking part in a cryptocurrency transaction may find its bank account closed, its directors' bank accounts closed, and a ban on opening an account again. Money service businesses are similarly targeted. The reason is that if a bank knowingly facilitates the undocumented overseas transfer of funds, especially if those funds are to UNSC sanctioned entities, the bank is liable for heavy fines, even though a customer of the bank committed the offence.

Designated Service

AUSTRAC regulates what are referred to as designated services: financial, gambling, bullion providers and money service businesses. Insurance intermediaries (including motor vehicle dealers) and solicitors also need to enrol with AUSTRAC. As a result of the Digital Currency — Game Changer or Bit Player inquiry[58], digital currency exchange services were added to the list of designated services. A designated service needs to provide an AML/CTF program and enrol and/or register with AUSTRAC.

Identification

One of the early measures AUSTRAC took was to establish identification requirements for account holders. This was the 100 Point Check. The more authoritative the document, the greater the number of points with no single document providing all 100 points so several documents were required to prove identity. From February 1991, all bank accounts in Australia have had to comply with the 100 Point Check.

Now known globally as Know Your Customer (KYC), identity checks are a cornerstone of AML/CTF regulations.

While Australia was one of the first countries to implement such a strong regime, some weaknesses have emerged in the current system; for example, lack of electronic validation of biometrics, regular updates, confirmation of change of address and a lack of mandatory photo identification. The system fails to sufficiently prevent mules and other fraudulent acts.

---

[58] Dastyari

Key Reports

Designated institutions or organisations must submit an AML/CTF program report to AUSTRAC for review. The report must demonstrate:

- How KYC procedures will be performed.
- Procedures for identifying suspicious activity.
- Procedures for identifying UNSC sanctioned entities and FATF blacklisted and greylisted entities, Australian identified terrorist organisations, etc., and screening payments to these entities.
- Procedures for screening politically exposed persons (PEPs); that is, high-risk people that could be subject to fraud and blackmail, and may accept or provide bribes and launder money.

AUSTRAC also requires the following key reports to be filed:

- Threshold transaction report (TTR). This reports transfers of over AUD $10 000 or the equivalent in cash.
- Suspicious matter report (SMR). This reports transactions that are suspected of being linked to a crime.
- International funds transfer instruction (IFTI). Any international movement of funds to or from Australia must be reported. Card transactions are, however, exempt from this rule. It is not clear whether IFTIs are required for cryptocurrency exchanges.
- A cross-border movement (CBM) report, like a TTR, is filed when moving AUD $10 000 or equivalent in notes and coins or bearer negotiable instruments such as traveller's cheques across Australia's international border.

Designated services require an AML/CTF program and must complete annual compliance reports.

Solicitors must file Significant Cash Transaction Reports (SCTR) for transactions over $10 000.

》 NOTE

Many organisations require a AML/CTF program, but there is limited guidance on how to create one. AUSTRAC advises one of three types: standard (for most reporting entities), joint (where the AML/CTF program is centralised between reporting entities), and special (for Australian Financial Services License holders including banks). Essentially, AUSTRAC needs to know how an organisation manages AML/CTF risk.

Read the Guidelines

AUSTRAC's response to questions is often to read the guidelines and seek independent legal advice. In some cases, as exposed in parliamentary inquiries, they have offered individual and specific advice to the big banks. Treatment of financial institutions is inconsistent. The guidelines are often insufficient, and legal advice can be vague with most lawyers recommending a very cautious approach, avoiding uncertain risks. This helps fuel the fear and perceived risk of non-compliance, stifling innovation.

AUSTRAC's favouritism was not unique among regulators. Due to limited resources, it was difficult to provide extensive advice and risky as well. A wrong instruction could have serious consequences, so reading approved guidelines was often the safest course of action however unhelpful it turned out to be.

Payment Systems Board

In 1997, the Wallis Report recommended that the RBA set up a Payments System Board.

There were many problems with payments; in particular, a lack of competition and high costs and fees. Additionally, in the new regime where critical assets were held with the Reserve Bank, if a bank were to fail, it would fail while settling a payment, likely one that had already been cleared.

The Reserve Bank Act of 1959 was amended, and a new Payment Systems and Netting Act 1998 was established, defining the functions of the Payment Systems Board as:

- Controlling risk in the financial system.
- Promoting the efficiency of the payments system.
- Promoting competition in the market for payment services that would be consistent with the overall stability of the financial system.

Australian Payments Council

The 1985 Australian Payments Systems Council was set up by the Treasurer, Paul Keating, in response to the Martin Review, in the hope to get the banks to self-regulate payment. It was reported as a failure.[59]

This, in turn, led to the formation of APCA in 1992 (AusPayNet — see below). Gradually APCA broadened in membership and deviated in agenda so, in 2015, the Australian Payments Council was formed to work with the Payments System Board to achieve strategic objectives for the industry.

[59] "The maiden report of the Australian Payments Systems Council will stand as a monument to that organisation's failure to solve the major problems concerning the access to, and operation of the electronic payment system." Stephen Hutcheon; Marshmallow Monument on EPS; Sydney Morning Herald, 28 October 1985.

In 2020, the members were the RBA, the Big Four banks, Macquarie Bank, one payment ADI (Cuscal), one supermarket giant (Coles), one telco (Optus), the Australian Payments Network, BPAY, NPP Australia (NPPA), and one international scheme (Visa). Notably absent are eftpos Australia as well as smaller banks and credit unions.

The council is drawn from the larger Payments Community, a group established by the Council, open to "any organisation with a significant interest in the Australian payments system." It is unclear what "significant interest" means. The community boasts barely more than 30 members, a small number, considering the number of interested parties in payments in Australia.

The group has largely been a white elephant. The failure of the group to get early traction with the NPP and insubstantial push of ISO 20022 illustrate this, along with a thin set of press releases over five years of operation.

Australian Prudential Regulation Authority (APRA)

Established in 1991 as the Australian Financial Institutions Commission, APRA, in its current form, began in 1999 as an amalgamation of the state supervisory authorities in an effort to standardise and federalise financial institution governance. This role was extracted from the RBA to allow the RBA to focus on monetary policy and system efficiency.

Authorised Deposit-taking Institution

An authorised deposit taking institution (ADI) is an institution allowed to hold, on behalf of a customer, $1 000 or more. Under the Financial Claims Scheme, the government currently backs such deposits so regulations need to ensure that the AD is properly managing that money. Even without the Financial Claims Scheme, good governance is important for the stability of the economy.

There are three types of licenses:

- Full ADI (banks, credit unions):
  - Australian-owned banks, building societies and credit unions
  - Australian banks owned by foreign banks
  - Branches of foreign banks.
- Restricted ADI (new banks).
- Providers of Purchased Payment Facilities (this is currently exclusively for PayPal).

APRA's role is to ensure that risk, information technology processes, and operational processes are managed efficiently and effectively through the setting of standards, and that ADIs adhere to these standards. Standards have legislative power; however, APRA consults with banks and releases drafts before the standards are enacted officially.

Capital Adequacy

A bank accepts deposits and gives out loans. In order to ensure that there are sufficient assets to cover their activities, banks require sufficient capital. This is referred to as *capital adequacy*.

Basel Accords

Basel is a town in Switzerland where the Swiss, German and French borders meet. It is the location of the headquarters of the Bank for International Settlements, formed in 1930. The Bank for International Settlements is currently owned by central banks.

In 1974, after an international financial market crisis and bank failures, the Basel Committee was formed to improve banking stability.

Since 1988, the committee has published the Basel Accords, which recommend capital adequacy requirements. The second accord was published in 2004 and the most recent Basel III Accord, in the aftermath of the Global Financial Crisis, was published in 2010. Each accord has strengthened regulatory supervision and asked for increased capital adequacy. The 2010 accord is expected to be implemented by all participants by 2022.

》 NOTE

The subprime mortgage issue that sparked the GFC was based on a series of mortgages in the US that were highly leveraged. These were securitised, a practice where a parcel of assets is packaged into tradable instruments such as bonds. In an environment of higher interest rates and increasing prices, the value of these assets goes up so they may be sold for more than their face value. In turn, the gearing increases (in the US by up to 48 times, compared with 14 times more recently). When the value went down, the loans were no longer performing (i.e., they were defaulting), and holders of subprime mortgage bonds were left with a geared loss. This brought down the Lehman Brothers in the US and caused the sell-off of Merrill Lynch to the Bank of America. It impacted banking regulation globally and led to the Basel III Accord.

Australia implements the principles of Basel III with some customisations, which we will focus on here.

In essence, the Capital Adequacy Standards (APS 110) state:

1. $$\frac{CET1}{Total\ RWA} \geq 4.5\%$$ ***The ratio of CET1 capital to total risk-weighted assets must be at least 4.5%.***

2. $$\frac{Tier\ 1\ Capital}{Total\ RWA} \geq 6\%$$ ***The ratio of Tier 1 capital to total risk-weighted assets must be at least 6%.***

3. $$\frac{Total\ Capital}{Total\ RWA} \geq 8\%$$ ***The ratio of total capital to total risk-weighted assets must be at least 8%.***

Common Equity Tier 1 (CET1). A bank starts off with shareholder equity. It actually needs a lot of it. This comes from shareholders when the company first floated (so for old banks this was a long time ago, and the original amount was probably quite small in today's value). Every year thereafter, hopefully, the bank makes a profit. It may pay some of this out to shareholders as dividends, which keeps them happy or it may retain earnings (or losses). The sum of shareholder equity and retained earnings is the value of the company, CET1. If the bank were to liquidate, in theory, CET1 is all it should have left. For APRA, more CET1 is good.

After the GFC, during the phasing in of Basel III, banks had lower than comfortable common equity. APRA advised them to take measures to improve it. Most banks issued shares to increase their CET1 and received more funds thanks to good share prices.

Additional Tier 1 (AT1). Tier 1 capital is made up of CET1 + AT1. AT1 generally includes preference shares and convertible securities. AT1 is problematic, as any losses incurred by a bank are not easily applied to these instruments, and some of them (especially overseas instruments) are complex so they are not as highly regarded as CET1. APRA limits AT1 to a maximum of 25% of total Tier 1 capital. APRA is also allowed to ask banks to increase their Tier 1 countercyclical capital buffer from 0 to 2.5% more than the 8%, taking the Tier 1 capital ratio up to 10.5%. This Tier 1 buffer, specified in 2016, has not been invoked. The idea is that, during a positive cycle, this capital is available to provide a buffer to a negative cycle.

Tier 2 Capital includes subordinated debt; that is, essentially, unsecured loans or bonds issued in the bank's name. It can also include other allowable instruments, such as corporate instruments of the bank, as specified by APRA, but never debt that is part of the customer-bank business relationship such as deposits. This subordinated debt could be defaulted in the event of a wind-up to pay out deposit holders and secured creditors so it acts as a buffer.

Total Capital is Tier 1 capital + Tier 2 capital.

Risk-Weighted Assets (RWA). When a bank takes money as a deposit, this is a liability as the bank owes someone money. If a bank lends money to a home buyer, this is an asset to the bank. With a loan, the bank has a guarantee from the customer to pay the sum back over time, and they have a mortgage on the property just in case. (The mortgage gives them the right to own the property in the event of a default.) There is a risk that this asset does not return its full value (e.g., if the loan defaults or the market collapses and the bank can only recover a portion of the loan). Depending on the quality of the loan (e.g., if the loan is for less than 60% of the value of the property, it is considered low risk) the RWA weighting varies. For mortgages, it can range from 35% to 100% of the value of the loan (less is better), depending on how risky the loan is. When looking at the loan to value ratio (LVR, covered in the next chapter), lower LVRs have a lower RWA weighting.

When a bank takes money from an individual (e.g., as a term deposit, or through a savings or transaction account), it has a few options of what to do with it. If it keeps the money in a safe instrument, the RWA weighting is 0%. This is a good thing from APRA's point of view, and these investments are not counted in the RWA.

Example of 0% weighted RWA instruments:

- Cash in ESAs
- Notes and coins
- Gold bullion held by the ADI or in depositaries
- Australian Government instruments (treasury notes and bonds, etc.)
- Overseas central bank bonds, state government bonds and local government bonds (those rated AA- or higher, about 30 countries, all Australian states and territories).

More risky investments have lower credit ratings and higher RWAs.

The disadvantage of low RWA instruments is that there is no return on investment. So to increase income or to make a profit (which is good for share prices and helps increase CET1 due to retained earnings and the capacity to get more equity), banks tend to balance their investments with riskier lending.

Big banks, under the authority of APRA, use alternative modelling to derive their total RWA. This is called an internal ratings-based (IRB) calculation. The Murray Report (2014) criticised the method as it led to the big banks assessing their risk weighting at a considerably lower weighting than those that used the standard model. This could have had a negative impact on big versus small bank competition, and also lower capital adequacy that was already regarded as insufficient by international standards. The report urged regulators to encourage better risk management of loans and requested they raise the average internal ratings-based calculations of the big banks to be in line with standard risk weightings used by the smaller banks. APRA found that banks using the IRB model were weighting residential mortgages at an RWA rate of 16%, much lower than banks using a standard weighting, so they asked IRB banks to increase their RWA average on mortgages to 25%.

In July 2019, APRA asked the so-called systemically important banks (i.e., the Big Four) to raise their total capital ratios by 3% by 2024. This may increase to 5% thereafter. In addition to this guidance, APRA placed specific risk mitigation measures on the CBA as a result of its prudential inquiry (below), asking it to increase capital by $1 billion in 2018, and instructed ANZ and NAB to increase their capitals by $500 million in 2019 based on self-reported assessments, as the three sought over the years to improve their risk management. It is likely that Westpac will be impacted heavily as well, particularly due to its IFTI failures in 2019.

Capital funding, particularly of the big banks, has been increased by the need to increase capital ratios. In 2019, equity made up 8% of the Big Four banks' funding (see *Figure 8*). The banks were required to issue shares, resulting in a lower return on equity. The Basel requirements have meant that banks have needed to shift a portion of lending to lower performance home lending.[60]

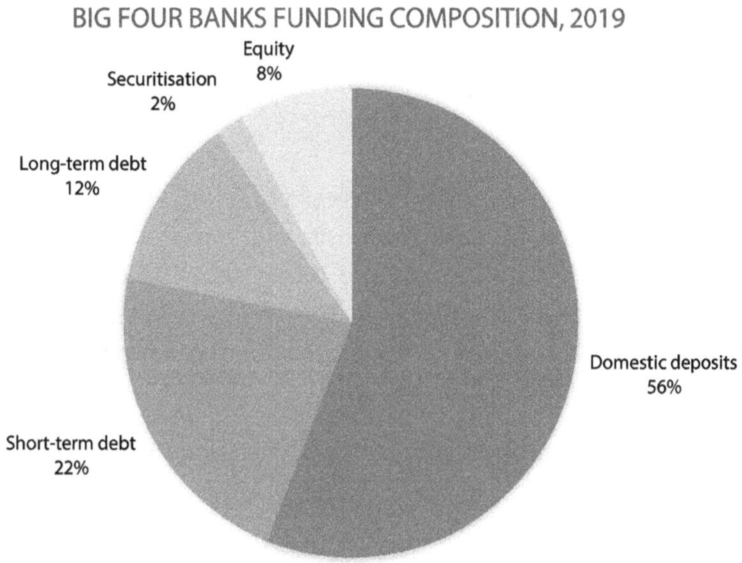

***Figure 8*. Funding composition of the Big Four banks (2019 estimate).**
Source: RBA/ACCC.[61]

Banks managed to find a way around the complex calculations involved in capital adequacy.[62] During the GFC, while maintaining adequate capital, banks leveraged around these ratios by exposing themselves to risks that were not included in the original adequacy formulae. Complex derivatives allowed the banks to conceal risks from the regulators. Basel III introduced a minimum leverage ratio of 3%. APRA defined the ratio as:

$$\frac{Tier\ 1\ Capital}{Exposure\ Measure} \geq 3\%$$

where Tier 1 Capital was essentially shareholder equity, and the Exposure Measure was a sum of the full asset exposure of the bank (e.g., loans), including balance sheet exposures, off-balance sheet non-market exposures, derivatives, and security financing transactions. Put simply, a bank can only lend out a maximum of 33 times its shareholder equity plus retained earnings. If the leverage ratio was lower than 3% after achieving capital adequacy,

---

[60] Atkin

[61] Wilson 2019

[62] BIS 2017

the bank needed to either exit from the exposure (over time), or increase shareholder equity, generally by issuing more shares. This further put negative pressure on the return on equity mentioned above.

As mentioned earlier, banks used an internal ratings-based (IRB) approach to risk-weighted asset (RWA) calculations which was criticised in the Murray Report (2014) as, in some cases, it could be used to obfuscate risk rather than exposing it. In 2018, ING joined Macquarie Bank and the Big Four as an IRB certified bank. APRA also announced in 2018 it was working with other banks that wanted an IRB system. Later, APRA, in an apparent attempt to dissuade banks from using the internal ratings-based approach to lower their adequacy requirements, set the minimum leverage ratio to 3.5% for these internal ratings-based ADIs.

Liquidity Coverage

Basel III also required banks to hold sufficient liquidity to cover 30 days of payments stress; that is, enough liquidity to cover cash payments and support settlements. As part of its liquidity guidelines, in APS 210, APRA required that smaller ADIs (those with low systemic importance, low liquidity risk or as otherwise deemed by APRA) have a minimum liquidity holding of 9% of its liabilities in APRA-sanctioned liquid assets and that for large ADIs, the full force of the Basel III recommendations apply:

- A three-year funding strategy that must be shared with APRA. ADIs should be ready to get funds when required.
- For local banks, a 100% liquidity coverage ratio (LCR) that was based on covering 30 days of payments in high-quality liquid assets (HQLA):
    - Minimum 60% in cash and ESA balances, and the highest quality unquestionably liquid sovereign assets.
    - Maximum 40% in other sovereign assets and corporate bonds that had a track record of liquidity even during stressed market conditions.

Net Stable Funding

The final major provision of Basel III was the net stable funding ratio, which ensured that prolonged liquidity pressures (greater than 30 days) could be met through more stable sources of funding.

In APS 210, APRA defined this as:

$$\frac{\textit{Available Stable Funding}}{\textit{Required Stable Funding}} \geq 100\%$$

Available stable funding is a weighted sum of liabilities (i.e., sources of funding such as shareholder equity or deposits) held by the bank. For example, regulatory capital (Tier 1 capital or shareholder equity) was weighted at 100%, term deposits for longer than a year at 95% (these needed to be difficult to break), term deposits for less than a year at 90%, and deposits used to make payments (i.e., transaction accounts) at 50%. Other liabilities, such as derivatives, short positions and open maturity positions, are not counted. The relatively high weighting of transaction accounts was reflective of consumer behaviour with consumers tending to keep money in these accounts longer (i.e., statistically, at least 50% of balances at any point in time would stay in the account for a year or more).

Required stable funding is a weighted sum of assets. For example, liquid assets of the highest quality that are unencumbered and have less than six months to maturity are weighted at 5% or 10%. The weighting increases for liquid assets of lesser quality and that have 6 to 12 months to maturity. For short-term retail credit card debt, the weighting is 50%, for mortgages over a year it is 65%, and for performing loans for a year or more (e.g., personal loans) it is 85%. For other assets that are encumbered for a year or more, such as non-performing loans, the weighting is 100%. Cash and central bank deposits do not count towards required stable funding.

APRA Prudential Inquiry into the Commonwealth Bank of Australia (2017)

After a string of issues with CBA, including the Storm Financial margin loan issue in 2008, financial planning controversies, the non-payout of insurance claims, the AUSTRAC IDM TTR issue, and credit card issues, CBA voluntarily participated in a review (conducted by APRA) into governance, accountability and culture. A number of recommendations were made in the APRA Prudential Inquiry,[63] which are also important for other banks, essentially with regard to the need for senior executives to understand risks and maintain a focus on details. The report is essential reading for executives in any bank.

The report was widely circulated among CBA staff, but feedback was that the problem was not reporting, raising or understanding risks, but in commercial decisions to accept risks made at the highest levels of the organisation.

As a result of the inquiry, CBA took general action to improve its reporting and was required by APRA to increase its capital reserves by $1 billion. Twenty-nine banks were asked to review both the report and their own risk management policies, and to identify any gaps. ANZ and NAB declared significant gaps and were instructed to hold $500 million in additional capital as they remediated their risks.

Criticism

APRA's attempts at a transparent framework, despite good efforts, have failed to provide consistency. Perhaps, this is the nature of the beast. A lot of regulation is subject to interpretation and variation rather than science or proceduralisation. The amount of discretionary power in legislation is significant in practice. For example, capital adequacy calculations of the Big Four banks are not published. The capital adequacy baseline is increasingly getting tightened, and the difficulty of starting a new bank in the current era is considerable. In 2018, the Productivity Commission criticised the inability of smaller institutions to properly assess the risk of their lending assets due to gaps in guidance from regulators.

[63] Laker

Despite attempts to allow flexible definitions of products, regulation has had the effect of standardising conventional products in the market. Banks are reluctant to introduce exotic or innovative products, due to the conservative approach of the regulations (which themselves are the result of banks overstepping safe practices and obfuscating risk, e.g., during the GFC). We have very little variety of core bank products in the retail market now compared to the 1800s.

The free market works best when there is no concentration of supply and demand; that is, a market with no monopolies. Nonetheless, regulatory restrictions and high compliance requirements make it difficult to establish competitive banks outside of the big banks. While APRA has explicitly raised the bar for big banks, the inability of smaller banks to achieve capital adequacy hampers their ability to make a profit. Without good profits, it is difficult to grow and without growth, it is hard to obtain shareholder equity, which, in turn, prevents growth of capital adequacy. This is a vicious cycle that impacts small Australian banks. In contrast, larger banks, which have a longer history of retaining earnings and demonstrating profits, are better able to get additional equity funding from the market, which frees their balance sheet to allow more profitable lending.

The long list of ADI license holders should not mislead readers into thinking there is broad competition. According to KPMG in 2018, 82% of lending was concentrated in the big banks. The senate Inquiry into Competition within the Australian Banking Sector noted banking was concentrated in the Big Four at 84% in 2008, among the highest within developed economies. Sure enough, they had the highest profit before tax too. The absolute value of lending continues to rise higher than Consumer Price Index or GDP growth, and the measures taken by regulators continue to drive a wedge between the well-established and less successful banks.

APRA regulations were reactionary — reluctant to implement change without a parliamentary or independent mandate, with an acknowledged limited ability to regulate. Perhaps they were reluctant to rock the boat — for, unfettered, APRA requirements could overwhelm banks, curtail lending, and not just impact bank share prices but the stock market and the economy in general. In banking, created as an adjunct to the RBA but without the broad public or legislative mandate to exert independent fearlessness as its counterparts such as the RBA, ASIC, AUSTRAC, the ACCC and the ATO, APRA was weak.

The Murray Report of 2014 found that Australian banks have low capital adequacy, which exhibits this weakness in plain sight. APRA should have protected against this. The penalties and capital edging are not as strong as they should be. Politically, however, a change in regulatory capital that drops bank share prices overnight and reduces superannuation balances is an unpalatable joust of bravery that few would appreciate and understand. No prime minister wants to suffer Ben Chifley's fate.

APRA's report into CBA[64] focused on the risk culture. Unclear accountabilities, a lack of sting in remuneration, too much collaboration and lack of oversight were some of the findings. The issues were much deeper and the report may not have had the desired effect. CBA, for example, removed collaboration from its core value statement as a result of the report,

---

[64] Laker

a bizarre outcome indeed, leading to the opposite effect of what could have prevented the issues. In addition, there were other causes,

- In the quest for profit and speed to market, risks are taken. More often than not (because risks generally have less than a 50% chance of realisation), the gamble pays off. People who take these risks are rewarded and, as luck would have it, they end up getting promoted, playing with higher stakes until their luck runs out — and it always runs out.

- Like gamblers, everyone knows the risks: in the case of a casino, the house wins 2%-10% of the money gambled, yet casinos are full of people who think they will not lose but come out on top, multiplying their bet. Banks have a mature risk process. Some executives just weighed personal elevation and saw their personal potential gain above the risk to the organisation's reputation. Like a child running after a ball down a street, risk analysis was not going to stop them.

- Organisations reward risk takers, and even if the project or initiative ends in disaster (like IDM, Storm Financial and credit card income insurance), the ultimate responsible executives can both accept credit and spin failures so there is little repercussion for bad judgement or expediency, in CBA's case, promoting these executives. It is disappointing this point was left out from APRA and the royal commission reports.

- The high levels of staff turnover lead to a loss of corporate knowledge. It is necessary for a sufficient quota of executives to have experiences to balance more innovative risk takers. Many executives came from growth-centric consulting organisations and failed to unilaterally exert this balance. Their input is useful but, if lopsided, can end in disaster as we saw. This experience is not just an issue at the top; loss of expertise has meant system knowledge has diminished as well, contributing to a lower ability to execute.

- A failure to properly architect and design solutions is a byproduct of rapid innovation — good design and architecture is a process that is increasingly being neglected in the desire to go-to-market quickly. This increases risks and creates technical debt, in this case, perhaps a debt of $1.7 billion that could have been avoided.

On top of AUSTRAC's fines, APRA imposed a capital penalty (a higher capital reserve). This was hardly a punishment, given the already low levels of capital reserves held by the banks, and the fact that eventually all the majors were subject to similar provisions.

In short, risks and rewards are a delicate balance, and APRA's job is not to achieve perfection but to make things a little better than before, for what is it that makes a capital adequacy ratio of 4.5% safe and 4% unsafe?

With the onset of COVID-19, acknowledging its limited ability to supervise, and perhaps a growing visibility of the tidal wave of risk that was approaching the market, granting new ADI licenses was suspended by APRA. Competition is nice to have but, in the final analysis, banking stability was more important.

Flaws in the Risk-based Approach

If we knew all the risks of crossing a road, perhaps we would never cross a road.

A risk-based approach, like that adopted by the FATF, AUSTRAC, Basel and APRA, sees the world as a series of risks that need to be mitigated.

One of the reasons for the stagnation in innovation in the banking sector is this risk-centric approach. Existing products were too entrenched to be taken off the market and new ventures were fraught with risk. The lack of a scientific method to measure and solution mitigations meant it was too hard to try new things.

One fundamental issue is that banks created new products. Not only was the risk obfuscated for the consumer (or buyer), but it was also obfuscated for the regulator. In turn, to compensate, the regulator codified the products and, while not preventing innovation, this discouraged a favourable risk treatment of new products and their integration so it discouraged innovative approaches.

Risk analysis is a good way to ensure there are no gaps in the system, but what is required (as will see later) is a low-risk system itself, and then risks can be analysed and reviewed, and improvements suggested for that system. Risk is never the ultimate basis for new activity; it is an aspect, albeit an important one.

If the low-risk system is rigid or mandated, like risk-weighted asset (RWA) calculations in the capital ratios or the Financial Claims Scheme, it limits the capacity to attempt new products and limits competition.

Further, as we saw, problems were very complex. A risk specialist cannot fix or know what the full implications of a complex Intelligent Deposit Machine bug are in the middle of the night. A risk policy that has worked for a century may not work for a black swan event. And black swan events happen more often in this time of significant change, increasing global commerce and mass disruption.

Many of the processes in payments have been stable for many years, and good measures have been instituted in the industry by the regulators. Yet, these days, many decisions are based on fear, uncertainty and doubt. Regulators eventually come up with a system and, rather than maintaining that fear and preventing innovation, perhaps it is ok to accept best efforts in the hope that better systems can be implemented over time through the process of continuous improvement.

Australian Securities and Investments Commission

In 1991, the Australian Securities Commission replaced the National Companies and Securities Commission. Prior to 1991, due to an omission in the constitution (intentional or otherwise), every state had its own company laws. This caused inefficiency and ambiguity, and needed to change.

In a rare move of solidarity, company registration was centralised from the states to the federal government and, while technically corporation law is the domain of the state, each state passed almost identical laws handing power to the Australian Securities Commission.

In 1998, the commission took responsibility for consumer protection in the financial sector and was renamed the Australian Securities and Investments Commission (ASIC).

ASIC's primary responsibilities include registering companies and business names, and the regulation of investment in them (through governing market operators, e.g., the ASX, as well as initial public offerings and crowdfunding). It is the broad-based regulator for the corporate sector, including auditors and the financial services industry.

Financial Services Regulation

How a financial institution engages with customers is generally covered by ASIC through its application of financial services regulation.

ASIC has a number of regulatory guides, and organisations are required to adhere to these in terms of policy, licensing and regulations.

An Australian Financial Services License is required by organisations that provide financial services as defined by the Corporations Act (2001). These organisations offer financial products, provide payment services and offer financial advice. License holders are generally required to provide a Financial Services Guide (FSG) outlining terms and conditions, rights and disclosures, fees for services, and procedures for handling complaints. If they sell products, they are required to issue a Product Disclosure Statement.

The National Credit Code (originally the Uniform Consumer Credit Code) was established by the National Consumer Credit Protection Act 2009. It has been active since 2012 and mainly covers lending to private consumers. ASIC oversees this code.

An Australian Credit License is required by organisations that provide credit, and also covers the Specialist Credit Card Institution(SCCI) licenses previously provided to ADIs by APRA.

Financial advisers need to be qualified and to have completed training in order to offer specific advice or recommend products. ASIC provides guidelines and registers advisers through an Australian Financial Services License holder. ASIC also oversees the Future of Financial Advice reforms.

ePayments Code

The Electronic Funds Transfer Code of Conduct, established in 1986 under the Trade Practices Commission, introduced a number of safeguards for consumers. These were later updated to form the ePayments Code in 2011, a voluntary code administered by ASIC.

In essence, the code provides a minimum standard for electronic payments and is intended to provide consumer protection. If, somehow, an electronic payment makes its way to an unintended recipient, either by mistake or by fraud, the onus is on the recipient to prove entitlement to that payment. If the recipient is non-cooperative, and there is no money in the account, the money may be lost. If more than seven months pass before a complaint is lodged, the recipient needs to agree before a refund is given. The ePayments Code is implemented separately by each electronic payment solution, of which there are many, including:

- Visa & Mastercard: Chargeback
- Direct Entry: APCA BECS Procedures

- NPP: NPPA Procedures
- BPAY: BPAY Procedures
- SWIFT: Payment cancellation process and messages as well as the GPI Stop and Recall facility
- PayPal: PayPal disputes (possibly the only solution that allows an end customer to lodge a dispute electronically).

School Banking

After a number of controversies in the school banking sector were exposed by the media, CHOICE, the Royal Commission into Misconduct in the Banking, and the Superannuation and Financial Services Industry, ASIC announced an Inquiry into School Banking in 2018.

In 2019, ASIC circulated a consultation paper to collect views on school banking. It wanted to know the benefits of teaching financial literacy, offset against the perceived benefits to a bank.

Within CBA (probably the dominant school banking provider with its famous Dollarmites account), school banking was viewed as a social service, a loss-making venture.

While there was an understanding that eventually young bankers were more likely to stay with the bank of their childhood, this foresight was well beyond the six-month, three-year or even five-year time horizons of most executives, so many in the industry felt that greater regulatory attention would be detrimental to this sector and to the cause of financial literacy.

Australian Competition and Consumer Commission

The Australian Competition and Consumer Commission (ACCC) was set up in 1995 after merging the Trade Practices Commission (1974) with the Prices Surveillance Authority (1983).

The ACCC's purpose was to ensure that fair competition exists in the Australian workplace. They do not have the resources to take up every issue, and generally focus their investigation and action on what is in the public interest, which is often shaped by political forces.

A number of inquiries were performed by the ACCC into payments and banking, as requested by the government.

The Residential Mortgage Price Inquiry (2018)[65] was initiated by the parliamentary Annual Review into the Four Major Banks inquiry, and found that headline interest rates were discretionary and frequently discounted, which led to opaqueness and stifled competition. It also found that new borrowers paid less, on average, than existing borrowers. The report identified accommodative and synchronised pricing behaviour (without the report using the words "pricing collusion" — collusion being against the law), and identified APRA's inadvertent use of an interest-only benchmark to further attract such behaviour. Non-Big Four banks had diverse approaches to pricing.

[65] ACCC 2018

The report noted that APRA's capital adequacy requirements had exacerbated challenges faced by smaller banks, preventing them from providing more loans to compete with the bigger banks.

The Foreign Currency Conversion Services Inquiry (2019) found that, while prices were difficult to compare, the Big Four banks charged consumers more for international money transfers and other foreign exchange products than other banks did. Payment cards (scheme debit and credit) are cheaper than travel cards, foreign cash notes and international money transfers. AML/CTF allowed banks to de-bank competitive providers and was a significant threat.

The Home Loan Pricing Inquiry (2020) found that, when home loan interest rates fell, banks received revenue from the time lag. Lower interest rates meant lower revenue for banks so, to increase profits, it was necessary to not pass on the full rate cut. The cost of funds was mainly driven by the official cash rate; however, there were also other components. In 2018, funding costs increased; these were initially absorbed but later passed on. These costs declined in 2019 but the decline was not passed on.

Australian Financial Complaints Authority

The Australian Financial Complaints Authority is the industry ombudsman. Financial services organisations in Australia (including banks) are required to be members and pay their dues, in accordance with ASIC regulations, giving the Australian Financial Complaints Authority legislative powers. Once a determination is made, it is binding subject to a court appeal.

The industry recommends that complaints initially be dealt with informally and directly by the financial institution then, if necessary, as an official complaint, following the organisation's processes. If an issue is unresolved, a complaint can be lodged with the Australian Financial Complaints Authority, which then attempts to negotiate and may make a binding determination and/or appoint an independent assessor. The Australian Financial Complaints Authority publishes statistics on their resolution outcomes, which is commendable. Most complaints are resolved through negotiation. If an issue proceeds to determination, over two thirds are in the favour of the financial institution. There remains a significant portion (7-14%) of complainants dissatisfied after going through the process. Whether the complainants have an unreasonable expectation, or the industry outcome is unsatisfactory, cannot be ascertained as, globally, few organisations are as open with their reporting.

Productivity Commission

The Productivity Commission, part of the Australian Treasury, was established in its current form in 1998. It has a broad remit, and operates essentially through inquiries and research. There have been three inquiries of note, described below.

Availability of Capital, 1991

A prior agency to the Productivity Commission, known as the Industry Commission, inquired into the Availability of Capital.[66] Prime Minister Paul Keating used the report to open the banking sector in Australia to foreign banks. In hindsight, foreign banks have had a limited impact on banking services in Australia with the Big Four well-entrenched 30 years later. The inquiry also recommended that the government pull out of providing financial services and supported the float of CBA.

Data Availability and Use, 2016-2017

The Data Availability and Use inquiry spawned the open data initiative and the Consumer Data Right (the right to access information). This is discussed below in more detail. The inquiry looked at how consumer access to data could improve innovation and productivity. Open banking was one aspect, with a view to looking at utility organisations and other industries.

Competition in the Australian Financial System, 2017-2018

The Competition in the Australian Financial System inquiry covered a broad range of topics including payments. Some of the recommendations were:[67]

- APRA's Capital Adequacy Risk-Weighted Assets (APS 112) schedule of products was light, and banks needed more guidance to support the variety of products in the market, especially for lending products.
- Card interchange should be banned. (This will be covered below.)
- ACCC and RBA's PSB should look into whether regulations favour three-party card schemes and whether merchant service fees (MSFs) should be regulated.
- Merchants should be able to choose how to route transactions (least cost routing).
- The ePayments Code should be made mandatory.
- Purchased Payment Facility regulation should be reviewed to introduce a tier that did not require APRA supervision.
- Access to NPP should be opened by the RBA PSB. Of fintechs surveyed, 80% were unconvinced they would be let in, and existing participants had a conflict of interest in allowing them into the system.
- The functionality of NPP should be improved. As we will see, banks were not interested in innovation using this platform and, as such, agreed functionality was lagging behind in implementation.

[66] Banks, Gary

[67] Harris

Office of the Australian Information Commissioner

The Office of the Australian Information Commissioner includes the Privacy Commissioner, who is responsible for ensuring organisations adhere to privacy laws and the Consumer Data Right (including freedom of information, open banking, etc.).

Significant corporate data breaches need to be notified to the commissioner as do complaints that have not been resolved by the ombudsman.

Australian Taxation Office

The Australian Taxation Office (ATO) is responsible for collecting tax revenue. The ATO affects the banks in a number of ways, as described below.

Tax File Numbers

Interest on bank accounts is generally taxable. Customers are required to declare their tax file number (TFN) to their bank. If no TFN is provided, the bank is required to withhold maximum tax and then pay this to the ATO. While TFNs existed in the back office of the ATO earlier, as a means of internally identifying customers, they were made more visible to customers around 1971 with the introduction of computers to aid in the processing of (at the time) six million transactions. With the failure of the Australia Card, a national ID scheme proposed in 1985-1987, Government Treasurer Paul Keating strengthened TFN laws, requiring that it be declared to various institutions, such as share registries, employers and financial institutions. (If undeclared, withholding tax would be deducted and would need to be claimed back.)

The purpose of TFNs was to match individuals to their unique tax identity. These days, with people requiring to be identified at banks and sophisticated data matching capabilities at the ATO, the ATO should be able to match identity through other means. The overhead of declaration and collecting TFNs may be unnecessary, and could be achieved through a more convenient centralised system through the MyGov initiative. A centralised system would also protect against non-declaration and identity theft where people could use another person's TFN. The non-declaration of TFNs, while attracting the highest tax rate, is little disincentive for the rich, who can use it to hide excess income, to avoid income and assets being picked up for income tests, spouse maintenance and other purposes.

» NOTE

In 1983, boat designer Ben Lexcen developed a winged keel for Alan Bond's yacht Australia II, which famously won the America's Cup race. The first time a nation other than the United States had won since 1851. The day was declared spontaneously an unofficial holiday by the jubilant Prime Minister Bob Hawke, who famously said,

"Any boss who sacks anyone for not turning up today is a bum!" Anyone and everyone who had anything to do with the 1983 victory was a national hero, especially the mild-mannered Lexcen. During the Australia Card debate, shortly before the next race in 1987, Lexcen, who had designed the new defending yachts Australia III and IV, said that if Australia introduced the card, he would leave the country. The debate ended. There were two things Australians never saw again: the America's Cup and the Australia Card.

Capital Gains Tax

Selling investments, such as managed funds, shares and property, attracts capital gains tax. These gains were generally declared by the taxpayer. The ATO is interested in such transactions of bank customers, and of the banks themselves.

Goods and Services Tax

The goods and services tax is a tax on most payments or services. When first introduced by the 1991-1993 opposition party leader John Hewson in his Fightback! initiative, it was ridiculed in an infamous example about cake baking. Food was exempt from the tax if not cooked. There were also exemptions for pastry chefs but not for food outlets, and there were complications with the decorations. These caused confusion among voters, and were successfully and entertainingly used by Paul Keating to help win the 1993 election.

The goods and services tax was later successfully introduced by Prime Minister John Howard and Government Treasurer Peter Costello, coming into effect in 2000. They were much better prepared with answers to the cake question; however, the GST implementation remains complicated. Raw food ingredients are GST-free, but bottled water sold in a restaurant incurs GST.

In financial services, the situation was more complex. Fees to maintain a bank account or a loan (including credit cards) are GST-free, but other charges such as interchange and merchant service fees (MSFs) incur GST.

Gold, silver and platinum as an investment (at or above 99% purity) are considered GST-free. Jewellery, however, is not regardless of the purity.

Goods and services tax, originally charged at 10%, could be used by companies to claim a tax credit and when they sold their products, they would pay the difference to the ATO.

›› NOTE

One scam was quite intriguing. Tax invoices were required for companies to get an input tax credit (i.e., a GST refund from the government). However, there was no onus on the payer company to check the invoice was genuine. So some criminal syndicates issued fake tax invoices for scrap gold to refiners

Gold Jewelry (GST)

Investment-grade Gold (NO GST)

that purchased the scrap. Scrap gold incurred GST, but once melted into an investment grade block it was GST-free. The tax invoices (which were paid for by cash) were used to claim tax credits, but the refiners sold the goods as GST-free, making money out of the scam through claiming back the GST, which was never paid by the crime syndicates to start with. It was alleged that the refiners had some part to play in the scam.

In a sign that the ATO policy is inexact, and evolving, for some strange reason cryptocurrency sales were originally subject to GST, before this ruling was reversed in 2017 after the Digital Currency — Game Changer or Bit Player inquiry.

Goods and services tax remains a difficult bookkeeping undertaking for many businesses. Often, each receipt needs to be checked for GST-incurring and GST-free amounts, and a big bill needs to be paid at the end of each reporting cycle.

Company Tax and Franking Credits

Large companies, including banks, pay about 30% tax on retained earnings. If a company pays out a dividend after tax, the tax paid by shareholders can be claimed as a franking credit to offset other tax or claim a refund. Banks normally pay franking credits.

Major Bank Levy

In 2017, a major bank levy was imposed on large banks that caught the Big Four in its net, plus Macquarie Bank. The levy was introduced at 0.06% of total liabilities (i.e., deposits) held by a bank. The levy was opposed by the banks, especially through the Australian Banking Association, who pointed out that, unlike other large Australian corporations, banks do not structure their affairs through offshore tax havens and already pay a relatively high company tax rate compared to other countries so do not deserve to pay higher taxes.

Effect of Tax on Payments and the Economy

In smaller segments of the economy, non-declaration of income can evade income tax and GST. In order to do this more covertly, cash is used, hence the terms *cash economy* and *black money*. This practice perhaps explains the high volume of large-denomination notes in the economy relative to the more useful smaller-denomination notes used for typical cash purchases. Goods and services are cheaper and receipts, if given, are with pen and paper.

Capital gains, dividends and interest income are treated similar to salary income, though longer-term investments that increase in capital value are generally favoured by investors over other forms of income (due to a capital gains tax discount of 50% for investments held for over one year). This practice tends to encourage long-term investments away from bank accounts and deposits. Net capital gains tax losses, on the other hand, do not offset income earnings and must be carried forward for most people. This is an inconsistency in the taxation system.

Goods and services tax (known as a broad-based tax) made sense as a rationalisation of a myriad of taxes that existed prior to its introduction. However, many of those taxes were narrow-based taxes used to recover government expenses, such as subsidies or other public costs on motor vehicles, clothing, fuel and cigarettes. Many of these items continue to be taxed and stamp duty on property still exists. Goods and services tax is not a direct tax on corporations, but discourages sale of goods and also consumption by consumers. (Perhaps this is a good thing as it encourages investment and saving rather than spending.) It impacts the poor (who spend a greater percentage of their income) more than the rich. On the face of it, GST acts against expansionist monetary and fiscal policy, and is cumbersome for businesses. It is a double tax on the earnings of workers.

Data Matching

In order to ensure that taxpayers are properly filling in their tax forms, the ATO collects data from a number of sources. In recent times, this collection also aids taxpayers to pre-fill tax returns.

One of the loopholes in the data matching capability is that the ATO has better data feeds from bigger institutions, and may not get information from smaller institutions on a regular basis though, by law, they are entitled to ask for it. This means transacting through smaller institutions is less likely to receive the attention of the ATO than transacting through bigger ones.

Major banks and fund managers provide information to the ATO about investment income. The ATO also receives information from merchant facility providers, administrators of specialised payment systems, cryptocurrency providers, shared economy providers (e.g., rideshare companies), online stores, contracting agencies and other sources of income.

The Foreign Account Tax Compliance Act

The Foreign Account Tax Compliance Act (FATCA) of the US 2010 is possibly the most internationally intrusive law of any single country. The act required foreign banks to identify and report on US persons, otherwise payments out of the US to that foreign financial institution would be deducted withholding tax at 30%. The costs for international banks to implement these measures were significant. Australia implemented reciprocal legislation recognising and enforcing the provisions of the US FATCA.

In 2018, as part of a sting operation, a Hungarian national working at a bank conspired to hide the identity of a US national (actually an undercover agent) and opened a number of accounts where the US national was not declared. The Hungarian was successfully extradited to the US without technically committing an offence in US jurisdiction, contrary to the norms of international law.

Clearly, it would not be scalable for every country to implement the same measures. The same year the law was passed, a more sensible international regime was established.

» NOTE

Most countries regard a taxpayer as a resident for tax purposes if they spent at least six months in the country in a given year. In the US, an individual needs to file a return if they are a US citizen or a Green Card (permanent visa) holder, even if they never lived in the US. In almost all cases, tax paid in another country can offset the tax needed to be paid in the home country. After the FATCA, many Americans surrendered their citizenship.

Common Reporting Standard

Tax sharing treaties have existed since before federations between Australia and other countries. Spurred to action by FATCA, through an initiative of the OECD and the G20, over 100 countries have agreed a Common Reporting Standard and many now share data between tax authorities. The ATO is part of this, and exchanges information about residents and their finances with other countries. In Australia, thanks to lawmakers and the ATO, FATCA and the Common Reporting Standard are largely identical for financial institutions and are intermediated by the ATO as part of a treaty with the US. Penalties for non-conformance are severe but, fortunately for Australians, prosecution and penalisation would take place in Australia.

The name, date of birth, foreign tax identification number, address, account number and account balance of each identified foreign person needs to be reported to the ATO, which will then forward it on to the relevant foreign government.

Another international standard of the OECD and the G20 is the Country by Country Reporting Standard. This standard was instituted to combat base erosion profit shifting after the GFC. A generally large multinational company will set up a nominal office in a low-tax country and move profits from its profit-making higher-taxation jurisdictions to avoid paying unnecessary tax. The Country by Country Reporting Standard applies to Significant Global Entities with a global income of $1 billion or more, which must provide a Country by Country Reporting Standard report detailing their local and global operations (through a local file and master file) to the local tax authority, which in Australia is the ATO. The files are then shared between tax authorities of countries where the company operates. The files use an XML format and, due to the large number of such entities in Australia, are a standard feature of many high-end accounting systems.

The general international tax philosophy is that the profit of a multinational company in one country should be taxed at that country's rate so as to avoid double taxation.

» NOTE

The Panama Papers of 2015, a leaked library of 11.5 million documents from a large offshore law firm, revealed how extensive offshore companies were with over 200 000 entities listed. One thousand four hundred of these entities were Australian and over one hundred of these were subject to compliance action by the ATO.

Banks and Tax

The big banks pride themselves on being good taxpayers. Besides their own tax levy, they are subject to corporate taxation like other businesses and, due to their public and political profile, they would rather not be known to be avoiding paying tax.

In 2019, CBA clarified its tax debt over a research and development claim during its core banking modernisation program, quietly paying back an undisclosed amount.

Administrative Appeals Tribunal

Decisions of government departments can have a significant impact on private individuals and companies. Often, they appear to carry the force of legislation, without necessarily being enacted with the same rigour or due process. The Administrative Appeals Tribunal acts to provide an accessible point of review where federal government agency decisions can be challenged. State governments have similar tribunals.

One decision was that, in June 2020, in reviewing an unfavourable decision made by the ATO for Seribu Pty Ltd, Seribu argued that the favourable tax treatment of foreign currency losses should be applied to cryptocurrency, which the ATO denied. The Administrative Appeals Tribunal followed the letter of the law as it stood on the day in supporting the ATO's decision with an indication that a more progressive treatment of cryptocurrencies "is a question for law reform that will be answered by others on another day."[68]

Courts

In Australia, all determinations made by a bank or regulator can be taken to or appealed in a court of law. Banks, like most institutions, generally avoid courts, and the Australian Financial Complaints Authority was designed to make it easier for consumers to take action and to remove workload from the court system, especially for smaller courts.

---

[68] AAT

Under state law, a number of courts exist including tribunals, local courts, district courts and supreme courts. Under federal law, there is the Federal Circuit Court, Federal Court and the High Court of Australia (literally Australia's highest court, since the Australia Act of 1986 removed appeals to the British Privy Council). There have been a number of cases in these courts involving regulators, schemes and the Big Four banks.

4.

BANKS

THE MOST IMPORTANT PART OF PAYMENTS, as we will discover, are the banks. Without them, in modern times, people would be unable to make payments. More than that, as we shall see, money itself became available largely due to private banks.

The technical regulatory term for *bank*, as we saw, is authorised deposit-taking institution (ADI), with the actual name bank generally reserved for the large ADIs.

Since 1999, there has been a net decline of over 50% in the total number of ADIs, but a marked increase in the number of banks (*Table 2*).

Appendix 1 illustrates the complex landscape of banks and rationalisations.

Table 2.

Changing landscape of ADIs (data courtesy of APRA)[69]

Sector	1999	2004	2009	2013	2017	2021
Domestic and mutual banks	15	14	14	21	33	48
Credit unions and building societies	241	188	125	95	58	36
Foreign bank subsidiaries	11	10	9	8	7	7
Foreign bank branches	25	28	35	40	44	48
Other ADIs	4	7	8	7	6	5
Total ADIs	**296**	**247**	**191**	**171**	**148**	**144**

The Big Four

Over time, a handful of institutions came to dominate the Australian financial scene. Around 1990, the government said that it would not approve takeovers that reduced the number of Australian retail banks below the current status quo. This policy became known as the Four Pillars policy and has been held as political policy for over three decades. The Big Four banks in question are:

- Westpac Banking Corporation (WBC):

  Founded in 1816 as the Bank of New South Wales, Australia's first bank. Headquartered in Sydney. Acquisitions included Bankers Trust (Australia) and St George Bank. Also spun off brands through a rebranding of St George branches outside NSW as Bank of Melbourne and BankSA. Acquired mortgage broker RAMS.

- Australia and New Zealand Banking Group (ANZ):

  ANZ formed from the 1951 merger of two banks originating in London: the Bank of Australasia (founded in 1835) and the Union Bank of Australia (1837). As we will see, this is often the bank to break ranks, especially with regards to payment systems and policy. Headquartered in Melbourne.

[69] Byrnes, APRA c. 2020

- National Australia Bank (NAB):

  NAB formed from the 1982 merger of the National Bank of Australasia (founded in 1858) and the Commercial Banking Company of Sydney. Acquisitions include MLC. Launched UBank as a digital bank. Also headquartered in Melbourne.

- Commonwealth Bank of Australia (CBA):

  Founded in 1911, CBA is Australia's largest bank and was originally the central bank. CBA became privatised in 1991 in one of the more rewarding Government IPOs in Australian history. Eventually, CBA took over Colonial First State, Auckland Savings Bank in New Zealand, Bankwest, Aussie Home Loans and others. Its Commsec share trading platform has achieved market dominance. CBA boasts a broad customer base as a legacy of being the first national savings bank. Headquartered in Sydney.

In the Productivity Commission's 2018 report into Competition in the Australian Financial System, the commissioner suggested the Four Pillars policy (which is separate to the ACCC and other controls) was redundant as it had the effect of protecting the weaker members of the Big Four.

» NOTE

While one could be forgiven for thinking that the Big Four are part of Australia's constitution; however, this concentration in banking is relatively recent. In 1990, a large insurer, National Mutual, attempted to merge with ANZ Bank. Treasurer Paul Keating blocked it, saying that there should be no mergers between the four banks and the two big insurers, National Mutual and AMP. This became known as the Six Pillars policy. In 1995, National Mutual and AXA merged operations in Australia; the following year, with the Wallis Report recommending an end to the policy, Treasurer Peter Costello compromised, reducing the Six to Four Pillars, covering the Big Four banks. National Mutual was acquired by AXA following the announcement and, in 2011, AMP eventually acquired the remnants of National Mutual after taking over the Australian arm of AXA Asia Pacific.

Wealth Acquisitions

Wealth management arguably provides a better return on invested money than traditional retail banking products. Transaction accounts earned a low rate of interest and investment in indexed funds, whether cash or shares, had a higher rate of return, even for balanced or low-risk investments. Insurance was also a component of financial security that banks were generally overlooking. Over the course of a few years, around 2000 to 2010, starting with CBA,[70] the big banks acquired sizeable wealth management capabilities:

- Colonial First State by the Commonwealth Bank
- MLC by NAB
- BT Australia (spun out of Bankers Trust Global) by Westpac
- ING Australia by ANZ.

Universally, wealth management never became fully integrated into traditional banking. There were several reasons for this. Firstly, distribution channels (bank branches) were not sufficiently incentivised to sell wealth management products. Cross-sell was clumsy. Secondly, the maturity of the wealth management arms to operate at retail banking volumes was just not there. Underinvestment dogged the divisions and procedures were not consistent, especially in financial advice, leading to controversies that resulted in a number of inquiries.

As a result of a series of inquiries, ending with the 2017-2019 royal commission into banking, many banks have attempted to exit from wealth management. While justifiable, it marked the integration of wealth management, tragically, as a failed experiment.

Share Trading

In order to round out their retail offerings, the major banks formed, acquired or partnered with retail equity providers:

- Commsec from CBA
- ETrade Australia from ANZ
- NABTrade from NAB
- WestpacTrade from Westpac.

ANZ announced in 2017 that they would be moving customers from ETrade onto a CMC Markets platform. Originally, both Westpac and NAB were powered by IWL, which was later taken over by CBA. NAB built NABTrade, and Westpac continued with the IWL solution now managed by CBA.

Special Attention

Bank-bashing, especially the Big Four banks is a favourite pastime of the Australian public, the media and politicians. Sometimes this is justified, other times not as we shall see. The Big Four do attract a great deal of official and unofficial attention, such as the Four Pillars policy and additional attention from APRA, due to their systemic importance (e.g., higher capital adequacy requirements as well as a banking levy, a special tax levied at 0.015% of a bank's liabilities).

---

[70] Phillips

The Tier 2 Banks

The next five banks are commercial operations with an established customer base. All five are listed on the ASX, and most have attempted a number of times to dislodge the Big Four so far without success:

- AMP Bank:

  Part of the AMP Group (an original member of the Six Pillars) formed when Australian Mutual Provident Society demutualised and became listed on the ASX. AMP Bank acquired various Australian and New Zealand mortgage providers and extended their banking offerings. It initially issued American Express credit cards. Payments are supported by Cuscal.

- Bank of Queensland:

  1874, third bank with the same name, with the previous banks failing. Queensland has a long tradition of independent regional financial service providers. As part of their expansion plans, BOQ franchised their branches. BOQ Specialist is an offshoot for medical professionals as well as accountants.

- Bendigo and Adelaide Bank:

  Formed from the 2007 merger of Bendigo Bank (founded in 1858 as a building society) and Adelaide Bank (founded in 1877). Bendigo Bank launched the first Visa Debit card in 1982 through its payment provider, Cuscal, and listed on the stock exchange in 1993. The Bendigo and Adelaide Bank Group acts as an umbrella bank to a number of brands: Community Bank (represented by 310 locally-owned companies), Delphi Bank (formerly Bank of Cyprus), Rural Bank (formerly Elders Rural Bank), and Alliance Bank (an amalgamation of social enterprise banks including AWA, BDCU, Circle, Nova and Service One). The group has also spawned a digital bank, known simply as Up, which offers transaction accounts and online savings accounts.

- Macquarie Bank:

  Registered in 1985. Established as Hill Samuel Australia in 1969. Popularly known as the Millionaire Factory, it is sometimes treated as the fifth member of the Big Four but, sadly, only when it comes to taxes (it is included in the bank levy tax). Macquarie has made numerous attempts to disrupt retail banking with limited success.

- Suncorp-Metway (Suncorp Bank):

  Acquisitions trace back in a complicated way to the Queensland Agricultural Bank (1902). The Metway Permanent Building Society (1959), then Metway Bank (1988), joined with the Queensland Government insurer Suncorp to form Suncorp-Metway (1996), part of the Suncorp Group, a large insurer.

- MyState Bank:

  Became a bank in 2014, tracing back to the 1970s Tasmanian Teachers, Police and Nurses Credit Union. Renamed the Connect Credit Union of Australia in 2000. Now demutualised. A subsidiary of MyState, a listed company. Payments are supported by Cuscal.

Neo Banks

There were no new private non-mutual banks in Australia between 1981 and 2018, which, as we shall see, precipitated the collapse of state banking and caused a major crisis. The regulators were naturally nervous about granting new licenses. In 2018, APRA granted five licenses, the first to be granted in 37 years. One unique feature of these neo banks was that they were almost exclusively digital banks; they were not branch based. Beyond that, however, the purpose of some of these new banks was questionable. A restricted license was also granted to in1bank, which claimed to be the first Australian owned, English and Chinese bilingual bank, a technical differentiation, unlike the more established and robust bilingual Bank of China (Australia) — which was an Australian bank owned by a foreign one. During the COVID-19 pandemic, APRA put a hold on new banking licenses. Licences were granted to:

- 86 400:

  Founded in 2019. Funded by Cuscal. Named after the number of seconds in a day. Supported by Cuscal for payments.

- Judo Bank:

  Founded in 2019. Targeted the SME market. Funding includes the Myer Family and Bain Capital. Payments are supported by Cuscal.

- Volt Bank:

  Founded in 2018, Volt Bank was the first neo bank to obtain a banking license. Investors include the Collection House Group, a debt collector and receivables manager. Payments are supported by ASL.

- Xinja Bank:

  Founded in 2019. The only bank to be equity crowdfunded. Payments are supported by ASL.

- Lutheran Laypeople's League of Australia (LLL Australia):

  Formed in 2018, quite different from any other bank, Australia's only charitable, not-for-profit ADI. A South Australian institution, the Lutheran Christian Church is named after and follows the theology of 16th century German protestant Martin Luther. LLL's members are the directors of the institution. In Australia, the LLL funds trace back to 1921. Payments are supported by Cuscal.

Mutual Banks

Most of the smaller banks today were born from mutual organisations, including building societies, credit unions and cooperatives. Originally, with deregulation in the 1980s, mutual organisations were encouraged to become banks; however, regulation at the time meant that they were required to demutualise. Some did so, including AMP. In 1999 and 2000, with amendments to the Banking Act placing regulation of these financial organisations under APRA, and then in 2000, with APRA harmonising regulations across all ADIs, the requirement to demutualise was dropped. Many credit unions required sponsorship from an ADI or took the leap in becoming ADIs themselves. To call oneself a bank, according to APRA guidelines, an ADI needs to hold at least $50 million in Tier 1 capital. The mutual banks are:

- Australian Military Bank:

  Founded in 1959 as a navy (civil staff) co-op, later to become the Army Defence Credit Union. It launched its new bank brand in 2015. Payments are supported by Cuscal.

- Australian Mutual Bank (also trading as Sydney Mutual Bank and Endeavour Mutual Bank):

  Resulted from the 2019 merger of Sydney Credit Union (founded in 1963) and Endeavour Mutual Bank (founded in 1953 as Transport Credit Union). Payments are supported by Cuscal.

- Australian Unity Bank:

  Formed in 2018 from the merger of Manchester Unity (1840) and various others. Initially offered student savings plans and now also broader financial services. Payments are supported by Cuscal.

- Auswide Bank:

  Formed in 2015 as a merger of Mayborough Permanent Building Society (1902) and Burnett Permanent Building Society (founded in 1966). Payments are supported by ASL.

- B&E (trading as Bank of US):

  A Tasmania-based bank founded in 2017, it traces its history back to Australia's oldest surviving building society, Launceston Equitable Building & Investment Society (1870). Payments are supported by ASL.

- Bank Australia:

  Originally CSIRO Co-op Credit Society (1957), eventually amalgamating with an astonishing 72 credit unions. Became Australia's first customer-owned bank (bankmecu — members and education credit union) in 2011, with the new name adopted in 2015. Payments are supported by Cuscal.

- Beyond Bank Australia:

  Formed in 2013, originally an Adelaide-based mutual bank, the Commonwealth Public Servants Credit Union (CPS Credit Union — SA & ACT, 1977), formed by an amalgamation of credit unions across Australia. Payments are supported by Cuscal.

- BNK Banking Corporation:

  Formed in 2019, started as Goldfields Credit Union in 1982, demutualising and listing on the ASX in 2012 as Goldfields Money. Renamed BNK — a shortened form of "bank."

- Cairns Penny Savings & Loans (Trading as Cairns Bank):

  Formed as the Weekly Cairns Co-op Penny Savings and Loans Bank (1899). Payments are supported by Indue.

- Defence Bank:

  Formed in 2012, originally the Defence Force Credit Union (1975). Payments are supported by Cuscal.

- First Option Bank:

  A Melbourne-based mutual bank, originally the TAB Employees Credit Union (1965). It became a bank in 2018. Payments are supported by Cuscal.

- Ford Co-operative Credit Society (trading as Geelong Bank):

  Formed in 1974 by Ford factory employees in Geelong. Renamed as a bank in 2018. Payments are supported by Cuscal.

- G&C Mutual Bank:

  Became a bank in 2014. It was a Sydney/Melbourne-based bank (1965), an amalgamation of public works credit unions. Payments are supported by ASL.

- Gateway Bank:

  Became a bank in 2017, formed as a CBA Staff Co-operative (1955). Payments are supported by ASL.

- Greater Bank:

  Renamed as a bank in 2016, named after the Greater Newcastle region, started as Newcastle and Hunter River Public Service Starr-Bowkett Building Co-operative Society (1924), formed on the basis of the Starr-Bowkett philosophy and lending formula and was interest free to members. Payments are supported by ASL.

- Heritage Bank:

  Became a bank in 2011 — the same year as the first of the mutual banks, formed by the 1981 merger of the Toowoomba Permanent Building Society (1875) and Darling Downs Building Society (1897). Largest mutual bank in Australia. Payments are supported by ASL.

- Horizon Credit Union (trading as Horizon Bank):

  Southern NSW credit unions, originally Illawarra County Council Staff Credit Union (1964), amalgamating Bega Valley Credit Union Ltd (1963) in 1980, both Wollongong City Council Employees Credit Union Ltd (1964) and Candelo Community Credit Union Ltd (1956) in 1982, Illawarra District Hospitals and Ambulance Employees Credit Union Ltd (1967) in 1983, Shoalhaven City Employees' Credit Union Ltd (1967) in 1995, and Eurobodalla Credit Union Ltd (1971) in 2009. Became a bank in 2019.

- Hume Bank:

  Became a bank in 2014. Originally the Hume Co-operative Building and Investment Society (1955). Payments are supported by ASL.

- IMB Bank:

  Named a bank in 2015, founded as the Illawarra Mutual Building Society (1880). Payments are supported by ASL.

- Maitland Mutual (trading as The Mutual Bank):

  Became a bank in 2018, a direct line from the Maitland Permanent Building Investment and Loan Society (1888). Payments are supported by ASL.

- Members Banking Group (trading as RACQ Bank):

  Renamed a bank in 2016 when it amalgamated with the Queensland Teachers

Credit Union (1961), famous for launching the first modern ATM in 1982. Payments are supported by Cuscal.

Members Equity Bank (trading as ME Bank):

Became a bank in 1995, owned by Industry Super Funds, which are themselves mutually owned. Payments are supported by ASL.

- Police & Nurses (trading as P&N Bank and BCU):

  Renamed a bank in 2013, originated as the Western Australian Police Union Co-operative Credit Union Society (1969). Payments are supported by Cuscal (P&N) & ASL (BCU).

- Police Bank (also known as Border Bank):

  Renamed a bank in 2012, started as the Police Credit Union in NSW (1964). Payments are supported by Cuscal.

- Police Financial Services (trading as BankVic):

  Became a bank in 2013, started as Victoria Police Credit Union (1974). Payments are supported by Cuscal.

- QPCU (trading as QBANK):

  Renamed a bank in 2016, started as the Queensland Police Credit Union (1964), services police, firefighters, and health and justice workers. Payments are supported by Indue.

- Qudos Mutual (trading as Qudos Bank):

  Became a bank in 2015, started in 1959 as Qantas Credit Union, one of the more successful credit unions turned bank. Payments are supported by Cuscal.

- Queensland Country Bank:

  Renamed a bank in 2018, originally Isa Mines Credit Union (1971). Payments are supported by Cuscal.

- Railways Credit Union (trading as MOVE Bank):

  Renamed a bank in 2018, formed in 1968, headquarters in Brisbane. Payments are supported by Indue.

- Regional Australia Bank:

  Became a bank in 2016. Traces back to Peel Cunningham County Council Employees Credit Union (1967). Payments are supported by ASL.

- Teachers Mutual Bank (also trading as Firefighters Mutual Bank, Health Professionals Bank, Teachers Mutual Bank and UniBank):

  Renamed a bank in 2012, formed from the Hornsby Teachers Association Credit Union (1966) and consequential amalgamations. Payments are supported by Cuscal.

- Unity Bank (also trading as Reliance Bank, Bankstown City Unity Bank):

  Renamed a bank in 2017, amalgamation from the Electricity Commission Employees Credit Union Co-operative (1958) and others. Payments are supported by Cuscal.

- Victoria Teachers (trading as Bank First):

  Became a bank in 2017, originally the Victorian Teachers Credit Union (1972). Payments are supported by Indue.

- Woolworths Team Bank:

  Formed in 1971 and still trading under the name of Woolworths Employees' Credit Union, the institution is exclusively for employees and family. Payments are supported by Cuscal.

Building Societies

A building society was originally a group of people or families that all wanted to save money and eventually buy or build a house. In its simplest form, the early building societies operated a kitty where, every month (or some other period), each member would contribute an amount and, randomly, one member would be able to build their house. Except for the last drawn member, everyone benefitted, and even in the case of the last member, forced savings allowed that member to save money for a house, money that would otherwise probably be spent on other goods. Once everyone had a house, the building society terminated. The property was used as collateral in the event that one member reneged.

Permanent building societies could take on new members when previous members completed their house or purchase and had paid off their loan. They became somewhat similar to banks.

In Australia, building societies were originally supervised by states. In 1974, a number of state building societies experienced runs due to rumours. Collapse was alleviated in part thanks to swift action, with the South Australian Premier pleading to queuing customers to not be hasty. In 1984, the building societies of almost all the states set up the Building Societies Share and Deposit Insurance Corporation, later to become the National Deposit Insurance Corporation (NDIC) to mutually guarantee funds. Victoria, under advice from the Victorian Building Societies Council, did not join this fund, despite the request of building society members, as they had their own funds ($23 million). In 1990, The Farrow Group collapsed losing almost $600 million. The Farrow Group included the Pyramid, Geelong and Countryside Building Societies. Only 51 cents in every dollar was returned to depositors. Regulations were tightened, with the establishment of the Australian Financial Institutions Commission (later to become APRA) and state supervisory board. Building societies were required to invest 50% of their deposits in home lending.

Building societies were mutually owned. Over time, especially in the 1990s after the above regulations came into play, building societies demutualised and their depositors (mutual owners) became shareholders. Some of the bigger societies became banks or were taken over by banks.

Today, building societies are regulated as ADIs by the Reserve Bank of Australia. There is only one left that officially bears the name, Newcastle Permanent Building Society, founded in 1903. However, it is now marketed simply as Newcastle Permanent. Its payments are supported by ASL.

Credit Unions

Credit unions, like building societies, were mutually owned. They differed from building societies in that they offered more lending options, not just for homes. Originally, they were designed for small deposits and loans.

Like building societies, they are now regulated as ADIs by the RBA and APRA, and are covered by the Financial Claims Scheme. Credit unions are no different to banks other than in the name, and many of them are banks, as shown in the list above of mutual banks. Technically, however, the term *bank* can only be used (according to APRA guidelines) if the ADI has at least $50 million in Tier 1 capital. The term is, therefore, a reflection of an ADI's size, rather than its quality.

The philosophy of the credit union dates to the 1850s, when German philosopher Hermann Schulze-Delitzsch envisioned a society of known, trusted people saving and lending money according to fixed rules.[71] Credit unions in Australia were generally associated with workplaces as most people held the same job their entire working life. Often, near the payroll window, when people would collect their money, the workplace credit union would encourage them to save a little, rather than spend it on a night out or on Thursday night shopping. In some cases, the credit unions were connected with trade unions. Building societies, on the other hand, were connected to a town or suburb. As job tenures became shorter, offices more distributed, and regulations more stringent, the original notion of the credit union became somewhat dissipated.

These days, credit unions are community-based social enterprises, and provide the workers or community they represent with a chance to connect outside of a work environment, often helping to solve problems outside of banking itself. In order to stay true to their base, they generally don't allow outsiders to join (but have varying levels of strictness to this policy). Consolidation of these organisations is likely to continue.

There are 37 credit unions in Australia. One, the Southern Cross Credit Union, supports its own payments, while, for the others, payments are supported by Cuscal, Indue or ASL. Those with payments supported by Cuscal are:

- Australian Central Credit Union (trading as People's Choice Credit Union)
- Central Murray Credit Union
- Central West Credit Union
- Credit Union Australia
- Credit Union SA
- Firefighters & Affiliates Credit Co-operative
- Fire Service Credit Union
- First Choice Credit Union

---

[71] Aschhoff

- Goulburn Murray Credit Union Co-operative
- Illawarra Credit Union
- Laboratories Credit Union
- Lithuanian Co-operative Credit Society Talka
- Lysaght Credit Union
- Macarthur Credit Union (trading as THE MAC)
- Macquarie Credit Union
- Northern Inland Credit Union
- Orange Credit Union
- Police Credit Union
- Pulse Credit Union
- South West Slopes Credit Union
- South-West Credit Union Co-operative.
- WAW Credit Union Co-operative.

Those with payments supported by Indue are:

- Broken Hill Community Credit Union
- Coastline Credit Union
- Dnister Ukrainian Credit Co-operative
- Hunter United Employees' Credit Union
- Maleny Credit Union (MCU)
- Traditional Credit Union:

  Founded in 1994, it is the only Indigenous-owned credit union and operates from Northern Territory. Payments are supported by Indue and Cuscal.
- Warwick Credit Union.

Those with payments supported by ASL are:

- Community First Credit Union.
- Family First Credit Union
- Summerland Financial Services (trading as Summerland Credit Union)
- The Capricornian
- Transport Mutual Credit Union.

Banks Owned by Foreign Banks

Once a foreign bank reaches a certain size and seeks to grow in the Australian market, rather than simply support expats and visitors, it is formed as a local entity and regulated as such. At present, there are seven such banks. All seven are governed by the RBA and APRA and covered by the Financial Claims Scheme:

- Arab Bank Australia:

  Based in Amman, Jordan, the oldest Middle Eastern bank still in existence, the local subsidiary in Australia provides home loans, personal loans and transactional accounts. Payments are supported by ASL.

- Bank of China (Australia):

  Boasts David Murray as a Chairman, this bank became licensed at the end of World War II. It issues a China UnionPay/eftpos joint scheme card. The bank does not tend to market outside of the Australian Chinese ethnic community.

- Bank of Sydney (owned by the Bank of Beirut s.a.l.):

  Bank of Sydney markets itself as a local bank and is supported by a significant ethnic Lebanese population in Sydney.

- Citigroup (trading as Citibank):

  A division of the US behemoth, a great deal of hope was placed in Citibank when it started operations in Australia; however, since deregulation, it has incessantly tried to disrupt the Australian establishment. After the GFC, investment in Australia froze, but the bank remains comfortable in the second tier retail market in Australia.

- HSBC Bank Australia:

  Another large international bank, initially based in Hong Kong and Shanghai but now in the United Kingdom, it has attempted to compete with local banks and remains a significant Tier 2 operation.

- ING Bank (Australia) (trading as ING):

  Previously ING Direct, one of the more successful challenger banks. Originally from Amsterdam, it now has shares listed in Europe and on the New York Stock Exchange. Associated with but separate to ING Australia, which was acquired by ANZ.

- Rabobank Australia:

  Rabobank's attempts to penetrate Australian retail banking have been disappointing, despite a clear mandate to do just that. Their focus both globally and in Australia is on agricultural business, and they offer products in this area, competing with Australia's largest agricultural business provider, CBA. Payments are supported by Indue.

Branches of Foreign Banks

As part of deregulation, and Australia's open policy towards banks, there are 48 overseas banks in operation in Australia. Some, such as ABN Amro, Deutsche, Bank of America (through Merrill Lynch), BNP Paribas and JP Morgan, have sizeable operations, especially in institutional banking. None of these banks are covered by Australia's Financial Claims Scheme, as they are not Australian entities (*unless they have a local subsidiary). As such, regulatory requirements are lower than for other banks in Australia, given that they are appropriately regulated by their respective national authorities. These banks are:

- ABN Amro Bank N.V.
- Agricultural Bank of China
- Bank of America, National Association
- Bank of Baroda
- Bank of China*
- Bank of Communications Co
- Bank of New York Mellon
- Bank of Nova Scotia
- Bank of Taiwan
- BNP Paribas
- BNP Paribas Securities Services
- Canadian Imperial Bank of Commerce
- China Construction Bank Co
- China Everbright Bank Co
- China Merchants Bank Co
- Citibank, N.A.*
- Co-operative Rabobank U.A. (trading as Rabobank)*
- Credit Suisse AG
- DBS Bank
- Deutsche Bank Aktiengessellschaft (which has a stake in Latitude Financial, an Australian specialist credit card institution).*
- E.SUN Commercial Bank
- First Commercial Bank
- Hongkong and Shanghai Banking Corporation (HSBC)*
- Hua Nan Commercial Bank
- Industrial and Commercial Bank of China
- ING Bank N.V.*
- Investec Bank plc

- JPMorgan Chase Bank, National Association
- KEB HANA Bank
- Mega International Commercial Bank Co
- Mizuho Bank
- MUFG Bank
- Northern Trust Company
- Oversea-Chinese Banking Corporation
- Royal Bank of Canada
- Shinhan Bank Co
- Société Général
- Standard Chartered Bank
- State Bank of India
- State Street Bank and Trust Company
- Sumitomo Mitsui Banking Corporation
- Taishin International Bank Co
- Taiwan Business Bank
- Taiwan Co-operative Bank
- UBS AG
- Union Bank of India
- United Overseas Bank
- Woori Bank.

(* Branch of foreign bank with a local subsidiary)

ADI-licensed Payment Organisations

In order to hold money for payments, ultimately an ADI license is required, especially for holding $1 000 or more for any one customer or for allowing settlement through an Exchange Settlement Account. The following organisations have an ADI to conduct their payments business:

- Australian Settlements Limited (ASL):

  Formed in 1993 as a mutual organisation to help facilitate the payments of credit unions and building societies, ASL has an ADI license to assist with settlement for its members.

- Cuscal:

  Formed in 1992 as the Credit Union Services Corporation Australia Limited, Cuscal was originally a representative body of credit unions. It has now less of a representative association, and focuses on payments and settlements on behalf of smaller financial institutions. Cuscal still supports the majority of credit unions. Cuscal invested in the bank 86 400, raising the question of whether they are competing with other ADIs or supporting them.

- Indue:

  Formed in 1992 as Credit Union Settlement Services Ltd and later Creditlink, a competitor to Cuscal. Originally an ATM provider, in 2016, Indue sought to become a bank, but only had half the Tier 1 capital required. In 2017, Stargroup (formerly Reef Mining NL) took over Indue, began operating Bitcoin ATMs and shortly after filed for receivership. Indue was spun off, providing payment services to smaller banks, it also issued the controversial government cashless debit card.

- PayPal Australia:

  PayPal Australia is a division of an international organisation which was spun off from eBay. They conduct merchant payments and P2P payments, and are the most popular consumer wallet on digital platforms.

- Tyro Payments:

  Tyro Payments was formed by ex-CISCO staff in 2002 in response to the RBA's directive to open up credit card schemes to new competitors. The RBA's primary intention was to open up the issuing side, while Tyro was more interested in acquiring, but they became one of two specialised credit card issuer (SCCI) license holders along with GE Money. This category has now been dropped and no longer requires an ADI license; however, Tyro has maintained theirs.

NOTE

PayPal is the sole holder of a newer ADI license type known as a purchase payment facility. A purchase payment facility is essentially a wallet. There is significant legislation and regulation authorising non-banks to have this type of arrangement. It is unclear to many observers why a new license type was needed, as other payment providers can have a normal ADI license, especially as APRA has the power to provide restrictive licences as it sees fit. Also, APRA has produced a brochure for the one institution that requires this license. In 2018, the productivity suggested simplifying requirements for this type of license to encourage purchase payment facility providers in Australia. There are a number of embedded payment solutions that provide similar services to PayPal that do not hold purchase payment facility licenses, supposedly as they have payment obligations under $10 million (the threshold for this type of license), though this is questionable.

Specialist Credit Card Institutions

Specialist Credit Card Institutions(SCCIs) were added to organisations that could be granted an ADI license as part of the Wallis Report and RBA credit card reforms of 2002, intended to allow non-bank institutions the ability to issue credit cards. Originally, these institutions were to be regulated by APRA, but this requirement was withdrawn by APRA and the RBA in 2014 after they noted that take-up was low. Tyro Payments (which never issued credit cards, but became a limited ADI to allow it to settle directly) and GE Capital (which eventually left the market, selling its operations to a Värde-led joint venture and becoming Latitude Financial) were the two remaining SCCIs. APRA advised that future SCCIs could be regulated through ASIC and granted Australian Financial Service credit licences.

Agency Banking

Prior to about 2009, agency banking provided an alternative to branch banking.

A corner store, for example, would act as an agent of a bank, displaying a sign, supporting opening accounts (origination) as well as making deposits and small withdrawals in the store. This was particularly useful in suburbs or towns with no bank branches and to take the demand off busy branches. The agent bank sign, as seen in *Figure 9*, was commonplace. Citibank used agency banking as a way of setting up in Australia without a branch footprint. Notably, in 1986, Citibank collaborated with MBF (Health Fund), and then in 1990 with Soul Pharmacy, to allow people to open and transact at their local chemist.

***Figure 9*. Agency banking sign, a metal sign that would hang below shop awnings.**

The fundamental risk with these agents was that AML/CTF and general fraud risks were high and, by around 2009, banks exited these arrangements. Today, Australia Post still offers agency banking through its Bank@Post offering, acting on behalf of CBA, NAB and Westpac (note again the absence of ANZ), and also supporting deposits and withdrawals from 71 other banks in Australia. Bank of Queensland's expansion out of state has been through a franchise model; however, all processes and systems are controlled strictly by the bank.

As the big banks continued to close less profitable branches, there was a resurgence in the agency model through Bank@Post when, in 2018, CBA agreed to pay $22 million a year to allow Australia Post to support the bank's customers in regional locations.

Different Types of Banks

The following lists the different types of banks commonly referred to in the market:

acquirer bank	A bank that acquires card payment transactions.
business bank	A bank that offers services to medium-sized or large businesses.
central bank	The regulatory bank of a country responsible for issuing money and setting monetary policy.
institutional bank	A bank that provides global markets (foreign exchange, commodity, and equity) as well as providing banking services to other banks and large corporations.
investment bank	An institutional bank specialising in markets.
issuer bank	A bank that issues cards. Normally a retail bank, but can be a business or institutional bank.
merchant bank	Another name for a business or institutional bank.
mutual bank	A bank owned by customers — usually originally a credit union or building society.
private bank	A division within a bank that offers services to high net worth individuals and medium-sized businesses through relationship managers.
retail bank	A well-known bank that offers services to the bulk of the population and to small businesses.
savings bank	An old term for what is now called a retail bank.
trading bank	An old term which can refer to what is now called a business bank or institutional bank, or to the treasury unit.

›› NOTE

The use of the word *bank* in a company name requires permission from APRA as do the following terms: ADI, authorised deposit-taking institution, banker, banking, building society, credit society, credit union and friendly society (the last in relation to the conduct of a financial business).

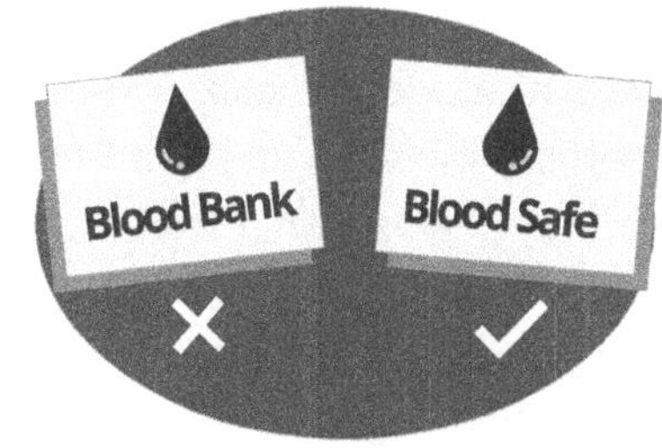

Australian Banks Overseas

Most of the Big Four banks have a subsidiary in New Zealand:

- ANZ New Zealand
- Auckland Savings Bank (owned by CBA)
- Bank of New Zealand (owned by NAB)
- Westpac New Zealand.

These four banks, along with New Zealand Post's Kiwibank, constitute the Big Five. The Reserve Bank of New Zealand created an outsourcing standard, BS 11, in 2006. Ostensibly, this was to reduce systemic risks in outsourcing, but it also prevented the Australian banks from consolidating systems and staff in mainland Australia, as the standards required service continuity in the event of an external (or offshore) failure. Australian banks took the initials BS (for banking standard) as a euphemism to mean something different, with the same initialisation. In defence of New Zealand's regulator, Australia copied the intent in APRA's CPS 231, in 2010. Both standards continue to be a headache for outsourcing bank systems on both sides of the Tasman.

Many of the big banks have overseas offices in London, New York, Japan, Singapore and/or Hong Kong, mainly for corporate and institutional banking services in the global market.

In the past, many Australian banks have expanded overseas: ANZ and Westpac into Asia, CBA into Fiji, Indonesia, Vietnam, India and South Africa, and NAB into the US and the United Kingdom. Many of the Big Four have retracted operations in recent years with smaller presences globally.

After the banking deregulation of the 1980s, with the early expansion strategy of the big global banks, it was thought in the future the world may have just a few global banks. The retraction of international banks since the GFC is a global phenomenon, and may point to high regulation and greater restrictions as well as market saturation in the Americas, Europe, Asia and the Pacific. A similar predicament befell airlines and telcos years earlier with once worldwide brands retracting considerably.

Business Units in Banks

Large organisations tend to divide themselves into smaller units. The purpose is to provide clear command and control lines. Working on the theory that any single person can effectively manage a maximum of eight people, an organisation of 30 000 people could only be efficiently managed if it had six levels. Level 1 is the CEO and Level 2 is the heads of business units, each with a staff size of 4 000 on average. The management levels continue, with all but the bottom two being "manager of managers". The key role at the top of this hierarchy is that of the CEO.

The chief financial officer is responsible for keeping the business unit heads honest and focused, and often manages treasury (money markets), the corporate money of the bank (internal expenses), and reporting of the consolidated profit and loss, assets and liabilities to shareholders and the market. The chief information officer and chief operating officer (sometimes the same person) have more than their fair share of people reporting to them. They are responsible for the background operations and technology of the organisation, and also manage vendors. The chief risk officer is responsible for risk and compliance in the bank. The chief legal counsel and strategy are smaller units, but with significant influence. Human resources is also a smaller unit. All of these are generally cost centres that are cost-driven.

›› NOTE

In a low-growth environment, profit can only be achieved by lowering expenses. The chief information officer and/or chief operating officer were always under pressure to reduce costs. But better technological capability often requires increased costs in technology resources in order to facilitate growth and efficiency. Without promised reductions in costs, the organisation gets impatient. In tightening times, these roles can be a hot seat.

The main business units that are responsible for profitability are:

- Retail banking (retail investors and small business, branches, retail products, online banking, retail financial advice, cards, etc.).
- Business banking and private banking (high net worth clients and SME corporations).
- Institutional banking (banking for other banks, large corporations and global markets).
- Wealth management (funds, superannuation, insurance and financial advice).
- International banking.
- A bank's other brands (e.g., overseas banks, or other local brands like St George, Bankwest and UBank).

Staff

Unions in banks formed soon after World War I with the Australian Bank Officers' Association and, later, the Australian Bank Employees' Union. The Australian Insurance Staffs Federation formed around the same time and later became the Australian Insurance Employees Union. Later again, it combined with the Commonwealth Bank Officers' Association to form the Finance Sector Union. Unions were quite strong and developed minimum wage standards that helped establish the Industrial Awards, the Wages Accord (under the Bob Hawke government), and the minimum wages of the Fair Work Commission. Each of the major banks is represented by their own section in the Finance Sector Union, which negotiates with the bank's executives for better conditions. In the 1980s, many senior officers and managers were members of the Australian Bank Officers' Association and were sympathetic to the union members' needs. These days, many bank employees, especially in IT and senior management, earn more than the award wage and tend to not be members of the union. In fact, in certain circles, it is frowned upon. Branch staff and operations staff tend to be members of the union. Little industrial action has been taken by the union in recent times (as in other sectors), due to tight regulation of industrial action.

Senior management staff and executives get paid a base salary, plus a bonus or short-term incentive. Long-term incentives kick in for more senior executive staff, and may be issued as shares or options. The most senior executives are the most highly paid in the industry with the CEO, chief financial officer and business unit heads getting paid the most. Interestingly, wealth fund managers, while not as senior, also attract high salaries; these must be reported on the annual report.

Large companies have sophisticated performance, feedback and review processes for staff, purportedly designed to develop individuals and assess them generally on a scale (sometimes one-dimensional, sometimes multidimensional). Sometimes, it can be useful as it provides a moment to mutually reflect and improve; however, in many cases, it acts to provide a procedural basis for a quite arbitrary limiting of salary review and performance incentives, or bonuses and promotions. In a modern workforce, in rapidly changing times, with unique problems and sophisticated workers, the ratings of "meets expectations" and "exceeds expectations" are almost entirely subjective. In almost all cases, salary increases, incentives and bonuses are relationship based, not so much driven by objective performance measures or job oriented ability. Younger workers tend to experience rapid growth and hit a ceiling, as the promotion opportunities dwindle in pyramid structures with an ageing workforce. This career stagnation, despite productive outputs discourages many workers, who find it more effective to find better pay and positions elsewhere than to remain in the same position indefinitely.

Further, out of work training tends to be poorly applied for various reasons: lack of time, lack of budget and lack of desire on the part of the employer. A fair amount of compliance training has been placed on workers to ensure the employer's compliance liability is managed.

In recent times, executive salaries and staff bonuses have been cut, despite increased profits. The reason for the cuts are due to poor risk management or bank customer failures that were exposed; for example, in the media or during the royal commission.

Women in Banking

In the 1960s, it was against banking regulations for CBA to employ married women so when women employees got married, they were required to resign or retire. This changed in 1968, when married women were allowed to continue working. In most banks, initially, women were employed as clerical staff and with more equal opportunity in banks, more senior positions were made available. The push for equal opportunity originated in the government sector, and CBA was an early mover, though other banks have caught up. These days, human resources encourages managers to seek women staff, and there is a push for more female representation at executive and board levels. Former CBA executive alumni include a CEO of Westpac in 2002, a premier of New South Wales in 2017 and a CEO of Optus in 2019.

Hours and Holidays

Normal working hours in Australia are 9:00 am to 5:00 pm with a break for lunch.

Traditionally, banks needed to spend time collecting overnight box deposits, applying overnight payments to ledgers and readying tills for the first customers at 9:30 am. Likewise, at 4:00 pm, the doors would be closed (customers already queuing would be served) and the backlog of ledger entries for the day would be completed, with cash reconciled and locked in the safe. These days, with centralised systems and greater automation, it is possible to attend to customers sooner and this has extended hours in some banks. Most banks are open later, until 4:30 pm or 5:00 pm on Fridays, and some branches open on weekends. However, additional work (ATM servicing, staff development, meetings) and fewer staff in branches has contributed to, in recent times, a reversing of the trend.

The Bank Holiday (observed by some banks in some states) was originally intended as a reward for working long hours in the lead-up to the end of the financial year on June 30. The first Monday in August was given as a day off in lieu. With greater automation, although head office staff are busy, the end of the financial year no longer adds a significant workload to others. Nonetheless, the holiday continues, and some state unions have agreed to move it to another day. The August holiday is observed in New South Wales and Australian Capital Territory, and is a state-wide Picnic Day in Northern Territory. Victoria observed the Bank Holiday on Easter Tuesday but later abolished it. Most states have additional holidays, namely Melbourne Cup Day (Victoria), Adelaide Cup Day (South Australia), Easter Tuesday (Tasmania), Western Australia Day (WA), Royal Queensland Show Day (Brisbane), Reconciliation Day and Canberra Day (ACT), and May Day (NT). New South Wales has the fewest public holidays and Australian Capital Territory the most. Contrary to popular belief, banks were rarely closed compared to other industries. Australia also has fewer public holidays than most of its trading partners.

While bank workers enjoyed the same number of paid vacation days as their peers in other industries, some banks required staff to take mandatory time off, supposedly to reduce risks of single person dependencies and, in the case of traders or operational staff, to reduce the risk of corrupt practices (altering ledgers, etc.). Like many industries, even the big banks requested head office staff to take mandatory leave during the Christmas period.

In batch payment systems (such as card settlements, cash, cheques, Direct Entry and HVCS) a public holiday is defined as a day when both Sydney and Melbourne have declared a holiday.

Indigenous Australians

Before European settlement, Indigenous people in Australia (Aboriginal Australians), Torres Strait Islanders, and Papuans had their own vibrant commerce, involving long-distance trade.[72]

[72] Balme; Connell

European settlement was devastating for the local population. There was little reward for the original inhabitants from the growing economy, acquisition of their land, the spread of disease and even massacre.[73]

As mentioned earlier, there was no reason to suspect that the absence of metallic money placed Indigenous society behind the European settlers for there would have likely been full employment and prosperity.

Until the 1970s, Indigenous people were largely excluded from the mainstream workforce, and the wages they did receive were managed by the government, referred to as *stolen wages*. Introduction of real wages was disruptive to the social order, where the younger, more employable members of the community would receive money and the older members would not. Possibly as a result, a culture of humbugging developed: a practice of "on-demand sharing, asking or pressuring a family member or other connection for money or other assistance in a way that can be bothersome."[74]

Therefore, it is not surprising that many Indigenous people are ill-equipped financially. In 2016, Indigenous people were 1.4 times less likely to be employed,[75] found it difficult to get loans from banks due to lack of modern forms of identity such as passports or driver's licences (therefore relying on unregulated and higher interest loans from loan sharks), and had poor financial literacy.[76]

The major banks have implemented a Reconciliation Action Plan, have attempted to increase staff numbers of Indigenous Australians, and support Indigenous businesses through Supply Nation and financial literacy initiatives such as the Indigenous Consumer Assistance Network (ICAN). In 2017, CBA trialled employing regional Indigenous youth as IT professionals, training them in IT and providing them work normally reserved for the head office, using regional branch locations to work remotely.

Better Indigenous cultural education is supported through organisations such as Black Card, with more banks and staff focusing on recognising and acknowledging Indigenous people and issues.

Controversial initiatives of the Australian Government to ensure Indigenous people spend benefits on appropriate goods were put in place, especially in Northern Territory, such as the Cashless Debit Card (CDC) trial of the Department of Human Services to prevent the purchase of alcohol and gift cards. This card is issued by Indue.

Indigenous Australians still experience the poorest financial conditions among the major demographic groups in Australia and more attention to this issue is required.

---

[73] Murray, R.; Carment

[74] Weier

[75] ABS 2016

[76] Hayne

Innovation Culture

Banks in Australia were responsible for a considerable amount of innovation. Genuine innovation took place from about 2007 to 2016, starting with CBA's modernisation of core banking and NAB's UBank, and culminating with a string of controversies and calls for a royal commission into banking.

In 2017, KPMG reported that Australian banks were ahead of their international peers in engaging with fintechs.[77] CBA took the lead as an innovative bank in this period, with more mentions of innovation in the news than any other bank. In its submission to the Productivity Commission, CBA could mention 38 instances of innovation and dozens of awards between 2011 and 2017, with Westpac not far behind. Digital capabilities of Australian banks were highly rated on the Apple App Store and Google Play compared to their overseas counterparts.

In 2014, the CBA Innovation Lab and NAB Labs launched with the other banks joining in; however, much of the investment was in external-to-bank initiatives, and many were designed to create a public image, especially for shareholders and analysts. These innovations were often not part of the mainstream bank. This golden era of banking innovation ended with the loss of innovation culture and of execution capability, due to considerable downsizing, both before and after the royal commission.

Account Types

The diversity of types of bank accounts offered by banks is substantial. These days, although many banks have been simplifying their account offerings, some old or legacy types still remain.

Party to an Account

A party to an account is a person, partnership, cooperative or body corporate that is associated with an account.

There are sometimes complicated arrangements of parties to accounts. There is the legal entity that owns and manages the account, the beneficiary, and the part authorised to operate the account.

Ownership of an account could be held by an individual or natural person, a married or de facto couple (or any form of partnership), a registered legal entity (such as a private or public company), a registered association, a registered trust, etc. An account can be opened in a registered business name if there is an entity behind it. Transactions and access may be granted to employees, parents, or authorised friends or relatives (normally natural persons). Authorisation can require that any one party can sign, any two, or all parties.

Corporate accounts are far more sophisticated with multiple levels of input and approval processes possible.

---

[77] Pollari

While some banks try to keep customer information in one place, the fact that an individual can have many roles complicates the situation, and can lead to duplication or incorrect information that is difficult to change. A person can be a direct customer, an employee with access or a person with access to an account they are not the owner of.

Banks tend to have sophisticated party models, but there are always limitations based on the policy of the bank. The big banks tend to have more sophisticated models to support diverse needs, but this is not always the case, with smaller banks offering flexible products to target a specific market segment.

One of the main limitations is that an account needs to be owned by a legally recognised entity, and that proper KYC procedures need to be completed for each party.

Since FATCA and the Common Reporting Standard came into effect, entities also need to identify if they are connected with a foreign nation and, in these cases, bank account balances and information could be shared with those governments as per Australian treaties and tax law. If a bank employee knowingly withholds information about a foreign person, they can face a criminal penalty.

Exchange Settlement Account

An Exchange Settlement Account (ESA) is an account held at the Reserve Bank, generally by a bank or a licensed settlement scheme. Originally termed Special Accounts during World War II (see above), these accounts hold excess cash, and are intended to provide all the money required to settle payments as those payments fall due. Banks can keep buffers and intraday amounts to support excess payments on an agreed upon basis; this money earns the official target cash rate in interest. Surplus amounts that were not agreed could be held overnight in an ESA and earn slightly less than the target cash rate (about 25 basis points, or 0.25% less). This is to discourage banks from using the ESA for anything other than to settle payments. Nevertheless, the ESA has a risk-weighted asset value of 0, the lowest risk rating.

» NOTE

When interest rates are low (near or below zero), the ESA rate may be discounted by less than 0.25%. This happened for the first time in March 2020, when the rate was reduced by only 0.15%. Low interest rates caused lots of technical problems so the regulators asked banks to confirm that their systems could cope with negative interest rates.

An ESA, like an overdraft facility, can also be used to borrow short-term money from the RBA. Instead of a reduced rate, the rate is increased by 0.25%.

ESAs are classed as either active or dormant. Dormant ESAs are used as a backup by ADIs using an ADI licensed settlement payment provider (another bank, ASL, Indue or Cuscal).

As we will see, access to ESAs is essential in order to provide the full capability of payments services, and their restriction to mainly ADIs prevented the entry of other organisations into the payments industry.

With the removal of Specialist Credit Card Institutions (SCCI) from ADI requirements and, given the need of other organisations to access ESAs, the RBA opened these up to non-ADIs.

Vostro

A Vostro is really a fancy term for a bank account, but instead of it being in the name of an individual, it is generally held by another financial institution. Key features of the Vostro are that, in some cases, the bank can transact on it based on written, verbal or electronic instructions; also the account is normally fully accessible by SWIFT. Banks generally treat these accounts as highly liquid. With balances placed with interest rates at near-official rates, they are often not very profitable, but allow other arrangements with the institutional customer and access to greater liquidity. Vostros are important in SWIFT correspondent banking (covered later).

The word *Vostro* is Italian meaning *your*, in this context: your money with us.

Nostro

Nostro is Italian for *our*. A Nostro account is our money with you.

Basically, a Nostro account is the journal or ledger a paranoid customer would keep — someone who just didn't trust the banks, recording every incoming and every outgoing transaction, and reconciling each transaction later. Based on their experience, banks don't trust each other or, rather, they accept errors can happen. It is good practice. A Nostro is this bank's representation of their account at another bank. (That other account would often be called, by that other bank, a Vostro.)

Nostro reconciliations happen when the other bank sends a Vostro statement over and the two need to match.

Savings Account

Account Type	**Savings Account**
Financial Claims Scheme	Yes
Deposits	Yes
Withdrawals	Yes
Payments	Generally no
Fees & Interest	Generally no regular fees. Transaction fees could apply. Low interest paid.

A savings account was the original consumer bank account. In fact, consumer banks were originally called savings banks. Most individuals used their account to save money and keep it safe while earning interest. Originally, savings accounts did not receive statements (often they were passbook-based) and did not have cheques issued. Fees were charged partly to recover costs and partly to dissuade withdrawals. Fees on savings accounts are generally low, and these days many savings accounts are fee-free.

When ATMs first came out, card withdrawals were permitted. These days, many savings accounts no longer allow ATM withdrawals.

The interest rate on a savings account is generally lower than the RBA cash rate, so in low-interest environments its primary purpose is as a safe haven as it is (like any other bank deposit account) covered by the Financial Claims Scheme.

Some institutions (outside the Big Four and other major banks) offer a much higher interest rate, likely to attract funds to improve their capital adequacy and to fund their lending activities. High interest rates on savings is loss-leading and serves to entice customers rather than to profit from them, at least not immediately.

Today's savings accounts are very different to the savings accounts of the past. New banks generally start out by offering savings accounts, as regulators understand them better and prefer these on the balance sheet rather than lending. Many banks allow these accounts to be created online and call them online savings accounts. They act as virtual accounts and can be used to siphon money away from transaction accounts to facilitate savings objectives. Online savings accounts have tools to encourage saving.

›› NOTE

While we have all heard since our school days that saving is good, many self-made billionaires will say they made their money not through savings via a piggy bank or savings accounts, but through heavy lending and gearing to the hilt. While successful for some, the latter path has led many to financial destruction.

From a payments point of view, most savings accounts accept deposits through Direct Entry and NPP. Money can be transferred to a transaction account online. A few savings accounts do allow debits through a debit card at ATMs and EFTPOS, Direct Entry (credits and debits) as well as BPAY.

For many, the savings account is an anachronism that is no longer worth maintaining as a distinct type of account.

Youth and School Savings

Originally, savings for children consisted of a money box. Over time, like the rest of society, a bank account, even for children, was a useful service.

In Australia, the Commonwealth Bank still successfully controls the market for children's savings accounts, having established, effectively, agency banking at many schools, known as School Banking. The product encourages children to save with a higher interest rate if regular deposits are made. Previously known as the Dollarmites account, this has now been merged with the youth product Youthsaver. The product would be loss-making; however, many banks have recognised the benefit of banking for life; that is, customers become captive, especially if they start early. In the case of the Commonwealth Bank, this is definitely the case and one reason they have the largest number of retail customers.

Despite the negative immediate returns of running a loss-making project, seeing the potential, many banks would target parents (especially mothers) with young children and try to sign them up. Some banks offered tellers incentives. In 2017, CBA offered $400 000 to schools in Queensland to get children to join.

In 2019, the Royal Commission into Misconduct in the Banking, Superannuation and Financial Services Industry revealed that tellers were pushing customers to open accounts using their loose change or with the tellers putting their own money into the accounts. In 2018, CHOICE criticised Dollarmites for cradle-snatching customers. The same year, ASIC launched a review into school banking.

The attention given to school banking was overkill. Despite the simple truth about capturing clients early, this is not the big battle that is discussed in bank boardrooms. Executives operate on a short timeline. Most business cases need to show a three to five-year NPV (net present value) benefit. Sure enough, school banking and youth banking are notoriously poorly funded.

Many in the banking industry were disappointed with the negative response to this business unit of the bank, seeing their school offerings not as cradle-snatching but as giving back to the community, and educating young people on banking.

In order to open an account, parental permission is necessary, and many parents will open an account for their children at their own bank. Saving money and spending less is a good lesson to teach children. Learning to value money results in less arbitrary spending, and spending less on discretionary items means more is left for more expensive items. For school children to get exposure to professions and industries, whether it be banking or manufacturing, is important. With banks forced to back away from school banking, few incentivised executives will shed a tear, but it will be a social loss.

Passbook

A passbook account was essentially a savings account. In the days of manual ledgers, it provided a way to give confidence to a customer that their account was properly reconciled. A passbook was required to deposit and withdraw money, and in the 1980s was computerised to allow printers to update the entries. Signatures were recorded on the passbook with ultraviolet readable ink for security (though these days, it is easy to get an ultraviolet light). Many banks transitioned passbook customers to savings or transaction accounts.

Account Type	Passbook Account
Financial Claims Scheme	Yes
Deposits	Yes
Withdrawals	Yes, though mainly designed for branch withdrawals
Payments	Generally no
Fees & Interest	Generally no regular fees. Transaction fees could apply. Low interest paid.

The Big Four banks still support passbooks, but due to the special printer requirements, not all branches do, and most banks will not issue passbooks to new customers. Many customers in an older age bracket are more comfortable with the simplicity of this account. Westpac still supports them for customers over 55. In order to allow savings account holders access to their money during the COVID-19 lockdowns, CBA issued a Debit Mastercard to passbook holders who did not have one, through a linked transaction account. This is potentially a way to wean them off the account, though the complex arrangement would have confused their target customers.

Transaction Account

Transaction accounts are the main source of profits for banks on the deposit side of the ledger. They operate on the behavioural economics of account holders. Investors put their salaries in a transaction account, and keep much of it there in the anticipation of making a payment.

Transaction accounts earn little or no interest, but banks can lend the money out and keep a portion of the money in liquid assets, making a profit on the difference.

Account Type	Transaction Account
Financial Claims Scheme	Yes
Deposits	Yes
Withdrawals	Yes
Payments	Yes
Fees & Interest	Monthly fees, transaction limit, excess transaction fee. Low interest paid.

The most common form of modern bank account, the transaction account originated with ATMs, cards, and later, phone and online banking. These days, a transaction account can be used to make electronic payments and has merged with the old cheque account. For those who still want it, they may be able to order a cheque book.

Fees were traditionally high to subsidise transaction costs; however, as transaction costs have come down, many accounts no longer charge a transaction fee and include a large or unlimited number of free transactions.

» NOTE

During the implementation of CBA's billion-dollar core banking modernisation program, the ability to price (charge fees), based on the bank's relationship with a customer, was intended to be part of the design; for example, no fees for home loan customers or high net worth individuals. While the project was in progress, NAB dropped its fees on transaction accounts. No sophisticated fee engine is required when fees are zero and this reduced the value of a core banking system, which now just had to calculate simple interest.

Overdraft Facility

An overdraft facility on a transaction account allows the account balance to go into the negative with interest rates comparable to those of personal loans or credit cards. This is classified as unsecured lending. There is sometimes a fee associated with an account having a debit balance, and an account may be overdrawn without applying for an overdraft (e.g., through a debit card transaction that may have been authorised in accordance with scheme rules without checking the balance) so it is important to keep sufficient money in an account that is being used to prevent these charges.

Business or Corporate Accounts

Business accounts are similar to transaction accounts, but may feature more payment facilities:

- Merchant facilities
- Direct debit
- Bulk Direct Entry (credits and debits)
- Unattended (automatic) access
- BPAY inbound (as a biller)
- Workflow-based payment approvals
- SWIFT electronic integration
- Accounting/ERP integration.

Cheque Account

Cheque accounts were originally personal and business transaction accounts provided with a personalised cheque book. With the advent of cards and electronic payments, cheque and savings accounts merged into a new type of account: the transaction account. With the usage of cheques declining, the use of *cheque account* as a market term for the account has declined.

A legacy of this era is the cheque button or option on EFTPOS or PED terminals.

Term Deposit

Term deposits or fixed deposits are deposits for a fixed period of time at a relatively high interest rate compared to savings accounts. Generally, the amount and periods are tiered and, in normal monetary conditions, higher amounts for longer periods earn more money than the reverse.

Account Type	Term Deposit
Financial Claims Scheme	Yes
Deposits	Initial deposit only
Withdrawals	Only at end of term, or with penalty fees
Payments	No
Fees & Interest	Early withdrawal penalty. Low to moderate interest paid.

Term deposits can be set to roll over (adding the interest paid into the new term deposit) or interest can be paid into another account. Breaking a term deposit often means forgoing interest, waiting a month and paying a fee. Terms vary from one month to five years.

Credit Card Account

Credit card accounts, and the cards themselves (covered in detail in the Cards chapter) were initially issued to any customer of good standing (positive account balances, regular credits). Later, application forms were largely self-assessed by the applicant, who would sometimes underestimate expenses. Over the years, the rules have tightened and, recently, with the National Credit Code regulated by ASIC, credit card rules are tough.

Credit cards are classed as a revolving line of credit. An unsecured loan, it is issued to customers with reasonable credit ratings.

Account Type	Credit Card
Financial Claims Scheme	No
Deposits	Yes
Withdrawals	Yes, cash-out at high interest
Payments	Yes, purchases at merchants. Cash transfers are at high interest.
Fees & Interest	Annual fee, interest-free period, loyalty points, high interest payable for unpaid balances, cash-out, or transfers.

On application, lenders seek to obtain a balance sheet of assets and liabilities (a customer needs to have more assets than liabilities), income and expenses (again, a customer needs to have a high disposable income). These days, expense estimates need to be validated against the profile of the customer — a high-income parent living in a large house with young children will have higher expenses than a low-income person living in shared accommodation with no dependents. The key ratio is the debt to income or loan to income ratio. A debt to income ratio of less than 36% is considered good. Higher ratios may be declined.

Originally, credit card accounts had a number of benefits that were subsidised by merchants through interchange fee revenue. This revenue has declined over the years and there is pressure to ban it altogether. How long the remaining benefits continue is questionable.

The main benefit was that credit cards were accepted by merchants for purchases at point of sale. Many cards offered an interest-free period. The cardholder would be sent a bill every month and had an additional 30 days to pay it off. So, in theory, it was possible (if a purchase was made at the beginning of the period) to get 30 to 60 days interest free. Most card providers gave five days leeway for a payment to be received (by cheque or through electronic payment) so this was officially advertised as 30-55 days interest free. Once that period was over, the interest rate catapulted, generally to an excessive rate, sometimes 100 times the official rates.

At this point, credit card accounts varied considerably. Some (as is now mostly the case) charged an annual fee. Most had loyalty schemes, with a dollar generally earning one point, but with a varying value on the points earned. Most credit cards teamed up with airlines to provide frequent flyer points or a conversion to them. High-end credit cards offered free travel insurance though terms varied. In some cases, the tickets and accommodation needed to be purchased on the credit card. In others, the customer had to register their intent to take a trip. Most cards required a minimum amount be paid back.

With the introduction of ATMs, cash withdrawals, or cash advances as they were known, were permitted on credit cards, but charged immediately at the full interest rate or close to it. At the discretion of the bank, some transactions could not be treated as purchases and did not receive an interest-free period, but instead the full interest or cash rate. These were generally gambling transactions, trading applications, etc. Transfers of money or payments through the bank were often treated as cash advances.

In order to entice new customers, some cards offered bonus points on sign-up as well as initial interest-free periods. Some offered initial or ongoing balance transfers with interest-free periods. A criticism of these offers was that many of them were not made available to existing customers.

One major controversy was the up-selling of credit card insurance, which insured against the inability to pay off a debt in the event of death, total and permanent disability, or loss of job. This insurance was an expensive type of life and salary continuance insurance for a relatively small benefit and a higher effective premium than more generic products. The fine print stated that (as is consistent with salary continuance insurance) the holder needs to have had a full-time job to be able to make a claim. This point was never checked with prospective clients at the time of sale, and CBA needed to refund the policy premiums as compensation. Many organisations offer some form of insurance with credit cards, and it is advisable to check the terms and conditions, and to compare them to more generic insurance products that can provide better and cheaper coverage.

Trust Accounts

Account Type	Trust Account
Financial Claims Scheme	Yes
Deposits	Yes
Withdrawals	Limited, based on trust account type
Payments	Limited, based on trust account type
Fees & Interest	Monthly fees, transaction limit, excess transaction fee. Low interest paid.

Under state and federal law, some professions and businesses are required to keep money in a trust account. These accounts were established by government legislation, generally due to the risk of misappropriation of funds. They are called regulated or statutory trust accounts, and include:

- Solicitors/conveyancers/settlement agents: for fees paid in advance but not yet incurred.
- Real estate agents: for deposits on houses or rent not yet paid out and expenses not yet incurred.
- Self-managed superannuation funds: for the cash component of the investment used to buy and sell assets, collect contributions and pay fees.
- ASIC managed investment schemes, such as fund managers: used to hold the cash component, and for applications, redemptions, expenses and fees.
- Collection agent (Queensland): for debt collectors.
- Motor vehicle dealers (Queensland and Western Australia): for example, deposits, purchases on consignment, etc.

Essentially, trust accounts are restricted, and specific reporting needs to be performed by the bank and submitted to the customer or to the government.

Trusts are a popular accounting structure in Australia as they have tax benefits. Non-regulated trust accounts are treated as normal transaction accounts by the bank and have limited specific regulatory requirements.

» NOTE

A famous mining magnate, Lang Hancock, created a trust, the Hope Margaret Hancock Trust, named after his second wife with his daughter as executor and grandchildren as beneficiaries. The purpose was most likely to divert asset income into a vehicle that would not incur excessive tax after his death and

save his daughter from a similar issue. With her children as discretionary beneficiaries, she could decide how much to distribute to herself and to the children, and how much to retain, reducing the total tax burden that one person would have incurred. Hancock did not envisage that there would be a falling out but there was. His daughter, Gina Hancock (for a time during the mining boom Australia's richest person) was taken to court by some of her children. The claim was that they were not getting their fair share and Gina was not acting as a trustee should, in the best interests of all the beneficiaries of the trust. The dispute is ongoing.

Personal Loan

Personal loans are a more sensible way of obtaining a loan for a personal unsecured expense debt that lasted more than a month compared to a credit card. It was unsecured and banks charged a premium interest rate, though not in the magnitude of credit cards.

Account Type	**Personal Loan**
Financial Claims Scheme	No
Deposits	Yes
Withdrawals	No (if at limit)
Payments	Yes
Fees & Interest	Monthly fee, moderately high interest payable.

Personal loans can be paid back in instalments with terms generally 10 years or less.

These loans have the most competition in the marketplace with non-banks offering products in this space.

As they have a bad risk weighting, compared to home loans, despite their profitability, banks are restricted in how much they push this product.

Mortgage/Home Loan

The mortgage, or home loan, is a mainstay of retail banking. Competition in this area since the mid-1980s, together with lower interest rates since the late 1980s, has made this product a critical driver of the Australian economy. The success of this product has resulted in higher house prices and increased the potency of monetary policy in the retail market. It has also pushed Australians into phenomenal debt. It is one of the most highly regulated products. Other than integration with PEXA, it does not feature remarkably on the payments landscape except in association with an offset or redraw account.

The implementation of these accounts varies so here we cover the classic home loan account.

Account Type	Mortgage/Home Loan
Financial Claims Scheme	No
Deposits	Yes
Withdrawals	No
Payments	No
Fees & Interest	Monthly or annual fee, low interest payable.

In addition to assessing affordability using debt to income ratio (see above), loan to value ratio (LVR) is an important measure with an LVR less than 80% being preferred. This meant a new home buyer required at least a 20% deposit. Higher LVRs required a Lenders' Mortgage Insurance product, or a similar low deposit premium, that added expense to the loan.

Maximum LVRs varied from 60% to 95%. Lower LVRs were required for riskier locations (e.g., a CBD) and for commercial properties. Non-Australian residents also required lower LVRs.

Due diligence has become tighter on lending with submissions checked independently by the bank's credit risk team (separate from the sales team). Where previously the sales team could exercise discretion to get the deal, now the risk team follows the book.

Interest rates vary, with low interest introductory offers (fixed for one year) and discretionary pricing available. However, according to the ACCC, discretionary pricing is opaque and hinders competition. Smaller banks were more competitive with their headline rates.

The rates also covered risk: riskier loans would have less discretionary pricing flexibility than less risky loans. Loans for owner-occupied properties had lower rates than those for investment properties. Interest-free repayments were lower than interest + principle, and had the added advantage that a higher debt could be claimed for longer if the investment interest was claimed as a tax deduction.

Over time interest-only loans were discouraged with banks pushing their customers to principal + interest.

In Australia, the standard home loan (principal + interest) was amortised over a period of between 20 and 40 years. This meant that, over time, the loan balance would decrease.

As shown in the charts below (*Figure 10*), the result of higher interest rates versus lower rates was not just lower repayments, but also a steeper pay-off at low interest rates, especially in the early years. Paying off extra in the beginning on higher interest rate home loans could cut off years from the loan, and many home loan products supported this. Given that there was no tax deduction for loans for owner-occupied properties, higher repayments were often a good investment strategy.

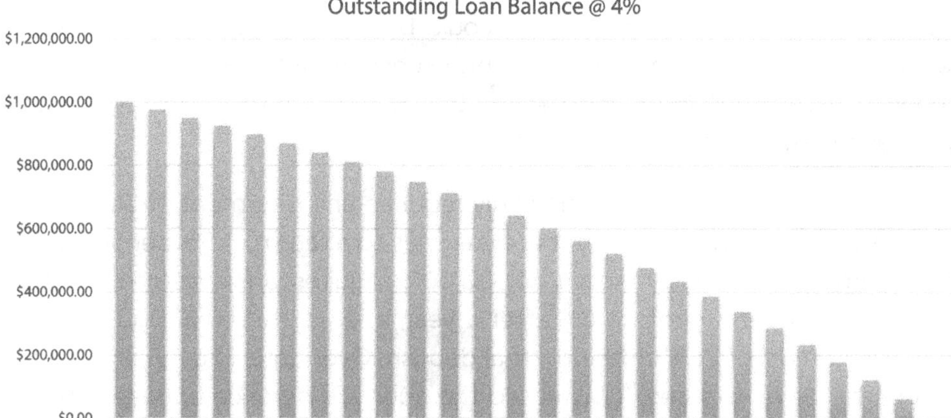

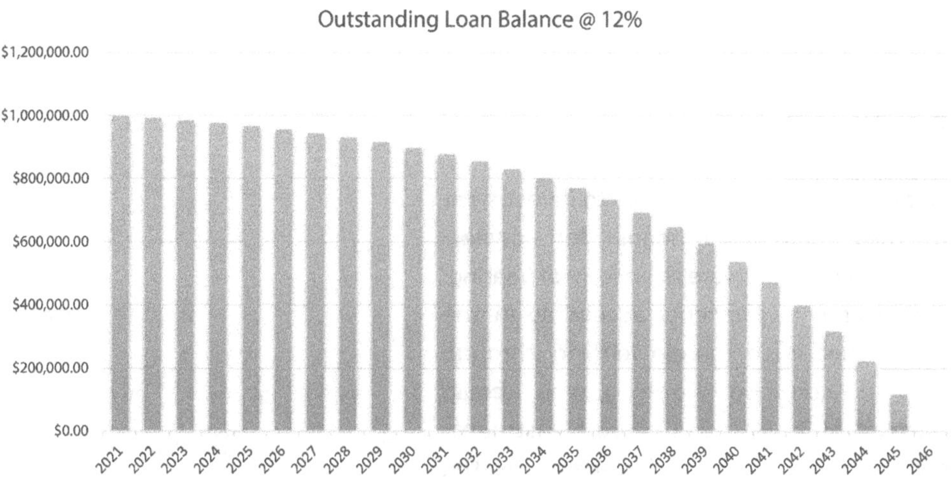

***Figure 10.* Principal reduction rates for low-interest and high-interest loans.**

Similar to credit card insurance, home lenders offered insurance to cover mortgage repayments in the event of death, total and permanent disability, or loss of employment. These policies are typically more expensive and less effective than general insurance policies, and consumers should consider generic insurance before making a decision.

Negative Gearing

Interest expenses for a mortgage on a residential owner-occupied property are not tax deductible in Australia; however, the increase in value of these homes was free from capital gains tax. One banker, asked about his expensive house, said that anyone in Australia who did not put the bulk of their wealth in their own home property was foolish, due to the capital gains tax treatment.

Negative gearing is often poorly understood. While it applies to an investment property, it applies to other investments as well. The key idea was that the rent (or income) obtained from the asset was offset against the expenses (mainly interest) so that the immediate tax impact was negative, which, for a wage earner, offset their total tax payable. However, as the property would increase in value, it could be sold after retirement when the tax payable would be lower. Property investment, especially with newer properties, had the added benefit that the building, and especially, the fittings, were depreciable; this could also be claimed as a virtual expense, adding to the tax benefits.

The gearing concept was that a property only required an investment of 20%, the deposit up front. The capital growth was therefore five times so a return of 5% per annum became 25%. For example, a property worth $1 000 000 requires an investment (deposit) of $200 000. If the property goes up 5% after a year, it is worth $1 000 000 — an increase of $50 000 or a return of 25% on the original deposit. Over time, in a rapidly rising market, as the property value increased, it increased the equity (difference between the loan and value of the property) to allow more borrowing. It was not so uncommon to hear people with modest incomes having several investment properties. However, a decline in property values, as seen in the US and United Kingdom in the lead-up to the GFC, would also have a significant negative impact. Real estate agents' claims that property never goes down in value were not entirely true.

» NOTE

Gearing was not just applicable to investment properties; traditional loans for owner-occupied properties were also a form of gearing. Other geared investments accessible in the retail market were margin lending through shares and commodity trading, which could be geared 500:1. Some of these investments required proper study and research as the losses could be as substantial as the gains.

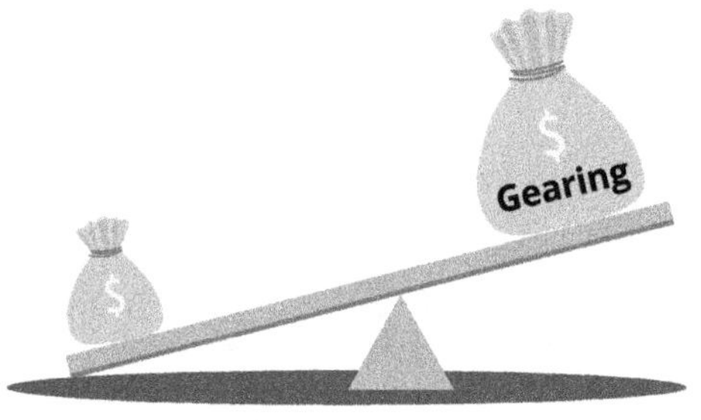

Fixed versus Variable Interest

Introductory mortgages attracted investors with a one-year fixed interest rate, which then reverted to a variable rate. Variable rates could be fixed for up to five years.

Breaking the fixed rate could result in a penalty charge and was inadvisable.

Most consumers thought that if rates were lowered, they may eventually be raised again. This fear was especially true for those who lived through the 1980s double-digit mortgage rate period. A fixed rate meant that the interest rate would not vary for a specified period. As it turns out, with a general trend of lowering interest rates, it may not have been effective to fix interest rates at any time between 1991 and 2020.

Variable rates had their problems too. New customers were attracted to an introductory rate. However, rates would increase as a loan got older and better deals offered to new customers. Old products with less favourable terms would be grandfathered (i.e., not offered to new customers). As we saw with credit cards, account holders and foreign exchange rates, loyal customers were at a disadvantage in terms of pricing. In 2017, all Big Four banks increased their interest rates on existing mortgages. This was ostensibly in response to APRA requesting that banks move customers to interest plus repayment, but this was a request for new loans only. Banks could profit from customers that were already locked in. The move was criticised by both the House Standing Committee on Economics and the ACCC, but there was no compensation or reduction of interest rates for existing customers.

Other Expenses and Rebates

Other expenses such as Lenders' Mortgage Insurance and low deposit premium, loan fees, mortgage stamp duty, state transfer stamp duty, legal fees and countless ancillary expenses were thrown into the loan. Sellers had to pay discharge fees and agents' commissions as well as their own legal fees. These fees were mostly dwarfed by the size of the loan and taken out at settlement. The government offered rebates and stamp duty concessions to some first home buyers.

All these fees dissuaded property speculation, but may have increased expectations of sellers, who wanted a better price than what they purchased their home for. This phenomenon also kept house prices high (but reduced the number of sales) during property cycle downturns.

Property payment and settlement is a complex affair, and is covered in more detail later.

Mortgage Brokers

While financial intermediaries are available for many financial products, mortgage broking is one of the most lucrative with significant broker fees.

Using a broker can be a useful exercise, with the broker making a preliminary affordability and lending value assessment before navigating the product marketplace.

Some brokers, as highlighted by the 2017-2019 royal commission into banking, did not always act in the best interests of customers, seeking loans that offered higher commissions.

Broker lending applications often use the electronic Lending Industry XML Initiative as an easy way to submit multiple applications, though many banks have their own platforms and forms. Customers should be aware that multiple checks on credit ratings (especially failures) can reduce scores, and that they should check with brokers before sending off too many simultaneous applications.

Repossession

If a loan cannot be repaid, banks offer a number of assistance programs through their collections department to assist customers, especially in the event of unusual circumstances (loss of job, injury, illness, etc.). Third parties also provide services to refinance debts in such circumstances.

Ultimately, with a mortgage or secured asset, a bank is entitled to sell the property. The exercise of repossession is an unpleasant one, and often does not recover the true market value due to costs being deducted. The owner is generally left with less of the proceeds of the asset than if they had sold the property themselves.

Redraw Account

A redraw account or redraw facility on a home loan is generally a line of credit separate to a home loan product that allows additional deposits to be made to reduce the loan amount, and then withdrawn into a linked transaction account or directly from the account itself. Unwithdrawn money reduces the amount of interest payable, whereas withdrawn money increases interest payable generally at the rate of the loan.

Account Type	**Redraw Account/Facility**
Financial Claims Scheme	No
Deposits	Initial branch deposit
Withdrawals	Yes
Payments	Generally not
Fees & Interest	Monthly or annual fee, low interest payable

Controversially, in 2020, during the COVID-19 pandemic, ME Bank (a bank owned by Industry Super Funds) prevented redraws to customers. Money that customers thought was available for redraw was transferred to mortgages without their consent. APRA and ASIC were concerned by the moves and asked for an explanation. The moves may have been illegal as, under credit law, changes to terms and conditions require 20 days' notice. The move gave the new bank a bad reputation in a market that was looking for ethical behaviour. It also led to consumers losing confidence in the product with many brokers not recommending it due to this precedent.

Offset Account

An offset account is essentially a transaction account, the balance of which offsets a mortgage, providing the benefits of savings and redraw in one account. With an effective interest rate higher than a term deposit, it is an ideal investment account for people with a home loan on the property they occupy.

Account Type	**Offset Account**
Financial Claims Scheme	Yes (though this could be a grey area, as the provider requires an ADI)
Deposits	Yes
Withdrawals	Yes
Payments	Yes
Fees & Interest	Interest offsets a home loan.

Retirement Savings Accounts

Originally, retirement savings accounts were savings accounts that could only be accessed after retirement. These days, they have largely been replaced with superannuation, though they do offer the advantage of security as they are covered by the Financial Claims Scheme if issued by a bank. The Big Four banks no longer provide new accounts with CBA being the last to withdraw its product for new customers. Smaller banks still offer retirement accounts; however, the interest rates are very low.

Account Type	**Retirement Savings Account**
Financial Claims Scheme	Yes
Deposits	Yes
Withdrawals	Only at retirement
Payments	No
Fees & Interest	Low interest rate.

Retirement savings accounts are covered by similar regulations to superannuation. Money can be contributed at concessional tax rates, earnings also have these concessions, and a pension can be taken out after statutory retirement.

Payments are made in conformance with the ATO SuperStream standard, ensuring that superannuation payments are correctly categorised for tax purposes and to prevent lost superannuation payments.

Commercial Lending

Lending products are varied and diverse being offered to high net worth individuals, small businesses, SMEs, and large corporations and institutions. A more comprehensive treatment is beyond the scope of this book.

Corporations have existed since ancient times, first being recorded around 800 BCE in India, and later in Mesopotamia and the late Roman Empire.[78] The early colony of New South Wales was already engaged with corporations, especially the East India Company. Today, under modern corporate law, organisations exist in several forms, including incorporated associations, cooperatives, no-liability mining companies, private companies (proprietary limited) and public companies (limited). In order to separate assets of shareholders or beneficiaries, these organisations have limited liability. This creates an additional risk in lending: the risk that the corporation goes bankrupt and is unable to pay its debts, despite the wealth of the individuals that own and have benefited from it.

[78] Khanna; Stern; Zwalve

Lending to corporations is contingent on the bank ensuring that the borrowing company can sustain itself, so a more detailed due diligence credit risk process is required than would be conducted for a loan provided to a natural person.

Generally, in Australia, directors cannot knowingly trade while insolvent; however, it is frequently the case that the declaration of insolvency lags behind actual insolvency as has been seen with some notable collapses, including Ansett and Dick Smith. For this reason, banks keep a close watch on the pulse of organisations to detect early signs of distress. In the case of smaller businesses, they may request a director's personal guarantee.

Banks try to ensure that, when lending money, they can recover their money in the event of a wind-up so they establish themselves as secured creditors. After the payment of outstanding tax, secured creditors get paid before employees, unsecured creditors and shareholders.

Business Loan

A business loan has similar features to a personal loan, but is often not secured by assets (though regarded as secured lending against the company). It attracts a moderately high interest rate.

Small businesses struggle to get these loans as they tend to pay their income out as modest salaries with little left for profits. Also, new businesses and startups (that are most in need of loans) need to show profitable company tax and accounting statements for one or two years, often ruling them out of bank financing.

During the COVID-19 pandemic, the Australian Government offered concessional rate loans to SMEs; however, these were issued to customers via the banks and private lenders who did not lower their credit risk requirements. Many SMEs failed to qualify after waiting weeks and submitting substantial amounts of paperwork in hope of acceptance.

Business to Business Lending

Business to business or B2B lending is very common, and in its simplest form takes place whenever a delivery is made from one company to another and an invoice is issued with deferred payment terms. Many small businesses struggle to obtain this credit, with suppliers often requiring payment on delivery or secured lending terms through strict contracts, including personal guarantees from proprietors.

Credit cards are often used to provide credit facilities for buyers. Banks offer receivables financing and trade finance to help on the supplier side.

Administration

Two stages take place when companies enter into or are nearing insolvency. The first is voluntary administration and the second is receivership or liquidation. Both follow similar processes, though the latter is generally more terminal with a low likelihood of shareholders recovering any of their investment. Several organisations have successfully recovered after entering into administration. In 2018, according to ASIC and ABS, 8 044 companies entered into administration, about 0.3% of actively trading businesses.

The appointment of an ASIC registered liquidator (an accountant or organisation with specific qualifications) is done by the company's board of directors (in the event of voluntary administration or director-initiated winding up) or by creditors (in the event of receivership). Courts can also initiate liquidation.

ASIC and corporate law generally permit a company to continue to trade while in administration, even though it may technically be insolvent. There are strict controls: the administration period is limited, and all creditors must be made clearly aware of the company's status and provided with regular updates.

Banks, as secured lenders, can trigger receivership, but tend to encourage the board of directors to seek voluntary administration before going down the liquidation path. The ATO has been known to request that a company enter voluntary administration if a reduced tax liability is requested.

The process of administration is one of the most mysterious practices in the life of corporations as there is often limited accountability and transparency in the process. Creditors, including the ATO and banks, have a say in the process, while smaller unsecured creditors and shareholders are generally sidelined. Some administrators may not always act in the best interests of the shareholders, company or creditors, but instead focus on satisfying their employers or appointers. This is a potential conflict of interest. The administrator has the power to assess a creditor and may give them more or less of a say in the outcome, based on their assessment of the creditor's statement of claim, and it may be possible for a block of creditors to game the system. For example, the landlord of a 10-year lease can claim they are a contingent creditor to the value of the 10 years worth of lease payments, even though that amount is not outstanding or in dispute. It is in the interest of that landlord to see that the business continues even if it means writing off debts incurred by other creditors, including the taxpayer through the ATO. It may be possible for spurious claims to be accepted by the administrator, adding weight to a creditor voting block. In order to silence a block, a liquidator may accept an applicant as a creditor but grant them a zero liability. There is an enormous amount of discretion in the administration process. An administrator appointed by the board of directors may also be less likely to look for evidence or expose the board to the charge of trading while insolvent.

Often during the administration process, the administrator is obliged to invite and accept external bids to take over company operations. Creditors can vote on the best bid, and do so without transparency. Even the ATO, as a creditor, has been known to engage in this practice without the transparency expected of a government agency.

A deed of company arrangement (DOCA) is often proposed by the new company owners and, if accepted by the creditors (who may also accept a reduced payout of their debts), the company is allowed to continue to trade, this time with solvency.

If no DOCA is accepted, then the company's assets are liquidated and the precedence of debtors is honoured, often leading to a lower asset value for the company than what was listed on the balance sheet prior to administration. The precedence is that the liquidators are paid first, then tax bills and government dues, then secured creditors, then priority unsecured creditors (employee entitlements), followed by other unsecured creditors (including bond holders and unsecured trade creditors), and finally shareholders, if there are any assets left.

DOCAs and liquidation proposals are voted on by creditors with two levels of voting: each creditor gets one vote at the first level, then a weighted vote (based on the amount owed to them) when finalising the deal. Once a DOCA or liquidation proposal is accepted, all creditors are bound to accept the outcome, often writing off debts even if they, as a minority creditor, did not vote in favour of the proposal.

Administration is a dissatisfying experience for a number of stakeholders as evidenced by class action lawsuits from shareholders and occasional criticisms from participants. During the administration of Virgin Australia in 2020, one external bidder felt they were not being properly assessed by the administrators. This is not an isolated occurrence.

The administration and liquidation process may work well for secured creditors and, in the interest of expediency, the administrator could see a payout of these major creditors and their own remuneration as a priority. However, the process may not work well for suppliers, shareholders, employees, other stakeholders (such as franchisees or customers), an often underestimated unsecured creditor base — and for the economy.

During COVID-19, the number of zombie companies — unsustainable organisations propped up by government aid — increased and, according to the Australian Restructuring Insolvency and Turnaround Association, the period saw a counterintuitive decline in the number of companies entering administration that would be reversed with the restoration of normalcy.[79]

Franchise liquidation is an example of the failure of the administration system, with franchisees as stakeholders not considered substantially in the liquidation of organisations, as was seen in the liquidation of Fogo Brazilia in 2020 and others.[80]

Administration remains a mysterious and opaque practice in Australia, and a review and overhaul of the process should be conducted to remove any potential for corrupt practices. Loss of money due to an inefficient administration process impacts bank profitability and banking risk, and increases the risk premium on the interest charged for corporate Australia. It could also contribute to money laundering, loss of tax revenue, asset stripping or siphoning, and fraud.

Dormant Accounts

After some time accounts that were not used became dormant. The period of inactivity could vary, say three to seven years or more, depending on the account, and access would be suspended and/or the dormant account would be closed. The bank would attempt to contact the holder and, if uncontactable, the money would be transferred to ASIC who administers "unclaimed money". A good customer/social contact pleaser is to look up the contact's name on the unclaimed money register and inform them of their potential windfall.

---

[79] Alberici

[80] Patty

Non-banking Products

Banks may offer the following products that are generally not regulated by the RBA and generally do not require an ADI license, but are regulated by APRA and/or ASIC:

- Managed funds: An investment vehicle that pools together funds and invests them in a basket of assets as per the fund manager's strategy. The funds are held in a trust.
- Superannuation funds: Generally similar to a managed fund, but regulated by laws that prevent early withdrawal and have concessional tax treatment. Superannuation is a significant, yet often overlooked product (due to compulsory superannuation regulation) and accounts for 29% of the total financial services offered in Australia.[81]
- Self-managed super funds: A superannuation fund without a fund manager. Not recommended by ASIC for investments under $500 000.
- Wrap accounts: A portfolio account that provides simplified reporting but has access to a range of financial investments.
- Markets:
    - Margin loans: A geared investment offering a loan of 50% to 99.9% of the value of the investment, held in the name of the institution.
    - Retail equity trading.
    - Global markets trading and derivatives.
    - Money market trading and derivatives.
    - Institutional equity market trading and derivatives.
- Corporate and institutional instruments.
- Life insurance (life, total and permanent disability, salary continuance, and trauma).
- General insurance (home, contents, landlord's, motor vehicle, assets, mortgage, workers' compensation, business insurance, public liability, indemnity, trade and travel).
- Health insurance.

Cash management trusts are a type of managed fund where funds are invested in money market instruments. Some are regulated through ADIs, while others are not.

» NOTE

Margin loans function by limiting the loss incurred in a geared investment portfolio to the value of the client's equity. For example, a client with funds of $1 000 could borrow another $1 000 to buy an investment worth $2 000 (50% margin loan). As long as the vestment was doing well (say its value went

Storm Financial

[81] Harris, 57

up to $3 000), everyone is happy. If its value went below $2 000, a margin call would be made and, if the customer did not respond, then investments would be automatically sold to get back 50% or more. If the investment's value somehow went below $1 000 (e.g., due to a severe crash or a failure in the margin call systems), then the margin lender could find themselves out of pocket. CBA was very conservative in terms of risk and only allowed its margin lenders to sell the product if the customer would allow the bank to recover losses from their assets; that is, the margin loan was a real loan. Corporate lawyers who read the fine print would reject the product; however, individuals failed to do so. There was a massive crash of the stock market on 29 September 2008 (known as Black Tuesday in Australia) and became known as the GFC. Storm Financial, an issuer of CBA margin loans to its customers, was exposed to the rapidly dropping market. Soon afterwards, it became apparent that margin calls had failed and CBA sought recovery of debt as per the fine print of the terms and conditions. Storm Financial became the first of a string of controversies for CBA. However, many regulators and inquiries criticised the risk policy: in actual fact, the problem was not risk, but the failure to visualise the ethical impact of implementing risk control.

Rewarding Loyalty

Like so many corporations, banks were poor at rewarding loyalty. Rewards were reserved for new or switching customers. Reduced introductory interest rates on loans or credit cards, bonus interest rates on new deposits, balance transfers and bonus loyalty points on credit cards and bonus cash incentives on new accounts were openly advertised as captive customers looked on. The only way to benefit was to switch, and switch again. While the practice may have had short-term benefits, not rewarding loyalty did not make sense from a relationship or a brand point of view. It could have impacted the negative sentiment towards these organisations.

Associations and Spin-offs

Australian Banking Association

The Australian Banking Association is an association representing the banking industry in Australia. Twenty-two banks are members including the Big Four. The Australian Banking Association's role is in political lobbying, representing the industry to the public, establishing a code of practice and setting industry standards (less so technical standards these days since the advent of other organisations and regulations).

Charge Card Services (BPAY)

Charge Card Services, eventually transforming into BPAY, have been a vehicle of collaborative payments for the banks. Owned by the Big Four but open to other banks, they were designed to extend efficient payment processing. They did this initially with credit cards (especially Bankcard), later with bill payments, and more recently with the New Payments Platform through Osko.

eftpos Australia Limited

eftpos Australia Limited (or EPAL) was formed in 2009 as a brand of the Australian debit card scheme. Similar to Visa Debit and Debit Mastercard, but a lower price, it now has a hub to enable transaction switching, a role that was centralised from the cumbersome bilateral system dating from the 1980s.

Property Exchange Australia

Property Exchange Australia (PEXA) is owned by CBA and various non-banks, and provides an electronic settlement service for properties known as e-conveyancing.

Australian Payments Network

Complaints that the Big Four were limiting access to payments led to Paul Keating's formation of the Australian Payments Systems Council in 1985. This kicked off reforms in the coordination of cheque processing, Direct Entry and the emerging EFTPOS systems and integration. The council was criticised for being ineffective.

Originally known as the Australian Payments and Clearing Association, the organisation in its present form was incorporated as a not-for-profit organisation in 1992 at the insistence of the RBA. This was to foster technical cooperation between banks to facilitate streamlined payment processing. It did so through a number of clearing systems and groups:

- Australian Paper Clearing System (APCS), covering cheques and the old paper credit transfers.
- Bulk Electronic Clearing System (BECS), covering Direct Entry, direct debits and direct credits.
- Issuers and Acquirers Community (IAC), previously the Consumer Electronic Clearing System (CECS) — formerly dealing with interchange of card messages between banks (which has now mostly moved to eftpos and the eftpos Hub). IAC now focuses on certification of PIN entry devices in the Australian market.
- High Value Clearing System (HVCS) for SWIFT and RTGS payments.
- Australian Cash Distribution and Exchange System (ACDES) for distribution of notes and coins.
- COIN — Community of Interest Network for the interchange of payments messages.

Today, AusPayNet or the Australian Payments Network boasts over 100 members, including banks, credit unions and building societies as well as schemes, payment providers and large merchants.

Either due to its large membership, or otherwise, AusPayNet has failed to drive payment modernisation since the turn of the century. Many functions that should have been driven by this representative body have been funnelled elsewhere such as to BPAY, eftpos, NPPA, PEXA and the Australian Payments Council (which AusPayNet itself spawned).

NPP Australia

The New Payments Platform organisation (NPP Australia or NPPA) controls the roll-out of the NPP solution. It is covered in more depth in the New Payments Platforms chapter.

Mergers

In 2020, discussions began on a possible merger between NPPA, eftpos and BPAY. There is only one logical outcome of the merger: the eventual extinction of eftpos and BPAY and rolling up their offerings into one solution. While shareholdings of the organisations are similar, an immediate merge is unlikely. Conway's Law is part of it with political lines being well established and no one keen to lose their job. Second, the two earlier schemes still have a significant legacy footprint that will stay around for some time. AusPayNet is a logical addition to this merger, though no proposal has been publicly aired.

Monetary and Fiscal Policy

Monetary policy controls the supply of money in the economy to achieve certain economic outcomes. Monetary policy is distinct from fiscal policy, which also seeks to achieve economic outcomes, in that the former is limited in the number of levers it has at its disposal.

In the classic sense, in the absence of a banking system, monetary policy was just the printing of money. The more money that is printed (and spent by the government), the lower its value becomes and, as a result, more money is spent and more economic activity takes place. This can also result in inflation or even hyperinflation. The less money that is available (due to higher taxes, or lower government spending or accumulation), the more the economy slows, potentially leading to a recession or depression.

As we have seen, monetary policy was put in the sole hands of the Reserve Bank, which has a clear transparent mandate that does not often change.

Australia lives in a global economy. Having a floating currency means that, in a free trade market, the value of this currency is consistent with the value of currencies elsewhere. Ideally, the price of a bicycle here (for example), if we were to exchange currencies, is the same as in another open economy. Increasing the supply of money in an economy inflates prices.

Money and How it is Made

The reason a knowledge of the banking system is so important in payments is that there are only a few ways to effect a payment today: cash, which is becoming less and less important, and electronic payments from a bank account or a loan facility (like a credit account or line of credit). For most of us, cash comes from an ATM connected to our bank account so bank accounts are an essential part of the picture.

When we deposit money into our bank account, many of us think this is cash that can be spent. We get a statement, look at the closing balance, or open up our Internet banking app to see the balance. We feel that that is our money. In a sense, it is. However, if everyone went to their bank to withdraw their money on the same day, the banks would collapse and, until 2008, most customers would be left penniless. The balance on the screen is little more than information held in a database, the same way a phone number is stored on a phone's contact list. So how does this data become so powerful in the economy?

According to the RBA,[82] paper notes make up 95% of currency in the economy. Coins are the remaining 5%.

The RBA treats the notes as a liability as, even though they no longer say so, they are treated as a promise to pay.

›› NOTE

The RBA's assets are essentially gold (and, as we mentioned earlier, there is proportionately less of it than there used to be), foreign currency reserves, instruments issued by foreign institutions, and loans to the Australian Government. So when we go to the RBA and ask for our note to be cashed in, what would we get? There is no requirement for the RBA to produce anything now that our currency is fiat though, theoretically, if the RBA were liquidated, all its assets would be sold. In 2019, the total assets of the Reserve Bank were valued at $176 billion. Normally, the ratio of gold and foreign instruments to Australian Government loans is 1:1. During the COVID-19 pandemic, assets were increased to $257 billion. Sale of gold and foreign instruments, and purchase of Australian Government securities, as well as a $20 billion increase in the money base (aka printing money, in this case as ESA deposits) changed the asset ratio to 3:7.

There is a notion that banks (including private banks) create money. The story goes like this: a bank takes a deposit, say $1 000, from *person one*. The bank then gives this money as a loan to *person two*. Then that person buys something from *person three*, who deposits it in the same bank and, like this, the same money is borrowed and invested ad infinitum, so that every odd numbered customer has $1 000 in the bank, and every even numbered customer has a $1 000 loan, leading to an infinite amount of deposits and an infinite number of loans. The only money that really exists is the original $1 000.

This is partly true.

First, *person three* may not have come to the same bank, but instead have banked elsewhere. Second, we saw that banks must maintain a total capital adequacy ratio of 8% (which for the major banks may increase to 11% or 13%). This means that, even in the simple model we had, the 8% acts as a limit on how much money is lent out. The bigger the bank, the more it can lend out. If a new bank was started with $40 million, it could lend $500 million maximum (in risk-weighted assets), less than 1 000 home mortgages. From that point on, any money it received as a deposit would need to go into safe assets such as 0 risk-weighted

[82] Doherty

asset (RWA) government bonds. Third, every time a person pays off a loan, the creation of money is reversed. In order for a bank to lend, it needs to have money so, over time, naturally, there needs to be more depositors than borrowers, which reduces the ability to multiply money. Fourth, if a bank cannot pay out its payment obligations for the day it is in trouble. Every morning, net settlement obligations from the previous day and, throughout the day, intraday settlement obligations need to be met in a timely manner. If one of the Big Four banks were to fail, it would be catastrophic for the banking system and possibly for the economy.

Money Measurement

When measuring the money in an economy, there are six types of money:

- Currency is legal tender in notes and coins outside of the banking sector. Currency in a bank is considered to be out of the economy and it can be counted as a secure 0 RWA asset by the banks.
- Money base is the debt of the Reserve Bank. This is currency plus bank deposits with the RBA, plus any RBA debt issued to private, non-bank institutions.
- M1 is currency plus private money in transaction bank accounts; that is, money that can be used immediately to make a payment. Accounts that have a card attached, or allow BPAY and transfers to other accounts, fall into this category even if they are called savings accounts.
- M2 is M1 plus near money. Near money is private, non-ADI money in banks' savings accounts (thus cannot be used immediately to make a payment), term deposits, and certificates of deposit that can theoretically be cashed in within a day or two. They are classed as liquid but not as readily available as cash.
- M3 is M2 plus all private non-ADI money in any ADI, including credit unions and building societies.
- Broad money is M3 plus all deposits in appropriately licensed institutions that can be converted to cash, such as foreign exchange accounts, cash management trusts and money markets instruments. It includes all financial institutions (AFIs) and is, as the name suggests, a broad definition of money. It excludes shares and AFI deposits in AFI accounts.

Some interesting observations:

- After the GFC in 2009, M3 and broad money merged (*Figure 11*) indicating that cash-like deposits have moved to more regulated entities.
- Increased supply of money historically corresponded to an increased GDP, but this correlation has weakened with financial deregulation and the increased availability of credit.

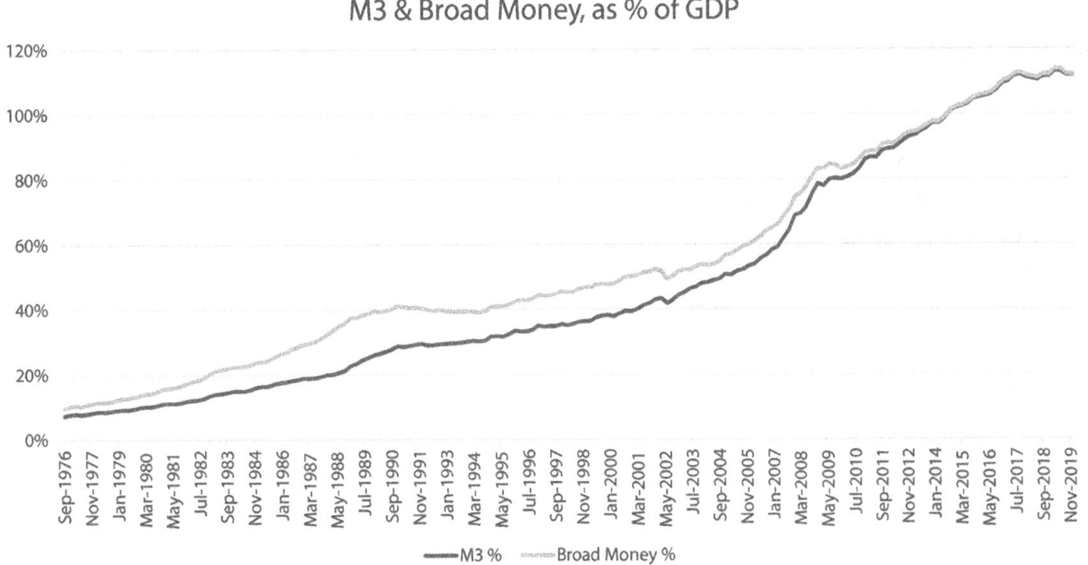

***Figure 11.* M3 and broad money as a percentage of GDP.**
Data courtesy of the RBA and the Australian Bureau of Statistics.

Money base, the money that the government (through the RBA) creates, is a fraction (6%) of broad money in the economy. If anything, money base has declined relative to broad money since 1976, when records started (*Figure 12*). The biggest contributors to broad money are the private ADIs, specifically the banks (especially the bigger banks), through their lending activities. To put this 6% another way, broad money is almost 17 times as large as money base.

Figure 12 shows two later spikes in money base, in 1996 and 2014.

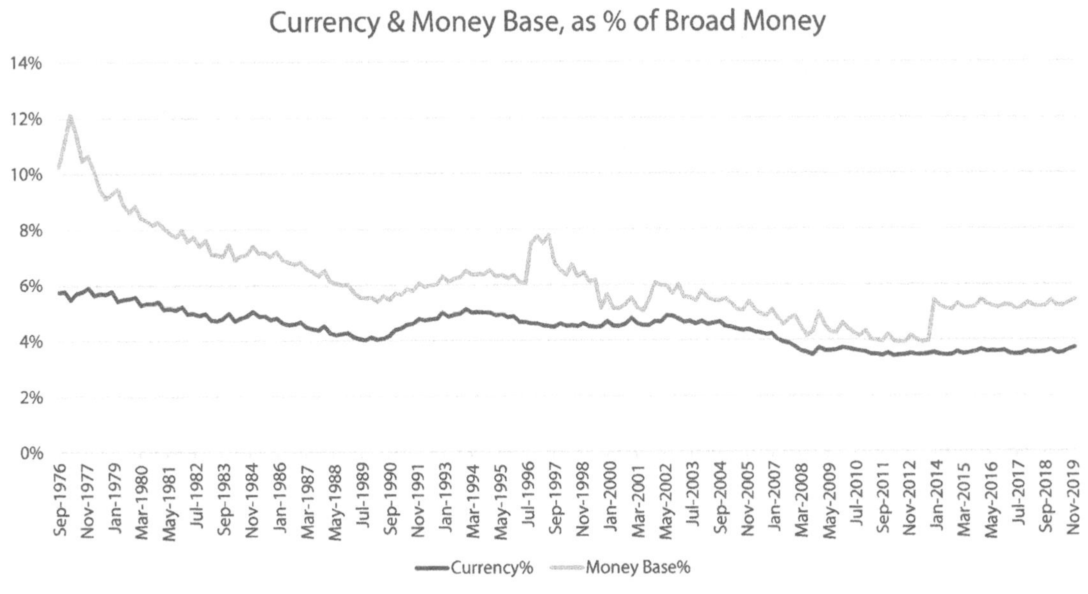

***Figure 12.* Currency and money base as a percentage of broad money.**
Data courtesy of the RBA.

Correlation of Money to Inflation and Nominal GDP

Nominal (inflation adjusted) GDP is an indication of how active an economy is, and ties in with the goal of the RBA to improve the economic prosperity of the country.

Studies by the RBA,[83] as well as other studies,[84] have shown that there is no real correlation, in recent times, between increases in money and the GDP. There was a universal spike in the OECD, including Australia, with the introduction and growth of credit and financial deregulation, though this has subsided. These studies also show little evidence of an impact on inflation in Australia, but they do show an impact in other less-developed countries pointing to the fact that interest rates are a better control of inflation in countries with a disciplined monetary policy. Also, recently, money velocity (the rate at which money is spent, i.e., GDP:money, the inverse of money:GDP) has declined over the period of deregulation with a slight stabilisation in recent years.

Liquidity Management

The science of making a profit in banking is all about how to invest cash deposits. It is a balancing act to meet payment demand with liquid assets. Depositors think they have their money on call, and there has to be enough available to ensure payments can be made.

Every day, liquidity operations teams in banks receive a list of accounts with large balances. If they do not recognise an account, that means more liquidity is required, generally in ESA accounts. They keep a calendar of when corporations make big dividend payments, pay days and special occasions (such as the days before and after Easter and Christmas holidays).

Getting it right means optimising profits. Longer-term investments return greater yields. Less money in ESA and secured deposits means more loans and more profits. Too little, and instruments would have to be sold on secondary markets (losing margins) or, worse, the bank could not settle its payments.

These days, especially for big banks, higher capital adequacy and liquidity coverage ratios mean more money in cash and safer deposits (0 risk-weighted assets). Liquidity management is not as much of an issue but, with tight margins, every dollar counts so this means earning more interest on high-quality liquid assets (HQLA).

---

[83] Doherty

[84] Feldstein & Stock; Ershad & Mahfuzul; Ahmed

5.

INFORMATION TECHNOLOGY

THE TECHNOLOGICAL INSTRUMENTS OF PAYMENTS and money during Australia's early years were pen and paper. Today, payments take place using sophisticated information technology. Information technology facilitates activities and commerce that were not possible 100 years ago and, likewise, a failure in a system can bring parts of the economy to its knees. An understanding of payments would be superficial without a look into how the technology works today.

Computers and computer scientists were originally used in banking to perform complex calculations, pushing in lots of data and calculating things that were difficult to calculate. Eventually, the real benefit of technology became apparent: the storage, manipulation and retrieval of large amounts of data. The information technology era was born around 1960.

Mainframes

The mainframe was a large computer that was generally housed in a purpose-built room. It could be accessed externally through terminals. Terminals were screens with keyboards that did not have much computing power themselves, but instead relied on the mainframe to execute commands, programmed by professionals.

》 NOTE

Early computers were very unreliable. Vacuum tube technology would blow out regularly. The origin of the term *computer bug* was literally a bug; that is, an insect causing a vacuum tube to short circuit. Finding the inactive piece was often a needle in a haystack scenario, which meant that the system could be down for quite some time. Transistor-based computers (using semiconductor technology) were an improvement but still failed often.

These early mainframe vacuum tube-based systems (e.g., the IBM 700 series) gave way to the more compact (but still large) transistor-based systems (e.g., the IBM 7000). Tandem NonStop hardware was developed to handle high redundancy, and it was only in the early 1990s that high redundancy mainframe architecture had matured in the banking world.

Assembly and FORTRAN code eventually gave way to the popular COBOL programming language. The challenge with early mainframe programming is that programmers had to do everything themselves. There were no, or few, libraries available — and without the Internet, and tools such as GitHub for code sharing and Stack Overflow for programming tips, programmers needed to rely on their own learning. Transaction handling, for example, (locking a file to write data, and unlocking it when finished to ensure two users did not corrupt the information), all had to be done through code from scratch.

Newer mainframe systems included CICS software, OS/360 hardware and IBM Z-Series mainframes.

» NOTE

Bank executives who had gone up the ranks from being a teller were highly regarded as they knew how banking works. The balance of knowledge has gradually shifted to IT. In fact, a former CEO of the CBA, David Murray, began his career as a bank teller and another, Ralph Norris, started off as an assembly card switch programmer at what would later become a subsidiary, Auckland Savings Bank, before making their way to the top of the organisation. Ralph Norris was known to personally grill technologists about their solution if he was concerned with over-complexity or cost.

Data Centres

The need to keep many computers in a managed environment gave birth to data centres. These buildings are purpose-built to house many machines. They are cooled, and dust and humidity are minimised. In the event of a fire, instead of water, inert gas (argon, nitrogen or CO2) is used to suppress fires. The room is locked down, access is restricted (even for staff), and can only be entered after clearing multiple checks.

Personal Computers

While a number of micro-computers were developed in the 1980s and earlier by Commodore, Apple Computers, Tandy Radio Shack and others, many of the personal computers (PCs) of today can be traced back to the IBM PC and Microsoft operating systems (disk operating system, DOS and later Microsoft Windows). They ran on Intel chips, originally the 8086 model, now manufactured by others as well (such as AMD), and collectively known as x86 chipset systems.

These computers and their software transformed banking and had a major impact on civilisation generally. For the first time, branch staff had access to computing power and, with the aid of a word processor or spreadsheet, people could use a computer productively without knowing how to write software.

x86-based Servers

PC hardware, facing greater competition and greater sales volumes, was becoming commoditised. At the same time, memory and hard drive space were becoming bigger, cheaper and faster to access. With minor peripheral changes, these PCs could be mounted in racks, the shelving used in data centres. Organisations started using x86-based machines as servers in data centres. These machines either ran Microsoft Windows (known as Wintel) or Linux, a version of Unix designed initially for the x86 family.

Cloud Computing

With the advent of the Internet, it was possible to access a computer anywhere on the planet provided it was accessible over the Internet. Originally starting with Amazon with Amazon Web Services, Microsoft with Azure, and Google with Google Cloud, organisations started offering space in their data centres for external customers to access. Cloud computing was intended to reduce the costs of running software.

There are several levels of cloud or outsourced offerings available:

- Infrastructure as a Service (IaaS), where rack space, machines and cables are rented out on an on-demand basis. An example is the Amazon Web Services (AWS) original offerings.
- Platform as a Service (PaaS) is the development of software on a platform without the need to worry about infrastructure; for example, Microsoft Azure's Integrated Azure DevOps.
- Software as a Service (SaaS) is a fully-deployed software suite ready to be configured and used. This was previously known as an application service provider (ASP). An example is Salesforce.
- Managed service is a fully managed service that provides a certain business outcome; for example, cheque processing from Fiserv (now run by Genpact).

Software Development Life Cycle

The implementation of projects, especially software, is an area of science in itself. Called the software development life cycle, there are several disciplines in this area outlined below.

Waterfall

The Waterfall method of development generally involves a long period of incubation followed by a sudden release. The steps and artefacts include:

1. Concept: An idea that is circulated to seek sponsorship.
2. Architecture: The high-level solution and components used to understand requirements and design.
3. Project planning and management.
4. Business case: A formal request for funding that includes expenses for the first year, expected benefits over a three to five-year period (expressed as a value in today's dollars), net present value and risks.
5. Risk management plan and execution.
6. Business requirements and analysis: The requirements of the system.
7. Non-functional requirements: Throughput and availability requirements.

8. Detailed design: This includes software, security, infrastructure and processes.
9. Building: The actual building of the solution.
10. Testing: This includes planning and execution of unit testing, system/integration testing, non-functional testing and user acceptance testing.
11. Deployment plan and deployment.
12. Production support and warranty.

In the Waterfall model, requirements would be set, and (as is usually the case) things took longer and were more expensive than expected. To contain costs, scope and quality may be reduced, and, together with differences between what is imagined, what is said, what is written down and what is delivered, business owners and sponsors were almost always disappointed.

A common criticism of the Waterfall model and the full software development life cycle was that it was slow and expensive. "Analysis Paralysis" was an oft-cited jibe. Faced with such criticism, it was often possible to cut corners and avoid steps at the expense of quality, and often the push to cut these corners came from the top. Nevertheless, failures would often be blamed on the implementation team not the expediency.

Cyclical Development

Cyclical development is similar to Waterfall in that there is a big project that results in a sudden software release.

The key difference is that, in cyclical development, work on version 2 of the product would begin even before the first version hit the markets. This method helps maintain the primacy of the product in the eyes of the consumer, and is common in software or hardware institutions. Various versions of Microsoft Windows are one example. Apple iPhone releases are another.

Banks loved to announce releases of something new. Version 1 of some new product was impressive and they left the best for version 2. Unfortunately, the team was disbanded, the executive who announced the product got promoted, and nothing ever came of the product again, primarily because it had not been established for cyclical development and enhancement. Examples of these new products include CBA's KeyCorp and Albert terminals, XPOS's Kaching, Westpac's Databank and Presto (with the name being relaunched for a new organisation: mx51), ANZ GoMoney, and NAB's Talk to MLC. It is unsurprising that many big launches are made, with the lack of success not publicised at all in the hope that the media and customers forget. The absence of information or a broken link on a website is the only hint that a product was a one-hit wonder. This is a clear sign that many products in banking are not set up for cyclical development. Although business cases are structured this way, permanent product owners and teams are rarely set up to support them. It was hard to set up a new product. But the real secret was that it was harder to set up cyclical development to support it.

Iterative Development

Some Waterfall projects were big and long — they needed to be as they only had one stab at achieving the business case. The iterative development process used in smaller technology teams and in innovation showed that breaking down projects allowed for more focused development, and allowed the team to change direction at the end of each iteration based on their learnings.

Agile, which popularised iterative development, was effective in bringing technologists and business owners together. It introduced the concepts of a fortnightly *sprint* and a daily *scrum* meeting where business product owners, managers, and technologists would identify what would be done and then deliver it in two weeks to show an outcome. The advantage is that for the first time, the business had a visualisation of what was happening through a system of resource and requirement allocation called *kanban*, from a practice called *lean* which tries to maximise value and minimise waste. Requirements needed to be traded off based on available resources, often on a daily basis, so that any issues to do with resource availability and budget could be visualised and sorted out immediately.

Unlike the Waterfall model, the business was taken along on the journey and, after the end of a program of work, stakeholders were more satisfied.

Agile was a necessary step in unifying the two segments of the bank: bringing technology constraints into the full view of the business. Agile was also more suited to a cyclical development process, though the Agile cycle was two weeks while a traditional cyclical release could be a year.

However, Agile, like Waterfall, could be corrupted. First, the scrum meetings needed to be small. The agile team would only do what was possible within the team. Members of the team became comfortable with each other, which is a good thing and meant accepting limitations as given but, unlike Waterfall, there is often a reluctance to raise issues. A team tended to operate at the average pace of its members. The two-week cycle often meant just scratching the surface and not taking on difficult challenges. In 1962, John F. Kennedy spoke about travelling to the moon by the end of the decade. (Sure enough, they did it in 1969.) It was difficult to use Agile to solve deep tech problems in two-week sprints. Some problems took months to solve. Sure enough, there were few transformational programs completed in Australian banks during the age of Agile. Despite its popularity, there is limited (if any) empirical evidence that Agile is more efficient than other methods. In fact, it is possible, that despite better communication, an Agile project can deliver less than a Waterfall project, but with the improved dialogue leading to greater stakeholder engagement and satisfaction, which is its core advantage. Perhaps a new model will be developed that facilitates both business engagement and deep technical development.

Continuous Development

For a bank, a software release would be a big deal: months of planning, even more development, and a big day when the software would be released. Sometimes, if the software failed, it would need to be rolled back and the process repeated.

Continuous delivery (or continuous development) is the notion that changes can keep being released as they occur. It generally requires automated testing, automated deployment, strict source code management, and moving quality to the left side of the timeline (shift to the left) or testing earlier. Continuous development facilitates and empowers small Agile teams and benefits customers due to regular updates.

By far the greatest benefit of the scrum meeting is a daily chance for team members to stand up and say what they have done, what they are working on and what is stopping them. It improved communication compared to other methods, where people would not speak unless spoken to.

Continuous development is also referred to as DevOps from a technology perspective, where the development lifecycle is automated on demand.

Configuration versus Customisation

Configuration is where a non-expert business user can modify a system without going through the full software development life cycle of specification, testing, and so on, the latter being known as customisation. Because configuration is cheap, a business case is not needed. The danger is that some configuration is so complex it requires an expert (paid much more than the salary of a programmer), defeating the purpose of its claimed efficiency. Some configuration changes have been known to stop a bank's operations, so often these complex configuration changes are as expensive as software development, and are included in the software development life cycle after all.

Design Thinking

Originally, software requirements were pulled out of an executive's head, based on their ideas and inspiration. Senior staff were sometimes treated to an overseas trip, a perk of the office, colloquially known as a *junket*. These trips were the source of many ideas. Often an idea would become a project and, two years after its inception, it would be discovered to be unsuccessful.

Human-centred design (HCD) and design thinking are a discipline involving understanding customers through empathy, experimenting with ideas, and testing them on customers before investing in them.

›› NOTE

Often attributed to Henry Ford (an early mass producer of motor vehicles) is the line, "If I had asked people what they wanted, they would have said faster horses." Although he may not have said it, it could have been true. We see this behaviour all the time. People are stuck in their way of thinking and disruptive change takes time to settle in. Some inspiration is necessary, but design thinking is not just about asking people what they want; it is about understanding their needs, and prototyping and testing solutions.

User Experience Design

User experience design (UX design) looks at how a user interacts with a channel or system — making the interaction usable, useful, accessible, valuable, etc.

Accessibility design includes making a service accessible to particularly disadvantaged users, but also users not in the top percentile of vision or technology savviness, or those in challenging environments such as with loud background noise, a silent environment, or in the dark or bright sunlight.

Service Design

An overlooked problem in many projects was how to provide excellent and sustainable service. Service design attempts to do just that for all participants, not just the end user, but also for employees, suppliers and anyone else involved in providing the service. In reaching a sustainable steady state, it looks at customer experience, employee experience and partner experience, both end-to-end and holistically.

Conway's Law

Conway's Law was coined by computer scientist Melvin Conway in the late 1960s to describe how system architecture mimics organisational structure and not always functional or technical requirements.

The need to get products out to market often meant taking shortcuts, with inexperienced or greedy software developers seeking to win business at a low cost and so neglected fundamental analysis design and efficiency. Often these solutions would create a new legacy that needed to be replaced or improved to be able to scale. The counter-argument was that the old organisation was slow and deliberative, meaning that the delay in time to market could cause the loss of an important opportunity. The trade-off between decentralisation and centralisation, and between agility and strategy, has been contentious and will continue to be for years to come.

Enterprise Architecture

"We've got to continue to push that enterprise architecture is about designing the way this company will do business, and that it's far beyond the scope of IT alone," said Jeanne Ross, Director and Principal Research Scientist at MIT's Sloan Center for Information Systems Research.[85]

The enterprise architecture of a bank provides, firstly, a blueprint of how systems and processes in the organisation are connected together. It provides a target state for the future, and standards to ensure the adoption of technology, business and processes are streamlined to allow the organisation to have lower IT and operational costs and, at the same time, achieve innovation and customer service objectives. It should also support the regulatory and security constraints of the organisation.

[85] Gardener

Sometimes, the need to be quick to market avoids this standardisation and simplification, and creates what is known as technical debt that, like all debt, needs to be repaid or will result in risk.

The enterprise architecture is broken down into domain architectures and solution architectures. These are the building blocks that have a business-focused outcome and attempt to achieve a greater vision for the organisation.

Figure 13 is a simplified view of a typical bank's architecture.

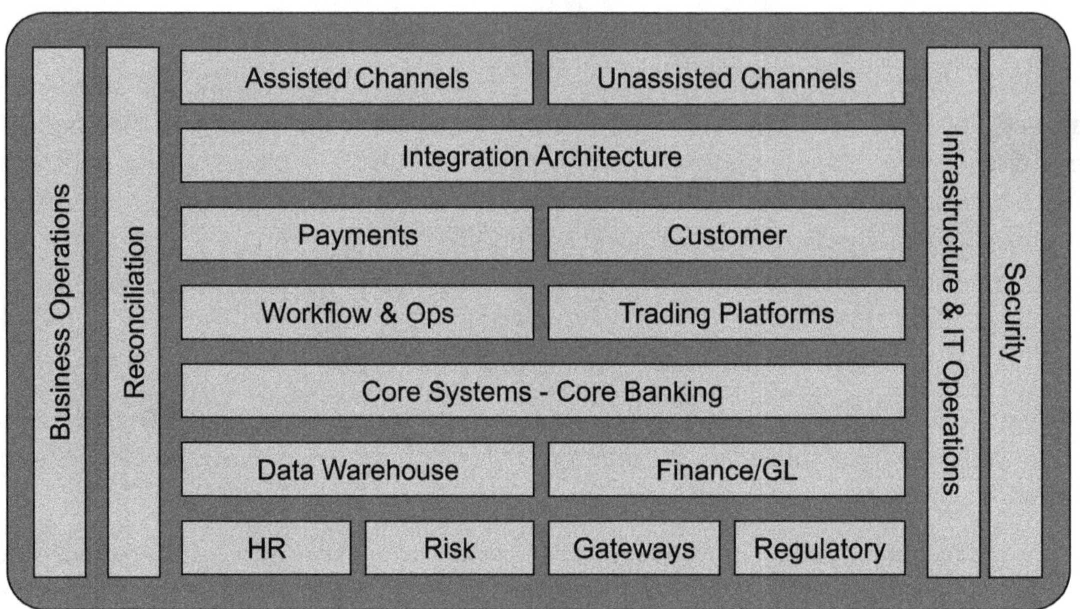

Figure 13. **A simplified high-level view of the enterprise architecture of banks.**

A good enterprise architecture tries to standardise platforms, and simplifies the environment, so it is easy to maintain, and is more consistent and compliant with standards and regulations, and to operate at a lower cost.

Table 3 describes the elements and the enterprise architecture opportunities.

Table 3.
Enterprise architecture elements.

Element	Description	Opportunities
Assisted channels	This includes tellers, phone channels and relationship-managed clients (e.g., personal bankers, relationship bankers and financial advisers).	By providing the front line with powerful digital tools, banks can do more things for their clients without handing over customers to different people, and requiring the front line to have manageable training.
Unassisted channels	These are new digital channels (such as mobile apps) as well as Internet banking. Corporate customers can integrate with the bank directly by using corporate Internet banking, Direct Entry files and, more recently, APIs. This layer also includes ATMs and merchant PED devices.	Multiple wallets may be confusing for customers, and the inability to perform the same functions on mobile and desktop software has dogged this area for many years. Standardisation of the backend of unassisted channels using APIs is one solution; however, even user interface elements can be standardised.
Integration architecture	The glue that holds all systems together is the API layer. Implementations split this middleware into several areas: the API gateway (with APIGEE, Mulesoft, and WSO2 being popular vendors), orchestration and integration technology, API standards and caching.	Providing APIs for everything in a bank is easier said than done. APIs need to be accessible and usable, and require authorisation, authentication and entitlements must be implemented before they can be rolled out. A one-stop shop is useful here.
Payments	These are the payment integration systems that allow payment requests from gateways and channels to be applied to core banking. This layer includes transaction monitoring and implements compliance policies. It supports both clearing and settlement.	A payment hub can help standardise processing and, if it is modern and real-time, can facilitate the agility of the organisation in meeting requirements. A good payment hub allows diversification of core systems so a bank can provide more products to customers.

Element	Description	Opportunities
Customer repository	The customer information repository contains key information about customers and the organisation's relationship with them (i.e., customer relationship management).	Having a single customer repository helps organisations understand customer relationships in full, and provides convenience to customers (e.g., with changes of address occurring in one place, not 10). De-duplication and Know Your Customer information can be centralised here for reuse across the organisation.
Workflow and operations	In the end, to pull everything together, some manual work is required. Backend business operations and workflow tools help streamline the bank's operations, and the back office provides the glue between system gaps. It is a poorly understood area, and few solutions provide real end-to-end automation here.	Enterprise architecture should provide tools to automate manual processes, but also help to document and define them so future projects can involve less manual work.
Trading platforms	Trading platforms are where decisions are made to invest and exchange. This could include foreign exchange, equities or commodities.	Trading platform standardisation helps downstream processes such as payments and settlements as well as regulatory reporting.
Core systems and core banking	Traditionally the be-all and end-all of technology in the bank, the core system is still important as it maintains customers' ledgers. It can be seen as the heart of the bank, rather than the limbs.	While having one core is a good vision, banks have (and will tend to have) a few core systems. Allowing all these systems to be equal citizens of the architecture through a common payments engine, a common integration layer, and a common customer repository goes a long way in ensuring the flexibility and agility of a bank.

Element	Description	Opportunities
Data warehousing	Large databases were originally held by finance and marketing departments. Technical challenges or organisational Conway's Law issues often meant there was no single database though, over time, information in many banks has been aggregated into one database. This trend was reversed slightly with the advent of big data.	Data warehousing before big data was a futile exercise in standardising data, with an excessive amount of data normalisation. Thanks in part to big data, it has now gone the other way, into a laissez-faire process of collecting everything and putting it into a data lake. There may be a return to a middle ground, and the standardisation of payment messaging (in the payments world) could be a good opportunity to standardise data. Reducing and rationalising reporting is a good opportunity for cost savings. Perhaps the centralisation of data and the federalisation of reporting is the best solution, if the technology allows it.
Finance/GL	A bank runs as a business and attempts to make a profit. Systems such as the general ledger, procurement (SAP Ariba is popular here), and payables are generally managed by the chief financial officer, who takes input from all business lines.	While financial systems are generally well centralised, one interesting observation can be made: banks mix the money of their customers with that of the business of running the bank. Separation of transactions and reporting could help resolve this issue, and maintaining separation of these concerns should be an important objective.
Human resources	Recruitment, onboarding, performance management, training, workers' compensation and payroll are standard functions of any organisation. These interrelated functions are generally grouped under human resources.	The human resource functions of a bank are no different to those of any other organisation, and there is a move towards using external software to manage all aspects. This is a good thing for banking because it reduces costs and allows the organisation to focus on core values. There will always be custom aspects to this as, like in any organisation, staff are a key and differentiated asset.

Element	Description	Opportunities
Risk	Risk management includes risk reporting, mitigation, control, limits and monitoring of positions (for trading), and authorisation limits and controls (for banking). Auditing functions may sit here or be separate.	There has been attention placed on risk management culture by making risk reporting accessible to all staff and making it as robust a framework as possible in all contexts.
Gateways	Connections, particularly to payment gateways, allow a bank and its customers to interact with the world.	One of the objectives of gateways is to centralise connections so that exchanges can be properly monitored and compliance is consistently applied. This means that connectivity should be reserved for certain interfaces, such as from payments or the integration layer.
Regulatory systems	Regulatory and compliance reporting are key functions of any bank. These systems, while not critical from a customer operations point of view, could result in significant action if not properly carried out.	By ensuring that data and information flows are standardised and less bespoke, common processes can ensure all regulatory frameworks are applied consistently.
Infrastructure and IT operations	One of the big expenses in the IT business is computers and data centres. In addition, service software and service staff from desktop support to incident management are a core component of IT infrastructure and operations.	One of the recent challenges is the use of cloud computing providers and the outsourcing of managed services. Clear standards and processes help to make it easy to implement these measures.
Security	Security ensures that cyber attacks and internal fraud are not possible. Authentication and authorisation for customers and staff, and intrusion detection and avoidance are critical features.	Security is becoming more and more important. It needs to encompass every element of the enterprise architecture.

Element	Description	Opportunities
Reconciliation	Reconciliation ensures consistency of the books of a bank and that all systems are properly aligned and no transactions are missing.	Good system design should not leave transactions unreconciled. Unfortunately, transactions in complex systems do go astray, and reconciliation is a way to audit and check that everything works correctly.
Business operations	Not everything can or should be automated. When things fall through the gaps, or manual work is required, business operation services do the last mile.	Workflow management, CRM and other tools are used in this space. These days, screen scraping and desktop automation tools are used to help manual processes complete faster. While this area has the greatest potential for cost savings, premature downsizing can have a negative impact on customers' perceptions.

⟫ NOTE

Surprisingly, after big fines, inquiries and royal commissions, the failure of organisations to implement the key checks (transaction AML/CTF, IFTI, TTR, and SMR in the payments layer) have been overlooked. Standardised processing would have saved much hardship. For example, with all payments flowing through one capability, a $10 000 TTR report would have been easy to implement and errors would not have occurred: nothing would have slipped through the net. Enterprise architecture always battles with individual projects rushing to get something out to market quickly, and overlooking essential measures that end up costing an organisation dearly in the long run. It is a pity the royal commission did not interview the architects.

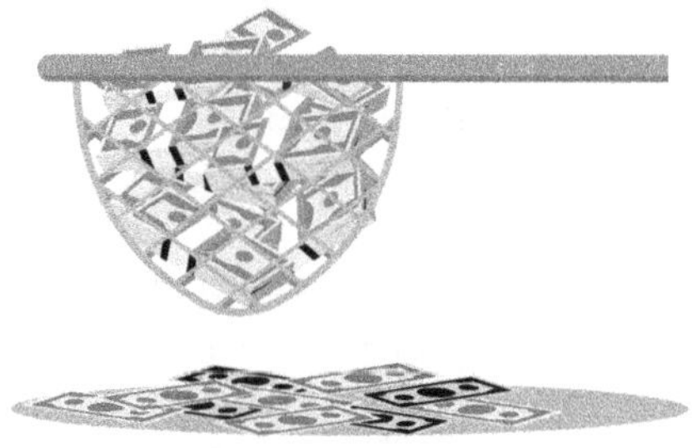

When discovering a solution (solutions architecture), the big decisions are documented and solutions are implemented in line with the enterprise architecture. Often, a reuse before buy, buy before build approach is advocated, unless a capability is new to the market and a differentiator. The choice of platforms and computer code languages attempts to utilise platforms with good market penetration so it is easier to find experts. Popular languages these days include Microsoft .NET, Oracle Java, JavaScript, Python and others.

Core Banking

Computerisation of bank ledgers, and eventual centralisation, resulted in a key system, the core banking system. Banks tended to have multiple core systems for deposits and lending, and for different lines of banking products.

Custom-built mainframe products and, in the 1980s, Hogan (a brand owned by DXC) have gradually been replaced. ANZ now uses Infosys Finacle overseas (but not in Australia), NAB and Suncorp use the Oracle Banking Platform, and CBA and Macquarie Bank use SAP's core banking software.

TCS BaNCS is used by the RBA and some smaller ADIs in Australia, and Temenos T24 is deployed at second tier banks.

Westpac and, to some extent, ANZ have avoided a core banking replacement.

Core banking replacements were expensive affairs costing hundreds of millions of dollars, sometimes even over a billion dollars (as in the case of CBA).

〉〉 NOTE

BaNCS was a successful Australian innovation, developed as a mainframe COBOL application by the New South Wales State Building Society. Called the Bank Automation and Network Control System, it was run at a number of credit unions and building societies. NCR acquired worldwide marketing rights in 1987 from the New South Wales state government. Eventually, the software was acquired by TCS, replatformed onto Java, and now TCS BaNCS powers some of the world's biggest banks: Bank of China and State Bank of India to name the top two.

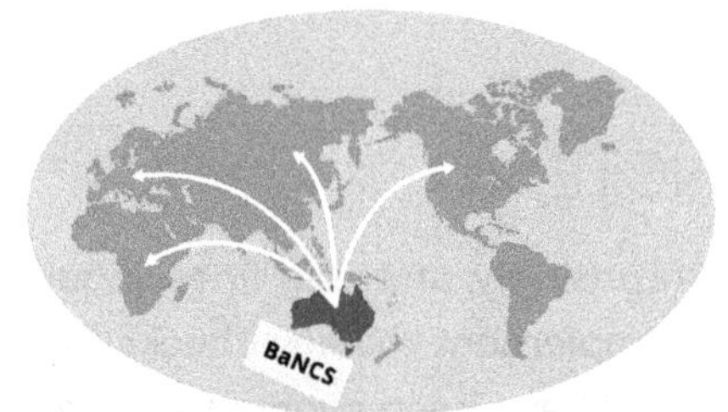

Core Banking Fallacy

Traditionally, core banking has been the central part of banking when viewed as a replacement to the ledger. In the early days of central computerisation (around 1980) this was true: tellers, mainframes and other systems were wired almost directly to the core bank.

The common fallacy, employed by even new or old modernising banks, is that this is all there is in banking.

This focus on the core has changed over time with cross-system integration, particularly payments and channels, needing their own technology stack outside of the core, and increasingly with a functional capability and cost magnitude well beyond the core banking system alone.

Online Banking

Online banking was born initially as a B2B file transfer capability direct to the bank, and later through bulletin board solutions, Teletext and Videotex, such as Telecom Australia's (now Telstra) 1985 Viatel service. To connect to the bank, it required either an X.25 link or, later, a modem over telephone lines (POTS). Through Viatel, before the Internet, it was possible for retail customers to buy online airline tickets from Qantas (at full price) and perform online banking — CBA's Telebank provided this service.

By the late 1990s, most banks had a rudimentary online banking service on the booming Internet, allowing account balance and transaction history access, transfers between accounts and, later, Direct Entry and BPAY.

These days, almost all banking functions can be performed online, though, strangely, there are inconsistencies with the functional capability on computers and mobile devices using Apple or Android apps.

Security risks remain a concern, especially for older users. Inside a bank, security risks are traded off for functionality and usability improvements. This trade-off often frustrates security professionals — with one head of online security for a bank refusing to use online banking for his personal needs.

The almost total reliance on the mobile in recent times is cause for concern. It has been possible for hackers to take complete control of a mobile device. High-definition cameras can capture mobile sign-ons. While banks are sympathetic to customers that encounter breaches, and the ePayments Code supports retail customers, businesses and individuals should be wary of keeping significant assets in one online basket.

Payment Systems

Payment systems were originally an adjunct to core banking; however, with the introduction of cards and SWIFT, purpose-built software was required.

Many banks take to payments once their budget has been spent on the core banking system and channel capability. For this reason, they often take a philosophy of building before buying. This trap has led to high IT costs and inefficiencies, the reason being that simple payment use cases are easy. But as things get more complex and the original team rolls off, internal building can turn out to be one of the costliest mistakes a bank can make in IT because what may seem like the last 20% of functionality is 80% of the work.

Payment systems in a bank are now a critical part of customer and internal operations, and an outage in any part of the system that prevents a customer from making a payment for greater than an hour needs to be reported to the RBA with an explanation. A big bank's payment systems failing will hit the headlines in Australia very quickly.

Frontend versus Backend

Another fallacy perpetuated by those new to banking or with less experience is the notion that a payment system is simply a card, a website or a screen that someone sees.

With modern technology, User experience (UX) designers and graphic designers can design a screen in minimal time. User experience tools are available to make this task easy and, after seeing the screens, many thought the job was done. But now it had to be built.

However, like an iceberg, what was visible on the surface was just a small part of the body of the work.

Building systems is complex. Not only does every permutation of events need to be taken care of, backend systems from different organisations need to be found and staff need to be paid/cajoled into modifying them. Integration is always the largest cost component of any system.

Conversely, a long period of complex development appears fruitless until exposed to an application somewhere.

Backend developers who did the heavy lifting for banks were poorly rewarded and rarely seen until something went wrong.

High Availability

Contrary to popular belief, high availability of payments was not really that big of a thing until the end of the first decade of this century.

As mentioned, mainframes were originally unreliable and ATMs would sometimes be down for days at a stretch. Internet banking was frequently down and, even now, many banks bring it down for maintenance in the early hours of Sunday morning.

Thanks to smoke and mirrors — namely batch processing and stand-in processes — customers did not always know there was a problem before real-time banking.

Transactions at an ATM would not always be reflected by the core system until a batch job ran overnight. If connectivity was down, a store floor limit would be invoked for ATMs and EFTPOS machines (and, before that, the voucher system), and transactions would be backed up until the systems were back online.

This changed gradually between 2000 and 2010. In the days leading up to 9/11, Westpac's Internet banking went down. By this time, many customers had started banking online and branches were beginning to close. The failure of Internet banking meant that the bank did not have enough capacity to deal with their online customers coming to a branch to make withdrawals all at once. There could be a run on the bank. A few days later, the tragic loss of life at the World Trade Centre and loss of systems, had a huge impact on the financial sector. The United States Securities and Exchange Commission and the Federal Reserve noted that, while the financial system was substantially intact, delays in clearing and settlement in payments led to a bottleneck in the availability of liquidity.[86] It could have been worse. This incident highlighted the need for high availability of systems and processes, better disaster recovery and business continuity planning.

With real-time banking and higher customer expectations, issues of availability were exposed to customers. There was no longer a batch to hide behind, and problems would be exposed immediately if there was a disconnect between payment systems and core banking. One example is when payment systems go into stand-in because they cannot get through to the core. These days it is more apparent.

» NOTE

While most systems are real-time, some systems, like cheques and cards, are not. Many banks display "pending" on some transactions and wait up to a few days for the settlement to come through, which is a more accurate transaction (e.g., a cheque may bounce, a credit card transaction may not settle), before displaying the final transaction.

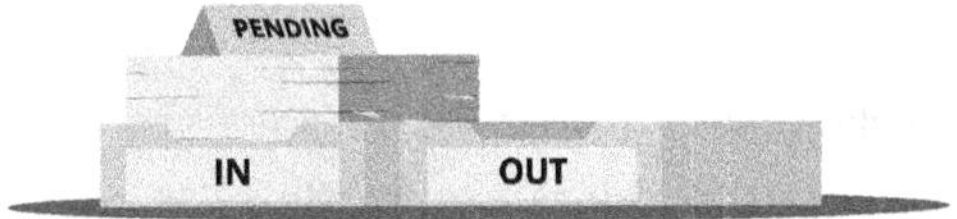

Year 2000 computer failures (the Y2K Bug) were raised as an issue in the years prior to the date, when many COBOL or assembly-based systems used two-digit dates to represent the year, so 00 would be treated as 1900 as the new century ticked over. Airlines, hospitals and governments were nervous, and people were reluctant to take flights or book elective surgery as the year transitioned. A big fear was that financial systems would fail. Regulators (the RBA and APRA) put in a concerted effort to mitigate the risk and banks checked all their systems. While publicly the transition happened without incident, before 2000 there were real issues and bugs. Luckily, all these were detected, fixed and tested. CBA encountered a 10-hour outage on 29 February 2012, possibly due to a leap year bug, indicating that date problems were real, and it was thanks to diligent focus and testing that the Y2K issue was averted.

Increasing Availability

With customers seeking greater availability, some key design philosophies were put in place. To a large extent, reliability was a function of software stability. If software remained unchanged, it was less likely to fail. However, as time went on, with the loss of key experts (job rotation, retirement, etc.), failures became harder and harder to fix.

For example, Direct Entry was designed for transactions less than $100 million. When the first transaction greater than $100 million came through, the transaction was truncated by removing the first digit.

As time went on, one particular system that was 40 years old had an original design that catered for a batch size 10 times bigger than the biggest of the day. Forty years later, this limit was breached, causing an outage on the day after Boxing Day when four days of transactions blew the limit.

[86] Ferguson

New software, as much as it is tested, does not experience the same stresses and environment as the real world.

In one release, a card deployment was well tested. However, it was not tested in Tasmania, where there was a higher use of automated fuel dispensers. Once released in the region, the system failed, as it did not cater for a reservation of funds before the final transaction. In another, South Australia, which is 30 minutes behind the time zone of the eastern states, would lose 30 minutes of real-time data every day due to a software oversight. Leap year bugs are also quite common and it can take up to four years to find them.

Therefore, new software has a tendency to be riskier than older software.

As mentioned, high availability is relatively new in banking.

Software glitches happen all the time. When we cannot see an update on Facebook that we thought we just posted, when a system is inaccessible, while we often think it is our fault we might refresh or try again and everything seems ok.

Banking and finance can be quite sensitive to glitches. Duplicate data (like a duplicated payment) or a lost transaction can have a significant financial impact on customers.

More than banking, health system failures or airline flight control system failures could result in injury or death. These industries have better availability and quality control systems, and banks will continue to lag.

Traditionally (perhaps before 2000), systems had an availability of two nines (99%) and sometimes three nines (99.9%). This meant the probability of the system working was 99.9% or, for about nine hours a year, the system would be down. A glitch with a credit card could be quite embarrassing for a customer.

The introduction of no single point of failure meant that everything was redundant, so if one item were to fail the system could continue to handle the full load; for example, by having two data centres, two servers and two databases. The challenge with data storage and retrieval was that it was relatively slow. To replicate information in two databases could double the time it took to commit a transaction. So high availability came at a cost.

Despite full redundancy, if each component in a 10-component chain had five nines of reliability (99.999%) due to the redundancy, then the total reliability would be only four nines (99.99%). It was very common to have a 10-component chain: frontend, network, switch, firewall, application server, database, and so on. Sometimes, something that goes wrong with one system can trigger the same issue with the redundant twin so no amount of redundancy can guarantee protection from issues.

One typical pattern to ensure availability is stand-in. Similar to a limited flight mode, if everything were to fail in the mainstream (including redundant servers), stand-in ensures that a function can continue to be performed at some level of customer satisfaction, rather than expose a complete failure.

Given that high availability in banking and payments is new, astute customers are benefited through having their own backup, such as a secondary account with another bank, a backup credit card, or access to unbanked cash in the event of an emergency.

›› NOTE

Limited flight mode was introduced in aircraft when fly-by-wire was first implemented. No longer could the aircraft be controlled manually through levers and pulleys. Fly-by-wire meant that everything was controlled by electronic signals from computers. Normal flight systems were incredibly redundant with up to four duplicate systems, each capable of dealing with the full load. Despite extensive testing and design, there was always a chance that the same issue could be replicated in every instance. Limited flight mode was designed to operate a minimal number of systems to allow passengers to survive. A drop to 10 000 feet means pressurisation can safely fail. Non-essential systems like heating could also shut down, with the only function required being maintaining flight and landing. The design of this system had to be so independent. It is said that even discussions and fraternisation between the two teams were banned lest they discuss a common problem and solve it the same way, and introduce the same defect. Generally, banks are yet to implement this level of availability.

Card Switching

FIS's Connex and BASE2000, and ACI's BASE24 supported cards from both a switching point of view, and, for credit card processing, the core system. Many of these applications ran on mainframe or midrange systems, usually IBM systems, but with Connex popular on Tandem (now HP) Non-Stop Hardware.

Outsourced Card Processing

Card switching, and credit card processing in particular, became a commodity capability with multiple financial institutions offering it, especially before the credit crunch associated with the GFC. In Australia, Certegy (taken over by FIS), FIS (through their Base Global offering), EDS (later HP/HPE, largely used by CBA), and Cuscal take care of processing for many financial institutions.

Real-time Banking

The challenge with many early core banking systems was that they were batch-based processes. Tapes would be loaded, calculations performed, transactions updated, balances and interest added, and the process repeated each day.

With the advent of cards, the mainframe was updated with an interim balance (an approximation of the balance). This was, in some banks, called the real-time masterfile. The file was a running copy of the core bank system, technically a spin-off to support payments. Every night, the proper settlement file would be run and the masterfile would be refreshed. For many organisations this continued and, even today, some organisations persist with this paradigm. Over time, a more robust solution was required as the core banking system needed to be updated in real-time, and payment orchestration needed to be dealt with independently. The advent of real-time banking was a significant improvement to banking and its systems.

Payments Hub

Critical to the design of a payment engine is the flexibility to add new payment methods and technologies, while maintaining standard backend processing.

With the unification of payment messaging (ISO 20022, see below), the utility of a single payments capability gained traction.

The benefit of a payment hub was demonstrated after CBA's core modernisation program implemented the world's first ISO 20022 real-time cross payments hub. This enabled real-time payments for customers, and allowed CBA to take the front foot with bank-to-bank payments, mobile payments, everyday settlement, and a lead role in the MAMBO and NPP real-time initiatives. There is debate on the merits of a payments hub, but the consensus is to be careful with how much happens in the hub and how much does not as some functions belong in core banking and channels.

Modern hubs tend to be Java applications such as TCS BaNCS payments, FIS Clear2Pay and ACI's Universal Payments. Finastra, SAP Payments and Intellect Design Arena are some providers in Australia.

Figure 14 illustrates a payment execution capability.

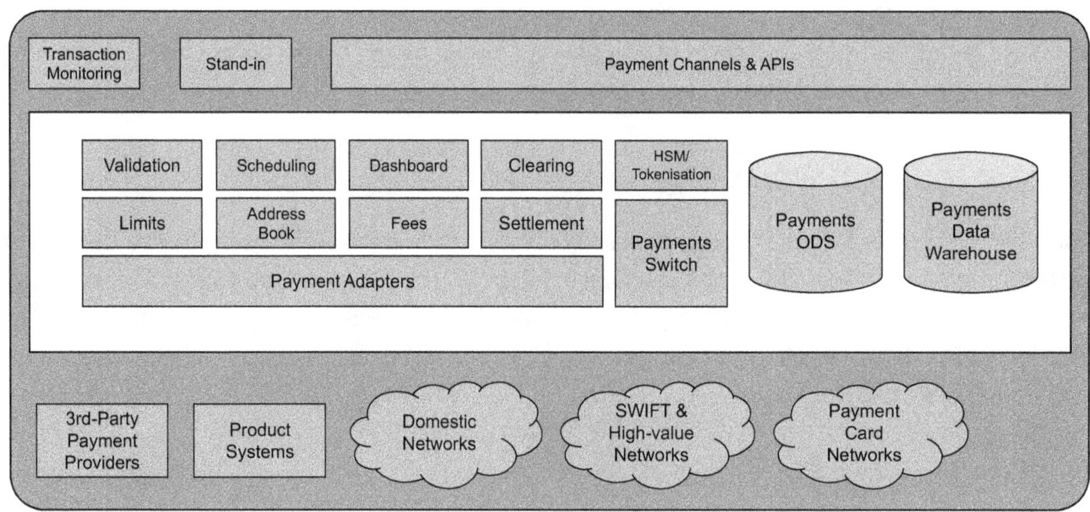

***Figure 14.* A view of payments execution capabilities.**

Intelligent Deposit Machine AML/CTF Breach

CBA introduced Intelligent Deposit Machines (IDMs), a type of ATM, into its fleet in 2012. From an architecture point of view, this was a new payment channel. These machines had the capability of validating notes and cash and, unlike deposit ATMs which took envelopes that would be processed later, often the next working day, IDMs could accept notes (and sometimes coins) and deposit them as cleared funds for immediate withdrawal.

As mentioned, deposits of $10 000 or more needed to be reported to AUSTRAC in threshold transaction reports. The deposit could be broken into smaller deposits, but if they take place over one service, and happen in succession, they should be considered as one transaction. The rules were clear and this capability should be a feature of the architecture. CBA failed to report such deposits for several years, and was spectacularly charged in 2017 for an AUSTRAC breach.

While the immediate cause of the breach appears to have been a coding issue, deficiencies like this are often due to many reasons. A good payment execution architecture that treats transactions consistently and has one place for TTRs (transaction monitoring), despite a myriad of channels, would have avoided this problem. Surely, CBA would have had such an architecture. Yet, in the public domain, to our knowledge, no information technology architect was summoned to the consequential royal commission, nor was system architecture addressed in the extensive APRA report that was published.

›› NOTE

When investigating an incident, there is a technique known as Five Whys or Nine Whys: keep on asking why a fault occurred until one could go back no further. Often an issue caused by a simple flaw is symptomatic of a deeper and broader problem that should be identified and fixed.

The surprising failure and oversight of CBA may not be a cover-up, but more likely an oversight of non-technology executives, regulators, and legal professionals to see what was obvious to an IT architect. While sophisticated big data, regtech and AI/ML claim to have a solution to the problem, a more fundamental system design and architecture analysis would have satisfied the needs.

The cause of this event was likely the desire to get to market quickly, a failure to implement a good payment architecture, which bypassed standardised checks and balances and, as often seen, the failure to repay technical debt.

Good architecture is important and could have saved the payment of the largest fine in Australia's history.

Outsourcing

Outsourcing, in its simplest form, is a recognition that another specialist person or organisation can better deal with a solution than the outsourcer (in this context, the bank).

For example, banks are good at managing risk on investments, not at manufacturing computers, so they would outsource the manufacturing process and buy from those providers.

Things that could be outsourced would increase over the years. Some examples are:

- Desktop computing
- Service desks
- Data centre operations (including cloud providers)
- Software:
    - Packages
    - Development
    - Maintenance.
- Building management
- Project management
- Testing
- Business operations:
    - Call centres
    - Processing centres.

Several organisations provide outsourcing arrangements. For software, these are too many to name; however, for cross-functional capabilities these are: TCS, Accenture, HCL, IBM, Infosys, DXC and Mahindra Tech. These are also termed systems integrators as they do the heavy work of integrating different systems into the organisation's environment.

Outsourcing has been contentious for many years. Euphemisms such as *right-sourcing* and *co-sourcing* have been short-lived with most accepting that outsourcing is here to stay.

Procurement

Procurement in a bank is a strict process governed by regulations. First and foremost, fairness is required in the process of procurement. This means going out to tender and conducting an evaluation process. Some common services like printing or management consulting have a panel which has gone through a vetting process in the organisation, and a streamlined solution is available for the organisation to acquire from them. For more complex and new acquisitions, a tender process needs to be followed and vendor due diligence needs to be completed. A number of APRA and regulatory requirements also need to be fulfilled.

Agreements

There are a number of contracts involved in outsourcing. First and foremost is a non-disclosure agreement. Outsourcers are normally not allowed to divulge any information about their customers and vice versa. A governing contract is normally put in place. This is called a master services agreement. It does not always specify the work but rather the broad costs, obligations, commitments, rate cards, protocols, and so on, when work is ordered. Ideally, the master services agreement is designed to make it easy for individuals in both organisations. Finally, there is a statement of work which, for a particular piece of work, provides the details of the work that will be done, and needs to be signed off before work starts and before invoices are issued and paid.

Indigenous suppliers are encouraged through the Indigenous industry representative body Supply Nation.

Fairness

In government, strict probity in procurement is required, ensuring vendor selection is above board, fair and transparent. The process is somewhat looser in banks, though procurement departments attempt to enforce high standards. In 2015, two CBA executives were charged with bribery after allegedly receiving payments from a vendor they selected to implement solutions in CBA. The vendor was consequently acquired by CSC (now DXC), partly (it is believed) on the basis of the implementation at CBA and other places. Bribery was a serious offence and both executives faced jail time. At the lower end of the scale, vendors often treated clients (bank staff) to events and gifts. Bank policy was that a gift greater than a certain threshold should be declared on a register and approved before the employee could accept it.

Corporate credit cards are sometimes used for small payments. This process is discouraged for significant purchases as it bypasses the procurement process, which uses SAP Ariba and a standard financial accounts payable process to pay vendors. Vendors are assessed based on their risk to ensure they are bona fide and appropriately managed.

For regular services, banks have a panel of vendors for different purposes, where each has a master services agreement for a defined period.

In the vendor selection process, small vendors can be brought on board with minimal due diligence; however, major acquisitions need to go through a request for information and request for proposal process where a broad set of vendors are approached, and assessments are made through responses, demonstrations, proofs of concept and pilot implementations.

» NOTE

Corporate credit cards are used to make general purchases such as entertainment. Usually a line manager needs to approve the expense and, in some cases, a manager would ask a subordinate to pay a bill so the expense could escape independent managerial oversight. This practice was a sackable offence in most organisations, with a policy that the most senior manager attending an entertainment event needed to pay for the expense.

Offshoring

Offshoring is where jobs are performed overseas and may or may not be associated with outsourcing.

There are two major types of offshoring. One is the use of captive centres. A captive centre is a building or office in an overseas location that is owned or branded with the Australian bank brand. Staff could be employees of the Australian company or an outsourcing organisation.

The other type is general centres, which are generally located in a corner of an offshore outsourcer's premises, where the employees move between clients with no specific tie (other than by contract to the Australian bank).

Technology Regulation

APRA and the RBA are interested in understanding how an organisation's IT systems are implemented and integrated. There are some specific regulations that are monitored:

- Outsourcing: APRA, through APS 231, requires that certain risks be mitigated. First is the identification of a material outsourcer where a critical part of a bank's function is outsourced to that party, who comes under greater scrutiny. One concern is how a service will be restored, if the provider is no longer able to provide the service (e.g., due to bankruptcy or war).
- Business continuity plan: APRA, through APS 232, seeks to understand how a bank will recover in the event of a severe outage and loss of systems, and how it ensures it is ready for such a day (i.e., disaster recovery and business continuity testing).
- Information security: APRA, through APS 234, seeks to ensure that institutions are protected against cyber attacks that extract or modify information held by the bank. Audited reports, such as SOC or ISO 27001 compliance reports, help in ensuring standards have been met.
- Data risk: APRA, through APS 235, looks to ensure that data integrity and safety are protected against loss and fraud.
- The payment card Industry PCI DSS standard is for dealing with card numbers and associated information.
- APRA's data security and general data protection guidelines.

Big Data

Originally, databases were just lists and later tables. Eventually, the relational database management system took off and SQL allowed data to be discovered. Data was well-structured, sometimes overly so, with each element having parents and children, and being related to other records. A simple shopping inventory could consist of 16 of these tables, all interrelated. Finding information meant storing it properly and this was a science in itself. It required an expert with great technical expertise. The data eventually made its way into a data warehouse. The amount of analytical skills required to use this aggregated data was immense, with few able to understand what data they needed and how to get the insights they needed, or did not yet know they needed.

A remarkable feature on the Internet is search engines, in particular, Google. They enable a user to search vast amounts of data held openly on the Internet to find key information by typing into just one box. They appear to do this successfully in a short amount of time.

Finding information in corporations, especially in a bank, has been a challenge. So, for a few years, applying this new Internet search engine technology to enterprise data became a big deal. The data scientist was a new role and it paid well. Universities caught on and we soon had an army of data scientists in corporations promising to solve all our problems. National Information and Communications Technology Australia (NICTA), a joint venture between the University of New South Wales, Australian National University and their host state governments, was foremost among the big data evangelists. Initial signs were promising as, for the first time in a long time, we had attention put on the data. Perhaps we could get insights that we could never get before?

However, in practice, few problems were solved and there were many reasons for this.

Big Data is a Long Haul

For years, IT systems have been collecting data. Doing things with those data has always proved difficult. The information was gathered, yet relatively little was done with it. Then, around 2016, big data specialists came to the industry, starting with the banks. Most promises in banks can be given a year or two before they need to bear fruit. Big data promised to find undiscovered insights in the data. Unfortunately, the initial promise did not lead to major actionable insights and, if there were, they were not produced at a rate that satisfied the insatiable pay masters.

Big data, rather than being a new science, is an evolutionary step forward, a new tool. Databases in banks were divided into online transaction processing and online analytical processing. The two cannot mix, because a complex query on an online analytical processing database could slow down or prevent transactions from being written to the table. It is a technical limitation that currently stalks the data industry. Indexing is also different. Online analytical processing databases needed lots of indexes to help speed up queries, but lots of indexes slowed down inserts.

Big data was designed to be used in the online analytical processing space. It dealt with unstructured data. Financial data is more structured than unstructured Internet information but, at the same time, it is possible to get some interesting insights from unstructured data; for example, the number of people who complained about fees to call centres versus in the media.

Big data did not really help with precise structured data analysis; for example, calculating the total deposited funds held by the bank or the total Financial Claims Scheme liability. For that, we needed old-school structured data analysis and systems.

In the journey to merge online transaction processing with online analytical processing, NoSQL systems and caching repositories are assisting in solving some of the problems. Tools like MongoDB, Apache Hadoop and Google BigQuery are popular in the NoSQL and Big Data space as are tools from other vendors. Another problem that is being solved is high availability through non-centralised clusters. Traditional database technology really only worked well with one database. High availability requirements compromised performance and increased the risk associated with a failure. Some big data technologies deal with high availability better.

In the end, big data will help, but not as soon as was first thought. It has elevated the poorly recognised data analyst or engineer who, rather than take requests from people who do not understand data, can (with additional expertise) deeply understand the business context of the data and, over time (it is a generational change), gain new insights.

Artificial Intelligence

Early computers were electro-mechanical devices. Some of these devices were quite amazing. One such device was the Bombe developed at Bletchley Park by the British attempting to decipher the German Enigma code (itself generated by an electro-mechanical device) during World War II. Bletchley Park intelligence is credited with hastening the end outcome of the war.

One of the scientists at the time was Alan Turing. Turing reflected on the almost human-like ability of machines to solve problems and, while acknowledging that a machine had a long way to go, came up with what is called the Turing Test. The Turing Test simply states that if a device (behind a wall), through a defined set of inputs and outputs such as typed text, can convince a human that it is another human that has responded, then it has passed the Turing Test.

Over the years, as computers have become more and more capable, we seem to get closer to passing the Turing Test.

Since 1950, most computers have operated based on procedural rules. If this condition is met, then do that, and so on.

When Apple Siri, Microsoft Cortana, Amazon Alexa and Google Assistant first came out, they seemed almost human-like in their ability to converse. Very quickly, however, they have been relegated to being tools (albeit useful ones) seemingly unable to take the place of a human. Amazing as they are, they failed the Turing Test.

Through artificial intelligence, the development of more and more capable machines has been ongoing and evolutionary.

Machine Learning and Modern Artificial Intelligence

One critical ingredient humans have over machines is the ability to learn by themselves. In computers, this ability is known as machine learning.

One particular branch of computer science has associated specific solutions with artificial intelligence and machine learning (AI/ML) through a set of algorithms. Many of these algorithms go back decades, and academic work on them has been impressive, and will continue to aid the evolutionary development of computers. However, for a while, people in the corporate world had the impression that we had arrived at the end goal of artificial intelligence.

In reality, the new technology failed to live up to expectations.

In one presentation, a technology company suggested that since we know the market history of shares, we know whether the market went up or down on any given day, and so we should be able to use the same data to predict where the share market would land tomorrow. Suffice to say that, despite this presentation, no one has cracked the problem.

The issue is several-fold. First, the technology was over-hyped. Not taking away from the great work of academics, AI/ML technology has developed slowly and will continue to do so. Applications such as image recognition seem to be the best applications of it today and, when the algorithms are combined with some commonsense (such as, in the case of facial recognition, looking out for key features and distance ratios between the eyes, nose and mouth) and lots of hard work, the technology can be quite robust. Voice recognition is also similarly mature.

The issue with machine learning is that the requirements for vast data and lots of training make it difficult to learn many problem spaces.

If a small automated vehicle were to learn to get from A to B using machine learning in a room full of obstacles, it would be involved in millions of collisions, whereas a two-year-old child could navigate the path successfully the first time without his or her parents acknowledging any major accomplishment.

Second, some traceability is required about why an organisation (or a machine, in this case) made the decision it did. If a machine learning system somehow came to the conclusion that people whose surnames were short had more likelihood of being false identities, and a computer rejected a financial services application on that basis, it would be unacceptable to customers, to the bank and to regulators.

Throwing data at AI/ML has been spectacularly unsuccessful in solving problems in the financial services industry. Many vendor tools claim to include AI/ML to increase sales, but the technical team will reveal that the real magic comes from procedural code. It is telling that no real insights came from big data, AI or ML that were not apparent through commonsense when COVID-19 hit the world by surprise.

This is not to say that AI/ML is useless, simply that the path to success will be a long and hard one. Technology will get closer to passing the Turing Test not through any one algorithm, but through the combination of many tools, and through the painstakingly diligent work of people who understand the problem: computer programmers and experts.

Consumer Data Right: Open Banking

Access to information has been a concern in the community with organisations and, initially, the government, making decisions without transparency. This led to the Freedom of Information Act in 1982. Private organisations were not covered by this and it was unclear what information they were sharing. In 1988, a Privacy Act was introduced; this would eventually cover private organisations in 2000. One problem remained. While people could see some data, they could not, for example, access electronic transactional data from a bank. The open banking initiative was born.

In 2017, the Productivity Commissioner commenced an investigation and inquiry on data availability and use.

Off the back of the inquiry and report, the commissioner recommended that access to data was not just useful for consumers, but a right. The government accepted this. So eventually, at the end of 2019, the Consumer Data Right Bill was passed, amending the Competition and Consumer Act 2010, Australian Information Commissioner Act 2010 and Privacy Act 1988. Data would be opened, starting with banking data, then move to other sectors such as energy, telecommunications and airlines.

The move to open banking was initiated in Europe, where it was called the Payment Service Directive 2. Payment Service Directive 1 had created the Single Euro Payments Area (SEPA). The most robust implementation, known as open banking, was in the United Kingdom.

The government charged the ACCC, the Office of the Australian Information Commissioner, and the Data Standards Body with developing and implementing the Consumer Data Right. In turn, these bodies charged a newly initiated division in the CSIRO, Data 61, with implementing open banking. The proposal was to use application programming interfaces (APIs).

Open Banking: A Lost Opportunity

The implementation of open banking was plagued from the outset. First, the banks were not interested in losing business so no encouragement came from that quarter. Instead, there was a subtle attempt to push a much less potent implementation, which provided only generic information. Threats that a complex solution was unworkable came from the sector. It was the oldest magician's trick in the book: "Nothing up my sleeves," focuses attention just where the magician wants it.

Second, the focus was on data rather than transaction execution. Around 2016, big data was all the rage. NICTA had sold the big data potential to a number of institutions. At some point the CSIRO merged NICTA into a new entity, Data 61. NICTA and Data 61 had been to the banks. After running dry there, they got the ear of the Productivity Commission. It was curious why the title of the initial request for the review was *Access to public and private sector big data*. Transactional bankers and IT professionals were puzzled about that. For reasons mentioned above, the banks were not going to correct the misdirection. Banks, by this time, knew that the problem society needed to solve was never in a bank's big data. There was nothing much in there. If there was, then good luck finding it because the banks had milked it dry. If there was a data problem, it was a small data problem and, interestingly that is exactly the problem Data 61 ended up solving. The proposed standard allowed data to be shared, but only one customer at a time with one provider at a time.

The problem with giving everyone the data was privacy. If the data was summarised too much, it was useless to people who wanted to perform their own analytics. Anonymisation of data had the problem that, no matter how well-anonymised the data was, it was always possible (with meaningful row-level data) to identify individuals or small groups. Useful analytics required raw data. But without permission, it could not be widely used.

Nevertheless, everyone in the know knew the core power of the bank was not its data. Tools such as Yodlee and Mint had been in use since the late 1990s. Banks encouraged it. ANZ and, more recently, Westpac tried them. Almost every bank and every decent accounting package had seen the data for decades before, and for bookkeepers it does help reconciliation. The sad truth was that customers were just not that interested in the data or its aggregation. Perhaps at tax time there was a utility, though many banks added categorisation to help with tax, and the ATO was busy getting the raw data into tax returns anyway. Maybe one day, access to transactional data may take off, but for now it is a 20-year-old idea that has essentially gone nowhere.

In 2017, the Australian Payments Council attempted a hackathon to illustrate. Without transactability, there was a limit to what the ideas could do. The winner in Melbourne, emFund, came up with an app to allow friends to pay each other in the event of a natural disaster (a good idea for the COVID-19 pandemic). Core to that, was one critical API that was missing.

The core power of a bank is to hold, move and give money. To be able to transact on an account was the holy grail. The European Union knew this: this is why the Payments Service Directive mandated APIs for payments, and why the United Kingdom included payments in its open banking core mandate.

The list of APIs the Data 61 group came up with is a technical list, published on GitHub and Swagger (the tech tools of the API trade). Any developer worth their metal would tick that off. It looked substantial to the politicians and regulators. Everyone around the table seemed happy: the technologists, the regulators and the banks. Big data people were satisfied with a small data problem solution in so far as they had all the data that the limitations of privacy laws would allow. As shown below, the big data problem of getting bulk data was their contribution to getting data in volume. Mission accomplished.

The APIs in *Table 4* needed to be implemented by each bank in a prescribed technical format. There are speed and volume requirements. Also, a third party (i.e., a service provider to a customer of the bank) needed permission to use these APIs through another set of APIs.

Table 4.

Open banking APIs from the Consumer Data Right initiative.

No.	API Action	Description
1	Get Accounts	Returns a list of accounts.
2	Get Bulk Balances	Returns all the balances for a set of specified accounts the provider has permission to access.
3	Get Account Balance	Gets a single account balance.
4	Get Account Detail	Gets specific attributes for an account.
5	Get Transactions for Account	Gets the transaction history of an account.
6	Get Transaction Detail	Gets more information on a transaction.
7	Get Direct Debits	Lists the direct debits on an account. (Traditional direct debits are held by the payee so the payer's list, as per the bank, is not going to be accurate. NPP will eventually solve this problem in a different way.)
8	Get Bulk Direct Debits	Lists all the bulk direct debits on the specified accounts (using a filter) the provider has access to.

No.	API Action	Description
9	Get Direct Debits for Specific Accounts	Lists all the bulk direct debits on the specified accounts the provider has access to.
10	Get Scheduled Payments for Accounts	Lists the scheduled (push) payments on an account.
11	Get Scheduled Payments Bulk	Lists all the scheduled payments on the specified accounts (using a filter) the provider has access to.
12	Get Scheduled Payments for Specific Accounts	Lists all the scheduled payments on the specified accounts the provider has access to.
13	Get Payees	Lists the address book or list of payees the payer has.
14	Get Payee Details	Gets detailed information about a payee.
15	Get Products	Lists standard products available on the market.
16	Get Product Details	Lists specific information about a product (product type, interest rate, etc.)

Missing was the most powerful API action of them all: Make Payment. Make Payment creates the data, fills the account (or removes money from the account) and provides transaction history. Transactions, payees, direct debits and scheduled payments are all secondary to payments. If someone could access payments, they had all the useful data.

Somehow, the banks convinced the open banking standards development teams that payments should be out of scope. This is because the New Payments Platform (NPP) was already looking at it.

Open banking, however, persisted with some payments related information: transactional data and, indirectly, payment related read-only APIs (which make up 10 of the 16 APIs). Without expertise in banking, however, the developers neglected the ISO 20022 model. The United Kingdom claimed to follow the model, but failed to do so in practice, while Australia neglected it all together. The Australian standard refers to SWIFT addresses for international payees that will soon (in 2021) be mandated to be ISO 20022 compliant. We will see later how Australia helped create ISO 20022. With open banking, Australia reinvented its own formats; it mixes in US and United Kingdom banking codes while neglecting others, and neglects NPP rich information.

If hope for data sharing is with the New Payments Platform, it has its own problems. NPP was not a mandate like open banking, but an encouraging nudge by the RBA, under threat of a heavy hand, operating as a gentlemen's club to date. So far, no proposal to have NPP APIs accessible by third parties has been substantially implemented by any of the big banks. So the only really useful service that open banking could benefit from, a payments API, was neglected by them and, sadly, with or without NPP it is not going to happen for a long time. CDR was a lost opportunity.

In an acknowledgement of the fact that open banking was not going anywhere, the treasury commissioned another review into write access (rather than read access) in 2020. Once again, the simple fallacy that banking was about static data persisted and the treasury truly failed to consider the core issue — the opening up of payments.

Encryption

In order to keep information safe, private and secure, and to prevent alteration, encryption became important, first in the military and government, and later in banking and finance.

Symmetric encryption, where a common algorithm or key is known to both the encrypter and decrypter, is ancient. Alluded to in India's Kama Sutra, it was probably in use long before this text and continued to be a common technique for centuries (*Figure 15*).

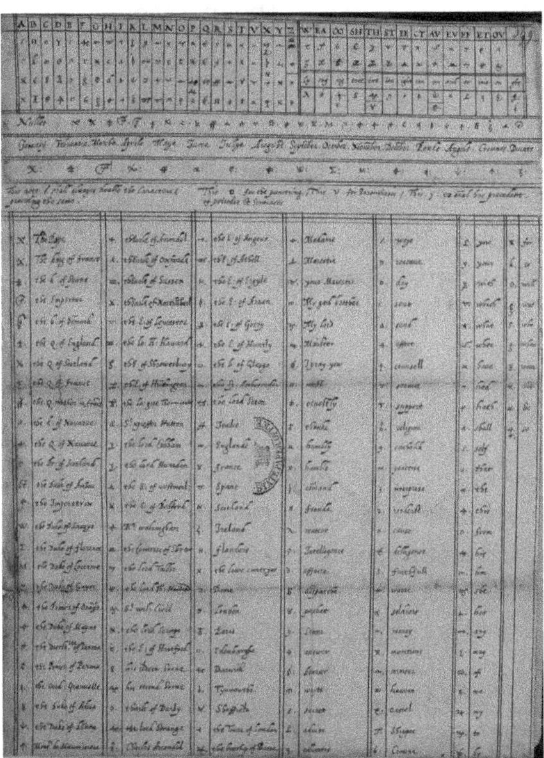

***Figure 15.* 1586 symmetric encryption used by Mary, Queen of Scots.**
Courtesy of National Archives, United Kingdom.

The problem with this symmetric method is that first the key needs to be distributed widely and, if one key is compromised, the whole network is compromised. Maintaining multiple keys for a bank with millions of customers could become complex, or at least was complex during the birth of the Internet. The Internet required a better solution that could scale.

Public key infrastructure (PKI), using public key encryption, was invented by Ron Rivest, Adi Shamir and Leonard Adleman in the late 1970s. Their commercial system was named after their initials: RSA. The solution was asymmetric encryption. One key (the public key) was used to encrypt the data and another key (the private key) was used to decrypt the data. It was important to keep this private key locked away.

PKI and asymmetric encryption are used in banking around the world to facilitate the movement of money from card payments, to Internet and mobile banking, to institutional payments.

The principle of modern PKI encryption is that it is easier to solve a specific mathematical problem in one direction than the reverse. For example, if you took two very big prime numbers, it is easy to multiply them together, but hard to figure out what the original factors are.

So, if we gave the number 111172687 to people and asked them to factorise it, most would give up. It would take quite some time to get the answer: 10601 x 10487. Think of 111172687 as the public key, and 10601 x 10487 as the private key. Modern keys are 600 digits in length. A further more recent example of asymmetric key algorithms is elliptical curve cryptography. It uses the mathematical difficulty of reverse engineering an elliptical curve relationship.

Another use of PKI is the reverse scenario. A sender encrypts data using a private key. The public key can be used to decrypt the data that only the holder of the private key could encrypt, thus validating that the sender sent the message.

Hashes

A hash is a one-way encryption that generates a seemingly random result, generally of fixed length. One popular algorithm is SHA-256. If one were to type an entire encyclopedia, a hash sequence of 64 hexadecimal or base-16 symbols (0-9,a-f) could be generated. If typed again, but this time with just one change (say a full stop instead of a comma), the hash would look totally different but still be 64 digits long.

For example, the SHA-256 hash of "The quick brown fox jumps over the lazy dog" is ef537f25c895bfa782526529a9b63d97aa631564d5d789c2b765448c8635fb6c.

Changing just one letter will give a totally different hash. There is a possibility of two different texts giving the same hash, but the probability of that is almost impossible in the human universe. Hashes are used in cryptography to scramble passwords or PIN numbers so they cannot be read. They are also used to summarise large amounts of text for digital signing, and to check that stored data is complete and not missing anything.

Digital Signatures

In its general sense, an electronic signature is the representation of a signature in electronic form with the objective of indicating acceptance or authentication.

In the US, an electronic signature can be applied electronically by just typing a name to indicate intent. To really electronically prove a document or message has been sent, and to ensure non-repudiation (the claim, "I did not sign that document"), a more robust solution was required.

PKI allows this, in a simple form, through a digital signature.

First, a public key is shared along with the document. The document is then hashed and encrypted using the private key. The result is sent along with the document. Only the holder of the private key can decrypt the document.

Public Key Infrastructure

PKI is made up of certificates, certificate issuers, certificate authorities, hardware security modules, private keys and public keys (*Figure 16*).

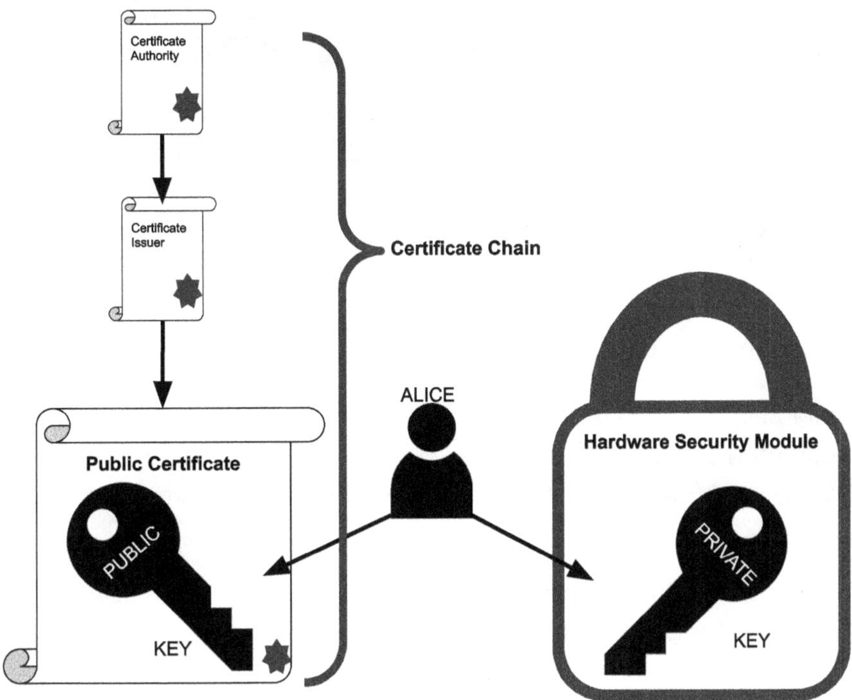

***Figure 16*. The components of PKI.**[87]

Hardware Security Module

A hardware security module is a highly secure way to store sensitive information such as private keys. They are designed to allow data to be stored securely without even the network knowing what it is, and to restrict direct access to the data.

Hardware security modules can be as large as computers and stored in data centres, or as small as a chip on a smart card (where it is called a secure element), including bank/credit cards, RFID cards, SIM cards and secure tokens.

Certificates

A certificate, in its simple form, is a public key and a digital signature from the issuer. It generally has some identifying characteristics such as a website address.

The certificate validates (if one trusts the issuer) that it is genuine.

Certificates can be checked offline but, these days, online checks to ensure the certificate has not been revoked are also made.

[87] Alice is a fictional character used as a placeholder name in cryptology.

There are different certificate types. Some just validate that the certificate is a genuine public key for some private key. Others are only issued to individuals or companies after a proper identification check so we can be sure we are dealing with the right entity.

Root certificate authorities are the highest level of trust in certificates. These authorities are generally installed on computers by the operating system and periodically updated.

In closed networks, like in banks, only certain certificate authorities are trusted.

Root certificate authorities issue certificates to intermediate certificate authorities, which issue certificates to certificate issuers, and so on. This is called the certificate chain; it forms a series of trust relationships. For efficiency, certificate chains are often kept shallow to avoid excessive network use.

Transport Layer Security

Transport Layer Security (TLS) replaced the old Secure Sockets Layer (SSL), and is a way for systems to communicate with each other securely. In a Web browser, https:// indicates the use of TLS, while http:// (which is less secure) does not. TLS requires that the server has a certificate.

In banking systems, to secure both ends, often a mutual TLS (mTLS) is used. Here both sides have a certificate that is generally pre-shared between the parties.

Authentication

Authentication is the process by which a user (e.g., a bank customer) securely logs in to a bank.

A login ID and a password are used to log in. In order to stop software that logged keystrokes, some banks, like Westpac, St George Bank and Citibank had a screen keyboard that moved, which must be used to enter in the password.

Banks were among the first sites to have logins and, for this reason, often have weak password systems today. By using common words in lowercase, it is easier for systems to guess passwords. These days, more complex passwords are recommended and changing passwords often is also recommended. Many banks supplement log-ins with more cyber security and fraud detection features.

Phishing Attacks

Simple phishing attacks involve an email asking a victim to log in to their Internet banking site as an urgent matter that needs to be attended to. Sometimes these emails can seem quite genuine. The user is directed to a website that looks like their bank's login page but isn't and, after logging in, the scammer uses the authentication credentials to steal money from the victim, or for identity theft or account takeover.

Banks advise to never click on links in emails; instead, they direct customers to their home website, a necessary inconvenience for bank marketing strategies.

Two-factor Authentication

Many banks allow their customers to enrol in a form of two factors of authentication. A mobile SMS, a token code or a code on a phone app is used to authorise a transaction.

>> NOTE

While two-factor authentication reduced fraud, it did not eliminate it with some fraudsters pretending to be an online bank, getting a mobile token from an unsuspecting user, and using it to make another, fraudulent transaction at the same time. Some phones became compromised and allowed fraudsters to take total control of what was displayed. Banks started scanning their customers' phones to ensure that none of this software, including malware, was running.

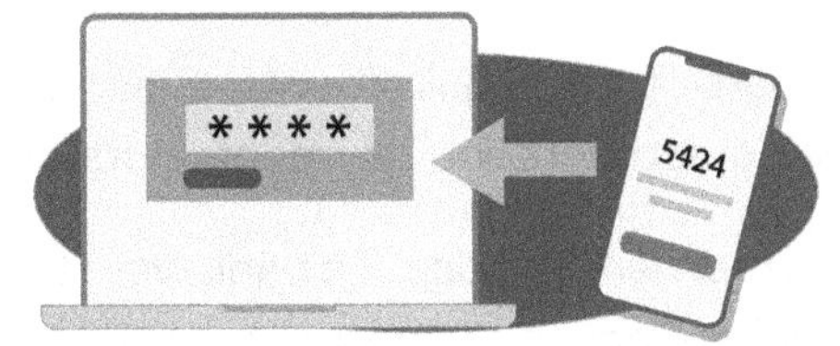

Risk Readiness

Understanding risk is a critical function of any bank. Risk impact and likelihood are measured to determine which risks need to be prioritised for mitigation or, if accepted, highlighted to executives, the board or regulators.

There are many risks in a bank and all of them impact its stability and, collectively, financial systems. This is why risk management is so important.

Disaster Recovery and Business Continuity

High availability is designed to keep systems running. Despite the best efforts, one or many systems may fail, and a process to re-establish them using the minimal amount of existing infrastructure is called disaster recovery and business continuity planning. Scenarios that could require disaster recovery include a loss of people or property at the head office, multiple data centre failures and major vendor failures.

Many banks have a backup site that may be used by non-business as usual staff (such as project staff) to relocate their core workers. Systems should have backups and documented processes for recovery. Many banks conduct regular disaster recovery tests of subsystems during quiet periods.

>> NOTE

Another high availability test, popularised by Netflix, is the Chaos Monkey. A system that randomly turns off components to check if the organisation is still functioning. This has not generally been implemented at banks.

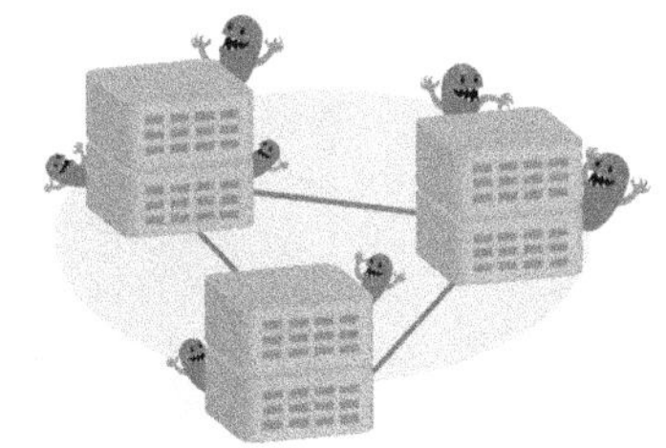

A good disaster recovery plan is one that is well documented and regularly tested. It should be possible to restore normal operations in the minimum amount of time. For this reason, banks regularly practice disaster recovery on weekends (when customer impacts are minimised).

APRA regulates disaster recovery through its standard APS 232.

Financial Claims Scheme

During the GFC, the Kevin Rudd government instituted the Financial Claims Scheme to provide a government guarantee on the first $1 000 000 (later reduced to $250 000) held by each customer with an Australian ADI.

As part of the requirements, every bank must be ready to submit all account ledgers for their customers and payments outstanding to regulators.

At a moment's notice, if a bank were to fail, once payments in flight were settled, all balances could be moved to another bank. ESA balances would be transferred (and topped up by the Financial Claims Scheme) and, theoretically, the customer of the defunct bank could still withdraw their money.

6.

CASH

CASH PAYMENTS involve the use of notes and coins to facilitate a payment. Also known as currency, this is traditionally what people think of as money.

In Australia, currency was originally backed by gold. It is now a fiat currency and is well regulated and efficiently managed. While the relative volume of cash payment is in decline, we have more notes and coins today than ever before. They are still used in many places.

》 NOTE

Previously, workers' salaries were paid in cash. Payroll would advise their cash supplier and yellow envelopes would contain the employees' fortnightly wage, which they picked up and signed for from the company cashier.

Payday was typically every second Thursday. In some states, late night shopping was permitted on Thursdays until 9:00 pm to allow families to spend their newly issued wages and, in the process, boost the local economy.

Features

In modern times, with electronic and card payments becoming more popular, cash, as a percentage of payments in Australia, is declining.

According to the RBA, the average Australian makes one ATM withdrawal per fortnight (probably coinciding with payday). This number is declining at 4% pa.

One of the key advantages of cash is that it is off the books. Not being recorded means being charged less tax.

》 NOTE

Contrary to popular belief, it is getting harder for small retail businesses, especially those that offer non-cash payment mechanisms, to hide cash transactions for a variety of reasons:

- **Cash on small purchases counts for less than 50% of sales (compared to card payments).**
- **Reducing official sales by a significant amount can raise eyebrows.**
- **Unless the owner is performing the sale, the failure to run receipts through the system could tempt theft by employees.**
- **System integration is becoming so useful that having a shadow book is not really feasible.**
- **In order to sell their business, many shop owners would rather declare true sales on the books. They don't pay much tax anyway and a few extra dollars of income can be easily offset against a legitimate expense.**

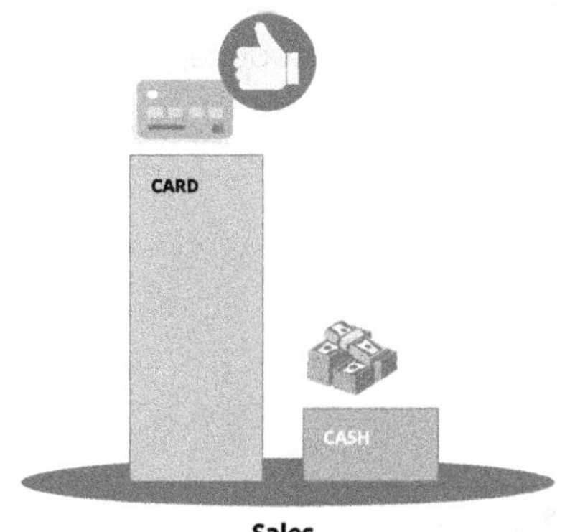

Older people feel more comfortable with cash. They may have had bad experiences with cards or have a mistrust for the new mechanisms. Retirees without an income often live on a budget. Cash is the ideal payment method for those on a budget, young or old. It is true that if we restrict the cash in our wallet and only spend cash, we will save money.

The key disadvantage of cash is that it is not convenient for phone, mail-order or online payments. Cash on delivery is offered by some couriers, but has not been popular with either sellers or buyers.

Plastic Notes

Immediately after the decimalisation of Australia's currency, the search was on for a better-than-paper note. The challenge was taken up by the CSIRO with the introduction of polymer notes in 1988 (Australia's bicentenary — see *Figure 17*). The technology was developed by the RBA and the CSIRO. The polymer notes were longer-lasting and more secure (i.e., more difficult to counterfeit). These were replaced again with an even more secure design, starting in 2016. Australia was the first country to have a man and a woman depicted on every note.

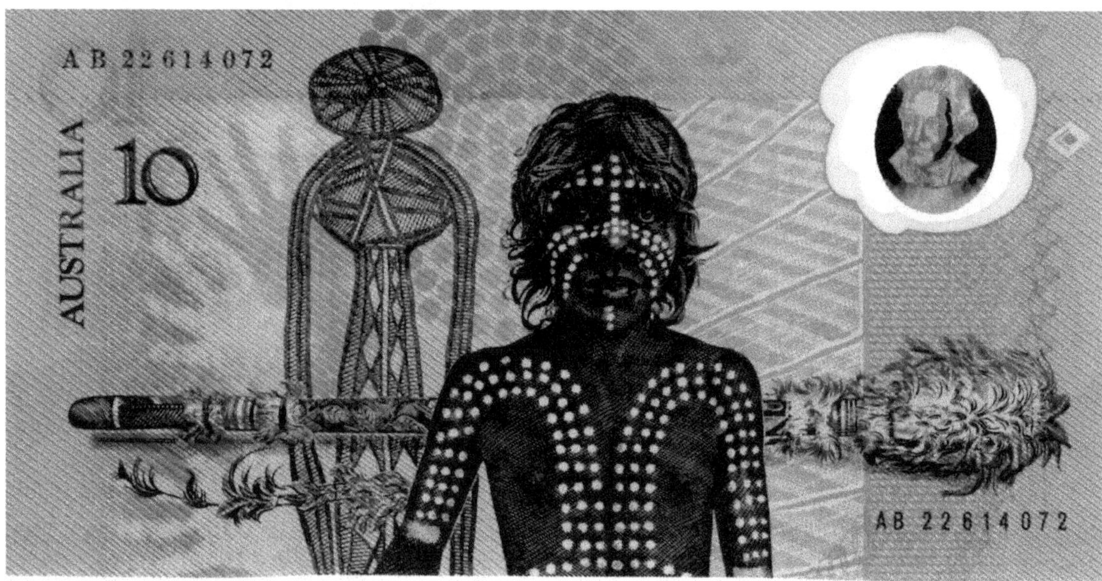

***Figure 17*. First polymer note, 1988.**

Polymer notes have proven to be a success: they are longer-lasting and, despite being more expensive to produce, generate a profit for the RBA, thanks to seigniorage (see below).[88]

[88] Wakefield

Spin-off

The success of polymer notes led to the spin-off of the note printing business to Note Printing Australia and Securency (now CCL Secure).

Securency was involved in a scandal, where bribes were paid by an employee to foreign officials to secure contracts for printing notes. While note production and security was never under question, the issue tainted the organisation, which eventually changed its name. To date, notes have been printed in 140 denominations. In some cases, they were trialled but not established as standard legal tender, notably, the US and United Kingdom.

》 NOTE

The US dollar is the most popular currency in the world, yet its notes are among the least secure. The refusal of the US to replace their note substrate with polymer,[89] despite a clear business case on printing costs alone and alleged evidence that nation state players like North Korea are creating high-quality counterfeit United States supernotes,[90] using sophisticated production equipment, is unfortunate.

In 2020, George Floyd was arrested for allegedly passing off a counterfeit US $20 note at a convenience store. There is no allegation that he produced the counterfeit himself. After his arrest, a police officer placed his knee and the weight of his body on Floyd's neck for nearly nine minutes, resulting in his death. The act was captured on mobile phone video and triggered a global protest on Black Lives Matter. There were many issues and forces at play, and similar events have taken place against other individuals for a variety of other alleged crimes. However, passing off counterfeit notes is a crime that can easily be removed from police charge sheets. The sometimes immeasurable cost of counterfeiting notes is significant.

[89] King

[90] Mihm

Circulation

In June 2019, the RBA reported the following cash on issue (before the COVID-19 pandemic), as shown in *Table 5.*

Table 5.

Banknotes on issue, June 2019, courtesy of RBA.

	Value		Count	
Denomination	$m	%	(millions)	%
$5	1 003	1	201	12
$10	1 340	2	134	8
$20	3 337	4	167	10
$50	38 201	48	764	47
$100	36 144	45	361	22
Total	80 024	100	1 627	100

An interesting observation is the large number of high-denomination ($50 and $100) notes on issue, indicating a high-value cash economy, and this is counter-intuitive if 80% of the cash purchases in Australia are under $25, as reported by the RBA.

This profile changed remarkably during the COVID-19 pandemic (*Figure 18*). Despite the lower use of cash, there was a similar hoarding of cash, as seen in the Great Depression.

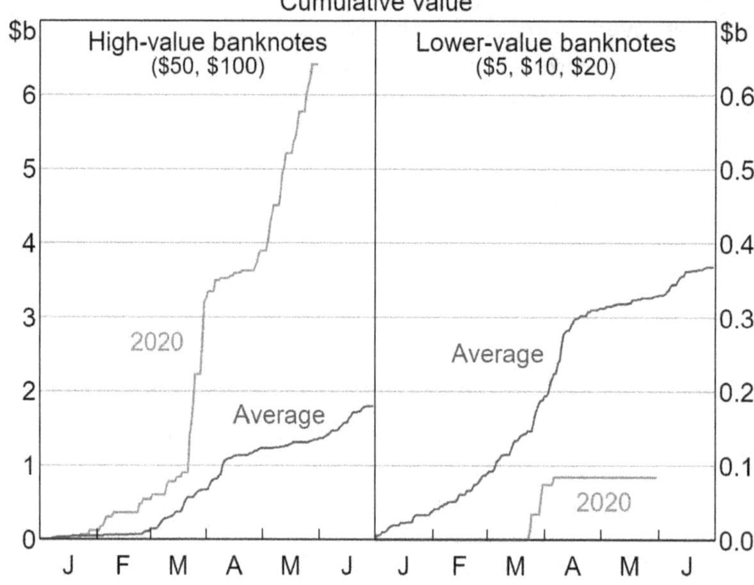

***Figure 18.* Banknote purchases before and during the COVID-19 pandemic.**[91]

[91] Delaney

Australian Cash Distribution and Exchange System

The Australian Payments and Clearing Association (APCA, now AusPayNet) formalised the Australian Cash Distribution and Exchange System (ACDES) procedure for the distribution of cash as its last clearing system in 2001 — Clearing System 5 (CS5).

A declining use of cash has meant little change since then, as few banks see an advantage in participating in the core of the ACDES. They generally obtain their cash through another bank or a cash centre operator.

Settlement in ACDES is deferred and takes place over the RBA's RITS the following morning (on business days).

Logistics

The ACDES procedures define a number of players and processes (*Figure 19*). Cash movements are included in the RITS settlement process.

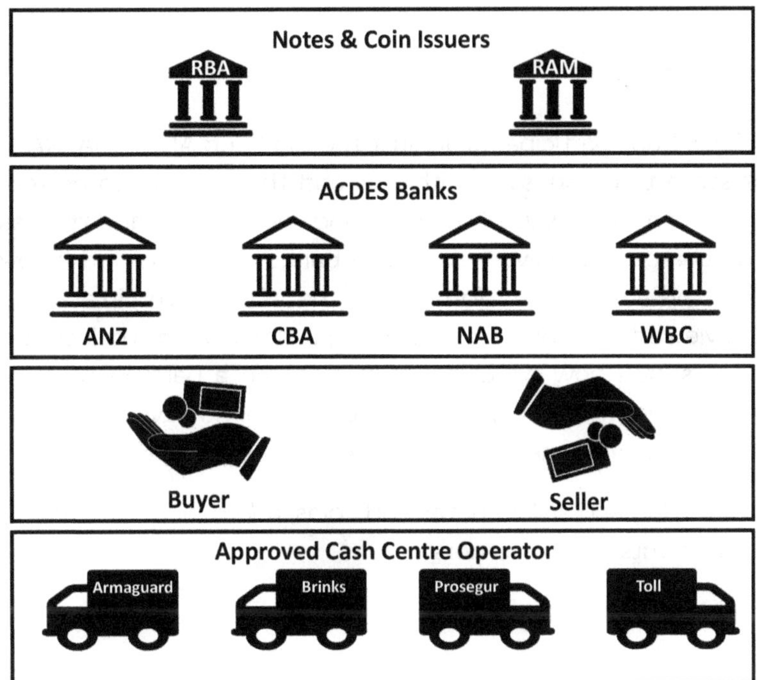

***Figure 19.* Participants in ACDES.**

Notes and Coin Issuers

Physical money is exclusively issued and monitored by the RBA (notes) and the Royal Australian Mint (coins). Their role is to assess the quality of doubtful notes and coins, and to acquire excesses or provide shortfalls, either from existing pools or through new issues.

» NOTE

Damaged notes need to be removed from circulation, but the RBA will pay out a note's value if 80% of it is intact. One needs to apply for this facility to make use of it and most banks support it. Smaller portions of notes (between 20% and 80%) are paid out to the nearest dollar of the surface area remaining. Traditionally, when giving notes as a gift, people would iron the paper notes to straighten them. With the new polymer notes, this damages security features and, in fact, ironing notes is a counterfeit technique to avoid detection of the lack of security features as the note looks worn. It is important to note that heat-damaged notes are rejected by intelligent ATMs and could be rejected for replacement by the RBA. In practice, they should also be rejected by payees.

Bank Participants

For cash, the ACDES bank participants are just the Big Four: ANZ, CBA, NAB and Westpac. There does not seem to be an issue with this, and there has been no recommendation of note called out in any inquiry. Cash is becoming less popular, and the cash distribution system only really charges for delivery, so neither banks, regulators or the government have complained about this arrangement (other than the ACCC noting in a 2015 determination that it has not reviewed or approved ACDES regulations). Nevertheless, a reading of the ACDES regulations shows how difficult it is to become a participant. Whether this has contributed to the strength of the Big Four is unknown; however, a decline in the use of cash may diminish this advantage, if it exists at all.

Banks operate by buying and selling notes and coins, and deal directly with smaller banks, ATM providers, merchants and customers.

» NOTE

Collectors' coins, which are minted by either the Royal Australian Mint or the Perth Mint, are often technically legal tender with a nominal face value (but usually less than what the coin is worth as a collectable). Sometimes the coins do find their way into circulation, and CS5 regulations require that they be given to the Royal Australian Mint for assessment or destruction.

Approved Cash Centre Operators

Cash delivery is a risky business, with large amounts of cash being moved around and the interface between vehicles and destinations being subject, even in recent times, to theft and shootings resulting in death.

For many years, Armaguard and Chubb were the main providers of secure cash delivery. In order to keep a competitive market, both operators have been supported by banks and the members of CS5 to continue to provide this essential service. In 2013, Chubb sold its cash delivery business to Prosegur. In 2015, Brinks sold their business to Armaguard and Toll has never really been a participant except in coin delivery. Fully armoured vehicles are a big expense that few organisations venture into.

In recent years, Armaguard has diversified and, in 2019, acquired Cuscal's RediATM scheme. It now controls the ATMs for 30 financial institutions.

One advantage of being an approved cash centre is that the Reserve Bank pays interest on money held in storage at these centres. This is to encourage the availability of sufficient cash for distribution.

In turn, approved cash centres can distribute their safes to merchants and banks, and money in these safes can earn interest even as they sit there.

Seigniorage

Originally, only a lord (seignior) could mint money. The profit or loss incurred in issuing material currency (notes or coins) is known as seigniorage. When minting a gold coin, the value of the coin is only the value of the gold, but there is a cost to the process (these days about $50 for a one troy ounce coin) so minting a gold coin incurs a loss of $50. On the other hand, circulated coins have a lower metal value than their face value (to avoid people melting coins) so there is hopefully a profit in making coins. In addition, when coins are circulated, unlike for money held in the Reserve Bank, the Reserve Bank does not pay interest, increasing the seigniorage profit.

According to the Reserve Bank, seigniorage profit (returned to the state) accounts for 20% of its total profit, a sizable amount.

Cash Regulation

Cash and its uses are regulated.

Legal tender remains largely undefined in Australian law so its common law definition is used though, with modern payments, it is not entirely clear what this is. The Constitution of Australia simply states that "A State shall not coin money, nor make anything but gold and silver coin a legal tender in payment of debts." From this, we can infer that legal tender is used to pay debts. There appears to be no law that legal tender must be accepted when paying a debt and, in the case of online stores, many do not have cash acceptance facilities.

The Perth Mint, a Western Australia state institution, has minted legal tender coins in metals other than gold and silver. Currency (Australian coins) determinations from the Federal Treasury recognise these coins; therefore, they are constitutionally permitted as legal tender. As mentioned, as part of ACDES, collectors' coins are removed from circulation once they hit the inter-bank cash clearing system.

Coins are issued by the treasury through the mint as authorised by the Currency Act 1965.

Legal tender of small denomination coins can only be used to pay small amounts:

- One cent and two cent coins (no longer in legal tender) to pay amounts up to 20 cents.
- Five cent, 10 cent, 20 cent and 50 cent coins to pay amounts up to $5.
- Coins with denominations up to $10 to pay amounts up to 10 times their face value.
- Higher denomination coins to pay any payment.

» NOTE

In the US, the president is permitted to issue coins, notes and other forms of money, and governance of monetary policy is the responsibility of Congress. During the GFC, when the US was instituting quantitative easing, some measures were being blocked by Congress. It was a joke that it may have been possible for the president to mint a $1 trillion dollar coin to overcome the impasse. This was never seriously considered, though some argue it is a loophole in the US. Fortunately (or unfortunately), no such loophole exists in Australia without an act of parliament.

Notes are issued by the Reserve Bank in accordance with the Reserve Bank Act 1959.

All states and territories have legislation to reinforce the federal Proceeds of Crime Act (2002) that allows the police or courts to assume that the assets, including cash, of a convicted criminal, drug trafficker, etc. are as a result of crime, unless proven otherwise (reversing the onus of proof, which normally is on the prosecutor). In fact, it was in one such operation that the police found $3 million in banking receipts, triggering the IDM/ATM scandal that would see CBA pay hefty fines.

In 2019, the Currency (Restrictions on the Use of Cash) Bill was put forward, restricting the use of cash to make purchases worth $10 000 or more. However, second-hand purchases (cars, for example) between individuals, and the holding of cash as well as family gifts were still permitted.

7.

PAPER INSTRUMENTS

AFTER CASH, the next type of payment is paper, these days, mainly cheques. Again declining in usage, every now and then we may still come across one. They were an important instrument in payments before the age of computerisation, and facilitated the evolution of the electronic age.

Stamp Duty

It was the British Stamp Act of 1765 that set in motion a series of events that caused the American Revolution,[92] which then led to the British settlement of Australia. Australia, however, swallowed it and, unlike the independent Americans, continues to pay stamp duty a quarter of a millennium later.

The original purpose of stamp duty was to collect tax on any paper instrument, from a declaration to a transfer of property. Initially, a small nominal fee was charged but, like many taxes, it gradually increased. A postage-like stamp (*Figure 20*) would be applied to a document and cancelled by signing that stamp over the paper so that it could not be re-used or transferred.

***Figure 20.* A 10 shilling stamp duty stamp.**

With the increases in volumes of transactions, witnessing became rather loose, and the focus was more on revenue with the value of the stamp increasing with the value of the transaction. For example, property transaction stamp duty today on an average house sale is around $40 000, far more than the nominal fee originally intended and with e-conveyancing, more than the cost of it being scribed and filed on registers.

Even after federation, stamp duty was largely applied by the states (and was one of the few taxes to be collected by states). After the introduction of the goods and services tax in 2000, stamp duty has been gradually removed from many transactions including cheques.

[92] Morgan

Credit Transfer

Over time, as processes to transfer amounts between banks were streamlined, an inter-bank transfer form was required. Like a cheque, this debits a local bank account and credits an account at another bank, but travels in the opposite direction to a cheque (i.e., debtor to creditor). The credit transfer form had two copies (with carbon paper) so a copy could be retained by each bank.

The form would be stamped by the debiting bank and, once the account had been debited, a copy was taken and given to the crediting bank along with the settlement proceeds. The paper credit transfer is no longer in general use.

Personal or Business Cheques

Cheques are a particular form of promissory note and have a long history. The key feature of a cheque, however, is that it is drawn on a bank account (generally an account held with the bank of the payer).

Defined nationally in 1909 in the Bills of Exchange Act, the processing of cheques remained a secret business. It was difficult for non big banks to issue and deposit cheques. This was a problem as cheques were the main non-cash payment instrument at the time, outside the store. The Martin Review and the consequential deregulation changed this and, in 1986, the Cheques and Payment Orders Act opened up cheque issuing and processing. This was later renamed the Cheques Act. Cheque processing became an RBA recognised settlement system in 2004.

Personal and business cheques are issued to a customer blank. Each cheque required stamp duty to give the instrument legal recognition; however, over time, this became a revenue stream for the government.

Once presented to the issuing bank, the bearer would be credited funds withdrawn from the issuer's account.

Cheques would be issued in cheque books. When one of the last cheques were issued (the trigger cheque) a new cheque book would be printed and dispatched by the bank. Individual cheques could also be stopped so that before settlement, a lost or stolen cheque, or a withdrawn cheque could be prevented from being honoured through a cheque-stop made through the branch and later, in some cases, online.

Frequent criminal issues with cheques included forgery or alteration and, in the event that the issuer had insufficient funds, bouncing. Where a cheque issuer was a distant bank, it took time for the cheque to be cashed so there was risk involved in giving goods with a cheque as payment.

Fees

In addition to stamp duty, depending on the type of account, payments by cheque would be charged to cover the cost of processing. Often a periodic cheque limit would be placed on an account and additional cheques would incur a fee.

Float Revenue

A float is when funds are in transit between a payer and a payee. One issue with floats is determining who receives interest as a cheque weaves its way through processing.

Banks generally tend to avoid float revenue on transient payments. With cheques, the depositor gets credit for value on the day it is deposited. The funds are called uncleared funds so the ledger balance goes up (for interest calculation purposes), but the available balance remains the same for a number of days (the clearance period) and then goes up. The available balance controls how much can be withdrawn at any point in time. In some cases, banks may allow customers to access deposited cheques immediately.

Dishonoured Cheques

Cheques can be dishonoured for various reasons, such as mismatched signatures, outdated cheques, cancelled cheques, insufficient funds, cheque-stops or closed accounts. These days, in Australia, every attempt is made to honour a cheque unless fraud is certain.

In some countries, issuing a cheque as payment, which later bounces on account of insufficient balance is a criminal or civil offence. This is not the case in Australia, although a bounced cheque serves as evidence for a broken contract to pay.

Processing operates on the principle that cheques are assumed to be valid unless found otherwise. Cheque processing time is a risk measure to give the bulk of cheques enough time to process though, in practice (when considering remote branches and agents), it could take even longer for a cheque to make its way through the system. So, technically, a cheque could be cleared but still bounce. The bounced cheque would then reverse the depositor's account (and interest credited would be deducted) and the issuer would be charged a dishonour fee. In addition, non-bank recipients of a bounced cheque often charged the payer their own dishonour fee to cover the costs of reversal and payment recovery.

Cheque Guarantee Services

A number of third parties attempted to provide a level of guarantee to a cheque recipient that the payment was good so that the payer could walk away with the goods. Payday lenders, merchants to businesses (like hardware suppliers), and the like would utilise their services. This was done by the guarantor doing credit checks and through contracts that allowed recovery of bounced cheques. TeleCheck Payment Systems (part of an American company, now owned by First Data/Fiserv) and Transax Australia (part of a European/global company, now FIS) were two providers of this service.

Cheque Printing, Endorsements and Marks

Cheques are printed on secure paper, such as with a background that could reveal alterations, watermarks and, later, heat sensitive ink. They are signed by the payer.

With the streamlining of processes, cheques were embossed with a stamp, and later printed with a simple text box reading "stamp duty paid," rather than a traditional stamp. As alternative electronic debits emerged, this stamp duty was abolished by state governments (New South Wales in 1990 and Victoria in 1992). This tax revenue was replaced by a state financial institutions duty and an earlier federal bank accounts debit tax, both of which were, in turn, abolished with the introduction of GST in 2000.

The key components of a cheque are the bank and branch issuing the cheque, the payee, the amount (in both numbers and words), date and signature. At the bottom of the cheque is the account number, name of the account holder (the payer), their account number and a cheque number. Generally, cheques would be deposited at the payee's bank into the payee's bank account.

Cash Cheques

A cash cheque could be used to take cash out over the counter. The cheque simply was written out to "cash."

Crossing a Cheque

Crossing a cheque (drawing two parallel transverse lines on the front of the cheque) prevents the funds being taken out as cash; they had to be deposited into an account.

Not Negotiable

Two lines and the words "not negotiable" mean that only the addressed party is entitled to the funds and they cannot be given to another party. Banks can be requested to preprint this on cheques.

Not Negotiable A/C Payee Only

Two lines, the words "not negotiable," and "A/C payee only" mean that only the addressed party is entitled to the funds and they cannot be given to another party. In addition, they can only be deposited into an account under the payee's name as written.

Endorsements

A negotiable cheque (one that is not stamped "not negotiable") can be endorsed to be given to another party. In practice, however, many banks discourage this, especially if the endorser cannot be identified.

Dates

The date on a cheque is generally ignored but, in theory, the cheque should only be processed up to 15 months after issue. Post-dated cheques are generally processed ignoring the date.

Validation

Most validation is done at the depositing financial institution, to check that the name of the account matched the payee as written to ensure the cheque was clean and valid.

» NOTE

While a lot of attention in recent times has been put on the security of electronic banking, cheques are a high fraud risk instrument with numerous avenues for deception and fraud. Signatures, in practice, are rarely checked, and issues with the paper can be easily overlooked. The movie *Catch Me if You Can* tells the exploits of a fraudster who used cheque fraud as his primary modus operandi. Many of these exploits are real and several remain exposed today.

Bank Cheques

Bank cheques, cashier's cheques and bank drafts are essentially the same instrument.

They differ from personal cheques in that they are drawn on the bank, and are often accepted as being as good as cash as they are guaranteed by a bank.

Traditionally, bank cheques solved the delivery versus payment (DvP) problem for in-person transactions and were popular in property transactions.

Unlike cash, they have an added security feature as only the payee can cash them in.

In some cases, banks offered cheque disbursement services to corporate customers, where they would mail out bank cheques to the company's payees along with payment advice.

Today, with electronic payments, if there is a failure of the real-time gross settlements system (see below), a bank cheque could be used to pay institutions.

Bank cheques often attract a significant fixed fee.

Float on Bank Cheques

Somewhat uniquely in payments, float revenue on bank cheques is significant; the reason being, when issued, the money is withdrawn from the payer's account and held in a clearing account, awaiting presentment of the cheque, which could be days, weeks or months after the date of the cheque.

Overseas Bank Draft

Where a cheque needed to be sent overseas, a cheque drawn on an overseas bank was issued, known as an overseas bank draft. Another similar type of instrument was the demand draft, that requested a partner branch and bank in the overseas country to make the payment, which would be returned and settled with the overseas bank.

» NOTE

Bank cheques are almost as unreliable as personal cheques. They could be faked, legitimate cheques could be cancelled before presentment, and they did have an (albeit small) risk of the financial institution collapsing before the cheque was cashed.

Letters of Credit

In trade finance, a letter of credit is issued by a bank and provides a guarantee of payment to a payee if certain conditions are met. It was not a payment itself, but ended up in one once the payee could prove that the conditions had been met.

Postal Money Orders

To overcome the need to post money, with the convenience of purchasing a stamp, the local post office could issue a postal money order. Similar to bank cheques, these attracted a fee. Other private organisations, such as American Express, were known for issuing money orders; however, these do not appear to have taken off in Australia. Uncashed postal money orders would be revenue for the post office.

Travellers Cheques

Made famous by Thomas Cook and American Express, travellers cheques were a more convenient method of payment for international exchange than a letter of credit in many circumstances. They continue to be used today, though are in decline.

Bank Guarantees

Commercial leases (among other endeavours) require a guarantee of funds if things do not work out as intended. This could happen if the lessee defaults on payments, or if a builder fails to complete work. Generally, this was enacted as a letter from a bank, called a bank guarantee, which would hold funds in a term deposit (or some other negotiated surety) under the guarantor's name. It could only be released on advice of the party to whom the guarantee is provided (the favouree), provided the favouree had the original guarantee paper. The guarantee was provided at a significant cost to the guarantor.

» NOTE

Bank guarantees were subjects of fraud (photocopying) so security features were added to the paper. Checking the validity of a guarantee remains a challenge, and a common solution is that the recipient (favouree) checks with the bank that the guarantee is genuine. This created confusion and complexity within banks, and the process of validation was not always fail-safe.

Processing Cheques

After cash, cheques were the most popular payment method for most of the 20th century. A large number of cheques needed to be processed daily by each branch, sorted by payer bank and branch. The cheques and direct transfers needed to be returned to the destination bank head offices, along with a net payment or request to pay (settled again by a cheque) and then distributed to the branches to process against each account. This was a long process so it was no surprise that cheques took so long to clear.

Cheque processing challenges were not unique to Australia, and many other countries had to deal with much higher volumes of cheques. Adoption of equipment to help sort cheques was the first step. A bank sort code, as used in the United Kingdom, and eventually a bank state branch (BSB) number that uniquely identified every branch was used to prefix the account number.

Magnetic Ink Character Recognition

Each cheque was printed with the payer's account details in magnetic ink, scanned using magnetic ink character recognition (MICR) devices. These came in various shapes and forms, from desktop readers to conveyor belt subsystems that allowed cheques to be sorted. Each character had a different magnetic footprint (*Figure 21*) and, before the age of optical character recognition, these could be used to sort numbers electro-mechanically. The numbering was introduced in the 1960s, with cheques preprinted with MICR account numbers, and operators typing in the amount appended to the end of the bottom line using a special MICR typewriter. It was the early days of computers and the challenge with the non-decimal currency, as shown in *Figure 22*, may have contributed to decimalisation.

0 1 2 3 4 5 6 7 8 9

***Figure 21.* Sample MICR numbers.**

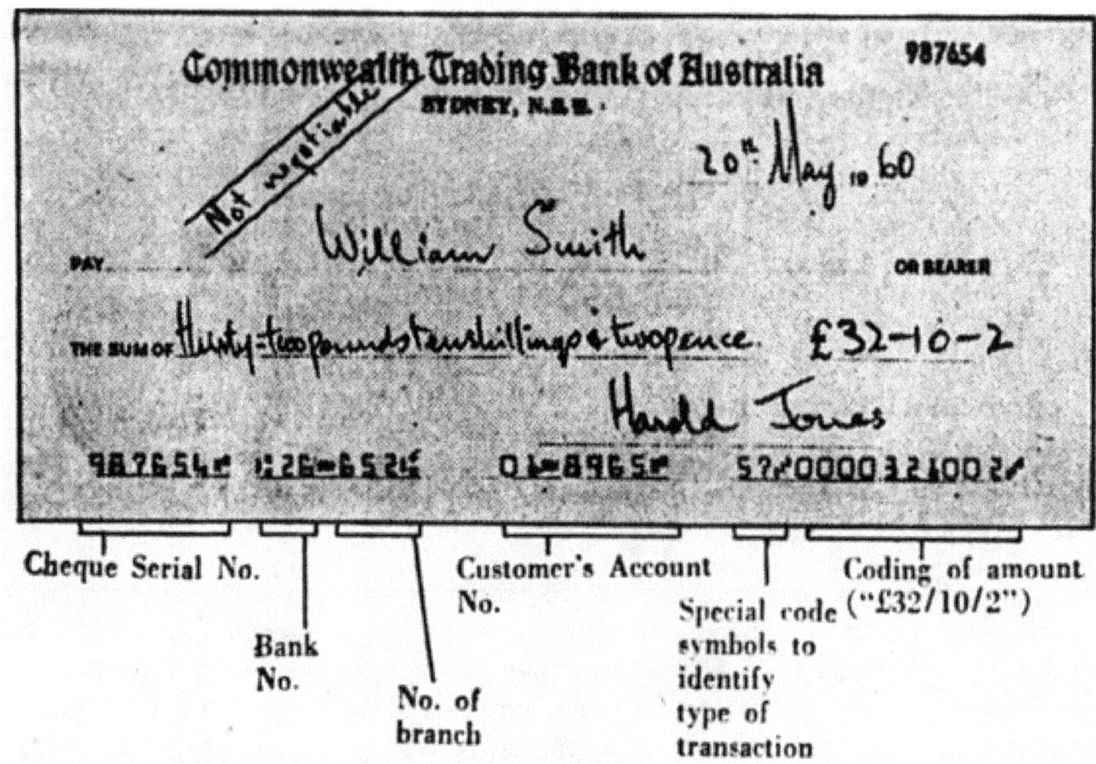

***Figure** 22.* **Cheque of the Future**

courtesy of the Sydney Morning Herald, 20 May 1960.

Australian Paper Clearing System

As payment volumes continued to grow, the government regulators grew concerned with the lack of accessibility in processing payments. APCA (now AusPayNet) was formed to streamline the clearing of payments and the first message system, or Clearing System 1 (CS1) as it was called, was the Australian Paper Clearing System (APCS).

APCS consisted of files informing a bank about cheques that had been presented. The bank had a few days to validate the details or to dishonour the cheque.

Cheque settlement initially operated on a deferred net settlement basis. Totals were agreed upon and, at around 9:00 am the next day, banks were netted off.

Cheque messages were originally exchanged bilaterally, but now take place through the COIN network (see below).

In 2015, a cheque image exchange was introduced for settlement. Before this, cheques were physically exchanged between banks as per APRA/AusPayNet rules.

Decline of Cheques

Due to the use of credit cards and the accessibility of alternative electronic means of payment, cheque use per capita has been declining year on year. Active measures were taken in various industries to help wean them off reliance on the cheque system. In the mid-1990s, an average of 50 cheques were written per person each year. This has declined at a considerable rate, to barely more than one per person in 2020.[93]

›› NOTE

While cheque use was declining, and bank executives wanted to put the last nail in the coffin, technologists were going crazy. One bank's team had real-time cheque-stop functionality on their Internet banking site, and the ability to retrieve images of cheques. This took a fair bit of effort to develop, but a call from upstairs put an end to it. There was no need to encourage people to use cheques; instead, they were to be actively discouraged.

Cheque usage

The Fiserv Cheque Processing Centre

Being a leading banking technology organisation in the US, Fiserv had lots of experience processing cheques. By 2005, it was clear that cheques in Australia were on their way out and processing them was not an expense that banks wanted. Fiserv saw an opportunity in the market: cheques were still going strong in the US and there were no signs of slowing down. A $600 million deal for 12 years was signed with Fiserv to centralise processing of cheques from CBA, Westpac and NAB. As is often the case with interbank cooperation, ANZ had its own ideas.

This was a significant step. Each of the three banks could outsource its paper processing to the same place as many of the recipients. Paper still had to be exchanged and archived. By 1998, the official cheque processing time had dropped to two days. Fiserv could process cheques, reconcile them, and exchange them with the relevant parties. Eventually, images could be exchanged, obviating the need for paper transfer.

---

[93] RBA 2020

» NOTE

At 500 million cheques per year, the Fiserv deal put a price of 7.5 cents on processing a cheque. This was a good deal at the time, but potentially not sustainable. The banks were doing their bit in driving volumes down, but regulatory action needed to be taken to end their use. The United Kingdom tried to set a target date of 2018 to end the cheque, but reneged in 2011. Poland and Finland have stopped cheques, and other countries in Europe are down to almost zero. There was a joke that when the last old lady writes the last cheque to pay her gardener, that cheque would cost $50 million to process! They needed to end cheques fast, but no one wanted to pull the plug. On the other hand, cheques were still strong in the US, and US-based tech companies like Fiserv and Genpact saw domination of the Australian cheque market as a real prize; however, there was a difference between the way cheques were viewed in the US and Australia.

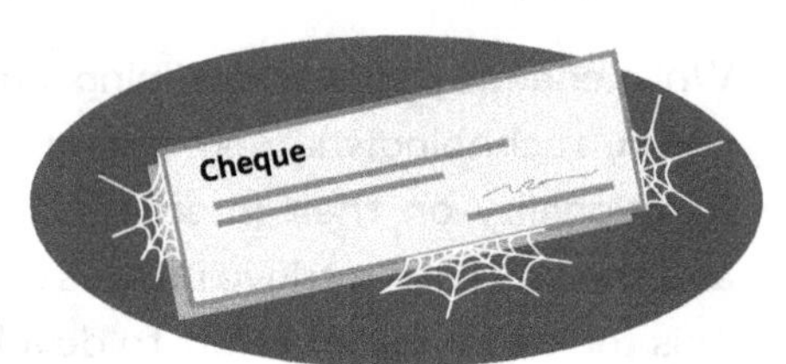

When Fiserv's contract expired in 2017 (perhaps with Fiserv discovering they had a raw deal), Genpact took over. Genpact had been spun out of General Electric 20 years earlier.

Cheque Settlement

Originally, cheques were settled bilaterally; however, with the introduction of the Low Value Settlement Service (LVSS), the RBA calculated the deferred net settlement and payment of cheques the next day, through the RITS system, applying transfers directly to the bank's Exchange Settlement Account (ESA). The settlement happens before the cheque is cleared (to give banks time to decline) and the convention is to credit accounts on presentment.

Cheque Payment System Operation

Cheques, while they were initiated by the payer, they were technically a pull payment as money was debited from the payer. Cheque processing operates as follows (*Figure 23*):

1. A cheque book is issued by the drawer's bank to the drawer, who fills in a cheque, signs it and has it delivered to the payee.
2. The payee deposits the cheque into their account at the payee bank and receives credit for interest from that day. The cheque is in an uncleared state and the amount cannot yet be withdrawn.
3. The payee bank either scans the cheque (on an IDM) or sends it to a processing centre in a major city. The cheque is either received digitally or imaged and archived.
4. The processing centre can validate the cheque and the image is sent to the drawer bank along with a clearing file.

5. The drawing bank has a day to dishonour the cheque; if no message is received, the cheque is assumed to be cleared.

6. Both banks send a Low Value Settlement Service message to the RBA.

7. The next day, at start of business, the payment is settled on the ESA account.

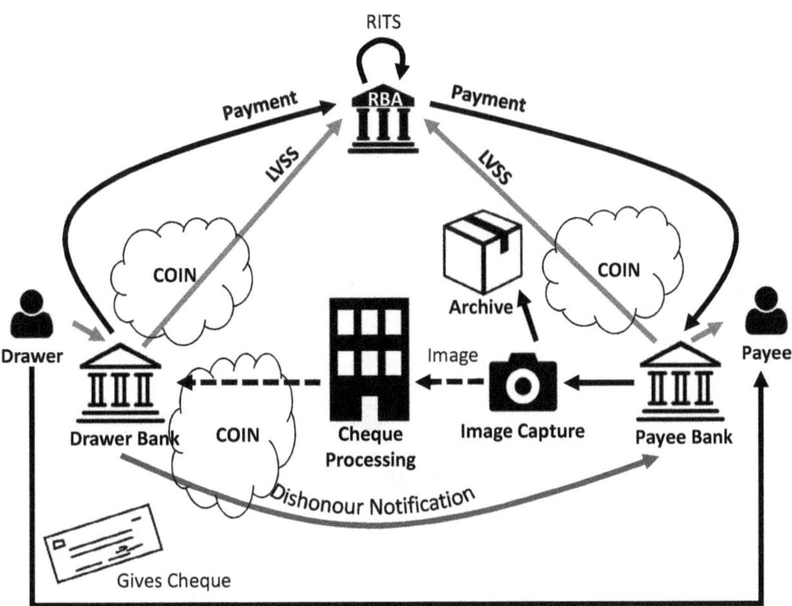

Figure 23. **Cheque payment system operation.**

8.

CARDS

CARDS, ATMS AND EFTPOS remain as part of the core of consumer payments today. The history of cards goes back to times before computerisation, yet today, they have evolved to be at the forefront of electronic payments on the Internet and through mobile devices.

In this section, we shall look at all things to do with cards. Like a complex river system with a number of tributaries, cards have many facets: in shopping, at ATMs, in person and online. It is impractical to cover the topics in a purely chronological way so, while the sequence is broadly time-based, in completing the story for each topic it may be necessary to jump ahead slightly and return again, just as we would if we were to survey the tributaries of a complex river system.

Store Credit and the Credit Card

Store credit is perhaps as old as stores themselves. Originally, credit was recorded on a small ledger card held by the store.

There has often been talk in recent times of a seamless payment experience: a utopian situation where we walk in, and walk out with our goods, and payment happens in the background. This existed long ago. Driving up to a fuel station, telling the attendant to, "Fill 'er up, thanks, mate. Put it on the account," without getting out of the driver's seat is a lost experience in this modern anonymous transactional world. Corner stores, butchers and grocery stores would keep accounts for local residents. In Australia, this would have started with the British settlement in 1788, all the way to, ironically, the arrival of the credit card in the mid-1970s.

The invention of the credit card was initially an elegant and simple idea that meant, for decades to come, we could avoid the problem of real-time integration with the banking ledger. However, back then, necessity was the mother of invention, for it was in an era before computerisation.

The simple idea was this: an identification card, initially cardboard, sometimes metallic, and later plastic, would bear the customer's name, perhaps address, an account number and a signature. It would be issued by a *scheme*. A scheme was an organisation that administered the issuing of the cards and settlement logistics and was, primarily, the brand of the card.

Initially, these cards were given to wealthy, well-established people, often recognisable, if not publicly, at least in the store. Rather than keeping a store account and the store having to deal with chasing the customer for payment, the bank would do the work.

At the time of payment, the card details would be transcribed by the merchant onto a voucher (eventually on a triplicate slip: one for the customer, one for the merchant and one for the scheme or bank). The merchant would then dispatch the voucher to the scheme or to their bank, known as the acquirer bank (the bank that acquired payment vouchers). The scheme would then collate all the slips, dispatch them and request payment from the cardholder, either directly through the scheme or through their bank, known as the issuer bank (the bank that issued the card).

A merchant service fee (MSF), usually around 3%, would be imposed on the merchant to cover administration costs, and, later, risks of non-payment or fraud.

Charge Card

Early credit cards were technically charge cards. This meant that bills were sent to the cardholder and had to be paid by the due date (generally monthly). It took time to collate all the bills, which meant that the customer did not have to pay their bill for around two months.

The first charge cards (issued in the US) were Diners' Club (1950), a paper card, as shown in *Figure 24*, later named Diners Club (without the apostrophe), mainly for the restaurant industry, and American Express (1958) for other stores.

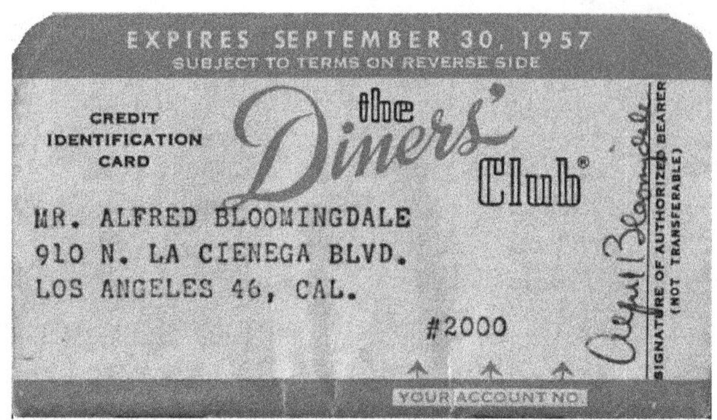

***Figure 24.* Early Diners' Club card.**
Courtesy of the Smithsonian Institute.

Credit Card: Revolving Line of Credit

A revolving line of credit is basically a standing loan or credit limit that could be drawn down and is payable (without interest) on a monthly cycle. This meant that a bill did not need to be paid for 30-60 days, depending on when the purchase was made. Missing a due payment meant using up the credit limit and incurring, generally, a high interest charge.

The first such credit cards were in the US: BankAmeriCard (later Visa, 1958) and Master Charge (later Mastercard, 1966). By 1970, 100 million cards had been mailed out, unsolicited, to bank customers. This practice was quickly banned.

Australian banks heard of this success and established, with regulatory approval, Charge Card Services in 1974, which launched Bankcard. Attempting to copy the mass market tactics of the US, but with more responsibility and a drive to encourage consumer spending during the 1970-1975 recession, customers were assessed for suitability before receiving (still unsolicited) a $300 credit limit credit card.

While Bankcard and the credit card revolution were considered to have caused modern consumerism, they also enabled real-time cashless payments in an era when merchants were not computerised or networked. The interest-free period was initially simply to allow time for the bills to flow from the merchant, and to be tallied and statemented on computers at the bank.

The implication of non-payment of these bills was severe. Interest would rack up (at 18% or more per annum), and many naive consumers would find themselves bankrupt over relatively small debts.

» NOTE

In one case, in 1979, one individual had 11 Bankcards and used them to take cash out for poker machines. He declared himself bankrupt with $2 000 in debt. The cards could be obtained from different institutions by filling in a form and there was no way that other banks could know about this. Average debt had climbed from $100 in 1976 to $350 in 1979. There were claims that, in this era before identity and credit checking, 16-year-olds were being given Bankcards.

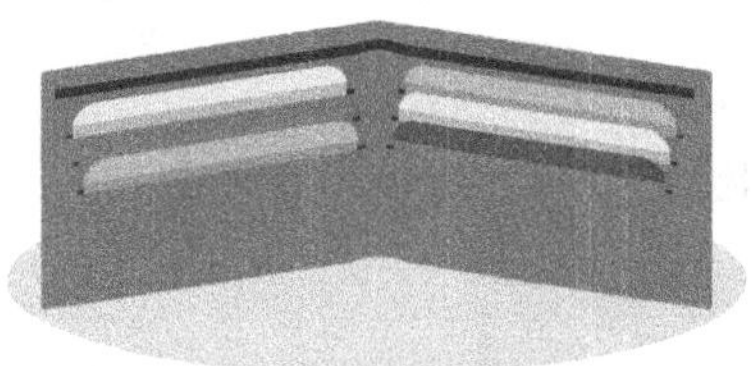

Over time, credit checks were imposed using agencies such as Equifax (part of Veda Group), Experian and Illion. In addition, due diligence, checking income, expenses and balance sheets, and general affordability and suitability have been under greater regulatory visibility so institutions are much more rigorous when accepting applications. Regulators have also been tightening lending policies.

Similar to a personal loan, credit cards offer unsecured funds that can be charged interest. The key difference is that with a credit card, once the loan is paid off, it can be reused; hence, it is called a revolving line of credit. Failure to pay off a credit card bill eventually invokes the bank's infamous collections division, one of the only bank divisions that takes our calls immediately.

Store credit ledgers were replaced by a card similar to a credit card. Over time, due to more uniform credit laws and risk, many store credit cards were issued by credit card issuing organisations.

Automatic Teller Machines

The phrase *automatic teller machine* in its literal sense, especially in the 1970s or 1980s, invoked the concept of a robotic teller. In fact, a 1978 headline says just that: "Bank Robot: swallows cards, spits out cash! New South Wales credit unions may soon introduce 'robot tellers' used in Queensland."

In reality, this has been a slow journey and the functions of ATMs remain limited even today.

While there are examples of ATMs from the 1960s (there is an amusing video on YouTube of an ATM-like device in an ABC report from the late 1960s), these machines were largely uncomputerised electro-mechanical devices and, in practice, it took years for the technology to mature. Computers were new and high availability of systems did not really exist.

The first useful ATMs were computer terminals: the mainframe was at the backend as were the device drivers. Basically, this meant the machine was relatively dumb and needed to get every instruction, from what to display on the screen to what to print, from the head office.

In the original machines, cash was provided in boxes with a conveyor belt to remove the notes. Tightening or loosening the tension on the belt was required to ensure one and only one note came out at a time.

It was not infrequent that an ATM would be offline for days or intermittently fail when a customer really needed it. The first *real* general-use ATMs appeared in the late 1970s with ANZ claiming a Night and Day ATM in 1985.

The initial machines were closed loop so a customer needed a proprietary card from a bank to access their funds; this card could only be used with its own bank's ATMs.

In order to access ATMs, a personal identification number (PIN) or, in effect, a secret passcode, needed to be entered. This deterred card theft.

Over time, ATMs became more sophisticated. One could deposit notes and cheques (originally the notes and cheques would be collated by staff and manually deposited). Rather than dumb terminals, they became full-blown computers with offers and advertisements. In other countries, they often took over the role of a bank. One could open a new account, buy phone vouchers, withdraw foreign currency or contact bank staff. In Australia, ATMs were a type-cast transactional device: money in and money out. In recent years, being able to deposit and withdraw money without a card (using a code from a mobile banking app) and cash recycling (cash deposits would be credited to an account in real-time and the same cash could be given to the next customer who withdraws funds) were added to the ATM arsenal.

The Card Schemes

The payment card industry consisted of many participants: banks, merchants, hardware developers and information technology companies. Central to them were the schemes, many of which are covered below.

Credit Card Schemes

Credit card schemes are some of the most profitable organisations in the world, when measured in terms of profit per employee.

Visa and Mastercard are the dominant schemes, both in Australia and globally. In Australia, other schemes exist too and have had their share of success.

» NOTE

An application of Hotteling's Law is that the most profitable place to locate two ice cream stores on the beach is back to back in the middle of the beach. So it is with Visa and Mastercard; they are almost identical offerings on the surface and, where they have collaborated, they have both excelled. Is it collusion or free market economics that has led to the two cards being almost identical? Perhaps the reason for their similarity is to attract the merchant: one process makes it easy for them to be accepted. However, the schemes do operate very differently and diverge significantly when comparing many of their failed innovations.

Visa Inc.

Visa grew as a Bank of America spin-off through a mutual ownership arrangement with other banks. Many Australian banks were shareholders of Visa, even before Visa's IPO. The CBA sold its shares in Visa in 2016 for gains of $278 million, a profit of over 100%.

Visa cards were issued early in Australia through Bendigo Bank (then a building society) in 1982, which offered both credit cards and debit cards. Their market penetration was slow, especially with the establishment of Bankcard as the domestic scheme for credit and proprietary cards for debit. Nonetheless, they grew a slow organic base of merchants. After the split with Bankcard (see below) they were unable to use the Australian Charge Card Services acquiring network, and turned to private companies, Electronic Funds Transfer Services and Austnet to process vouchers. In 1984, Austnet claimed to process the first electronic intercontinental card transaction in the world.

Visa cards have traditionally been issued by the Melbourne banks: NAB and ANZ.

Mastercard

Mastercard started as a joint venture, known as Interbank Master Charge, between the Californian banks: Wells Fargo, Crocker National, United California Bank and Bank of California. Later, New York-based Citibank joined this venture. Like Visa, Mastercard was mutually owned by banks, including some in Australia.

Mastercard has traditionally been issued by the Sydney banks: CBA and Westpac. As with Visa, there is always competition between the schemes and a contract with the Big Four is not always guaranteed. All the banks have been known to issue cards (e.g., travel cards) under the rival brand.

Mastercard has had a close relationship with CBA, which was the gateway of their network into Australi, through the Mastercard Internet Gateway Service, and which conducted settlement activities on behalf of Mastercard, before granting this capability to Mastercard directly.

American Express

Born from express mail and travellers cheques, American Express charge cards were available in Australia before Bankcard. They required a high income and were not widely accepted by merchants, other than high street city stores.

One of the challenges for a customer was knowing their credit limit and, in the early days, there was nominally no limit. However, with computerisation, the head office did have sophisticated rules, and if a large payment that did not match a customer's spending habits was made, it would be declined.

American Express and the other second tier schemes have had a challenge in the Australian market. While initially a closed operation, American Express eventually teamed up with banks to market their card.

The American Express mail service was very fast and, in the US, was used to transport vouchers from the east to the west coast. For many years, the company could return charge forms to a cardholder for them to verify expenses, even in Australia. It was a similar convention to personal bank cheques in the US.

Around 2000, with the introduction of GST in Australia, American Express, through their independent acquiring solution, could collect more data. For taxis, they could collect journey information, and with GST in 2000, they tried to itemise it on a statement (*Figure 25*).

The advantage was short-lived as, eventually, American Express succumbed to standardised acquirer devices and messaging, losing the rich information that keying in dockets gave them.

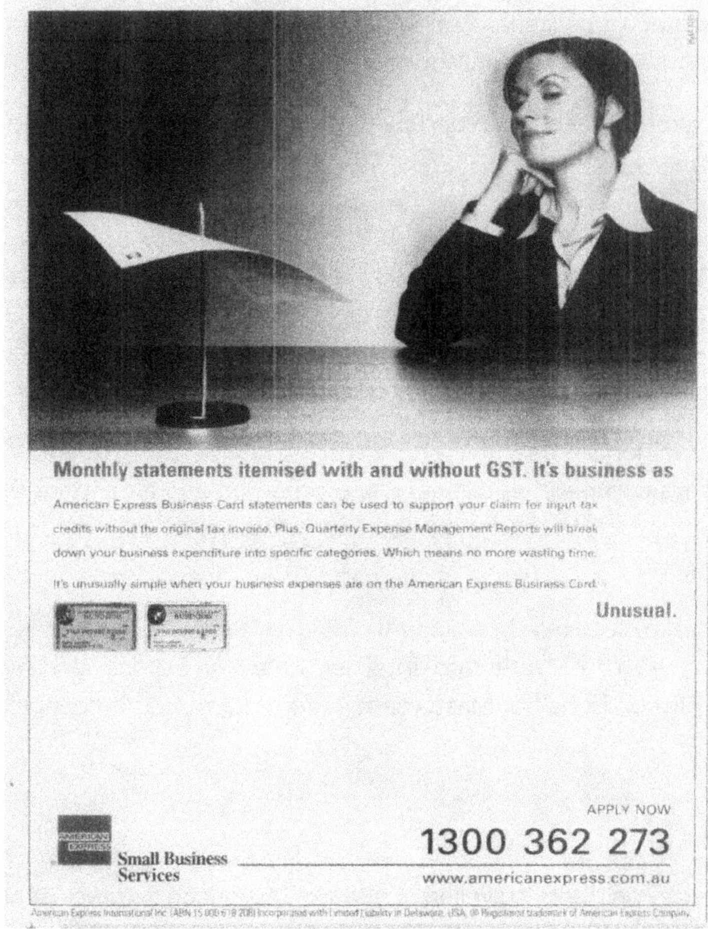

Figure 25. American Express statements could sort out GST, Sydney Morning Herald, 15 October 2001.

Copyright American Express.

American Express merchant fees were higher than competitors, which dissuaded merchant acceptance. Their argument was that they were charging not just scheme fees but also doing all the acquiring and issuing work themselves.

American Express is quite different from Visa and Mastercard, as it has more interchange revenue (as we will see) per transaction and can provide generous loyalty offers to its members. With the introduction of merchant surcharges, many expected American Express to fade from the Australian marketplace, but it remains strong.

American Express settlement times for merchants remain sluggish. With many banks in Australia providing same-day settlement (on non-American Express transactions), American Express payments tended to take relatively longer to settle. This is somewhat ironic, given it was originally an express delivery service for conventional mail.

Diners Club and Discover Card

Diners Club remains a niche scheme in the Australian market. Discover Card is not issued in Australia, but is accepted through the same network.

Originally formed in the US for the restaurant industry and wealthy clients, Diners Club was taken over by Citigroup and, more recently, Discover Card. In some markets, including Australia, Diners Club is still owned by Citigroup and distributed under license by Discover; in turn, Citigroup supports acquiring for both Diners Club and Discover Card through the same network.

The Voucher System

Original credit card systems relied on a voucher system at point of sale. The details of the card, the merchant, the purchase (and purchase amount) as well as the signature of the account holder, would be recorded on triplicate paper and then distributed for payment.

Over time, plastic cards that had embossed names were issued. Credit card imprinters, or click-clacks as they were informally known, would be used to easily transfer the name onto paper. They did this by applying pressure with a roller over the carbon paper and card.

These vouchers were then tallied by the merchant and sent to the acquirer, who would distribute them to issuers, who would, in turn, request payment from the cardholder, hopefully for a payment they recognised. In the meantime, settlement would occur (at different times) through the issuer paying the acquirer, the cardholder paying the issuer, and the acquirer paying the merchant.

›› NOTE

To this day, some banks offer imprinters, known colloquially as "click clacks" as a backup if electronic systems fail. However, the imprinters were problematic. Inexperienced staff would incorrectly complete the voucher and it would be rejected by the bank, resulting in loss of revenue. Store management, therefore, had their staff circle the card number (to confirm embossing had worked) and the expiration date of the card, and tick the signature to ensure all steps to validate the slip were completed.

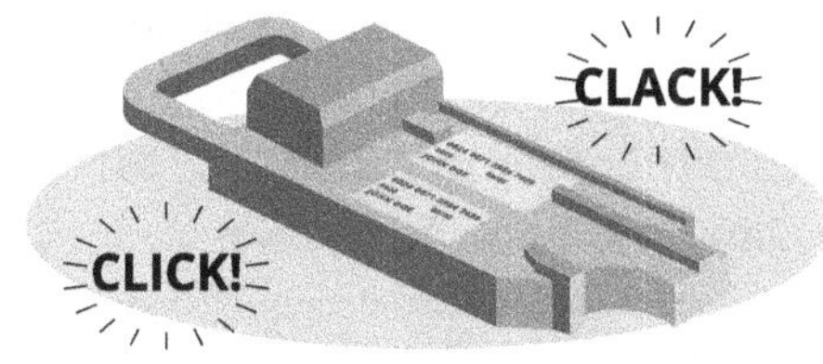

Verification

In addition to the normal checks, one of the issues with the manual process was lost, stolen and cancelled cards. Cards could have been stolen or used after cancellation without the merchant knowing. For this purpose, Bankcard, Visa and Mastercard published a list of unusable cards. It was the merchant's responsibility to check this list to ensure the card was valid, otherwise the voucher would be declined and the merchant would lose payment.

Further, above a certain limit, an authorisation check was required. The merchant would call up Cardlink for authorisation to process the voucher if it was over a certain amount.

›› NOTE

It was reported that around Christmas in 1990, Cardlink had 250 staff answering 50 000 calls for authorisation checks in two weeks.

Debit Card Schemes

Debit card schemes began with the advent of the ATM. A card was used to obtain money from the device. The technical challenge is that, while a credit card could be continuously charged (with limited checks to ensure that the holder did not go over the limit), the debit card had a fixed balance and needed checking in real-time to avoid overdrawing (which many bank accounts did not support). Debit cards were mass market instruments and generally given to any transaction account holder who wanted one. Without any identity or credit check, there was little or no certainty of repayment if the holder had insufficient funds.

What was required was a seamless and automated real-time check on funds. ATMs, wired to the head office, could do just that. Eventually, a solution was required at merchants, and that would come within a couple of years in the form of EFTPOS.

›› NOTE

The terms and conditions for banking products (like for many products in the market) are complex and generally go unread so few people realise what they sign up for. In the case of debit cards, consumers sign up to conditions that allow the bank to recover money, even if they spend over their balance due to a technical fault (or otherwise) in the banking system. So what is the difference between a debit and credit card? Either way, the bank knows where the customer lives and does get its money back.

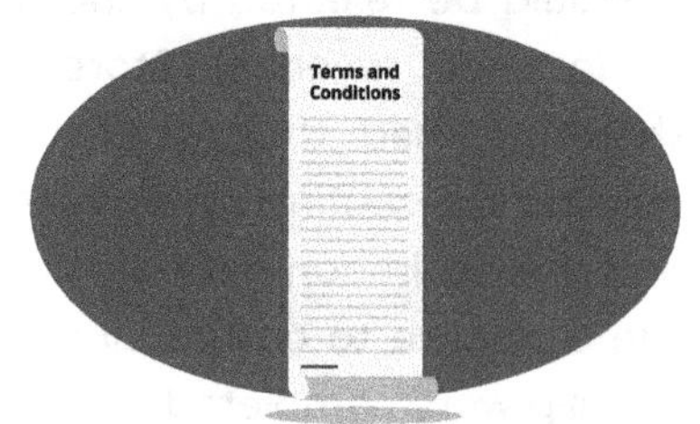

Proprietary Cards

Early debit cards in Australia were proprietary cards that were first issued to allow customers to withdraw money from ATMs and to help identify them at bank tellers. There were some non-bank applications of plastic cards, such as store cards, gift cards and loyalty cards though, these days, many of these are issued by banks or schemes.

The connectivity of these cards relies on a closed loop, in which all messages and rules are controlled and distributed by one party.

At some point, the benefit of ATMs accepting cards from other banks became a necessity, and banks started integrating bilaterally.

Each bank marketed their card with pride and each had a unique name: CBA's Keycard, Westpac's Handycard, NAB's FlexiCard and ANZ's Access Card. Other smaller banks joined forces to create Cashcard.

Cashcard connected these institutions through Austnet in the early 1980s, with First Data acquiring Austnet in 1992 and, later, Cashcard itself in 2004. Meanwhile, RediTeller was launched by Cuscal and later replaced by RediCard for RediATMs. These physical ATMs and their network are currently owned by Armaguard. CueCard and, later, Indue networks were another card network for small institutions.

Bankcard

Bankcard was formed in 1974 to provide a credit card scheme to Australian and New Zealand residents. It proved to be a major success for two decades.

Managed by Charge Card Services, operations were centralised. After a restructure, Cardlink Services took over in 1987 and would become Australia's largest credit card authorisation processing centre. Over time, as Bankcard usage declined, this function would be moved to the banks.

In 1979, Bankcard teamed up with Mastercard (then Master Charge) and Visa. Under an agreement, member banks would issue Bankcard for domestic use and Visa or Mastercard for international use. Charge Card Services (i.e., the banks) became a member and soon a shareholder of Visa and Mastercard, and they peacefully coexisted for a few years.

In 1980 and 1981, the Trade Practices Commission (now ACCC) took an interest in Bankcard. In granting permission to continue what may amount to a restrictive practice that stopped member banks issuing Visa and Mastercard cards domestically:

- It ruled the 18% interest charged by all banks was anti-competitive. (It is interesting to note that, since this time, while RBA interest rates have gone down, credit card interest rates have not.)
- It allowed merchants to discount non-Bankcard (i.e., cash) purchases.
- It forced banks to admit non-banks to the Bankcard scheme.
- It allowed Bankcard to issue Visa and Mastercard cards for overseas use.

In 1990, after Bankcard failed to accept a number of new banks, the Trade Practices Commission revoked Bankcard's monopoly permission, and this opened the way for banks to split from Bankcard and allow alternative credit cards. This led to the eventual demise of Bankcard.

The Bankcard brand was shut down in 2006 as most banks had moved to international schemes, especially Visa and Mastercard. The corporate organisation would live on under the brand of BPAY.

›› NOTE

In 1982, a new bank, Australian Bank, challenged Charge Card Services (which controlled credit card acquiring in Australia) to accept Visa cards domestically. Charge Card Services was acting against Visa's rules and uncompetitively, they said. Eventually, this resulted in a split between Visa and Bankcard, with Visa using Australian Bank as their local issuer. At the time, 20 000 merchants in Australia accepted Visa, compared with 100 000 that accepted Bankcard.

After the split, which initially turned out to be disastrous for Visa (they only secured Australian Bank and Bendigo Building Society (now Bendigo Bank) through CUSCAL), three major banks (CBA, Westpac and NAB) aligned with Mastercard. ANZ (always the odd one out), however, eventually aligned with Visa.

Australian Bank's success made it the target of a bidding war with both the State Bank of Victoria and the Australian property and construction company Lendlease. Lendlease was looking to get into banking, and later established outsourcing partnerships with EDS, IBM and Telstra, and attempted share acquisitions with Westpac in 1993. In 1989, Lendlease lost to the State Bank of Victoria. Lendlease was lucky, for the acquisition set in motion a train of events that crippled the state bank, spawned a state royal commission and contributed to the loss of government. The State Bank of Victoria and the remnants of Australian Bank were acquired by CBA.

While Australian Bank's reign was short-lived, its entry either caused or coincided with an enormous impact to the banking sector: deregulation, the entry of the international card schemes, the rise of Cuscal and Bendigo Bank, and the development of international electronic card authorisation.

Alternative Credit Providers

While banks continued to provide the lion's share of credit cards, other organisations came into the picture, especially to support retailers.

The Australian Guarantee Company (later the Australian Guarantee Corporation) was formed in 1921 as a credit organisation providing loans, especially car loans. Initially, through their AGC CreditLine product, they provided store credit (a buy now, pay later system with several years interest free) through a model where the retailer was charged a larger fee to encourage more sales. This card eventually became a credit card. The Australian Guarantee Company's credit card business was eventually taken over by General Electric, and the traditional equipment finance business was taken over by Westpac.

Store credit cards were challenged in terms of maintaining operational efficiency and running a business that was not core to their operations. In 1995, The Coles Myer Group spun off the Australian Retail Financial Network, their store credit arm, to the multinational GE Capital Finance. The group continued to grow, providing credit in Australia including credit cards. It was later renamed GE Money. In 2015, recognising the core business of General Electric was in manufacturing, Global GE sold its capital and money businesses. In Australia, the business was taken over by a consortium of Värde Partners, KKR, and Deutsche Bank, later to become Latitude Financial.

Retailers and airlines issuing cards tended to do this off the back of bigger issuers. Woolworths and Myer used Macquarie Bank, and David Jones switched to American Express from its internal offering. Coles, which originally used GE Money, now uses Citibank. Virgin and Qantas Money also use Citibank.

Standardisation of Cards

In order to allow merchants to consistently process cards, schemes started to standardise card formats:

- ISO/IEC 7810 defined the size of a card (length, width and thickness) as well as other physical characteristics.
- ISO/IEC 7811 defined how cards are embossed: the raised printing on older cards to allow them to be transcribed easily by manual imprinters.
- ISO/IEC 7812 defined a numbering system (also known as primary account numbers or PAN), in which different schemes have different prefixes (or bank identifier numbers, BINs). This allowed manual and, later, electronic sorting (or switching) of payments to the correct bank. Like phone numbers and IP addresses, the numbers are running out and will need to be extended by two digits. The last digit is a check digit (explained in the BPAY Bill Payments chapter) that ensures when transcribing no errors were made.

Magnetic Stripe

Magnetic tapes were the original mechanism for the exchange of digital information between computers (originating before floppy disks, CDs and USB drives). The tape would allow binary information to be stored. Each digit would be coded like a miniature magnet. Each bit of the tape could be magnetised in a north-south orientation, or a south-north orientation. The difference between a 1 and a 0 was not the orientation, but the length of the magnetisation, because a north-south followed by a north-south would just become a long north-south (like joining two magnets together to make a longer magnet). A long magnetisation represents a 0 and two short magnetisations represents a 1 (*Figure 26*).

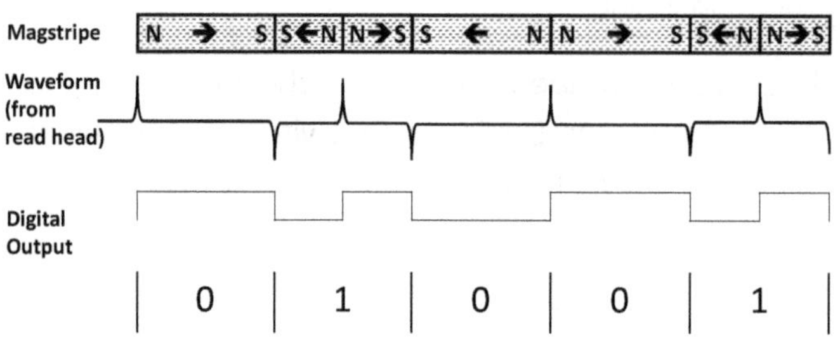

***Figure 26.* Encoding of binary data on a magnetic stripe.**

It was possible to embed a short magnetic stripe on a plastic card, which was done for Australia's proprietary cards in order for ATMs to read them. Australia was one of the early adopters, with the manufacturing technology developed in Australia in 1978. Eventually, magnetic stripes were used by merchant terminals (PEDs) and embedded in all cards. They are defined by the standard ISO/IEC 7813.

In the early days, magnetic stripes had one track of data. This included most of the data on the front of the card, but often included a scrambled version of the PIN as well. Eventually, this was removed. Additional data to ensure the security of the card and to provide additional information was encoded on a second track of the magnetic stripe.

›› NOTE

Crooks were always on the lookout for new opportunities. By copying the magnetic information from a card, a duplicate card could be fashioned and used to withdraw money from the cardholder's account. Initially, thieves would recruit merchants, who would have a card reader under the counter. Later, in a more daring escapade, thieves would install these readers in front of ATM card readers. Along with a camera, they could get the PIN and use the card elsewhere. Measures were taken to avoid this type of theft; for example, physical changes to ATMs to avoid reader attachment and new magnetic stripe encoding technology.

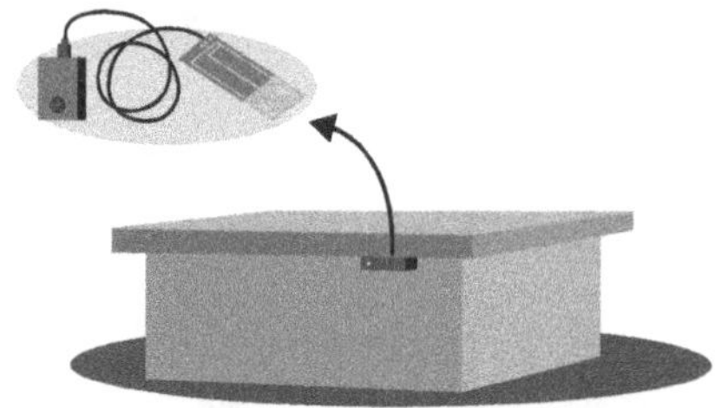

EFTPOS

Many innovations in payments took place at fuel stations. The old store paper-based account paper card system did not scale, and perhaps there was a significant number of patrons who would realise they did not have enough money on their person to cover rising fuel costs after they had filled up. Electronic Funds Transfer at Point of Sale (EFTPOS) was born when, in 1984, ANZ teamed up with Shell, Westpac with BP, and CBA with Mobil to roll out new terminals for fuel stations: the EFTPOS machines. NAB joined ANZ in EFTPOS trials.

Like ATMs, EFTPOS machines at the time were bulky (*Figure 27*) though not as large as they did not have cash in them. They also used the same PIN system.

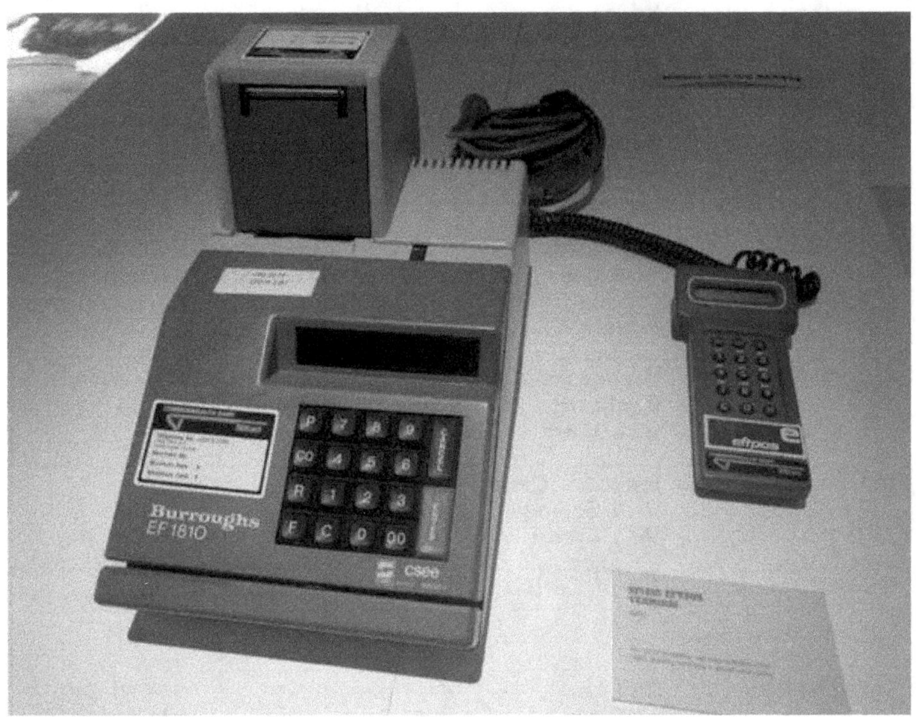

***Figure 27*. Burroughs Electronic Funds Transfer, circa 1985.**
Courtesy of ITNews. Copyright ITNews

In 1984, Westpac, with its growing list of merchants, including BP, Woolworths and Foodplus, teamed up with CBA and their merchants: Mobil, Caltex, Liquorland, BBC Hardware and Safeway.

Gradually, the networks became somewhat of a mess, and customers struggled to know where their cards were accepted as demonstrated in *Table 6*. A long list of card logos would be displayed in stores, at fuel stations, and at ATMs to allow customers to choose which card to use or where they could shop. Wallets, in turn, grew thicker, as customers needed to carry several cards to ensure they could use funds when needed.

Table 6.

Where You Can Use Your Card, courtesy of the Sydney Morning Herald, 5 July 1989.

WHERE YOU CAN USE YOUR CARD

Institution	Cards	Network access	Type of service	Main retail outlets
Westpac	Westpac Card MasterCard	all	debit debit/credit	BP, Food Plus, Sportsgirl, Caltex, Shell, Mitre 10, Lowes Manhattan, Ampol, Mobil, Woolworths, Esso
Commonwealth	Keycard MasterCard Bankcard	all	debit debit/credit debit/credit	BP, Food Plus, Sportsgirl, Caltex, Shell, Mitre 10, Lowes Manhattan, Ampol, Mobil, Woolworths, Esso
NAB	Flexicard Bankcard MasterCard	all	debit debit/credit debit/credit	BP, Food Plus, Sportsgirl, Caltex, Shell, Mitre 10, Lowes Manhattan, Ampol, Mobil, Woolworths, Esso
ANZ	Tranzaction Bankcard Visa Card	all	debit debit/credit debit/credit	BP, Food Plus, Sportsgirl, Caltex, Shell, Mitre 10, Lowes Manhattan, Ampol, Mobil, Woolworths, Esso
Advance Bank	Advance Card	all	debit	BP, Food Plus, Sportsgirl, Caltex, Shell, Mitre 10, Lowes Manhattan, Ampol, Mobil, Woolworths, Esso
State Bank	Greencard Bankcard Visa Card	all	debit debit/credit debit/credit	BP, Food Plus, Sportsgirl, Caltex, Shell, Mitre 10, Lowes Manhattan, Ampol, Mobil, Woolworths, Esso
St George	Freedom Card Visa Savings Visa Credit	ANZ	debit debit credit	Mitre 10, Sportsgirl, Shell
NRMB	Client Card	ANZ	debit/credit	Mitre 10, Sportsgirl, Shell
Credit Unions	Redicard	Westpac ANZ	debit	Shell BP Mitre 10 Sportsgirl Food Plus Woolworths

These complications triggered the Martin Review to recommend an Australian Payments Systems Council, and later resulted in the establishment of APCA (now AusPayNet) to standardise messaging.

Cheque, Savings or Credit

A unique feature of the Australian cards landscape was the choice of using cheque, savings or credit accounts. Unfortunately, none of these buttons reflect the original intention and can be quite confusing for overseas visitors.

Originally, on a credit card, the credit button referred to the credit account that belonged to the issued card. Cheque and savings buttons were linked to accounts and, as the name indicated, covered the two common types of deposit bank accounts available at the time.

Today, though, the credit button can be used on a scheme debit card to refer to the primary debit account attached, or on an EFTPOS card to refer to a bank account.

Cheque accounts are no longer marketed as such, and most savings accounts these days do not allow card withdrawals.

Instead, banks can link each button to a different account, with some banks allowing customers to change the configuration in real-time. Linking to a different rail is not really possible, as rails are set up at the BIN level (i.e., a whole card range) through a manual process run by AusPayNet's IAC (previously CECS) that takes months.

With non-EFTPOS cards, like American Express, the cheque and savings buttons will either fail or be treated as *credit*, depending on the machine.

The cheque and savings buttons normally switch via CECS (or, now, the eftpos Hub, see below). AusPayNet is informed whenever a new card is issued and the credit button switches to the issuer, CECS, the eftpos Hub, or the scheme (Mastercard, Visa, etc.).

›› NOTE

eftpos Australia used to advertise "Press CHQ or SAV," (*Figure 28*) and gave out cufflinks with the two abbreviations. With contactless payment, there is no button, so the merchant can choose in some cases how to route the card if it is a debit card. This practice is called *least cost routing.*

"CHQ SAV or CR" has been a point of confusion for many cardholders. ATMs especially may order them differently, and people forget how the bank has mapped their account. Some customers may have a transaction account that is neither cheque, savings nor credit. Hint: especially for visitors or debit card lders — if in doubt, choose *credit.*

***Figure 28.* A campaign to encourage the use of eftpos.**

Copyright eftpos Australia Ltd, Chemist Warehouse.

eftpos Australia

In 2009, eftpos, a successful brand for the Australian debit card network, was formalised into a company in order to provide consistency between proprietary cards and to market the Australian network. The following organisations are members:

- ANZ
- CBA
- NAB
- Westpac
- Australian Settlements Limited
- Bank of Queensland
- Bendigo and Adelaide Bank
- Cashcard (First Data)
- Citigroup (Citibank)
- Coles
- Cuscal
- Indue
- Suncorp Bank
- Woolworths.

The new company would gradually take over bilateral exchanges with the eftpos Hub completed in 2017.

Electronic Funds Transfer Services

Electronic Funds Transfer Services, later known as EFTEL, and operating the Austnet network, took on the processing of EFT transactions on the Visa network, and Credit Union and Building Society ATM transactions. First Data, the US acquiring giant, took over EFTEL in 1993.

Credit Union Services Corporation (Australia) Limited

Credit unions, left out in the cold by the banks and separate from the building societies, were surprisingly early and effective adopters of technology. Some examples being the Queensland Teachers Credit Union with the first ATM, and a collective effort to implement ATMs before the banks — through the Automated Financial Services organisation, and before that via the Australian Federation of Credit Union Leagues.

Credit Union Services Corporation (Australia) Limited (Cuscal), formed in 1992, was originally a representative body and eventually became a Tier 1 payment provider, now supporting all types of financial institutions, both banks and non-banks.

Cuscal took over electronic card switching, which had originally been outsourced to FDI.

Opening Closed Loops

Proprietary cards were in abundance across the globe. However, while banks wanted to compete domestically, they wanted to collaborate internationally.

To meet these needs, certain networks were established by Mastercard and Visa.

Mastercard Maestro and Visa Plus were the first proprietary cards that could function as open loop cards when used overseas, like normal Mastercard and Visa cards.

Shortly after, the Mastercard Cirrus and Visa Plus ATM networks allowed previously closed loop ATMs to switch cards to the Mastercard and Visa networks, to charge their respective cards. This was particularly useful, as it allowed Australia's domestic ATMs to accept foreign cards, with a high fee providing an incentive to rewire.

Cashcard

In 1981, credit unions and building societies announced the launch of a cooperative card system which allowed them to roll out ATMs, Cashcard. The company was owned by Gresham Private Equity, Suncorp, St George Bank, Ken Gaunt, Piers Hill and Adelaide Bank.

Backend switching was originally provided by Austnet but, in 2004, First Data took over the network. Eventually the network died, with many of the credit unions moving to RediATM and First Data.

RediCard

Originally an ATM fleet used by some credit unions, RediTeller was renamed RediATM and became managed by Cuscal.

The proprietary card, RediCard, is still supported today and operates on the EFTPOS network.

Visa Debit and Debit Mastercard

In certain areas, Australia was one step ahead of the market so local solutions were developed before international schemes came up with an alternative. Visa and Mastercard were not generally available as a debit solution, although Bendigo Bank (then Bendigo Building Society) became the first in Australia to issue a Visa branded debit card via Cuscal, hot off the heels of Australian Bank's Visa credit card. It used local bilateral card links to integrate it with the electronic ATM link. There were, as yet, no electronic credit card links, so the card operated over the credit card paper voucher system for purchases at 8 400 merchants in Australia, and also overseas, settling to a transaction account instead of a bill being issued. Clearly, a lack of funds, if not picked up through a phone authorisation process, could result in a debit balance — and Bendigo would have attempted to recover such funds, charging a high interest rate.

It would take 20 years, to around 2004, before Visa Debit and Debit Mastercard cards took off. They had the benefit over proprietary cards of being used at more shops, both online and on the street.

Stored Value, Prepaid and Gift Cards

Stored value cards recorded money in either an open loop or a closed loop system. Prepaid cards are essentially stored value cards.

The distinction between stored value cards and gift cards was slightly fluid, as gift cards were often simply stored value cards given as a gift. For this reason, KYC requirements on the cards were lax and, even today, they can be purchased over the counter with no identification. As a security measure, some merchants activate them only after 24 hours to reduce the risk of fraud (24 hours being a reasonable time period for people to report significant fraud events).

Due to the lack of identity checks, these cards were treated with great concern, especially by AUSTRAC. What added to the risk was the ability to top up the balance on a card and to exchange the cards without any identity. In many cases, they could be used online so the payment credentials could be transferred across the globe.

Most large ADIs avoided issuing these cards due to the risks. (The bigger the bank, the bigger the fines.) Those that did issue them were sometimes lax with monitoring top-ups; in theory, once $1 000 was deposited or recycled through a card, the issuing party required an ADI license, at least like PayPal's purchase payment facility license. Open loop gift cards were often more risky than closed loop ones, though Apple's iTunes was a large enough market that its closed loop system seemed quite open.

According to some economists, giving gifts was often seen as a dead loss, as a purchased item has a value of 30% less than its original value in the eyes of the recipient. A more economically efficient gift was cash, though many saw this as a lazy gift requiring little emotional engagement. Gift cards were a solution, with merchants offering nicely presented certificates and, in the case of David Jones (*Figure 29*), a gift-wrapped, boxed, silver alloy token.

***Figure 29.* David Jones' gift token, courtesy of Downies.**

Gift cards were a big profit source for issuers. They had an expiry date and many gift cards were left unspent. The balance left from unspent expired gift cards, known as breakage, was a profit for the chief financial officer. From late 2019, Australian Consumer Law requires gift cards to have a minimum expiry of three years.

During the receivership of bookstores in Australia (both Borders and Angus & Robertson), as well as electronics store Dick Smith, gift cardholders discovered that their cards were potentially worthless and that they were unsecured creditors in the wind-up of these organisations.

Foreign Exchange Cards

Many banks issued foreign exchange cards. These cards were stored value cards, but could hold money in different foreign currency sub accounts and, when used overseas, could use the local currency first. They allowed consumers to lock in exchange rates before travel. Often the exchange rate was a retail rate and the value of this product was questionable, given that consumers could not reasonably predict the fluctuation of the currency; however, it may have helped travellers on a fixed budget.

The backend system was quite sophisticated, and generally not managed by the banks, so it was not normally possible to deposit United States dollars in cash over the counter into the card.

Many big banks issued the cards in pairs, sometimes without embossed names, giving the impression that they could be used by a traveller and a companion, relative or friend when, in actual fact, they were only officially usable by the KYC-approved holder.

Foreign exchange agents also issued these cards, as did Qantas with a Mastercard Travel Money Card (issued by Heritage Bank) and Virgin with GlobalWallet (Issued by Rêv Australia, part of Rêv Worldwide, under Cuscal's ADI). Proper KYC procedures were generally required once stored value exceeded $1 000.

Mastercard Send and Visa Direct

The idea behind Mastercard Send and Visa Direct was to make P2P payments from a debit card. (Generally credit cards could be treated as cash-out and incur a higher interest charge, so this P2P payment did not make sense for credit accounts.)

Due to AML/CTF concerns (and perhaps others), banks in Australia have not implemented this, though the schemes may have mandated that issuers in Australia accept such payments.

With solutions like Beem It and NPP (see below), the value proposition of these real-time payments is questionable.

Taxis

Taxis had their own scheme. Cabcharge dockets or vouchers and cards had a monopoly on corporate payments in taxis and hire cars for some time. The advantage of Cabcharge was that the invoicing system could capture taxi pick-up and drop-off information, to allow categorisation and audit by the accounts department. Dockets could be given out on an ad hoc basis if, for instance, someone was going home late one evening.

Other International Schemes

Other international schemes in Australia, from an acceptance point of view, are China UnionPay and Japan Credit Bureau (JCB). Similar to Bankcard/eftpos in Australia, these cards are largely issued in their respective countries, but are accepted at many stores in Australia (primarily to support tourists and other visitors). The Bank of China (Australia), a fully locally regulated bank since World War II, offers a dual-branded eftpos and China UnionPay card that can be used in both Australia and China.

BIN Sponsorship

Banks that were members of a scheme (originally acting as both issuer and acquirer) were known as BIN sponsors, named after the bank identification number, the first few digits of a card number. Under scheme rules, card issuers and merchant acquirers are required to be sponsored by a scheme-approved BIN sponsor. In Australia, these are ADIs, including Specialist Credit Card Institutions (SCCIs) like Tyro (allowing them to be merchant acquirers). Although, in recent times, the SCCI category of ADI has been disbanded in favour of ASIC regulation, many schemes still favour ADI BIN sponsorship.

The regulators were keen to step out of acquiring licensing and, as much as the schemes were reluctant to separate issuing from acquiring, they were pressured to lower the bar and allow acquirer-only organisations into the fold. In order to become an acquirer, the schemes issued an acquirer licensing procedure.

Electronic Funds Transfer at Point of Banking

Electronic Funds Transfer at Point of Banking (EFTPOB) was designed to allow banks and their agents (especially Australia Post) to transact on a card. The functions of an ATM were available over the counter with some banks allowing signatures to be collected on digital devices. Cash deposits, bill payments, cash withdrawals and cheque transactions were all available. Over time, with the banks exiting from agency banking, Australia Post has been the only organisation to make use of this feature, marketing it as GiroPOST and, these days, the functionality has been subsumed by eftpos and marketed as Bank@Post.

As post offices have full access to credit cards, bill payments made through their system may be processed as cash advances, and charged at full interest rates from day one, something to be wary of.

Card Messaging: AS 2805 and ISO 8583

In the mid-1980s, a Westpac card could be used at BP fuel stations but not at Shell. Other merchants started getting interested in the new devices but they wanted to attract customers from every bank, and having four of these machines would be cumbersome.

The first question from these customers to their acquiring banks was whether they could accept other cards. This was a simple question, but technically difficult to implement.

It was becoming a global problem, but Australia needed an answer immediately.

Well-connected to international standards bodies, Australian bank technologists developed a communication protocol to allow an acquirer to transact on an issuer's card. The Australian Standard AS 2805 was first published in 1985. In 1987, the international version of this standard, ISO 8583, was introduced. The two are similar and interchangeable on a switch, with ISO 8583 used for international schemes like Mastercard and Visa.

EFTPOS is a single message system. Clearing and settlement would happen in one message. If there was a problem at the acquirer end, the payment would have to be reversed.

Visa and Mastercard are dual message systems. The dual message was a legacy of the pre-terminal days, when a phone authorisation was given and settlement happened once the bank received all the dockets. These days, automatic electronic authorisation (BASE I) takes place at the point of sale in real-time, and delayed settlement (BASE II) takes place at the end of day, allowing the signature to be checked and a tip to be added (two features of the US system that Australia did not require). EFTPOS transactions were verified by a PIN.

In order to get the information from the acquirer to the issuer, the messaging standard was machine-readable. The traditional format for these messages was fixed width, with each message having fields at defined positions. Space was limited with these messages (and data was costly in time to transmit and money to pay for bandwidth and storage) and, given that every message did not need every field, a bitmap was used to inform the other side which fields were being sent and which were truncated from the message.

EFTPOS uses what are called 200 messages to notify the issuer of a request to debit. The card number, security information from the card as well as a secure rendering of the PIN is sent to the issuer. The issuer responds with a 210 message to approve (or decline) the transaction.

Mastercard and Visa used so-called 100 messages. These messages put a hold on funds, but the settlement message would come later. The issuer would respond with a 110, accepting the request. However, when the settlement did come, the issuer was obligated to pay.

Schemes introduced more sophisticated messaging such as:

- Pre-authorisations that put a hold on an account for funds and that would be followed up later by the real transaction (e.g., for hotel bookings).
- Incremental auths, frequently used on cruise ships, that would increase (or decrease) the original authorisation but only settled later.
- Automated fuel dispenser (AFD) transactions that would reserve money to unlock the pump, and then update the authorisation with the real amount once the nozzle was replaced.

The key message types in ISO 8583/AS 2805 are:

- 100 message: An authorisation (auth) request, the most common message. This is a request to debit an account and place a temporary hold on it (seen as pending on some Internet banking sites). Used in dual message systems like Visa and Mastercard. Due to the delay before settlement, an authorisation can be pending for up to 10 days unless the merchant releases it. In many cases (e.g., hire car deposits) the debit sits on the account for a number of days before expiring, causing inconvenience, especially for travellers who find their funds locked.

- 110 message: A response to a 100, which accepts or declines the request, and, in the latter case, provides a reason, such as the account being closed or declined, or a technical error.
- 120 message: A forced authorisation, when a previous pre-authorisation has already been requested for a higher amount and this is the actual, lower amount say, for an automated fuel dispenser transaction. It can also be used as a stand-in message where the scheme has authorised the message, due to some system error in communicating with the issuer or a delayed response.
- 200 message: A request to debit an account. This is used in single message systems.
- 210 message: A response to a 200, which accepts or declines the request; again, like the 110 message, providing reasons.
- 220 message: A forced settlement. This is used by some dual message systems to confirm a transaction that was previously authorised through a 100 or 120 message, and requests a settlement. The original 100 or 120 authorisation generally expires at this point.
- 4XX series messages: These are used to reverse a transaction; for example, if an ATM gets jammed after an authorisation as it is releasing notes.

Refunds are generally processed through a settlement message, so they can take days to clear. However, 100, 120 and 400-series messages can also be used to refund a transaction. Several other services, such as tokenisation, ATM management and mobile phone provisioning, use ISO 8583/AS 2805 messaging to effect transactions.

The emerging ISO 20022 unification initiative uses a more modern XML messaging standard; however, this is not yet in wide use. Its messages are better organised:

- caaa: Card acceptor (e.g., terminal or ATM) to acquirer card transaction messages
- caad: Card administration messages
- caam: ATM management
- cain: Acquirer to issuer card transactions.

Consumer Electronic Clearing System

Banks had developed their own ATM and card networks, including EFTPOS, at merchants. In order to allow them to interoperate, a new clearing system was set up: Clearing System 3 (CS3).

The Consumer Electronic Clearing System (CECS) was a process whereby card transactions could be exchanged (cleared) in real-time and settled between banks later. CECS was supervised by the Australian Payments and Clearing Association (APCA) and later the Australian Payments Network (AusPayNet).

Australian domestic transactions were switched locally. This began to change for various reasons. Initially, the core network used X.25 links, and later the COIN network. International

Mastercard transactions were sent to CBA, and Visa transactions were sent to their first supporter, ANZ. In order to open up, accessible payment gateways were established. Eventually, CBA's Mastercard gateway was taken over by Mastercard, with most new connections going to Mastercard Internet Gateway Service (MIGS), Mastercard Payment Gateway Service (MPGS), or later to Mastercard New Payment Gateway (MNGS). Likewise, Visa's VisaNet and later CyberSource was the preferred network of Visa card processing.

Eventually, eftpos created its own eftpos Hub and, with Visa and Mastercard establishing direct points, the CS3/CECS network became redundant over time. Most core acquirers sent their credit transactions through the bilateral links. New banks dealt exclusively with the eftpos Hub, MNGS/MPGS or VisaNet. Settlement of eftpos was still bilateral and cumbersome, with eftpos moving later to deferred net settlement (with each participant only needing to pay/or receive upon payment).

Today, the Issuers and Acquirers Community (IAC) continues the task of certifying PED machines and ATMs for the Australian marketplace. The certification is in two parts: hardware and software.

At the time, Australia's early adoption of the personal identification number (PIN) at point of sale meant that APCA still had an important role to play. The ATMs, EFTPOS machines, and PED machines were designed to protect the PIN from being compromised. It has been an uphill battle as technology has compromised the sanctity of the PIN. Initially, the PIN was so secure, even the ATM or EFTPOS computer did not know what it was as it had been scrambled (encrypted or hashed) at the point of entry. Eventually, online applications started asking for PINs for other purposes and many users used the same number as their card PINs. New devices came on the scene, and Visa and Mastercard moved certification to the independent Payment Card Industry (PCI) organisation.

It is questionable how long this will continue, as a similar function is conducted by the Visa/Mastercard schemes (through EMV/PCI, and generally outsourced). eftpos Australia Limited (EPAL) may be a better organisation for this functionality. If they adopt similar outsourcing arrangements and align with EMV/PCI, this could help streamline a messy arrangement. However, the main reason this function has not been taken up by EPAL is likely due to the limited resources and funding of eftpos, as APCA/AusPayNet were associations, not commercial operations, and much of the time and work on APCA's agenda was offered by the members. Also, for a long time, the requirement to support the eftpos scheme and have cheque and savings options (two words that have little meaning today) on the PEDs was best pushed by an independent, more authoritative organisation.

Cards and the Internet

One of the resilient features of the schemes, particularly Visa and Mastercard, was their innovative ability to remain relevant. Looking back at the paper-based cards, signatures and voucher system of the 1950s, the schemes are barely recognisable. There is one essential element that keeps them relevant: their cards provide a level of real-time guarantee of payment.

By 2000, the Internet had gained mainstream attention with businesses seeing its potential. Ultimately, the demand of commercial organisations was to make money on it and this eventually meant taking payments.

>> NOTE

Despite the appeal between 1994 and 2001, few organisations could directly cash in on the Internet. This may have contributed to the dot com bust of 2001. People were simply not yet comfortable buying things on the Internet and, in hindsight, rightly so: few sites had encryption, even for credit card payments. Human behaviour takes time to change. Pizza Hut attempted PizzaNet in 1994, which allowed orders to be made online, but payment had to be made in cash on delivery. This was possibly the first thing sold to a market on the Internet. It was largely unused. Was the order correct and what if a pizza needed no cheese? The early Internet screens were rudimentary and unsatisfactory by today's standards when compared with human interaction. It took a decade before Internet sales would pick up. Card schemes had an opportunity to re-invent themselves.

At an almost global level, international card schemes were uniquely suited to the Internet.

Due to security issues, fraud became problematic early on and measures were taken to reduce it, such as, in the US, collecting billing address details and comparing them to what was entered at the time of purchase, as well as checking a card's expiry date, not just to see if the card was valid, but to ensure the cardholder was genuine. CVV codes (see below) were introduced by the schemes as a result of the Internet revolution.

From 1999 to 2000, Internet companies became quite popular, especially for investors. In payments, eWay, QSI Payments and GPayments were established, and succeeded in getting significant business in the early days of payment gateways. eWay boasts 25% of the Australian market and was acquired by Atlanta-based Global Payments Network. QSI Payments developed a strong relationship with Mastercard and was acquired by News Corp. GPayments focused on 3D Secure solutions (see below) and remains a provider in this space today.

Card-not-present Transactions

Card-not-present transactions are transactions conducted remotely, where the card was not available to be physically imprinted or (later) swiped through a terminal.

Originally referred to as mail order or telephone order (MOTO) transactions, these transactions were a subset of credit card transactions. The Internet provided a new channel for transactions, potentially surpassing card-present transactions in volume.

In Australia, only the overseas scheme cards and Bankcard could be used for MOTO. EFTPOS or proprietary cards could not, until recently, be used over the phone, by post or online.

Today, one of the issues with card-not-present payments was high fraud rates. With globalisation and the Internet, it was possible to use a card online, obtain services and then disappear.

Particular services are high risk. These do not require delivery of goods:

- Electronic gift cards, especially iTunes
- Cryptocurrency transactions
- Gambling transactions.

Other transactions are also risky, such as online jewellery and electronic goods purchases. However, the need to mail the purchased item generally gives a compromised payer time to stop a transaction, and a merchant can avoid some fraud losses by allowing a small delay.

Under scheme rules (and as per the ePayments Code), if a cardholder disputes a card-not-present transaction, in many cases, the merchant has the onus of proof and needs to refund the money unless they can prove the transaction was made by the cardholder. This has led (indirectly) to merchants including fraud risk in their pricing.

Rewards

One of the benefits offered to credit cardholders, other than the short interest-free period, is loyalty points and rewards. The programs are designed to encourage the use of cards, though unlike the name suggests not necessarily long-term loyalty to the issuer.

The system operates by offering points for spending, normally one point for every dollar spent, but this could vary depending on the issuer of the card.

Loyalty points are redeemed either through frequent flyer program partnerships or an internal gift system. Smaller issuers partner with privately run, white-labelled providers, including the scheme themselves.

Some credit card programs, such as American Express and Summerland Credit Union, offer cash back.

Most credit cards offer rewards though, these days, with tighter interchange regulation (see below), much of the cost is increasingly covered by the annual fee and interest profit, with low-cost credit cards often providing low loyalty benefits.

Only a few debit cards offer rewards (their interchanges, as we shall see, are low). Bankwest and Australian Military Bank are the two banks that offer rewards on debit cards, according to Canstar.

Some organisations and publications such as CHOICE publish rewards comparisons by ranking, taking the purchase power of points earned per dollar spent. Few big banks rate well in these comparisons.

Card Security Measures

With the information age, cards became inherently insecure for online transactions and, with readily available card emulation technology, they were insecure for in-store use. They should have died. However, innovative steps by the card schemes, and the absence of an alternative global, bank-based payment method meant that, like the mythical phoenix, cards were reborn.

CVV

Card verification value (CVV), card verification codes (CVC) or card verification numbers (CVN) were used to dissuade or stop card skimmers and cloners. Imprinted vouchers could be copied by hand. However, a non-embossed number was printed on the front or back of a card. This number (CVV2) was only known to the issuer.

Over time, for certain transactions, merchants accepting card-not-present transactions were required to collect the CVV2 number.

For in-store purchases, typically unknown to either the merchant or customer, an additional number (CVV1) appeared in track two; this was sent to the issuer electronically for verification. This prevented a photocopied card from being cloned. CVV1 and CVV2 were different, so it was generally not possible for a card skimmed at a store to be used online (though, of course, the CVV2 could be noted down by an unscrupulous merchant).

EMVCo

Ten years before Bankcard, a Swedish businessman established Eurocard. Eventually, Eurocard joined forces with Mastercard to create a single European brand, Europay. (In 2002, Europay merged with Mastercard.) So, the three big card schemes in the world in 1993 were Europay, Mastercard and Visa, which eventually counted for at least 80% of cards on issue in most regions outside of China. These schemes together formed EMVCo. EMVCo was eventually extended to include American Express, JCB and China UnionPay.

›› NOTE

China UnionPay, largely issued in China, counts for 45% of cards issued worldwide, beating any other scheme. In China, the card is issued to almost every bank customer. The organisation's preferred branding is simply "UnionPay". The card is accepted in 179 countries according to its website. It remains however, a card essentially for Chinese residents.

EMVCo was established to counteract the problems of card number theft and skimming, as the signature was no longer a satisfactory means of authentication.

Security was a baseline concern for the industry, not a differentiator, so industry members were happy to collaborate.

EMV Chip and PIN

The development of a chip for plastic cards proposed to eventually solve the problem of card compromise, at least for card-present transactions.

The technology used PKI encryption technology and embedded a private key on the chip's secure element (a sort of hardware security module).

By challenging the chip, an acquirer could test if the card was genuine. The chip contained certificates issued by an EMVCo member, and the certificate chain could be verified. Further, using an Authorisation Request Cryptogram, a secret message is generated by the card and sent to the issuer. Only the issuer can check this response. If the cryptogram is not valid, the transaction will be declined.

Getting an EMV card chip encoded is a lengthy process, and the encoding needs to be signed off by a certifier approved by the scheme. A small mistake often means the process needs to be repeated.

〉〉 NOTE

One scam is, with a stolen card, to damage or cover (with tape) the chip. On some terminals, the customer will be asked to use the magnetic stripe which, in some cases, does not require a PIN, but the less secure and often unchecked signature. This technique is used to pass off stolen cards.

In one case, a fraudster used just such an altered card, and in paying for coffee took the PED terminal from a small business café, and changed the amount from $4.90 to $490.00. He swiped the card without entering a PIN, as the chip was detected as faulty. The transaction approved with the operator not checking the amount. The fraudster returned back later after the shift to claim the previous operator had overcharged. The new operator was apologetic, and offered a refund. However the fraudster claimed the card was his partner's who had gone to work, and if he could have the refund in cash instead of the usual practice of refunding on the card. This scam is often a trap for inexperienced small business checkout operators. All refunds should be processed to the same card.

One of the advantages of a chip is that, almost like a computer, it can store programs. A chip could retain bank balance information or automatically cancel itself if the PIN was incorrectly entered. In the end, few of these features were used by card issuers.

Chip and PIN are used throughout the world; however, the US and a few other countries have been slow to adopt it. In 2016, eftpos Australia licensed the technology from EMVCo so that EFTPOS can coexist on scheme cards (Mastercard, Visa, etc.) or by itself.

EMV chips continue to be upgraded, primarily to improve security, though there have been few (if any) breaches of EMV since inception.

Organisations such as Giesecke+Devrient, founded in 1852, turned their focus from banknote printing to card and chip manufacturing (and later mobile phone SIMs) in 1981 and thrived in the new world.

3D Secure

3 Domain Security (3D Secure or 3DS) was originally implemented independently by various schemes. The three domains were the merchant/acquirer, issuer and payment system (though, in reality, there are more than three players involved and the name is no longer an appropriate reflection of the solution). 3DS was implemented in order to avoid the risk of personal account numbers (PANs) and associated data being fraudulently compromised. The result of a compromise would be a charge being levied on a victim's account.

The original implementations, from 1999, were branded by the schemes as Mastercard SecureCode and Verified by Visa, among others.

Essentially, before authorising a transaction, the scheme would send a message to an issuer to check that a transaction was being authorised by the cardholder. Some implementations would display a code word and ask for a password. Eventually, most banks used SMS to validate the transaction.

EMVCo introduced 3DS 2.0 to merchants as a better and less obtrusive way to check that a transaction was valid. Personal data would be sent to the issuer, and a decision could be made if the transaction was risky (e.g., whether the transaction was taking place at the home location of the customer, any identifying details, etc.). A risky transaction would result in a step-up, whereas a less risky one would result in an approval. The approval code would be sent back to the issuer to validate the transaction and hopefully approve it.

Australia was one of the first countries to introduce 3DS.

Payment Card Industry Security Standards Council

The Payment Card Industry Security Standards Council (PCI SSC) was formed in 2006 by American Express, Discover, JCB International, Mastercard and Visa. In hindsight, PCI SSC and EMVCo should have perhaps been one organisation; however, at the time, EMVCo had excluded American Express and the others.

The focus of PCI was on data security outside of the card, while EMVCo was focused on chip and PIN on the card itself.

Altogether, there are 15 security standards:

- Overarching: Data Security Standard (DSS)
- Issuers: PIN security

- Issuers: Card production — physical
- Issuers: Card production — logical
- Issuers: Token service provider
- Issuers: PCI 3D Secure Core
- Acquirers: PIN Transaction Security Point of Interaction
- Acquirers: Payment Application Data Security Standard
- Acquirers: PIN Transaction Security Hardware Security Module
- Acquirers: Point-to-point encryption
- Acquirers: PCI 3D Secure Software Development Kit
- Acquirers: Software-based PIN entry on COTS Standard
- Acquirers: Secure software
- Acquirers: Secure software lifecycle
- Acquirers: Contactless payment on COTS.

We shall cover a few of these in detail below.

PCI DSS

The fundamental issue that needed to be solved was the use of personal account numbers (PANs) and associated data to make a payment. The compromise of this data would result in loss of money to a cardholder or merchant, and threatened to weaken the confidence the public had in their cards.

PCI Data Security Standard (PCI DSS) was an initiative to keep card data safe. Looking at every aspect, from collection to transmission to servicing, PCI DSS created a standard of security that every participant in the card ecosystem (other than the cardholder) had to adhere to.

PCI DSS also created a new industry, with two new professions or service providers: qualified security assessors and approved scanning vendors. In order to achieve PCI DSS compliance, organisations needed to secure the services of a qualified security assessor and/or an approved scanning vendor.

Every participant, including merchants dealing with card data (small merchants that just use a terminal or an online payment gateway do not touch the data so are generally exempt), card payment providers, merchant acquirers, and issuers need to be compliant or be subject to a scheme sanction (warnings, fines or exclusion).

To become PCI DSS compliant is onerous. Systems need to be locked down, and data needs to be encrypted in transit and at rest. If people need to access card data, they need to do so from a secure workstation at a secure location, and could not use common Internet applications, phone cameras, or pieces of paper to potentially copy data outside the organisation, and the room itself would be locked down. Organisations need to ensure the risk of theft of this sensitive information is reduced to near zero. Access to the data is limited, and needs to be logged and audited. Staff need to be trained, and systems segregated and monitored.

Many organisations outsourced this capability so they would never see a card number. If PCI DSS was required, it could be an expensive exercise, the least of which included the qualified security assessor. Once an organisation is compliant, regular reviews need to be completed.

PCI DSS breaches are serious. In 2013, Target (in the US) suffered a breach that resulted in between 40 and 70 million customer records being compromised. Two banks sued Target for USD $19 billion.

There have been a number of criticisms of PCI DSS. First, the whole problem of PAN compromise was created by the schemes and could have been solved by them. In stores, through the use of EMV chip and PIN, in countries where it is mandated, like in Australia, the risk of compromise of PAN data in-country is basically zero. It still exists overseas, principally in the US, as those geographies have not been placed under similar mandates. 3DS for online card-not-present transactions also reduces the risk; however, schemes have dragged their feet on mandating this globally. With or without these measures, industry participants still need to go to the expense of obtaining PCI DSS certification.

Second, issuing banks (and some acquirers/issuers) tend to ignore the mandate without any repercussions. Perhaps this is for two reasons. First, the data that could be lost are largely their own customers' data for which they are willing to take the risk (primarily reissuing cards to affected customers). Second, the scheme's direct customers are the issuing banks and they are hesitant to rub them up the wrong way. Nevertheless, PCI DSS compliance for a bank is a significant task, as PANs are everywhere: on systems, correspondence, statements and screens. Locking them down is not a task for the faint-hearted. This does not stop them from requiring merchants or integrated payment systems to have PCI DSS compliance.

By outsourcing the collection of payment data online, many merchants can avoid the costs of PCI DSS compliance. This is done by using a hosted payment page (in Web technology terms, an iframe) for a PCI DSS-compliant payment service provider.

PCI Payment Application Data Security Standard

The PCI Payment Application Data Security Standard is designed for software applications. It is similar to PCI DSS but, rather than applying to an organisation, the assessment is limited to software.

PCI PTS

PINs are essentially numeric passwords, originally four digits long, now up to 12 digits (though few banks support this), according to the ISO 9564 standard which governs the handling of financial PINs.

PIN entry devices (PEDs) appear on card terminals used by shops and are referred to as EFTPOS machines or terminals, PIN pads, and so on.

The PCI PIN Transaction Security (PCI PTS) standard requires approved PEDs to have implemented security measures, including measures to prevent compromise of a PIN.

These PEDs were originally required to be approved by the major schemes (Mastercard, Visa and eftpos). American Express generally accepted Mastercard and Visa approval, and eftpos continued to rely on AusPayNet's approval for these devices. From 2006, the major schemes started accepting PCI PTS/EMV approval processes. AusPayNet still maintains its own approval process through the Acquirers and Issuers Community Framework.

While a seemingly innocuous requirement, this one standard has created its own industry.

KeyCorp

Long before the development of PCI PTS, original PEDs were dumb terminals connected to a mainframe. Mainframe manufacturers were responsible for these, and early machines used by the banks were, like the mainframes, large and bulky. Burroughs, NCR and Ericsson supplied the major banks with acquiring terminals that were installed at merchant locations. In Australia, in the mid-1980s, EFTech, which supplied Verifact machines, joined the club. These devices were large, bulky and cumbersome. Leased telecommunication lines (X.25) were required, so EFTPOS was not really a solution that could scale. Australia was relatively unique as one of the few countries that required a secure PED. In the US, signatures were sufficient, and the card could be swiped on a simple mag-stripe reader, no PED required (yet). But the world was changing.

Seeing the potential, CBA engaged (and later invested in, eventually with a 40% stake) KeyCorp. KeyCorp had already developed a solution that used dial-up (aka plain old telephone service or POTS) telecommunications lines. In 1992, KeyCorp was contracted to develop a new generation of PEDs based on the Commonwealth Bank's requirements. It was during the "recession Australia had to have", and while most banks were contracting, CBA was grabbing new market share. It took four years before these were widespread and profitable, This would establish CBA's market lead in the acquiring space for decades. KeyCorp attempted a world expansion, securing Unisys to market the terminals globally. A takeover was attempted by Telstra, initially for $515 million; however, the investment was declined, due to the telco/dot com crash of 2001. What seemed to be a promising innovation for the world turned into a fizzle.

CBA continued to order KeyCorp devices until 2005, peaking at almost 100 000 terminals. Soon afterward, CBA switched to Ingenico.

Super Pay acquired KeyCorp in 2014, which Bambora acquired in 2015 (ironically, not so much for the terminal business as for the online IP payments product, which Super Pay acquired the same year), which, in turn, was acquired by Ingenico in 2017.

KeyCorp, as a local manufacturer, was never able to significantly break into the global market and compete with the now dominant European Ingenico or American Verifone (taken over by private equity in 2018).

Bambora, part of the Ingenico group, acquired KeyCorp in 2017.

Pi-Albert

Until the announcement of CBA's Pi-Albert solution, PEDs needed to have a mechanical keypad that would encrypt the PIN on the pad itself so that no other application could accept it.

The problem with the keypad was it took out a big chunk of the surface area of the device. The user interface was aged, mostly without touchscreens. In the era of tablets, it was a relic.

The Commonwealth Bank came up with an idea. Using the international design agency Ideo, they developed Pi-Albert. Pi was to be a family of PEDs, referring to the irrational number π and Albert was after the scientist Albert Einstein.

The idea was a touchscreen device that could encrypt the data, and an ecosystem that could make the device a powerful point-of-sale instrument.

The device was initially promising when it was announced to the public in 2012. In partnership with German manufacturer Wincor Nixdorf (now Diebold Nixdorf), it was sure to be a success. It had a built-in camera/scanner, integrated printer, Bluetooth, Wi-Fi and USB connections. Apps could be installed on it as it ran the Android operating system. It was, on paper, the perfect PED.

The device unfortunately took three years to launch to market. Getting it secure, PCI PTS and APCA certified, and workable took longer than most had anticipated. Due to the highly locked-down environment, it was not really possible to install a custom application, and few applications were written that made use of the platform. It was heavy and cumbersome and, without an ecosystem, its bulk gave little benefit to users beyond any terminal on the market at the time.

Another complication was to do with difficulties for vision-impaired people in entering the PIN on a touchscreen. CBA was taken to the Federal Court over the issue. (They settled out of court in 2019.) The Australian Banking Association had introduced new standards for accessibility to help in the design of banking services, in light of the issues.

Diebold Nixdorf no longer markets the device or any derivative of it, and CBA has switched vendors to Verifone PEDs.

Poynt and Competitors

The Albert device, at the time of inception, was a revolution: a tablet that ran the Android system. Google must have been aware of it, having just launched Google Wallet. Soon after Pi-Albert was announced, Poynt was kicked off as a Google-funded venture in 2013. Pre-orders of the device were announced in 2014. A founder of Poynt was previously part of the Google Wallet team. Poynt still sells its device with PCI PTS, PCI DSS, and EMV certifications.

Square and Software-based PIN Entry on COTS

Perhaps the nail in the coffin for the tablet PED concept came from Squareup. Their product, Square, was already big in the US. A simple coin-sized square that plugged into the headphone jack of almost any smartphone, the device could read a magnetic stripe from a card and take payment. Great for taxis and smaller merchants, it really took off. Due to there being no EMV chip/PIN mandate in the US, it did not require PCI PTS certification.

Around 2015, Square attempted to enter the EMV market with a similar solution, but this time it wanted to accept PINs on a PED. There was no way PCI PTS standards would allow it, many thought, as there was no way to ensure PIN entry on the device was secure. What if some software was reading the key taps on the phone and could compromise the security?

There was a key difference with Square. Visa had a 10% stake in the company.

Cuscal, a non-bank acquirer, jumped at the opportunity to acquire Square and pushed for certification on their behalf.

Rather than seek PCI PTS certification, Visa allowed it as an exemption. This was a trial, they said. Similarly, not to lose market share to a potential disruptor, Mastercard provided a similar exemption, and American Express followed suit. The new Square device accepted Tap and Go payments so, for many transactions, PIN entry was not even required. APCA and AusPayNet, which were to certify the device on behalf of the eftpos network, rejected the certification of Square, in keeping with the original principles (or with pressure from the banks?). This move was criticised in the Productivity Commission's Inquiry into Competition in the Australian Financial System. AusPayNet submitted that the fault was with the schemes, not itself.

The decision to allow Square was hypocritical and, like PCI DSS, gave the impression that the PCI PTS standard is applied selectively to outsiders. Having developed a new standard, software-based PIN entry on COTS, to effectively allow Square-like solutions, the PCI PTS standard seems unfair. However, having been accepted by the big schemes, the cat is out of the bag, and it would be in the best interests of eftpos (and AusPayNet) to accept it for small merchants, given that the risks of losing both the PIN and card with EMV are low.

Square uptake has been low in Australia. It is convenient for occasional merchants, as there is no monthly fee, but not for heavy use as the merchant service fee (MSF) is high.

By 2020, Pi-Albert had instigated a flood of Android PEDs into the global market. In Australia alone, Bolt, PAX, Ingenico, Verifone, and Castles provide these terminals.

Contactless Payment on COTS

Contactless payment on commercial off-the-shelf devices such as smartphones is very much a possibility that we will see soon. While mobile phones can already make payments, this will allow them to accept payments too like a merchant.

Together with the software-based PIN Entry on COTS Standard, this may see the end of the PED.

Tokenisation

Organisations, in order to avoid PCI compliance, would sometimes tokenise card numbers so that they could be identified but, if compromised, would pose less risk. Mobile payment solutions such as Apple Pay used this service. Mastercard Digital Enablement Service and Visa Token Service implemented tokenisation for merchants.

Tokenisation for merchants allowed them to store a token of the card rather than the card itself, and allowed features such as continuing payments after expiry and stopping payments through a bank.

Merchant Solutions

For merchants, the core of the card ecosystem is the equipment, systems, and processes to help them acquire payments.

Merchant Acquiring

Many banks offer direct solutions to merchants. This requires a risk assessment of the merchant. Banks have sometimes been liable for merchant failures, where money is taken, and goods and services failed to be delivered, either due to illegal practices of merchants or company failure. Cards are generally a real-time payment mechanism. The merchant may be subject to a higher than normal risk, due to the goods and services they sell, and how they sell them. Merchants with international activity are riskier than domestic ones (as many scams are perpetrated through overseas corridors). Online card-not-present transactions are riskier than in-person transactions. A stolen credit card can be used to purchase expensive goods (or services) that maintain their resale value, like gold or jewellery. Merchants who sell these items are at more risk than others. Gift cards, especially electronic gift cards, can be sent overseas and spent in seconds. Providing or dealing with cryptocurrency is also a high-risk activity. While officially card issuers and merchant acquirers do not accept liability, they could be found liable in some cases, and this risk is assessed when bringing on a new merchant.

For online merchants or small merchants, rather than go through the difficult process of being onboarded directly by a bank, third-party organisations which have a strong relationship with banks offer to onboard merchants directly. These are called payment facilitators. (They acted as a merchant of merchants from a compliance point of view.) While the bank has ultimate oversight, some of the risk and red tape is given to the payment facilitator to manage (at a cost to the merchant). PayPal, Square and Stripe are famous examples of these.

» NOTE

A common scam involves criminal enterprises calling unsuspecting victims and claiming that the call is from the ATO, federal police or a similar agency. The victim is threatened with prosecution. The victim is then asked to keep their mobile phone on the line, continue to talk to the caller, make their way to a supermarket and purchase gift cards, especially Apple iTunes cards. The victim is asked to pay by telling the caller the code(s) on the back of the card. (The electronic codes on cards are then sold to unsuspecting buyers, potentially in another country, perhaps at a discount.) It is little wonder why AUSTRAC sees these stored value cards as risky.

In-store

Today, due to deregulation, a number of payment solutions are available in stores: bank devices, Tyro Payments, Quest (hardware only), and First Data (now part of Fiserv) and, for smaller occasional merchants, Square and PayPal offer entry-level solutions where no monthly fee is required. For larger volumes, these solutions are not cost-effective as they charge a higher MSF.

Many merchant acquirers offer simple pricing. This puts a standard price on almost all transactions. This means overcharging debit cards and perhaps a good rate on premium cards. For most merchants, they will find the interchange plus model works out to be more cost-effective (though they should review their market profile and the terms and conditions of the provider before finalising a decision).

» NOTE

Before the entry of low-cost PED devices, a number of small merchants took in-person payments using a payment gateway, or by swiping the card using an unauthorised device, then acquiring the transaction as a card-not-present payment. This practice was banned by banks and schemes, due to the likelihood of increased fraud. A good practice is to never let the card out of one's hands.

In 2003, CBA introduced XPOS, a way of selling numerous electronic products like fishing licenses, movie tickets, phone cards and prepaid mobile phone top-ups. There were over 100 products. Touchcorp and E Com provided the solution.

PED Manufacturers

Manufacturing has been a difficult industry in Australia, yet Australian companies have had a significant role in the development of PEDs. Australian innovations such as KeyCorp and CBA's Albert (Wincor Nixdorf) are mentioned above; however, there were several more. EFTech, one of the earlier players, was listed on the stock exchange in 1985. In 1989, Norton Ofax attempted a failed takeover with EFTech delisting in 1993. Quest remains active supporting a number of banks and large corporations (particularly winning the New South Wales Government contract). SmartPay, an Australia and New Zealand-based company which acquired Provenco/Cudos, is a supplier of merchant terminals to Bendigo Bank and several large Australian merchants as well as a large part of the New Zealand market. More recently using PAX hardware, they now have a phone-sized merchant terminal (PED) with a touchscreen PIN pad. Card Access Services partnered with Nayax, a US-based company, to provide unattended vending machine solutions. Hypercom (formed in 1978) supplied NAB and Westpac, and was acquired by Verifone in 2010.

International solutions are led by Ingenico and Verifone, but also include BBPOS Wisepad (Stripe, a small Bluetooth connected PIN entry device), Banksys/Worldline (Tyro, a mobile and desktop application), Thumbzup (ANZ Blade Pay, an Albert-like solution) and XAC (First Data). Ingenico was subject to an acquisition by Worldline in 2020.

Integrated PED

Most merchants have a POS system that takes orders and sales at the item level and, in a shop, integrates with a barcode scanner. The PED is located nearby and, if it is not integrated, the operator must key the grand total from the POS into the PED and take the payment. This could lead to a few problems: first, there could be a transcribing error and second, a declinement may be missed and customers could walk away without paying. For this reason, integrated PED (or, from the PED point of view, integrated POS) is a recommended solution. In Australia, PC-EFTPOS was the major provider of integration software in this space. PC-EFTPOS has become Linkly after being acquired by private equity.

Online

Online solutions are also known as payment gateways and by using hosted payment pages (iframes), a merchant does not need to worry about PCI DSS compliance, which is left to the provider (known in the industry as a payment service provider, PSP). Originally PSPs required the merchant to be onboarded by a merchant acquirer before they could use the PSP solution; these days, many PSPs either partner with banks or payment facilitators in their own right.

The major banks offer solutions, along with other providers. Some of these are:

- PayPal
- Braintree (also from PayPal)
- BPoint (CBA)
- Qvalent (Westpac)
- NAB Transact
- ANZ Secure Gateway/eGate
- IP Payments/Bambora
- Premier Payments/Merchant Suite
- Fat Zebra
- Checkout
- Stripe
- Square (online)
- eWay
- WorldPay (now FIS)
- Assembly Payments/Presto
- Authorize.net (now Visa)
- CyberSource (now Visa)
- 2Checkout
- Allied Wallet
- Tyro
- ePath.

The Mobile Generation

Digital Wallets

Digital wallets were primarily a way of storing card details securely so they could be used online to make payments. It saved the customer from taking out their card every time they needed to make a purchase.

The first mainstream digital wallet was probably Microsoft Wallet in 1997 (not to be confused with a later implementation by the same name) and Microsoft Passport in 1999, which allowed desktop browsers to store credit card information securely. In 2003, flaws exposed in Microsoft Passport that allowed hackers to get credit card details led to the product being shut down in 2005.

PayPal

Around the same time, in 1998, PayPal was spun out as a separate company from eBay. Unlike the Microsoft solution, PayPal stores credit card details on its servers. The Internet had not taken off and, in the early days, the use of encryption was rare, and people were reluctant to enter credit card details online. PayPal provided a secure way of doing this. eBay was founded in 1995 and became the premier online store, especially allowing the trading of second-hand goods at auction. In order to facilitate payments, it needed a sophisticated payment provider and PayPal met their requirements. Eventually, eBay would acquire PayPal and later spin it off again. PayPal allowed a seamless checkout experience as it stored address details and credit card information. Regular payments could be set up with a minimal amount of effort. The main advantage for smaller stores (and eBay was really a collection of many stores) was that they could accept payments without being a fully accredited merchant acquirer. PayPal allowed anyone to accept payments by card.

In addition to cards, in Australia, PayPal supported Direct Entry payments (direct credit and direct debit). A penny test (see earlier) was used to validate that the account belonged to the PayPal account holder.

» NOTE

PayPal fees were high, around 3% for most merchants, about double the rate of competitive offerings. PayPal knew the customer better than competitors so they were taking less of a risk. This did not stop them from taking more profit. When PayPal introduced direct debits in Australia, they maintained a card backup. Direct debits could take two business days to clear and, in case the debit failed, they could revert to debiting the stored card through the normal means. No matter the outcome, PayPal still charges about 3% despite the low costs of direct debit. However, the customer was forced to use direct debit as a default payment once this had been set up and had to explicitly change the payment method if they so desired. This had the effect of pushing up profits. Eventually, this default was changed to allow the customer to set the default payment method.

In addition to their online checkout, PayPal diversified into P2P payments (though, strictly speaking, transferring across borders is only allowed if paying for goods or services).

PayPal trialled a pay with face solution called Check-in, where a user could pay using an app, and the merchant would see a picture of the customer's face and approve the transaction.

PayPal allows requests for payments and invoices to be sent after a payment is made. It has a dispute management service that is essentially automated, and offers a payment guarantee where a payer, if they did not receive goods or services as requested, can obtain a refund from PayPal.

In addition, by having a view of receivables, they provide working capital lending to businesses.

PayPal, however, has always acted on the edge of banking. In Australia, for accepting deposits over $1 000 and for transferring money overseas, it has been required to obtain a unique banking license (Providers of Purchased Payment Facilities, see above). In 2019, AUSTRAC ordered "the appointment of an external auditor to examine ongoing concerns in regard to PayPal Australia's compliance with the AML/CTF Act 2006."

Other Wallets

Visa and Mastercard attempted a number of digital wallets over the years. In 2013, Mastercard launched PayPass Digital Checkout with CBA (not to be confused with the contactless solution of the same name). A few months later, Visa Checkout launched a similar solution. These wallets were similar to PayPal in that credit card details were stored on their servers. The key advantage of PayPass and Checkout were that credit card details for some cards could be validated with the bank for added security. This provided more certainty to the merchant and reduced payment repudiation risk.

EMVCo QR Codes

QR codes were used by a number of initiatives in Australia, eftpos digital and other merchant solutions. EMVCo developed their own QR code solution in 2017.

Click to Pay

Just as Mastercard and Visa had developed their own extended 3D solutions and tokenisation, they had their own wallet solutions too. Click to Pay was introduced to reduce the plethora of wallets and payment mechanisms at online merchant checkout. Card payments, online Mastercard PayPass, and online Visa Checkout were combined in one tokenised offering from EMVCo so at least those payment methods would disappear. Originally a security-oriented feature, called Secure Remote Commerce, the idea was one wallet to rule them all. It is unknown whether PayPal, Google Pay, second-tier schemes, and domestic schemes will join this all-in-one wallet system so it may make the checkout experience more confusing.

Mobile Phone Payments

Telcos were into payments before mobile phones. Telstra issued phone cards for pay phones and many telecommunications companies had phone cards (or, really, stored value systems) for international calling.

With the take-up of mobile phones, prior to smartphones and contactless payments, telecommunications companies explored the idea of using mobile phones to pay.

Telcos did a form of customer verification through issuing a subscriber identification module (SIM) card. Telcos also collected money primarily for paying or prepaying phone charges.

Many telcos put two and two together, and attempted to set up low-value payments in their networks.

SIM cards, like EMV cards, could run applications. Before the advent of smartphones, rudimentary applications could run on even the most basic mobile phones and, using the Short Message Service (SMS) or Unstructured Supplementary Service Data (USSD), a phone user could interact with the network.

In Kenya, unique in that mobile phone networks developed faster than the banking network at a time of considerable domestic economic growth, Vodafone's M-PESA solution was and continues to be the most successful example of mobile phone payments. Despite numerous attempts, telcos and banks elsewhere in the world have been unsuccessful in repeating the success of these types of payment systems.

›› NOTE

Telstra still runs a payment service using USSD in Australia called CreditMe2U. It allows transfer of phone credit. Dialing #100# provides access to the service. Optus had a similar service Me 2 U that is now discontinued.

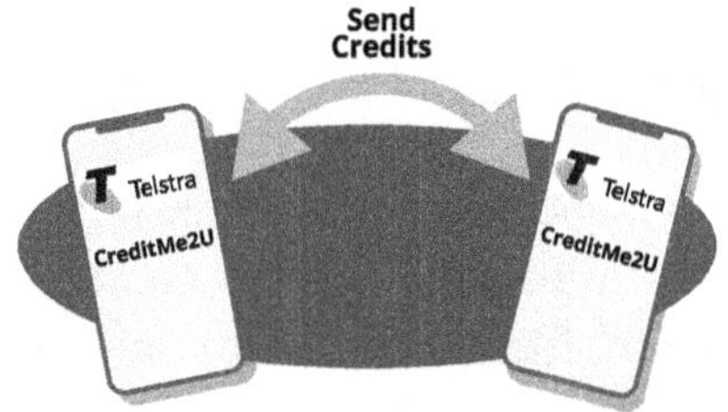

Contactless payments

In 1831, Michael Faraday discovered that a magnetic field could induce a current in a wire. This discovery gave rise to a whole series of technologies including electricity generation, electric motors, transformers and wireless communication. Contactless payments (Tap and Pay or Tap and Go) operate on the same principle.

Radio-frequency identification (RFID) was developed as a way to provide electronic remote information from an object to a reader. This technology developed the near-field communication (NFC) standard.

An antenna, basically a coil of wires, runs around near the edge of a card. These wires are connected to the EMV chip. A variable magnetic field generates a current in the coil and powers up the chip. Using a signal over that electromagnetic field, data can be exchanged between a terminal and the card. The specifications for this protocol are designed by EMVCo and standardised through ISO/IEC 14443.

Tap and Go on EMV is a type of near-field communication. Other standards in the area include ISO 18092 and the NFC Forum's NFC Data Exchange Format (NDEF) that allows peer-to-peer (P2P) communication over the air.

The solution was branded Mastercard PayPass and Visa payWave. American Express, a relative latecomer to Tap and Go, used the simple symbol of concentric arcs and the term "contactless" with Mastercard and Visa following suit as the offering became standardised.

Introduction in Australia was a multi-staged deployment from 2007 to 2012. Canada had shown some success, which inspired action in Australia. First was the gradual replacement of cards with the new technology. Initially, rather than change terminals, an additional reader (ViVOTech was one brand of NFC reader) was connected to the old one to allow the terminal to read the card via NFC. Westpac partnered with McDonalds and ANZ with 7-Eleven. CBA went all-out. The results were staggering. Over time, Tap and Go (which, in Australia was permitted for purchases up to $100 without a PIN, and during the COVID-19 pandemic by some banks for more) accounted for about 95% of transactions.

Initially, many merchants were still on dial-up (POTS), so Tap and Go would have been tap, wait and go. Some merchants allowed some cards, especially credit cards, to be authorised offline, allowing up to five purchases per card (tallied in memory on the chip) to be made before needing to go online.

With the increased use of debit cards, many banks forced the merchant to get an authorisation online. Newer terminals were designed to work using Wi-Fi or Ethernet connections to the Internet in real-time.

Mobile Phone NFC Payments

The first widely usable mobile phone NFC or contactless payment system was implemented in Australia as part of the Kaching application by CBA in 2011. A hardware cradle for the iPhone 4, it allowed the phone to make payments, and designate which account to use for the payment. The cradle was cumbersome, and needed to be redesigned and replaced every time a new iPhone hit the market and, with Apple launching parallel models, this would become an expensive exercise. A number of banks implemented alternative form factors.

Later, CBA developed a sticker that could be used to pay. The payment account could be controlled via an app by reconfiguring the payments switch to point the sticker's PAN to the customer's desired account in real-time.

Google Pay

Later in 2011, Google announced, as part of Google Wallet, a solution on NFC-enabled phones.

The issue with the initial solution was that it locked the ISO/IEC 14443 protocol (secure element) to Google, so only Google could control payments using the app. This meant a user had to use Google Wallet and not their own app to pay.

While Google locked down the secure element (in pretence for security purposes, but many speculated that it was to build up Google Wallet's market share), they allowed developers to develop non-payment NFC applications like NDEF.

Google's approach was not necessarily to make money but to collect data. This is their core business. When a user searched for something online, then walked into a store, or made a purchase online, for Google, the user was invisible. They had no idea what was happening; this explains why users receive annoying targeted ads for items they have already bought or when they have chosen a competing product. After having bought an LG TV, the last thing on the customer's mind is a competing brand, yet Google knows no better. If a customer paid using Google, they would know about the purchase and could start to do a lot of useful things, such as showing more relevant advertisements, have better analytics, and calculate the effectiveness of ad campaigns. This was the vision. However, their closed approach when developing Google Wallet, both by initially refusing to partner with other banks and locking down the secure element, was not yielding the penetration they expected, and they were breaking their open architecture approach that allowed developers to use all the features of the phone without Google's corporate greed or unfair restrictions, perhaps even breaking their "Don't be evil" motto of the time.

In 2013, CBA applied for a patent for a push payment mechanism that used Android's NFC/NDEF or QR codes (on any mobile phone) to push rather than pull money from the bank to merchants. eftpos trialled a similar mechanism with Coles and CBA in 2014.

Telcos, wanting a piece of the action, sought to have the secure element of the SIM used rather than the phone. Google Wallet backed off from a secure element. Much earlier, in 2011, a host card emulation idea was demonstrated on a RIM (Blackberry) device where, instead of the phone security element being used, the card information was stored on the server and the phone stored a token. The phone would store tokens that looked like card numbers or PANs (these are also called dynamic account numbers), but were not easily usable outside of the transaction. These tokens would be used to make payments. The merchant acquirer, instead of sending payments back to the acquirer, would send the payment to the token service provider. Mastercard Digital Enablement Service and Visa Token Service are two token service provider services today, though there are others.

Eventually, Google opened up payments using NFC. Whether it was due to the lack of uptake of Google Wallet, or in keeping with their philosophy of open technology, together with pressure from handset manufacturers, banks and developers. The development was a welcome one. Google Wallet was later renamed to Android Pay and then Google Pay.

Android is a shared ecosystem. Attempts to control it are looked at negatively by handset manufacturers. Samsung had developed a phone; why should Google restrict how it is used? Visa and Mastercard opened up their solutions for device-based contactless payments. Samsung eventually developed its own contactless payment solution, as did a few other manufacturers (including Huawei, Fitbit, and Garmin) both on and off the Android platform.

Off the heels of Google's approach, both Microsoft and RIM (aka Blackberry) developed NFC payments with a more open approach. Microsoft still wanted to control its product, Microsoft Wallet, whereas RIM was more open.

Apple Pay

In 2011, Apple was not interested in NFC. It was already possible for an app developer to allow in-app purchases through a stored credit card similar to the digital wallet solution above. Physical credit cards were dead and Apple thought they could change the ecosystem with the introduction of Apple Passbook (now Apple Wallet). Apple had developed a framework to allow alternative payment systems. They thought that, as an Apple executive put it, "Passbook does the kinds of things customers need today."

As Apple saw their attempts to introduce an alternative payment system failing, they started a secret project in 2013 to go mainstream with an NFC payment solution. To do this, their devices first required NFC support and secure element capabilities. This was easy to do as they were not the first.

Apple's motivation, unlike Google, Samsung, Microsoft Windows or RIM, was not data collection or good functionality. They wanted to get a piece of the pie. In the Card Economics section (see below) we will see the complex world of interchange and acquiring service fees. For now, suffice to say, the issuer and the scheme gets a big part of the revenue.

Apple inserted themselves into the message flow. While this added some value, it was technically unnecessary for effecting payments. But what it meant was that Apple could extract a fee. In many cases, this fee was 0.15%.

They prevented access to NFC payments by any app, perhaps under the pretence of security, but more likely to force applications to use their new offering: Apple Pay, which increased revenue.

The Apple Pay solution used tokens and a token service provider. This is like host card emulation but with one difference: it stores the tokens in a secure element. While this is technically more secure than a software-based host card emulation solution, it is overkill as even when accessing tokens the probability of theft is low. The risk could have been given to issuers. One drawback with the Apple solution is that for most implementations, it demands that the real card number be divulged to the Apple software, even for a short time, either through direct provisioning (where the card number is entered into the phone) or in-App provisioning, where the card number is provided by the bank's app.

Apple's card solution is quite complex. However, they found, as suspected, that this did not dissuade banks from implementing it and providers came to the party with solutions. When a user adds a card, it uses new messages on the card rails to negotiate provisioning. Banks can provide an SMS verification to confirm the customer is the user. In order to protect against security flaws on the phone, Apple assesses the account holder on the phone and may recommend the issuer step up their checks, for example, by direct customer contact. All these messages take place over the old ISO 8583 card communication rails.

In order to work in Australia, for the first time banks had to switch their own payments to Mastercard and Visa. In addition, to access the token scheme, a fee would be payable per transaction.

Australia was leading the world in contactless payments and some banks were the first to implement mobile contactless payments. Nevertheless, they pushed back against Apple on what they saw as clearly unfair behaviour on Apple's part: limiting access to NFC and charging high fees. ANZ took a different approach and embraced Apple Pay. In April 2016, they announced themselves as the first Australian bank to launch Apple Pay.

ACCC and Apple Pay

Collective bargaining by independent businesses with a significant market share is regarded as cartel behaviour and not allowed in many countries. In Australia, such behaviour requires the authorisation of the ACCC or it may be deemed illegal.

In July 2016, CBA, Westpac, NAB, and Bendigo and Adelaide Bank (with potentially others to follow) requested the ACCC to allow them to collectively bargain with Apple regarding Apple Pay. With the iPhone being the most popular phone in Australia, Apple was in a strong position to extract fees from issuers.

As we will see, the ACCC and the RBA had come down heavily on credit card fees demanding transparency and openness. Apple was not open. In fact, their dealings with banks are subject to non-disclosure agreements. Other competitors do not charge on a transaction basis. The banks argued that Apple was in a monopoly situation and able to dictate terms.

The group said, "Apple's refusal to provide third-party apps with any access to the NFC functionality of its devices sets it apart from other hardware manufacturers, operating system providers and third-party wallet providers such as Google, Samsung and Microsoft. It is also inconsistent with Apple's treatment of most of the other hardware and software features it has developed. For example, app developers are able (with the user's permission) to make use of the iPhone's camera, microphone and accelerometer, its cellular, Wi-Fi and Bluetooth transmitters and its touch ID fingerprint sensor, but not its NFC functionality."[94]

In what was clearly profiteering behaviour by Apple and restrictive practice on the NFC front (though later Apple would open up non-payments to NFC, but leave payments NFC restricted). The ACCC accepted Apple's position and, in balancing competition interests (with Apple stating that they would be disadvantaged against Android if their Apple Pay model was changed), the ACCC did not allow the collective bargaining application. Over time, it would be clear that the security mechanism of the different models (Android, Google, Samsung, Apple, etc.) were not sufficiently different to have any bearing on consumer decisions. Further, almost every other application of payments does not extract a fee. The 0.15% fee is a significant revenue cost and, in the end, all bank consumers pay for this directly or indirectly. Denying the bank's application (to act as a cartel) was probably a fair one; however, the failure to prevent anti-competitive behaviour by Apple has not been beneficial to the industry. Apple yields significant market share in Australia. The ACCC decision stopped many providers investing in Apple payment solutions, even outside the card application use case. In short, it was detrimental to competition, and sent the wrong signal to the market and encouraged the wrong behaviour.

Within a short period of time after the decision, most banks in Australia implemented Apple Pay.

The Battle of the Wallets

The original goal of card issuers, whether they were loyalty cards or payment cards, was to ensure that the consumer would carry around their card in their wallet. It was to ensure that the store, bank or scheme was front of mind (and front of revenue). This frustrated consumers, especially men and light-travelling women, who, due to the general lack of a handbag, wanted to carry less bulk in their pockets. This battle carried on into the digital age, but this time organisations wanted to be the wallet themselves.

---

[94] Gilbert + Tobin

Starting from the early Internet wallets like Microsoft Passport and PayPal, through to Internet banking and, later, mobile banking phone apps, then Google Wallet and Apple Pay, the battle for which could be the app that rules all apps has been raging.

Everyone wanted to be the one-stop wallet, and the collateral damage was consumers with dozens of financial apps they need to do what they want.

Today, there is a truce of sorts. Phone and device manufacturers, phone operating system developers, schemes and banks need each other so they all have the power to be *the* wallet. Interest has somewhat waned in recent times, due to an acceptance of the proliferation of apps and the fact that best of breed beats jack of all trades.

The Resurrection of eftpos?

A number of nails were driven into the Australian domestic card schemes.

The introduction of the big schemes in Australia, especially the extended roll-out of their debit card solutions, the global online market, where only international cards could survive, and, finally, the use of Tap and Go, where there was no tap, press cheque or savings, and then go, was leaving eftpos firmly out of the picture. Finally, a home goal for the Australian regulators was to push interchange, especially debit interchange, to zero. All these changes should have killed off the Australian debit scheme.

Marketing of eftpos began in 2009. An initial focus on digital online payments was subsumed by a desire to take on the central switching of the banks. While this would have made sense several years earlier, the implementation of Connex, an old-school switch, seemed to head them in the wrong direction. A theme of playing catch-up continued with their implementation of the EMV chip and, later, contactless payments. After some trials with CBA, work finally started on a digital online solution, 20 years after the dot com boom. Was this too little, too late?

Basic Card Operation

The unique proposition of cards is that, at point of sale, the payer can create an obligation to pay strong enough for the merchant to accept. The payment takes time to make its way over the network: originally months, now days or even less than a second.

Before the card era, we had the payer and payee (or, in this case, a merchant). The payer made a payment and the merchant supplied the goods.

In modern card networks, we have a scheme. The scheme (like American Express, Visa or Mastercard) provided the logo on the card and set the rules of the game. In this case, the rules of use and acceptance of the card. As time went on, there would be a lot of rules.

The issuer is the corporation that gives the payer the card. The payer needs to pay the issuer when a bill is due. If the issuer is a bank, the money will be deducted from the payer's account.

A payer commits to paying for goods. They effectively give the merchant an IOU.

The acquirer takes the IOU and underwrites it, provided everyone is playing by the scheme rules.

If any rule is broken, the transaction needs to be declined before the customer receives the goods otherwise, one of the participants could be out of pocket.

In an ATM scenario, the ATM acts as the merchant and the ATM's bank is the acquirer.

Four Parties

In the case of Visa, Mastercard and the eftpos scheme, there are said to be four distinct parties (ignoring the scheme and the RBA, which are recent additions for domestic transactions):

- The issuer (the party that issues the card: a bank, ANZ, for example)
- The consumer, payer or cardholder (the customer)
- The acquirer (another bank, NAB, for example), the party that acquires the transaction from the merchant and pays them
- The merchant.

These schemes are called four-party schemes. Where the issuer and acquirer are the same entity (which both takes the transaction and issues the card) there are three parties, and this is known as a three-party scheme. Examples are American Express and Diners Club.

When looking for the issuer, look at who sends out the bill or takes the money off the account. When looking for the acquirer, look at who (in the old days) got all the charge slips and underwrote the payment. In modern times, it is hard to find the acquirer. In most cases, it is the bank or brand on the card POS machine. For three-party systems, the acquirer is the scheme as they get the message and underwrite the payment.

On Us

For any given transaction, if the bank or institution that acquires the transaction through an ATM or point of sale is the same as the issuer of the card, that transaction is called an on us transaction, and is generally favourable for institutions as external fees and integration are not required. There are also more innovation opportunities with these payments.

On the other hand, where a transaction is acquired by one bank and sent to another, it is called an off us transaction.

Card Transaction Flow

Card payments were a pull payment, i.e. payment was pulled from a payer's account. In modern four-party systems, a simple card payment operates in the following way (see also *Figure 30*):

- The issuer institution issues a card to a payer, who is responsible for funding their account with the issuer and presents the card to a merchant, either online or at a store terminal (completing all security verification processes, e.g., PIN or CVV).

- The terminal sends an authorisation request (e.g., ISO 8583, a 100 message or, for a single message system, a 200 message) to the acquirer bank.
- The acquirer forwards the message to the scheme after checking for fraud. (In Australia, previous conventions required a bilateral connection, i.e., directly to the other bank.)
- The scheme switches the message to the issuer.
- The issuer checks for fraud, applies the transaction (either in a pending state or, in a single message system, in a final state) and responds with a confirmed authorisation (or a declined transaction).
- A message is sent to the terminal, which approves (or declines) the transaction.
- In dual messaging systems, at the end of the day, the acquirer sends settlement messages for confirmed transactions to the scheme (adding tips, etc.). The scheme then forwards these to the issuer, who applies the transactions in a final state, replacing pending transactions.
- The total invoices (the schemes being exempt from tax invoicing) are sent to the banks and the final figures to the RBA.
- The payments are settled on a net deferred basis the following morning by moving ESA money on the RITS system.

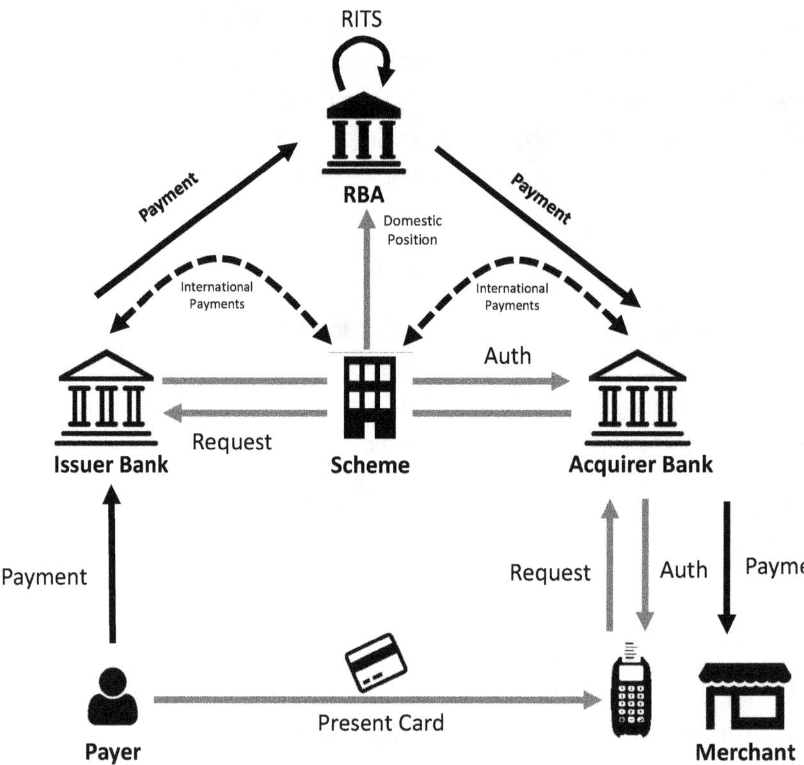

Figure 30. **The key participants in a modern simple card transaction.**

There are sometimes a few modifications to this model:

- The picture is complicated by legacy bilateral links that are slowly being phased out. Here, scheme messages bypass the scheme and go directly to the banks.
- In the case of three-party systems (American Express and Diners Club), the acquirer and issuer are generally the same party.
- International card payments for all schemes (including three-party schemes and overseas schemes such as JCB and China UnionPay) are settled through the respective scheme. The scheme gives or receives a local RTGS or Direct Entry payment to settle the transaction.
- eftpos is a single message system and uses 200-series messages to confirm the transaction, which may be declined. Mastercard sends a settlement file and Visa sends a 220 message (aka BASE II message) that cannot be declined.
- In some cases, in a dual message system, such as where a pre-authorisation has already been provided and there is a downward revision, an acceptable tip has been added, or the scheme has acted in stand-in mode, due to technical problems in accessing the issuer bank, a forced authorisation is sent using a 120 message. These cannot be declined.
- Refunds follow a similar path.
- If the consumer or bank has a problem with the transaction (and sometimes parties do break the rules) a chargeback can be initiated.

Cards: Impact on the Economy

There is a clear correlation between the use of credit cards and consumer spending. An MIT study observed a 100% increase in spending associated with cards.[95] Australia witnessed the increase in consumer spending from the mid-1970s, coinciding with the mass adoption of credit cards.

It is fair to assume that the current trend of tightening credit and discouraging interchange (thereby discouraging credit card use) could have a gradual negative impact on spending, maintaining downward pressure on interest rates through responsive monetary policy (to encourage spending). While the demise of credit may make sense economically, to reduce what could have been crippling household debt, the direct impact of some retail and merchant groups pressuring regulation of credit cards could have a negative impact on discretionary household spending.

Card Economics

The study of card economics is one of the more complicated exercises in banking with benefits flowing between five parties (the consumer, merchant, acquirer, scheme, and issuer

[95] Prelec

and back again). It was the subject of regulatory action that took four years of study to suggest just one change, and decades of inquiries, recommendations and regulation. Even courts have avoided diving into its details. As the Federal Court of Australia put it, "[This] is because much of the subject matter includes controversial economic issues which, as the evidence demonstrates, are the subject of strong and sharp differences of opinion between economic experts."[96]

Card payments were originally free for consumers. However, payments cost money. The cost of sending a message and processing it is an expense. In the modern era, moving data is cheap. Payment data is small: 320 bytes for a card payment or even 4 kilobytes for an ISO 20022 MX SWIFT message. If we made 500 payments in a year that would be 2 megabytes of payment data for the whole year. (Compare this with a high-definition movie of 4 gigabytes.) The cost of moving that data through the network (assuming an expensive mobile plan of 50 GB for $30) is 0.12 cents to cover one person's payments for a whole year, whereas the typical charge to a merchant for a $50 payment is between 60 cents and $1.50. How and why does this happen? This is a good question and, in Australia, a topic dear to regulators' hearts.

A Basic Example

A simple exercise in estimating costs can help us understand how payment fees work.

First, there is the cost of moving a payment around. As we have seen, the cost of getting the data from one end of the network to another is negligible; we can say $0 per payment. However, there are systems and processes involved in switching the payment to get it to where it needs to go: acquirer and issuer switches, fraud detection engines, and so on. In many of the banks, these systems are 20 years old (sunk costs, as they are called) but, nevertheless, data centres, associated hardware and maintenance need to be paid for. Every now and then, there needs to be an update. Every three to five years, cards need to be replaced and mailed out. Let's say a large bank with 5 million regular customers spent $100 million to support its payments per year. (This is a generous amount.) This is $20 per customer per year or about 4 cents a payment. Not all loyalty points are cashed in efficiently and there are loyalty system running costs, but we will let these cancel each other out. Whether the payment is a small one or a big one does not make any difference to the cost: data are data and is all treated the same.

Bigger payments, however, have a bigger risk. But thanks to EMV and other measures, fraud is declining, even with (or partly thanks to) contactless and mobile payments. AusPayNet reports fraud at less than 0.1% so, on our $50 payment, the cost of fraud is 5 cents.

On top of this, interchange is a fee that an acquirer pays to an issuer and is intended to cover all the issuer's costs: system fees, fraud risks on their side, scheme fees and loyalty fees.

Many credit cards offer loyalty points to cardholders. The cost of this is included in the interchange fee. Typical loyalty programs offer 1 point per dollar spent; however, $20 from popular retailers grants 5 000 points, which puts the cost at about 0.4%.

---

[96] FCA

In 2018, Visa made $21 billion gross revenue from $11 trillion worth of transactions. This means their fees are about 0.2%. This fee is paid by both issuers and acquirers. As mentioned earlier, card schemes are among the most profitable organisations in the world (when measuring profit per employee) so, while this may or may not be excessive for what they do, it contributes to the cost of acquiring.

Credit cards provide an interest-free period between 30 and 60 days, depending on whether the payment was made at the end or beginning of the billing cycle. The cost to a bank of this money is the cash rate, let's say 1%.

Finally, the merchant acquirer needs to provide equipment and support to a merchant customer. Let's just say a typical terminal sees 8 000 customer transactions per year (at the low end); that's 22 customers per day, and the equipment and support costs $300 per year per terminal. This is about $0.04 per transaction.

So, when we add this all up, we get the charges as shown in *Table 7*.

Table 7.

Rough estimate of costs and charges in card transactions.

Charge (excl. GST except bottom line)	Per Transaction	$50 on Debit Card	$50 on Credit Card
Network charges	$0.00	$0.00	$0.00
System charges (issuer and acquirer)	$0.04	$0.04	$0.04
Fraud risk	0.1%	$0.05	$0.05
Loyalty (varies)	0.4%	-	$0.23
Scheme charges	0.2%	$0.10	$0.10
Interest-free period (1% pa.)	0.1%	-	$0.05
Merchant equipment	$0.04	$0.04	$0.04
Total	0.8% + $0.08	$0.23	$0.51
Total inc GST	**0.9% + $0.09**	**$0.25**	**$0.56**

The table above, which used our rudimentary calculations, roughly lines up with the fees that are charged to merchants by low-cost acquirers, with a little room for some (limited) profit.

Merchant charges were not always this low. Before regulatory action in 2002, they were almost double.

As *Table 7* shows, the biggest component of the fees is loyalty. This varies from card to card (standard cards less, premium cards more). While from a merchant perspective, the fees may seem excessive, from a cardholder point of view, it is a charge that benefits them in the form of rewards or interest-free purchases. A case of robbing Peter to pay Paul, or robbing Peter to pay Peter?

Often, in addition, an annual fee (larger for premium cards) is charged to the holder. Some cards offer travel insurance as well. So, for our basic calculator, let's use that fee to cover the costs of running the loyalty program and travel insurance.

Credit cardholders also pay a high interest rate if they exceed the interest-free period. These customers are known as revolvers.

Fraud Risk

As we said, fraud risk is 0.1% of the value of the payment. This assumes good fraud measures are already in place. EMV in stores, PCI DSS compliance, and 3D Secure online have helped the cause as have the anti-fraud systems implemented by banks such as ANZ Bank's Falcon, which was advertised on television to provide cardholders with a sense of security, even though banks considered the fraud cost low relative to interchange revenue.

The scheme rules are such that either the issuer, acquirer, merchant or cardholder takes the risk when something goes wrong. The scheme generally does not take risks in transactions.

Let us look at some scenarios in *Table 8*.

Table 8.

Liability shift in card payments.

No.	Scenario	Who's liable	In practice
1.	A card is stolen and used before it is cancelled.	The cardholder is liable up to a certain amount, generally $150. If the PIN was compromised, and this is the cardholder's fault, there could be more liability. If the card is left at an ATM, the cardholder is liable. (Fortunately, ATMs swallow the card after a few seconds of inactivity to avoid theft of the card.)	Issuer banks take a substantial risk in this space, as payments over $150 may be payable by the issuer.
2.	A card number is stolen or a card is fraudulently duplicated.	If the card is used without EMV, or if it is used online without 3D Secure, the merchant (or acquirer) is liable.	It can take some time to get the money back. The bank will stop the card and reissue it once compromised. This is the largest component of fraud risk.

No.	Scenario	Who's liable	In practice
3.	A card is used by a merchant in an unauthorised way (e.g., card charged for a monthly subscription after a free trial, or a merchant charging $1 230.00 instead of $12.30).	Negotiated between cardholder and merchant.	This is not always clear if a settlement can't be reached. The issuing bank may write it off and treat it as a compromised card. Lesson: When giving out credit card details: caveat emptor, buyer beware.
4.	A merchant is liquidated before they fulfil an order.	The cardholder is an unsecured creditor. Ultimately, the merchant acquirer may be liable.	Again a grey area. Cardholders, in some cases, can get their money back from the bank.
5.	A faulty merchant acquiring machine clears a payment that should have been declined, e.g., if the merchant systems are down and manual dockets are used at the bank's instruction, or an EMV chip cannot be read, and magnetic stripe/signature are used.	The merchant acquiring bank is liable.	This is quite rare, but worth knowing.

The ePayments Code may provide some additional protection, though it may be difficult to access its provisions without a fight. The mechanism most schemes have for dispute resolution is called *chargeback*. A chargeback costs money to lodge, but the money is returned if the claim is successful. Chargebacks are orchestrated by the scheme, and involve the exchange of information between the issuer, the acquirer and their customers. It is possible that a chargeback may fail but, if a payer invoking the ePayments Code succeeds, especially in the case of an international payment (as foreign banks are not signatories to Australia's ePayments Code), the Australian issuing bank often takes liability. If a chargeback and the ePayments Code do not resolve the issue favourably, ASIC, the banking ombudsman, the tribunals and, ultimately, the courts are an option though, in most cases, the matter should be resolved through the procedures.

» NOTE

During the COVID-19 pandemic, gym membership fees were initially deducted from cardholders' accounts in advance of the service being provided (as was previous normal practice). Given that no service could be provided, gyms were liable for a refund under common law. Some gyms continued to charge based on their terms and conditions. Their merchant acquirers, however, stopped the payments as there was a risk of the gym going broke and the acquirers may have had to pay. This is why some credit due diligence needs to be applied to merchants by their acquirer.

Interchange

Interchange is the fee an issuer charges a merchant. It does not include the merchant fees (system fees, equipment, and fraud risk), so the interchange fee is lower than the merchant service fee (MSF).

In theory, interchange is meant to cover scheme royalties and marketing, and issuer costs. It also covers the loyalty program and the interest-free period of credit cards. It is debatable how many other charges it should cover, but the fee is not generally bank-specific but set by the scheme. As we will see below, these fees are highly regulated and are required to be transparent so they are published on the Web.

Some examples of interchange fees (based on Mastercard published rates of 2020; Visa was slightly cheaper):

- Debit cards charge a maximum flat 16.5 cents for transactions over $20
- Charities: 0%
- Corporate cards: 0.88%
- Government: 0.25%
- Strategic merchants (these are large merchants the schemes try to attract): 0.28%
- Discounts for petrol and transit
- Consumer standard card in-store: 0.22%
- Consumer premium card online: 0.88%.

Apple Pay, Samsung Pay and Google Pay generally charge 0.88%. Do you recall how Apple takes a 0.15% cut? Here is where it comes from. Google and Samsung are effectively subsidising the Apple profit grab, a price fix with the ACCC's blessing. American Express fees can vary from 1.6% to 2.3% plus 10 cents, depending on the transaction. Large transactions take a bigger fee. (It is unclear why, given economies of scale should mean the opposite.)

Due to regulation, Australia and Europe have low interchange rates compared to the US. The argument for high interchange rates is that it encourages spending, and the argument for low interchange is that high interchange rates disadvantages merchants and non-issuer acquirers.

» NOTE

American Express, as a three-party scheme, takes on part of the merchant acquiring cost and risk, and provides greater loyalty and service benefits to consumers and merchants. While this may not fully justify the high cost, given it is a premium product and less regulated (see below), American Express gets away with it. As punishment, few merchants accept it and those that do, charge a premium surcharge.

Merchant Service Fee

The merchant service fee (MSF) is the charge from an acquirer to a merchant.

First, it should cover the interchange fee (depending on the plan, the relationship may not be direct and many plans are simplified). Second, it covers the terminal and support costs. Third, it covers the network processing and connection costs.

There are several fee models for MSFs. The main two are interchange plus and fixed rate. In the interchange plus model, a fixed fee is charged per month (sometimes waived on high volumes), plus the interchange charged by the scheme, plus merchant charges, generally as a percent of the fee. In the fixed rate model, either a fixed rate is charged per month up to a certain volume, or just a terminal rental fee plus a flat rate percentage for each transaction.

Large merchants can substantially do their own acquiring (though they do require BIN sponsorship), and then pay interchange without incurring the full MSF markup. Supermarkets Woolworths and Coles have their own switches and terminals. Other large retailers, like fuel stations, government departments, and others have their own terminals and connect them to banks at a lower cost, accepting much of the risk themselves. These options are not readily available to smaller stores as the infrastructure expertise and setup would dwarf any benefits. Further, smaller stores do not have the same wholesale bargaining power of the large merchants.

Merchant Surcharge

The merchant surcharge is a fee charged by the merchants to recoup the cost of accepting a credit card (and these days, almost any scheme card). The fee is a controversial one. It is designed to recoup the cost of the merchant accepting a card as payment.

By default, schemes and banks banned merchants from surcharging. It was a condition of acceptance. This was to encourage use of the card; from a consumer perspective, it was designed to appear free.

It has gone back and forth over the years. Originally Bankcard disallowed it. Then, in 1981, the Trade Practices Commission allowed a discount for cash. Then again, in 1990, with the revocation of Bankcard's exclusivity, schemes were allowed to enforce no-surcharging (though Bankcard never did). In 2002, surcharging was reinstated for all schemes, including Visa and Mastercard by regulation, and by American Express and Diners Club by coercion.

(The RBA made these two three-party schemes guarantee no action would be taken or the RBA would regulate the respective payments, and possibly limit interchange fees in the process — killing those schemes.)

The controversy with the surcharge is that card use does increase spend. As mentioned in some studies, many individuals are twice as likely to buy something thanks to a credit card. As a merchant, it is not sensible to charge the fee as it inhibits spend, and many savvy merchants understand this, with some notable exceptions.

When surcharging was first discussed in 1981, the Australian Retailers Association felt it was pointless. Shops would compete to offer fee-free Bankcard transactions and there would be a race to the bottom.

Some savvy merchants used it as a way to add income on a heavily discounted item. Airlines, for example, forced to drop prices due to competition, would start charging for basic items such as headphones, check-in luggage and, yes, it all started after we had found our desired flight and were about to check out. The credit card surcharge was about adding revenue to the bottom line for airlines. It was also used by captive merchants, where the customer had no choice. For a government agency or strata scheme, there was no competition so an additional revenue stream was a golden opportunity.

For online immediate purchases, there is a strong argument against surcharging as there is really no other option but to use card payments — especially if real-time confirmation is required (which it normally is), yet the charge was applied anyway.

Many surcharging venues do not differentiate between debit and credit cards so debit cards end up paying an excessive surcharge.

Cash handling has a merchant cost associated with it: for miscounting, cash leakage, robbery (and associated injury/death risk), counterfeit risk and damaged notes. (A heat-damaged note is worthless, yet many circulate in cash tills.) During the COVID-19 pandemic, many merchants stopped accepting cash as contactless card taps were safer. Reconciliation of cash is also an expense, as is banking it, topping up change, maintaining a till/float, etc.

From a government/regulatory point of view, especially the federal government, reducing the hidden cash economy means more tax revenue (GST and company/individual tax) — so credit card payments should have been encouraged above cash.

›› NOTE

Many tradespeople offer a 10% discount for cash payments. Once, a tradie offered someone a 30% discount. "How come?" asked the customer. The tradie said, "Well, if I don't declare the income, I don't need to pay GST. I don't need to pay income tax and, if my ex-wife doesn't find out, I don't need to pay spouse maintenance. I can save a fortune!"

Some merchants used it as a way of extracting additional revenue. So regulators required that surcharges be justified based on actual expense (cost of acceptance). This regulation was tightened and extended to small merchants from 1 September 2017. Also, if a merchant has a "One size fits all" card surcharge, they need to choose the card with the lowest surcharge.

It is difficult for a merchant to know which card will be tapped. Online it may be possible, but in-store it is not practical. So under the new regulations, the merchant has to choose the lowest interchange card.

The RBA is effective at regulating banks. It is not set up to regulate merchants, and politically and economically it is not a priority for the ACCC, so these merchant directives are substantially toothless, except for the largest of merchants (e.g., airlines).

There is now clear evidence to suggest that card surcharging has had a negative impact on the use of electronic payments, expenses for the economy,[97] GST revenue[98] and spending.[99]

When weighing up the benefits of card payment, the now low cost of interchange and merchant acceptance fees, and the inconvenience and poor customer service of levying the fee at checkout, the merchant surcharge did not make sense for so many reasons. Yet it persists.

Banks versus Regulators

A number of measures have been taken to limit the profits and charges of cards, especially credit cards. Banks have been equally adept at coming up with ways to circumvent the controls.

Some have pointed out that, given the correlation of card payments and spending habits, regulators have taken action against card schemes in times of monetary tightening, giving them an extra lever to enact monetary policy.

The two major schemes, originally owned by and currently largely representing the issuing banks (Visa and Mastercard), have been in the middle of a proxy war between the banks and the RBA.

In 1980-81, off the back of the Campbell Committee, the Trade Practices Commission allowed merchants to provide discounts if customers did not use a Bankcard. In 1990, this restriction was removed, though Bankcard did not prevent the discount. Visa and Mastercard did stop merchant surcharging in their terms and conditions of acceptance.

In 1989, the voluntary Electronic Funds Transfer Code of Conduct of 1986 (now the ePayments Code) was modified to stop annual fees being charged on credit cards. The banks responded by increasing interest rates.

In 1993, the Prices Surveillance Authority (now ACCC) pushed the banks to reduce interest rates by 6%; in return, the annual fee would be restored.

---

[97] Bolt

[98] Hondroyiannis

[99] Schuh

After the Wallis Report of 1997, with the formation of the Payments System Board and the passing of the Payment Systems (Regulation) Act in 1998, a study of interchange fees was commenced by the RBA and ACCC in 1999. The result of this study was published and some ideas put forth, which were responded to by the industry.

In August 2002, the RBA introduced a number of reforms. Bankcard, Mastercard and Visa were formally designated as payment systems by the Reserve Bank as per the Payment Systems (Regulation) Act and were directed to:

1. Allow merchant surcharges on credit cards
2. Allow APRA-supervised Specialist Credit Card Institutions (SCCI) to participate in credit card schemes, and to allow non-issuer merchant acquirers equal treatment (the scheme rules required/encouraged banks to issue more than acquire).
3. Limit interchange fees.

American Express and Diners Club escaped designation as a card scheme, given they were three-party card schemes. However, they gave an undertaking to the Reserve Bank not to take action against merchants who surcharged to avoid regulation on their interchange.

In December 2002, Visa International mounted a legal challenge in the Federal Court to have the reforms overturned. The RBA was disappointed and they said so. Mastercard joined in later. In 2003, the Federal Court found in favour of the RBA.

The only two surviving SCCIs, Tyro and GE Finance, were removed from APRA regulatory control in 2015 when the Productivity Commission noted that APRA control was too restrictive to support increased access to credit card networks.

The schemes were forced to implement the measures.

The Interchange Fee Game

A cat and mouse game was initiated by the schemes and the banks to try to regain lost issuer revenue.

While interchange fees were limited, the task of administering them fell on the schemes. Each bank was required to submit financially accurate numbers (in accordance with accounting standards) that would be independently reviewed by an expert agreed to by the RBA.

The first part was to calculate the cost of issuing for the top issuers, who provided 90% of a scheme's issuance by transaction value — basically, the big banks. Allowable costs from these top issuers were:

- Issuers' costs incurred principally in processing credit card transactions, including the costs of receiving, verifying, reconciling and settling such transactions.
- Issuers' costs incurred principally in respect of fraud and fraud prevention in connection with credit card transactions.
- Issuers' costs incurred principally in providing authorisation of credit card transactions.

- Issuers' costs incurred in funding the interest-free period on credit card transactions, calculated using the average of the cash rate published by the Reserve Bank of Australia over the three financial years prior to the date by which the cost-based benchmark must be calculated.

While scheme fees were permissible in the calculations above, notably missing from the list were the loyalty points and loyalty program. The Reserve Bank felt that the loyalty program could be run from annual card charges, and why should a merchant fund the points? If merchant loyalty is required, merchants have their own cards and can run their own system.

Once the costs were established and divided by transaction value (to get a percentage cost-based benchmark), the scheme was required to determine the weighted average sum of interchange fees.

Interchange fees vary based on the type of card and the type of merchant: basically, the total interchange anticipated revenue of the (new) interchange table, using the previous year's numbers, divided by the total transaction value. This rate had to be no more than the cost-based benchmark. The table was required to be published. Sure enough, the interchange rate fell from 0.9% to 0.55%. The calculation had to be repeated every three years or whenever the table changed (and it stopped changing so often).

Several attempts were made to claw back the lost interchange revenue.

First, was card creep. Standard cards had a lower interchange than higher cards. So, at the beginning of the three-year period, issuers would upgrade standard cardholders to gold or platinum — premium cards. This also meant merchant acquirers made less profit over the three-year cycle. At the end of the three-year cycle, premium card interchange would need to drop, but a new category could be added with a higher interchange, and so the cycle would continue.

Today, Mastercard has standard, premium, super premium and elite cards. Visa is similar; however, their Visa signature cards take the elite position. The consequence of premium card creep is that every three years the interchange has to drop. This meant less revenue for the issuers, and eventually it impacted the loyalty programs, so issuers would have to rejig their programs to the disappointment of astute customers.

Another attempt for the banks to regain revenue was to issue American Express companion cards alongside their Visa or Mastercard programs — one account, two cards. American Express was not under the same interchange regime. Sure enough, in 2015, RBA designated the American Express Companion Card System (excluding American Express cards) as a designated payment service. In addition to American Express, Debit Mastercard, Mastercard, Visa and eftpos prepaid cards were added to the designated payment systems list in 2015. (Visa Debit was designated in 2004.) Regulation was soon to follow.

In 2016, to limit premium card creep and to put the nail in the coffin for American Express companion cards, the RBA put a cap on weighted interchange at 0.55% for credit (8.8 cents for debit) and an absolute cap on any single rate to 0.88% credit (16.5 cents or 0.22% for debit). Sure enough, banks withdrew their companion card offerings.

In April 2019, Westpac came up with an idea. The wording of the companion card regulation defined the arrangement as having a card with American Express's logo that is issued "by an entity other than American Express Australia Limited or a related body corporate of American Express Australia Limited." Westpac issued a card bundle — similar to the companion card. This time the American Express card was not issued by the bank, but by American Express itself. Both American Express and Westpac did a credit check as it was legally two different debts. It is unknown what the arrangement is between American Express and Westpac; suffice to say, there surely must be a substantial interchange kick-back from American Express to Westpac. With widespread acceptance of China UnionPay, the game of cat and mouse may not be over.

Another trick that the schemes and banks attempted was a rebate or incentive. Both acquirers and issuers paid the schemes a fee. Acquirer to issuer payments were counted, but an incentive payment from the scheme to the issuer was not. To counteract this, the RBA, in 2016, introduced the net compensation rule: "Under these provisions, benefits received by an issuer (excluding interchange fees and some other payments) that have a purpose or effect of promoting the issuance and use of credit cards cannot exceed the payment of benefits by the issuer to the scheme or acquirer in a reporting period."

The Productivity Commission in 2018 recommended that interchange should be banned by the end of 2019. This did not happen. It also recommended that merchants should be able to choose a cheaper routing. The RBA introduced the *least cost routing* initiative. Rather than regulate, the RBA encouraged merchant acquirers to choose the cheapest route to send a debit card transaction. Some cards were dual network or dual scheme connected (Mastercard and eftpos or Visa and eftpos). The Mastercard and Visa networks were more expensive (due to both merchant fees and interchange). Least cost routing would, according to the RBA, encourage lower merchant service fees for debit cards and create more competition. Least cost routing was often implemented as a *switch to issuer* — a merchant acquirer would send the transaction directly to the issuer (bank or scheme) to minimise interchange and network charges. This routing technology was simplified with the rationalisation through the eftpos Hub and the mandated scheme interchange for Mastercard and Visa.

After 40 years of card regulation, card payment fees are approaching zero in Australia. Whether the schemes will survive this is yet to be determined.

Profit in Cards

Profit in the cards ecosystem has largely been on the scheme and issuing side and that too is dwindling. In the hallways of banks, the merchant acquiring division is not generally a profit centre — but often acting as a loss-leading segment. The leaders there often complain about their continual subsidy of either the issuing business of the bank or the corporate banking division that can attract customers — with a merchant acquiring a Trojan horse for other business.

Despite the losses, merchant acquiring has seen the most competition from outside players.

The schemes continue to make money though, as we have seen, this is under pressure in Australia.

Ultimately, the profit in card payments is largely in the underlying account as retained interest (for debit cards) and interest income (for credit cards).

Profit in the cards ecosystem has largely been on the scheme and issuing side and that too is dwindling. In the hallways of banks, the merchant acquiring division is not generally a profit centre — but often acting as a loss-leading segment. The leaders there often complain about their continual subsidy of either the issuing business of the bank or the corporate banking division that can attract customers — with a merchant acquiring a Trojan horse for other business.

Despite the losses, merchant acquiring has seen the most competition from outside players.

The schemes continue to make money though, as we have seen, this is under pressure in Australia.

Ultimately, the profit in card payments is largely in the underlying account as retained interest (for debit cards) and interest income (for credit cards).

The push to zero interchange and credit tightening (perhaps also due to competition with buy now, pay later schemes covered later) resulted in a clear move away from general credit card use. In 2020, small purchases with credit cards were just 20% of all card purchases.

ATM Direct Charging

Originally ATMs were free to use — they only accepted bank cards issued by themselves. Over time, and with the implementation of CECS and EFTPOS, the ATM card network was connected domestically and cards could be used in other ATMs. There was a cost, obviously associated with installing a machine, renting the space, and replenishing cash and receipts.

ATMs began charging fees for withdrawals. The fees could be quite sizable and were not clearly visible to the customer. Private ATMs took this as an opportunity to charge customers extra. Shops installed private ATMs and had no EFTPOS facilities. Pubs, bars, casinos and racing tracks did the same. (Many banks would not install ATMs at these locations.) The fee would only be apparent when the customer saw their transaction history.

In 2007, the RBA asked banks to explain the fee. Many banks did not have a good answer. In 2009, an ATM direct charging mandate was issued. ATMs had to declare the fee before charging the customer. This ATM direct charging mandate was a significant change to the old ATMs, which were difficult to modify.

In 2018, as a gesture to non-bank customers in the wake of a damaging royal commission, CBA dropped its fees to zero. Other banks followed. Private ATMs, some of them in locations not serviced by banks, closed down as cardholders could now go to competitive banks for free.

Eventually, seeing less profit, the big banks started closing their ATMs too, despite the ever-increasing demand for cash. (As mentioned, cash continues to increase, at an ever-declining rate relative to electronic payments.) This, along with COVID-19, may put absolute downward pressure on the need for cash generally with the number of ATMs in Australia declining by 12½% by 2020.

9.

DIRECT ENTRY

THE FIRST WIDELY USED computer-based electronic payments in Australia were interbank transfers (transfers from a client of one bank to a client of another). Every country had their own electronic domestic clearing system. Australia's was called Direct Entry.

Tape Swaps

In the early days of computerisation, organisations centralised the function of interbank transfers rather than have them run out of each branch. Then, someone came up with a great idea. Rather than exchange bits of paper between the banks and re-key information, what if they just ran off the tape from the machine that had fed in all the data? So every day, from the head offices, one bank employee would drive over to the other and exchange tapes — in the garage. This mechanism of exchange was called Direct Entry — a direct entry on the ledger of the account holder.

Eventually, the tape drop-offs were replaced with X.25 (packet switched) network links between banks. Established by Telecom Australia (now Telstra), initially these links served to avoid the physical movement of tapes and made it possible for not just one but several exchanges per day. When branches were computerised, the links allowed mainframe traffic to go from the branches to head office. The links also allowed the connection of automatic teller machines to head office, and provided the backbone EFTPOS and ATM interbank link in Australia. These links allowed the networking of systems within and outside an organisation in an age before the Internet.

These dedicated links became a spaghetti network of interchanges. Taking the Big Four banks, and adding a fifth, increases the network and system costs for all participants (*Figure 31*).

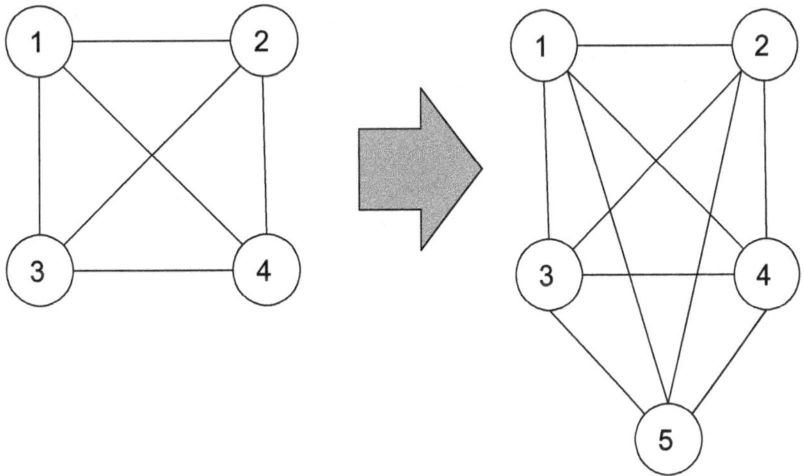

***Figure 31.* Network complexity in an X.25 linked network.**

Every time a new bank needed to be connected, the complexity of adding a new participant meant that a new link needed to be established with all the banks. Each existing bank would charge for the privilege and this cost became larger over time. A new entrant could bypass the complexity by sitting off the back of a Tier 1 player; however, as that entrant became more significant, it introduced risk to the system. There was limited competition for this service so the charges were not as competitive as they could be. Four banks connected to each other would require six links. Five banks would require 10 links, 20 banks would require (19 + 18 + ... + 3 + 2 + 1) 190 links. So, rather than connect directly, some smaller banks would connect to a larger bank and rely on that larger bank to feed it into the rest of the network.

By 2005, even the telco Telstra was growing tired of this X.25 network, and urged the banks to consider an Internet Protocol-based virtual private network (IP VPN).

The issue also extended to CS3 (CECS) ATM and EFTPOS clearing, which used similar links.

So, in 2008, the RBA noted that:

> "While the Board supports the current reform package it nevertheless sees a need for more fundamental reform of the architecture of both the ATM system and the EFTPOS system. In particular, the bilateral nature of these systems means that potential new entrants need to establish connections with each of the existing participants, rather than being able to join the systems through a single point of access. The Board notes that the current technology underpinning the ATM and EFTPOS systems will need to be updated over the next year or so. This provides an opportunity for the industry to improve the architecture of these systems in a way that promotes efficiency and supports more open access. If the industry does not make substantive progress in this direction by March 2010, the Board will consider taking a more active role, perhaps through setting technical standards or using its own operations in the payments system to facilitate reform."

In 2010, the Community of Interest Network (COIN) was formed: a virtual private network most of the banks joined. Telstra could decommission their X.25 links. ANZ, always different, insisted on using SWIFT. RBA was open to the idea and established a Low Value Clearing Service (LVCS) or clearing interconnector that allowed ANZ to use SWIFT FileAct (see below) to send DE messages to the other banks.

This exchange of payments became known as Direct Entry — because it was a direct entry on the ledger. It was also known as BECS or the Bulk Electronic Clearing System. This clearing system is the backbone of payments for businesses and individuals. It is how many workers get paid their salary. Simply address the payment with a BSB and account number, with an account name also required and, while not generally checked, it should represent the legal holder of the account. Payers can add an 18-character description to help the payee identify and reconcile.

The format is fixed-width files. The top line has a header and the bottom line a footer. The dates, totals and counts are contained in the header and footer.

The modern Direct Entry flow is illustrated in *Figure 32*.

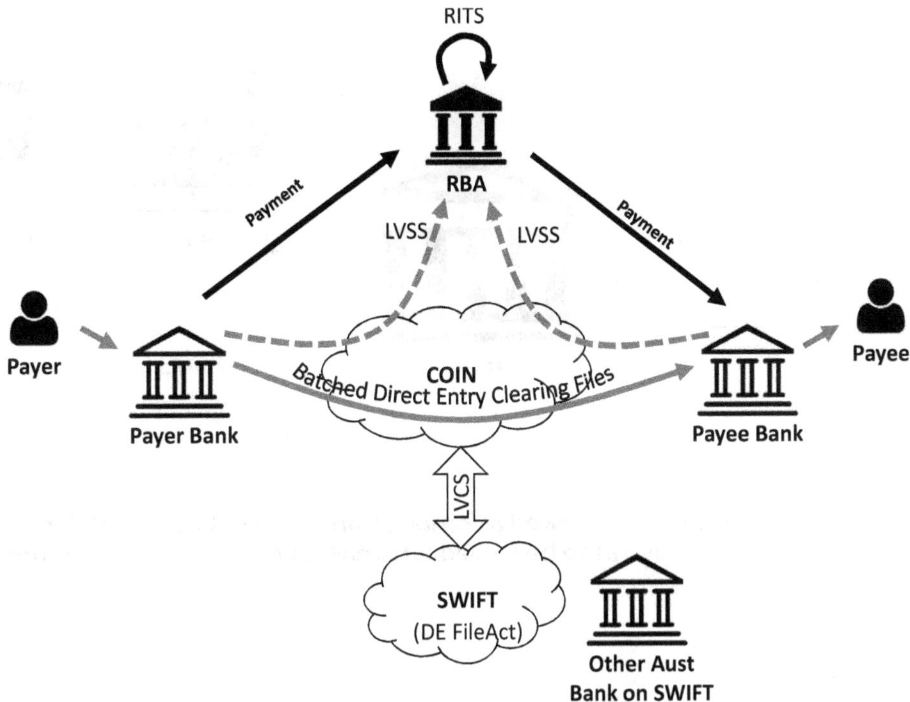

***Figure* 32. Modern Direct Entry, with the COIN, clearing files, Low Value Settlement Service (LVSS) and the SWIFT Interconnect LVCS run by the RBA. Settlement takes place on each Low Value Settlement Service batch on RITS — moving money from one ESA to another.**

Bulk Electronic Clearing System

The Australian Payments and Clearing Association (APCA) in 1994 published the standards for interoperability of Direct Entry files, known as Bulk Electronic Clearing System (BECS) or Clearing System 2 (CS2). In practice, the standard had been used for many years prior, perhaps dating back to 1970.

The number of file exchanges has increased over time. Today, the files are exchanged at 10:00 am, 1:00 pm, 4:00 pm, 6:30 pm, 8:45 pm and 10:30 pm. Government files (pensions etc.) are processed at 7:00 am, 6:15 pm and 9:00 pm and have specific processing dates. Non-government files generally have a processing date of the same day except the 10:30 am file, which is for next-day processing.

Corporate BECS Users

Direct Entry files could be submitted by corporations to their banks for accounts payable and payroll purposes. They also allowed, in custom applications, the generation of cheques, bank cheques, and payment advice letters to be processed by the bank, then the Direct Entry payments (normally direct credits, i.e., pushing funds from the corporate to the recipient) were extracted from the file and sent for inter-bank clearing through BECS.

Banks offered this value-added service as a payables service (*Figure 33*).

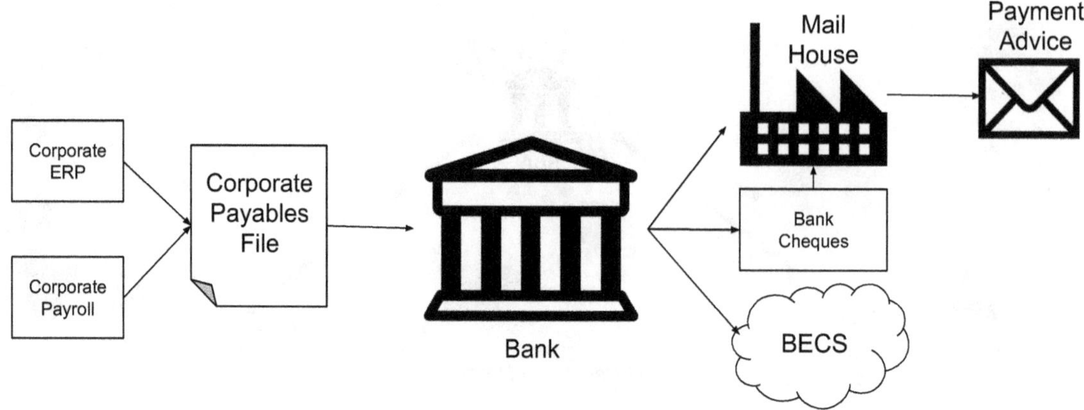

***Figure* 33. Corporate payables files allowed a combination of Direct Entry, bank (or corporate) cheques and payment advices to be mailed (or emailed) to recipients of payments.**

Direct Debit

Direct debit was also supported by the banks through BECS. This allowed a corporate to debit a bank account and credit their own. Corporate participants in Direct Entry, especially direct debit, required an APCA ID or Direct Entry ID to be obtained. This allowed the receiving bank to block a corporate's direct debits, if so instructed by the payee.

While the direct credit was a push payment, the direct debit was a pull payment. This did not mean (contrary to popular belief) that a payee had a permanent debit mandate to take money from an account. The direct debtor was required to keep a record or authority to debit an account by the payer.

» NOTE

While a lot of attention was placed on the security of the credit card number as it could be used to effect a payment via phone, mail or online, Australian account numbers were no less sensitive. A malicious party with access to account numbers could, in theory, run direct debits without strong authorisation processes from those accounts.

BECS Data Exchanged

The BECS data allows the exchange of the following information:

- Payer name, 16 characters
- Payer BSB (6 digits) and account numbers (9 digits)
- Payee name, 32 characters
- Payee BSB and account numbers
- Description, 18 characters
- Amount, up to $99 999 999.99. i.e., less than $100 million.

The payer and payee name should correspond to the legal name of the respective parties. In practice, few banks do check the name, and the restrictive length of 16 characters often means that the name needs to be shortened.

» NOTE

The description on a payment could provide a means for payees to reconcile payments and many organisations use it for this purpose; however, it is generally a manual process as one customer may send a payment in as "Invoice 123", whereas another may use "Inv 123" or just "123." One organisation, Payment Adviser, now part of the ASX listed company InPayTech attempted to put a tiny URL like bit.ly/33g4EC8 and encouraged the recipient to retrieve the details of the payment from that URL.

The limitation of $100 million was based on the fact that payments were not envisaged to go over that amount in the 1960s when the standard was developed. There are stories of organisations missing payments because their large payments over $100 million got truncated.

BSB

Bank, state, and branch (BSB) numbers were the Australian domestic bank and branch identification convention. Consisting of six digits, BSBs are managed and issued by AusPayNet.

Used to identify a specific customer's bank ledger and account on Direct Entry, but also more recently on SWIFT and NPP, the number is made up of several parts. This dates back to times when each branch kept a ledger and the payment needed to be quickly routed, either visually or with basic computers, within a bank to the right place. The first two digits identified the bank and the third digit represented the state. The last three digits of the BSB represented the branch. For example, the Commonwealth Bank was 06, New South Wales state was 2 and Miranda Branch was 204, but internally called 2204 with the BSB being

062-204. Most account numbers at CBA were eight digits, for example, 10000001, but were only unique within a branch. Unlike card primary account numbers (PANs), these numbers had no check digit so transcribers needed to beware. If the BSB number was incorrect, the money could find itself in an account at a different bank branch. If a customer moved residence, they originally needed to move their account to a different branch in order to make withdrawals with the BSB pointing to the new branch.

In order to accommodate more than 100 banks (with some banks having more than one bank number due to acquisitions), AusPayNet started using the first three digits (including the state identifier) to identify the bank.

These days with IT systems, centralised ledgers and online banking, the branch number makes little sense. New banks ignore them using larger account numbers to identify the account across its bank network. Volt Bank used 517-000 for all its accounts with a full nine-digit account number. The branch number these days is used to identify different ledgers, products or core banking systems, and is also used for off-system BSBs (see below).

Government Direct Entry System

The Government Direct Entry System (or GDES) is similar to BECS files (predominantly Centrelink) and originated from the RBA or a large corporate bank.

They are generally exchanged at a certain time, as mentioned earlier. Government files are generally for processing the next day.

》 NOTE

The story with the government delayed processing date is that originally the government file was given to one bank. That bank could process it immediately but would take a day to send it to other banks. So as not to disadvantage customers of other banks, the government requested that payments be held a day. Now every bank gets it at the same time, but the tradition continues.

The Penny Test

One recent way organisations, particularly online organisations, verify that the owner of an account is the person at the end of a screen is the penny test. A small amount or a number of small amounts, less than $20 or less than $1, are secretly sent to an account. The account holder needs to validate the amounts. As only someone with access to the account can validate the amount(s), the online organisation can prove the online entity is the same as the account holder. This is especially useful when obtaining direct debit consent.

ABA File

The ABA file, named by the Australian Banking Association, was a simplified version of the BECS Direct Entry files for use by small, medium, and large organisations to send their payments to the bank for BECS processing. The file did vary slightly from bank to bank, with some banks offering a full payables solution. The payables file included not just the ability to send BECS, but also payment advices, by post or email, automated check, or bank cheque printing.

Sub Accounting

Some banks, especially Westpac, offered the ability for corporate customers to have sub accounts with their own credit limit or balance. They sometimes issued an off-system BSB (OSBSB), which allowed Direct Entry payments to directly hit this virtual account. It was useful for superannuation funds and other managed funds, making reconciliation for corporate customers easy. Customers could also control sub account budgets through the banking system.

Settlement in Direct Entry

Originally Direct Entry was finalised through deferred net settlement. For this reason, some banks delayed crediting the account until the settlement had occurred.

The RBA felt that there was systemic risk in low-value payments, especially Direct Entry and EFTPOS debit card payments (including ATM withdrawals). There was a risk that a bank would fail in between the clearing file being received and the inter-bank settlement completing at the RBA. The RBA also wanted to speed up Direct Entry.

To reduce settlement risk, the Low Value Settlement Service (LVSS) and Low Value Clearing Service (LVCS) was introduced in 2013. Settlements were settled six times per day on Direct Entry.

Float on BECS

Interest on an account for that day is generally calculated as the closing balance of the day. For most of the BECS non-government batches (except 10:30 pm), settlement occurs on the same day and accounts are credited on that same day. This means that at any point in time, payments made before about 6:00 pm are credited to the recipient's account — so there is generally no float revenue for banks.

Costs of BECS

The total cost of Direct Entry to banks in 2008, according to the RBA, was 8 cents for credits and 10 cents for debits.

10.

BPAY BILL PAYMENTS

WITH THE INCREASE in uptake of automatic phone banking (intelligent voice response or IVR) — where a customer could call a bank, an automated machine would voice-guide them through steps and they could enter in data on the phone — a new innovation was trialled with BPAY.

The issue with transferring funds over Direct Entry was that it was not always easy for corporations to know who the money was from and what the payment was for. In the 18-character description, a user could type in the wrong description. A biller receiving an incorrect description could attribute the payment to the wrong bill, and it would be difficult to spot the mistake and get the money back.

Further, the bank account number was cumbersome to enter.

So, in 1997, a scheme was set up between the banks called BPAY, short for bill-pay.

Billers would be assigned a biller code, a four-digit number. (Later, to cater for more billers, the size increased.) Behind the scenes, these mapped to a BSB account number.

Also, the bill would have a customer reference number (CRN) to define a customer. It was followed by a check digit.

Check Digits

Check digits feature in credit card numbers (PANs) and BPAY CRNs. The idea is that if a user makes a single error in typing a number, it should be detected. Note that if two numbers are incorrect, the probability that a check digit algorithm will pick it up is reduced.

There are different algorithms for check digits. The simplest one is called a mod 10 check digit. For example, take the number 12345 . 1+ 2 + 3+ 4 + 5 = 15. 15 mod 10 (the remainder of 15 divided by 10) = 5. So the number, with the check digit, would be 123455.

A simple error like using 2 instead of 3 would be picked up (e.g., 122455); however, a swap would not be, for example, 124355. BPAY allowed billers to come up with their own validation check digit algorithms.

BPAY Credit Card Payments

Initially, all credit card account payments of bills were treated as cash advances and charged at the higher rate from day one. BPAY eventually allowed some billers to accept credit card payments (at a higher cost to the biller, including interchange) that would allow credit card customers to treat the transactions as purchases and get the interest-free benefits and credit card rewards. Customers needed to be vigilant as to which method was used when paying bills by credit card through their bank.

Costs

The cost of each BPAY transaction to the bank was estimated to be 51 cents per transaction, over 10 times Direct Entry or BECS.

Reconciliation

Initially, having individual bill transactions appear on the bank statement was cumbersome, so BPAY introduced files that were sent to billers that aggregated all the day's takings (or all the batch takings) in one to the biller for reconciliation, with only the grand total of the batch listed in the biller's bank statement.

Eventually, BPAY took over the sending of bill payments to biller banks. Today, banks send their BPAY outbound files to BPAY, which distributes the records appropriately to the billers' banks.

BPAY Operation

There are only a few biller banks: the big banks and some of the payment providers with some non-ADI providers providing solutions through bigger banks (like Assembly Payments, eziDebit, redPAP, etc.).

Almost every ADI, on the other hand, supports BPAY bill payments for payer customers.

BPAY periodically issues biller master files (with the biller codes representing the different billers) and check digit formulas to validate the bill reference number.

Different billers have different risk profiles; some bills, once paid, cannot easily be reversed, and have a greater risk of money laundering, so some level of bank-based transaction monitoring is advised.

As shown in *Figure 34*, the steps are summarised as follows :

1. Biller sends a bill to the customer through the mail, electronically or via BPAY View (described below).
2. Customer logs into Internet banking and enters the biller code, customer reference number and amount. (This process could be automated by BPAY View or QR codes, and some banks have implemented intelligent bill scanning through a mobile phone.)
3. Periodically, several times a working day, the payer bank sends a bulk file of bill payments to BPAY.
4. BPAY splits received files and sends them to biller institutions.
5. BPAY sends the RBA positions of all the banks (on a net basis).
6. The next day, the RBA moves money through RITS to settle bill payments.
7. Biller institutions credit billers and send them the biller statements.

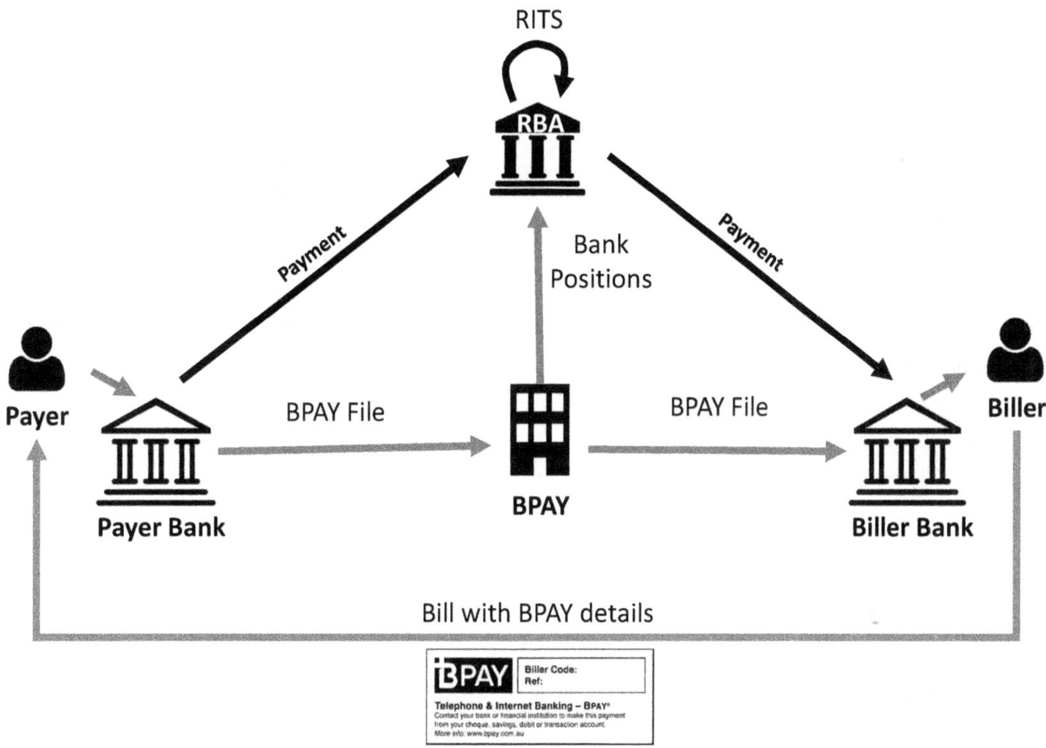

***Figure 34.* BPAY operation for a simple bill payment.**

BPAY View

With the advent of Internet banking around 2002 and with Internet adoption still early, banks were among the first organisations with an electronic channel to customers. To save posting statements, organisations could host an image of the bill and have it delivered to their customer through that customer's Internet bank account. This system was called BPAY View.

The bill was added using the CRN and biller code, with the customer's details sent to the biller who would check that the name matched, and enabled the sharing of bills.

Over time, automated payment of a biller would be enabled through BPAY View; however, as more and more corporations established direct connectivity with their customers over the Internet to provide better online service options, the need for BPAY View diminished. These days, many bills link to the biller's bill portal with providers providing multiple options for bill delivery.

MAMBO

Around 2006, with the success of BPAY View in delivering bills, the Cardlink organisation proposed an electronic replacement to Australia Post: Me At My Bank Online (MAMBO or M@MBO) . The idea was to allow people to address correspondence securely to their Internet banking account using an email-like address or even an email address. Bills and correspondence could be directed in this way.

Interest in the concept was low so a modification was proposed: a real-time, rich information payment scheme, using simple (email-like) addressing. The Reserve Bank took an interest in the project through the Payments System Board.

While initial take-up of all four banks was positive, when the costs came forward, the two Melbourne banks (ANZ and NAB) pulled out. Westpac pulled out as well soon after and the project collapsed.

The RBA had been supportive of the initiative, and the failure of MAMBO left a gap in the objectives of the Payment Systems Board that would result in a new payments solution for Cardlink (later renamed BPAY), Osko.

Competitive Bill Payments Solutions

Some competitive solutions to bill payments were introduced by other providers.

Australia Post

MAMBO's attempts to put Australia Post out of business was reciprocated. For many years, Australia Post was an agency of CBA and continued to play a role in banking through Electronic Funds Transfer at Point of Banking (EFTPOB), Bank@Post and bill payments on behalf of corporations. Over time, they introduced an online bill payment mechanism, Post Billpay, that allowed the payment and retrieval of bills on the Internet. The capability went through a few iterations along with their Digital Mailbox. Most of these ideas failed to get market share and, these days, Post Billpay is a simple payment gateway supported by an in-person solution at post offices.

›› NOTE

Australia Post's history with banking started early. Before federation, some state-based post offices operated post office savings banks, some of which were subsumed by the Big Four, mainly CBA. Along with Telecom Australia (later Telstra), the Postmaster-General's Department had a powerful position in building Australia's infrastructure. Speculation that Australia Post would resume banking was rife during the 2017-2019 banking royal commission until it was officially denied. As we will see, Australia Post has, and continues to play, a prominent role in payments.

Once

Once credit started in 2004, attempting to facilitate bill payments by aggregating them and charging the customer *once* per month or for some defined period. They moved into credit card/line of credit financing for bill payments, then buy now, pay later and became part of flexigroup. The brand is no longer active, having been relaunched as a store credit card scheme, Skye Mastercard.

DEFT

Macquarie Bank's DEFT payments is a one-stop solution that allows bill payment integration to credit cards gateways, bank transfer (through an off-system BSB — OSBSB or direct debit) and, more recently, BPAY. The solution was strong in the property industry: real estate rent payments and strata payments, with good backend integration to key systems in those industries. With better offerings from BPAY and other competitors, DEFT has not really progressed in the market and is now a niche offering.

Later Innovations

BPAY continued to innovate their core product. The addition of QR codes on bills allowed customers to scan their bill rather than type information in. In addition, there was the integration of BPAY View and automated bill payments, and better reconciliation at the invoice or bill level to allow automatic matching for corporate customers.

iCRN (intelligent customer reference numbers) were introduced to allow payments of a bill to expire or to validate the amount. Their use in Internet banking confuses regular payers as the number keeps changing, and often the bank would ask for another second factor authentication validation.

BPAY View lost its popularity as more and more corporations digitised, providing a preferred direct-to-consumer billing service. For small businesses, accounting software such as MYOB, Xero, and Quickbooks from Intuit provided online bill delivery, viewing and payment services. Many merchants utilise PayPal for the payment and delivery of invoices, or other online payment gateways such Square or Stripe. The top end of town developed their own or used industry-specific solutions, ERPs, or customised capabilities from payment service providers such as IP Payments (now Bambora or Ingenico).

BPAY settlement is recognised and effected by the RBA as a RITS settlement; however, it is on a deferred net settlement basis.

The slowness of BPAY as a batch-based solution, and the decline of BPAY View, has probably led to another pivot for Charge Card Services: NPP's Osko overlay as we shall see later. Potentially a major threat to incumbents, action on this front remains slow in keeping with the lack of interest from the big banks.

11.

INTERNATIONAL PAYMENTS

INTERNATIONAL TRADE required the movement of funds between jurisdictions, normally payable in the local currency according to an exchange rate.

A promise to pay had many risks, and the exchange of goods added additional risks. Systems were established to reduce these risks. If anything, over time, the risks grew and traders, banks, and systems became more sophisticated in dealing with them.

The risks increased the expenses of the transaction and, while card schemes eventually established international payment solutions in the retail market, business-to-business transactions and person-to-person transactions continue to take place over different rails. These transactions are called International Money Transfers (IMTs)

Telegraphic Transfers and the Telex

International transfer orders would make their way to banks, where clerical staff would transcribe them on large electric precision typewriters that recorded ledger entries just in the right place on large cards or ledger papers that represented Nostro and Vostro accounts. A paper order would then be transmitted, sometimes by post, sometimes by wire as a telegraph.

Original wire transfers were in Morse code, or similar, over copper wire. A fluctuation of the voltage would indicate a signal. Eventually, with telephony, came the automatic telex machine. A typewriter-like device, it could automatically transcribe a signal into meaningful text over cable or radio waves. It was still text, and someone had to read it to make sense of it.

Sometimes they did not make any sense.

Telegraphic transfers (TT) were essentially notes between banks. While there were conventions and standards, these promise-to-pay letters were loosely formatted, and could be misinterpreted and were error prone.

SWIFT

In order to improve the accuracy of cross-border payment instructions and automate the process of making international payments, in a remarkable act, several banks in the world self-organised into an association. Four years later, in 1977, the Society for Worldwide Interbank Financial Telecommunication (SWIFT) started sending automated computerised messages. Telegraphic transfers and, later, telex, were common globally until the early 1990s. Even today, TT is used to describe these payments, long after the retirement of the last telegraph operator, and decades after the decommissioning of the last telex machine.

Essentially, the core payment message of SWIFT is a promise to pay.

The SWIFT organisation, like the card schemes, was owned by the banks. SWIFT was legally structured as an association, though these days it provides many services and has a very corporate sales model.

SIBOS

SWIFT International Banking Operations Seminar (SIBOS) was initially an international seminar to aid technology and operations information dissemination for SWIFT functionality. These days, it is one of the more expensive public conferences in the world with tickets costing €3 200, and banks and tech companies spend much more to showcase their capability. Run annually, it is a showcase of banking and payments. Nowadays, banks use it as a chance to establish correspondent banking arrangements at the institutional level. Countries take turns in hosting the event, booking out a city's best conference centre. (In Sydney, it has been held at the International Exhibition Centre.) Tech companies and banks will hire square spaces, normally 4 metres by 6 metres, sometimes up to eight of them, and construct a booth or exhibit often costing $100 000s in construction alone, complete with private meeting rooms, exhibits and showcases or gimmicks to attract passersby. Ironically operations staff are the last people to be invited to SIBOS these days.

Correspondent Banking

SWIFT payments generally are a promise to pay. With more than 11 000 banks worldwide, of varying reliability, risk management of payments could be unmanageable for any single bank.

Some large banks, with global operations offer correspondent banking facilities.

In each country, there is normally at least one bank that acts as a global intermediary bank. Intermediary banks are almost synonymous with correspondent banks from a functional point of view, with the main difference being the number of payee currencies and countries that the bank can deal with. Basic intermediary banks tend to be single country, providing USD and local currency support, with correspondent banks supporting several currencies and a number of countries/sub continents. One of the reasons for the blurring of lines is that, to support intermediate bank functions, a bank needs accounts in several countries and this could enable correspondent banking. For example, the Big Four banks in Australia act as intermediate banks for Australian payments. They all have New Zealand offices, and many have branches and strong relations with Asia, the United Kingdom and the US. A few of them are strong in the Pacific Islands, and have Vostros in Europe and South Africa. At SIBOS, they all sell their capabilities as correspondent banks.

The purpose of correspondent banking is to underwrite or cover a payment between two mutually unconnected banks. For example, if a customer of Westpac wishes to send a payment to a customer of the US bank Capital One, it would do so through JP Morgan Chase. Westpac holds a Vostro account with JP Morgan Chase which can be used to fund the payment. Capital One trusts JP Morgan Chase; with US banks regulated through the United States Federal Reserve, their payments to each other are honoured. Even if the balance is low, JP Morgan Chase trusts Westpac to settle or top up its Vostro account.

In some cases, a correspondent bank could be in a third country. Also, there may be no Vostro accounts. In such cases, the correspondent bank may cover the payment and settle the payments at the end of the day. Also, in some situations, more than one correspondent bank could be used to complete the payment.

Like everything in banking, nothing is free. Correspondent banking came with a fee. This will be covered later.

Series versus Cover Payments

The correspondent/intermediary international banking networks supported two modes of payment. Series payments followed a customer instruction with an interbank payment as it made its way through the network, with each step taking place through the intermediary and the transfer (or the institutional promise to pay) travelling along with it. They often took longer (for multi-step payments) as each bank in the chain needed to check and validate the payment, and ensure it could be funded.

Cover payments allowed payment messages to be sent more directly to the recipient banks, with the correspondent bank sending the transfer (interbank IOU) in addition to the customer transaction.

Cover payments could become quite complicated. Consumer payments could take place, netted off or aggregated so that the institutional payment became disconnected from the original.

Post-FATF, 9/11 and AML/CTF measures, it was discovered that it was possible for large banks to be implicitly involved in money laundering through their funding of a payment between two banks that, in the end-to-end flow, may involve the funding of UNSC sanctioned entities.

To close potential gaps with cover payments, generally, cover payments were separated from institution-to-institution payments, the latter being the funding and settlement of bank global markets trading activities or funding Vostro accounts. Cover payments were required to echo the payer and beneficiary information of the transfer, and local regulators of the correspondent bank generally required those banks to monitor these payments for AML/CTF compliance.

AML/CTF in SWIFT

We mentioned earlier the international FATF initiative.

Within a country, money laundering and terrorism financing is controlled by monitoring the bank accounts of residents, proper KYC procedures and, in Australia, through suspicious matter reporting (SMR) and threshold transaction reporting (TTR) to AUSTRAC.

Like with any payment, SMRs and TTRs had to be filed by banks. In addition, AUSTRAC asked for a unique report, the international funds transfer instruction (IFTI) to be supplied for any payment going overseas.

Initially, only SWIFT was targeted. Somewhat inexplicably, card payments were excluded. Perhaps at the time, card merchants were less risky. Also, all the major schemes used by US citizens were US schemes, and the US Government felt they could control and monitor them and, given the US was pushing the AML/CTF agenda after 9/11, most countries have overlooked these payments.

AML/CTF introduced the largest fines for banks and, sure enough, national regulators have issued them. In just four months in 2019, USD $7.7 billion in fines were issued globally. In Australia, AUSTRAC initiated action for all four AML/CTF vehicles, including against CBA for not filing TTRs for IDMs, against Westpac for failing to lodge IFTIs on bulked international transfer distribution, on TAB Corp for failing to lodge SMRs in cases it knew could have been potentially fraudulent, and on NAB for discrepancies with its KYC process.

Primarily due to this fear factor, banks are reluctant to let customers do external international fund transfers, and many ban money service businesses using bank accounts as part of their business. This is beacause if a bank knowingly participates in an international fund transfer without declaring the beneficial recipient and ultimate payer, they can be fined. Even if the money service business does declare the IFTIs, banks are still reluctant to participate.

Of all the AUSTRAC breaches, Westpac's IFTI breach was terrifying and not just because of an AUSTRAC fine. Executives could face jail time and, due to the international nature of the failure, Westpac could be under the US regulator spotlight as well and other national regulators. Westpac's correspondent banking partner was JP Morgan and, if JP Morgan exited the relationship, no bank would pick up a hot potato. Together with the potential loss of a banking relationship, there was also a chance of a ban from US AUSTRAC counterparts, FinCEN (United States Financial Crimes Enforcement Network) and OFAC (United States Office of Foreign Assets Control[100]). This possibility could spell disaster for Westpac.

For these reasons, SWIFT is generally the only bank-supported international funds transfer mechanism today, with innovation in international non-card payments being frozen since 9/11.

AML/CTF requires banks to impose a number of checks. The originator needs to be properly approved following KYC procedures. (If they have an account, they already have been.)

The payment instruction must include identifying information of the sender and recipient, including residential address. Both are run through a sanctions check to ensure there is no fuzzy match with UNSC sanctioned entities. If there is, a payment is stopped for manual checking and could be returned. If suspicious, an SMR is triggered to AUSTRAC. If the bank suspects money laundering, terrorism financing, tax evasion or fraud, the account can be closed. A bank need not disclose reasons for closing an account and, in some cases, is not required to advise if a payment has failed. Screening lists are generally available from FATF lists. In addition, Australia has its own list of terrorist organisations.

There are several issues with this system. First, names are abbreviated on payments so this makes false positives or false negatives more likely. Second, many banks do not check that the recipient name matches their books, if they are acting as a payee bank. Given FATF countries share largely similar lists, this risk is lower; however, this gap should be tightened in the next few years. Third, the quality of KYC processes varies by country. Australia's KYC process is weaker these days despite an early tough policy; however, as few, if any,

---

100 Counterparty to the Department of Foreign Affairs and Trade/AUSTRAC, administers sanctions. Reports to the United States Treasury.

international UNSC sanctioned entities are based here, the risk may be low — though expect action here in the coming years. Fourth, the sanction lists are very vague. Sometimes just a name, and a common one, is enough to get an innocent person caught up in the process. There is not much recourse sadly.

Speed of SWIFT

SWIFT was an apronym, an acronym that spelt a contextually meaningful word. It was meant to be fast. Indeed, SWIFT messages are literally lightning fast, travelling over wire at the speed of light, basically instantaneous. Yet it could take days for a SWIFT transfer to hit the other account.

Historically, with telegraphic transfers, SWIFT transactions were a drawn-out affair. A customer in a bank would have to fill in a form, that form would be express delivered to head office, entered on a Nostro and Vostro, transmitted by wire. The process would then be reversed at the other end with the money recorded in the branch ledger days later. It was faster than surface mail, but slow by modern standards. While many banks have automated the processes since the emergence of SWIFT, smaller banks still have manual processes, with some branches sending faxes to head office for re-keying, even relatively recently.

The other problem is settlement risk. Banks generally are reluctant to release money for an IOU (which, in essence, is the consumer SWIFT message) until they have actually been paid.

The new AML/CTF measures following the 9/11 attacks introduced additional processes that required some or all payments to go through manual checks. Too often, due to the free form of SWIFT messages, and complications in addressing them, payments would need to be corrected. All this slowed payments down (and added to the costs) so these days, SWIFT can take normally up to two business days, sometimes longer.

Bangladesh Bank Cyber Heist

In 2016, Bangladesh's Central Bank's payment applications were compromised by malware or viruses running on workstations. On Thursday 4 February 2016, attackers accessed the payment systems in the bank. SWIFT software was compromised. The attackers generated SWIFT messages, authorised by Bangladesh Bank and transferred, from their account with the Federal Bank of New York, money to various parties in the Philippines, Sri Lanka and Asia. The attackers transferred almost USD $1 billion. The bank was unable to get the SWIFT printer working on Friday due to a computer malfunction, possibly caused by the hackers. Eventually, after a few days, the bank could determine what had taken place. Most of the transfers were stopped and recovered, but $81 million remains unrecovered, siphoned through a bank in the Philippines, laundered through dormant accounts, and promptly transferred to gambling entities. A bank manager in the Philippines was convicted for money laundering in 2019.

» NOTE

The Nigerian letter scam was a letter purportedly from a public figure or official seeking to launder money out of the country. The recipient victim would be offered a share of the money if they assisted. The exercise would be drawn out over a period, with the trickster gaining the confidence of the victim, eventually resulting in a request for the victim to deposit a so-called nominal amount (but in general a large amount of money, the money to be defrauded) to an account to facilitate a bribe or activate an account. Eventually, the victim would discover they had been swindled, but often too late. Originally, these scams took place over SWIFT, but as banks tightened controls on these through FATF (and thanks to the relatively slow speed of SWIFT), Moneygram and Western Union were used. They work through significant criminal operations, targeting one gullible person out of thousands so, even though the vast majority of people don't fall for the trap, the volume of attempts means that some will. These days, the letter has moved online and to social media. The scam is sometimes a proposed romance and, every year, millions are stolen from unsuspecting victims.

Addressing SWIFT Payments

SWIFT payments are addressed using a bank identification code (BIC), also known as a business identifier code. It is an eight-character code followed by a three-character branch identifier (if unused, then "XXX").

The BIC is defined by ISO 9362, and the two-letter country code, not to be confused with the Internet domain country code, ISO 3166 (e.g., US, GB or AU). SWIFT issues BICs as per ISO 9362 (and charges for them).

The first four letters of the BIC are the bank code. Some examples are the Big Four CTBA (from Commonwealth Trading Bank of Australia), WPAC, ANZB and NATA. The next two letters are the ISO 3166 country code; for example, AU for Australia. The seventh and eighth are generally the location 2 for New South Wales, 3 for Victoria, and a city code S for Sydney and M for Melbourne. In many cases, the last three digits are not used. Most Australian banks have one SWIFT BIC for retail customers to avoid confusion; for example, our Big Four again: CTBAAU2S, WPACAU2S, ANZBAU3M and NATAAU3303M. They use other BICs for trading purposes.

A SWIFT message needs to include an account number. There is some confusion with this. Each country has a basic bank account number or BBAN that is normally registered with SWIFT by the clearing authority. To send a payment to Australia, the standard is to include the BSB six digits to the left of the account number.

In Europe, the international bank account number or IBAN is used for an account number. IBAN is defined by ISO 13616, with SWIFT again acting as the registration body for the format of IBANs in each country. The IBAN starts with a two-letter country code, like the BIC, defined by ISO 3166. The remaining digits include the bank, branch number (in some cases) and bank account number.

Construction of the BIC and account number messages to other countries can be complex but, essentially, just these two fields need to be filled in so the recipient should check with their bank what their SWIFT BIC and SWIFT account number is. Some online banking sites in Australia try to make it easy by copying the domestic electronic clearing system of some countries as if we were in that country and, behind the scenes, populating the SWIFT BIC and account numbers:

- United States — Fedwire routing number
- United Kingdom — Bank sort code
- New Zealand — National Clearing Code
- India — Indian Financial System Code.

In addition, the payment needs the name of the beneficiary and their residential address, and often the purpose of the transfer.

Like the postal mail system, as SWIFT fields are freeform, sometimes it is hard to locate the destination account automatically so manual corrections are required. Some banks use sophisticated software to autocorrect (called straight-through processing or STP), and some intermediary and correspondent banking partners charge extra for these poorly formatted messages as they require manual effort. For this reason, banks try and fix the messages themselves, and sometimes need to go back to the customer. All this adds time and cost. Worse, it could result in a lost payment to the wrong address.

SWIFTNet

Originally, just like Australia's electronic payments networks, connectivity to SWIFT was via X.25 links. Every bank needed to connect directly. Clearly, and not just in Australia, this grew complex and expensive, and the technology was eventually superseded. SWIFT replaced these links from 2001 with a modern, Internet Protocol (IP)-based network.

›› NOTE

Use of the Internet Protocol refers to how computers talk to each other in an environment where there could be lots of computers from two to potentially billions. Using the protocol does not always mean that the computers are on the Internet. The standardisation of the use of this protocol has revolutionised how computers and devices can talk to each other as so many machines and systems are designed to support it.

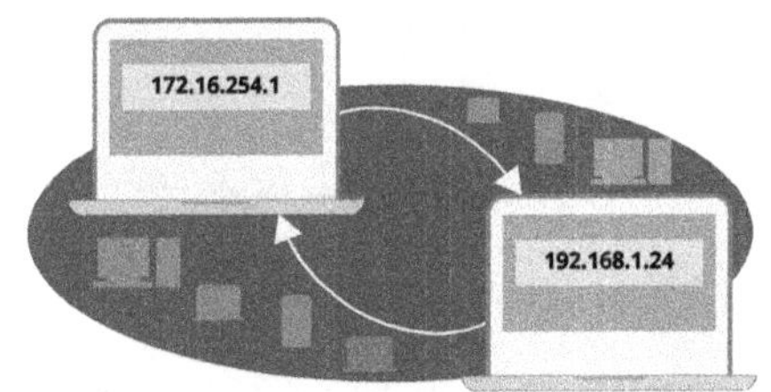

SWIFT, over time, established three data centres: in the US, the Netherlands and Switzerland (*Figure 35*). These were linked with dedicated lines, including dedicated submarine cables. All three centres are designed to handle global load and the loss of any two centres can be sustained by the third.

Multiple options exist for institutions to connect to SWIFT. From connecting to a bank that already has a connection to connecting to one or more SWIFTNet data centres, either through some form of direct link or an Internet-based virtual private network. By connecting to more than one data centre, a bank can ensure resilience if one link or data centre were to fail. In practice, most highly available banks have multiple data centres so the connections are still complex.

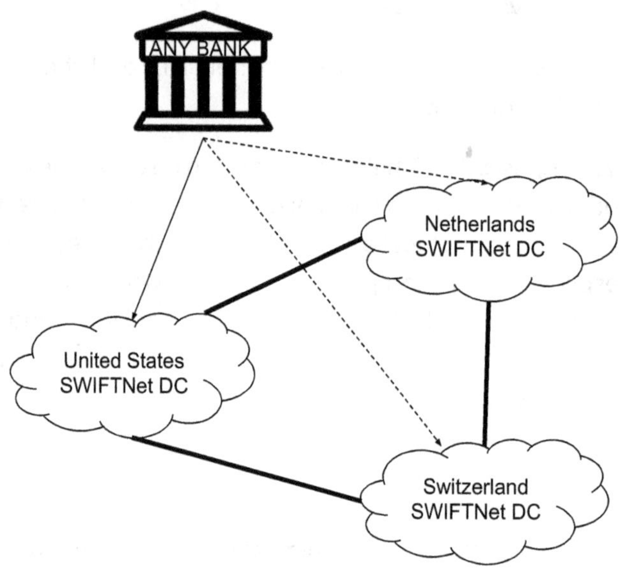

***Figure 35.* Architecture of SWIFTNet.**

SWIFT gpi

SWIFT gpi (global payments initiative) was originally designed as a corporate solution to allow a bank's corporate customers to send and receive SWIFT payments efficiently through the SWIFT network. It is now also used by second-tier banks to effect SWIFT payments. It includes a number of tools to trace payments and fees.

SWIFT FIN

SWIFT FIN is the primary financial message that is the backbone of SWIFT.

By 1988, *SWIFT I* was processing 1 460 member banks in 68 countries and passing a million messages per day worth $246 million. The market had outgrown its systems and *SWIFT II*, which was in development for nine years, was unreliable and did not recover well after failure. It was only in late 1990 that just 39 banks migrated[101] to what is called SWIFT FIN and, for good reason, SWIFT did not want to rock the boat again for over 30 years.

[101] Scott

SWIFT MT Messages

Originally, MT (message type) messages followed what would be called ISO 15022 standards. These were fixed-width messages like the card ISO 8583 messages, followed by specially defined text fields. Interestingly, they looked quite similar to the standards used in telegraphs and telex.

Common messages are:

1. MT 103: A credit transfer initiated by a customer. This could be a series transfer (so the bank IOU is contained in the customer IOU) or it could be a covered transfer, where the bank IOU and customer IOU travel their own routes to the destination bank.
2. MT 101: Generally only used if a corporate is on the SWIFT network. Rather than use the IMT form on their bank's corporate Internet banking site, the corporate can send a payment request directly to the bank of their choice where they would generally have a bank account. That bank essentially converts the MT 101 to an MT 103.
3. MT 202 COV: A message to or from an intermediary (or correspondent) bank covering a customer's credit transfer. It was introduced by AML/CTF to identify the ultimate recipients of an institutional payment.
4. MT 400: Advice that a payment is coming.
5. MT 700: Letter of credit (followed by a suite of messages, to release or not release, and to make payment).
6. MT 940: A statement of an account in electronic format.

A full treatment of MT messages would fill another book so we will leave it here. Suffice to say that the messages covered foreign exchange, money markets and derivatives settlement, securities, commodities and paper instruments (cheques and travellers cheques).

Fixed-width had its limitations: extending fields for new functionality became problematic, and repurposing fields (e.g., address lines used for email) led to interbank inconsistencies, somewhat similar to telex challenges). A new standard was required. MX was designed to solve these problems.

SWIFT InterAct

SWIFT InterAct replaces SWIFT FIN for the new message types. The new message type MX was designed to overcome the limitations of the old, and provide better interoperability between systems, banks and organisations. The solution was ISO 20022.

ISO 20022

SWIFT was in need of a better message format that could provide richer information.

Australian Connection

Australian superannuation payments were complicated. Contributions needed to be sent to the correct account, and there were different types: employer contributions, salary sacrifice, personal contributions and spouse contributions to name a few. Often payments went missing or went to the wrong account or were taxed incorrectly. The industry through the Investment and Financial Services Association (IFSA), later the Financial Services Council (FSC), formed a number of working groups to assist in the development of standards to facilitate managed funds and superannuation transactions:

- Superannuation Electronic Commerce (SuperEC)
- Managed Fund Electronic Commerce (MFundEC)
- Superannuation Wealth and Investment Management Electronic Commerce (SwimEC).

SuperEC and MFundEC were set up to address inefficiencies and payment reconciliation issues in the Australian wealth industry. Transactions (e.g., contributions and rollovers) were sent as paper with payments sent separately. Also, there was no industry product registry to allow payers to send the documents and payments to the correct entity (e.g., the specific superannuation product).

MFundEC had worked with the FIX standards body to expand their standards to incorporate managed funds. SWIFT saw this move as a reason to expand their standards; they saw FIX as a competitor. FIX remains very big in the US, especially for equities and markets trading. Around 2000, SWIFT identified that they wanted to extend their footprint by expanding into markets other than just payments. They identified wealth management (which they called collective investment vehicles or CIV) as a big opportunity.

SWIFT saw the work being done in Australia with the industry associations. They invited an IFSA representative, Dr Andrew Blair, to become a member of their group to create a common standard.

A small team of four people started looking at the development of the next version of the SWIFT MT messages, version 2 of ISO 15022. This would be later called SWIFT ISO 20022. These Australian-initiated wealth management messages were the first message standards in ISO 20002.

UNIFI

The ISO 20022 universal financial industry message scheme (UNIFI) was designed to bring together message formats from all over the financial services arena. The new messages replacing MT messages were dubbed MX.

A simple idea at first was: what if we could standardise every payment into one format? What if we could use that format everywhere: for international payments between individuals, between banks, for domestic payments, card-based payments, institutional payments, central bank payments, for B2B, for everything?

The vision was good, and most executives and managers bought into it. The problems were several fold. Essentially, the devil was in the detail.

This new version of SWIFT was XML based. XML was an extensible markup language. Inspired by the Web and HTML, it used tags instead of unlabelled fixed positions to define each field.

If later, another field was required, it could be added in without older systems getting too fussed. XML, in a simplified format, looked like this:

```
<payment>
        <sender bank>ABC Bank</sender bank>
        <sender account>1234</sender account>
        <recipient bank>XYZ Bank</recipient bank>
        <recipient account>2468</recipient account>
        <amount>123.00</amount>
</payment>
```

It was easy to read and easy to understand. The vision was clear. The executives and futurists left the room, and the designers took over.

However, as the standard developed, so did the challenges.

Competing Standards

ISO 20022 was a slow-moving beast. Other more proprietary protocols were being developed in the industry:

- Financial Information eXchange (FIX), a US-based standard for trade business
- IBM Information FrameWork (IFW)
- Open Financial Exchange (OFX), an Intuit/Microsoft initiative
- IFX/Nacha standards in the US for domestic clearing (ACH, automated clearing house), health and government benefits
- Financial Data Exchange (FDX), another US standard
- Banking Industry Architecture Network (BIAN), initiated by SAP.

The low blow was our own ATO. Australia had assisted in starting the ISO 20022 global movement (which may prove to be one of the great payment innovations of the century). The initial use case was superannuation payments. The FSC took the idea and business case to the ATO. ISO 20022 was now being looked at by MAMBO and then NPP, who urged the ATO to await a better solution that integrated with payments. The ATO decided to institute its own standard, SuperStream. Most payments are considered as paid the moment the funds leave a bank account. The ATO could change the rules, and they did, with a bizarre regulated benefit afforded to their own solution. SuperStream payments needed to come through a clearing house. The clearing house adds delays to the payment. Unless that clearing house is the restricted ATO Small Business Superannuation Clearing House, the funds were not considered paid until they hit the fund. This rule continues to trap businesses wishing to clear super payments on a deadline or before the end of their financial year, generally 30 June, with the expense only registered the next financial year. SuperStream was overkill. A simpler solution could have sufficed in the interim as NPP came online.

Nevertheless, despite the competition, ISO 20022 ploughed on. No other standard had widespread adoption in the industry.

Some Drawbacks

There were a few drawbacks or traps for new players. XML was all the rage when they started working on the standard around 2007. By then, the father of XML, HTML, was almost 30 years old. Like all technologies, it started falling out of favour for all sorts of reasons. The current favourite is JSON REST APIs. The United Kingdom used JSON in their open banking standards, including for their payments, claiming it was aligned to ISO 20022. This was a substantially misleading claim, in fact, almost scandalous, and it is surprising the technologists got away with it though they were trying to do the right thing (for the reasons here and below). In truth, there is no easy way to transpose the two formats.

Second, XML is quite bloated. Tag names get duplicated; for example, above, "sender bank," is repeated. Bandwidth costs time and money and, in the fast-moving world of payments, storage can be an issue too.

The third reason is complexity. "A payment is a payment is a payment," was a famous catch cry. In reality, they are all quite different. Mastercard uses multiple messages to effect a payment: an authorisation followed by a financial message. New Zealand domestic bulk payments literally settle before interchange (called SBI). EFTPOS in Australia, from a user point of view, looks and feels like a credit card transaction, but it is a single message system. Australian domestic payments on the New Payments Platform look up an address and check the account before making a payment, and settlement is simultaneous. Faster payments in the United Kingdom have settlement happen soon after and, in RTGS, the clearing message is the settlement message. In payments, there are debit requests and credit transfers. There could be a single payment or multiple payments, instructions, and notifications, messages and statements, and the list goes on.

There are, so far, 25 different business domains within ISO 20022. Consider these as totally different message families, as shown in *Table 9*.

Table 9.

Top-level business domains of ISO 20022.

No.	Code	Purpose
1	acmt	Account Management
2	admi	Administration
3	auth	Authorities
4	caaa	Acceptor to Acquirer Card Transactions
5	caam	ATM Management
6	cain	Acquirer to Issuer Card Transactions
7	camt	Cash Management

No.	Code	Purpose
8	casp	Sale to Point of Interaction Card Transactions
9	catm	Terminal Management
10	catp	ATM Card Transactions
11	colr	Collateral Management
12	fxtr	Foreign Exchange Trade
13	head	Business Application Header
14	pacs	Payments Clearing and Settlement
15	pain	Payments Initiation
16	reda	Reference Data
17	remt	Payments Remittance Advice
18	secl	Securities Clearing
19	seev	Securities Events
20	semt	Securities Management
21	sese	Securities Settlement
22	setr	Securities Trade
23	tsin	Trade Services Initiation
24	tsmt	Trade Services Management
25	tsrv	Trade Services

In addition, each domain has different messages. Take payments initiation; for example, (pain), as shown in *Table 10*.

Table 10.
ISO 20022 pain (payment initiation) messages.

No.	Code	Description
1	pain.001	Customer Credit Transfer Initiation
2	pain.002	Customer Payment Status Report
3	pain.006	Payment Cancellation Request
4	pain.007	Customer Payment Reversal
5	pain.008	Customer Direct Debit Initiation

No.	Code	Description
6	pain.009	Mandate Initiation Request
7	pain.010	Mandate Amendment Request
8	pain.011	Mandate Cancellation Request
9	pain.012	Mandate Acceptance Report
10	pain.013	Creditor Payment Activation Request
11	pain.014	Creditor Payment Activation Request Status Report
12	pain.017	Mandate Copy Request
13	pain.018	Mandate Suspension Request

Cutting the cake in ISO 20022 was done by slicing according to business domain, an application of Conway's Law. Business domains were controlled by organisational members of the ISO standards group. SWIFT had gone crazy with their messages and everyone left them alone. The card representatives did the same with the card messages and SWIFT was left out. One payment type could span multiple domains. NPP, for example, covers more than six. How much of the complexity was intrinsic and how much was overdesign is a valid query.

Fourth is the length of time to implement. Despite the apparent speed of innovation we see in society today, it is getting harder and harder to kill old technologies. ISO 20022 was proposed and developed in 2007. Yet, the first implementation will go live in 2021. Even optimistically, the MT messaging will be decommissioned at the earliest in 2025. That is an 18-year implementation lag before it can be widely used.

Fifth is interpretation. As much as the standard was intended to standardise, there is a lot open to interpretation. For an organisation seeking to supplement information and add to ISO 20022, it is not practical to go back to the organisation for guidance. Even with the most basic element, such as target bank account number, one internal paper suggested five ways of implementing the standard to carry the account number. In Australia, two initiatives were attempting to do substantially a similar thing. BPAY's MAMBO (which failed for the non-technical reasons mentioned earlier) and RBA's NPP were seeking to replace the simple message of Direct Entry (six core fields, 25 fields for the full file) with something that was faster, and initially extended the description from 18 to 280 characters.

Sixth is verbosity. Put this all together and we get 189 lines for a simple payment that was one line in the old telegraphic transfer world.

Seventh is interoperability. The challenge with conversion from one standard to another is that details are often lost in the conversion process. This will dog the industry, especially when old and new systems need to coexist, in particular, for cards, which have millions of merchants on old technology not changing anytime soon. We may see the death of the card before we see message modernisation.

So what does this mean? Yes, there is one standard, sort of like one set by the United Nations, an umbrella group that recognises most. Any attempt to code or to switch a payment for one system will not enable that switching to be reused for another. Populating the message is not intuitive. Reading a manual will not provide sufficient information to expect that a payment will work. Samples are required and they must be tested against every scenario. It is more an art than a science. ISO 20022 utilities can be designed, but they will only work for that use case not for others. A payment by card to a merchant, a transaction at an ATM, by SWIFT or by NPP may seem the same, but use very different payment messages.

So how did this happen? Is the world too complex to allow a simplified standard to work? The old system ain't broke so why fix it too much? Is the payment world fragmented by organisational divides and, politically, Conway's Law comes into play out of an instinctive need to survive? Are there two classes of people: those who know how things work and those who instruct, and the two do their own thing? It could be all of those things.

An Alternative

As challenging as it sounds, now may be the time for a slight improvement to ISO 20022, a small change to a 20-year-old standard.

What if we made a minor modification to the payment message? What if we created an envelope: where the payment came from, where it is going, how much, a short description or reference, a unique reference and, within the payload, the full ISO 20022?

This would allow us to implement standardised switching and basic processing, making payment messaging more accessible to the public.

Hopefully, over time, payments will be simplified so that simple messaging can suffice for most transactions in the future.

ISO 20022: The Best Solution for Now

Despite all the issues, ISO 20022 remains the best initiative to allow payment messaging to interoperate. It is a start, but not the end. Any future initiative will probably build on ISO 20022. What we need now is a universal simplification of payments. This will allow greater innovation and interoperability between systems.

SWIFT FileAct

SWIFT supports a file transfer protocol. These files are used to transfer bulk files. For example, in Australia, Direct Entry files are sometimes passed through SWIFT (from corporations or the ANZ Bank). New Zealand and some other countries use it to exchange domestic payment files. Bulk payments are sometimes issued through SWIFT FileAct to avoid bank IMT charges, though banks should be careful with AML/CTF screening, as Westpac discovered when AUSTRAC took action in 2019.

SWIFT Operation

SWIFT operates like an Internet network, sending messages between banks with SWIFT infrastructure maintaining resilience and adding value-added services. *Figure 36* shows a covered payment flowing through the network.

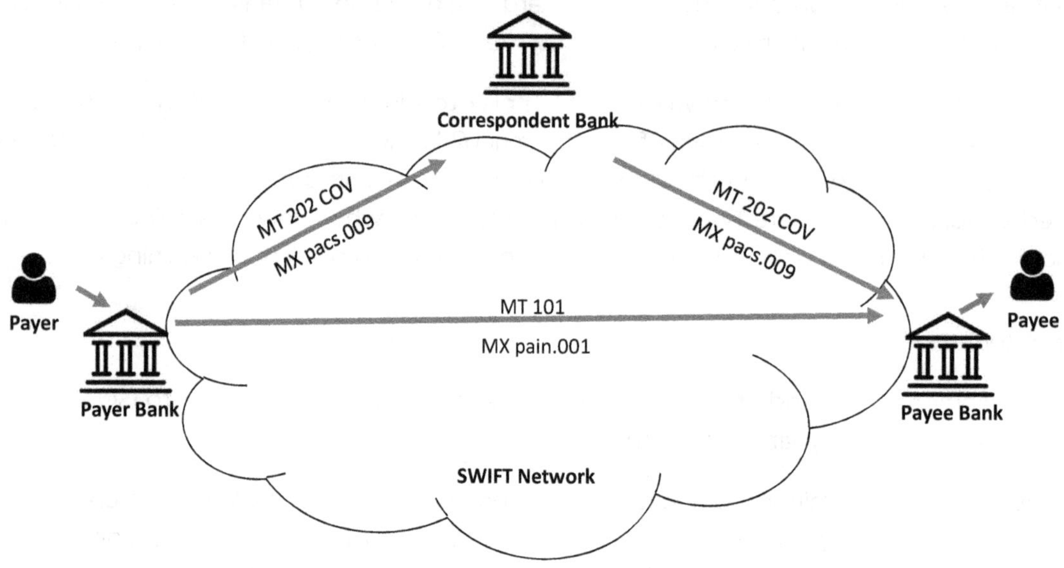

Figure 36. **SWIFT clearing messages: MT and MX formats for a simple transfer.**

SWIFT Connectivity Software

SWIFT provides a number of software and a few hardware solutions. Some are required to access SWIFT, others are value-added products that are sold/licensed by SWIFT for ancillary purposes. Some of these are included in *Table 11.*

Table 11.

SWIFT connectivity and integration solutions.

Solution	Description
SWIFT Alliance Access	A messaging level application that supports the creation of various SWIFT messages (MT, MX, and Files) and allows the management of them.
SWIFT Alliance Entry	An entry-level solution instead of SWIFT Alliance Access.
SWIFT Alliance Messaging Hub	Extending/replacing Alliance Access, a messaging and workflow engine allowing orchestration of business processes.

Solution	Description
SWIFT Access Lite 2	The cloud version of SWIFT Alliance Access/ Entry/Hub using the SWIFT Community Cloud.
SWIFT Alliance Integrator	SWIFT's middleware is used for message transformation and integration between SWIFT and/or other systems.
SWIFTNet Link	The direct SWIFT access link, network protocol level solution.

Foreign Exchange

Foreign exchange (Forex or FX) under the Bretton Woods system was straightforward. The rates were fixed by the central banks, pegged originally to gold then to a basket of the top currencies. Essentially, central banks could exchange currencies at the determined rate and, due to balanced payments, whatever went out came back in again.

This system broke down, and the so-called free market was not organised like it was in domestic trading floors, with regulations and governance. It was largely free-for-all.

Banks would trade directly, shop for a good deal and make the payment.

Some banks would be known for certain currencies. When Australia made its way into a floated currency, CBA, with its trade banking business, still had a strong connection to the government and became a major AUD liquidity source. And remains so until this day, with Citibank and Deutsche Bank for the USD and EUR.

Over time, trading banks and corporate banking trades were dwarfed by institutional or speculative trades by 20% to 80% or more.

Like most trades, in FX, there is no buy or sell price. There is one price: the deal price. There are no fees on trades in the core market.

Trades were made and any profit was not between banks, but from their clients.

Small trades would not be handled by the trading desk. Retail Smalls, as they were known, would be bulked up and traded as a whole in the millions, or tens of millions or more. Sometimes, the bigger the deal, the better the price. On the other hand, clearing a big transaction, like the purchase of an Airbus A380 for $500 million, will send markets crashing if not done carefully, so the trader would break the amount down.

Calling around was cumbersome. Brokers were inefficient at finding the best price.

Paul Reuter established a telegraph office soon after the dropping of the English Channel submarine cable between London and continental Europe. By providing regular stock prices, traders could get early scoops. The company Paul Reuter founded, Reuters, became and continues to be a markets and news provider. In the late 1980s, Reuters was trying to publish the now fluctuating FX price through new computerised messaging services. It discovered a potential solution in the market to allow traders to trade directly. The D2000 system allowed bilateral trading and recorded trades in real-time so the rates could be published (and subscribed to for a fee, of course!). Reuters had established a marketplace.

All this did not help the retail investor. Every morning the retail bank gets the latest exchange rates from the market. They would add a margin, (a) if the rate fell sharply or (b) if the rate rose dramatically over the course of the full day. Added to this was profit margin and instrument risk (fraudulent travellers cheques or notes), with exotic currencies (non-majors), attracting higher margins, and a list was prepared with a wide gap of 12% (*spread* or retail margin, the money that a consumer would lose if they bought and then sold the currency immediately). This was faxed to the branches in the morning, transcribed on the FX board in the branch and, in the evening, the FX deals in branches would be faxed back, collated and sent to the dealing room. The retail bank kept the profit. If the currency fluctuated too much, they could always fax the banks during the day or withdraw the currency.

These days, FX rates are electronically wired and can change instantly, reducing FX fluctuation risk. However, despite technological advancements, the wide spreads are still maintained by banks. The ACCC noted in the 2019 Foreign Currency Conversion Services Inquiry that customers of the big banks were penalised for their loyalty.

›› NOTE

A good way to find out if we are getting a good rate is to subtract the buy rate from the sell rate and divide the answer by the average of the two. If the rate is 12%, it is a bad deal. Credit and debit cards are generally 2%, which is good, but banks sometimes add their own fee, say 2% or more plus sometimes an international transaction fee. Yet even then, if we are willing to accept currency fluctuation risk (and most people, even good traders, have no idea where it will go over the length of a holiday), being slack and just spending off a credit or debit card is probably the best thing to do.

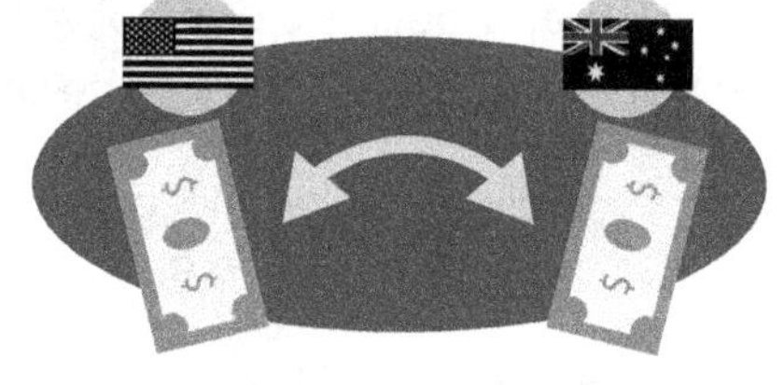

FOREIGN EXCHANGE

For large amounts of money — $10 000 or more — banks may be permitted to ask for a dealer rate. The dealer books the trade and locks in a rate. This allows them to trade the risk on the market immediately, and the bank is no longer subject to currency fluctuations. Settlement in FX spot markets (as they are called) settles two days later (known as T+2). Global markets traders in the big banks always wondered why the retail bank was so inefficient and did not sympathise with the profit margin. If a consumer did get put through to the market's FX sales desk, the dealer was more than happy to give you a good rate.

Corporates have access to dealer rates in real-time through their bank. Corporates access multiple banks and portals to get the best rate, often at 20 basis points or less (0.20).

With increased electronic access to the FX market, anyone can trade. FX margin lending and contracts for difference (CFDs) give retail investors up to 500:1 leverage. So a $1 investment allows a trade of $500. Some Australian providers, like CMC Markets, Trade Direct 365, and Pepperstone give a spread of 0.2 basis points or 0.002%. Compare this with the 12% spread of a retail bank when next planning a holiday.

International payments, when cross currency is concerned, build FX into the pricing of these international money transfers, yet another cost of doing business.

International Trade and Payment Risks

International payments and trade was risky business. The DvP problem was complicated by terms of trade, distance, the lack of cross-border regulation, and the difficulty to apply for legal recourse in such matters.

So many things could go wrong with the shipment: goods were not as described, goods were lost in shipment, customs duty was unpaid (in India, Velcro tape was subject to import customs duty) and goods were seized. (In Australia, uncertified cordless landline phones were contraband. Lithium-ion batteries are restricted as well and could be seized by the carrier.)

In addition, the payment itself was risky. The payment could be misdirected, or stopped due to a fraud or sanctions check. The payment may not be made at all as agreed.

» NOTE

International trade would involve warehousing — some unscrupulous warehouses would unilaterally increase the rent and seize the goods for non-payment. In other cases, so-called trusted counterparties would purchase goods and claim they were destroyed on delivery etc. Often shipments worth hundreds of thousands, or millions, would be lost/defrauded in this way, and there was very little that could be done. Bank products and insurance companies attempted to assist the process, yet this added expense and complexity, and cunning players were always one step ahead.

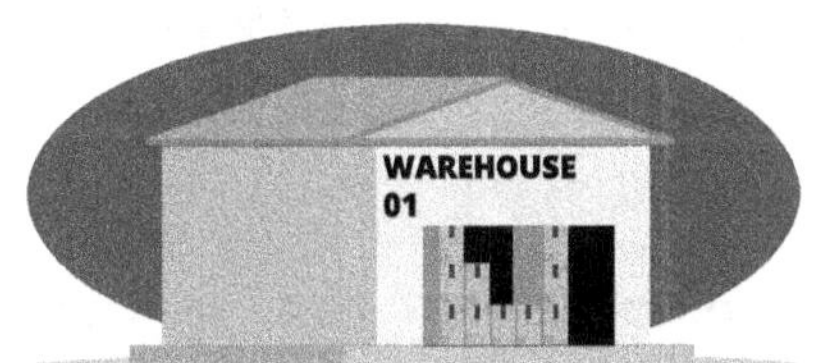

Some of the trade and payment risks are listed below.

Credit risk was the risk associated with the payer. Primarily, would the payer be good for the money?

Cost of delivery risk was where the cost of delivery could vary from initial estimates. A provider may only deliver goods to the dock, with moving the goods from the dock to the buyer costing thousands. These include demurrage and dispatch charges. Customs charges, levies, and taxes could add to the expenses of the sender or receiver. In agreeing to terms, a whole library of delivery conditions are used in the industry. Each has inclusions and exclusions of its own:

- Ex Works (EXW): A formal name for what is known as pick-up in eBay; basically, the buyer needs to organise shipment and delivery from the seller's premises or some agreed location.
- Free Carrier (FCA): Slightly better than EXW, the seller will put the goods on the first carrier. This ensures correct packaging and reduces some of the shipment risks for the buyer.
- Free Alongside Ship (FAS): Basically gets the goods to an export dock.
- Free On Board (FOB): Similar to FCA, but the carrier is a ship.
- Delivered At Terminal (DAT): The goods are delivered to a terminal; unloading and customs is the responsibility of the buyer.
- Cost and Freight (CFR): Goods are sent to an agreed location, generally a port. The buyer needs to pick them up from the port and may need to pay customs.
- Cost, Insurance and Freight (CIF): Like CFR but formalises the risk of loss to the seller.
- Delivered At Place (DAP): The seller sends goods to an agreed point, but the buyer is responsible for unloading and payment of customs etc.
- Carriage Paid To (CPT): The seller sends the goods all the way to an agreed point near the buyer. Customs charges are the buyer's responsibility.
- Carriage and Insurance Paid (CIP): The seller sends the goods all the way to the buyer, covering insurance. The buyer needs to unload from the carrier. When buying goods online, this is the default mode normally for retail international purchases though insurance is not explicit. The buyer could be liable for customs duty. As a courtesy, the courier (or postal service) will normally deliver goods to the door.
- Delivered Duty Paid (DDP): The buyer only needs to unload the goods from an agreed point. All costs, including duty, are paid. eBay international purchases (if duty is paid) fall under this category.

Legal enforcement risk was the inability to enforce term(s) of trade. An order for A+ goods, being provided at A- quality or, worse, non-delivery and non-payment was difficult to enforce cross-border. The system tended to favour the perpetrator for it was difficult and/or expensive to bring a law case forward from a foreign land. Legal enforcement was not always used, but acted as a deterrent. The deterrent capability in foreign trade was dampened.

Time risk was the length of time to complete a transaction were the goods perishable or time sensitive (e.g., COVID supplies). The length of time the payment was outstanding incurred interest, or the length of time the goods took to ship would lose interest expenses. Goods stuck in limbo could add to costs. Manufacturing time, shipment, banking, customs, etc., all contributed to this risk.

Foreign exchange risk was where the fluctuation of the foreign currency between the time of order, time of payment, and time of delivery could impact the cost of the transaction.

Regulatory risk was risk associated with moving goods within a country, and regulations between countries added a further dimension, as to who was liable for deficiencies, customs bills, etc. UN sanctions could apply if dealing with UNSC sanctioned entities or restricted goods.

Intellectual property, security and privacy risk was where, for example, the import of a large shipment of the soon-to-be released version of iPhones should not be divulged to competitors or the market. There were many people involved in a shipment, and even sealed containers could be opened by many authorised people for any number of reasons. Goods needed to be declared openly. A shipment declaring it was for spice number 6 to KFC could give away a trade secret.

AML/CTF as an international payment was a risk. AML/CTF restrictions applied to trade payments. For whatever reason, SWIFT did not control payment messaging so without checks by sending banks, it was possible to send money to UNSC sanctioned entities. These payments could be stopped, or could result in significant fines if regulations were breached. In Australia, compliance required the submission of an IFTI report on each transaction. This process was inconsistent with card transactions, nevertheless, banks were required to comply. SWIFT eventually sold a separate software, Sanctions Screening, to help banks comply.

›› NOTE

Mistaken payment was another risk. Some fraudsters would discover typical bills of institutions and send a fake invoice with real SWIFT bank account identifiers belonging to the fraudster. Sometimes companies would pay the invoice, especially if it looked familiar. In some cases, even government agencies were duped. Like we saw in the Bangladesh case, it was possible to get the money back thanks to the non-swiftness of SWIFT, but payers needed to be quick and vigilant to avoid loss.

Mitigation

In the face of all this, the financial services sector came to the party with a number of solutions that could reduce the risks. They all came at a cost and sometimes introduced their own risks.

Trade finance mitigated the time risk (delay in receipt of payment) for a producer to provide a large order to a buyer. By giving the invoice to a bank, the bank could fund the cost of manufacturing while the goods were being made and shipped. Once shipped and payment was received, the debt could be repaid. Some risks with this were the duplication of invoices. (The manufacturer could go to two banks to obtain finances for the one order.)

A **letter of credit** could be issued to provide security to a seller that they would be paid, subject to specific conditions such as a delivery receipt.

A **bill of lading** is a document used to provide definitive ownership, a shipping contract and terms, and the status of a shipment. Delivery as per the bill of lading could trigger a release of payment on a letter of credit.

Escrow is a financial service where a trusted third party takes the payment from the buyer and releases it to the seller once conditions are met. These conditions were generally more complex than a simple delivery receipt and often required inspection of goods. In Australia, livestock agents are used to facilitate escrow payment for buying and selling cattle and sheep. Alibaba and Escrow.com for eBay offer this service to online buyers. There is a cost and also a risk as, often, acceptance of goods can be subjective.

Insurance. While a sender is generally responsible for delivery of goods up to their agreed drop-off point, and couriers are responsible for the safe delivery, issues in shipment can get complicated, especially as the goods become more expensive. Insurance provides some definitive protection; however, like all insurance products, it is important to understand the conditions to ensure all risks are covered.

Sanctions screening, KYC and AML/CTF programs. Banks provide AML/CTF programs and monitor payments for compliance. However, buyers should ensure, before sending or receiving goods overseas and before the payment, that their counterparty (or a courier route) is not in the list of UNSC sanctioned entities as payments, refunds, or the return of or seizure of goods could become an issue.

SWIFT Costs

To its credit, SWIFT is an association and, while it has sizable profits of around EUR €50 million, these are dwarfed about 200:1 by the far more profitable major card schemes. For the calendar year 2018, SWIFT claimed 7.8 billion transactions and a total revenue of €822 million. While SWIFT has other revenue streams (like SIBOS and software), this puts the maximum cost on a SWIFT message at well under €0.10, a fee anyone would be happy to pay for an international money transfer.

However, SWIFT is not a scheme. Other than impose standards on messaging, it is just a pure payment rail, moving data from one point to another. Charges and fees are up to the member banks.

Many of these banks charged hefty fees, dating back to when telegraphic transfers were manual. However, with the passage of time, improvements in IT and greater efficiency, many of these fees still remained the same.

The first fee is the sender bank fee. In Australia, the major banks charged $20-$30. These fees were dropped in recent times, if the transfer was made in foreign currency (as they received foreign exchange retail margin) to as low as $6.

The other fee was the correspondent banking fee. Each bank could charge a fee as the transaction made its way through the network. Often banks would negotiate a good deal and build the fee into their own charge, but sometimes it would be passed on. Correspondent bank charges went up if, as mentioned, manual corrections were made, and to support smaller countries and less common banks.

The third fee was when the receiving bank sometimes charged the sender or the payee a fee when the money hit their account.

To top it all off was the FX fee up to 6% i.e., half of the spread for some retail customers of the Big Four.

Corporates and institutions could negotiate lower fees than retail customers.

The fees were to cover the SWIFT costs (low as they were) and the software, systems and operations of the bank, and provided a lucrative profit stream for the IMT division.

If the payment went missing, there was an investigation fee of over $50.

It was not uncommon to hear horror stories of transfers of $20 costing $60, and going missing or much worse.

All up, SWIFT payments were expensive, and continue to be so; however, contrary to the common misconception, the cost is not because of SWIFT, but due to the profiteering of banks around it, and a complex network in the international banking system.

Alternative International Transfers

SWIFT or, rather, bank-based international money transfers, over which the SWIFT system and consequential network had a monopoly, were due for disruption around the time of the Internet revolution, 1998 to 2001. The recovery post-dot com crash saw a significant upheaval of merchant solutions in the cards space and global payment solutions, and the rise and rise of card schemes. The 9/11 event dampened this in 2001 with the hard line AML/CTF policy that followed.

In the early days, alongside American Express were Western Union and Moneygram, born as payment systems in the US, using telegraphs, money orders and, later, travellers cheques.

» NOTE

There is an interesting story around the interrelation of American Express, Western Union, Moneygram, Wells Fargo, First Data, Thomas Cook, Travelex, Ant Financial, and other card schemes of partnerships, acquisitions and spin-offs that is worth researching.

By 2000, Western Union and Moneygram were offering transfer services in Australia.

A number of alternative remittance providers entered the market later. In order to access money in the electronic age, they needed to work with a bank. Unfortunately, due to tough AML/CTF regulations and the real fear of large fines, many of the big banks refused to work with money service businesses, as they were known, and would de-bank them if they discovered a customer conducted the service. There was no outsourcing of AML/CTF policy for the big Australian banks, and it was not just the fines from AUSTRAC they were afraid of. US or European fines and loss of banking reputation could isolate them in the world and bring Australia into disrepute. It made total sense for the Big Four to stay away from the sector. While this resulted in high fees for bank-based IMTs, as noted by the ACCC in its Foreign Currency Pricing Inquiry (2019), the recommendation to establish a "due diligence scheme for access to banking services" is likely to have little impact, at least, on most of the Big Four.

Some banks agreed to bank more compliant alternative transfer services. These days, some of the international services accept Visa and Mastercard, though, caveat emptor (buyer beware). A credit card payment may not be treated as a credit purchase, but incur a high interest bill from day one as cash-out. Other remittance providers accepted BPAY and sometimes POLi Payments (though in many cases, these could take one to two days to clear).

The big brands still had a hefty foreign exchange margin, 9% or more, with smaller, more nimble providers being more competitive

World Remit, Remitly, Oz Forex, WorldFirst, SendFX, XE, CGM, OrbitRemit (which, in Australia, offers a local BSB account for overseas remitters), and InstaRem are a few of the many regulated providers with offerings lower than the big banks. State Bank of India, Sydney (an overseas bank branch) offered 2% or lower retail margins, and low fees, especially to India. Bank of China, Australia offers a dual eftpos/China UnionPay card with IMT services to a number of countries at lower rates. Citibank and HSBC similarly offer better rate IMTs.

TransferWise was early in the market with a possibly naive claim that it could avoid SWIFT by using demand and supply dynamics to have payers in one country settle domestically with an unconnected receiver, if there was a corresponding payer and receiver in the other country, i.e., netting off. While netting off may have some advantages at scale, the FX cost was never about the underlying expense in moving the money, a problem few institutions had. The problem was the sending of small transactions over the banking network. With bulk settlement, especially if the transfer agent had liquidity offshore, SWIFT could be used effectively to net off the gross settlement amounts. TransferWise, through a partnership with NAB and other banks globally, offers a solution that lets them receive money in local currency globally through domestic clearing and pay out to the recipient in real-time.

While the smaller providers offer good prices, they do not cater for all currencies or countries. Some have better networks in certain countries compared to others. Europe, the United States, major Asian countries, South Africa, New Zealand and Fiji are generally better serviced than others.

Regulated providers needed to be registered with AUSTRAC and have ASIC financial services licenses. They needed Financial Services Guides (FSGs) and Product Disclosure Statements, and to have an AML/CTF program which, for a client, meant proper KYC procedures or identity verification, often using third-party providers.

Bulking Solutions

Individual IMTs were expensive. By bulking payments up and sending one big transaction, organisations could save fees on payments.

Global pension payouts were one application. The United Kingdom, Germany and many other countries paid pensions of former residents even if they lived in foreign countries. The payments were small and frequent, and could have been more expensive if the foreign governments needed to pay for the IMT, even at institutional rates. So instead of sending several SWIFT FIN messages, they sent a SWIFT FileAct, which is basically a file full of many smaller payments.

These payments were picked up by agreeing banks and then split into smaller payments using the local clearing system — in Australia, Direct Entry.

Earthport attempted to provide a similar solution to banks in Australia, bulking payments up and using domestic clearing to disseminate them. In 2019, Visa acquired Earthport to provide their B2B Connect solution.

There was, however, one catch. AUSTRAC still wanted its IFTI reports. Payers and receivers had to be properly identified.

When sending a domestic payment, the recipient and recipient bank needed to be advised that it had received an international payment.

In 2019, Westpac, using a similar solution (and with the use of off-system BSBs, in sending payments overseas) was subjected to a statement of claim from AUSTRAC, and fines for breaching IFTI reporting requirements.

Unregulated Remittance Providers

There is a long list of smaller regulated remittance providers that one may come across in small stores and through accountants or other professionals. Many offer good rates, but are at the edge of regulation and, in many cases, due to insufficient or lax AML/CTF policies, were banned or fined by AUSTRAC.

Unregistered remittance service provision is illegal under Australian law. It does still happen, for example, the Hawala network. This system predates banking by possibly 700 years or more, and operates on a trust system where trusted counterparties would exchange money to get value to the destination. It was originally a legitimate system. As it evolved alongside the banking system, the practice was eventually overshadowed by mainstream banking and, over time became unregulated, focusing on unbanked corridors. Often, there was no paper trail and, despite claims of reliability, there were cases of fraud by people falsely claiming to be in the network or by agents themselves. The method, or similar, is used these days to get money out of countries in Africa, Arab countries, the Indian subcontinent and Southeast Asia, countries with FX restrictions, or in an effort to launder money.

Sometimes a similar activity takes place through friends of friends to get money across. The practice avoids foreign exchange markets, often through domestic netting, which became less efficient due to the infrequency of transactions and the difficulty of matching in what needed to be a tight circle. Due to the complexities and the high level of monitoring, such activities are extremely risky and, under Australian law, could find participants in criminal proceedings, especially if the transaction is implicated in terrorism financing. Nevertheless, it is not uncommon for individuals to seek social media contacts to enable a mutual AUD deal in Australia and a corresponding one abroad with FX rates generally set at market.

Real-time Gross Settlements

After computerisation, the Reserve Bank, like any bank, had a core banking system that kept a record of funds and settlements, basically a ledger. There was one difference. For a bank, these ledger lines, while representing money, were actually just information. For the Reserve Bank, they were real money: there were no notes or coins behind them; that was it. The Reserve Bank Information and Transfer System (RITS) was the core banking system for banks.

One of the sub ledgers of RITS was each bank's cash account. This was the Exchange Settlement Account or ESA.

In 1995, real-time gross settlements, RTGS, was integrated into RITS ESA accounts. RTGS was essentially a set of domestic SWIFT messages between Australian banks flowing through the RBA, a real-time payment. The banks were the customers and RBA was their bank. An RTGS message would be initiated by one party, move money from one account to another in the RBA (from one RITS ESA to the other) and inform the other bank.

It was very powerful and, by law, irrevocable. If a bank were to make an RTGS payment at 10:15 am and the bank failed at 10:16, its assets in liquidation would exclude the RTGS payment and courts would be bound.

The primary purpose of RTGS was to gross-up smaller payments of the previous day and settle the next. Over time, RTGS payments became more frequent to reduce the systemic risk associated with banks agreeing to pay before they settled.

RTGS was used between corporations to guarantee large payments. In many cases, an RTGS payment was expensive, only operated during banking hours, and needed manual banking support to effect.

Retail customers could avail themselves of RTGS by sometimes using IMTs or SWIFT to send a payment to an Australian bank account domestically. With NPP, this does not make sense, but some banks use RTGS as a backup if Direct Entry fails.

CLS Bank

Continuous Linked Settlement (CLS) was introduced as a way of reducing systemic risk between banks overseas. Australia, through the RBA, joined CLS in 1999.

In a very simple scenario, assume two banks: Bank A (Australia) and Bank B (US) wish to exchange Australian dollars for US dollars. The settlement problem is the payment versus payment issue. At any point in time, if any one organisation has both AUD and USD, there is a risk, for example, of that organisation failing.

The solution that CLS Bank International offers is:

1. It is owned by 76 shareholders, largely the settlement member banks, and is monitored by the world's central banks.
2. It holds an account like any bank in each of its supported jurisdictions with the equivalent of an exchange settlement account in each nation. Today, it operates in 18 nations directly and others indirectly.

3. It first attempts to net each bank off with each other without the need to access its own funds. In the example above, there may be a Bank C and a Bank D trying to do the reverse transaction. CLS attempts to net off transactions (essentially enact a domestic deferred net settlement) without putting any money down. In the end, the netting-off may require some funding (due to the international nature of the settlement). CLS has claimed it can, with a minimal amount of input funds (0.5 % of total settlement value in one case study), complete the process with minimal funding.

Ultimately, CLS accomplishes its objectives by facilitating the equivalent of RTGS transactions with each bank. The settlement transactions are final and irrevocable. Within each CLS account, sub accounts are kept for the various members with the goal of the starting and ending balance being zero.

The example in *Figure 37*, the situation is simple In the real world, it is much more complex and that complexity leads to risk. CLS Bank solves that international currency settlement risk and, as such, is favoured by banks and central banks.

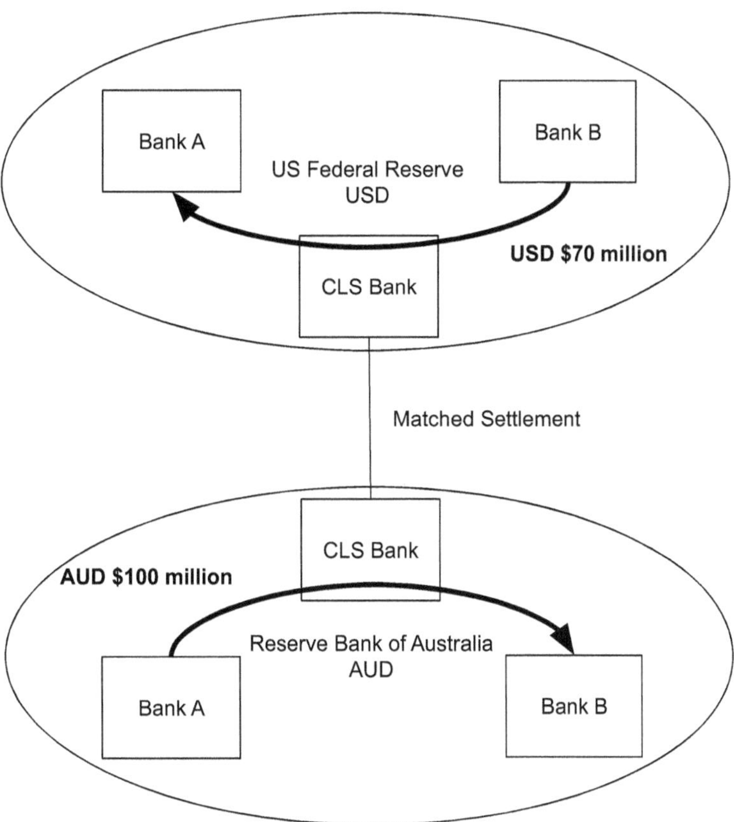

***Figure* 37. CLS Bank operation.**

CLS generally operates on a deferred net settlement basis: this requires all central banks across the world to be open at the same time from roughly 6:00 am to 11:00 am Central European Time for Australia (Asia-Pacific Banks), with settlement continuing until 12:00 noon for European banks. This tends to be into the evening in Australia.

Settlement: The Core of Payments

We previously discussed clearing and settlement. One of the key reasons that SWIFT is so entrenched is the integration with CLS for settlement. Many new international payment solutions tend to leave out this aspect of the solution, as it is complex and requires central bank liquidity to support. As a result they often end up using SWIFT to net off positions (which in turn uses CLS Bank).

High Value Clearing System

The Australian Payments and Clearing Association (APCA) or now the Australian Payment Network's Clearing System 4 (CS4), was established in 1997 as part of the move to RTGS. RTGS could be used by customers of banks to clear high-value amounts, where the systemic risk of the banking system was an issue, or the real-time settlement of funds for delivery versus payment (DvP) was required for high valued transactions.

The High Value Clearing System (HVCS), as it is now known, defines the use between banks of both SWIFT and RTGS.

12.

NEW PAYMENTS PLATFORMS

A SIMPLE IDEA captured the hearts of Australian payment progressives. What if we had a single payment system that had all the features of an ideal payment system? These are:

- Electronic real-time payment.
- Rich information.
- P2P: Anyone could pay anyone, from a person to a business to a bank.
- Any value, high or low, so it had to have a low cost and needed a solution to the settlement problem.

In 2007, there was nothing that could do the above when looking at all the alternative payment types, as shown in *Table 12*.

Table 12.

Searching for an ideal payment: Australian payment method comparison.

Payment method	Real-time electronic	Rich information	P2P	Any value
Direct Entry	✗ Batch cycle	✗ 18 characters only	✓ But account number is cumbersome	✓ Less than $100 million
Cards	✓ Real-time notification, settlement may be delayed	✗ This is why we get two receipts when we pay by card	✗ Merchants only	✓
BPAY	✗ Batch cycle	✗ CRN only	✗ Billers only	✓ $100 000
SWIFT	✗ Many banks take too long to post	✗ Not visible to customer	✗ Not easy to use or practical for domestic	✗ Too expensive for low value
RTGS	✗ Real-time but only during banking hours, and not generally posted immediately to retail	✗ Not visible to the customer	✗ Expensive, not a real-time solution	✗ Too expensive for low value
Cash	✗ Real-time but not electronic	✗ Can attach documents but cannot be sent remotely	✗ Real-time but not electronic	✗ $10 000 restriction

Payment method	Real-time electronic	Rich information	P2P	Any value
Cheque	✗ 2 days of clearing and not electronic. Bank cheques have less risk of bouncing, but the same clearing time and are non-electronic.	✓ Attach documents	✓ If the payee can wait for it to clear	✓
The ideal payment	✗ Real-time notification at least	✓ ISO 20022 standard	✓ Email or mobile phone addressing	✓ Initially to cover retail payments, payroll etc.

As mentioned earlier, the idea was taken in 2007 to BPAY (Cardlink back then, a company owned by the Big Four banks). The MAMBO project was transformed to deliver this for the banking industry.

Eventually, the project failed, starting with the Melbourne banks (NAB first, then ANZ in 2011), followed by Westpac, leaving CBA, the major instigator of the initiative, to officially close it. The other banks could not see the business case to justify the cost.

The Reserve Bank, through its Payments System Board, was a keen observer. Disappointed with the outcome, they eventually pushed the banks to implement a cross-industry solution. The Australian Payments and Clearing Association (APCA) kicked off the New Payments Platform (NPP) in 2013.

KPMG was selected to run the program and, after a competitive tender, SWIFT won the contract to implement the solution. Fiserv was subcontracted by SWIFT for the P2P part of the solution, the addressing service.

NPP turned out to cost the industry much more than MAMBO, and with BPAY eventually taking over the marketing, it was a déjà vu experience with real-time payments coming full circle to where it started. In hindsight, the decision of the three banks to pull out was financially disastrous for their shareholders and a bad outcome for the industry.

Emerging P2P Payments

As MAMBO was shutting down, the mobile app market was picking up. The year before ANZ pulled out, they launched ANZ GoMoney offering the same P2P real-time capabilities that MAMBO was proposing.

Resistance

Several banks resisted the implementation once the costs came out. The failure to comprehend the implications and size of an impending project or a decision is a symptom of overly large enterprises and lack of executive sponsorship and engagement. Quite rightly the central bank was annoyed. Alternative systems, such as using eftpos rails, were proposed, and rejected. The RBA's point was: you had your chance, your people were involved in the development, now deliver.

The eftpos Solution

The use of ISO 8583 or AS 2805 (card payment rails) for faster payment solutions was not new. In fact, recently in the United Kingdom, their so-called faster payments solution used this message standard.

eftpos was unique in that most banks were connected to it and, also, thanks to a previous implementation (Mediclaims, direct consumer payment for medical bills from Medicare), the refund functionality had already been used to push funds to a consumer.

Changing this system to have a frontend that could do all the things required could have saved money, proponents claimed.

The idea was put forward at the beginning of MAMBO and, later, at the beginning of NPP, through a bid from eftpos Australia Ltd (EPAL). The idea was rejected both times, based on the second requirement: the need to have rich information, pointing towards the ISO 20022 standard. The counter-argument was the use of a reference number in AS 2805 and a separate subsystem for the extended description when required. The counter-argument was rejected.

The eftpos idea was put forward once again, once the costs came in and, after the final RBA rejection, the big banks (ANZ again, the odd one out) proceeded to implement Beem It.

Beem It

Around the same time as NPP was being developed, a secret project was kicked off by the banks, led by CBA.

Perhaps out of spite, or perhaps in a last-ditch attempt to stop further expenses in NPP, some of the banks got together and spun off Beem It.

The idea was to implement an eftpos-based solution using the rails, but put a mobile frontend on it. All the customer needed was an eftpos card, and they could create a new wallet and transfer money to friends and, later, businesses.

Beem It: A Good Idea, 10 Years Too Late

There are a number of reasons Beem It is destined to fail.

First, Beem It came out at the same time as NPP, and there is no reason why NPP could not have been used to accomplish the same use cases from within the traditional bank app. Current NPP implementations clearly lack inspiration. If the creative energy put into Beem

It (including the marketing budget) had been put into the NPP solution, NPP would be more attractive. The big banks have dragged their feet on NPP debits and QR codes, yet have implemented it in earnest in Beem It.

Second was the high cost of acquisition. Banks already had a big market share of wallets. Beem It required a new wallet. To get people to move, a lot of money had to be spent on acquisition. Initially, they gave away cash, $5 to $10 per wallet, with incentives to "Bring your friends."

Third, there are only three banks involved and it is unlikely a customer would change banks just for Beem It. Further, this could be seen as a clear attempt by some big banks to exclude smaller players from a real-time ecosystem.

Fourth, the target marketing and application convenience has been successful in attracting youth; however, it is relatively unused in the more established market, and the NPP solution is proving to be more robust in the P2P market.

Fifth, the merchant solution is relatively light and does not scale. Currently, a mobile app is required and there are few, if any, point-of-sale devices integrated with it. As a result, merchants bigger than sole traders have not generally implemented the solution.

Sixth, the system only works with debit cards currently, even if a credit card is linked to a debit card.

Finally, low-value payments between known people or parties, as Beem It is generally used and marketed, has never really been an issue for those people have a trust link. The use of a receipt or screenshot to prove a payment was sent (and will eventually be received) acted sufficiently to prove a payment even if their word was insufficient.

Beem It, sadly, is destined to fail, or roll into a wider NPP solution. It is tragic that the energy put into the initiative was not spent on a more strategic outcome that would have better benefited the market and accelerated adoption. Perhaps in this instance, ANZ's resistance was well placed.

In late 2019, the RBA called out CBA for resisting the implementation of NPP. It is ironic that CBA should resist, given its digital accomplishments and real-time capability.

For many banks, investing in a payment method they cannot own or control makes little commercial sense. Investing in Beem It, however, does, and this is one of the tragedies of the NPP implementation.

NPP Australia Limited

NPP Australia Limited (NPPA) was the organisation set up to implement and operate NPP. The current 13 members are the Big Four banks, the RBA, Macquarie Bank, Citibank, HSBC, ING and Bendigo banks, and the payment organisations (on behalf of their members): Indue, ASL and Cuscal.

There are five ways to access the system:

- As a full participant: Only full participants can connect directly to the NPP. They need to be an ADI with an ESA, tested and certified to be compliant, and are reported if they are down for even short periods.
- As a settlement participant: Getting many of the benefits of a direct participant in terms of settlement, but they sit off a full participant who integrates with the network. They need to be an ADI and settle on their own ESA, and are less exposed in terms of system risks and outages.
- As an identified participant: Can be a non-bank but, again, need to go through a full participant who takes the settlement risk.
- As an overlay service provider: Providing extended services (e.g., addressing service) to the NPP.
- As an end user: Through the use of ISO 20022 APIs or a bank's UI, an individual or business can send payments and receive notifications of payments via their bank.

Each participant needs a SWIFT bank identification code (BIC) as well as BSB identifiers. The need for a SWIFT BIC, while cumbersome to obtain and technically redundant (the BSBs could have been used for routing), is a part of using a SWIFT-based solution for messaging and may future-proof the messages when SWIFT moves to MX messaging from 2021 to 2025 (though there is some scepticism of any interoperability, based on the ISO 20022 discussion earlier).

NPP Payments Access Gateway

In order to connect to the network, an NPP payments access gateway (PAG) connector is required. This is analogous to the SWIFT Alliance Gateway (SAG) used in SWIFT, and SWIFT claims that the same SWIFT connection components can be reused for NPP. The backbone of the network is the local SWIFT network, though it is unclear in public documents how much (if any) of the traffic needs to be routed to the core data centres in Europe and the US, or whether the NPP is autonomous.

Settlement in NPP

One of the problems in electronic payments is that in most systems it is a *promise to pay,* not really a payment.

The instruction — a promise — is over a wire, but there is no way to move coins or notes over that wire.

Over time, with the requirement that banks keep their excess deposits with the Reserve Bank (World War II), and with the implementation of RITS and, finally, in 1995, with the implementation of real-time interbank payments through RTGS, something changed. Between banks, it was possible to actually move money by wire, provided the money in RITS Exchange Settlement Accounts of the respective banks was moved. Traditionally, for low-value payments, settlement happened the next day and then, over time, more and more frequently (the Low Value Settlement Service).

With NPP, settlement happens from exchange settlement funds almost simultaneously. Like RTGS, it is irrevocable. The subsystem on RITS that facilitates this is the RBA's Fast Settlement Service (FSS).

Core Operation

In Direct Entry, a single credit transfer (SCT), which NPP is primarily designed to replace, is principally one message. NPP has seven messages to affect the same thing. They are across the ISO 20022 pain, camt, and pacs business domains.

NPP transactions take place over the NPP basic infrastructure, which includes the RBA's new RITS Fast Settlement Service, an addressing service built by Fiserv (who were contracted by SWIFT), and the SWIFT NPP messaging service and a distributed switch. In SWIFT's words, a "Domestic Messaging Channel supported by SWIFT's established network partners in Australia."

The process for a simple credit transfer message, as illustrated (*Figure 38*), is:

1. If using an alias (email address, mobile phone number, ABN or company name), the payer bank looks up the alias on the addressing service using a pain.a11 message (especially created for the NPP).
2. The addressing service responds with the details of the institution's holding account.
3. The bank sends an attempt (clearing message pain.) to pay using a pacs.008 message.
4. The receiving bank responds that it is/is not acceptable. A credit message can be rejected if the account does not support NPP or if it is closed etc. The sending bank may then choose to route the payment to Direct Entry instead. If successful, a clearing notification message is provided, pacs.002.
5. The payer bank sends a message to the RBA to settle the funds using the message pacs.009.
6. The RBA, using its RITS Fast Settlement Service (FSS), settles the transaction by quickly moving money from a sub account of the bank's ESA to the other bank's ESA. This completes the payment, with funds settled.
7. The RBA sends both banks a message confirming the settlement took place using a pacs.002 message.

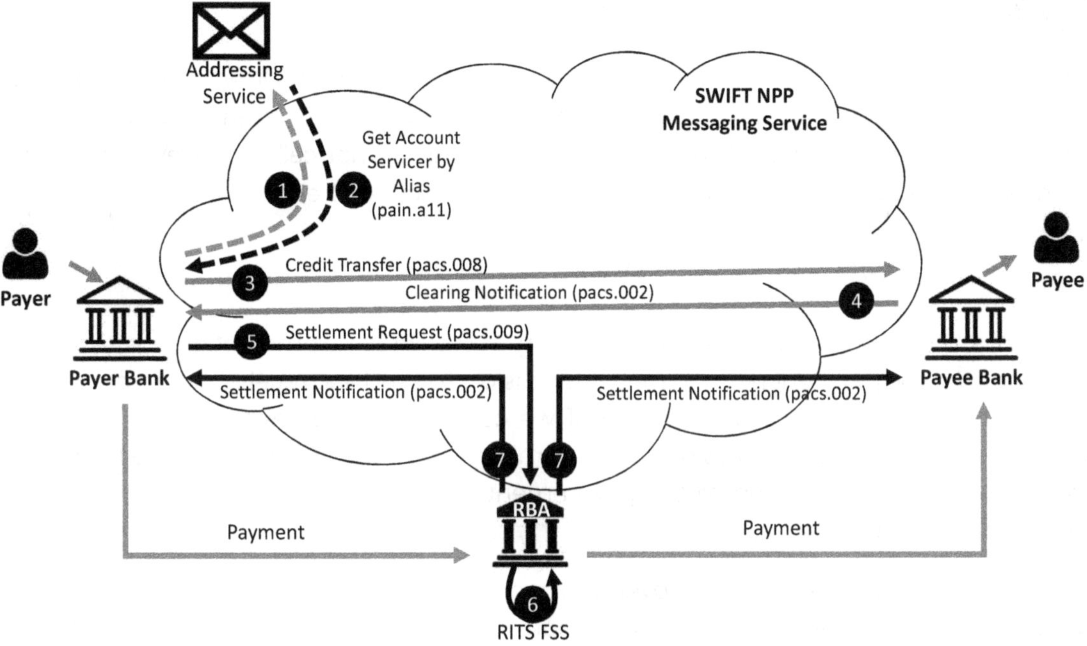

Figure 38. A basic NPP credit transfer message.

Early Security Flaws

Early implementations of NPP exposed some security flaws in the design and in the implementation of the addressing service.

In 2019, Westpac and Cuscal were separately attacked by an enumeration attack. Compromised bank accounts were used to look up an identity, like a reverse phone book lookup. In NPP, typing in a mobile number looks up a shortened name of the holder so a legitimate payer can ensure they have the right mobile. In the case of Westpac, 600 000 lookups were made from seven compromised accounts, with almost 100 000 of them being successful. This could have been sold on the black market as a contact database for telemarketing or to perform a scam. The privacy commissioner and bank regulators were generally required to be informed of a breach like this. Later that year, Cuscal had a similar breach through a financial services client; however, due to their exposure of APIs, the data released not only included the shortened name, but their full name and account number, according to reports.

Measures to limit lookups to a maximum of two or three counterparties at a time were instituted by most NPP banks, which meant that, in the event of multiple NPP payments, a mistype or error, it was easy for genuine customers to get temporarily blocked.

In 2020, NPP was used by some customers to send explicit messages. At least one bank changed its terms and conditions to de-bank such users. This issue made little sense, as, with the holder's mobile or email, a message could be sent directly, and in many states it was a criminal offence. It was possible to commit a similar offence using Direct Entry.

Overlay Services and Extensions

The original intent of NPP was to supply a core payment service. Organisations were free to bilaterally or unilaterally add services onto NPP to enhance the system. These extensions were called overlay services. Some of these extensions are not called overlay services, but unimplemented parts of the core offering. They are described below.

PayID

PayID is not really an overlay as it was mandatory in the core implementation. It is technically distinct from the payment network, and it is possible to send and receive payments without PayID. The PayID idea was simple. What if we could address a payment, as proposed in MAMBO, using an email address or mobile number? This overlay was attractive to the RBA Payments System Board and to the government, not just for its convenience, but for its ability to facilitate portability.

Unfortunately, it was considerably over engineered and implementation by the big banks varied. To date, for many reasons, account portability is an unlikely, distant dream. BSB and account numbers are still in wide use and, to start with, Direct Entry would need to be turned off to make it effective.

Besides a mobile phone number and email address, we had BSB account number addressing already also supported in NPP. NPP added an ABN number and organisation ID so, in future, a customer may be able to type "Qantas" to pay for their airline ticket.

It was up to the banks to validate that an address was valid; for example, a mobile number needed to be the one on file and to be verified (by sending an SMS, say). Some banks allowed customers to create multiple addresses, others gave no option, and others invented one; for example, customer@acmebank.com.au.

In order to port the bank account, the original bank has to release the payment account identifier. The ease with which this is done varies from bank to bank.

Osko

One of the problems with NPP is that it is a framework—a "Build it and they will come" approach to a solution. The banks were dragged kicking and screaming into the implementation, and their reluctance to make it usable and slick is demonstrated by the contrasting solution of Beem It. In the end, the truth is that NPP is actually a far more robust solution and has the support of more banks. NPPA had very limited success marketing its solution. PayID fell flat. Perhaps reflecting on this, looking at the sunk investment and how to recoup costs, and perhaps with a little bit of pressure from the RBA, the banks looked at what they could do to help market the solution and turned to BPAY for help.

BPAY's Osko is really a service standard on NPP. First, messages are as fast on NPP as the banks choose to make them. Osko put stricter requirements in place. The payments needed to look real-time to customers. Second, the marketing pitch was considered. How do we market the rich information feature of NPP? Osko advertised that people could send emojis on a payment message. NPP supported it, and every Osko-compliant bank had to support it. Osko certification was required and banks paid a fee for it. They needed to display the Osko logo to assist marketing efforts.

The confusion in the marketplace as to what the difference is between PayID and Osko may persist but, hopefully, most banks will implement Osko anyway so the difference may remain technical.

QR Codes

QR codes at point of sale were originally trialled by XPay, eftpos's digital payment solution. CBA applied for a patent in 2014.

The idea was that a merchant displays a request to pay in the form of a coded barcode. These could either be static or dynamic. Static or fixed codes would often be preprinted on card or paper, simply have the pay ID of the merchant and some lodgement reference text. A dynamic, changing code would display on a screen and may include the amount of the transaction, and a unique transaction identifier and expiry time. Dynamic codes are more secure and could not be reused, whereas static codes are reusable and may be open to fraud (e.g., someone placing another QR code over the top of a legitimate one that redirects payment to the fraudster's account).

Implementation of the QR code is not just at the merchant's end, but requires banks to implement it in their apps. Sadly, despite being able to implement the QR code in Beem It, banks have dragged their feet on the NPP implementation. As the card schemes develop and expand EMV QR Codes, the NPP opportunity may be extinguished.

» NOTE

Quick response (QR) codes are essentially similar to barcodes found on grocery or store items. Bar codes are one-dimensional, whereas QR codes are two-dimensional and can contain exponentially more information than a one-dimensional barcode of a similar size. The QR code can contain numbers and text, and today is defined by the standard ISO/IEC 18004. While they were developed by a Toyota subsidiary, the trademarks and patents associated with QR codes have not been enforced, in order to encourage take-up; however, it is worth mentioning this as a risk as at any time Toyota may seek to take action against QR code implementations, and who better to sue than the banks!

International Funds Transfer Instruction

Before NPP, the only bank payment method that supported the AUSTRAC reporting requirement for international transfer was SWIFT. The report is called an international funds transfer instruction (IFTI). Banks are reluctant to implement alternative international payment solutions, primarily because they are unable to easily file an IFTI and provide it to the receiving bank.

Under AUSTRAC rules, banks are required to file IFTIs and, if they deposit the funds in another domestic bank, they are required to inform that domestic bank that they have an international payment on their hands, and the customer of that bank needs to be advised of the details of the transfer, who the sender was, etc.

Australian banks have been fined for switching international payments domestically without the proper measures. In November 2019, Westpac was taken to the Federal Court for 23 million breaches of the regulation. In theory, the fines could exceed Westpac's market capitalisation. The third charge is of particular importance: that Westpac failed to "pass on information about the source of funds to other banks in the transfer chain. This conduct deprived the other banks of information they needed to understand the source of funds to manage their own AML/CTF risks."[102]

NPP allows the exchange of rich information, and has developed an IFTI solution in line with SWIFT conventions. However, for it to be used widely, it needs to be implemented by most, if not all banks. The reasons for this are:

- Even though a bank may receive an IFTI in XML, if it does not show it to the customer it is useless.
- If the receiving bank does not recognise and process the IFTI, the information is useless.

Once again, banks have been reluctant to implement this change, perhaps to avoid loss of revenue on SWIFT rails or maybe they have overcapitalised on NPP.

Debit Mandate

Another overlay proposed by NPP is the debit mandate. These extended the push payment of the single credit transfer to a pull payment.

Designed to replace direct debits, the idea of the debit mandate is to:

- Use pay IDs to allow billers to send a mandate (permission to pull funds) to a customer.
- Allow customers to manage all their mandates within their bank (approve, cancel, move).
- Allow automatic debits once a mandate is in place for fixed or variable amounts.
- Allow portability of the mandate from bank account to bank account.

The direct debit mandate is powerful and could, in the domestic world, replace many point-of-sale use cases.

Again, the debit solution is useless without widespread implementation. As we have seen (with the early sluggish implementations of single issuer EFTPOS at fuel stations and Visa by Australian Bank), it is inconvenient for billers or merchants to implement solutions that cater only for a small subset of their customers.

The debit mandate, if widely implemented in consumer digital wallets, could compete with cards in the world of retail payments.

---

[102] AUSTRAC 2019

Request to Pay

The request to pay is a digitised version of BPAY View. It allows an invoice or a bill — a request for payment — to be sent using the NPP via a PayID address to a recipient. That recipient can then see it in their inbox and pay it if required. Again, at this time, the request to pay has generally not been implemented.

Payment Notifications

A payment notification is a message back to a corporate customer indicating a successful payment has been received. Ideally, it could be used by a system to automatically act on a receipt of payment. Implementation of this message, while defined by SWIFT, is outside the scope of the NPPA core and up to each bank to implement.

ISO 20022 APIs

Like a payment notification, it is, in theory, possible for corporations to send an NPP-based application programming interface (API), though few banks have implemented this. A number of other corporate APIs exist that may be implemented by the banks over time.

Rich Information

With the use of XML, it is possible to attach more detailed information to messages. This has a number of applications. The extra data can be in the payload of the message (up to a certain size) or as a reference to data held elsewhere.

Some applications of rich information are:

- eInvoicing: The invoice, as an image or digitised, allows the integration of data related to the purchase. Earlier, we saw taxi invoice information on American Express and Cabcharge payments. With eInvoices, it would be possible to track the purchase of goods at an itemised level, what price was paid, how much is in stock, etc. Integration between businesses could save a lot of manual work.
- Tax information: Including GST and non-GST amounts, and tax treatment of the invoice allows for easy integration with accounting packages.
- Payroll: A payslip is often sent in a separate mail to an employee. With NPP, the payslip can be combined with the payment.
- Superannuation: Lost superannuation was a major issue in the industry. As we saw, solving this problem initiated ISO 20022, until the problem was solved in a siloed manner by the ATO. Super funds were not clear about what to do with a contribution, and sometimes funds did not know where it came from and who it was for. NPP can facilitate information about a contribution being conveyed to the super fund, and avoid lost super and excess processing.

NPP Costs

The RBA noted that the costs of running NPPA would put the real costs of transactions at 20 cents per year. In order to encourage NPP over Direct Entry (BECS), charges are competitive (potentially around 10 cents) though the cost is not publicly disclosed.

NPP: An Unloved Payment System

Despite strong backend capabilities to facilitate real-time payments and an extensible design, banks have again dragged their feet on implementation.

Despite open APIs, and what seems to be a genuine attempt by the RBA and SWIFT to open the platform up with API sandboxes for outsiders to test their applications etc., for some inexplicable reason, like cards, DE, and SWIFT, official documentation remains poor, with the few documents redacted and sections labelled "confidential".

In the early days of NPP and PEXA (covered in a later chapter), the RBA was keen to develop much of the software. One seasoned private bank executive said after a meeting, "They love to build model trains!" Both NPP and PEXA solved a systemic risk problem of intraday bank payment failure that no one else saw the need to solve (especially as the balances of most accounts were guaranteed anyway through the Financial Claims Scheme). If the train builders were right, only time will tell.

The chattiness of the messages means that some real-time scenarios, like transit payments, may be too fast for the system. Perhaps a simplified version may become available.

The user experience is bad and inconsistent. Two years after implementation, many big banks did not support flexible addresses (e.g., email ID) for their customers to receive money. Regular payments were not available, and the capability was hidden away for many, who continued to use the less efficient DE due to ignorance, with few Australians recognising "Osko" and "NPP". In December 2019, the RBA was reported as slamming CBA for their lethargy.

All this was clearly avoidable and contrasted with the continued investment and elegant user experience of Beem It, all of which could have been accomplished better on NPP.

The problem with industry initiatives is that organisations fail to see the long-term benefit for them. They do not own the IP, and any innovation is short-lived in an accessible solution as a larger pool of competitors quickly catches up.

In Australia, investment in domestic payments is divided between eftpos, NPP, BPAY and the big card schemes, with the national systems unable to attract the willing investment of the latter. NPP is not a scheme and eftpos is under invested. To their credit, NPP was only initiated by the RBA in response to a failure of BPAY/MAMBO; however, with the creation of PEXA and the failure of integrating eftpos, the end result was a complication of the environment. Today, NPP is not really a scheme, with BPAY's Osko marketing overlay providing a Clayton's scheme and, as a result of this, the market enthusiasm remains subdued.

Nevertheless, despite all the issues, NPP remains a fundamentally robust payment method that could replace domestic alternatives, if given a chance.

Recognising this, in 2020, NPPA recommended discussions begin on a possible merger between eftpos, NPPA and BPAY. The result would be the natural extinction of the latter two, which would be resisted but, given the common owners and the robustness of NPP's strategy and potential, it made sense.

13.

OTHER REGULATED PAYMENT SYSTEMS

OTHER RBA REGULATED PAYMENTS generally come under the delivery versus payment or DvP functions. While important within the industry (markets and property), for the most part they remain hidden from public view but occur between institutions. They are a critical part of making some of the economy's fundamental transactions work.

Delivery versus Payment

Delivery versus payment attempts to resolve the stand-off between delivering something and paying for it. Picture buying a car on the second-hand market. The seller has the keys, the buyer has the money. DvP states that neither party should have both money and goods at the same time.

In keeping with the adage: "There's many a slip between the cup and the lip," the Reserve Bank has taken a pessimistic view of the risks. Even with the best solution that timed everything precisely, there is always a systemic risk that a party could fail (i.e., go bankrupt), or a court could apply some order that means settlement is not complete and this risk adds cost, uncertainty, and hesitation to the system, impediments the RBA wanted to remove.

In each of the clearing systems discussed previously, eftpos, IAC (previously CECS), Direct Entry, APCS, ACDES, and HVCS (excluding the international schemes and BPAY), payment is final and irrevocable at the wholesale level, by law though, to date, no challenge has been taken to the Federal Court. (Of course individual customer payments can be refunded as per the ePayments Code and various implementations of this code across the clearing systems.) CLS Bank for international payments is also similarly privileged, which provides a payment versus payment clearing capability. These systems are either RITS members or approved multilateral netting arrangements.

Delivery versus payment is slightly different in that, rather than just move money around, it also seeks to move entitlement to an instrument; namely debt instruments (Austraclear), derivatives (Chicago Mercantile Exchange), interest rate swaps (SwapClear, LCH), exchange instruments like shares (CHESS/ASX settlements) and property (PEXA).

The RBA regulates these DvP parties through the Financial Stability Standards (FSS) for central counterparties (the CCP Standards), with the exception of ASX Settlements (which is an approved multilateral netting arrangement) and PEXA (a RITS member).

Austraclear

Austraclear was originally created by the banks to facilitate debt instrument settlement.

Debt instruments are bank bills, bonds, debentures, etc. issued by various institutions.

When a debt instrument is settled, the payment is made over RTGS.

In meeting the CCP standards, Austraclear is run independently, though it is part of the listed company Australian Securities Exchange (ASX).

It does not offer credit and settles immediately, reducing risk in the system.

CHESS/ASX Settlement

The DvP problem for share trading is that shares are traded on a particular day and a few days later, simultaneously, the money and shares change hands.

Historically, due to batch processing, settlement of trades would take three days (T+3). In 2016, this was reduced to T+2, thanks to better automation.

Shares are traded on a stock exchange. The ASX is Australia's largest and primary stock exchange (itself now listed on the exchange) and has a market license from ASIC. It is the only domestic stock exchange to have a special real-time settlement capability with the RBA, though other systems can use RTGS or alternative payment systems.

Companies are free to use their own registries. Shareholders can access and manage their shares through those registries. When trading shares at the ASX, or before settlement, shares should be moved to the ASX Clearing House Electronic Subregister System (CHESS). CHESS could also work for other competitive market providers. On the settlement date, the agreed value would be transferred from the buying broker to the selling broker, and the shares would change name from the seller to the buyer at the same time.

In theory, it should be possible to perform real-time settlement of trades, the key issue being availability of funding. As CHESS operates on a deferred net settlement basis, it is possible for multiple trades to complete without settling, reducing the amount of money required to trade. Since 2000, the RBA has permitted some CHESS transactions (large institutional trades). Trades may be mutually agreed to settle on RTGS, reducing the net deferred risks.

›› NOTE

Stock exchange trades are not included in the calculation of broad money; however, in this microcosm, short-term money is created that probably exceeds the value of money that will actually get settled. Similarly, share value, which can quickly be exchanged for cash is also not included in broad money. Conversely, if everyone wanted to sell all their shares simultaneously (at $2 trillion), there would not be enough free broad money (again $2 trillion) in the economy to complete the purchase. So broad money and payments can only scale to a percentage of the entire private wealth of Australia (about $10 trillion) at a point in time, enough to cover a moderate amount of commerce. Another way of looking at this is that 20% of private wealth is held in money.

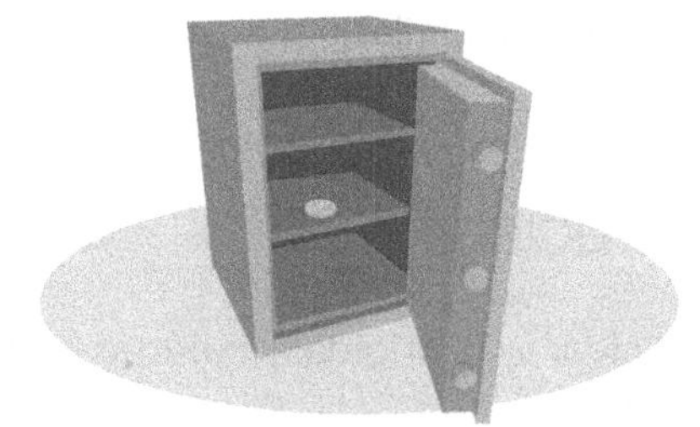

PEXA

Around the time the NPP was gathering steam, a long-running inefficiency in the payment system was in the delivery versus payment (DvP) part of property settlement, known as conveyancing.

Originally the sole domain of solicitors, it was an expensive and inconvenient component of what was the largest personal purchase most people ever made in their lifetime. Eventually, states issued conveyancer licenses to paralegals and non-solicitors, and legislation and regulations were passed to make contracts and processes standard and simple.

Often a home purchase would be accompanied by a home loan so the process of purchasing was quite complicated. It involved real estate agents and commission, final inspections, mortgages on titles, our old friend stamp duty, transfer of property, update of registers, payment of legal fees and other outgoing allowances, drawdown of mortgages, a list of bank fees, paying off of loans, vacant possession, exchange of keys and the trade of the property. Behind some of these tasks were complex processes such as mortgage broking, lending real estate management and conveyancer tasks.

Many people wondered why it took so long and, while e-conveyancing was an easy concept to imagine, the road to this destination was a slow and complicated one. While to this point, the normal four-week settlement (depending on the state) gave plenty of time to be ready for settlement, there were many failures in the process. There are horror stories of missing the settlement date, even at the last minute, when one critical component was missing such as a bill payment for electricity. The process could be improved.

Sure enough, a decision was made by the Council of Australian Governments (COAG), in November 2008, to start work on a National Electronic Conveyancing System (NECS). The decision was published as 2½ lines alongside other decisions and notes in a 33-page communique of a meeting of one day. The project was due to complete in 2010. How hard could it be?

The challenge fundamentally was not technical, not even from a payment perspective. It was behavioural, and perhaps political, but many of these challenges were overlooked and Australia ended up with a technically over-complicated, anti-competitive solution. The first transaction occurred in 2013, almost five years after the COAG decision, and that too was for a discharge of a mortgage, not generally a task for a conveyancer.

The original non-electronic process (where two mortgages were involved, originating and discharging) required two banks, two solicitors (representing each party or, and not recommended for novices, the parties themselves), and the land titles office. They would book a room, normally at the land titles office in the capital city.

The purchasing bank/party would show up with a series of bank cheques, normally including one large one, land title papers would be ready to be signed and handed over, solicitors would check the cheques and paperwork, the transfer forms and mortgage forms would be submitted to the land title office's officer, who would review them (not process them), and the cheque would be handed over. The solicitor would advise the agent to release the key and the house was legally sold.

» NOTE

Some solicitors or conveyancers required bank cheques be written for even $5 to cover small bills such as electricity bills to cover settlement disbursements. While some did accept trust accounts, others, being abundantly cautious, did not want a bounced cheque to void settlement. The banks charged up to $50 for each cheque so they were happy, and the unsuspecting customer just paid up.

The first hurdle to overcome was the DvP problem. In essence, the delivery versus payment problem is that the payment and transfer of titles should be simultaneous, with no party walking away with both title and money.

However, the approach taken was somewhat erroneously directed at a problem that was not that big an issue from the point of view of the solicitor. A great deal of the effort of the initiative was to remove systemic risk from the banking system: bank failure in between the time of transfer and time of payment. The solution took care of the payment, but not really the transfer.

A design was constructed with the aid of the Land Titles Office, RBA, solicitors and banks. They formed a company owned by the four largest states, the Big Four banks, Macquarie Capital, and (oddly) unconnected investors, property organisations Little Group and Landgate, and share registry Link. The company, named National E-Conveyancing Development Limited (NECDL), engaged Accenture and started work on a system: Property Exchange Australia (PEXA), which eventually became the popular name of the company.

In order to get PEXA over the line, the initiative had to convince the lawyers and conveyancers that the new system was better than the old one. One part of the changes was to get rid of the cheque system. In the end, that is all that was really replaced.

The advantage with a bank cheque was that it could be viewed, but not handed over. In the DvP world, this meant that the seller could see the cheque, sign the papers, have them accepted by the land title office, and then receive the cheque. But even then, there were many things that could go wrong. A bank cheque in a banker's hand was generally accepted as good as gold. In reality, a bank cheque, like any other cheque, could bounce. It could bounce if it were cancelled, it could bounce if it were fraudulent or obtained through fraudulent means, if it were damaged or had a defect or discrepancy, largely at the discretion of the issuing bank. It would take time to clear.

Further, the acceptance of the papers by the land titles office was not, in itself, a transfer. That would happen later. In Africa, it was known for properties to be double-sold, due to inefficiencies and delays in the system. The big problem was automation of the land titles office, and this was not part of the scope.

All sorts of things could happen but, as a safeguard, Australia had a court system to hopefully dissuade unfair action and reverse decisions.

Next door to where PEXA met, or not far from it, the RBA was working on NPP. NPP was solving a number of problems. One problem NPP solved, in addition to the main ones of the use of email addresses and mobile numbers, real-time and rich information, was the systemic risk of a bank failing during clearing and settlement. On another floor was another real-time payment system, RTGS, whose only deficiency was that it operated during working hours only, similar, though, to property settlement times. In the history of property settlement, this had never happened — or at least, was never an issue. The banking system operated on "My word is my bond", and even today, larger settlements take place in financial markets, especially in foreign exchange markets, with a longer, two business day window for settlement. Letters of credit are similar. To solve the problem at hand, the banks could have issued letters of credit.

Ironically, despite all the complex engineering, DvP was not solved, and the land titles offices only issued a lodgement advice before payment needed to be completed. (They would take time to complete.) Also, even after the bank has their money, the money is not disbursed to the customer (seller) who, in theory (again, this will probably never get tested in court), may not be entitled to the Financial Claims Scheme. The only real advantage of the process was a standard online workbench/workflow: the ability to do the settlement online, without being in the same room at the same time.

It could be argued that reducing this systemic risk was forward thinking, to the days when non-banks could settle properties and offer mortgages, but it certainly was not a burning problem at this time. The fact that the customer did not receive money in their account immediately made it worse than NPP, RTGS, and even the bank cheque system. It did not force the land titles organisations to automate. They could, in theory, still reject the payment, and a court could challenge the transaction. Nor did the solution remove many of the causes of delayed settlement,

Nevertheless, the RBA built a new payment system, and integration to RITS to handle the reservation of funds and payment directly from ESA accounts, a duplication largely of something that could have been solved by RTGS, NPP or even Direct Entry. While the systemic payment risk was reduced, a bigger risk of non-transfer of titles was introduced. Surprisingly, despite the involvement of the law societies, and every state and federal government agency, PEXA and the Electronic Conveyancing National Law was just a new way to accept forms, and did not alter the process of processing them after the fact. A completed form was not evidence of property transfer.

To its credit, PEXA managed to successfully move a lot of mainstream settlement to its platform. Though PEXA does not publish adoption statistics, we can assume that it has taken a step in the direction of digitisation. However, given this was supported by the taxpayer, the fact that it largely failed to achieve a reasonable level of digitisation or improve the system and, given the large expense required to facilitate this system, it barely scratched the surface of the problem.

So it was largely a failed opportunity, right under the noses of the COAG. The RBA settlements were moved from an open market to a closed solution, a permanent monopoly owned by a private consortium, without an open market tender. A solution that now acts as a barrier of entry to smaller players, whether they be mortgage financiers, banks or settlement solutions.

Sure enough, eventually, after an unsuccessful IPO, PEXA sold to a consortium of CBA, Link and a Morgan Stanley managed fund before being listed on the stock exchange. To their credit, the office of the New South Wales Registrar General (the land titles office of New South Wales) was reported as attempting, somewhat unsuccessfully, to restrict the private monopoly that had been created. Conveyancers also resisted. Nevertheless, PEXA, with the building blocks in place, with a monopoly mandate, is in a powerful position to move forward on the journey of automation of property settlement.

Competitors

In 2018, the ACCC chairman noted anti-competitive behaviour in property settlements, and named PEXA and state land title organisations as potentially causing the issues.

InfoTrac, Simpli, and LEXTECH entered the market as competitors, attempting to automate the workflow. It was unclear if they would be granted access to the RBA PEXA solution and land titles registries. The PEXA solution was a mess, and the federal and state governments as well as the RBA, were to blame for this failing.

14.

EXTERNAL INNOVATIONS IN PAYMENTS

A BIG PART OF THE STORY of innovations in payments happened outside the traditional banking system. Some were successful, some were not, and some were adopted by banks and will continue to evolve.

The Investment Ecosystem

Many large organisations invest in new ideas. Recognising the benefit of hard work and passion, the initial investment is often attached to entrepreneurial individuals. It is often difficult to innovate within a large organisation. Conflicting interests, such as cannibalisation of an existing cash cow, can lead to a conflict of interest that implicitly or explicitly dooms an idea to failure before it gets off the ground.

Even after proper due diligence, careful research and external advice, possibly only one in 10 ideas can be continued after the initial investment. Very few of them become successful, yet the small minority, say 1% of successful ideas do pay for themselves and the failed ideas by several factors, and this is the economics of research and development (R&D).

Many innovations are driven by a desire for fame or fortune. An entrepreneur is highly motivated for success and, to motivate such attitudes, and to allow a competing idea to grow freely, organisations will often externalise innovation. This could be accomplished several ways, through venture arms, spin-offs, etc.

Other investors include venture capital or private equity investors. Many of these investors, dissatisfied with the wholesale returns on investment, sought portfolios that funded several startups and ventures with the idea that most would fail, but at least one would be sure to succeed and become the next unicorn (a privately held startup worth more than $1 billion).

Some global venture capital organisations include Intel Capital, Andreessen Horowitz, Sapphire Ventures (formerly SAP Ventures) and GV (formerly Google Ventures).

Australia is often criticised for lacking venture funding, though there is some. Blue chip companies entering this world include Telstra Ventures, Reinventure (Westpac), ING Ventures, Venture Studio (Macquarie Capital), NAB Ventures, ANZi and CBA's X15.

» NOTE

One criticism of the top end of town, particularly banks, investing directly in startups is that, ultimately, their shareholders chose to invest in a specific company in a specific industry. If these shareholders wanted to invest in a startup, they could have done so directly. Investing in startups could change the risk profile of a business and distract an organisation from its core agenda. Is a bet each way indicative of uncertainty with an organisation's strategy? Or is this just a manifestation of uncertainty?

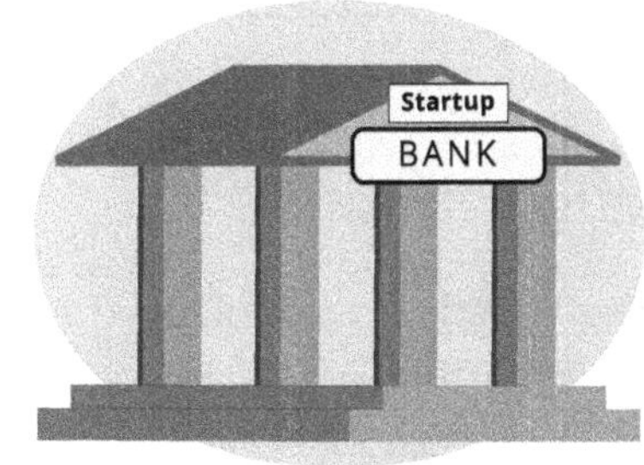

Big Techs

The big tech companies, like Apple Inc. (founded 1976), Alphabet Inc. (Google, 1998), eBay Inc/PayPal Inc. (1995), Facebook Inc. (2004), and Amazon Inc. (1994) are significant US-based technology companies that have attempted to innovate in the world of payments. While maintaining a technology culture, they have been seen as a threat to banks.

Through sizable commerce activities, all four of these companies have developed their wallets as a mechanism to pay for goods and services on their platform. App stores, advertising, online shopping, eBooks, etc. see substantial online flows of payments.

Two of these companies, Apple and Google, having ventured into the mobile phone market (through iPhone and Android respectively), implemented a contactless card payment solution. Neither of these innovations can be regarded as revolutionary for they were not the first and the technology was well established. Other than the fact that Apple succeeded in obtaining a revenue cut, and they both dragged their feet on implementation and opening up, the feature was under-inspiring.

The lack of innovation has not, however, been from want of trying. Apple's passbook of 2012 was designed to bypass other modes of payments with Starbucks, an early adopter. Initial take-up of Tap and Go in the US was low, which prompted Google to issue a secondary physical card in 2013 to access the Google wallet. This card had a magnetic stripe, usable at the bulk of merchants in the US.

PayPal extended its credit card gateway, with *pay with face,* also known as Check-in.

More recently, Apple and Google have been attempting to issue debit cards. Facebook, and recently, their WhatsApp, have trialled payments on their platform.

Amazon's Just Walk Out innovation at point of sale (cashierless payments) uses cameras and AI/ML to detect what goods have been taken from a store, and automatically charges the customer without a cashier. It does require the shopper to check in and out using the payment account, Amazon Pay, which generally charges a card. It was one step ahead of the self-service checkout systems elsewhere.

In many cases, the actual payment capability of the big tech companies has been under-inspiring, and really just a layer on top of card payments, embedded payments.

One exception is the Chinese super-tech company, Alibaba.

Social Media Payments

US social media platforms have struggled to provide a viable social media payment solution (Facebook and Twitter in particular). Beyond embedded payments for other services, take-up has been low.

CBA attempted a Facebook payment solution with Kaching in 2011 that was later withdrawn. Australian startup GroupTogether provides a solution for social collectives online. Facebook has proposed the Libra cryptocurrency, and its WhatsApp solution is trialling P2P payments in some countries.

Alibaba and Alipay

Alibaba was formed in 1999 by Jack Ma. Interestingly, he visited Australia in his youth in 1985, and was mentored by a Newcastle (New South Wales) based electrical engineer. His visit may have inspired his future endeavours.

With the rise of eBay, a few early attempts were made in China to emulate the online auction model. Heavy regulation, especially of foreign-owned companies in China, prevented external entry, and Alibaba developed the Taobao marketplace in 2003. (Coincidentally, this coincided with the outbreak of SARS coronavirus, SARS-CoV.) China, like many countries in Asia, has a significant number of languages, about 300. Communication across China was difficult. Being a communist country with centralised education, in 1952, the Chinese Government embarked on the simplification of the written language to ensure that, at least in writing, what was written could be understood from one end of China to the other. Simplified Chinese was a written language, not a spoken one. Fifty years later, a whole generation of Chinese citizens could read and write in a consistent way. Along came the World Wide Web, a written medium. Now, a merchant on one side of China speaking Mandarin could communicate online to a customer on the other side, speaking Cantonese, without the need for translation. While SARS-CoV ended up not being severe, for various reasons, East Asia tends to be overly cautious during disease outbreaks. In 2003, people stopped going out. They still needed to buy things. The Internet was now everywhere. Taobao took off.

American tech companies knew the potential of a 1 billion person market. Yahoo bought into Alibaba in 2005. Later, SoftBank joined in, owning 75% of the organisation.

Like eBay and PayPal, Jack Ma implemented a payment capability in Alibaba: Alipay. At the time, it was difficult for Chinese consumers to pay online. China's UnionPay had just started (2002) as a classic card scheme. Alipay was directly integrated into bank accounts (mainly through proprietary card links), and was granted an exclusive license at the time by the Chinese Government for online payments. With increased competition in China, much of the profit for the online transactions was skimmed by Alipay (up to 3% of the transaction value being charged to the merchant).

At some point, eager to see profits, Yahoo asked about Alipay. Jack Ma responded that it was a separate company. Yahoo and SoftBank were furious. Alipay, the almost exclusive profit vehicle behind their majority holding, had been taken from under their noses. Corporate regulation in China, still a communist country, at the time was nascent. It was also clear the foreigners would lose a battle in China against a native player. This was Wild West frontier territory, and Yahoo and SoftBank were alone. Not even the United States Government stepped in to save them. In an alternative timeline, Yahoo, an early player in the dot com boom, could have been a much more successful tech company and assisted in better Chinese tech company integration into the rest of the world.

Alibaba rebranded/restructured Alipay as Ant Financial, now the biggest fintech in the world.

Australia has implemented Alipay and Alibaba solutions for trade to and from China (or with Chinese tourists) so, in most cases, one party (buyer or seller) remains Chinese. Alibaba (under its core brand) is a popular business-to-business marketplace globally in the small to medium enterprise (SME) segment.

Another large online Chinese company is Tencent, owners of WeChat, which offers payments online. Again, WeChat is used for communication in China and, globally, mainly within Chinese communities.

» NOTE

Restrictive trade practices of the Chinese Government are often reciprocated by trading partners. While they do seek to grow internationally, penetration or growth of Chinese tech giants into mainstream overseas businesses, even within Asia, has been weak outside of pure investment plays. Their main strength is that they are a window to China, one of the largest consumer markets that many would want exposure to.

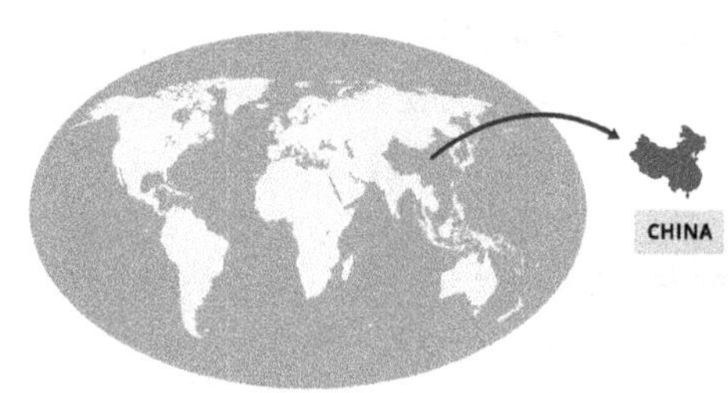

Alipay and Tencent have implemented a number of concepts online. WeChat allows people to pay each other over their social media chat, and Alipay innovated with facial recognition payments (no phone required) and pay by sound (sound waves used to transmit payment information).

Accounting Systems

While larger corporations used enterprise resource planning (ERP), general ledger (GL), and other accounting software to manage their corporate finances and payments (accounts payable and accounts receivable), like SAP, Peoplesoft/JD Edwards/Oracle, Microsoft Dynamics, Sage and others, smaller merchants used Microsoft Money, Intuit, MYOB and Xero. MYOB (developers from Teleware/Sage) was founded in Australia in 1991, and Xero was founded in New Zealand in 2006. These organisations developed interesting payment solutions. SAP, and their procurement platform SAP Ariba, as well as the SAP Ventures (now Sapphire Ventures) startup Traxpay, provided solutions for supply chain finance. ERP payments made it easy to pay from a platform, receivables financing, etc. With PayPal, MYOB, Quickbooks, and Xero offering financial services, Microsoft and KPMG supported an Australian startup, Wiise to deliver a competitive offering in the space. Originally, Wiise started off as a set of financial calculators, and pivoted once the two stakeholders became involved. CBA also supported the initiative to help penetrate the SME finance space. However, Wiise has struggled to get market share.

Alternative Payment Methods

On the Internet, a common term used is alternative payment method (APM). Some examples are coupons, non-scheme gift cards, PayPal (which is actually usually a card), or another card-based wallet, direct debit, BPAY, NPP, and others. These can also be innovative alternatives to paying by card, such as Alipay, POLi Payments, cryptocurrency, and buy now, pay later schemes. Some of these are covered below.

The Adoption and Hype Cycles

Traditional technology marketing textbooks talk about the technology adoption lifecycle. For any new technology take-up is slow, then it peaks and is then dropped as the next best thing arrives, and the cycle continues.

An example in written communication is surface mail to airmail, airmail to telexes, telexes to faxes, faxes to emails, emails to online chats.

For each technology, there are early adopters and late ones, and the late majority outnumbers the early adopters, as depicted in *Figure 39*. Older fundamental technologies tend to have a longer cycle and never really die. The first technical invention was the tool or wheel. Both are still around, though the flint has been replaced by carbon-tungsten, and the wooden wheel by inflatable tyres.

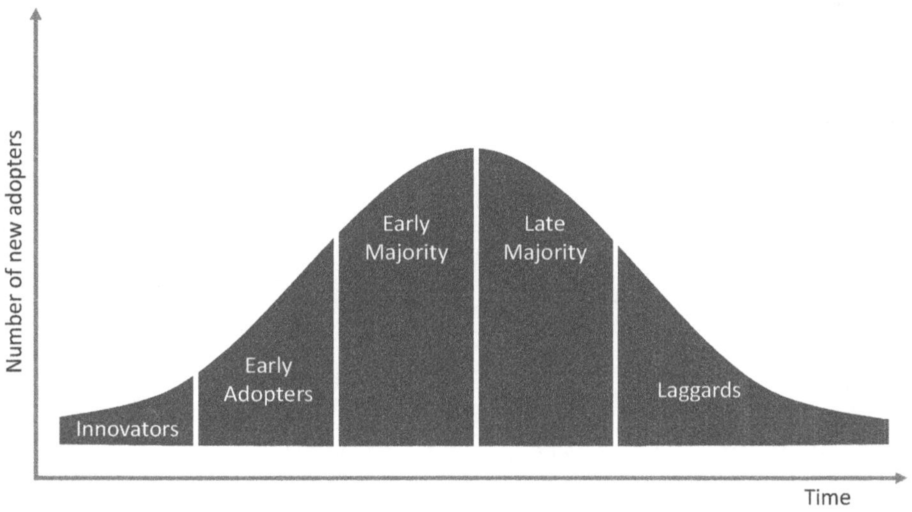

***Figure 39.* Technology adoption lifecycle.**

In the early stages of adoption, technology goes through a hype period. This has been attenuated in recent times due to global, real-time and sometimes viral media.

Gartner identified the hype cycle (*Figure 40*). A long period of incubation, research, and development grabs public attention one day, often with a premature claim, and suddenly, at least in the small tech universe, the technology reaches a climax. Sadly, outside the tech community, the sales do not reflect the excitement, primarily because the technology is still in its infancy, and behaviourally or technologically, people are just not ready to use it. *Vapourware* or *brochureware*, a play on *software*, are sarcastic terms used to describe solutions that only exist in ideas or marketing and not in the real world. Somewhat savagely, the technology gets dumped when the reality hits home. This dumping (or *trough of disillusionment*) is often unfair, but is marked by investors and internal company executives regarding the technology as a has-been or non-starter.

In so many cases, however, innovation needs time. Time for the mainstream population to catch up, time for the technology to work for real problems, and time for trial and error to yield results.

» NOTE

In the scientific world, premature claims are frowned upon. Every now and then, an over-enthusiastic researcher may claim the cure for cancer or to have discovered perpetual motion, cold fusion or some such discovery. Very rarely, have sweeping breakthroughs happened overnight through one person. Likewise, in the engineering world, the path to innovation is often a slow, multi-faceted process, with no one hero that can ever claim full credit. A deeper study of the invention of human flight and the electric light bulb may deflate the popular notion that the Wright brothers or Thomas Edison were the creators. In fact, they stood on the shoulders of giants, who made sometimes more remarkable breakthroughs, and their own inventions were improved to such an extent that their work is barely recognisable today. Similarly, Apple did not invent the smartphone, nor did Google come up with the Web search engine. The roll of names of innovators is a long trail of silent workers, most of whom will never know fame.

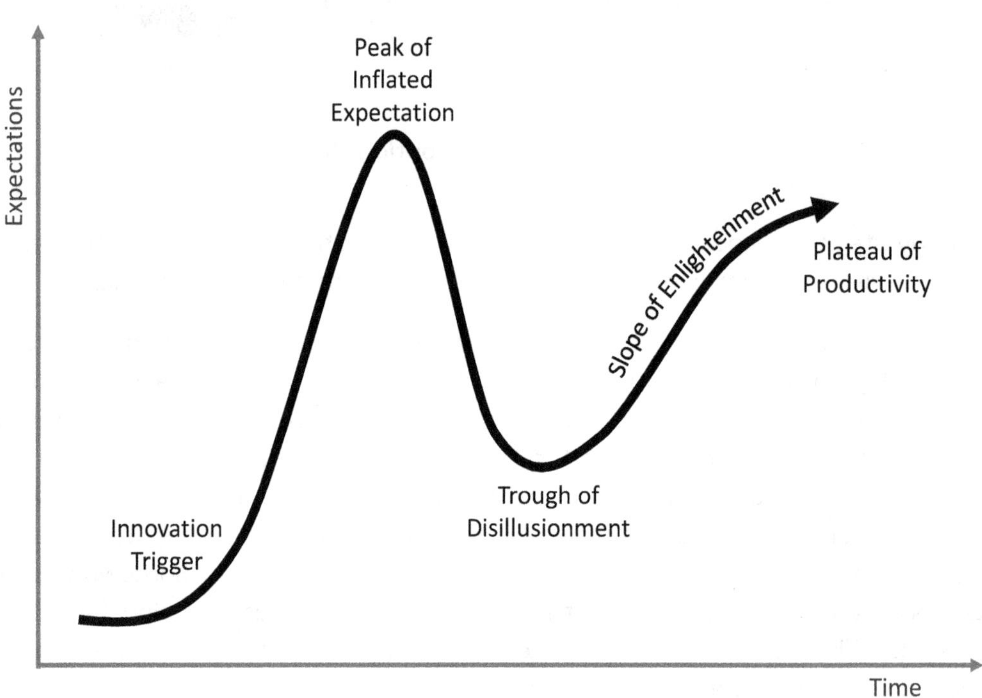

Figure 40. **Gartner's hype cycle.**

Geoffrey Moore identified the *chasm*[103] (*Figure 41*) as the biggest issue in innovation. Surprisingly, it remains a continuous trap among non-technologists who often provide investment money for new ideas.

In modern innovation circles, *fast failure* became popular as an innovation management technique to stop investment in ideas that were going nowhere. While it is true that the opposite strategy of dogmatic persistence could result in lost investments, many of Australia's successes are attributed to perseverance, sometimes against significant resistance, to attain success. The compromise between the two extremes is a commonsense, patient and non-reactive approach that is open to improvement and changes, not necessarily pivots in strategy, but adjustments. Sadly, most investors have little time for this approach, leaving a window of opportunity in innovation wide open.

While there are ideas like snake oil or the tulip surge of the 17th century that never come back, many successful concepts do exhibit this chasm before mainstream adoption.

The chasm or trough of disillusionment is the short period of stagnation before take-off. After the dot com crash, the NASDAQ recovered in five years and continued to grow. Many of the early ideas of the Internet were dumped early on, but are now mainstream (e.g., grocery shopping, video conferencing).

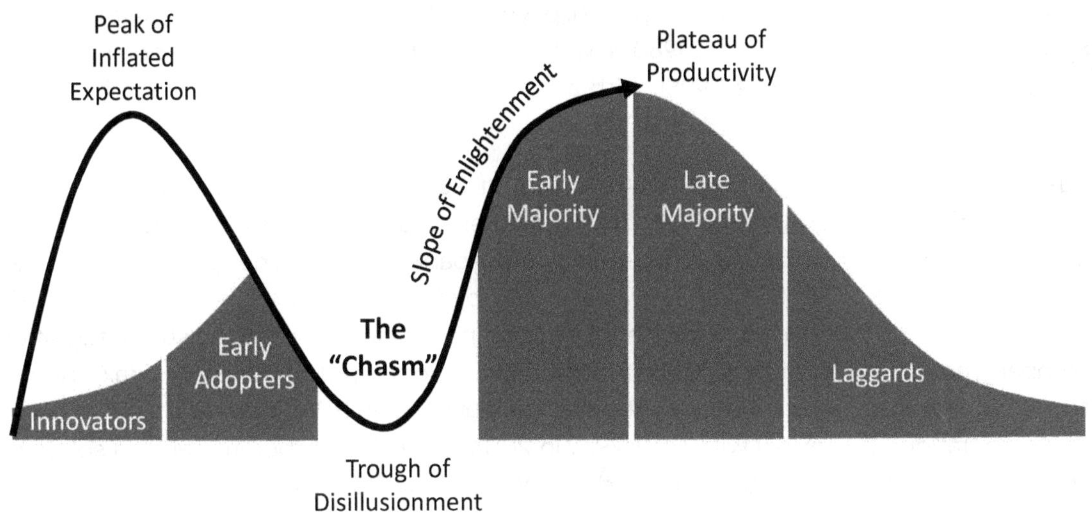

Figure 41. The superimposition of the hype cycle on the technology adoption lifecycle.

Many great innovations have fallen through this chasm: digital photography, developed by Kodak, early computer technology by Xerox and, in payments, the compact disc by Philips, and some promising ideas with potential from Microsoft and IBM. The rediscovery or repurposing of these concepts by other organisations, without the political and investment baggage, has led to market success as the newer solutions ride the wave of mass adoption. Working through the trough is hard and unrewarding at first, yet the benefits of perseverance could be significant.

---

[103] Moore

Startup Fintechs

Financial services technology companies, or fintechs for short, and specifically startups, have been the scene of some interesting innovations.

Fintechs cover a range of financial and technical activities.

Often associated with fintechs are the regtech (regulatory technology) providers looking at supporting compliance. While there was a fair bit of hype surrounding the automation of compliance, few organisations have succeeded in automating what is still a very human activity. This is not to say that technology is used in compliance, just that the notion of outsourcing compliance to a system or solution is a long way off.

Fintechs support financial information and trading, and provide software to the financial industry for various purposes. Specific to payments, we have a few fintechs of note. Many of these are payment service providers (PSPs) and, more specifically, Internet payment gateways. Some offered much broader services.

Some original Australian startup fintechs were, as previously mentioned, Hypercom (1978, acquired by Verifone in 2011), initially computer data to voice for the blind, and pivoting to credit card acceptance terminals and PEDs, in the early 1980s, exporting to Japan, Austnet (early 1980s, acquired by First Data), KeyCorp (keyboards, then merchant terminals, acquired by Bambora/Ingenico), Premier Technologies (1986, later a payment gateway provider), Card Access Services (1987), flexigroup (1991, payments/credit provider) and Quest Payment Systems (1991). In New Zealand, 1980 saw the establishment of PED provider Provenco, which later acquired Cadmus (1998), with a significant clientele in Australia, and itself was taken over by SmartPay NZ (1986) in 2009.

Australian PSPs were SecurePay (1994), which, in 2002 acquired eSec Payments (1995), a Cashcard-owned venture. Also in 2002, SecurePay acquired 1997 startup DirectOne. SecurePay became the largest independent (non-bank, non-scheme) payment gateway PSP in Australia. In 2010, SecurePay was acquired by the government enterprise Australia Post. PC-EFTPOS, the PIN entry device (PED) to point-of-sale (i.e., cash register) integration company, now Linkly, was formed in 1998. Sienna Technologies (2000), formerly Udax, entered the world of transactions and payments, eventually providing BPAY View solutions to banks and corporations. It merged with Clear2Pay in 2004, providing corporate banking solutions and payment hub solutions to banks, and was acquired by FIS 10 years later.

Startups were popular around 2000, with the dot com boom, and continued to attract investors and attention over the next 20 years. The chances of success for many of these organisations were exceptionally slim; however, many persisted and some have succeeded in becoming significant players today. At the start of the dot com boom, there was Distra (payments switch), acquired by ACI Worldwide in 2012, eWay, QSI Payments (payment gateways), and GPayments (a 3D Secure solutions specialist). Intellect Holdings (2000) later spun off the PED division as Tafmo/Touchcorp in 2004, which merged with Afterpay in 2017. Later, Paymate (2001) successfully challenged eBay/PayPal for anti-competitive behaviour in 2008 (acquired by flexigroup 2008), IP Payments (2004, acquired by Bambora/Ingenico), and ePath (2004, Payment Gateway).

Later, Fat Zebra (2011), a payments gateway, formed. SmartPay NZ, which earlier acquired New Zealand PED providers Provenco/Cadmus, moved to Australia (2011) attempting to sell its sizable New Zealand portfolio to Verifone. A delay by the competition regulator during the COVID-19 pandemic allowed Verifone to trigger a withdrawal, suggesting lesser terms. The updated proposal was rejected by SmartPay. Till Payments/SimplePay (2012) provided merchant payment solutions. Assembly Payments (2013, a payment gateway, merchant terminal integration and split payments solution), a Westpac investment through Reinventure, partnered in 2020 with Standard Chartered Bank in Singapore to take the Internet payments gateway offshore. The remnant in the terminal space, initially called mx51, was spun out as Presto, previously Westpac's terminal brand (not to be confused with the defunct Australian online video site), promising to take on Tyro and CBA's Albert, but more accurately initially competing with PC-EFTPOS/Linkly. Another startup, Beyond Payment Systems (2014) offers complex merchant surcharge calculations to pass on the cost of acquiring to the consumer so the merchant pays no merchant service fee (MSF).

Buy now, pay later organisations formed one after another: Openpay (2013), Zip Money (2013, later Zip Pay) and, later, the more popular Afterpay (2014). Startup Bolt Payments began PED development in 2015. In 2016, Slyp talked to a few banks about online receipting, with NAB investing in 2018 and CBA signing up in 2020. In 2017, Frankie Financial provided solutions in the KYC and fraud space in Australia and abroad. In 2018, DataMesh aimed to build and deploy Australia's first solution-based, independent financial switching network (Unify), and The Payment App to facilitate merchant payments oriented at improving the customer experience. 2019 saw Azupay, a PayID solution that allowed merchants to accept NPP payments through a QR code, reconciling the payment to a transaction automatically.

Square, Stripe and Braintree are some of the more successful PSP/payment gateway startups globally.

One interesting story is about the formation of Tyro. One of most successful companies in the US dot com boom/bust cycle was Internet appliance provider CISCO. Three Australian technologists, returning home with a fair amount of wealth, were greeted with an announcement. The RBA wanted to open up banking licenses. Tyro obtained one of two Specialist Credit Card Institution licenses (SCCI) though, oddly, they never really got into the business of issuing credit cards. Instead, they used the license to become a BIN sponsor, focusing on merchant acquiring. They continue to be a vocal opposing force to restrictive practices in the merchant acquiring space with regulators, especially the RBA and federal politicians, having a soft corner for them. Initially utilising Belgium-based Banksys (now French Worldline SA) for its box-like merchant terminals or PEDs, the technology focus of the organisation has led to a strong integration with point of sale. Tyro remains a sizable second-tier acquirer, with a lower cost offering compared to other issuers. Like many merchant acquirers, it still continues to run at a loss, listing in 2019. It is questionable how long it can sustain itself in the traditional merchant acquiring space where it operates.

Regtech

Regulatory technology (regtech) is an area of considerable hype.

Technology that can automatically assist compliance, machines understanding legislation, AI, etc. (and, as we will see, smart contracts) are a long way away.

As was the case with CBA's IDM issue, the regulatory problem is often not complex. It is often an omission of fundamental and simple architecture and design standards, or a failure to follow procedures that leads to problems.

Barcodes

Barcodes were introduced widely in stores in the early 1980s, as a way of saving the effort of tagging and retagging stickers on goods to indicate the price to consumers and checkout staff. Governments were going to ban this efficiency as prices could deviate between the shelf label and the point of sale. A code of conduct was adopted by many stores that said, if the price of the item was higher than the indicated price, the first item (if under $50) was free.

QR codes were a modification of the barcode concept.

Loyalty Cards and Offers

Loyalty cards were issued to customers of merchants, offering them points to return. Some of the major programs had complex offers, such as bonus points on specific items that required email or mailbox diligence on the part of the consumer to make use of such offers.

Open loop programs were generally not attractive to merchants (as, for example, the credit card loyalty system, though some merchants like Myer allowed credit card points to be redeemed in-store; nevertheless, they had their own MyerOne loyalty program). They were unattractive, because merchants liked their loyalty to be spent with themselves.

Flybuys was initiated through a joint venture between the Coles Myer group, NAB and Shell. The scheme changed owners, though Wesfarmers (Coles) remained the main controller throughout. One of the criticisms was that initially, by the time enough points were earned to be useful, they had expired. Woolworths also issued a rewards card, which went through a few modifications. Eventually the cards offered cash back at point of sale.

Airlines also offered a frequent flyer rewards program. In Australia, their card was sometimes combined with a foreign exchange scheme card. Points allowed holders to redeem them for more flights, and these airline points became the most popular currency in loyalty programs (including credit card loyalty programs), with most of the major loyalty programs offering points in one of the two major airlines (Qantas or Virgin). These airlines partnered with banks to issue credit cards with a high-earning points system. In 2001-2002, then Australia's second top airline, Ansett collapsed. This came as a surprise to frequent flyer points holders, who lost sometimes hundreds of thousands of points. Despite the parent company, Air New Zealand, continuing on, there was no redemption of the lost points.

Another aspect of loyalty programs, similar to gift cards, is that they are largely unregulated. The failure of the parent company through bankruptcy or even voluntary receivership (or due to a policy change at head office) can render an investment in these points worthless.

Qantas frequent flyer points were one of the most successful programs. Based on the large number of ways they could be earned and spent, they were almost an open loop system. During COVID-19, like most grounded airline programs, there were less options to redeem the points.

There has been talk, and startups have attempted loyalty point currencies. In addition, a number of semi-open loop schemes were established by startups, such as Rewardle, Stampii, CoffeeClub and Loyalty App. The value of the open loop to the merchants was questionable, as loyalty from other places could be used to cash in at the store. Some ideas, especially overseas, were interesting, like stamps that could be uniquely applied to the screens of phones, in a similar way to the old-school coffee card stamp.

Loyalty cards were issued with a barcode or, in some cases, a magnetic stripe. These were not secure, in the sense that they could be cloned though the risk was deemed minimal. Many merchants sought to insert their card in the holder's wallet; however, many consumers would not have carried all of their loyalty cards with them so the checkout experience involved looking up the card — a cumbersome process.

By obtaining the holder's contact details, offers could be targeted at the individual either through mail or email.

Over time, with the advent of mobile phones, loyalty cards became phone apps, and many loyalty apps used a barcode on the screen to allow payment to be taken. Initially, due to barcode scanner technology, many readers could not read phone screens; over time this improved and, today, most readers can read them. Apps allowed offers to be pushed to customers.

Offers online, often implemented as coupon or voucher codes, could reduce the price of a sale.

Shopa Docket, from the late 1980s, printed offers on the back of receipts at some major retailers. The offers were for smaller stores.

Some startups began offers on mobile phones. They would use the location of the device to push discounts to the holder. Groupon, a US company, eventually dominated the space in Australia.

Gaming and Casinos

Gambling can be traced back to the early convict days in Australia. Though banned, makeshift gambling tokens were discovered in the archaeological surveys of the Hyde Park Barracks in Sydney.

While two-up (coin tossing), horse racing, and pokies have been a central feature of Australian culture, the first Australian casino was opened in Tasmania in 1973 in a bid to increase local tourism. A more commercially successful operation started in 1985 with Conrad Jupiters on the Gold Coast, Queensland. The chips or gambling tokens from the casino were implicated in crime syndicate money laundering, acting as a pseudo currency in the black market. Chips could be taken out and brought back by another person and, if asked, the recipient of money could claim they won the money at a casino. Globally, casinos turned a blind eye to the practice as they did not need to pay out chips that were in circulation. In 2011, fake chips were seized at an airport, resembling Melbourne's Crown Casino's $500 chips. Poker and gaming machines in clubs and casinos introduced cards that could be used to store value.

Online games on the Internet started offering bonuses that could be purchased, and even local currencies. Second Life achieved a big mainstream following from 2003 to 2009, when banks, including Westpac, set up a presence. Many of them have since exited. The Second Life currency, the Linden dollar, was interchangeable with conventional currency approximately

250:1 to the US dollar. During its peak, Second Life had a significant GDP. Second Life inspired banks to philosophise on virtual currencies and this was seen as a potential disruptor. Virtual currency was the precursor to digital currency and cryptocurrency.

These days, many online games on the Internet and on smartphones attempt to monetise their platform by including purchasable virtual currencies, or allowing payments for their token system. They do this as embedded payments by integrating with a payment gateway to take money generally off a card, or utilising the phone stack, Apple Pay, Google Pay, etc. There have been stories of children racking up large bills on their parent's credit card account to pay for online games or gaming tokens. Technically, these platforms may require an ADI license if they exceed a threshold though few, if any, have applied for one in Australia.

Vending Machines

Originally, mechanical vending machines were operator-less devices that allowed a customer to insert coins and obtain goods.

Over time, these became more sophisticated. In Asia, and to a lesser extent in Australia, some shops were established near commuter terminals that only contained several vending machines, a low-cost 24x7 unstaffed store. Some vending machines accept notes and cards. With the Internet, it was possible to use a smartphone to make a payment from an online wallet to a vending machine. Due to the low value, some of these charges were authorised offline, and others would reserve funds and charge for what was vended at the end of the transaction.

Account Aggregation

Another startup born during the dot com boom was the Australian origin eWise. Founded in 2000, with input from a 1980s Australian tech company, eTeam. eWise developed personal financial management solutions and account aggregation services, based on the store of multiple logins, and what many called screen-scraping technology to combine data from several institutions in one. The more famous competitors in this space were 1999 US startup Yodlee/Envestnet and Mint/Intuit. eWise later moved to the US to access larger markets.

Initially in 2008, ANZ MoneyManager (a Yodlee based solution) and later in 2015, Westpac Live (through an eWise based integration) implemented personal financial management solutions.

Account aggregation services could see accounts from other banks and to initiate transfers. This meant it was possible to provide real-time notification of the transfer of money. POLi Payments, a 2006 startup and an offshoot of eTeam/eWise, did just that.

By logging in on a payer's behalf, the service can advise its merchant customer of a transfer in real-time, even though the payment may take a few days to make its way to the merchant's account.

There was a risk with POLi Payments. A consumer could unilaterally stop the payment by contacting the bank, without the merchant's knowledge or authorisation (as it had not gone out the door). For this reason, merchants took a risk. Alternatively, they delayed acceptance until money hit their accounts, making it similar to Direct Entry or BPAY in these cases. POLi Payments was cheaper than credit card acquiring, but came under pressure from NPP and lower debit card interchange rates. It was popular with airlines looking for a lower cost real-time payment option, margin lending Internet sites (foreign exchange etc.), and licensed money remitters. Many banks wanted to ban it, ostensibly due to security concerns; however, perhaps more likely due to the threat of disintermediation. With the advent of open banking standards, the banks pushed their case. Regulators did not act though they allowed banks to warn their customers and, in certain circumstances, may have voided their right to recourse through their bank. Bank opposition to POLi Payments became subdued when, in 2015, POLi Payments was acquired by Australia Post's SecurePay. Two years after the introduction of NPP, surprisingly, the service remained popular.

P2P Lending and Crowdfunding

A number peer-to-peer (P2P) lending facilities re-emerged around 2010.

Microlending, as it was often called in the developing world, allowed investors to provide sometimes interest-free or low-interest loans to individual small projects for as low as $25.

The infiltration of criminal elements and the potential for money laundering hampered the efforts, as many of these providers were frowned upon by regulators.

In Australia, Society One established a P2P lending platform. It struggled to get investment for lending activities as the investors, under Australian regulation, effectively needed to be corporate/high net worth investors. In 2014, Westpac bought a stake in it, and today it resembles any other NBFI (non-banking financial institution) credit provider, providing personal loans.

Tight regulation means P2P lending is looking more like traditional B2C lending.

Equity crowdfunding, a form of P2P lending, was attempted by Indiegogo and others. Today, again due to regulations (United States Securities and Exchange Commission), it has stepped away, with funders offering gifts, cheap beta or early release produce, or just accepting donations for individual health or legal needs.

Buy Now, Pay Later

Buy now, pay later is a concept older than money itself, as we saw in prehistoric debt systems. Store accounts were a form of this concept.

In the late 1800s, time payments were a way to pay instalments for an item; originally, sewing machines, then pianos, furniture, and even a wedding trousseau could be acquired, and the item gradually paid off. The time payment man would collect a part payment from households, normally £1 or £2.

>> NOTE

Time payment men were initially a curiosity to prying neighbours and, over time, became more popular. Time payment men were protected in law. In 1905, in NSW, the Landlords and Tenants Act of 1899 was amended to ensure that if a landlord were to dispose of the goods left by a defaulting tenant (called distress), the landlord would first need to pay the time payment man the outstanding debt.

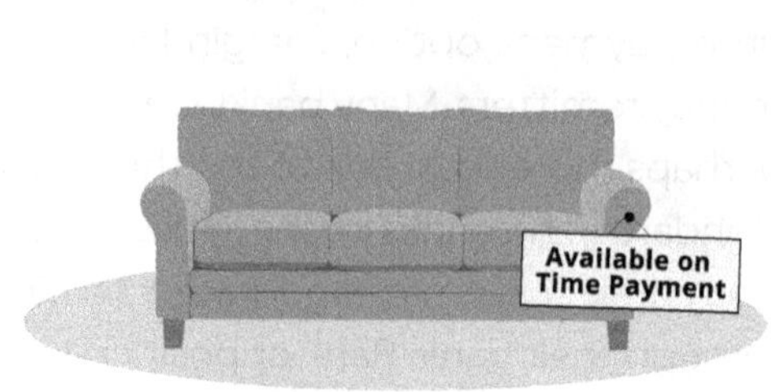

Around 1910, stores in Australia introduced the lay-by system. A unique offering in the world, goods could be reserved on payment of a deposit and, after regular instalments, the goods could be purchased at a later date. The system became very popular, even during World War II, with rations used to pay for goods on lay-by.

More recently, in mainstream banking through asset finance, credit cards, personal loans, and store schemes. It has been popular for decades.

Through better information technology systems and with the use of digital identification, it has been possible to speed up the credit process and reduce the transaction amount to make solutions viable at the lower, mass-adoption end of the market.

With the substantial withdrawal of AGC and GE Capital from the market, a gap needed to be filled. Tighter credit controls through the National Credit Code led to a credit crunch at the low end of the market. An inflexible product and credit card surcharging allowed for innovation in the area.

In 2013, in an attempt to improve the now 100-year-old lay-by system, Openpay, an Australian startup, invented electronic transactional buy now, pay later. Solutions like Openpay, Afterpay, Zip Pay, Latitude Pay, LayBuy and flexigroup's Humm and Bundll allowed those without bank credit to pay for things over a period of time, and applications and payments were easier to obtain online at a store. The key difference between these products and credit cards was that they were offered by the merchant, who would generally pay or subsidise the interest charges and fees. Ironically, many merchants surcharged the less expensive offerings when they accepted credit cards.

Some institutions, such as Citibank and credit specialists MoneyMe and Prospa, introduced more sophisticated revolving lines of credit.

Westpac invested in Zip Pay in 2017, and in 2019, CBA announced that it would partner with Swedish bank Klarna to offer the service in Australia.

Payments on Behalf of

The challenge with innovations on payments is that, at some point, an ADI license and capability is required, either for regulatory purposes, or in order to access the restricted core systems of payments in Australia and the world.

Payments on behalf of (POBO) is a concept that allows a bank or ADI to be the agent of the payment, which is actually performed by a non-ADI for their customers. Due to the AML/CTF risk, many large banks shy away from this type of arrangement; however, neo banks and smaller ADIs are open to this business. This type of arrangement is developing and can assist organisations execute payments such as embedded payments, described below.

Embedded Payments

The storing of credit card details allowed a number of offerings to just charge a card through their own authorisation mechanism. Starting with eBay/PayPal and Apple Pay, and within its ecosystem, Google, Uber, and so on, these days, many organisations use embedded payments to accept a payment.

Some issues have ensued, such as inadvertent payments, children using their parent's account to make in-app purchases (purchases within an application), and the most infamous free trial scam. The free trial scam was probably initiated in Australia by the US giant Internet service provider, America OnLine (AOL) during the dot com boom, where a free trial would be offered. To validate that the recipient was over 18, credit card details would be requested. After the free trial ended, the card would be billed, often without the knowledge of the holder. The ePayments Code was to no avail as the terms and conditions were very clear in their fine print. Over the years, the scam has become mainstream, with some merchants making it difficult to cancel the free subscription so people should be wary of this practice.[104]

Hospitality

In the hospitality industry, initially, food ordering and payment on delivery was enhanced by middle agents who clipped the ticket by taking card-based embedded payments, such as Uber Eats, Menulog, Deliveroo, and DoorDash, and in return, offered an online marketplace and organised delivery. PayPal Check-in was unsuccessful for ordering ahead but eventually Menulog offered this service. During the COVID-19 pandemic, Zomato launched the capability in Australia to order at a table or to order takeaways.

Beat the Q was a Sydney-based startup formed in 2011 that allowed coffee orders on an app to be picked up later. It was renamed Hey You and invested in by Westpac's Reinventure. Initially, the founders would beat the streets looking to successfully grow the merchant base; however, since the takeover, and despite good efforts by Westpac (who paid $5 to credit new customers' coffee accounts), the app faced challenges with the onslaught of global food ordering apps a couple of years later.

In the hotel industry, agent or directly booked hotels were replaced with innovations such as dot com era lastminute.com (in 1998) and, in 2000, the Australian export Wotif.com (taken over by Expedia in 2006) online hotel marketplaces. Airbnb disrupted the market when, in

[104] While some may not regard this practice as a scam, it is listed on the ACCC Scam Watch subsite.

2008, it allowed people to hire a home or hire one out for short periods. This centralised payments away from the provider to the marketplace, which also charged a fee for access to the marketplace.

Clipp, a bar tab application, allowed people to securely shout a drink in a pub. The application was taken over by The Payment App in 2020.

Travel Payments

Payment on transport systems was a unique challenge. Frequently used, with fast interactions, travel payments are a special case for consideration.

Taxi Payments: Cabcharge

With the rise of Bankcard two years earlier, taxi drivers needed a way to accept payments, as cash was getting more and more cumbersome, and the taxi driver and environment did not lend itself to big-store merchant acquiring. Taxis were somewhat unique as their clientele were the top end of town, yet many taxis were a small business (often sole trader). A sophisticated payment solution was needed to support these small operators. The taxi industry established Cabcharge in 1976.

The solution was developed in Australia and later exported to the world. Two major products were offered: first, a charge card issued to corporate employees, second, a cheque-like voucher that could be given to corporate employees for one-off trips. These two have been replaced with closed loop NFC cards FASTCARD and eTicket. These payment methods have the advantage of the accounts department or manager verifying the details of the trip, something not possible with credit cards (though, at one point, American Express attempted such a solution through a partnership with Cabcharge).

Cabcharge and taxis were challenged with competition from a number of sources. Initially, a 10% surcharge was charged on top of the fare to cover the payment solution. Over time, with the widespread acceptance of electronic merchant solutions, Cabcharge's surcharge was seen as a merchant surcharge and their hold on the taxi industry a monopoly. The ACCC and RBA raised concerns. Some companies and individuals attempted to offer acceptance of other cards to avoid the surcharge, but the taxi companies, which owned Cabcharge, resisted.

The overcharging practices of the taxi industry (little of which ended up in the pockets of drivers) succumbed to free markets, as rideshare solutions such as Uber and the Australian GoCatch were eating revenue. With the development of compact mobile cellular PEDs, organisations such as Suncorp started providing solutions directly to taxi drivers. Ingogo developed an integrated ride booking and acceptance application, and merchant acquiring device. When a customer used an app to book, payment through the app meant no exchange of money was required at the end of the journey.

Cabcharge was listed on the ASX in 1999 at a good profit, and became A2B Payments in 2018. As competition ate into revenue, the share price collapsed.

Airlines

Paying for airline tickets online has been a controversial matter with large surcharges levied, up to 12% or more, before the RBA stepped in. There was really no way to pay other than by a card, which made the surcharge implicitly unfair. Not only this, but the traditional ability for agents to reserve tickets without payment led to considerable overbooking — an expense for the industry — and the advent of direct marketing should have reduced the risk and cost, not increased it. Fundamentally, however, airline competition was cut-throat, and any opportunity to grab back some margins was taken in a bid to lead with a low advertised rate.

As most of the airlines in Australia had at least a few international segments, they were exempt from needing to have APCA compliant terminals in the air, but were unable to accept EFTPOS payments, only scheme cards, largely through the magnetic stripe. A significant security hole but lower risk, as all passengers had, in theory, been identified. In-flight purchases, even for domestic routes, were made on disconnected terminals, so it was possible that transactions would decline once the aircraft landed. Thanks to Internet connectivity during flights, this loophole has been closed.

One interesting behavioural development was the airport departure tax. After a number of unpopular and unsuccessful attempts to levy a departure tax to recuperate the increasing costs of running a government airport, a $10 tax was imposed in 1978 (*Figure 42*). The initial deployment was delayed in order to construct staff booths across the country. Applicants paid $10 at a booth in an airport, and a stamp was placed on the cover of the paper ticket and checked by customs. There was an outcry against the inconvenience of this new tax. There was a big outcry again in 1981 when the tax was extended to the 12-18 age group, and doubled to $20 for all passengers.

Airports are much more commercial operations these days and, with enticing shops and expensive parking, revenue is significant and, unlike in 1978, they run at a profit with Sydney airports making $1.3 billion EBIT in 2019 (before COVID-19). A Productivity Commission report noted the high profits, especially of Sydney, but noted it was within bounds. While the original tax, now called the Passenger Movement Charge, has gone up only slightly higher than inflation. It has been supplemented with airport head taxes, noise taxes and other airport charges with relative acceptance by paying passengers. This contrasts with an industry that is struggling to make a profit. By moving taxes and charges from the view of consumers and making airlines pay for them, few complain about the charges these days, yet they make up a higher portion of the cost of travel.

Figure 42. **An advertisement advising travellers of a new tax in 1978.**

Copyright Commonwealth of Australia.

Toll Payments

Similar to airport taxes, road tolls, a user-pays tax, were imposed originally to help fund the roads. The Sydney Harbour Bridge was completed in 1932, with requests to remove tolls originating from before 1950, yet tolls continued for decades, long after the original costs were covered. Every time there was a price rise, there was an outcry.

Human-operated booths were replaced with automatic coin collection booths and, later, with the introduction of RFID, long-range tags (generally battery powered, stuck inside to the top of the windscreen) allowed the payment of tolls through an account system: a deposit was paid and a card was automatically charged as the balance became low.

The main toll collectors each issued e-TAG technology developed by Transurban under different systems: in Melbourne, Linkt (Transurban) and Eastlink; in Sydney, E-Toll (New South Wales Government) and E-Way (Interlink Roads); and in Brisbane, Linkt again. All other states and territories had no tolls, and a tag from one scheme could be used on all the others, making it perhaps the most efficient toll collection system in the world.

Attempts at using these tags for non-toll payments, for example, at fuel stations, were discussed but never eventuated.

Parking

Seamless parking payments greatly sped up the traffic at parking stations and reduced staffing requirements. Ironically, the convenience card payments brought was negated somewhat by a surcharge charged by many operators on the same cards, despite the difficulty in handling cash. These low-value payments, transacted without a PIN, also contributed to the efficiency of the process.

Pay at Pump

Payments at fuel stations have been an unexpected source of innovation in payments. Sadly, the consumer convenience of the days when accounts were kept and the driver did not need to exit the car has not been surpassed. Originally people avoided service station shops, which were an extension of the auto-mechanic's workshop. Self-service pumps changed this. Fewer staff meant cheaper fuel and, perhaps to keep the visit to the cash register short, fuel stations saw the first EFTPOS machines. Later, automated fuel dispenser payment solutions were developed.

Gradually fuel stations discovered cross-sell, which transformed many fuel station shops into general stores/mini cafes and, to encourage sales, the customer was encouraged to walk into the store. Pay-at-pump PEDs were welded shut.

Many companies introduced closed loop corporate credit fuel cards, which had the added advantage (similar to taxi cards) of tracking kilometres for tax and corporate compliance purposes.

The archaic warning to not use mobile phones (there had been no known accident involving a mobile phone igniting a fuel explosion at a pump) was dropped, and a number of stations offered app-based payments: Seven-Eleven/Mobil (for fuel lock-in), BP (for pay-at-pump), and Caltex (for Caltex card payments only).

Urban Transport Payments

Contactless payments proved enormously successful in Hong Kong (Octopus, 1997, almost like an alternative payment rail/debit card with a deposit-taking license) and the United Kingdom (Oyster, 2003).

Monday morning queues, when most passengers would buy their weekly tickets, required long lines of staff.

Australia, a leader in payments, was somewhat slow to catch up, partly due to a failed implementation of T-Card initiated in Sydney in 1996 due before the Sydney Olympics and before Hong Kong's world-leading Octopus solution had hit the markets.

Gradually, contactless payments were rolled out from 2006. Most of these used the NXP MIFARE protocol.

- Smart Rider (Western Australia, 2006) MiFare Classic 1K
- Go Card (Queensland, 2008) MiFare Classic 1K
- Green Card (Tasmania, 2010) MiFare Classic 4
- MyWay (ACT, 2011) MiFare Classic 1K
- myki (Victoria, 2012) MiFare DESFIRE

- metroCARD (South Australia, 2012) MiFare DESFIRE EV1
- Opal (New South Wales, 2012) MiFare DESFIRE EV1
- Tap and Ride (Northern Territory, 2014).

metroCARD doubles as a senior's card for eligible holders. myki supports use on Android phones. (Apple's historic lock-down of the NFC protocol prevented its use in a big iPhone market.) The Opal network (through the US Cubic Corporation) accepts standard credit cards for adult fares, a convenient alternative that they should have led with, especially for occasional travellers and tourists.

In order to support Opal and similar initiatives globally, the schemes needed to overhaul their switch to support faster micro payments. Mastercard and American Express developed transit solutions; Visa outsourced it. Essentially, rather than do a full authorisation, the card is checked against a deny list and the passenger is allowed to board. Later (during or at the end of a trip), an attempt is made to take payment and if the card fails due to a low balance, it is added to the deny list.

Shared Economy

The shared economy is moving payments from individual providers to marketplaces. While economic theory suggests that open and accessible global markets are good for the economy, the marketplaces we have today have led to monopolies. eBay, Airbnb, Uber, Experian, SAP Ariba, Alibaba, and Aliexpress are examples of online marketplaces, all of which intermediate payments and take a higher-than-market charge for them, often along with a market charge. While the economic benefits have ensued from the removal of intermediaries, the new intermediary has also squeezed the providers with drivers and hospitality providers complaining of smaller margins. The emergence of a lower-tier more local online marketplace may provide better service and competition to these international networks.

Electronic Money

As previously mentioned, with the computerisation of bank ledgers, much of the money in the economy (broad money) exists as little more than information on a computer server somewhere. So, generally speaking, most money these days, with the exception of cash, is electronic money. This money has the feature, however, that it is centrally controlled and regulated by the Reserve Bank.

There are solutions where the ledger is distributed. Passbooks were a distributed ledger: every holder had a mini-ledger; however, in fact, this was a copy of the ledger of the bank.

Mondex (eventually owned by Mastercard) launched in 1995 and, two years later, Visa Cash (a slightly different solution) enabled money to be stored on the newly developing EMV chip. The chip contained a secure element and was a mini computer once powered up. Money could be moved from card-to-merchant-to-card to make payments with balances stored in multiple currencies. This idea became known as digital currency. The transaction could be anonymous, and there was no external settlement; it was integrated with the payment and stored on the card. If the card was lost so was the money on the card. The idea never extended beyond a trial as, within a few years, banks became more concerned with anti-money laundering.

Bitcoin

While debate continues around who created it and what was the first cryptocurrency, Bitcoin took off like nothing else before it. Around the time of the GFC, quantitative easing was instituted. The popular fear was that with printing money, and that too for the pseudo international currency, the US dollar could diminish the value of people's savings.

A paper written under the name of Satoshi Nakamoto proposed *Bitcoin: A Peer-to-Peer Electronic Cash System*. This author also published the source code.

Using a relatively simple application of the hashes and PKI cryptography mentioned earlier, a scheme of transfer was developed that allowed a Bitcoin to be transferred from one owner to another, not dissimilar to electronic money solutions of the past, though this was a true Internet payment that only existed as data on the Internet (*Figure 43*).

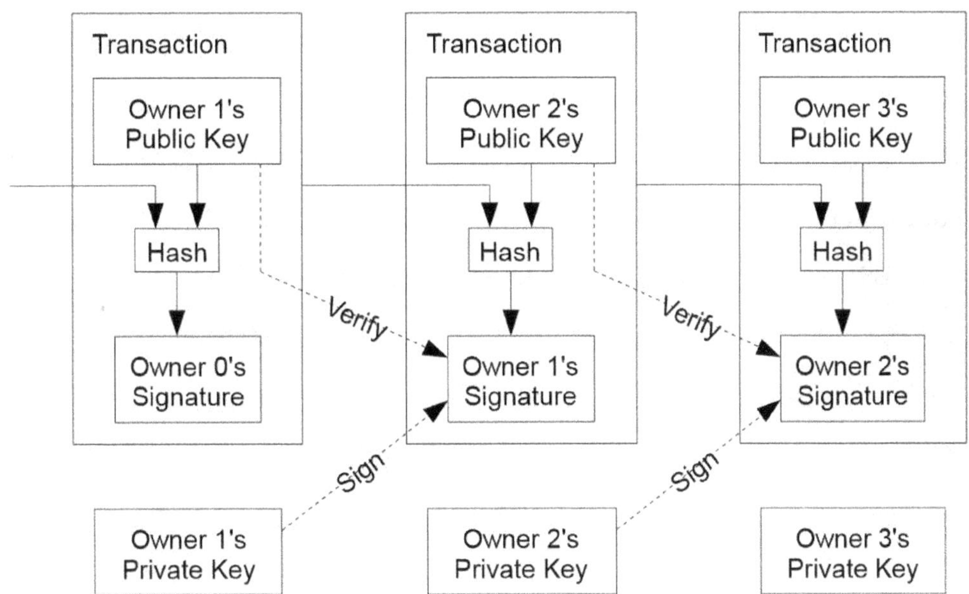

***Figure* 43. A Bitcoin transaction chain, courtesy of Satoshi.**

The critical difference with Bitcoin was that the ledger was distributed or shared and not centralised, nor was it decentralised, like on Mondex. Everyone knew where the money was all the time.

In order for a transaction to get stored on the ledger, the owner was required to pay a fee to the successful node.

Each node was called a miner. Like gold mining, it required effort to find the nugget, but once found, the miner would be rewarded with fees and newly minted Bitcoin.

A miner would pick up that transaction (if it so desired) and attempt to add it to the chain. A number of miners would work to solve the problem. In the 10-minute period, the miner with the longest block (first) succeeds and all nodes accept that as the new chain.

Bitcoin introduced a proof of work. A new transaction could be added to this shared ledger, if sufficient computing power could be expended. As time goes on, the computing power required to be expended would increase so that, according to Satoshi, a new block always took all the machines in the Bitcoin network an average of 10 minutes to compute. As more computing power was added, the difficulty of computing the answer would get harder. The accepted block would be added to the blockchain: a series of linked blocks.

To compute a block, the SHA-256 hash would be calculated twice. In the early days, it was easy to mine a Bitcoin; the SHA 256 hash needed to start with only two zeros. A miner would take the old chain, add the new transactions, add a nonce (a number that the miner could keep incrementing) until the hash started with the requisite number of hashes.

For example, to mine for just one leading zero from the nonce (starting point) 1 and incrementing each time, the hashes would be:

1. 6B86B273FF34FCE19D6B804EFF5A3F5747ADA4EAA22F1D49C01E52DDB7875B4B
2. D4735E3A265E16EEE03F59718B9B5D03019C07D8B6C51F90DA3A666EEC13AB35
3. 4E07408562BEDB8B60CE05C1DECFE3AD16B72230967DE01F640B7E4729B49FCE
4. 4B227777D4DD1FC61C6F884F48641D02B4D121D3FD328CB08B5531FCACDABF8A
5. EF2D127DE37B942BAAD06145E54B0C619A1F22327B2EBBCFBEC78F5564AFE39D
6. E7F6C011776E8DB7CD330B54174FD76F7D0216B612387A5FFCFB81E6F0919683
7. 7902699BE42C8A8E46FBBB4501726517E86B22C56A189F7625A6DA49081B2451
8. 2C624232CDD221771294DFBB310ACA000A0DF6AC8B66B696D90EF06FDEFB64A3
9. 19581E27DE7CED00FF1CE50B2047E7A567C76B1CBAEBABE5EF03F7C3017BB5B7
10. 4A44DC15364204A80FE80E9039455CC1608281820FE2B24F1E5233ADE6AF1DD5
11. 4FC82B26AECB47D2868C4EFBE3581732A3E7CBCC6C2EFB32062C08170A05EEB8
12. 6B51D431DF5D7F141CBECECCF79EDF3DD861C3B4069F0B11661A3EEFACBBA918
13. 1A252402972F6057FA53CC172B52B9FFCA698E18311FACD0F3B06ECAAEF79E17
14. 9A92ADBC0CEE38EF658C71CE1B1BF8C65668F166BFB213644C895CCB1AD07A25
15. 238903180CC104EC2C5D8B3F20C5BC61B389EC0A967DF8CC208CDC7CD454174F
16. E6C21E8D260FE71882DEBDB339D2402A2CA7648529BC2303F48649BCE0380017
17. 54183F4323F377B737433A1E98229EAD0FDC686F93BAB057ECB612DAA94002B5
18. 7EE29791FC17E986B97128845622B077FB45E349FDB80523FAC9DBA879B4AD60
19. F8FF18F5091484C8D789F909FABD899138A7140F4FDB5921DFF67F77FF6A4A5E
20. 075E7674A969687957CE158D8A9BC659C9110FDD1DB4CEFCA59359002CDD9880

In the above example, it took 20 attempts to get there. We were unlucky; the average is about eight.

As the degree of difficulty gets harder, with the need to find more leading zeros, it takes more effort. In essence, this is mining. The amount of computing power it takes to get to 20 leading zeros within 10 minutes is significant.

As all participants were anonymous, Bitcoin required that the majority (more than 50%) of nodes be honest. The rules could change, but 50% of nodes would need to agree.

Disagreements have resulted in two networks called a *fork*, with different networks giving a new name to the fork; for example, Bitcoin Gold and Bitcoin Cash. A holder of one Bitcoin can claim ownership of the original as well as the forked Bitcoin (though both would be on a different network and have different values).

New Bitcoins are generated at a slower and slower rate, according to the rules. According to these rules, currently only 21 million Bitcoins can ever be mined, the bulk of which have already been mined. In future, miners' rewards will only be the transaction fee.

Mining hardware is generally purpose-built machines with multiple application-specific integrated circuits (ASIC chips).

A lone miner with even a dozen machines will take a very long time to find a coin. For this reason, mining pools with the workload spread across multiple miners, offer to distribute a divided award if and when they find a coin.

One of the advantages that attracts people to Bitcoin is that it is an accepted asset, highly liquid.

Second, like electronic money, settlement and clearing happen in one go.

Third, as long as one trusts the majority of miners, the number of Bitcoins cannot increase; the asset retains its value.

Fourth, there is no central ledger; it is shared and open. A corollary to this is that it is theoretically possible for individuals to make transactions with no middle party.

Fifth, transactions are anonymous. Anyone can open an account or wallet and there are no ID checks. All one needs is a private key (or password).

A simple calculation of the potential value of Bitcoin is that if the top 1% of wealthiest people in the world put just 1% of their assets in Bitcoin, each coin would be worth USD $500 000.

Criticism of Bitcoin

The work of Satoshi Nakamoto, or whoever was behind the name, is a work of genius, and its implementation demonstrates not just great theory, but a practical mind.

Bitcoin and the revolution that followed was the biggest challenge to conventional payments and money this century and remains unsurpassed. It has created an industry, opened people's thinking to new possibilities and inspired millions of people.

Like all challengers, it has been criticised, and what follows are some arguments that potentially explain why it may not succeed.

First, philosophically and politically, Satoshi took a paranoid view of the existing monetary system. While it is true that the government, through the central banks, has the power to create money at their whim, thereby reducing an individual's wealth, and while we do criticise the government's perceived lack of genuine concern for its people, the fact is, in democracies, we the people voted them in or at least 50% of us did. Satoshi still maintains this 50% control but, for technical reasons, he does this through CPUs (1 CPU = 1 vote) rather than citizens. The CPU count already separates the tech-rich from the tech-poor. So at the outset, it is replacing one form of democracy with another lesser egalitarian form. Other cryptocurrencies have attempted to fix this proof of work deficiency through central governance, distributed governance, or proof of stake systems, the latter giving the owner of a coin a say in the adoption of change.

Further, what motivates miners? More rewards? So, hypothetically, if Bitcoins were to run out and a miner were to come up with a proposal to add more Bitcoins to the network, it could be in the best interests of all the miners to agree. It would give them access to more wealth, and diminish the holdings of existing Bitcoin holders who have no vote. The miners would, however, be slightly reluctant to do this, only because overissuing Bitcoins could backfire and remove trust in the network. They would need to tread carefully. This conflict is not fundamentally different to the conflict of governments and central bankers when dealing with monetary and fiscal policy. So really, we are back where we started. The difference is that, at least, governments are answerable to the people. Anonymous miners are not.

To further illustrate this second point, we can see in a pie chart of mining pools (*Figure 44*) that four mining pools control well over 50% of the mining capability. All four of these pools are China-based. While it is true that the pools may be made up of individual independent miners, voting rights are generally controlled by the pool, and it is in this context quite possible that the Chinese Government could have unilateral control of what happens to Bitcoin, if they so choose, not that they would, but definitely worth considering. Alternatively, the four miners could collude to implement an undesired change to the network.

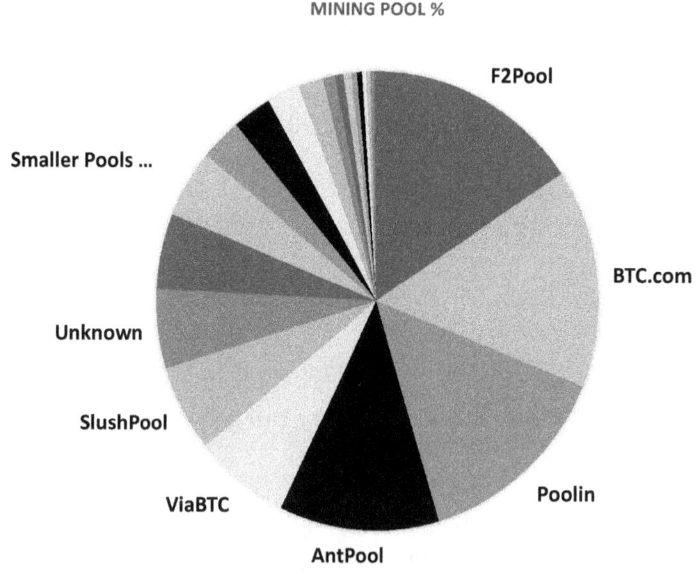

Figure 44. **2020, one year's percentage of blocks mined.**

It is interesting to compare this with a similar pie chart (*Figure 45*) of the shareholdings of an Australian big bank, in this case, Westpac. Other banks will yield similar results.

Thanks to superannuation and managed funds locally and globally (e.g., the US 401(k) superannuation equivalent), the so-called large shareholders are custodians or proxies for millions of smaller underlying individual fund holders.

Even discounting these fund holders (custodians HSBC, JP Morgan, Citicorp, National, BNP Paribas, Blackrock and Vanguard), the majority of shares in the big banks are owned by the insignificant shareholders "Other" with stakes much lower than 1%.

As can be seen, listed banks offer a more distributed model than Bitcoin, with a larger number of entities needing to cooperate to enable a takeover.

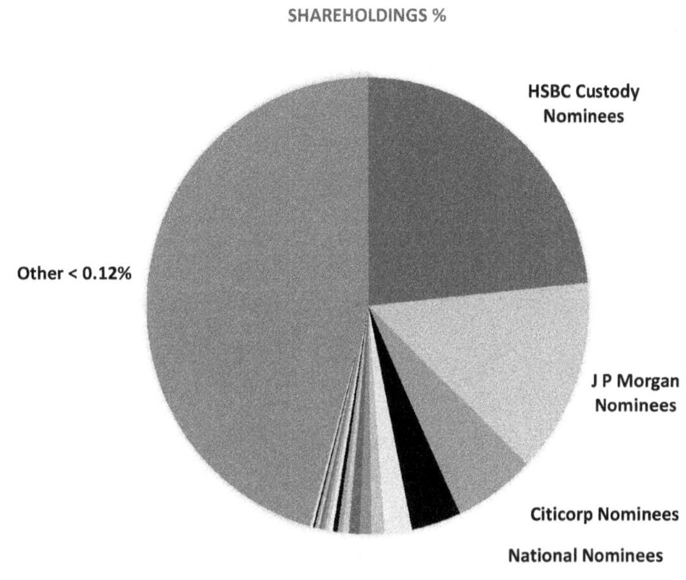

***Figure 45*. Shareholders of Westpac. Source: 2019 annual report.**

Third, while Bitcoin transactions are unique, as the electronic instruction is both the clearing and settlement message in one, confirmation of payment can take some time. It takes 10 minutes for the block to be confirmed, but that is only if a transaction gets picked up by the successful miner. Further, once confirmed, there is still a chance that a rival chain defeats the main one, and a fraudster could easily double-spend the Bitcoin in an attempt to defraud an unsuspecting payee. Over time, there is greater and greater certainty that a transaction is accepted. The worst known case was a fork that lasted four blocks (40 minutes approximately), where two ledgers existed simultaneously. During busy periods, it has taken a day or more to have a transaction confirmed. This makes Bitcoin by itself, in its current form, an inconvenient payment mechanism in the world of real-time transactions. Imagine waiting 10 minutes, 40 minutes or three days to get confirmation that a payment in a store has gone through.

For this reason, Bitcoin is not an effective payment vehicle.

Fourth, the need to mine was a technical quirk. Today, the amount of electricity required is substantial, which makes Bitcoin a potential pariah in a world that is environmentally and greenhouse gas conscious. The cost of mining a Bitcoin is proportional to the cost of electricity. Countries with cooler climates where air conditioning requirements are reduced, coupled with areas with cheaper, renewable electricity such as western China and Iceland, with Iceland having the added incentive of a restrictive currency that is devalued, have significant Bitcoin mining operations.

Fifth, maintaining a wallet is essential to ensure the security of coins. While one could build one's own, in the mass market adoption part (made up mainly of people who can't or won't write their own wallet software), users need to trust a third-party wallet provider almost like they trust a bank. Direct wallets are dangerous, as loss of a password can mean loss of coins. Managed wallets exist, like Coinbase; however, these have been subject to fraud, and it is not clear what happens if the organisation fails, as the balances could become an asset of the managed wallet provider.

Sixth, while Bitcoin was designed to be anonymous, therein lie two problems: it is and it is not. The ledger is open so it is possible to trace every transaction ever made. By tracing footprints back in time to 2009, it is possible to somewhat trace identities back in time. The term *pseudo-anonymous* was used to describe identities on blockchain. Further, cryptocurrency providers in Australia and other countries are coming under regulatory attention. In Australia, any organisation that swaps money for digital currency or vice versa needs to be registered with AUSTRAC, identify individuals and report transactions. This effectively means that any AUD payment to a cryptocurrency is monitored and can be identified.

Due to the ability for a person to effectively make a cryptocurrency payment from a Bitcoin wallet to UNSC sanctioned entities, banks have been reluctant to bank cryptocurrency providers. Often, a cryptocurrency provider would walk into a branch and attempt to open an account. They would trade on that account. If an astute bank found out, action was swift and severe. CoinJar, an Australian startup crypto wallet, reported that when CBA found out, in a process known as de-banking, their accounts were closed, and notice received that the personal accounts of directors would be shut down too with no reason given. Several other providers suffered the same fate.

Further, cryptocurrency transactions can attract fraud, money laundering, and terrorism financing, as transactions from legitimate sources can quickly be transferred anonymously and liquidated at original value. It is the payment of choice for darknet marketplaces such as Silk Road, which was shut down by the FBI in 2013.

Bitcoin is arguably more liquid than cash. Cash can only move by hand, whereas cryptocurrency can move at lightspeed over the public Internet from one end of the world to the other.

» NOTE

In an episode of Judge Judy (an American reality court show),[105] a former cryptocurrency dealer is sued by a plaintiff who was attempting to buy a pick-up truck on eBay from an unknown fraudster. The fraudster gave the bank account details of the cryptocurrency provider. Meanwhile, the fraudster opened up a cryptocurrency wallet with the dealer (the defendant) online, and was required to deposit money before a transaction could be made. The fraudster was given an account number which was handed over to the plaintiff. The unsuspecting dealer received the money, and returned cryptocurrency, which was promptly transferred elsewhere. The plaintiff got the bank account details via a police warrant from the bank, who promptly closed the empty account. The defendant claimed he did nothing wrong and, Judge Judy, new to the world of cryptocurrencies, was unable to make a decision. This pattern is a classic man-in-the-middle attack, where both ends think they are talking to one individual, but are being brokered by a fraudulent actor.

Bitcoin, despite its revolutionary approach to payments, was largely seen by most people as an alternative store of value. It was one more speculative commodity to add to the list so, for monetary activists, it never quite ticked all the boxes.

Cryptocurrency

While Bitcoin is popularly considered the original cryptocurrency, other currencies soon developed, either to cash in on the cryptocurrency hype or to improve on the technology.

Digital Currency

The generic name for cryptocurrency became *digital currency.* Electronic money was conventional money stored and moved electronically on a bank ledger. Digital money was the property of the holder, held in a separate wallet, and generally existed outside central banking. Mondex was an example. Cryptocurrency utilised a distributed ledger and cryptography to secure the money.

Some examples of cryptocurrency include the following.

Ethereum

Ethereum introduced a simpler mining algorithm that utilised graphic processing units (GPUs) rather than the emerging application-specific integrated circuits (ASIC chips, not to be confused with the regulator) emerging in Bitcoin. It also developed a programming capability

[105] Judy

that allowed *smart contracts* (discussed below). Ethereum also transitioned to *proof of stake*, perhaps a fairer form of control than proof of work. A controversial software flaw caused the theft of coins, and the branching of Ethereum into Ethereum and Ethereum Classic.

Litecoin

Litecoin was a variation of Bitcoin. It is designed to be less memory intense in mining; however, it has a more complex ASIC chip solution than Bitcoin. It has a shorter block confirmation (2½ minutes, making it more payment friendly) and more coins than Bitcoin.

Ripple

Originally Ripple was developed as a cryptocurrency. Ripples (XRP) were produced en masse by Ripple Labs, 100 billion, a pool almost 5 000 times larger than Bitcoin. Rather than mining, the coins were released to the network by Ripple Labs to facilitate the use of the network and to maintain the value of the currency, currently at around USD $0.20. Ripple Labs makes money every time a Ripple is sold. The Ripple consensus model was based on nodes allowed in the network by Ripple. So, largely, the value, profit and rules of the network are entirely controlled by Ripple. The value of XRPs increased during the 2017/2018 cryptocurrency boom to almost USD $3.00. Investors probably thought it was good value and an easy way in, compared to the peak Bitcoin price of almost USD $20 000. While Bitcoins (and XRP) are divisible into smaller units (1 Bitcoin is divided into 100 million units, called Satoshis), psychologically, 1 XRP felt like more than 0.0001 Bitcoins, even though it was less in dollar value.

Thanks to a simplified almost centralised consensus model, Ripple transactions were faster, and the network was closed and more controlled. This appealed to banks, desperate to get into the crypto-action. Australian and New Zealand banks were among the first, if not the first, to perform legal cross-border transactions using Ripple.

In order to attract the top end of town, Ripple developed a payment solution, more through its blockchain technology rather than its coin, XRP, though the two were inseparable. Every time a payment message was sent on the Ripple network, it would destroy XRPs of the sender. (This was the profit model to cover Ripple's fees.) The central idea was that the Ripple network could be used as a network to transfer value from one person to another internationally, using the liquidity held in corporate accounts.

The problem was that this simply used the Ripple network as a transport layer to convey IOUs. The same end could be accomplished through the Internet, a COIN or via SWIFT FileAct.

The issue with using corporate so-called lazy money to facilitate payments is that it effectively doubled the liquidity requirements of each payment. Lazy money was used by banks to facilitate lending and to add to broad money, as discussed earlier. If that money were to be taken by a corporation to facilitate payments, a bank would need to keep that money in their Exchange Settlement Account (ESA) to have it ready for payment settlement. This, in turn, would reduce the money available for the bank to lend to other customers, reducing money in the economy.

The main advantage claimed was lower fees; however, Ripple did not offer a scheme to control bank pricing, and the network fees of SWIFT were relatively low. As we saw, costs came from banks in the chain, something that Ripple was not going to fix.

Ripple Labs, as a corporate entity traditional banks understand, remains a preferred partner for an impressive number of banks and financial institutions.

Other Coins

There are over 1 000 cryptocurrencies on the market, though many of these are not readily exchangeable. There is no easy way to classify them with each offering a unique value proposition. Some are designed to be better currencies like Bitcoin and others offer extended functionality. Auroracoin, for example, was issued to all Icelandic citizens with a national ID.

Initial Coin Offerings

An Initial Coin Offering (ICO) is a play on the more mainstream Initial Public Offering (IPO, where shares in a company are first listed to the general public). ICOs are cheaper, and originally, unregulated. Many cryptocurrencies are issued as a representation of a share in such a company. It is a form of crowdfunding, where investors are gathered online, and often limited information is provided about the investment. The investment is made available globally through the Internet.

Regulators, while initially open to the idea, have largely failed to give ICOs a regulatory tick. ASIC (the Australian regulator) published INFO 225 as a guide to such endeavours, listing current regulations requiring an ICO to have a number of licences, including a markets license, currently held by a few organisations like the ASX. For all intents and purposes, an ICO was illegal. The big concern for ASIC was the lack of governance, transparency and information, including risks, potentially exposing susceptible investors to scam investments.

Cryptocurrency Exchanges

These days, most cryptocurrencies are largely unusable in their raw form until they are turned into conventional money. And the reverse is true: most cryptocurrencies require another cryptocurrency (or money) to be purchased. Entities that convert between the old and new currencies are called exchanges.

Cryptocurrency exchanges (or digital currency exchanges, DCEs) are required to register with AUSTRAC and have an AML/CTF program. This means they need to properly identify customers and report suspicious transactions and threshold transactions (the latter when dealing with cash). Curiously, a purchase of cryptocurrency can go offshore very quickly, yet AUSTRAC clearly does not regard it as a international funds transfer instruction (IFTI), making it a chink in the AML/CTF armour, and one of the reasons banks are reluctant to have anything to do with cryptocurrency providers. All this came at the expense of the exchanges, now required to follow AUSTRAC guidelines, but still often unable to get banked.

Some initiatives to make cryptocurrency safer included a walled garden, where wallets were managed by regulated entities (e.g., banks), and transfers could only be made to other identified members of the walled garden.

ATO treatment was an issue. Initially, the ATO charged a goods and services tax (GST) on Australian cryptocurrency sales, which disadvantaged Australian providers. From the 2017-18 financial year, cryptocurrency was GST exempt, but was subject, as before, to capital gains tax. There is a strong argument that losses, in particular, should be treated like foreign currency losses; this was (as mentioned) denied by the ATO and the Administrative Appeals Tribunal.[106]

Sovereign Cryptocurrency

Central banks have looked at implementing cryptocurrency as the central currency. These became known as central bank digital currency (CBDC). It was possible to not use cryptocurrency but, instead, a digitally signed record that could be transferred on ledger with the advantage being that digital currency movement can be properly tracked. One disadvantage (or advantage) is that if deposits are held with identified and reserved digital currency, then this would potentially reduce the capability of private financial institutions to create broad money, with central banks having greater control. At a macro economic level, it is unclear what monetary policy advantage this would have over the present system. With a reduction in cash, it may bring about better controls over money laundering and terrorism financing.

Cryptocurrency Wallets and Exchange Providers

Several wallet options exist: hardware wallets like Ledger Nano, a USB key device, keeps the keys safely away from hackers. Software wallets allow currency to be transferred in or out, but do not act as an exchange to enable withdrawals or deposits in traditional currency and, as such, do not need to be licensed or regulated. Examples of software cryptocurrency wallets are Trezor and Electrum. In general, lose the keys and the coins are lost forever.

Most people do not have the ability or desire to write their own wallet code. For this reason, there is an implicit trust relationship with the wallet provider. If the wallet provider goes out of business or loses interest, the software may not get updated, and a holder might find themselves in their own fork unable to access their coins.

Exchanges allow buying and selling of cryptocurrencies. Generally, they keep the private key so, as a wallet, they have the advantage that a customer can recover lost passwords. With their ownership of the coins comes risks as they are not ADIs. If the company enters bankruptcy, secured creditors have legal rights over the coins. (Mt. Gox famously collapsed, losing investors' coins to theft or fraud.) Exchanges are generally regulated for AML/CTF (as mentioned) so they need to get a real identity and validate it. Some big international exchanges are Coinbase (which allows AUD deposits from a scheme debit card), Kraken and Bitstamp. International bank transfers to some of these providers may be prevented by banks.

CoinJar (offering an eftpos card in Australia), Bit Trade, BTC Markets, CoinSpot (offering a wide selection of cryptocurrencies), Independent Reserve, and BitRocket are some of the Australian cryptocurrency exchanges.

---

[106] AAT

Merchants and Payments

As previously mentioned, Bitcoin, in recent times, has not been an effective method of payment, due to the delays in mining and the risk of unconfirmed ledgers.

Bitpay is an Australian wallet provider that facilitates cryptocurrency payments in stores or online to merchants. With both the buyer and seller having the same managed wallet provider (themselves), they can exchange Bitcoins in real-time.

Bartercard

Bartercard deserves separate treatment. It was an odd innovation, a closed loop payment system that stored value as a unit of account without being a fully transferable medium of exchange.

Basically, someone could pay for services in the B2B world with notional trade dollars (which were identical in value in Australian dollars) and receive credit for them in a closed loop scheme. Those trade dollars could only be used to spend trade dollars with another cardholder. On signing up, Bartercard would charge about $1 000 per year and give 5 000 trade dollars to the new customer. Bartercard started in 1991, but struggled with a weak point of acceptance capability.

While the ATO was clear about the tax treatment of barter transactions (GST was payable as for a normal money trade, and a barter service rendered was income), perhaps some businesses overlooked this.

Bartercard expanded with solutions globally and moved into cryptocurrency with its Qoin offering in 2019.

Bartercard has some positive feedback, though the benefits of freeing up cash are offset by the limited marketplace available for buying and selling Bartercard goods and services. Bartercard has somehow escaped ADI regulation.

Blockchain

One of the features of Bitcoin was the use of an open ledger, that was simultaneously visible where it needed to be and cryptographically secure with private information: the blockchain. While many organisations were sceptical of cryptocurrency, the open ledger was interesting.

A common shared ledger that everyone had access to was a paradigm shift, and Australian financial services organisations were in the middle of it.

Ledgers were older than money, predating coins, as was mentioned at the beginning of this book. While some ledgers were initially made public, through engraving stones in temples, the invention of paper meant that the ledger became private. They were kept securely within the walls of institutions to prevent alteration and for convenience. This practice continues today and, had it not been for Bitcoin, it may have gone on for a few more decades.

The Bitcoin ledger contains public keys. No one knows who these keys belong to except the owner of the private key. The private key signs over Bitcoins from the owner to another person without ever being revealed. That transfer is broadcast and stored in a ledger without any other record of who did it. A coin is signed from one person to another, and from that person to yet another, and so on. This is the chain.

So, some information is public, like which public keys own which coins. Some information is private, such as the identity of the owner.

Extrapolating this idea: with an open public ledger or, at least, a shared one, it should be possible to maintain the integrity of a ledger without giving everything away, for privacy reasons etc. All this is thanks to modern cryptography.

Bitcoin itself allows a limited amount of information to be stored with a transaction. As with Direct Entry, it has a limit, though it is larger.

So, when storing information for posterity, information can be kept with the transaction. For example, a payment of 1 Bitcoin can be accompanied by the text: "Happy Birthday Mum!" In order to maintain the privacy of the message, the text could be encrypted or hashed.

An example of an application of this privacy was the poor man's patent. A provisional patent could be kept secret for one year before needing to apply for a full patent and revealing it to the world. However, writing a provisional patent is expensive as it requires specialist lawyers. So for those who could not afford a lawyer but wanted to record the priority date (the day when they came up with an idea), they could file the poor man's patent: basically, in the old days, writing the idea down on paper, putting a copy in an envelope, sealing it and mailing it to oneself. The post office would cancel the stamp with a date ink stamp, so if an inventor ever needed to prove that they had the idea first, the sealed, dated envelope was proof.

Similarly, private information such as a secret formula could be hashed (using SHA 256, as before) to be this:

03b680eab659c430a16c7f515928d31a4e46fb60e668543ca4d080390bfd0aaf

With only the creator knowing that the message was "$E=mc^2$," they could prove to chosen people the date they came up with it through the blockchain.

In 2017, the New South Wales office of the University Admission Centre published their Australian Tertiary Admission Ranks (the main score for school leaving students) on the Ethereum blockchain. So, by sharing a copy of their ATAR with another person, though the text could be forged, the data could not as it was stored on the blockchain seemingly forever.

〉〉 NOTE

After each cycle or block, older transaction histories get summarised in their entirety into a single hash to keep the current block size small and workable across the Internet. Some sites, such as blockchain.info, maintain a history of every block, so it is possible to go back in time to validate it. However, this is a private service, not part of the standard, and again relies on an element of trust to ensure longevity of the data.

Similar to the two examples above, people around the world began thinking about what was possible beyond coins — records of ownership of a diamond, for example, exchanging other assets, marketplaces, international trade and payments.

Soon blockchain solutions became another hype. It was said that technologists started conversations with: "Your solution is blockchain. Now tell me, what is the problem?!"

Outside the cryptocurrencies or, adjacent to it, in the case of Ethereum and Ripple, a number of blockchain ledgers were proposed.

Banks were the most afraid of the potential disruption, for what was a bank other than a set of ledgers? A group of banks, including the Australian majors (NAB and Westpac, with ANZ once again the odd bank out) started by CBA, and international banks, formed a global consortium: R3CEV, or R3 for short. The consortium remains the best bank-funded and supported distributed ledger organisation. R3 developed Corda blockchain. Arguably, Corda is not an open ledger. It exists, like Ripple, between trusted organisations only, whereas anyone can be part of the Bitcoin or Ethereum networks. Some argue it is not a blockchain either, as it does not batch transactions, though this deficiency is its major asset as it can confirm transactions in real-time. Corda is sometimes described as a *permissioned ledger*.

Hyperledger was a more open blockchain started by the Linux Foundation, led by IBM, Intel and SAP Ariba. Australian bank ANZ (always the odd one out) backed this ledger, rather than R3.

Digital Asset Holdings received a significant backing from the Australian Securities Exchange (ASX), with its digital asset platform and Digital Asset Modelling Language. ASX has a plan to move CHESS to the blockchain; however, this move could be much more efficient if all registries used the same ledger,

Countless blockchain startups globally and some in Australia were formed from around 2015. BBiller, Identitii and Monecatcha (in payments), Bloxian (education and enterprise solutions), TBSx3 (combating fake products), E-nome (electronic health records on the blockchain), and bron.tech (identity on the blockchain), to name a few.

Australian banks were quick off the block, with prototype blockchain-based trade finance solutions, bonds on the blockchain.

In 2020, the Department of Industry, Science, Energy and Resources published the paper *The national blockchain roadmap: Progressing towards a blockchain-empowered future*. It said, "There are opportunities across our economy which can be seized and enabled by the use of blockchain technology: to create jobs, to create new economic growth, to save businesses money, and to improve our overall productivity. In addition, the combination of blockchain technology with other technologies, and the digital data underpinning blockchains, can add enormous additional economic value."

Smart Contracts

Besides data, Ethereum popularised the use of standardised computer executable code on the blockchain.

What this meant was that if certain conditions were met, an outcome could be processed. For example, if the code said to only pay the recipient on a certain date, that recipient would receive money on that date and not before. It was possible to externalise certain functions; for example, only pay a recipient if it rains in Brisbane. This requires an external oracle, like the Bureau of Meteorology, to report to the blockchain that the condition is met before the payment can be made. Extrapolating this idea, it would theoretically be possible to write a contract on the blockchain in code rather than on paper with words. These contracts were called smart contracts.

The idea grabbed the attention of many and a number of solutions were trialled.

Development of smart contracts for mainstream applications is still in a dormant state, while many proofs of concepts continue, some internal applications are using the technology with limited utility at the present time, and mass adoption some time away.

Digital Identity

In the beginning, the problem that money and payments tried to solve was the loss of identity. In simple societies, within a closed family or community, there was less of a need for payments — it was probably a sharing economy or a simple debt-based system of exchange. Everyone knew each other and everyone knew who was indebted to whom, and often it was not explicit. One good deed would be returned for another. Over time, with distant trade, a common currency was required. We recognised the currency more than we recognised the payer.

With banking, identity became important. In the world of payments and commerce, unknown people traded with unknown people, but both people were known by their banks and banks trusted each other. Fundamentally, this was how bank-based payments worked. Early paper instruments, such as cheques, identified the payer, as did the original credit cards and electronic transactions. Identity became important. Transacting in a branch required that the customer furnish a passbook or account number and signature and, later, card and sometimes PIN to confirm identity. This was the birth of digital identity, the ability of machines to independently confirm identity. Online this was replaced with an ID and password, and sometimes a second factor of authentication was required to confirm identity. In fact, by law, banks were required to know your customer (KYC), which is why identity was so central to their processes.

Privacy

An important aspect of the age of information is the need of people to maintain privacy. In Australia, organisations are bound by law to the Australian Privacy Principles. Under the Privacy Act 1988, certain organisations must have a privacy policy, and maintain confidentiality of private information and clarity of how it will be used. The Consumer Data

Right (CDR) covered open banking. Both of these initiatives are overseen by the Office of the Australian Information Commissioner (OAIC). In the European Union, a General Data Protection Regulation (GDPR) introduced a *right to be forgotten*. Cookies (website tracking of users, and storage and sharing of information) were notorious for being able to track people's Web behaviour from site to site. The GDPR required websites to have a warning on the use of cookies, and they needed to be clear about what they were used for.

Legally, or as a matter of good practice, organisations in Australia are careful with what they do with information and are restricted in sharing it.

Data Sovereignty and Sovereign Access to Data

In 2013, Edward Snowden, contracting through Booz Allen Hamilton, revealed the PRISM Program of the United States National Security Agency (NSA), where the agency collected information, not just of American citizens, but of information passing through American companies and networks concerning foreign nationals.

Project ECHELON and the Five Eyes (a cooperative global surveillance initiative of the US and core US allies: Australia, Canada, New Zealand and the United Kingdom) were claimed to collect private information on citizens and non-citizens worldwide.

While Australia has not confirmed or denied the existence of the program, many people accept that their information is not private from the government, at least. The same is true of residents of most countries in the electronic era.

For its part, APRA recommends bank data and services hosted in Australia eliminate a number of additional risks which can "impede a regulated entity's ability to meet its obligations; or impede APRA from fulfilling responsibilities considered necessary in its role as prudential regulator".[107] This principle is known as data sovereignty.

Credit Scoring

Knowing an identity is one thing, trust is another. Someone with deep pockets is more likely to be credit worthy than someone without. Someone who may appear to be rich but has lots of debts should not be offered more loans.

Credit rating agencies in Australia, like Equifax (formerly Veda), Illion and Experian have credit scoring systems. These were generally secretive systems; however, they have been opened up due to privacy and credit regulations.

Every loan application (but not every loan) is recorded by these agencies as well as defaults. A credit score can be obtained online in real-time by an individual or, with their authority, a financial institution or credit provider, such as a telco or real estate agent on behalf of a landlord, or a buy now, pay later provider.

[107] APRA 2018

» NOTE

A failed credit check also appeared on a credit report. Some banks would let a potential client know if they were going to fail before running a check, and others ran the check before doing an assessment, so it was worth speaking to someone before application to ensure an unnecessary negative scoring inquiry was not put on file.

In Australia, credit agencies score a person based on the number of inquiries they have made in the last five years. (Each inquiry has a loan amount.) Many loans are stored on file, with credit limits and dates, and, if still active, are updated regularly. Driver's licence details, passports details and addresses are also stored. Company directorships and any adverse events, such as defaults, fines, etc., are also kept.

Credit scoring is an important part of identity in the world of banking and payments.

Online Identity

Establishing identity was difficult. It required one to show one's papers in person. To open a bank account or apply for a passport, this was fine, but something people found inconvenient for less essential tasks.

To top this off, without carrying a passport around, proof of identity in Australia was weak. Driver's licences were popular for simple matters, though not everyone had one. Proof of age cards were issued to those who could not get a license. Tax file numbers uniquely identified taxpayers; however, could not be used to confirm identity outside the ATO. Long before the digital age, in 1985, the Australia Card, a national ID, was proposed. It was extremely unpopular and suggestions of its return haunt politicians even now.

However, through stealth, the Attorney General's department, which, incidentally, houses AUSTRAC, kept a data link (technically not a database but a cross-link to systems of record) of the major identification documents in Australia. State-based driver's licences and proof of age cards, birth certificates, national passports, immigration visas, high-definition photographs from the various photo documents, and voice biometrics (courtesy the ATO) are all held by this Document Verification Service (DVS) and Face Verification Service (FVS). Some functions have been made available to private organisations to facilitate digital validation of identity. The vendors include IDMatrix/Equifax, VixVerify/GreenID/GBG, PrimeID, RapidID/Xref and Verifi.

A number of initiatives were attempted to establish an ID easily online. DVS, in conjunction with email or SMS verification to maintain a consumer link, was often used by third parties. Unlike some other countries, a strong online identity or digital identity solution does not exist in Australia.

» NOTE

Originally, online authentication for the government was specified by the Australian Signals Directorate. This was a high bar, requiring hardware certificates. Eventually, email, SMS, and app-based security was permitted to connect, due to political pressure, to make government online services more accessible.

Australian Signals Directorate

Identification on mobile devices has been facilitated by state governments through the digitisation of driver's licences. Australia Post, which also provided KYC services through passport applications, outsourced KYC services for banks and other institutions and issued a Keypass card, and later a mobile app with Keypass, photo ID and a digital iD. The digital ID could be used to establish identity online.

One of the big issues with establishing ID online was that often a stolen photocopy of a driver's licence could be used to establish an identity. Without a robust solution, online services, like online neo banks, could be targeted by criminal syndicates. Many of the modern technologies, such as AI/ML (as mentioned) and live image capture technologies, could be compromised and many vendor offerings were little more than gimmicks.

Australian online crowd tasker, Airtasker, wanted to ensure safety of users by identifying workers. Initially, it trialled three-legged authorisation with CBA (looking to monetise their large identified user base), but eventually turned to Australia Post digital ID.

The federal government introduced the MyGov portal and later a mobile app, MyGov ID, that was used by government agencies to facilitate authentication using three-legged authentication. Three-legend authentication is often implemented as a standard OAuth 2.0. If a customer has a relationship with organisation A, and organisation B has a relationship with organisation A, with the customer's authorisation, the customer can be authenticated to organisation B using organisation A's credentials without the password etc. being compromised. It is also used as a form of single sign-on. This is typically seen when trying to log in to third-party websites, where Google or Facebook credentials can be used.

Blockchain solutions were proposed and implemented on Sovrin, Corda/R3CEV, IBM Verify Credentials, the Decentralized Identity Foundation, and others.

Originally, online authentication [illegible] government was specified by the Australian Signals Directorate. This [illegible] high bar, requiring hardware certificates. Eventually, email, SMS and app-based security were permitted to connect [illegible] to [illegible] pressure, to make government online services more accessible.

[illegible]

15.

THE JOURNEY SO FAR

HAVING GAINED a deep understanding of how payments and the banking system works — the landscape of payments — let us take stock of what we know.

What is Money, Really?

We saw the evolution of money into what economists classically describe as having three attributes that today have been wound up into one thing: a widely accepted medium of exchange, a unit of account and a store of value.

Today, the availability of money is controlled by the government through regulation, essentially, monetary policy, by the setting of interest rates and the printing or issuing of money called the money base.

We saw the different ways individuals can deposit their money with financial institutions, which then lend this money out, creating more money, broad money, in the economy. The regulation of these financial institutions is controlled by the government.

The large amount of currency held as $50 and $100 notes is indicative of the behaviour of people to hold money. The even larger amount of broad money, accounting for more than our entire GDP for a year, is further proof of this behaviour.

And What is a Payment?

A payment is the exchange of value between two parties, normally for goods and/or services one way and money in the other direction.

We saw how payments in modern Australia started as coins and notes and, later, came cheques. Eventually, banks discovered information technology and, over time, banking became a technology industry. The infrastructure was important to facilitate reliability and accessibility of payments. Initially, early payments were exchanged by Direct Entries on account ledgers; electronic bill payments saved us mailing cheques. The introduction of cards and the Internet led to more convenience and global commerce when buying from merchants. International payment transfers facilitated large-value trades and allowed the movement of money across borders between individuals and companies. Australia's New Payments Platform promises to add convenience and speed to local payments.

Payments, for most people, are a message on a network, a promise to pay, are a change in some numbers on their bank account statement that is nothing more than another promise to pay. Strong banking regulation by the government simply strengthens that promise, but whether your money is in a bank account or stashed under a bed, it remains simply a promise to pay.

External payment innovation, while having lots of hype, has really been an adjunct to bank-based payments. Cryptocurrency, blockchain and smart contracts may offer promise; however, for the common person (or for any major corporate), no real benefits have been realised.

The government not only regulates money but regulates payments. It is keen to see innovations in payments to make them seamless, to encourage innovation and entrepreneurship, but it also wants them to be low in cost to consumers, if not free.

Differential Value

There is a common notion that a dollar is a dollar. As we will see, a dollar in Australia is actually worth less in buying power than in most other countries in the world.

Further, we talk about the Consumer Price Index (CPI) as a measure of inflation. The CPI is calculated on a basket of goods. Within that basket are a number of goods and services. Some of those items have been subject to more inflation than others.

The price of goods and services should, theoretically, be a function of cost to produce, and demand and supply. There is another dimension to value created by the payments and banking system which leads to the differential value of certain goods.

An example is a global phenomenon, acutely experienced in Australia,[108] where the value of a residential property, a home, has substantially increased against household income. This increase in price can be attributed to a number of reasons. First, there is the demand-supply dynamic, increased (and later regulated) foreign investment interest, increase in real household income (due in part to both partners working), positive tax treatment of investment properties, and a lowering of the average number of residents in a home from 3.5 to 2.5 since the 1980s.[109] Increases in property prices have outstripped annual household income from about three times income to seven times, as shown in *Figure 46*. This could be more for houses in capital cities, particularly Sydney.

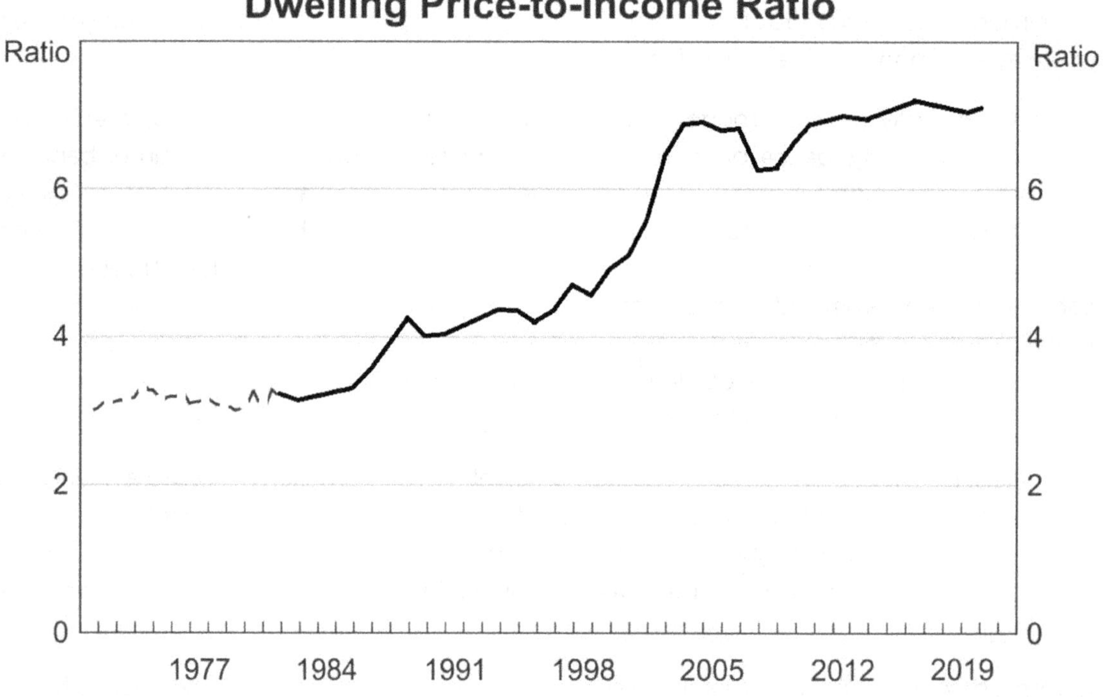

***Figure 46.* Median dwelling price to median household income in Australia.**[110]

[108] Fox

[109] Kohler

[110] Data based on surveys, and extrapolated, courtesy of CoreLogic and Fox, Kohler (RBA)

One explanation for the staggering increase in prices is a low interest rate environment, better access to lending since the mid-1980s and bank deregulation. As we saw, availability of broad money is driven by lending and, due to the favourable treatment of safer mortgage loans in the risk-weighted assets, money seems to have less value when used to buy homes.

Fortunately, the increase in prices is compensated by a lowering of interest rates, so when we look at the value of mortgage repayments over time, especially since the 1980s, we have a generally stable average value of repayments as a percentage of disposable household income, as shown in *Figure 47*.

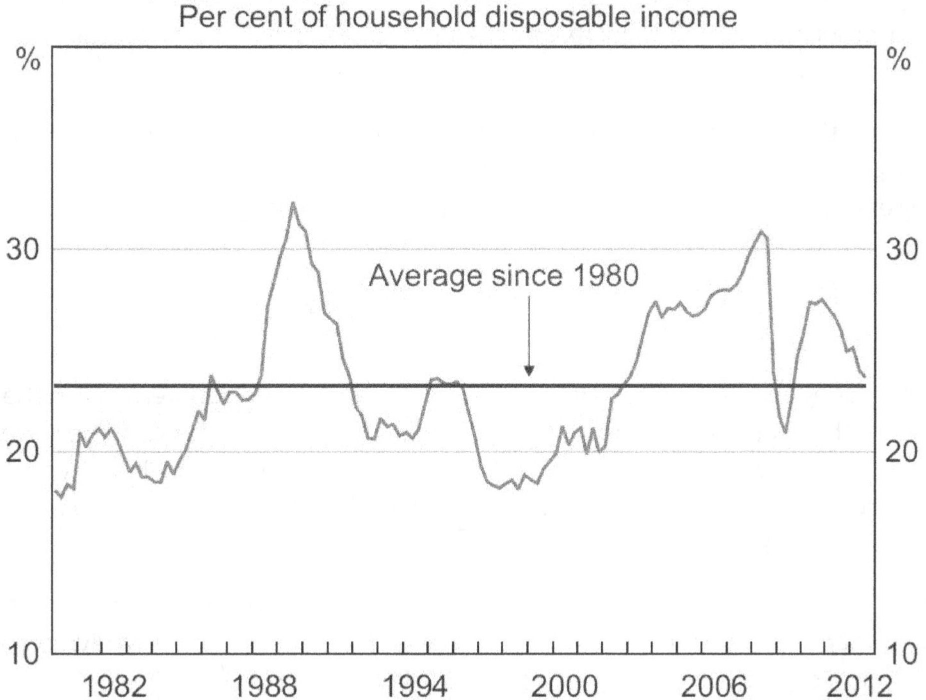

***Figure 47*. Repayments on new housing loans, courtesy of RBA (Fox).**
Copyright Reserve Bank of Australia.

This later repayment amount (and not the former, actual value) is included in the CPI calculations to give us our inflation numbers. An increase in home prices puts pressure on inflation, and feedback pressure on wages to grow. The phenomenon of increasing house prices against income, if continued, could further limit monetary policy to a narrowing band of interest rates. These days, any increase in home loan rates will have a sharp and contractionary impact on the economy. This indicates, at least for the foreseeable future, low interest rates could be around for a while.

It is for these reasons that money and its value (through monetary policy) are greatly shaped by the property market.

Australia has among the highest incomes in the world, yet we do not always feel this way, due, in part, to our mortgage repayments. To counteract this, after the COVID-19 pandemic, and extended Internet availability throughout regional Australia, thanks to the National

Broadband Network (NBN), with the widespread use of remote working, there may be an increased move away from urban centres for some jobs. As much as increasing prices are good for an investor/owner, more subdued prices are better for the economy.

There are other assets that exhibit a similar behaviour. Commodities, foreign currency and equities, as well as other tradable market instruments in general: as they can be secured, their monetary value increases. Superannuation forces the spending of money (a good thing), with much of the value going into equities. How much of this value is returned to the pockets of speculators, versus how much of it contributes to an investment in uplifting the means of production is a separate discussion. However, it is fair to say that more money is available for such investments than for other goods and services.

The fungibility of an asset also impacts its value. It attracts more producers (who may have produced other goods) and it increases demand (as buyers and marketplaces see more value in fungible items).

Extrapolating this idea, the ability to securitise and leverage an asset, whether it be property, shares or other assets, changes the demand and the price of that asset. So we find that these assets have a differential value when compared to other goods.

Trust

Central to money and payments is trust. Whether it is trust in the counterparty, in the seignor who minted the coin, in the authenticity of the coin or note, in the bank, in the government to retain the value of a customer's savings, in the security of an app, in a cryptocurrency wallet or the community of anonymous miners, people trusted their debt to be honoured and trusted that their money would not be lost or lose its value.

Asking a friend two questions reveals a paradox. First: "Where do you keep your money?" Second, perhaps a little bit later: "Do you trust banks?" The answers reveal a division between what we think, say and do.

The discrepancy is reflective of a conflict of interest in banks that we can all sense but few articulate. It is a conflict of interest that is unlikely to be declared on any Financial Services Guide (FSG) or Product Disclosure Statement, but is fundamental to the problem. First is the need to be prudent with a customer's money. The second is a desire for profit. This profit could be an organisational desire to profit, or it could be an employee's desire to get promoted. It could be the recklessness of a well-meaning individual trying to do the right thing but without the experience or knowledge to know the risks and implications of what they are about to do.

Without articulating it, trust has withered away slowly over time. The Guardian lists over 60 scandals in the nine years preceding the last royal commission.[111] It is no wonder that so much trust has been lost: consumer trust in the system, trust among staff that their voice will be heard, trust in the system not to reward those responsible for failures, trust that the systems will work the way they need to, and trust that the thirst for a quick launch would not compromise good system design and architecture, like it did in CBA's IDMs or Westpac's IFTIs.

---

[111] Guardian

Regulation

What the government giveth, the government taketh away. CBA and Westpac were government creations. The stringent regulations by which all the banks operate, the fees and interest they charge, and the way the payment systems operate, whether through direct action, or through the RBA and other regulators, are controlled by the government. Creating in one moment and admonishing the next; for example, PEXA, payment systems, surcharging and fees, the Four Pillars etc., in a manner similar to the contrary actions of raising a problem child: providing freedoms, only to have those freedoms abused and retracted, and the cycle continuing. How else can one explain inquiry after inquiry, leading to legislation and regulation, followed by shocking revelation and inquiry again?

Incrementally better regulation is not unique to payments and banking. However, in few other industries have we seen such velocity of change over such a long period.

Why has this been the case? Why has the problem child not matured? Perhaps Ben Chifley was right. Perhaps payments and banking are so important and fundamental to society that one can profit and earn money from everything, but not from money itself. Or perhaps the industry is inherently corrupt and, if we are to become civilised, we should banish it from human activity. For now, the solution is to give it one more chance. This time, it has learnt.

Regulatory Homogenisation

Great ideas for innovative products, when hit with regulation, end up looking the same. Society One looked at the inspiring world of P2P lending; however, the regulator saw the first peer as an investor and required that proper diligence be applied, and that the investor was high net worth or a corporation and, before we knew it, Society One became a B2C financial intermediary,[112] offering personal loans, much like the myriad of other private lending organisations. New banks are forced to offer deposit accounts in the form of savings, transactional, and term deposit accounts, building up their Tier 1 capital and HQLAs before they can start lending. Getting an exotic product through the regulatory process is next to impossible for an ADI, though many new institutions have dreamt of it, before they turned the pages of APRA's APS 110 and 112.

This is not a criticism of regulations, for these regulations have been crafted to avoid serious deficiencies, investment scams, and issues uncovered from the past, many of which we have touched on here.

The shortfall of product innovation is due as much to the complexity of regulation as the fear of institutions capable of providing that innovation taking a risk. Clearly, this is an opportunity for new players to enter the market.

---

[112] In 2012, Society One claimed to be working on P2P lending. In 2020, their website stated: "Our platform is currently open to Sophisticated or Wholesale Investors." Canstar stated that the minimum investment was $100K.

Competition

We saw previously how regulation has inadvertently tended to favour the large established Big Four banks, which, contrary to political and government policy, still maintain over 80% of the market, and retain the highest profits before tax of financial institutions in the developed economy.

Besides access to better shareholding funding to meet capital adequacy requirements, as previously mentioned, the big banks have better access to money markets and funds to obtain loans at a lower cost than smaller banks. The RBA's official rates and action in the money markets impact short-term instruments, but less so longer-term rates.

Further, the benefits of enormous scale mean greater efficiency and lower costs. So, newer banks and smaller banks are challenged with higher costs of borrowing and higher expenses and, in order to compete, they need to lower their already low profit margins.

This scale advantage is not unique to the banking industry but, coupled with other advantages, it further skews the industry and entrenches the big banks.

Stronger regulation also saw the practical death of building societies and credit unions, which exist in name, but are now smaller banks and capital adequacy etc. acts to limit how much lending business they can do. The bar was now so high that competing with the big banks was unrealistic.

The other challenge, as we saw, especially in cards, is the historic tight coupling between payer banks and payee banks: issuers and acquirers, or consumers and corporations. Unlike other countries, Australia's dominant banks (the Big Four) control both sides of the payment. In order to establish a new payment capability, one of the Big Four operating alone will not work, for the solution needs to be rolled out to both payer and payee. A bank with 25% or ¼ of the market share has only a 6.25% (being ¼ times ¼) share of the market for a given unilateral payment method, in the best case. This is why most initiatives (Bankcard, EFTPOS, BPAY, NPP, Mastercard, Visa, PEXA, Direct Entry, SWIFT, Beem It, etc.) were initiated or adopted by at least three of the Big Four at the outset.

At the consumer level, big banks continue to have deeper supply, especially in lending, which is a big contributor to broad money in the economy. A corollary to this is that to access this broad money, to make a payment, one needs to access, generally, a payment facility supported by a big bank. For this reason, as we saw, it is the big bank payment methods that dominate the landscape, whether they were invented by them or they were forced to adopt them through regulation or the threat of competition. Hence, many innovations in payments outside the banking sector tend to scratch the surface of an underlying bank payment. As we saw in the technology overview, they were the frontend, not the backend.

For a while, the threat of big global banks: Citibank, HSBC, Deutsche Bank, etc. taking over the developed world was significant. A few things prevented this. First was the global financial crisis. The global banks eager to shore up their own balance sheets and maintain their offerings in established markets, did not want to invest heavily in emerging markets. Second, standardised IT at the frontend ended up being a liability as the digital age and domestic payments evolved. They did not have significant investment dollars to improve their offshore capabilities, and IT was centralised. Meanwhile, the banks, especially CBA, were focusing on IT with others keeping step. This created a wedge between the local and international banks. The pattern was repeated globally, with the international banks facing increased local competition, and a head office unwilling or unable to invest. Third, while branch numbers were declining and moving to the Internet, most people preferred a bank that was located close to home. This favoured local banks with a branch network.

Continued intent exists to increase competition, and there have been numerous attempts to curtail the monopoly, either directly or indirectly. APRA's higher threshold for capital adequacy, the federal government's bank tax of 0.06% on liabilities was introduced in 2017 and applied to the Big Four plus Macquarie Bank. These banks have been excluded from benefits during the COVID-19 pandemic that have applied to other enterprises.

As the Productivity Commission's Inquiry into Competition in the Australian Financial System (2017-2018) noted, the explicit Four Pillars policy, which prevents cross-takeovers, also protects the weaker of the Big Four (NAB and ANZ). Also, foreign takeover of one of these may improve competition.

The big banks, however, are facing a turning of the tide. Consumer sentiment against them, tax profits reduced by regulators, regulatory control of fees, and tighter restrictions on credit as well as tougher capital adequacy requirements all act against their future.

Their ability to grow without acquisition (the ACCC will no doubt frown on it), in a country with a low GDP growth and low population growth, means income remains stagnant and a lack of growth in the stock market is death.

The only way banks can increase profits is to reduce costs. Offshoring may be close to its optimal level, and reduction of staff through reduced branches will lessen their appeal as the local bank attraction dissipates. In an organisation that is already highly automated, reduction of staff will only mean poorer service and a lessened ability to execute on change and further modernisation. We have not seen major bank-led innovation in recent times. All this points to what chief financial officers call *narrowing jaws* in a graph that plots income and expenses, something that analysts and the shareholders that read their reports do not like to see.

ANZ: The Odd Bank Out

In the course of our reflection in this chapter, if there is an opinion that the banks are colluding to conspire against their customers, it may be worth noting the one that has consistently taken a contrarian route: ANZ Bank. Perhaps it has stronger ties to New Zealand, at least, in name, or just has a different culture. Whatever the reason, it has resulted in ANZ often being outside the establishment. This is not to say that the others have not been different too. NAB has frequently gone out on a limb, challenging account fees, and they advertised in 2011 that they were breaking up with the other members of the Big Four. CBA has ploughed ahead with unilateral innovation (though, to their credit, they are often the instigator of cooperation in the industry), and Westpac, Australia's first bank, has challenged the status quo all the way to the Privy Council as we saw and, more recently, trying to take on interest rate pressure with the banana smoothie campaign.

ANZ is unique. It has ventured into Asia at a scale like no other Australian bank, and if circumstances and luck were more favourable, it could have been a very different bank.

Throughout this book, we have pointed to a significant number of cases where it has been quite different, sometimes a thorn in the side of the other Big Four members. Sometimes it has made the right call, sometimes an inconvenient one. The interesting observations we saw were:

- The only Big Four bank to have its founding banks registered in London.
- The only Big Four to start operations outside Sydney/Melbourne (Launceston, Tasmania).
- As Bank of Australasia, during the South Australian gold rush of 1852, accepted gold deposits.
- Attempted to merge with National Mutual in 1990, disturbing the status quo, and instigating the Six Pillars, and, later, Four Pillars policy.
- The only Big Four not to share common cheque processing via an industry solution.
- The first Big Four to attempt to pull out of the Bankcard arrangement.
- The first Big Four to join Visa (others joined Mastercard).
- The first bank, and the only Big Four to not use COIN for Direct Entry, but to use SWIFT — forcing the RBA to build the Low Value Clearing Service (LVCS) interconnector between the two networks.
- In 2008 unconventionally at the time, implemented Yodlee personal financial management software to aggregate data (screen-scrape) from competitor banks — ANZ MoneyManager. The initiative was later implemented by Westpac. The practice may have been in breach of other banks' terms and conditions.
- Launched ANZ GoMoney in 2010 as an intrabank P2P payments app, just as industry focus of interbank P2P is on MAMBO.
- Joined NAB in pulling out of MAMBO, then causing RBA to push NPP — a more expensive solution to the same problem.
- In 2011, it decided to break the mould and change interest rates on its own calendar, not on the RBA's, perhaps to avoid the first Tuesday of the month media circus and escape pressure. The policy was dropped in 2014.
- The only Big Four to initially accept Apple Pay, while the others took Apple to the ACCC.
- The only Big Four not to join Australia Post's Bank@Post to support branchless communities.
- Failed to join the Big Four payment initiative Beem It.
- The only Big Four not to join the R3CEV blockchain consortium, choosing instead to join Hyperledger.
- Despite serious issues found in all the Big Four in the royal commission, the only bank to have retained its CEO.

Shifting Paradigm

We have said that money has been an important social component for as long as any of us, anywhere on Earth, can remember. Consumerism (the acquisition of goods and services in ever-increasing amounts), though, dates from the introduction of mainstream credit, the credit card (in Australia, in the 1970s). Direct global commerce is still in its infancy despite mass adoption of the Internet from 2000.

The term *paradigm shift* was coined by physicist Thomas Kuhn, who basically suggested that revolutionary ideas required that the old school die off before the new ideas take hold. He was referring to the science of non-solid matter and probability, rather than the stationary states that were proposed by Albert Einstein, Erwin Schrödinger, and others in quantum physics. It turns out that he was probably optimistic about the timeframe. As we have seen, change happens slowly. The chasm, or trough of disillusionment, takes a long time to work through. Sometimes it takes a long time before an idea takes off.

In money and payments, this paradigm shift is a move away from physical money to a new state, which we do not yet know or understand.

That paradigm shift was from metal to notes, a foreign currency issued from afar, to our own. Physical money transformed into electronic money. Something we could touch became just data: balances with institutions, virtual currencies, stored value on a card and cryptocurrencies. The shift was slow settlement (colony bills drawn on the treasury in 1788 could take a year to cash in) to real-time settlement. We shifted in our notion of an asset, from something we owned to something we hired, through a mortgage or via the shared economy. We shifted in our desire to possess and realised it is often cheaper to rent than to buy: that access trumps ownership.

We shifted in so many ways, yet we persisted with some age-old structures around banking, payments and money.

Australia's Impact

We have seen that Australia's impact on world payments has not been insignificant. Australia was open for business with open trade before and at the time of colonisation. Australia shaped Bretton Woods and set a standard on the global stage for full employment. For over half a century, the Australian dollar has been in the top five most traded currencies.

Australia invented the polymer note and took it to the world. Australia was one of the first countries with a widely adopted credit card, propelling itself into the consumer age and electronic money. We were one of the first countries to implement and mandate the chip and PIN. We implemented contactless payments at an adoption rate like no other. We had a high adoption of fintech technology, number 5 in the world. Our fintech startups were successful on the world stage, many of which are providing solutions to the world, or have been acquired by what are now the world leaders. We processed the first intercontinental card transaction in the world.[113]

---

[113] First Data

From the lay-by system to buy now, pay later, Australia has led the world in innovations in alternative methods of purchasing in instalments.

We have participated in and accelerated the world adoption of the shared economy, welcoming providers like Uber and Airbnb, and exporting our own, like Freelancer and Airtasker.

Australia had a fast and early adoption of much emerging technology, the Internet, smartphones and blockchain payments. We have the world's most liked Internet and smartphone banking applications. We have a powerful and modern domestic real-time payment capability, the first major bank with a mass-market mobile contactless payment capability, the inventor of the world's first touchscreen PIN pad, with Australian standards and development leading the implementation of a new wave of Android PEDs flooding the marketplace. We are a world leader in cryptocurrency and blockchain technology.

We established AS 2805 card messaging two years before the ISO 8583 message, the core of Visa and Mastercard messaging today. We were instrumental in the early development of the current emerging standards in payments, ISO 20022. We were quick to see the potential of real-time payments and banking, and were among the early countries of the world to get there (and we could have been faster if we had collaborated better).

We inspired the founder of the largest fintech in the world, Jack Ma, and our core banking technology, TCS BaNCS, powers the world's largest banks.

A highly regulated environment, with over 20 major inquiries setting up over 10 major regulators, Australia has, for the most part, balanced enterprising spirit and innovation with economic safety and security. We have had our problems and, for the most part, there has been redress. Australia was one of the first countries to regulate the efficiency of its payment systems.

Australia has also led standardisation and internationalisation initiatives in banking and regulation, making the world a safer place at a number of levels, and was an early adopter in both word and intent of the Basel accords, FATF, and action against money laundering and terrorism financing — OECD/G20 Common Reporting Standard for tax information exchange — and a signatory and active member of almost every international standard and treaty.

Australia has had and will continue to have an enormous ability to shape and change the world of payments here and globally. We are small enough to implement change quickly and large enough to make it worthwhile and noticeable. Most importantly, we are open to the world of ideas, and, as a player in the world economy, we can be the genesis of a new future of payments and money.

16.

DISRUPTION

THE SHIFT OF A PARADIGM is a slow one. While big and rapid changes appear to have occurred, generally, they were the fruits of a slower shifting change in behaviours. So many changes we see are evolutionary rather than immediate, especially when viewed several years later with a wider lens.

Nevertheless, the move from one way of doing things to another, to utilise a quantum physics analogy, is like jumping from one quantum level to another, and does appear sudden, with old structures dying and new ones emerging seemingly overnight. The early use of Bankcard, not needing to worry that there was not enough cash in a wallet, was disruptive for consumers and retailers. Getting out of an Uber, like being chauffeured, without needing to fumble for cash was disruptive.

In innovation circles, sometimes three categories are used to identify the speed of change. **Evolutionary change** is the slow, gradual, often imperceptible change from one way of doing things to another; for example, in the history of money, the move from sharing to barter. **Transformational change** is generally a deliberative move from one practice to the next; for example, the introduction of Basel III, and the need to retain more shareholders' equity — definitely perceptible, but not fundamentally or, at least, immediately, impacting existing banks or institutions. **Disruptive change** is a ground-shaking change that can bring existing institutions to their knees and make giants out of new ones.

The difference between one change and another is subjective. We have had parents or grandparents who turned to the Internet late, and may have seen the sudden disruption it caused in their lives decades after the Internet was old news.

From saplings to bottles of wine, it can take five years for a virgin vineyard to have impact. As we saw earlier with the hype cycle and adoption chasm, sometimes it is the old, boring ideas that can cause the most disruption when they finally come of age in the minds of the mass market. So many future disruptions may not be new ideas, but simply ideas that have not yet had their time in the sun.

To claim or pretend to know the future is an act of arrogance and, if proven correct, it is simply coincidence for there are so many things that can happen in the affairs of the world. The inability to see the future fruit after the first sign of green from an emerging sapling is a deficiency of a botanist as much as that of a novice.

Nevertheless, the fruit of what will be reaped has probably been sown so, with that qualification, we can look at the possibilities.

Innovation as a Science

Innovation inspiration, like any form of scientific inspiration, is and forever will have an element of mystery — from before the time of Archimedes's "Eureka" moment to today. Nevertheless, there are benefits to making the innovation and design process more scientific.

Design science is an emerging scientific field.[114] It differs from natural science, in that this field "tries to understand reality, design science attempts to create things that serve human purposes."[115]

[114] Puffers

[115] Simon

It is notionally made up of six stages:

1. Identify problem and motivation.
2. Define objectives of a solution.
3. Design and development (produce an artefact to test, experimentation).
4. Demonstration of the artefact (e.g., a proof of concept testing).
5. Evaluation (testing results collation, analysis and conclusions).
6. Communication (similar to other sciences, so others can benefit from learnings, and we build on human endeavours).

A design science research methodology attempts to apply research to at least one of four areas:

- Problem-centred initiated research looks at stage 1 and attempts to isolate the problem using surveys, published research, etc.
- Objective-centred solution operates at stage 2 and isolates the metrics to measure the success of a solution.
- Design and development-centred approach operates at stage 3. This is often where detailed requirements are obtained to design a successful solution. Or it could also look at the best development methodologies to achieve the goal.
- Client context initiated research is instigated at stage 4, and is similar to experimental research in natural science and the social sciences.

Sadly, mature design science principles are often missing from the information technology industry and from banks. The big deficits are the inability to learn from failed or successful implementations. Many organisations keep the result secret for commercial reasons. This is not to say that an academic approach (with publications of methods and results) solves the problem itself — for it is often difficult to find material, and many academic papers remain behind a pay-wall, requiring a commercial reader to purchase the paper.

Many people treat innovative ideas as a secret and, even if they did not implement an idea, the idea is kept locked away from public view lest a rival gain a competitive insight.

BankAmericard (forerunner to Visa) apparently unsuccessfully hid their success to prevent copy-cat implementations. They were forced to open up to gain market acceptance of their solution in order to compete with others. Ironically, BankAmericard is now issued on the Mastercard scheme. CBA's Pi-Albert device resulted in more robust implementations of Android PEDs in the marketplace, and the rapid decline of CBA's attempt, accelerating its obsoleteness, despite attempts at patenting it. We had seen a similar phenomenon with Kodak and their digital cameras, leading the charge into digital but restricting the IP, with its patents unable to save the company from filing for bankruptcy. The list goes on. The patent's central purpose is to publish a design so others can study and benefit from it. The lesson is that the restriction of access to innovative ideas is pointless.

Better sharing of design science findings will be disruptive to the industry, as people and organisations can more substantially and consciously build on each other's ideas.

Decentralised Settlement

The purpose of legal tender in Australia was never defined in legislation — perhaps for good reason. Fundamental terms are generally not defined, as they are part of common law, convention or commonsense. This gives us a hint at the problem money is trying to solve. As earlier stated, it is to *settle* a debt. Debts are as old as humanity, and only in relatively recent times has that settlement meant the exchange of cash and, even more recently, the movement of money on an Exchange Settlement Account (ESA). That ability to move money on an ESA brings power to the banks. Through gross net settlements, deposit products, and lending activities, banks can use their own IOUs to settle many debts, and to fuel the economy and its payments.

Mondex, and, later, Bitcoin and other cryptocurrencies, demonstrated how settlement can be taken away from the banking system.

The increased use of alternative global settlements, international trade, and foreign currency will dilute the power of single central banks and, particularly, of their banks to regulate money outside its real value, being the true value of that currency in the local market to, say purchase a basket of exportable goods, when compared to other countries.

The popular acceptance of a new currency may bring about this change.

On the other hand, these alternative settlement systems (like Ripple) will increase the demand on real money, or money base, which will reduce the amount of broad money in the economy.

Thanks to the credit card, people and the economy are addicted to the additional money it provides, so weaning off short-term borrowings provided by banks (overdrafts, credit cards, personal loans) will be slow and painful, if possible at all.

International Settlement Currency

During the final days of World War II, Keynes proposed the Bancor, an international currency for settlement. This currency was only to be in the hands of the central bank. Unfortunately, the idea was before its time, and the emerging economic superpower of the time, the US, successfully established its own currency as the central benchmark. The safeguard, a protection of currencies against devaluation, was that Bretton Woods required that currencies be pegged against gold. This system broke down, in the 1970s when, instead, a basket of currencies was used. Nevertheless, central banks, including the United States Federal Reserve, have been conservative with the monetary policy, not just to satisfy the international community, but mainly to maintain currency confidence and low inflation in the US domestic economy.

However, just as Bitcoin was created in response to a perceived threat of quantitative easing, resulting in the free printing of money, Zimbabwe style, devaluing money for everyone, a new emerging power was getting nervous as well.

China, previously a developing economy was, at the time of the GFC, an emergent powerful player in the world economy. Unlike other economies, China did not grow off domestic consumer demand fuelled from credit. Instead, it grew from exports and had a net trade surplus. Surplus money gained from exports needed to be invested, and the World Bank, the International Monetary Fund, the US dollar, and other major currencies were the logical choice. By the time of the GFC (which left China largely unaffected and, thanks to this, its demand for mining/raw materials fended off a recession in Australia), China was the major investor in US dollar assets. To pay off debts, all the US needed to do was run the note printers. In 2009, Zhou Ziaochuan, the Governor of the People's Bank of China, proposed a new international currency. Ziaochuan cited Bretton Woods and acknowledged Keynes. As an analyst from HSBC put it: "This is a clear sign that China, as the largest holder of US dollar financial assets, is concerned about the potential inflationary risk of the United States Federal Reserve printing money."[116]

No country followed the call of China. A few years later, China proposed the Asian Infrastructure Investment Bank. The bank was similar to the World Bank and the Japanese originated ADB, but this time on the table was China's massive investment and many of the debts had to be paid back in Chinese yuan (or local currencies). Few countries resisted participating on either side of a potentially enormous sovereign investment opportunity. Even Australia and South Korea joined in. The Asian Infrastructure Investment Bank now rivals the World Bank and ADB, with the highest credit ratings.

Like the US, Europe, Japan and China before them, new super economies will emerge, like India, which seek similar benefits.

The stage is set, finally, for the rebirth of the Bancor, with one critical difference. Technology will enable the new currency to be accessed by individuals and banks, and not just central banks.

Could a middle power, with good international standing and goodwill suggest such an initiative?

The disruptive impact of international settlement will be internationalisation of banking, payments and finance. It will reduce the power of individual countries to control the economy through monetary policy, but may bring about greater global monetary stability.

Alternative Settlement

A return to gold for settlement is possible but, essentially, in order to fulfil real-time exchange, the gold reserves need to be held by a trusted third party. Cryptocurrency settlement (Bitcoin) does not have this restriction. In both cases, though, a secondary market that offers lending can only succeed if we allow virtualisation of these currencies (i.e., accept IOUs in trade and money investments), which is essentially and fundamentally the system we have now.

The concentration of mining powers we have seen in Bitcoin is unlikely to go away and, for this reason and others, the likelihood of a new cryptocurrency taking its place (as a settlement coin) is doubtful amid all the noise of distant contenders.

More likely, gold and, to a lesser extent Bitcoin, will continue as commodity investments. Even in this case, given the absence of other accepted non-currency stores of value, the value should continue to rise, supplies being limited, as wealth and demand increases.

---

[116] Anderlini

» NOTE

For centuries, even respected scientists, including Isaac Newton, have proposed that it may be possible to turn lead or base metals efficiently into gold.[117] Similarly, quantum computing, as mentioned below, proposes to break current asymmetric encryption, which could impact cryptocurrencies. If either of these eventuate, or some other as yet unconceived possibility arises that shakes the value of these gold and crypto commodities in the minds of the public, it could spell the end of their tenure.

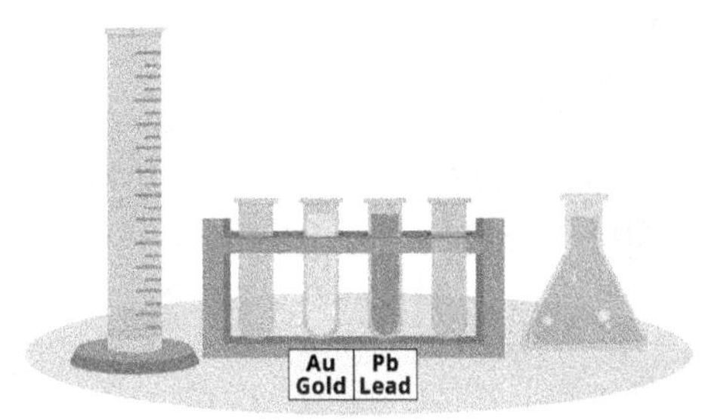

Power to the People

We saw the good ownership cross-section of the major Australian banks, with no block of shareholders controlling the majority of the organisations. There was a fear that at the time of the CBA float, company control would go to the dogs, with bitter elections like what had happened at the NRMA at the time. It did not, far from it. The board of director's nomination is rarely opposed. Most shareholders probably do not know they are shareholders (thanks to superannuation and other similar international schemes, like the 401(k) in the US).

It is ironic that bank-bashing is popular in Australia, as the ultimate responsible authorities are the bank-bashers themselves — the superannuation investors. No need for inquiries and royal commissions. People need to stand up and be heard.

Technology exists to give beneficial owners a say in the ownership of corporations and, eventually, managed funds should allow this. CBA's loss of $700 million in fines and $1 billion capital penalty should not have gone unchallenged, at least, not internally and at the shareholders' annual general meeting.

By allowing votes by fund holders, and with greater awareness of shareholders, corporate boards can be more ethical and accountable, and we should see less negative behaviour uncovered by the royal commission and other inquiries.

Will people care enough to vote? They will evolve to care for, in the coming era, intelligent, savvy, informed, and active citizens and shareholders will be key to continued success. An easy start is: if you are a shareholder or mutual owner, exercise your right to vote. Ask the tough questions. If you can, nominate yourself as a director.

---

[117] Northfield

Organisational Size and Structure

There is a tendency for people to be attracted to large brands, both consumers and employees.

As we saw earlier, large banks could have six or more levels of hierarchy and, for a worker, this puts the executive on an unnatural pedestal, so that it is commonplace for a veteran of the organisation to never personally meet the CEO or a director until their 40th anniversary in the organisation. Communication suffers and, whether the conversation is about progress, issues, risks, ideas, or innovation, the value and opinion of the individual is diminished.

Executives in these organisations yield enormous power that could corrupt their behaviour or, at least, make them seem aloof. The power gained by these executives is power ceded by the staff, as freedom and individuality seem to follow Isaac Newton's momentum law: the sum total remains the same. People accept this, often for years at a time, for the pay is good and, in the words of Thomas Jefferson in the United States Declaration of Independence, people "are more disposed to suffer, while evils are sufferable, than to right themselves by abolishing the forms to which they are accustomed."

Gradually a web and culture of conformity grows in large organisations and people learn to tow the line, to not speak up. Messaging is controlled, and people who speak up out of the chain of command are sidelined or pushed out.

Further, these large organisations yield large monopolies and, in many cases, can control public messages and information to the detriment of the industry and customers. With their large advertising budgets, commercial media organisations are reluctant to publicise negative issues. They restrict the flow of information, with staff prevented from speaking even on trivial matters without going through training and vetting. These restrictions limit the capability of the individual to express themselves.

Smaller organisations remain better able to maximise the value of individuals. We will see over time, as the means of production become more and more accessible to smaller players, that these organisations become more competitive. In the future, with opening up of access and data (and not just through the Consumer Data Right initiative, but through a realisation that open data has competitive advantage), we will potentially see greater competition from smaller banks. There is emerging economic evidence that smaller organisations contribute more per person than larger ones.

Further, six or more levels of hierarchy is unnatural, with the high ratio of managers to workers a clear mark of inefficiency and depersonalisation. Perhaps in the future, and a guide to new workplace entrants is to potentially avoid companies that have "manager of managers" roles, or organisations where it is not possible for all junior staff to know or meet the CEO.

» NOTE

Aggregated software or systems that take the opinions of thousands and organise them in one place, e.g., surveys, innovation boards, risk tools, and even hack-a-thons are useful engagement, but depersonalise people, and are designed often to convince workers that they are being heard though many see through this. Organisations bigger than a certain threshold fail to connect to individuals.

Mutual Banks and Neo Banks: Rebels without a Cause

By now, we have realised that the word *bank* is an arbitrary one, attached to a specific form of regulated financial intermediary of a specific and quite arbitrary size. There are a plethora of banks, even in Australia, and many of them use the phrase "not a big bank" to market themselves. Able to be much more nimble, to leverage individuals better, take risks without fear of loss of market share or share price, they will please customers and innovate once established.

Of this group, the mutual banks offer an overlooked but mature proposition. Controlled by customers, they are generally not-for-profit companies that are best positioned to be trusted by customers. The mutual banks and credit unions have been reluctant to take risks and innovate as much as their more corporate peers. The need to manage risks should not inhibit innovation and, hopefully, these institutions will discover this.

First and foremost, they must live true to the "not a big bank" promise. This will require better customer service and fewer complaints. The ME Bank redraw account fiasco cannot be repeated and should act as a strong warning.

On top of this, they need something more. Being able to create a bank may give the founders a buzz, as it did for Tyro and the neo banks. But what is their purpose for being? What do they offer the world?

Becoming an ADI is not required for everyone. Regulators have removed SCCIs from the need to have an ADI license. PPF licensing should be done through ASIC as well, and these organisations should be allowed to use an ESA account. Similarly, regulators should allow payment providers Cuscal, ASL, and Indue to operate more as technology integrators rather than requiring an ADI license to provide their services. ESA pooling can be accomplished by the RBA through technical means. This would allow the entry of technology companies to provide the existing smaller banks solutions that will allow these banks to innovate payments solutions outside the shadow of the ADI payment providers.

While there is concentration of business with the Big Four, today there is a glut of smaller banks (see Appendix 1). We do not need more, as much as we need some of these to thrive.

Any fintech interested in providing a solution to banks should seek out these lower-tier ADIs and banks, and partner with them on a solution. This will be a major source of disruption in the Australian banking space.

If, as a reader, you feel unempowered to effect any change suggested in this book, consider getting a better financial deal and supporting a mutual or neo bank, or a credit union with your business.

Separation of Manufacturing from Distribution

NAB's attempt to separate the distribution of products from manufactured ones was prematurely axed, and the Future of Financial Advice put the nail in the coffin of any emergent model in this area, at least for a decade.

Separating the two interests enables the proper prudential regulation of the funding, and less restrictive and more competition in presentation, marketing and payment systems.

Credit Crunch

The rules by which a bank or any financial institution can lend, and the now more coordinated credit scoring agencies keeping better and more complete records on individuals, meant that credit was harder and harder to obtain. Banks now knew the full picture of borrowings, beyond a simple summary credit score.

›› NOTE

One loophole in the credit scoring system was that it was possible to make two purchases of property at once, without informing the other bank of the second property, thereby only being assessed on each property in isolation. Some brokers would orchestrate this technique to maximise loan chances for customers who otherwise could not afford an investment property (and, in the process, retain more commission!).

With tighter controls on capital adequacy and measurement of risk-weighted assets, the system is moving away from credit. Added to the injury are the tighter controls on interchange, with a clear political and regulatory intent to reduce it to at or near zero. This means that *revolvers* (people who pay off their credit card bills on time) are less profitable for banks, which need to subsidise the 30 to 60 days' interest-free period.

Buy now, pay later feels like a reinvention of the credit card system, where merchants pay for the interest but, this time, more directly and at a higher rate than interchange. (Some buy now, pay later schemes charge 4 to 6%, more than even American Express, making these new schemes less viable for retailers.) The simple economics in a surcharge-free environment is that all consumers collectively pay for loans on purchases.

A lot of the push to bring interchange down has been from big acquirers (merchant groups) and alternative acquirers like Tyro. Unfortunately, this could have backfired; the benefits to acquirers and merchants of a less regulated market were probably greater. The reduction of interchange is leading to the notion of a reduction or regulation of merchant service fees (MSF), which will negatively impact organisations like Tyro that already struggle to make a profit, and could continue to struggle more in a race to lower MSFs. Also, lower interchange will have a negative impact on credit cards and, without alternatives, this will reduce spending at merchants and perhaps reverse somewhat the consumerism trend that started with the introduction of purchase credit. This may or may not be a good thing economically, but it will hurt challengers more than the establishment.

This credit crunch leads to two scenarios. The first is a move away from credit-based purchases. The immediate effect is a behavioural one, where people gradually transition from credit to debit. We know, psychologically, this will reduce spending. Fortunately, it will happen gradually, and may not have an immediate effect on market indicators. Over time, though, it will align with greater globalisation (direct or near-direct consumer purchasing from more production efficient countries), and also perhaps the move away from direct purchasing to more elements of the shared economy. The COVID-19 pandemic may aid this move.

The second scenario — and this is perhaps the immediate desire of regulators — is a move towards user pays for credit. Behaviourally, an individual would rather pay 6% more if the interest is embedded in the list price for an item (and the merchant pays behind the scenes), than pay 3% interest, a lesser rate, directly themselves so there will be free market resistance.

Personal loans are much more secure these days with robust credit checks and responsible lending practices. Non-bank participation in this industry, through the supply of lines of credit (revolving or otherwise) at lower interest rates, could assist competition and these products could take off. Many private financers, however, are reluctant to reach beyond the boundaries of safe lending, and are hampered to act only on the data that lenders provide.

Alternative credit ratings suggested by some startups have not really picked up. The idea was to use social networking as an indicator of community connection and responsibility.

A system of peer-to-peer trust, supplemented by third-party certification, could reduce the cost of credit, similar to the philosophies of Hermann Schulze-Delitzsch,[118] credited with founding credit unions. We will expand on this later.

Payment Unification

Ultimately, as we saw, a bank payment is an instruction to move money from a payer to a payee. Alternatively, a payer could give permission to a payee to take their money. That instruction needs to have the weight of trust behind it, as it needs to be followed up immediately or, soon after, with a settlement.

All of the payments we have looked at follow this pattern.

For the bank-based payments, there is no reason why they could not be unified.

[118] Aschhoff

ISO 20022 has established a standard for such payments (with the issues we mentioned). This is a good start, despite the deficiencies, or perhaps an improvement could be suggested.

This payment unification could happen domestically but, to be effective, given the growing global market (and we have barely seen the beginnings of it), this unification should happen internationally. With the success of international standards in fighting COVID-19, the Basel Accords, FATF and AML/CTF, the Common Reporting Standard, and base erosion profit shifting through the Country by Country Reporting Standard, as well as private initiatives such as ISOs, EMV, and PCI, there is a clear ability for the world to cooperate, and this should be led by governments and regulators. Could Australia lead this initiative?

This unification would simplify the landscape and allow providers to standardise solutions that will work in any country. It would also mean the end of dispersion of payments between competing schemes that will, due to regulatory pressures, bring down the costs of payment systems.

Securing Unsecured Assets

Mortgages on properties are secured through the Land Titles Registry. Vehicles, aircraft, vessels, shipment and machinery can also be secured, though with less legal authority, with third parties offering registration services. Few other assets are securable from a financial point of view.

Technology exists today to laser etch articles as small as diamonds, microdot technology in the vehicle industry and others, as well as old-fashioned serial numbers on most equipment and household items (that could be supplemented with microdots for the more valuable items). The low cost of producing unique barcodes and computerised printing means even perishables can be tracked. The development of tracking technology is promising, with the famed GPS dot, previously an object of science fiction, looking more and more likely and cheaper. Current dot-based location technologies require short-range Bluetooth or NFC; however, use of mobile networks, long-range Wi-Fi, LoRaWAN or satellites could assist. Embedded in manufactured goods, it can help locate goods. An Internet of Things (IoT) that extends our telemetry to the physical world will enable greater efficiency. CBA attempted to trial the tracking of a cotton shipment over a shipping route to assist in trade finance, as have others, and the usage will expand.

Through widespread use of centralised registers (i.e., ledgers), allowing transfer of goods from one owner to the next, honest users could be more certain of the provenience of their goods. Warranty support and recalls could be more effective, and the shared economy could be more accessible. If the average electric drill is used for 20 minutes each year, by checking in and out equipment from a register, it will be possible to track and insure goods at a lower risk and cost.

Taxation depreciation can be better monitored and calculated

» NOTE

Stolen vessels and ships are a global problem. Small to medium ships are pirated and then sold on the black market. With over 50 000 global ships worldwide, it is unsurprising how difficult they are to find. Through the use of tracking technology, large assets can be better secured.

By having a complete view of an individual's assets down to the micro asset, it could be possible to fund these items and facilitate better financing outside just home mortgage securities. Securitisation, currently the domain of financial services organisations, could be made available to everyone.

Account Unification

Essentially, as an individual migrates through life stages, their money needs to transition from small savings (school), to big savings (early employment), to borrowing (family home), to big savings again (wealth acquisition and retirement).

Essentially, if we add up the net balances of all accounts, we either have surplus money or are in deficit. As we spend our excess income, likewise, we should be either saving money or paying off our debt. Essentially, we have one financial position, yet so many of us have several. Banks like the US Wells Fargo encouraged this practice with "Eight is great". Australian banks tried to emulate this policy internally.

» NOTE

Even if someone is sufficiently wealthy, in order to save tax, they need to take out a loan e.g., to negatively gear. This is a bizarre tax rule in Australia and other countries. If tax laws were altered, the same benefit could be claimed if there was a notional borrowing from one's own assets, paying a notional market interest that could be deducted from tax, without needing to take out an actual loan. In the present system that forces people to take out loans to save tax, even if they have the money, the banks can come after an individual's assets anyway if they default, so the benefit of these loans is sometimes questionable.

Due to complexity and a general inability to challenge the risk-based approach, banks are locked into traditional products so this new concept of account unification seems out of reach: a lifetime account that uses the security of an individual's financial income to provide unsecured lending or, if there are assets that can be securitised, lower interest-secured lending. One account that can be used throughout an individual's lifetime could be disruptive. The portfolio should be easily swapped to another bank to facilitate contestability but, in the early days, first-mover advantage would be very profitable even without tax reform.

Payments and Banking as a Service

Cloud, application service providers (ASPs) and *as a service* providers have become popular in a number of industries. Except for card-based Internet payment gateways and merchant acquiring, banks do not offer this due to the complexity of compliance, especially AML/CTF. Credit and debit cards are the only retail products that are white-labelled but, even then, they tend to require the strong backing of a financial institution (SCCI or similar).

TransferWise, PayPal and other aggregation software sought bank partners that could offer headless banking and payment services beyond cards that they could white-label within their platform. NAB came to the party with Transferwise, which, using off-system BSBs, created a network of foreign currency bank account numbers around the world so, as a corporate, you could get paid locally and collect globally. Providing this wholesale service to non-FIs is a gap in the market.

An analogy is the mobile virtual network operator (MVNO), like Aldi and Woolworths (Telstra), Coles and Dodo (Optus), Kogan and TPG (Vodafone), where full service telecommunication providers wholesale their offering to retailers.

The lack of competition and the high compliance bar dissuade banks from providing payments or banking as a service in Australia. The inability to separate wholesale from retail impedes the banks as well. But if it did, this would be disruptive for the market.

Open APIs

For those in the industry, open APIs have been a dream for 20 years. Many would think they have been delivered several times over based on the claims of some providers.

Unfortunately, surprisingly, none of the payment APIs in Australia are open. They are, as we mentioned, excluded from open banking.

Visa and Mastercard API documentation is extensive, but only available to members or through members or banks. This applies to both the simplest payment and the more complex ones.

AusPayNet file formats, even the so-called-standard ABA file, are not available from the Australian Banking Association, and much of what has been published has been substantially deleted/redacted due to so-called confidentiality.

NPPA standards and roadmaps, likewise, are not open, and this prevents the development of ideas and solutions on the standard.

SWIFT similarly does not publish its original API and integration APIs. While ISO 20022 is a good start to publishing APIs, it is just one part of the integration.

A test for the openness of APIs is this: by reading and accessing publicly and freely available resources, is it possible to develop a solution that will work completely?

» NOTE

The confidentiality of APIs means that only tech companies with insider experience of the APIs have solutions that work with the same APIs. This brings about an implementation deadlock: how can a tech company get a contract with a bank if they have not implemented the solution before? Further, if they have done it before, are they not in apparent breach of confidentiality and non-disclosure agreements when they reuse this IP? This clearly limits competition, and solution vendors are unable to provide simple solutions to the marketplace. In practice, most of the payment solution vendors, especially the successful ones, got a foot in the door of a bank thanks to fast-talking salespeople, which enabled them to access information they required to extend their solution, which they later sold to other entities.

An argument for keeping information confidential is that it prevents hackers accessing payment systems. This notion, in security circles alone, is a fallacy. With modern cryptography and system access controls, there are better and more secure ways to prevent access to systems. Specifications, as we have seen, get around the vendor space with little restriction so their security is dubious. Further, the open source doctrine suggests exposure of source code and standards, and community detection of security weaknesses is a better defence than specification confidentiality. Regulators should resist calls for payment system specification restrictions as it is a barrier to entry.

Many organisations publish a Swagger (a simple API library/test bed) and call it an open API. Often this is a mimic of a real API without useful data, and does not allow a vendor to provide an effective proof of concept or an implementation-ready solution of their new idea.

The opening up of APIs will, over time, create a significant advantage for the payment method (as we have seen with PayPal and Stripe), to give that payment method market dominance.

As boring as it sounds, open APIs of core payments is still an unrealised dream that could be disruptive in the market. Many think we have it, however, we do not, and if some banks have provided it, it is not accessible to the market.

Open Ratings

For those who have seen the vast array of offerings in some of the emerging marketplace, the big emerging challenge is quality. The use of open ratings on eBay, Amazon, Alibaba/ Aliexpress, and trading platforms, shared economy services, and marketplaces like Uber and Airbnb, are just scratching the surface.

Shared ledgers, like databases of telemarketers and scammers that now pop up as "SPAM" or "SCAM" are helping us share trust as a community. This has a long way to go and will continue to evolve, perhaps not as bespoke solutions as much as add-ons to marketplaces or solutions with an already large market penetration.

Better quality ratings and the like for individuals and transactions reduces the element of risk pricing in money and payments. It increases the value of quality and gives a better dimension to credit ratings.

As obtuse as it sounds, better crowd-based rating solutions could be disruptive to commerce, payments, credit and the availability of money.

Shared Ledger

Satoshi Nakamoto's work on Bitcoin appears, to the best of our knowledge, a work of genuine selflessness. There was no way for him or her to know that this experiment would take off. That selflessness created an open ledger.

Some great inventions of our time have been acts of selflessness: the World Wide Web, the humble *Request for comments* of the Internet Society, SMTP or email, and many others.

Openness meant it was easy to start to use and that if an idea took off, there was no license fee to pay and one could not get sued. Basically, the idea, technique or source code could be used freely.

Open source, open APIs, the GNU General Public License and *Creative Commons* are part of the lexicon of this open community.

On the other hand, *intellectual property (IP), patent, copyright, trademark, non-disclosure agreement,* and *confidential* are the corresponding words used in the corporate sector. This ownership of knowledge is a key philosophical gap that needs to be bridged.

Almost every Bitcoin-like implementation post-Bitcoin (and even Bitcoin industry implementations themselves, post Satoshi), whether it be cryptocurrency, shared ledgers, blockchain, or smart contracts has been implemented with a degree of selfishness.

Initial Coin Offerings (ICOs) designed to make proprietors money, patents of blockchain ideas, control of ledgers, and centralised issuing of coins, are all examples of this control.

Fundamentally, the idea of the open or shared ledger is to relinquish control of what was a proprietary part of an organisation. And the core asset for a bank is the ledger, so it was going to be hard.

By opening up the ledger so much more is possible: other organisations can add value to each record, and integration and exchange of information surpasses any implemented open API.

But opening up the information of a bank means giving away its core asset, for does not the bank own the data? Customers would argue not, as are not these data theirs? The law (Consumer Data Right) may support the latter argument.

So, even if blockchain or cryptocurrencies do not pick up, if an entity genuinely attempts to open its ledger (with the permission of its customers and ensuring privacy), we could see some amazing innovations in the short term beyond what is possible today with blockchain.

Given that blockchain, even Bitcoin blockchain, suffers concentration issues, the key problem to solve may not be concentration of the ledger, but simply openness of the data model and replication of the data between trusted parties that adhere to a customer confidentiality and privacy pact.

Relational databases are great structured stores of data, the technology is mature, and they can be replicated between organisations. Or perhaps a trusted third party could maintain the database? The key feature required is an open data model and permissioned access but, most importantly — and this was never a technical problem — cooperation to a degree that has not happened before.

This new shared ledger technology could be the mass adoption part of the cycle that blockchain is waiting for.

Future of Cryptocurrencies

Unless there is a fundamental crypto compromise, Bitcoin will remain a commodity investment.

The use of cryptocurrency to make mainstream payments will continue to be hampered by regulators across the globe until a solution is found to reporting and tracing.

There are two obvious solutions.

There are serious flaws in both reporting standards. In Australia, which has better and more progressive regulations, by world standards, we nevertheless have a gap. A purchase of Bitcoin or digital currency with Australian currency should be reported in a manner similar to IFTI.

Given it is on the public ledger, it may be possible to allow transfers between wallets within regulated nations. The public key of a wallet should be declared to the state and transfers between regulated wallets should be permitted.

The other solution is a walled garden, as mentioned before, where managed wallets from regulated entities requiring KYC procedures allow the transfer of cryptocurrency to other managed wallets with similar regulation within the global FATF community. With proper reporting, as for normal currency, this would solve the regulatory issue.

The other issue to solve is greater payments efficiency with an open coin. Bitcoin looks unlikely to reduce execution time, and coins with better execution capabilities, like Ripple, do not have open coins.

Security and Encryption

Security and encryption are fundamental to banking, from Transport Layer Security (TLS) on the Web to EMV cryptography on cards.

Quantum computing using probability states (the probability of a quantum bit being in one state or the other, rather than an absolute bit position like in a vacuum tube switch or a transistor) has been theoretically proven to be able to break modern encryption in a shortened time. Quantum computing is itself at the start of a hype cycle, and initial expectations have been exaggerated, with a real challenge of whether it is possible to make a practical quantum computer, and an even bigger challenge of the adoption and implementation of the technology in useful ways, with much of the industry not yet utilising existing conventional technologies to their full capacity. However, the potential for quantum computing to break modern asymmetric encryption is real and could be disruptive, initially in a negative way. CBA, Telstra and the federal government invested in 2018 Australian of the Year, Professor Michelle Simmons, who led the University of New South Wales initiative in the development of components for a future quantum computer.

One solution is the distribution of private keys, and the use of less convenient symmetric encryption, the classical encryption mechanism that requires the keys to be distributed securely beforehand. Key distribution could be a logistic challenge, and solutions for this risk should start to be considered as an immediate loss of confidence in encryption could be devastating to payment systems as, like Westpac in 2001, electronic channels are now mainstream.

Another issue is the continued attempts by scammers to access online banking sites. Phishing attacks and other scams are being handled well through the use of mobile apps (and protections implemented by operating systems), Internet protection software and modern browsers. The use of second-factor authentication will need to be further improved; however, this is inconvenient for many users and disrupts efficient use of Internet banking sites.

Coupled with this, is the potential move away from personal devices. In 1996, Bill Gates said that one day, computer monitors (the single most expensive component of the PC) would be as cheap as wallpaper. In 2002, the movie *Minority Report* illustrated what could be possible with biometric recognition — personalised messages on billboards, something that Amazon demonstrated with Just Walk Out. Electronic SIMs (or eSIMs) will no longer tie us physically to our device. We will be able to interact anywhere. These technological changes will bring forward centralised biometrics. Unlocking a phone today with a face or thumbprint is a decentralised biometric solution, and tech companies are nervous about sharing personal information or storing biometrics centrally.

Despite the lack of trust, people have grown accustomed to big tech companies, governments, and banks knowing more about them than they should. In the interests of safety, after 9/11, many people accepted they were subject to biometric scans as they entered or left the country. During the COVID-19 outbreak, millions of Australians voluntarily downloaded the COVIDSafe app that could track their location.

Open biometrics, allowing an individual to be authenticated externally, is a significant area for disruption, and the pay by face (or similar solutions) trialled by Alipay and others is an area of disruption.

Digital identity is an extension of this. Initial emerging solutions at point of sale may gain short to medium-term traction. A long-term successful solution will need to be pushed by the government or a big tech company.

Regulation and Regtech

Regulations will continue to be enhanced, with governments gaining more and more information, and inter-government cooperation will likely continue the journey of information sharing.

Buoyed by the Common Reporting Standard initiative, governments may seek transactional information on multinationals and foreign persons.

The government can or does know everything about us, and people have or will gradually accept this, for they will choose safety over privacy. The popularity of COVIDSafe illustrates this. Are we in for George Orwell's *1984*, Big Brother government? We have been saved from *1984* for all these years and have been protected by democratic institutions. Fair use of the information should be protected by the law, our elected representatives and, ultimately, we the people. If that should fail, then it would be our *et tu, Brute?* moment.

Regulatory compliance is at a number of levels of maturity:

1. Vague rules (these days called risk-based) that a reasonable person could easily contravene with severe punishment (e.g., suspicious matter reporting).

2. Clearer rules but subject to human interpretation (e.g., negligence case law).

3. Clear rules that can be codified through computer code (e.g., threshold transaction reporting, TTR in its simple form, where a single transaction over $10 000 needs to be reported).

4. A system where it is not possible to break the law (e.g., collection of airport departure tax from the airlines, meant it was not an offence for a passenger to travel without).

5. A system where no laws are required and, therefore, there is no penalty (e.g., removal of the Stamp Act after the American Revolution).

As much as technologists love a good challenge, and startups have begun looking at level 1 problems, the better solution for the world and governments is a level 4 or level 5 regime, that takes the problem away. Let us provide an example.

International payments have been impeded by fear and uncertainty since 9/11, with AUSTRAC providing significant fines, yet vague guidance (level 1, as per the above). The regulations create a real deadlock and impinge on the growth of the global economy. All issues attracting AML/CTF fines (CBA, NAB, Westpac and TAB) are the result of ignorance, confusion, or internal regulatory compliance incompetence, not organisational malice. Few would allege that any of these institutions engineered the issues. The technology exists to allow AUSTRAC (and international regulators) to easily see all payments, and to directly or indirectly intercede. The problem of KYC (solvable through government digital ID), SMRs, TTRs, and IFTIs, including screening, can be largely taken away from private institutions and centralised in order to facilitate greater safety and compliance. It is time the risk-based system matured into a procedural one: computer code. Once the problem is solved centrally, history will judge these fines as unnecessary.

The same applies to ATO reporting and monitoring. With national tax departments having KYC information, sharing cross-country citizen/multinational corporate information, and reporting on it, there can be greater protections against tax avoidance and tax evasion, and more efficiency and competition in the private sector.

Unfortunately, regtech is best applied in the public sector, and the less of it the private industry sees, the better.

Today, there is no way for an individual to know whether their transaction will be reported, and to which regulatory authority it will be reported. Regulators might as well be allowed to see all transactions and have all these transactions reported to AUSTRAC, the ATO, etc. We have the technology to handle this volume of data. IFTI, SMR, and TTR requirements drop off, and the major fines would never have happened because *everything* gets reported. The regulators get a holistic view, the tax office can ensure better compliance, and the business activity statement (BAS) could be dropped if we include tax information in the transaction, using NPP/ISO 20022 additional data elements across all transactions.

The implementation of industry-level anti-fraud systems is also something that can lead to greater efficiency in the fight against criminal activity.

Too many times in the narration above, we have seen the restrictions that regulations place on new entrants (despite the regulator's stated desire to allow more competition), banks are unable to outsource AML/CTF, for example, and the regulatory rules are designed for a paradigm where banks control the full stack of manufacturing to retail. Either regulation compliance should be centralised, or compliance liability should be allowed to shift to retail providers; for example, KYC and data collection.

The next application of AI/ML would be to help discover the causes of correlations or anomalies and, with the causes discovered, either through this method or the hard way (trial and error), retaining learnings in an organisation, not through word of mouth, but through procedures and technology.

While regtech in its general form makes little sense in the private sector, it could be useful in specific areas, as below.

Refining the Fine Print

We saw how Product Disclosure Statements and terms and conditions obfuscated important aspects of products and services from the consumer. Very few people read them. In at least one case, someone reading the mandatory terms and conditions had their online session time out before they could agree to them. Few read these complicated financial industry documents. But an insurer can point to their terms and conditions to deny legitimate insurance claims, often oblivious to the loyalty of the customer. The fact this is common knowledge and practice is a travesty. It impedes the development of loyalty, trust and confidence in the industry, and impacts long-term revenue.

The problem arises from actuaries constructing limits that reduce the wholesale risk premium, hopefully without the consumer noticing. Perhaps they act under instruction from an unscrupulous or unconcerned product executive, who takes the product to market with a headline that does not mention the shortcomings. It is a practice that can only be described as implicitly dishonest.

Software licensing through GPL, employment contracts through Fair Work agreements and copyright through Creative Commons or via legislation take the stress out of worrying if one is covered or if the contract is fair. These "open source" standardised simple form contracts will be a useful innovation to restore fairness in the market. Technology that allows standard blocks to be applied and assessed publicly could assist in the understanding and acceptance of new products, restoring faith to the industry.

Suptech

The emerging supervisory technology, or suptech, enables regulators to better supervise; for example, to determine suspicious financial crime activity from the vast amounts of data they will collect. It also could assist in rapid forensic analysis after a breach. Unlike core regtech, this technology could be viable and could disrupt risktech.

Risk management technology, or risktech, that manages key risky components of a bank (products, technology systems, customers, projects, and staff), could help properly manage and mitigate risks. Use of AI/ML could help discover risky aspects of systems and business that could be used to inform risk management practices.

Opstech

Operations technology, or opstech, helps to proceduralise and automate end-user tasks, ensuring learnings and better practice are applied. Standard operating procedures (SOPs) are rarely documented and read, but more accessible SOPs could aid in the application of procedures so that efficiency, quality, risk management, and compliance are consistently and continuously improved.

Global and Local Marketplaces

While eBay, Wish, Aliexpress, and Amazon are giving consumers an opportunity to shop from global sources, and crowdsourcing websites such as the Australian online platform Freelancer and others allow consumer outsourcing, the fact remains the full capability of a global marketplace has not yet been achieved.

One useful indicator of this issue is the OECD Price Level Index (*Figure 48*), the for-adjusted cost of goods in each country relative to the OECD average.

Australia is among the most expensive with our goods costing four times the price of goods in India (at the bottom). This disparity is significant. In a true global free-market economy, we should see countries at the same level of prices as goods and services flow freely. So, despite all the talk, there is plenty of scope for more mass adoption marketplaces.

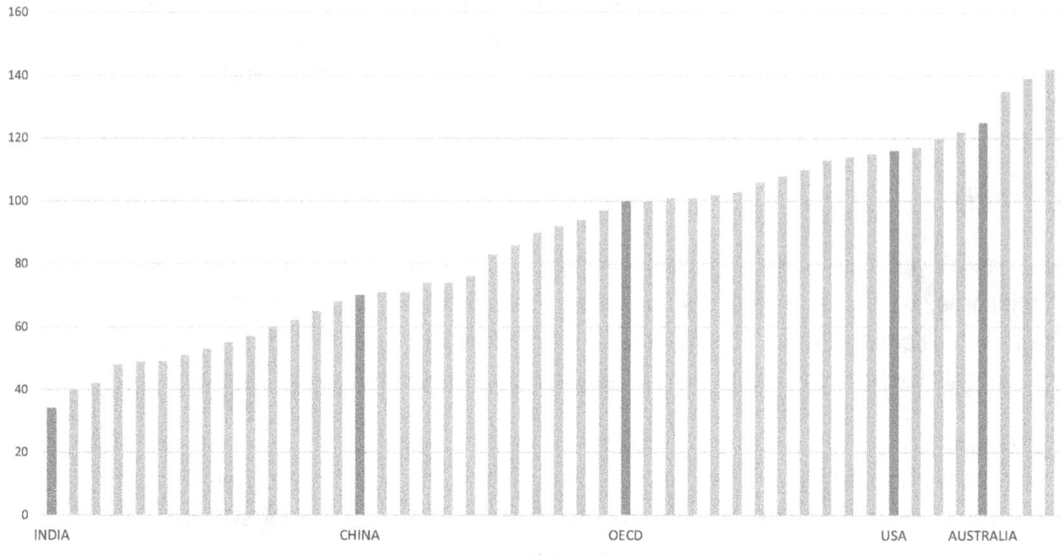

***Figure 48.* OECD Price Level Index (2016 data)**[119]

» NOTE

Other more suitable measures are manufacturing cost indexes that measure the cost of manufactured, exportable goods. BCG publishes one such index; however, the use of a standard baseline to cover 80% of "other" costs makes it a less accurate measure as it only looks at labour, electricity and natural gas costs. What it does demonstrate is the increase in costs in previously developing countries, like China and Brazil, illustrating that global parity is possible, a good sign for the world and Australia. Some other informal measures of price levels are the cost of a burger at McDonald's, or the cost of an iPhone in different geographies. The obvious problem with these later measures is that at the left end of the spectrum, these items are luxury purchases for more affluent people, even though they may be mass market products in other countries.

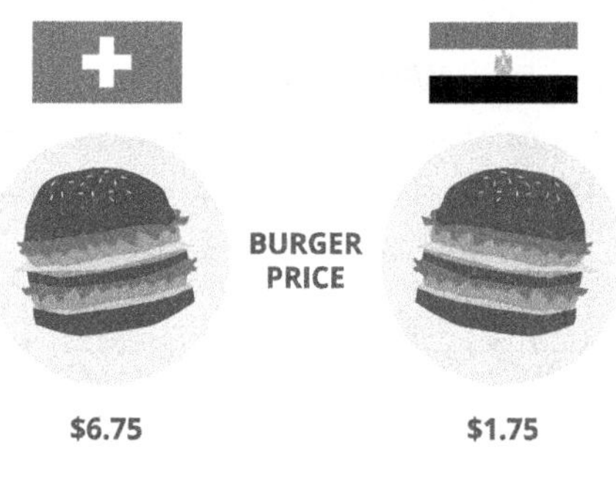

Some of the barriers to trade are efficient cross-border payments and accessible marketplaces. Postage is another issue, and customs/non-transportability of goods or services also acts as a barrier.

[119] https://data.oecd.org/price/price-level-indices.htm

This provides some evidence that a global market has not yet been fully established. A lower cost, accessible cross-border P2P payment system, coupled with marketplaces that can connect to them through wallets, should continue to be in demand.

Trust remains the biggest inhibitor — with buyers wary of unknown manufacturers, their quality and delivery. The next stage of the global marketplaces are local marketplaces using trusted local brands to provide a more personal touch to a transaction. Kogan in Australia, and other Australian brands, will soon start offering these services. Ultimately, an open marketplace is the solution, with effective feedback and quality assessment, where suppliers are not intermediated. This will bring about the utopic free market that has been theorised about by economists for so long.

NOTE

Some of the most violent demonstrations have occurred during World Trade Organisation summits, as in Seattle in 1999, yet all evidence since the beginning of modern economics[120] suggests free world trade is beneficial for all nations, especially the poorest. Australia can continue to benefit, even from manufacturing industries, because, as cheaper price level index countries achieve greater parity, our goods become more valued. Focus on quality has led to considerable demand of foreign goods in China. Automation and investment can bring our per unit costs down to a competitive level. Most importantly, we are exposed to a global market, meaning more demand and more exports.

Decommoditisation

Commodities and currency were largely created in marketplaces and allowed certain products to be fungible. This property gave rise to money and our modern payments system and, while at some point it may have assisted the evolution of modern commerce and society, we need to ask now, is it impeding it?

It is easy to trade when everything is the same, and before the age of information and communication technology we could cope with little more than ubiquity of goods and services. However, standardisation seems to go against the grain of nature and life. Every barrel of oil out of the ground is unique and does not always meet the benchmark of tradable "West Texas Intermediate". In order to meet commoditised quality benchmarks, most sheep are a specific breed of Merino (for wool) and dairy cows are mostly Holstein, Jersey or Aussie Red. Standardisation simplifies the market and supply chain. Surely natural demand should be as diverse as natural supply and commoditisation is limiting choice?

In the services sector we see the same thing. A master services agreement for thousands of workers slots them into a small subset of roles: junior analyst, senior developer, or project manager to name some. The use of Industrial Awards in minimum wage setting

[120] Smith

and measurement of work and experience is essential; however, it also standardises jobs. A café assistant today needs to serve coffee, light meals and operate online ordering systems. If the roof leaks or a customer falls, they need to use their extensive ability to deal with unique issues. Every one of them is unique and adds their own skill, ability and personality to their work. It is the same thing with job descriptions as we will see. We ignore the uniqueness of human beings. While it is one thing to be measurable, it is another thing to be the same. We saw how a fungible commodity may corrupt its true value. Perhaps only the most basic needs and components need be commoditised, and our quest to commoditise everything has and will be curtailed.

Money and liquidity are so tangled up with commodity trading so we do not know when one begins and the other ends. Many people and institutions who trade in the commodity market never touch the commodity. The derivatives markets have their benefits in risk management, in arbitrage (equalising prices), and in levelling demand and supply. It can also lead to corruption of pricing, with the strange phenomena we saw in COVID-19 of negative future contract prices on crude oil caused by the fact that traders who could not deliver were holding obligations they could not fulfil, and with the drop in demand, no one wanted to buy and fulfil the contract. It is also questionable if the action of speculators levels the price or makes it more volatile.

Technology, specification standards, and demand and supply should allow us to assess value more accurately without needing to standardise the product. A poor-quality phone charger and a good one is still difficult to discern in an online market, and many end up falling back on brand reputation — propping up power in the hands of the established organisations. Marketplaces and produce quality, discovery, and specification need to transform to allow product diversification at scale. Solutions like a scalable request for quotation (implemented on Alibaba and Ariba) need to enter mass market adoption and retail buyers need to become more procurement savvy, like their corporate counterparts.

The same principle of decommoditisation applies to services. Standardised jobs and professions will go or are going from the job market. If a job can be repeated, it will, in future, be automated. The work of people will need to be unique and varied, as it should be. It will not be possible to know the future of what a job entails and a job description will become increasingly fluid. The marketplace for work needs to transform to facilitate this new reality. Imagine a marketplace where every item is unique.

B2B Payments

The business-to-business (B2B) exchange of goods and payments is a considerable challenge. Small businesses cannot get good payment terms from suppliers without providing a personal guarantee. In many cases, businesses require supplies before they can sell their end product. Providers want payment or guarantees before they sell, and transactions are often lost and unreconciled. Construction and hospitality are two industries that are heavily affected by this productivity challenge — and there are few solutions to the problem. The Beat the Q founder established Ordermentum, a simple marketplace for restaurants and cafes that uses embedded payments and credit cards, a good solution that works for the seller more than the buyer. Openpay provided a B2B funding capability for businesses.

Could it be possible to attach a payment to the end product, through the Internet of Things or through an electronic chain of custody arrangement?

National and Global Biometric Online Identity

We mentioned the inconsistency and difficulty of establishing identity, especially for online-only institutions. This will continue to be a problem and issues will arise due to this gap. The need for ID validation on passports and immigration visas, and KYC procedures on banking products, could all be eliminated if there was a sovereign, potentially internationalised identity system that used biometrics, and/or an online authentication mechanism to validate and authorise an individual. The idea is highly discouraged by established banks and service providers as it is disruptive to many providers.

The Australia Card days are long behind us, and there is a public acceptance that identity is becoming harder and harder to keep secret with the Web, Facebook and others able to biometrically facially match against large repositories. Nor do we have a strong argument against it, based on the myriad of state-sanctioned programs and data-sharing initiatives. Government departments share hundreds of service links with each other, the ATO seeks dozens of industry data feed types from thousands of institutions, and the Attorney General's DVS system shares identity records across state and federal governments with private providers. Nor do many oppose the sharing of data; after 9/11 and the COVID-19 pandemic, safety has been prioritised over privacy.

This is not to say that the data should be open, just that identity and the validation of it should be a government service. The impact could be significant and is a building block that will enable other disruptions.

Bank Corporate Profitability

The increase in share price of organisations is driven by the market perception that a specific company will continue to grow its revenue. As we mentioned, in a market that is not growing, with the limitation of growth of the Big Four banks given the Four Pillars policy, added to tighter regulations and with large organisations that are less likely than smaller ones to risk their business, banks can only do one thing: reduce costs. This containment of costs is known as positive jaws, where the gap between income and expenses increases. In practice, this is not sustainable, as forced cutbacks mean less innovation and the loss of key resources to keep the machine oiled. Outages will become longer and more frequent, further eroding customer service in a very digital age.

Governments on both sides of the spectrum continue to squeeze margins on banks. Interchange is heading to zero. A low interest rate environment (which is here for a long time) means there is little profit in deposits or payments. With personal lending and credit card lending always a side business, home loans are the last bastion of profit. The ACCC 2018 Residential Mortgage Price Inquiry[121] and 2020 Home Loan Pricing Inquiry provide some valuable insights into the profitability of banks when it comes to lending, and it is not good news. For this reason, personal investment in the big banks should be questioned.

The ever-increasing desire for more and more profits cannot continue in environments of subdued growth and, like airlines and telcos before them, the days of high growth of banks in their current form must end.

---

[121] ACCC 2018

Banking Centralisation

For physical reasons, as mentioned, ledgers were stored in the home bank branch of the customer. With the first computers, around 1960, it was eventually possible to store information centrally.

» NOTE

In 1973, the Calcutta office of the Central Bank of India (not to be confused with the Reserve Bank of India, India's actual central bank) burnt down and, with it, the non-computerised bank ledger. Thanks to passbooks, the records could be recreated. Customers were invited back to the branch immediately to allow recreation of the ledger; however, few bothered, as they were confident their passbooks would be honoured whenever they returned.[122]

In 1957, an IBM 350 magnetic hard drive, part of the IBM 350 RAMAC suite (one of the first hard drives), was so big it needed a full forklift to carry it. It could hold 3.75 MB of data and cost USD $34 500. (This is about AUD $482 000 today.) It was still not practical to store everything centrally. Over time, Moore's Law prevailed (named after Gordon E Moore, the number of transistors on a semiconductor doubles every two years or, loosely applied, memory and processing power improve and prices come down over time) yet, even today, these electronic ledgers remain in banks.

Now it is technically possible to store all of Australia's bank account details on the memory of any modern smartphone worth $300 or more (holding 64 GB). On a good one, we can store two months' transaction history as well. So, if the bank was just a ledger, we could fit all of Australia's banks in our pocket.

Thanks to the Financial Claims Scheme, the banks need to be able to dump, with no notice, a record of the ledger position of all their clients with the Reserve Bank. This process is designed for a bank failure, but tested anyway just in case. So not only could the RBA get the technology, it could get the data as well. We heard the jibe about the RBA being model train builders. In fact, they have done a good job, now running the core Fast Settlement Service (FSS) of NPP payments for the entire country, and they did this with a budget that is a fraction of the big banks. A good start — why not finish it and move all of core banking to the RBA?

Further on the lending ledger, the banks' hands are tied, post-GFC and Basel III, with credit decisioning rules guided by regulators. COVID-19 introduced a new SME loan that banks were required to implement. The government would partially guarantee the loan. Risk-weighted

---

[122] Dadabhoy

assets tell banks exactly how to measure risk and, to a great extent, force the products they are able to sell by weighting some better or worse than others. Regulators are increasingly telling banks how they should lend money. So can the lending ledger be centralised as well?

Tight control of the assets of the bank means that much of the bank's assets in the retail sector are held by the government, either through the Reserve Bank or as mortgages on property titles with the state governments.

With almost every aspect of banking so heavily regulated and so government controlled, does it not make sense to end the pain and just take over banking centrally?

This idea has a lot of merit. Historically, it was called the nationalisation of banks and has happened in Commonwealth countries, including the United Kingdom, to a limited extent recently. As we saw, it was proposed by the Australian Prime Minister Ben Chifley in 1947, and almost actually happened.

The support or criticism of nationalisation tends to be political, with free-market proponents pointing to the innovation and entrepreneurship of free enterprise. However, with technology, it may be possible to please both sides.

To dismiss the centralisation of core ADI functions in an emotional or political way would be premature without a proper consideration of the reasoning. We are not talking about nationalisation any more.

The free market, without regulation, all sides would agree, has failed with respect to core banking functions: lending risk, core payment systems, and deposit security, all three of which are now heavily regulated due to bank failures in Australia: from the 1890s, to the run on the banks of the Great Depression, globally in the 1970s banking crisis, 9/11 with terrorism financing, and the GFC. With the COVID-19 pandemic, we did not give them the chance to fail: regulating from the outset and providing government funding to the hardest hit.

Maintaining core deposits, payment settlement, assets, mortgage titles, and even credit records and lending rules in a central place (which, let's face it, is almost the current status quo), and allowing the next generation of private banks to provide surface enhancements (or, to borrow the NPP term, *overlays*), with freedom to profit, could provide all the benefits we have seen in digital banking, versatile payments, good customer service, and innovation, without systemic risks in asset management, lending risk, payment settlement, and overcharging. It would remove the need for decentralised capital adequacy (which props up established banks relative to smaller competitors), and allow smaller players to compete. No ADI licenses would be required. This is the boring part of banking. Procedural and uninspiring, there are few decisions that can and do happen in this area.

Basically, the RBA becomes the central (shared) ledger, and individuals give permission to the new banks to intermediate, at the surface level. This concept would disrupt our notion of banking and provide a positive impact to society, with more competitive options and more options to pay.

Technically, the RBA would hold balances in a central ledger (bigger, hopefully, than our phone mentioned above) against our national ID. (Yes, we have many: tax file number, birth certificate number, immigration visa number, passport number, driver's licence or proof of age card number, Medicare number, Centrelink customer reference number and, sitting with the Attorney General is the ID number that ties them all together, a DVS ID.) It would also hold a ledger of our debts, one step better than a credit score agency that only sees some of the debts.

Non-bank credit and investment/fund accounts could continue as is. Many other functions of banks, such as global markets, can be completed without an ADI license today by accessing ADIs.

Using the previously described method of three-legged authentication, similar to the United Kingdom's open banking for payments, potentially possible with NPP, we would authenticate with our chosen provider via MyGov (or a similar government digital identity authentication service) and, from that point forward, transact through that chosen provider. This provider would be regulated, not as an ADI, but for security and privacy. For their efforts, they could extract a small fee. Likewise for lending, the regulators (APRA and ASIC) would apply the existing constraints on how much could be borrowed, with or without mortgage insurance, based on the e-conveyancing-controlled mortgagee property titles. Again, the provider is similar to a mortgage broker and takes a fee based on the government rate. ASIC has proven that non-ADIs can be regulated.

A simple centralised banking pilot could be initiated for a new type of non-ADI banking license with the RBA as the underlying ADI, through Australia Post or, for government accounts or government pension recipients by accessing RBA customer accounts through a more robust open banking API.

Consumer Innovation in Payments

Putting aside banking centralisation for the moment, many of the non-bank innovations, including cryptocurrency, have ultimately been surface innovations on the payments and banking system.

PayPal, Square, Stripe, Apple Pay, Google Pay and Samsung Pay are more convenient ways to access (generally) cards or other bank payments.

Alternative international payment/money service businesses make international payments cheaper and more accessible but, at the wholesale level, they generally ultimately need to settle on SWIFT, a regulated bank payment.

Even cryptocurrency has a similar reliance. Ripple, normally through an IOU protocol, and Bitcoin and others, do settle but, ultimately, the recipient needs currency and, for that, they need to access today's banking system.

It may be possible for a deeper innovation, but we have not seen it.

These innovations will continue to make payments more convenient, but we do need to acknowledge one thing: that today, if we have money, it is possible to pay anyone. Improvement of payments is a first-world problem. Access to money, however, is a different issue that we will cover later.

We should not dismiss payment improvement. Global marketplaces and access to better payments will help third-world countries elevate to the first world, and make first-world countries more competitive. While we can all make payments, fees, accessibility and slowness are niggling issues in the system.

Being able to walk into a store and smile or wink to make that payment will liberate us from our wallet and our phone.

Allowing anyone to be a merchant will restore the balance of small business, which is a good thing according to most economic modelling. Even a relatively smaller small business sector generates almost half of an economy's activity. Big businesses spend money on acquisitions and are less efficient, from a staff member to revenue point of view. Small businesses tend to spend a higher percentage of their income.

Further, the notion of innovation now being limited to big tech companies in the US is a fallacy. We have seen that China's Ant Financial is the world's biggest fintech. We are seeing tech incursions in the retail sector now of the Indian companies Ola and Zomato. US big tech firms have retreated or have never really executed on their payment capability, and are hampered by a slow and difficult to change regulatory and market environment: the US. Ultimately, many solutions fundamentally end up as card payments.

On the other hand, as we said, Australia has provided some impressive changes. Even if they do not classify as inventive ideas, the implementations have been innovative: early implementation of PIN, then chip and PIN at point of sale, early adoption of credit cards, fast adoption of tap and pay and of mobile payments, a national electronic toll system, and real-time domestic payments.

Let's have a look at some of these surface innovations that could be disruptive in payments.

Payment Handshake

Card payments are really made up of two components: the card rails and the use of the card (or, more recently, mobile phone) to initiate a payment handshake.

A payment handshake essentially could either let the payer know the payment details (account number etc.) — a push payment — or provide secure payment credentials using cryptographical means, the account of the payer, for the payee to debit, with the former being more secure than the latter. A consumer would experience the handshake either as a tap of the phone or a wink of an eye, or some less obtrusive innovative connection.

With alternative rails available (like NPP and eftpos, the latter technically being a card rail), it may be possible to invent alternative handshakes based on NFC, QR codes, Bluetooth, Wi-Fi, LoRaWAN or biometrics to initiate a secure handshake that allows the payment to continue via new or existing payment rails.

Global Sovereign Interconnected Consumer Electronic Payment Scheme

Here we invent the Global Sovereign Interconnected Consumer Electronic Payment Scheme, GSICEPS. Each country develops a local real-time clearing system (like eftpos and NPP in Australia) and interconnects them as a global scheme to allow international payments through an FATF, Common Reporting Standard/FATCA, and UNSC-compliant trusted circle.

The solution could use SWIFT ISO 20022 rails (like NPP), but requires a scheme mandating rules, costs, and user interfaces, which SWIFT does not.

Country regulators are responsible for compliance, with payments identifying the recipient as well as the payer through national identity systems.

This new system would allow low-cost international payments, net settled through SWIFT/CLS Bank/sovereign RTGS and distributed to local banks. It could be used as P2P, online merchant purchases or a small IMT payment system.

People could use their cards overseas, unifying eftpos, China UnionPay, India's RuPay, and New Zealand's Paymark, and allowing the resurrection of the Euro Alliance of Payment Schemes (EAPS), and others, operating as an online payment solution.

The initiative would require unprecedented international cooperation in payments, and may have a stronger initial business case outside the US and Europe. It would be disruptive to existing schemes and, in reducing the cost of payments and increasing safety and accessibility, could accelerate a global marketplace.

NPP

Turning to the Australian domestic systems, NPP is actually a core payment rail but, as mentioned, many of the proposed innovations have not been implemented, due in part to the lockdown of the NPP network by NPPA, something the Productivity Commission has called out in its inquiry into Competition in the Australian Financial System. The essential problem facing NPP, like SWIFT, is that it is not really a scheme, hence, Osko, which is really a no-frills scheme. Once available, due to the previously mentioned trough of disillusionment/chasm, it will take time for corporate access and for real-world implementations to emerge. In turn, the exposure of NPP could be disruptive outside the traditional banking system.

- True account portability: the widespread use of the NPP addressing scheme and turning off BSB/account number addressing. Easy to implement transfers that move all mandates and banking in one go. New players can now easily take over banking from the establishment.
- B2B and consumer bill payments have, surprisingly, not kicked off. Even with electronic Direct Entry, we still have the "cheque is in the mail" problem. Perhaps BPAY/Osko will start to push this as it is far more efficient to have bills paid in real-time than the current wait.
- Personalised addressing for bill payments, like Paul@bill.telstra.com or Sam@card.davidjones.com.au, could help corporate reconciliation of bill payments and immediately reject invalid payments.
- Real-time notification of payment could be used to electronically notify a biller or merchant that money has been received. In the domestic Australian market, this could disrupt scheme cards and alternative solutions like POLi Payments.
- The implementation of debit mandates could be used by consumer-trusted wallets to take money from bank accounts. Similar to credit card wallets, this would further encourage the dislodgement of cards and is a more secure solution. It would bring consumer control back to direct debits through customer-controlled mandates.

- The use of rich information flows to allow eInvoicing, eReceipts, and payment advice, peer-to-peer, business-to-business, or consumer and back again, could allow greater automation, automatic tax solutions, and machine-based ordering. Automatic STP to the tax office and super, as well as GST reporting, would make accounting so much easier.
- GST payments at point of sale, or at least GST reporting at time of sale, would save lots of bookkeeping work, especially for small businesses, and might even facilitate tax extraction at time of sale. While, as mentioned above, GST did not make sense, GST reporting at POS could be useful to help calculate and pay it. Consistent application of tax law levels the playing field for businesses.
- eReceipts can also help with warranty registration and recalls. SKU level receipting identifying each item could allow manufacturers to offer discounts directly to consumers. Parallel loyalty can be developed. The system could also warn consumers when they were paying too much, and assist retailers in becoming more competitive.
- IFTI on NPP, reporting of foreign transfers, and the NPP's core network SWIFT, could allow NPP to be globalised or, at least, facilitate cheaper, faster, information richer transfers with other countries, or even open up to local domestic distribution of bulked-up payments. It could remove the fear factor of international payments and allow less expensive players to enter the market at a lower cost.

〉〉 NOTE

Issuing receipts has been a global challenge. In China, receipts are printed on special paper, often by special POS printing devices, called *fapiao*. The receipt data is given to the government to ensure vendors pay tax. The system also facilitates variation of tax rates for smaller businesses. Cash payments in taxis, even for small amounts, require a *fapiao* preprinted receipt, like currency notes, all of which ensure every yuan is accounted for as every payment requires a receipt. In Greece, shops were threatened with temporary closure if they did not issue receipts. A policy of no receipt, no pay was instituted by some stores and governments to dissuade the non-recording of sales, by allowing consumers to get a full refund if they did not get a receipt.

One Domestic Scheme

Innovation and investment attention is divided between a number of scheme rails, many of which are attempting to accomplish the same things. It is not a question of competition, with the same banks providing funding to all. Competition can continue at the surface, allowing third parties to provide solutions using APIs or similar solutions.

Some serious effort, as was proposed in 2020, should be made to unite NPP, eftpos, BPAY, and Beem It (and actively decommission Direct Entry) to focus attention on what should be one payment rail and, with the establishment of a better-funded commercial scheme and focused investment, more could be possible.

Future of the Schemes

We have been challenging the schemes: Mastercard and Visa and, to a lesser extent, American Express and eftpos, with disruption, but now is their chance to fight back. As we saw, they introduced real-time payment acceptance before computerisation. They enabled the consumer revolution. They were the consumer payment of choice in mail, on the phone and on the Web.

Continued investment in genuine innovation has meant and could mean they remain one step ahead. Their international reach means that what they implement has the best chance of success, especially in the US, which, even today, still shapes the online world.

Visa's Visa Direct, which uses emerging real-time domestic payment networks, Visa B2B Connect and their open banking solution Visa Plaid, are looking into some of the areas mentioned in this chapter. Mastercard and Visa are on the lookout for acquisition opportunities.

eftpos is moving to a digital solution online. This is too little, too late, but it could unsettle local (domestic) online payments in some segments that are cost sensitive. The problem is that it does not support credit well, and the NPP solution on paper is more robust. eftpos is poorly funded and poorly empowered by its members, so our expectations and hopes are low. Beem It illustrates what can happen if just one bank gets behind an idea.

The End of Credit Cards?

Tighter controls on bank credit, as we said, could result in a slow and gradual weaning off credit purchases. Today, credit to debit card ratios, even for small purchases, are around 9 to 1, that is, there is nine times the volume of credit cards as debit, but the numbers are moving gradually to debit.

The replacement could be micro-credit (a further evolution of the buy now, pay later solutions we have today) and, if marketed well and integrated seamlessly into payments, it does offer a disruption opportunity. However, logically, a more robust solution is a user pays form of credit; this will need to be at a lower interest rate. Such solutions are true revolving lines of credit or just simple lines of credit.

The movement from credit rating agencies to better regulated solutions, or to shared credit ledgers, will be better for consumers. There are a dozen ways to implement this solution and, if it does happen, it will further enable a lower risk of providing credit. Digital identity that ensures the proper identification of recipients is essential in such a solution. Strong credit checking and better credit recovery practices, authorised by law, should result in the narrowing between unsecured rates of lending and secured mortgage interest rates.

In truth, the discrepancy between the two rates is not explained by risk alone and can only be attributed to lack of competition. This lack of competition, in turn, is due to the underlying interest rate of credit cards, in particular, being obfuscated or hidden behind the interest-free period, loyalty points, and initial introductory interest periods that expose the underlying rate only once the customer is locked in. The use of a non-open ledger means previous credit applications and inquiries impact the credit score, dissuading customers from moving financial service providers, clearly an anti-competitive behaviour that has not been addressed by the ACCC.

Alternative Investments

Payments are partly made possible by access to private sector broad money. As we saw, this has moved towards, not away, from traditional banks despite tougher regulation of ADIs.

Yet, the discrepancy between bank unsecured lending and deposit interest rates of more than a staggering 20% indicates an enormous under-tapped economic opportunity.

With the notion of P2P lending largely defunct, an opportunity to develop high-quality responsible personal lending products at lower than bank rates, and to offer investment fund products to finance them, can provide a good return on investments even in a low interest environment.

More generally, while many of us deposit our savings in the bank, this is the lowest return. While the balance is subject to the Financial Claims Scheme guarantee, this does not protect the money from inflation, and few people have become wealthy from bank savings, contrary to what we may have learnt at school (as mentioned earlier). We also mentioned that the profit a bank makes is from people anticipating to make a payment from their savings, but instead just keeping it floating in the account.

Consensus is that the best investment is not going it alone but relying on an indexed managed fund. There are many funds to choose from. The most mundane is the balanced fund, curiously, one of the better performing ones over time. In addition, there are the cash and bond funds for conservative investors, the Australian and global equities funds, property funds or agricultural funds for those who prefer a specific sector and, for risk takers, emerging markets and many others.

» NOTE

We have all had that friend that says they can beat the market, or have heard of a new fund manager who has their finger on the market pulse. Many people have self-managed super funds (SMSF). In some cases, it may make sense, if the holder wishes to make a specific investment and use the tax benefits of SMSF to save on individual tax. However, due to the high accounting and compliance fees, SMSFs are not as lucrative as they seem to be and, for many, underperform retail super funds, according to ASIC, at least, for balances less than $500 000. The science of funds management indicates that indexed managed funds are, over time, more likely to succeed than others due to:

1. **Economies of scale.**
2. **The diversity of the investment, less subject to a single failure.**
3. **The fact that markets tend to go up and an index is, by design, a good basket of the market.**

4. **Management in indexed funds is mechanical and does not require highly-paid fund managers, systems and analysts to figure out how to invest.**

Low fees are actually a good indicator of long-term success. However, listed indexed funds tend to have higher compliance fees.

Imagine we had the best of both worlds: an investment that earned a good return and that could make payments. Diversifying our portfolio would help us minimise the risk of failure so the Financial Claims Scheme may not be required.

A fund manager would simply need access to an ESA (directly or through a bank) and maintain a balance there to cover withdrawals (or redemptions, as they are called in the industry). A debit card could be issued against the fund, and a BSB/account number or NPP and BPAY could be added to facilitate the normal payments or, alternatively, the account could be connected to a regular transaction account through real-time transfers. Based on withdrawals and deposits, investments would be bought or sold.

This product is not only technically possible, but could disrupt the financial marketplace.

Investment Product Distribution

Investment product distribution is still poorly handled and has yet failed to attract mass adoption. The CBA IPO, the Telstra float, and others in the 1990s attracted new investors to the stock market — mums and dads as they were called. Even now, the dividend payment for these shares is a liquidity and logistical challenge. Superannuation, widely introduced in the 1990s, forced people to look at managed funds. However, outside this, for many people, investment products have remained substantially unchanged in Australia since the Bank of New South Wales opened its doors in 1817.

Wealth management was the domain of the wealthy. Private banks, investment, and merchant banks popularised by the Millionaire's Factory, Macquarie Bank developed exotic products, and complex tax minimising investments and strategies. Some of them were quite good. Payment accessible cash management trusts; for example, a Bankers Trust (Australia) wrap product that rolled several products into one managed portfolio with one annual tax statement, were some of the innovations.

The acquisition of wealth management companies by the banks around the early 2000s promised to bring some hope to the retail investment industry.

In 2005, NAB attempted to integrate MLC products into its retail distribution channel by creating a business unit called distribution, with the view of moving wealth distributors, and business and retail banking product distributors together so they could all cross-sell the one suite of products to customers where it made sense. However, the nearly 200 years of siloed operation meant it was almost impossible to insert outsider products into the retail branch network, even if those products came from the same company. The initiative failed before it could get traction.

Financial product sales was a shady business. Originally, poorly regulated, with origins going back to door-to-door salesmen, the now gentrified advisers would recommend products without proper application of investment science: without comparing products and without understanding customer needs. Further, it was clear that advisers were aligned to sell products from specific providers for which they would receive significant commissions. Unsuspecting investors were given poor investment choices and, as long as these investors were limited to the elite high net worth class, and the issues were few, the industry tolerated this activity. This changed with the attempt to scale up operations after the banks acquired them. Now every branch had access to a financial planner or adviser.

Due to poor behaviour by financial advisers, poor compliance by their employers, and the emerging mass market something was bound to fail. In a rising market, even bad advice can turn out good. When markets turned south, there was a perfect storm: small-time investors, mass-market corruption, big banks and politicians. Lawyers swooped on what had been an ongoing issue for many years, but now the top end of corporate Australia was implicated. A number of inquiries started — in 2009, the Parliamentary Joint Committee on Corporations and Financial Services. There were embarrassing current affairs television revelations. Future of Financial Advice reform regulations ensued. The other side of wealth was not immune. Insurance sometimes obfuscates its benefits in terms and conditions with headline product names that hide the true level of risk mitigation. One customer thought that he was covered for a heart attack — that was what was sold to him — but having a troponin level of 1.9 micrograms per litre instead of 2.0 voided the claim. Wealth management was not yet mature enough to hit the mass market and, after the 2017-2019 royal commission, banks had no choice but to throw the baby out with the bath water. Unfortunately, three simple truths remain: that Australians do not receive the right amount of financial advice, are underinsured and they do not invest their money the best way they can.

〉〉 NOTE

A common footnote on printed financial advertisements are words to the effect of: "This is general advice. Please read the Product Disclosure Statement and Financial Services Guide. This advice has not considered your personal situation, so please seek independent financial advice before acting on any investment presented here." Those words were often changed to remove "seek independent financial advice" to "consider your personal circumstances". The banks wanted nothing to do with financial advisers. Few people read the Product Disclosure Statement, and most are poorly written and unintelligible for lay people.

Heavy regulation, fear, and lack of competition have stagnated the alternative investment sector in Australia. There remains an enormous capacity of disruption, with fairer products, if non-bank financial institutions are willing to take the opportunity.

The Rise of the Expert

Classic academic education focuses on singular disciplines.[123] Many of us, when we leave school, have often invested so much relative time in one particular field that it becomes, for a time, an obsession. We have all come across an expert that claims they know everything, and has the solution to all the world's problems, viewing the problem, however, through one lens. The world is complex and, without an open mind, it is hard to solve the world's most

[123] Comte

difficult problems and convince others to buy into a potential solution. The ability to dumb things down became a quality, a relatable one, that helped win arguments in the boardroom, and helped convince customers, shareholders and voters. Simplicity became a science and expertise became a hindrance.

›› NOTE

Many of Australia's more recent prime ministers: Bob Hawke, Tony Abbott and Malcolm Turnbull were Rhodes Scholars, and many more were well-educated lawyers. Paul Keating, though not formally educated, remains one of the most intelligent, insightful and witty leaders in the country's history. Chairs of big corporations were very intelligent people. The recent trend away from well-read leaders, deliberating over complex issues and listening to experts, may be temporary, a reaction against an elite intelligentsia; however, a broad-based, educated, rising youth, as Barack Obama suggested in 2020,[124] may provide hope for the future.

A gap remains between old school bankers and technologists, though these days the line is blurring as one walks down the engine room of banks, with Agile and similar processes having much to be thanked for in bringing the two groups together. However, the relatively recent royal commission into misconduct, for example, failed to consider technology and technologists in its inquiry and findings — so there is a long way to go. The ACCC review of Apple Pay and other regulations and regulators further demonstrates this divide.

Auguste Comte identified the need for scientists with good knowledge of several disciplines, capable of applying, for example, physics to biology. The value of deep technologists who understand commerce and economics is already emerging in some fintech startups that apply technology to a narrow understanding of the business of banking. At the moment, there are more misses than hits so they may still need some time to mature. Nevertheless, mature they will be, and scientists, technologists, engineers and mathematicians (STEM professionals) who can apply their knowledge to the psychology of human trade may be the source of the next disruptive innovations. Already, we are seeing interdisciplinary courses at universities, and the investment of banks in technology startups.

Workforce of the Future

In 1960, an accountant would do accounting, a lawyer would take care of the law, and an engineer would tinker with machines. Today, if any two jobs are the same, that is an opportunity for downsizing, consolidation or automation. Continuing this trend, it is not hard to visualise that the workforce of the future will have only unique roles for individuals.

---

[124] Obama

The rise of the gig economy, like Freelancer, Airtasker, and Upwork and the shared economy with Uber, etc., may see the end of permanent staff. Globalisation through Internet communication and trade may make outsourcing more available to all sectors and businesses.

Despite the increase in automation, more people are employed in banking (and in the workforce) than at any other time in the past. Keynes explained it well almost 100 years ago in a prophetic essay:

> *"We are being afflicted with a new disease of which some readers may not yet have heard the name, but of which they will hear a great deal in the years to come — namely, technological unemployment. This means unemployment due to our discovery of means of economising the use of labour outrunning the pace at which we can find new uses for labour. But this is only a temporary phase of maladjustment. All this means in the long run that mankind is solving its economic problem. I would predict that the standard of life in progressive countries one hundred years hence will be between four and eight times as high as it is to-day. There would be nothing surprising in this even in the light of our present knowledge. It would not be foolish to contemplate the possibility of a far greater progress still."*[125]

Humans need to grow in capability faster than their machines. For those that remember, going to a bank or customer service, in general, 30, 40 or more years ago, was very different to what it is now. Then, it was an unpleasant experience — take a number, little information, the convergence of two strangers who could not see eye to eye: one who knew the process and one who did not. This has improved remarkably. Our customer service has improved significantly, with standard operating procedures that work and are well communicated, feedback, and surveys — continual improvement. Yet, we have a long way to go.

Systems, rather than just becoming smarter through artificial intelligence and machine learning, need to become more aware of the needs of people, like *conscious computation*, a machine that has been programmed to deeply understand what a user needs. Apple Computers were famous for this. From the Apple II to the iPhone, they were designed for real humans: from a mouse with just one button, to an iPad that can be operated by a toddler. Conscious computing is a program or a form that can reduce retyping information, a navigation system that can guess where you need to go, or an oven that can cook the inside and outside just right. This means more, not fewer technologists.

When Google hired operations staff, they did not hire operators that followed instructions. They hired engineers who could write programs that could automate a process so they did not have to repeat it.[126] A good programmer is a lazy one. The ability for call centre staff to solve a problem directly to the satisfaction of the customer, or to program a chatbot to answer a real question so that no one needs to answer it again is a long way off. Perhaps programming will be easier in the future, but we all need to become more aware and empathetic.

In the future, there will be mainly two categories of work: communicating with machines and communicating with humans. Those who can do both will be treasured.

---

[125] Keynes 1930

[126] Murphy

Diversity

Diversity in the workplace is important at so many levels. Gender diversity and indigenous diversity are important, and programs to encourage them are good and should continue. Discrimination still exists, due to what is now called subconscious bias, senior executives tend to hire people they see as friends (or people who could be friends).

Walking into the engine room of larger banks and seeing the diverse set of highly competent professionals, and then taking the elevator to higher floors, seeing a homogenous sea of executives: attractive people, quality suits, cufflinks, silk, where style matters more than substance, one could be forgiven for thinking they have stepped back to a time before the invention of plastic buttons. Many large private organisations continue to hire in senior roles a set of people limited in diversity, and even when people of diverse backgrounds are chosen to fill these senior ranks often their skin colour, gender, or orientation barely distinguishes them from the cultural and behavioural styles of their less diverse peers. In short, there is a culture of fitting in that limits an organisation to be disruptive, to try new things, to avoid groupthink — where everyone in the room agrees with each other. There are so many aspects to this diversity: racial, cultural, LGBTI, neurodiversity, professional, technical and educational diversity, physical ability and psychological diversity. The widespread use of psychometric evaluations — while proven and effective in measuring task aptitude for basic, repetitive work, could reinforce group think and may not be appropriate in more senior roles. Diversity has slowly shaped workplaces over the last few decades. Once an artificial environment with adopted behaviours, the workplace is more relaxed, with less of a distinction between home and work. In such environments, people can apply their whole personality to the office or can work from home. With this atmosphere comes a broader set of ideas, and more creativity and less mechanistic practices. For these reasons, a more diverse workforce can help disrupt organisations.

Culture Shift

The most disruptive change in society is not a technical one, but a change in the way we collectively think.

Innovation and Change Culture

Ideas, like those contained on these pages are cheap; as they say, execution is everything.[127]

The ability of large organisations to adapt has been impressive. However, the risk of losing reputation, getting fined, or impacting a large machinery through a single action makes them cautious. The advantage of market share and being able to grow an idea at scale is offset by bureaucracy. The Big Four are under an APRA risk watch. The big banks have capital reserve handicap penalties. This will slow them down. Risk management, as wonderful a science as it is, must be balanced for, without balancing it, one may never cross a road.

The new banks and new institutions have an enormous advantage. New accessible technology without the legacy, and with an emerging shared economy (cloud, managed

[127] Sacca

services) have demonstrated that they can achieve in a short time what the big banks took years to accomplish and can move ahead. Xinja, Volt Bank, 86 400 and U Bank are some of the examples. They may fail, but they will try, and out of that may come a breakthrough that will alter the banking and payments landscape.

Ethics

The recent royal commission and an earlier APRA report into CBA highlighted behavioural problems in banks. Indeed, our story of banks started with corrupt behaviour in the first months of the first bank.

We mused, in the previous chapter, about why big banks exhibit corrupt behaviours. Let us look at two causes and two analogies.

In the lead-up to the 2000 Sydney Olympics, if a prospective spectator was not quick, it was difficult to get cheap tickets. The women's 20 km walk was one of the last available, a chance to see the new stadium and witness a lifetime event for thousands of locals. On the day of the event, the home crowd was not disappointed. There was the rare opportunity to witness a potential Australian gold medal winner — rare indeed, as Australian athletes were not big track and field contenders (with the single exception in 2000 of the legendary Cathy Freeman).

The walk is a strange event. The winner is the first to cross the finish line, the one who (logically) is the fastest. Nothing unusual about this, apparently. However, human reflexes, in trying to get somewhere quickly, especially for those of us who are fit, speed up a walk into a run. This is not a problem for most of us, and has evolved as a reflex that probably saved many of our ancestors from death when pursued by wild animals or when trying to catch one to satisfy our hunger. Unfortunately, the same reflex can result in disqualification in the 20 km walk.

The walk is a long one, and most of the race takes place on the roads outside the stadium. It has been poorly adjudicated due to limited expert referees. Referees are experienced professionals: difficult to find, highly skilled, under resourced and underpaid. So, these referees need to compromise their efforts in light of their limited resources, distance between the leaders and the laggers, and the need to simultaneously observe so many contenders; so they logically focus on the leaders in the race. To maintain the lead and claim gold, athletes needed to walk faster than they ever had before, for this was probably the race of their lifetime. This meant doing one thing: compromising the walking gait, breaking the rules. Sure enough, leader after leader was disqualified in the final kilometres, still outside the Olympic Stadium finish line, until Australian Jane Saville was leading a pack that was about to enter the stadium. The crowd cheered. Unfamiliar with the refereeing nuance, many thought, "How could she not win?" The whole stadium was watching. But so were the referees. Sure enough, she was the fifth to be disqualified with just 100 metres to go.[128]

Like the women's 20 km walk, the Martin Committee in 1991 noted that, "There are limits to the number of organisations which the Reserve Bank has the capacity to supervise without diminishing the quality of that supervision." Limitations of supervisory capacity meant more

---

[128] Gavel

attention on the Big Four. Sure enough, more regulatory action appears to be directed at the bigger banks than the smaller ones. This pattern has been repeated in the media with many negative behaviours of the big banks making the news, while those in the industry knew of worse behaviour in smaller financial intermediaries. ME Bank's revocation of the redraw account was just one contrary example.

This observation is backed by statistics. With the big banks having a market share of over 80%, they have accounted for only 68% of complaints received by the Australian Financial Complaints Authority. Given the more extensive product range and greater touch points of bigger banks than smaller ones, we should have seen more complaints than the 80% market share of the Big Four, yet the statistics indicate that big banks are better behaved, perhaps due to better compliance, internal oversight, and complaint management that smaller institutions may neglect. So perhaps it is the nature of the industry.

Eyeing the revenue opportunity of handling money, even the otherwise noble big tech companies: Apple and, initially, Google succumbed to the temptation (much like the walkers changing their gait), treating a contactless payment fundamentally different from what it really was: just a message.

Our second analogy is the slowly boiled frog. The legend, reported by E. W. Scripture, is that "A live frog can actually be boiled without a movement if the water is heated slowly enough; in one experiment the temperature was raised at the rate of 0.002 °C per second, and the frog was found dead at the end of two hours without having moved."[129] Thankfully, the cruel experiment has proven to be incorrect,[130] due to recent tests that have shown the opposite. These days, the story is used as a metaphor for human behaviour, that slow change numbs us to negative environments that would normally shock newcomers.

For those who have witnessed obfuscation tactics in fine print of product disclosure statements — protection of ineffective products by those that would supposedly desire their customers' financial wellbeing — the slowly boiling legend may well hold true, if not for the frog, but for humans. Employees of banks are only people, like us. Why do we refuse to act when forced to sell a bad product? Peer pressure? The desire for wealth and success corrupting our good nature? Fear of losing our job and an income stream? Perhaps a more optimistic version of the slowly boiled frog is Thomas Jefferson's articulation, immortalised in the United States Declaration of Independence (which, indirectly, gave birth to not just the US, but Australia, 12 years later): "All experience hath shewn, that mankind are more disposed to suffer, while evils are sufferable, than to right themselves by abolishing the forms to which they are accustomed."[131]

Perhaps the time has come for us to abolish the forms to which we are accustomed.

---

[129] Scripture

[130] Kruszelnicki

[131] Jefferson

The Enigma of Central Banking

A central bank is somewhat of an enigma: neither political nor truly independent of politics and government policy of the day, neither bank nor uninvolved umpire, empowered with an ambitious goal but with limited tools to realise it, an existence that is built on the strange rules and conventions of a very arbitrary design. It is a strange, almost unnatural product of the evolution of human commerce. It is one of the most powerful institutions in every nation. Yet, it measures its response based on these strange rules that few would know, and even fewer would care if the rules were changed. The wording on our banknotes to no longer guarantee payments in gold, the floating of the dollar, all these rules can be changed.

One thing that most laypeople do not realise is the large amount of assets the central bank has. As the bank issues money, it balances its balance sheet with assets — government debt instruments, largely. (Japan has been in quantitative easing for a while, with negative interest rates; it has also racked up the highest debt.)

The need for governments to go into debt when issuing money is a commitment from Bretton Woods. In addition, this discipline maintains confidence in the local currency, for unguarded issuing of money could lead to hyperinflation, as we saw.

However, if the government could issue money in an inflation-responsible way, without racking up debt, would monetary policy be more effective?

The End of Money?

> *"Economics of the future are somewhat different. You see, money doesn't exist in the 24th century ... the acquisition of wealth is no longer the driving force in our lives ... we work to better ourselves, and the rest of humanity."*
>
> ***Captain Jean-Luc Picard***
> ***Star Trek: First Contact***

If aliens visited Earth today and observed human behaviour, perhaps one of the things they would notice the most is our fascination with money and how it makes the human world spin.

"What's all this about?" they could ask. And if we are fortunate enough to have read this book, we could explain how it works. "What a bizarre story! What a strange system!" they may say. Our question would be, "So how does your world operate?"

Fundamental to payments is money. We use it to get something we do not have. Economists talk about needs and wants. The line between them is a shifting one. For us to live the way humans did 10 000 years ago would be considered a violation of human rights today. Access to a toilet, clean running tap water, cooked food, electricity, education, access to good health and medication, and even computers, telecommunications and the Internet are considered emerging basic human rights today. Reasonable people on all sides of the political spectrum agree that no one should be denied these basic human rights.

Australia has, for the most part, honoured this philosophy with a relatively better minimum legal wage, free healthcare (Medicare), essentially free education and the higher education contribution schemes (HECS) to make higher education accessible to all. Perhaps central to our culture of mateship is that we take care of each other in a society where everyone gets a fair go and we despise the bludger, but our commitment is, recalling Bretton Woods, full employment. For those who want to work but cannot find it, there are JobSeeker payments (the dole), and for those who are physically unable to work or are retired there is the pension, and benefits for low-income workers who need to care for or support family. Essentially, in Australia, there is a level of minimum security.

When humans were secure, free from the fear of beasts, we could explore. When we were no longer in search of food, we had time for higher pursuits: art, literature, science and technology. Freeing us up from struggling for basic needs is what it means to live in an advanced society, and fulfilling these basic needs should be more fundamental than payments and money.

›› NOTE

An often cited measure of financial security is being able to access $1 000 in an emergency. Despite relatively high wealth, due to high debt levels, 26% of Australians have less than this amount of savings.[132]

Even in a society that fulfils basic needs, money can be a useful instrument of distribution as a unit of exchange and as a unit of account.

However, basic needs are not enough, for without wants society stagnates. We learnt this from communism, where the most basic needs were met, but wants were controlled by the state.

›› NOTE

Karl Marx's philosophies that led to communism were based on the notion that, in capitalism, the true value of labour was largely exploited by those with the means of production. The solution proposed was to give the means of production to the state. George Orwell prophetically predicted the outcome in the classic novel *Animal Farm* (where a revolution overthrows a regime, only to be corrupted by power, just like the old regime). Instead of the rich, communism had the powerful; the result was the same. Communism is now essentially defunct with many communist countries existing in name alone.

---

[132] ME Bank

Store of Value

Through money's store of value, we could save up for a bigger expense to fulfil our wants. Those with more wealth could own the means of production.

Industrialisation gave power to those with the means of production: in capitalism, to the factory owners and, later, large corporations and, in communism, to the government.

This intermediation of the wealth of labour, both in capitalism and communism, led to the phenomenon often cited as the aphorism: "The rich get richer and the poor get poorer."

Perhaps the Internet is decentralising the means of production, through accessible marketplaces where anyone can sell their goods and services, and market access where anyone can buy anything from anyone.

The means of production goes through renewal cycles, thanks to technology advancement. The old guard makes way for the new. Increasingly, the means of production is getting more accessible. A music recording studio or a movie camera, once a significant investment, is now in the hands of anyone with a mobile phone. A global publishing printing press is now on every desktop with the old equipment having antique value only.

So, while this means of production is being decentralised, we still need money to purchase it.

George Stephenson Beeby, an Australian politician, judge and author, reflected on the nature of money and credit towards the end of the Great Depression in 1933. Perhaps the times were simpler, and perhaps Beeby was more insightful than most; he made a few interesting observations reflecting on the cause of and solution to the economic calamity his era was facing. First, he observed that money is not wealth itself, but can be exchanged for it, and is a good measure, a unit of account. Money is an ineffective store of value. Second, he noted that credit (which creates immediate money supply, whether private credit or the printing of notes) is a loan that demands future productivity as a repayment. The capacity for credit to be used for matters other than production was the cause of the current problem.

Coincidentally, the same year that Beeby made his insightful observations, in the US, Irving Fisher, a Yale professor of economics, was making similar observations. He provided a different solution. People were reluctant to spend cash. Some local governments were issuing a stamp script.[133] The stamp script had real money value and needed to be stamped every time it was used or stamped once a week. At the end of the year, the paper, if completely stamped, could be redeemed for cash. The idea was that the note had to be spent and could not be hoarded, used as a store in value. The notion was supported by Keynes, who said proposers were on the right track and their ideas deserved consideration.[134] The proposal was actually tabled as a bill in the United States Congress unsuccessfully.

In recent times, Australian monetary activist, Dr Shann Turnbull, has published over 1 587 articles, many on this topic. Modernising the stamp script of Fisher, he proposes a few modifications. Government money is "air-dropped" to every person or household. He suggested doing this electronically via SIM credits (see our discussion on USSD earlier) and,

---

[133] Fisher

[134] Keynes 1936

more recently, the government cashless debit card (also discussed previously), MyGov[135] or even state government travel cards: a crypto coin that electronically takes care of the stamping, ensuring that unless the coin moves, it attracts negative interest. He also proposed a stable currency.

Unit of Account

First, a stable measure of currency value is difficult to find. Gold is speculative as is each of the major currencies. A basket of currencies was used to provide consistency and stability, as mentioned, by the IMF. Facebook proposed the Libra, a digital currency that was similarly based on a basket of currencies to provide stability.

The use of the unit of account, however, as Turnbull advises, has not been an accurate measure of the value of something and the free market does not always cater for it. The classic example he suggests is the burning of coal. This industry never accounted for the cost of greenhouse gas emissions.

One other inequality is the unit of work — say, one hour of effort and the discrepancy of value between the rich and the poor, with workers in the poorest nations getting paid a few cents for back-breaking work, and a top CEO over ten thousand dollars for a coffee meeting.

›› NOTE

One popular anecdote concerns a wealthy individual of the era (a Jeff Bezos, Bill Gates, Warren Buffett or Larry Ellison) and the time taken to pick up a $100 note from the ground. The short rewarding exercise for many is not worth the billionaire's time — they are better off doing whatever it is they do that earns them the billions. This contrasts with the world's poorest for whom the note could be their monthly wage.

This is not to ask that all labour be valued equally. The future will demand more efficiency from everybody. With accessible marketplaces, more of the gig economy, and better access to the means of production, the value of an individual's labour will be the unique value they provide.

A unit of account, like a weight or a measure, becomes simply a yardstick of value. Carrying it around in a wallet would be as bizarre as carrying a 2 kg weight in one's pocket to measure a purchase of bananas.

135 Turnbull

Exchange of Value

With the demise of physical currency from hard currency to a fiat currency, and from physical to electronic, the exchange of value is not really an exchange as much as an intermediate stage, and the value is not in the money but in the goods and services it buys.

Particularly when viewed as broad money, the value is often associated with debt. Essentially, over the last 100 years, the exchange of value property of money has gradually been eroded.

A More Efficient System

The property of money to be an intrinsic store of value died a long time ago. As Beeby put it, gold was useful insofar as, if melted, it could be used as jewellery, and paper notes were only wealth in the form of "a bizarre wallpaper of the study in which we reflect on human folly."[136] What to say of our virtual bank account balance today? It is little more than pixels on a screen, yet we continue to value it.

Technology has the capability to improve the system. We could replace the concept of money and wealth with a ledger, this time, an electronic one. With education, skill, experience and job fitness, we have the capacity to generate value through production. Our ID validates who we are and provides our good standing and history. Our debts are recorded, as is our ability to pay them back. And so are our assets.

Whether we call it the Internet or a future generation of it, cloud computing or open ledgers — the Internet, its evolution, and its technologies are a shared field of human knowledge and experience, where no one is too small and everything is known.

Cooperation is the key ingredient in the history and future of economic and collective human development. Barter was directly cooperative and money was too — we all cooperated to make it work, to exchange what we needed for what we could produce. The future solution, perhaps a virtual ledger will be the next, more effective evolution of our cooperation.

We can see the early signs of this virtual ledger in online marketplaces with embedded payments. Perhaps eBay tried this in the early days — as an online second-hand auction site, where buyers were sellers and sellers were also buyers. It will continue to evolve. Imagine if we could balance our payments on a marketplace: what we produced and what we purchased were equal in value. In that marketplace, on that virtual ledger, there would be no payment in the conventional sense. A global marketplace-of-marketplaces becomes larger and more cooperative, connected by a ubiquitous virtual ledger.

Picture this virtual ledger opened up when we walk up to the register in a store. The shop validates our ledger through biometrics and our good standing, gives us the goods and records the debt. The government (the agent of our generosity) underwrites our needs and, for that, takes taxes, and credit providers (the agents of our modest desires) underwrite our wants and, for that, take repayments and (hopefully lower) interest as an underwriting fee. The debts and taxes are repaid by the fruits of our labour. The dollar (or Bancor?) is the unit of account, a measurement like a kilogram, metre or litre. However, there is no store of value, and the exchange is the goods and services we produce and take, not a coin. There is no

136 Beeby

need for money and no need for monetary payment, as we know it; the ledger is a real-time system and, in a manner similar to deferred net settlement, our debts are regularly repaid overnight or periodically as we earn. We move on from a strict time-bound double-entry system.

Being able to share our ledgers through technology restores the power of individuals to maximise the value of their labour; it removes labour intermediation. Companies exist, but only profit as they would in a competitive environment through their ability to support outcomes, through their IP, processes and intrinsic non-labour assets. Non-monetary private wealth exists as well, secured by the ledger and available for hire, if desired, through integrated marketplaces. Assets become more affordable based on their utility value. Our wealth becomes collateralised and our debts can be secured against them, like a mortgage or a car today. We restore the trust system of the village market, but now at a global scale, thanks to information technology connecting the world.

"Fill 'er up," we say, as we approach the voice-activated electric station in our rented self-driving car. "Thanks, mate. Put it on the account!"

Appendix 1.

BANKS

(Note: Only primary building societies and credit unions that became banks are shown.)

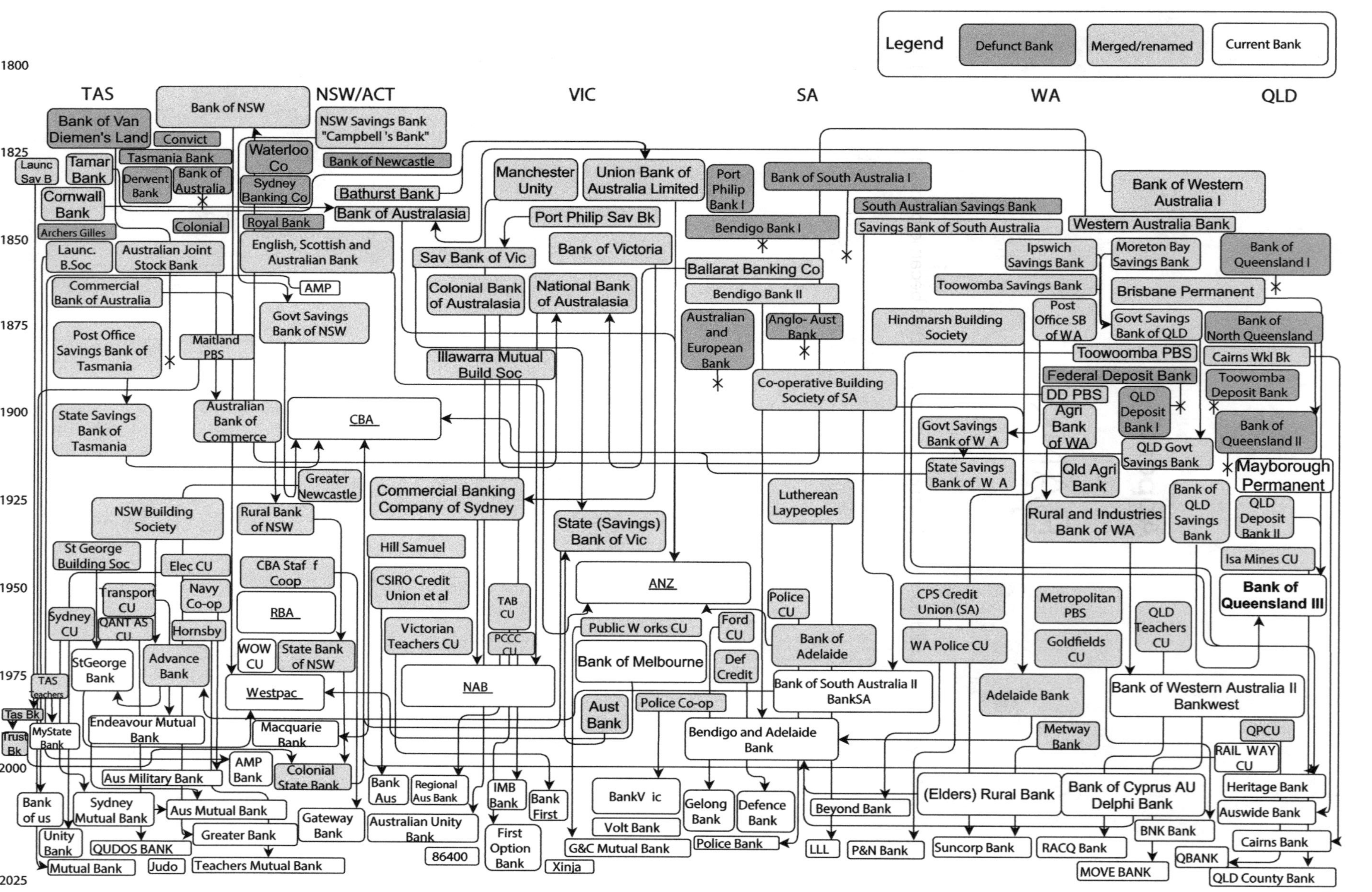

Legend
Defunct Bank
Merged/renamed
Current Bank
TAS
NSW/ACT
VIC
SA
WA
QLD
1800
1825
1850
1875
1900
1925
1950
1975
2000
2025
Bank of Van Diemen's Land
Tamar Bank
Cornwall Bank
Archers Gilles
Launc Sav B
Launc. B.Soc
Derwent Bank
Tasmania Bank
Convict
Bank of Australia
Colonial
Australian Joint Stock Bank
Commercial Bank of Australia
Post Office Savings Bank of Tasmania
State Savings Bank of Tasmania
Bank of NSW
Waterloo Co
Sydney Banking Co
Royal Bank
English, Scottish and Australian Bank
AMP
Govt Savings Bank of NSW
Maitland PBS
Australian Bank of Commerce
NSW Savings Bank "Campbell 's Bank"
Bank of Newcastle
Bathurst Bank
Bank of Australasia
CBA
Greater Newcastle
Rural Bank of NSW
NSW Building Society
St George Building Soc
Elec CU
Navy Co-op
Hornsby
Advance Bank
Transport CU
QANT AS CU
Sydney CU
StGeorge Bank
Endeavour Mutual Bank
TAS Teachers
Tas Bk
Trust Bk
MyState Bank
Aus Military Bank
Sydney Mutual Bank
Bank of us
Unity Bank
Mutual Bank
QUDOS BANK
Judo
Aus Mutual Bank
Greater Bank
Teachers Mutual Bank
AMP Bank
Macquarie Bank
Colonial State Bank
Gateway Bank
CBA Staf f Coop
RBA
WOW CU
Westpac
State Bank of NSW
Bank Aus
Australian Unity Bank
Regional Aus Bank
86400
Hill Samuel
CSIRO Credit Union et al
Victorian Teachers CU
NAB
Commercial Banking Company of Sydney
Manchester Unity
Sav Bank of Vic
Colonial Bank of Australasia
Illawarra Mutual Build Soc
Port Philip Sav Bk
National Bank of Australasia
Bank of Victoria
Union Bank of Australia Limited
TAB CU
PCCC CU
IMB Bank
First Option Bank
Bank First
Xinja
State (Savings) Bank of Vic
ANZ
Public W orks CU
Bank of Melbourne
Aust Bank
Police Co-op
BankV ic
Volt Bank
G&C Mutual Bank
Port Philip Bank I
Bendigo Bank I
Ballarat Banking Co
Bendigo Bank II
Australian and European Bank
Anglo- Aust Bank
Ford CU
Def Credit
Gelong Bank
Police Bank
Defence Bank
Bendigo and Adelaide Bank
Bank of South Australia I
South Australian Savings Bank
Savings Bank of South Australia
Co-operative Building Society of SA
Lutheran Laypeoples
Police CU
Bank of Adelaide
Bank of South Australia II BankSA
LLL
Beyond Bank
P&N Bank
Hindmarsh Building Society
Toowomba Savings Bank
Ipswich Savings Bank
Govt Savings Bank of W A
State Savings Bank of W A
CPS Credit Union (SA)
WA Police CU
(Elders) Rural Bank
Suncorp Bank
Adelaide Bank
Metway Bank
RACQ Bank
Metropolitan PBS
Goldfields CU
Western Australia Bank
Bank of Western Australia I
Moreton Bay Savings Bank
Post Office SB of WA
Agri Bank of WA
DD PBS
Qld Agri Bank
Rural and Industries Bank of WA
Bank of Cyprus AU Delphi Bank
MOVE BANK
Bank of Western Australia II Bankwest
QLD Teachers CU
BNK Bank
Brisbane Permanent
Govt Savings Bank of QLD
Toowoomba PBS
Federal Deposit Bank
QLD Deposit Bank I
QLD Govt Savings Bank
Bank of QLD Savings Bank
Bank of Queensland I
Bank of North Queensland
Cairns Wkl Bk
Toowomba Deposit Bank
Bank of Queensland II
Mayborough Permanent
QLD Deposit Bank II
Isa Mines CU
Bank of Queensland III
QPCU
RAIL WAY CU
Heritage Bank
Auswide Bank
Cairns Bank
QBANK
QLD County Bank

Appendix 2.

TIMELINE

~65 000 BC	First peoples in Australia.
Unknown	Songlines tell of trade routes of Indigenous Australians.
~2000 BC	First ledgers in the world.
~800-500 BC	First coins in the world.
~1000 AD	Age of coins found in Northern Territory, Australia.
~1700	Indigenous Australians already engaged in international trade.
1764	A series of trade taxes imposed by Great Britain raises the ire of settlers in the American colonies: the Sugar Act and, in the following years, the Stamp Act and the Tea Act.
1770	Captain James Cook lands in Botany Bay, Australia.
1775-1781	American Revolutionary War permanently prevented the practice of transportation of convicts to the American colonies.
1788	Great Britain establishes a penal colony in Australia, Governor of NSW is Arthur Phillip.
1788	Bills drawn on British treasury first official currency in Australia.
1795	John Hunter is Governor of NSW.
~1796	Commissariat established.
1800	Philip Gidley King is Governor of NSW.
1800	Second coin proclamation recognising a range of coins.

1806	William Bligh is Governor of NSW, bans the use of spirits (rum) as payment.
1808	Rum Rebellion, Australia's only coup d'état to date, Bligh deposed.
1810	Lachlan Macquarie dispatched as the new governor, signs a contract for the exclusive importation of rum in exchange for the building of Sydney Hospital.
1812	Macquarie stamps 40 000 pairs of the holey dollar and dump from a consignment of Spanish dollars.
1816	Australia's first bank, the Bank of New South Wales, is established (now Westpac).
1822	British coins enter circulation in Australia.
1835	Bank of Australasia established (now ANZ).
1849	Gold rush in California spreads to Australia in the following years.
1852	South Australian Governor stamps bullion from the goldfield to be used as bank reserves.
1854	First Australian telegraph.
1855	Royal Sydney Mint established for gold coin production.
1858	National Bank of Australasia formed (now NAB)
1870	Australia's oldest building society, Launceston Equitable Building & Investment Society, launches (now Bank of US).
1872	Australian overland telegraph connects Australia to the rest of the world.
1872	Melbourne Royal Mint established.
1893	Bank lending crisis triggers runs and institutional collapses.
1899	Western Australia, uncertain of joining federation, starts the Perth Mint.
1901	The Federation of Australia centralises currency, Edmund Barton is prime minister.
1908	Andrew Fisher is prime minister.
1909	Coinage Act specifies Australian coins similar to the United Kingdom.
1910	Treasury prints first federal notes.

1910	Federal government creates the CBA, a central savings and trading bank.
1914-1918	World War I sees a large part of the Australian working population head to the war front in Europe.
1916	First Australian coins produced in Melbourne Royal Mint.
1919	Treaty of Versailles signed asking for war repatriation payments from the vanquished Germany.
1920	CBA takes over note printing from the treasury.
1929	James Scullin is prime minister.
1930	A run on the banks triggers removing the gold standard from the Australian dollar, creating a fiat currency.
1930-1939	The Great Depression hits Australia hard.
1932	Joseph Lyons is prime minister.
1935-1937	First royal commission into banking looks at the banks and the depression.
1939-1945	World War II sees Australia at war in Europe and Asia.
1941	John Curtin is prime minister.
1941	War time establishment of Special Accounts, the forerunner to Exchange Settlement Accounts, begins centralised regulation of private banks.
1944	Bretton Woods International Monetary Conference, Curtin pushes Australian delegation to seek global full employment objective.
1945	Ben Chifley is prime minister.
1945	The Banking Act formalises central control of banks, away from states, requiring state and local governments to bank with CBA .
1947	As the Banking Act is activated, a High Court challenge is successful, striking out state and local government restrictions.
1947	Chifley proposes the full nationalisation of banks.
1947	John Cain, Premier of Victoria, loses election over bank nationalisation, Chifley withdraws proposal.
1949	Robert Menzies defeats Chifley, to become prime minister, in part due to bank policy.
1950	Diners Club launches first charge card (precursor to credit card) mainly for dining.

1956	IBM RAMAC launches a computer with a hard drive, bringing the prospect of practical computing to the commercial world.
1958	American Express issues the first charge card and, less successfully, Bank of America issues the first credit card (later to become Visa).
1959	Standalone ATMs in Sydney.
1959	The RBA is created, separating central banking and regulation from CBA.
1960	MICR cheques issued in Australia.
1960	First computers in use in banks.
1965	Royal Australian Mint opens in Deakin, ACT, and production starts in preparation for decimalisation.
1966	Menzies retires just as new decimal notes and coins are issued, replacing pounds, shillings, and pence with dollars and cents.
1972	Gough Whitlam elected prime minister.
1973	Global petrol crisis.
1974	Run on building societies.
1974	International bank failures establish the International BIS Basel Committee on Banking Supervision.
1974	Whitlam launched Bankcard credit card, launching an era of consumerism in Australia.
1975	Malcolm Fraser was appointed prime minister by the governor general, later John Howard is his treasurer.
1977	First SWIFT message sent by the then Crown Prince of Belgium.
1979	Global energy crisis.
1979-1981	Inquiry into the Australian Financial System (Campbell Committee), recommends deregulation.
1982	First modern ATM launched in Australia by Queensland Teachers Credit Union (now RACQ Bank).
1982	A new bank, Australian Bank and the international Visa scheme challenge Bankcard for its monopoly.
1983	Bob Hawke is prime minister, Paul Keating is treasurer.
1983-1984	The Australian Financial System Review Group (Martin Review) confirms the need for regulation.

1980s	Deregulation of banks.
1984	First EFTPOS transaction at a Shell fuel station, using an ANZ card.
1984	First global intercontinental electronic card transaction completed by Austnet.
1985	Paul Keating forms the Australian Payments Systems Council to aid better coordination of Direct Entry, cheque and EFTPOS processing between the Big Four and smaller financial institutions.
1986	Voluntary Electronic Funds Transfer Code of Conduct (now ePayments Code) established.
1988	Cash Transaction Reports Agency set up, precursor to AUSTRAC.
1988	First polymer notes released by the RBA/CSIRO, marking the bicentenary of European settlement.
1988	BIS Basel Capital Accord (later known as Basel I) approved by G10 and released to banks.
1989	FATF established.
1990	The "recession Australia had to have" (Paul Keating).
1990	State bank and building society failures.
1990-1991	Inquiry into Banking and Deregulation (Martin Committee) confirms Four Pillars policy and recommends allowing foreign banks to compete with locals.
1991	SWIFT II or SWIFT FIN finally rolls out after 11 years of development.
1991	100-point check made mandatory in Australia.
1991	Paul Keating is prime minister.
1991	Availability of capital report by the Industry Commission, supports floating of CBA and entry of foreign banks.
1992	RBA establishes the Australian Payments and Clearing Association (APCA) to open up interbank payments.
1996	John Howard is prime minister, Peter Costello is treasurer.
1996-1997	Financial System Inquiry (Wallis Report) recommends formation of APRA.
1997	BPAY launched.
1997-1999	CBA is the first major bank to launch Internet banking, other banks follow.

1998	Formation of the Payments System Board in the RBA.
1999	APRA established, taking over bank prudential regulation from the RBA.
1999	Euro currency launched in European Union.
2000	Y2K bug causes no significant issues in Australia.
2000	Australia launches a 10% goods and services tax.
2000-2001	dot com tech crash.
2001	9/11 attack on the US, initiates AML/CTF initiatives globally.
2004	Basel II released.
2006	Bankcard shuts down, end of an era, as international schemes Visa and Mastercard launch.
2007	House Inquiry into Home Loan Lending Practices and the Processes Used to Deal with People in Financial Difficulty, chaired by Bruce Baird, recommends better regulation of brokers.
2007	Kevin Rudd is prime minister, Wayne Swan is treasurer.
2007	BPAY MAMBO and banks commence work on real-time payments.
2007-2009	Global Financial Crisis.
2008	Inquiry into Competition in Banking and Non-Banking Sectors confirms the need for a better payment solution and credit card regulation.
2009	eftpos scheme launches as a domestic debit card system.
2009	Satoshi Nakamoto releases Bitcoin source code, mining starts.
2009	Parliamentary Joint Committee on Corporations and Financial Services recommends changes to financial advice after a number of controversies in the industry; committee kicks off reforms that become the Future of Financial Advice.
2009	Report on bank mergers looks at the takeovers of St George (Westpac) and Bankwest (CBA), and recommends retaining the Four Pillars policy.
2010	Julia Gillard is prime minister, Wayne Swan continues as treasurer.
2010	Basel III released in response to GFC.
2011	First mutually owned bank is licensed with the establishment of Bankmecu (CSIRO Credit Union, later Bank of Australia).

2011	Competition within the Australian banking sector looks at the GFC and suggests competition is more advisable than regulation, and also recommends retaining the Financial Claims Scheme permanently.
2011	Westpac is the third major bank to withdraw from BPAY MAMBO, ending immediate hopes of a real-time P2P payment system in Australia.
2013	Tony Abbott is prime minister, Joe Hockey is treasurer.
2013	In the US, Silk Road black market site, using cryptocurrency to transact, is shut down by the FBI.
2013	Work starts on NPP.
2013	Openpay launches in Australia, world first: buy now, pay later.
2014	Hockey requests David Murray to chair a Financial System Inquiry (Murray Report) recommending banning merchant fees and changes to tax system.
2014	Bitcoin price surges to $1 000, gaining market and regulatory attention, marking the beginning of the hype cycle.
2014-2015	Digital Currency — Game Changer or Bit Player, parliamentary inquiry and report encourages the safe support of cryptocurrencies by the regulators.
2015	Malcolm Turnbull is prime minister, Scott Morrison is treasurer.
2015	First cross-border Interbank blockchain payment performed from Australia.
2016	A series of controversies and media reports of the actions of the big banks builds up in the media.
2016	House of Representatives annual inquiries into the four major banks initiated by Scott Morrison, responses attract public attention and strengthen calls for a royal commission.
2016	Second edition polymer note issued by RBA.
2017	Productivity Commission releases report into Data Availability and Use, spawning the Consumer Data Right and open banking.
2017	AUSTRAC issues a statement of claim to CBA in relation to IDMs and failure to report threshold transactions.
2017-2019	Second royal commission into banking, looking at misconduct in the industry, sees the loss of four CEOs in the big financial institutions.
2018	NPP launched after 11 years of attempting to provide a real-time interbank P2P payment solution in Australia.
2018	Scott Morrison is prime minister.

2018	Productivity Commission's report, Competition in the Australian Financial System, is released, recommending changes and improvements to payments and the financial system.
2018	Residential Mortgage Price Inquiry report released by the ACCC, finding "accommodative and synchronised pricing behaviour" among the major banks, and recommends improvements to APRA's capital adequacy requirements for smaller banks.
2018	First of the neo banks, Volt Bank, to get licensed. No new bank had been licensed since Australian Bank in 1982.
2019	The ACCC Foreign Currency Conversion Services Inquiry finds that customer loyalty to the Big Four disadvantages these customers — as they had been overcharged for foreign exchange.
2019-2021	Senate Select Committee on Financial Technology and Regulatory Technology looks into fintech and regtech development and support.
2020	The ACCC Home Loan Pricing Inquiry reports on margin creep in residential loans to maintain profitability.
2020	COVID-19 impacts the world and the Australian economy.

GLOSSARY

9/11	On 11 September 2001, a coordinated terrorist attack took place in the USA, with targets including the World Trade Centre, New York and the Pentagon, Washington DC.
ABN	Australian Business Number
ACCC	Australian Consumer and Competition Commission
account takeover	A criminal act — taking over a legitimate account, generally to aid money laundering.
ACDES	Australian Cash Distribution and Exchange System, the fifth clearing system of APCA or AusPayNet dealing with notes and coins.
accommodative	The willingness to fit into another's needs without necessarily colluding.
account unification	Bringing together multiple account types into one financial vehicle.
acquirer or acquirer bank	The party (financial institution) that collects payment requests from a merchant (historically, the acquiring of credit card dockets).
ADB	Asia Development Bank, a regional version but independent of the World Bank.
ADI	Authorised deposit-taking institution
AI/ML	Artificial intelligence and/or machine learning, an area of computer science focussed on getting computers to exhibit human (or better than human) intelligence and learning characteristics.

alternative payment method	Normally used in the online context, the use of a non-card payment method to effect a payment.
Amex	Short form of American Express
AML	Anti-money laundering, see AML/CTF
AML/CTF	Anti-money laundering/counter terrorism financing. Measures taken by banks and regulators to prevent or detect flows of money concerning avoidance of tax, proceeds of crime, payment for illicit goods or services, or funding of terrorist activities in contravention of laws and treaties.
anti-competitive behaviour	Activities that prevent free market competition, and may be illegal in cases.
ANZ	Australia and New Zealand Banking Group
APCA	Australian Payments and Clearing Association, now AusPayNet
APCS	Australian Paper Clearing System, the first clearing system of APCA or AusPayNet, dealing with paper instruments such as cheques.
API	Application programming interface: the way two computer systems communicate with each other.
APRA	Australian Prudential Regulation Authority
AS 2805	Australian standard for card messages, used by Australian domestic payment cards, these days exclusively EFTPOS. Similar to ISO 8583.
ASIC	Australian Securities and Investment Commission
asset	Something that has value
ASX	Australian Stock (now Securities) Exchange
ATM	Automatic (or automated) teller machine, dispenses notes from an account, and sometimes supports deposits and other functions.
ATO	Australian Taxation Office
AUD	Australian dollar
AusPayNet	Australian Payments Network
AUSTRAC	Australian Transaction Reports and Analysis Centre
auth	Normally authorisation, especially in a cards context, sometimes authentication

authentication	The validation that a user is who they claim to be, often facilitated by a login, or use of a card and PIN.
authorisation	Generally, a bank allowing a customer to perform a certain task. If that task is a payment, then the target account's balance is checked.
B2B	Business-to-business, an interaction between businesses, such as high-value payments or trade finance.
B2C	Business-to-consumer, an interaction between a business and retail customers, e.g., merchant terminals.
balance of payments	Total value of exports minus total value of imports. Positive or surplus means exports are greater, negative or deficit means imports are higher.
Bancor	A universal currency proposed by John Maynard Keynes at Bretton Woods
bank	Can legally hold significant money on behalf of another. Generally an ADI that is permitted to take deposits. In general popular use, it excludes credit unions and building societies.
bank bill	A debt instrument issued by a bank
bank identification code	An 8 or 11-character identification used normally in SWIFT (and in RTGS and, now, NPP, both of which are based on SWIFT messaging) to identify the bank and (in the 11-character version) the branch.
BASE 1 or BASE I	The authorisation message in card messaging, Visa terminology, etymology supposedly Bank of America Systems Engineering.
BASE 2 or BASE II	The settlement message in card messaging, Visa terminology, etymology supposedly Bank of America Systems Engineering.
base erosion profit shifting	The movement of profit (generally by a multinational corporation) from the high taxing nation where the profit was made, to a lower taxing country, generally with the goal of reducing taxes.
basis point	One basis point is generally 0.01% or 0.01
BECS	Bulk Electronic Clearing System, the second clearing system of APCA or AusPayNet, dealing with bank-to-bank domestic transfers, known as Direct Entry.
BIC	see Bank identification code
big data	A discipline of information technology data management that deals with large amounts of generally unstructured data

Big Four	The four largest banks in Australia: ANZ, CBA, NAB and Westpac
big tech	A very large technology company such as Apple, Alphabet (Google), Microsoft, Amazon.
biller code	In BPAY, a short number, used to identify a biller.
bills of exchange	A note promising to pay someone, a promissory note.
BIN	Bank identification number, the first six digits of the card number.
biometrics	The use of unique human physical identification attributes to identify someone via a technology system.
BIS	Bank for International Settlements
black swan event	A very rare event that cannot be anticipated, originates from the ancient notion that black swans are very rare, before the European discovery of Western Australia's black swan.
Bluetooth	A short-range radio frequency protocol for connecting devices.
body corporate	An incorporated organisation, company or corporation.
BPAY	Bill payment scheme owned by the Big Four banks.
Bretton Woods	At the closing of Word War II, a global monetary policy agreement, the 1944 United Nations Monetary and Financial Conference, US.
broad-based	Wide-ranging, extensive, not narrow
broad money	A measurement of money in the economy: M3 plus deposits in all financial institutions.
BSB	Australian bank, state and branch identification number, six digits with the first two identifying the bank, and the third (often redundant) identifying the state, and the remaining digits identifying the branch number (also often redundant, especially for smaller modern banks).
bullion	Generally gold, silver and, more recently, platinum in the form of bars or coins, used as a commoditised store of value.
business bank	A bank that offers services to medium-sized or large businesses.
card	A payment card, a wallet-sized card that can be used to pay for goods and services at a merchant.
cash	Another word for currency.

cash cow	A business product or venture that continues to produce revenue and profit beyond the modest initial investment.
CBA	Commonwealth Bank of Australia
CECS	Consumer Electronic Clearing System, the third clearing system of APCA or AusPayNet dealing with cards, now defunct, see eftpos Hub or IAC.
central bank	The government-controlled bank responsible for issuing currency, regulating banks and monetary policy.
CEO	Chief executive officer
challenger bank	A non-Big Four bank that is in a strong position to compete for business.
charge card	A payment card that can be used to accumulate expenses, and generally should be paid off at the end of a billing cycle, usually a month.
China UnionPay	China's domestic card scheme
Clayton's	A non-alcoholic substitute drink popularised in the 1970s and 1980s: "The drink you're having when you're not having a drink." The expression is used to indicate a less potent substitute.
clearing	The stage in a payment where an instruction to pay, an IOU, moves between payer and payee bank. The instruction is agreed or rejected, and settlement of funds can take place.
clearing system	Usually one of BECS, APCS, CECS, HVCS, ACDES or some other institution-to-institution payment mechanism.
closed loop loyalty	A loyalty program where points earned with one merchant could only be redeemed at that merchant.
Closed loop payment	A payment system that is generally limited to a small number of banks, one bank or no bank.
cloud	The use of the Internet to host computer applications.
COBOL	The computer programming language of choice for early computer systems in banking, originated around 1960. (APL and FORTRAN were lesser used languages.)
coin	A small metal disk-shaped object, issued by the treasury as legal tender.
COIN	Community of interest network (the network for low-valued payments in Australia)

Common Reporting Standard	OECD/G20 initiative to share information on foreign persons. Global version of the FATCA.
Consumer Price Index	see CPI. A basket of goods, representing an average household's expenditure, periodically valued to measure inflation.
contactless payment	A payment, generally using NFC technology, between a paying instrument such as a card and a merchant device to effect the transfer of money.
Conway's Law	An adage, named after Melvin Conway, to reflect on the similarity between political structures and the architecture of systems.
core banking	The customer account record keeping system.
correspondent bank	An intermediary bank used to guarantee payments between two banks.
COTS	Commercial off the shelf. Could refer to a product or service, including software.
countercyclical capital buffer	In order to cope in times of stress, APRA required banks to maintain a buffer in positive times of additional Tier 1 capital.
cover payment	A bank-to-bank payment through known banks that covers a payment between other banks that otherwise do not have a relationship, allowing them to directly settle payments. see also Series payment.
CPI	Consumer Price Index, used to measure the value of money over time (to measure inflation or deflation).
CRM	Customer relationship management software
CRN	Customer reference number, on BPAY, used by the biller to identify which bill has been paid.
cross-sell	The selling of a different product to a customer in order to increase the banking relationship.
crowdfunding	Equity crowdfunding, a way of obtaining diverse funding for a venture.
cryptocurrency	Based on Bitcoin, a currency that exists in electronic form only, secured using cryptology.
CS1	Clearing System 1, see APCS
CS2	Clearing System 2, see BECS
CS3	Clearing System 3, see CECS

CS4	Clearing System 4, see HVCS
CS5	Clearing System 5, see ACDES
CSIRO	Commonwealth Scientific and Industrial Research Organisation
CTF	Counter terrorism financing, see AML/CTF
currency	Notes and coins
data lake	A large store of an organisation's generally unstructured data, used for analytical purposes.
data normalisation	A technique of structuring data so that data is properly related to other data.
data warehouse	A large store of an organisation's generally structured data used for analytical purposes.
DE	Direct Entry, a domestic low-value payment system, also called BECS or CS3.
dealing room	The physical or virtual room in an institutional bank where customers call up or electronically negotiate sales deals.
de-bank	The practice of banks removing services from a customer, generally due to AML/CTF risk.
decryption	The exercise of reversing encryption so encrypted data can be read.
demurrage	Charges payable for delayed collection of goods from a transport vessel.
demutualise	The practice of turning a mutual organisation into a traditional corporate. Members become shareholders and there may be an IPO or an offer to buy members out.
derivative settlement	A derivative being an indirect trade of an underlying financial product or commodity. Derivative settlement is the required settlement at purchase or sale to currency or to the underlying product or commodity.
designated service	A service that has been identified by AUSTRAC in accordance with legislation and regulation, requiring specific reporting due to potential risks with payments.
designated payment system	A critical payment system that is designated by the RBA — allowing the central bank to control the system in the interests of making it more efficient (and less expensive).
DevOps	The automation of development operations from design to build, test and deploy.

digital bank	A modern bank that has no branches or discourages branch use, using the Internet, mobile app, and cards to facilitate predominantly self-service banking transactions.
digital currency	Generally synonymous with cryptocurrency.
Direct Entry	The Australian low-value domestic clearing system, formally referred to as BECS.
document verification service	The Australian Government's Attorney General's data access system to verify the legitimacy of commonwealth and state issued documents to aid in the verification of identity.
double-entry bookkeeping	The notion that every credit should have a corresponding and immediate debit.
double-sided transactions	A transaction like a repurchase agreement or a deposit that transfers money one way and reverses at a defined point in the future.
DSS	see PCI DSS
dual message system	In card processing, two stages of messaging: the first is an authorisation (auth) that puts the funds on hold (or pending), and a second that commits the transaction, or scheme settlement, also referred to as BASE II in Visa parlance.
DVS	see Document verification service
ecosystem	A set of systems, processes and people that interact with each other.
email	see Electronic mail
EFTPOB	Electronic Funds Transfer at Point of Banking. An agency banking system, used these days primarily by Australia Post through the EFTPOS system, supporting deposits and transfers over the counter at postal offices.
EFTPOS	Electronic Funds Transfer at Point of Sale. The acceptance of a card at point of sale using an electronic acceptance device, a PED. Also the Australian proprietary domestic card scheme known as CECS prior to 2009.
eftpos	The domestic card scheme in Australia, previously referred to as EFTPOS. Incorporated as eftpos Australia Limited (EPAL) in 2009.
eftpos Hub	The central domestic eftpos card clearing system replacing CECS/ CS3.

electronic mail	Mail sent over the Internet using the Simple Mail Transfer Protocol (SMTP).
electronic money	The storage of money and the transfer of it using interconnected computer systems.
EMV card	A card with an EMV chip on it.
EMV Co	An organisation founded by Eurocard, Mastercard and Visa.
encryption	The coding of data so only systems entitled to read the information can do so, and someone sitting in the middle of the transmission cannot.
enumeration attack	The use of a random sequence of data to find an item that matches one of the inputs, in the hope of obtaining unauthorised information.
EPAL	eftpos Australia Limited (see eftpos)
ERP	Enterprise resource planning — generally referring to a software system.
ESA	Exchange Settlement Account, the central bank account held by banks to settle their payment obligations.
false negative	In fraud or AML/CTF, the failure to detect negative activity.
false positive	In fraud or AML/CTF, the detection of an activity, thought to be negative, turns out to be benign.
fapiao	Chinese receipt or invoice and system that is monitored for tax calculation, at a transaction level by the government.
FATCA	Foreign Account Tax Compliance Act, US law requiring foreign banks to provide information on US persons.
FATF	Financial Action Task Force
Fedwire	The US real-time gross settlements system for institutional payments, equivalent to Australia's RTGS.
fiat currency	A currency whose value is based on the monetary policy of the government alone, with no recourse to an underlying asset such as gold. (see Hard currency)
file transfer protocol	FTP, a way of transferring a large amount of data, stored in a file, through a network.
financial message	A message that contains financial information. Fundamentally similar to any other message but treated differently, for various reasons.

financial switch or financial switching network	A solution that allows financial messages to be dispatched to the correct destination, like a telephone switchboard but electronic and automatic.
fintech	A financial services related technology company.
float/floated	The opening of the free market to price a currency, commodity or company, e.g., float of the Australian dollar; float of the Commonwealth Bank.
float revenue	Interest earned on money held by a bank or payment provider as a result of a timing difference between the date of debiting the payer's account and the date of crediting the payee.
foreign exchange	The exchange of one currency for another at an agreed (or market) rate.
Forex	see Foreign exchange
Four Pillars	A policy that the Big Four banks should not consolidate (i.e., they should not merge).
freeform	In software systems, the use of unstructured, human-entered data that could be difficult to decipher by a machine.
FSC	Financial Services Council, a representative body of the financial service industry.
fungible	Generally applied to a commodity, the ability of that item to be replaced in commerce with another item of the same specification.
Future of Financial Advice	A government initiative, based on the Parliamentary Joint Committee on Corporations and Financial Services inquiry, and subsequent legislation.
fuzzy match	A text match that matches with initialisations and alternative spellings.
FIX	Financial Information eXchange, a US-based standard for trade business.
FX	see Foreign exchange
G7	Group of seven countries plus the EU, representing the world's advanced economies. Russia has been included (making it the G8) and excluded, Australia is an outside official invitee. G8+5 includes Brazil, China, India, Mexico and South Africa.
G20	A group of 20 wealthier countries, focusing on financial stability for both governments and central bank governors, includes Australia.
GDP	see Gross domestic product

gearing	The use of lending to get greater exposure to an investment. A small geared investment can multiply both gains and losses as the market moves.
general ledger	The financial records of an organisation (including a bank), separate to core banking.
GFC	Global Financial Crisis of 2007-2008
GL	General ledger
GNU	Recursive acronym for: GNU's not Unix. An open source initiative.
GPL	GNU General Public License, frequently associated with open source.
gross domestic product	The total produce of an economy in monetary terms.
GST	Goods and services tax
handset	Mobile phone
hard currency	Currency notes that are backed up generally by bullion reserves, being gold and silver. Compare with fiat currency.
hash	This scrambles a message so that it cannot be unscrambled. Often used in the storage of passwords or PINs.
headless banking	Similar to white-labelled, where a banking service is provided under the cover of another brand.
headline interest rates	The published interest rates of banks. These could be discounted, and often were, in the case of loans for customers.
high-quality liquid assets	Assets held by the banks that are generally easy to liquidate, including cash, ESA balances and short-term sovereign money market instruments.
High Value Clearing System	The fourth clearing system of APCA, now AusPayNet, dealing with SWIFT and RTGS.
HQLA	see High-quality liquid assets
HVCS	see High Value Clearing System
I owe you	see Promissory note
IAC	Issuers and Acquires Community, replaced the first clearing system of APCA or AusPayNet dealing with bank domestic transfers.

IBAN	International bank account number, an international account number that specifies the country, bank and bank account number. Used in Europe, but not generally in Australia, the US and other countries. Format managed by SWIFT.
IBM RAMAC	IBM's Random Access Method of Accounting and Control, from 1956.
ICO	Initial Coin Offering (compare with IPO), an issue, normally of cryptocurrencies, to the broad international public, as a notional share in a company. Generally unregulated.
identity theft	The criminal use of another entity's or individual's identity in banking, generally to launder money or obtain a loan.
IDM	Intelligent Deposit Machine
IEC	International Electrotechnical Commission
iframe	Inline frame: a portion of a Web page that comes from another website.
IFTI	see International funds transfer instruction
IIN	Issuer Identification Number or BIN, the first six digits of a card number.
IMT	International money transfer
institutional bank	A bank that provides global market services (foreign exchange, commodity, and equity), as well as providing banking services to other banks and large corporations.
Intelligent Deposit Machine	A machine capable of reading notes and cheques and depositing them for immediate value.
interchange	The fee that schemes charge merchants, the bulk of which is passed on to issuers.
intermediary bank	Similar to correspondent bank but supporting fewer payee currencies and countries (sometimes just one country and currency).
International Bank for Reconstruction and Development	The lending arm of World Bank Group, it offers loans to middle to low income developing countries.
international funds transfer instruction	A report given to AUSTRAC of an international funds transfer from a financial institution.
investment bank	An institutional bank specialising in markets.
IOU	see I owe you

IPO	Initial Public Offer to buy shares, normally before listing on a regulated public stock exchange.
IRB	Internal ratings-based calculation, used generally by the Big Four, Macquarie Bank and ING to provide a more sophisticated risk-weighted asset calculation.
ISIL	Islamic State of Iraq and the Levant, identified by authorities as a terrorist organisation.
ISO	International Standards Organisation
ISO 8583	International card messaging standard, similar to the Australian AS 2805. Used by most international card schemes, though heavily customised by each scheme.
ISO 9362	see BIC
ISO 9564	A standard for PIN management.
ISO 13616	see IBAN
ISO 15022	The classic SWIFT MT (message type) messages.
ISO 20022	The emerging global standard for payment messages, including SWIFT MX, NPP, and SEPA (Single Euro Payment Area).
ISO 27001	Framework and policies in IT systems.
ISO/IEC	Joint standards in the electrotechnical arena formed by ISO and IEC.
ISO/IEC 7810	A standard that describes how identification cards should be implemented, used almost universally for bank cards.
ISO/IEC 7811	A standard that describes how numbers are embossed (raised) on a card's surface.
ISO/IEC 7812	A card numbering system that specifies a numbering system for plastic cards. The first six digits, the IIN, are allocated to individuals.
ISO/IEC 7813	The standards for embossing and printing magnetic stripes.
ISO/IEC 7816	The standards for a chip on a card, aka EMV chip.
ISO/IEC 14443	Contactless standard for cards.
ISO/IEC 18092	A peer-to-peer contactless standard for cards.
issuer or issuer bank	The party (financial institution) that issues a card, which could be an SCCI or a retail bank, or other financial institution.

Java	A modern computer programming language.
JCB	Originally Japan Credit Bureau, now just JCB, Japan's domestic card scheme.
JSON	JavaScript Object Notation, a way of representing data, a modern alternative to fixed width (COBOL style) or XML. Often used with REST (representational state transfer).
KYC	Know Your Customer, a procedure of properly identifying customers.
ledger	A book, either physical or electronic, that stores financial or non-financial positions related to the notional holder of those positions.
legal entity	A body recognised by the law (individual, organisation, company etc.).
legal tender	Government money that can be used to settle debts.
letter of credit	A letter promising a payment on condition that certain conditions are met, used in trade.
lever	A controllable input that can effect a broader change.
Linux	An operating system similar to Unix but under GNU licensing.
liquidity coverage ratio	The amount (normally 100%) of HQLAs required to meet 30 days of payments.
LoRaWAN	Long-range wide-area network, Wi-Fi alternative.
LVCS	The RBA's Low Value Clearing Service, used to connect domestic SWIFT to COIN to allow clearing files to be exchanged across networks.
LVR	Loan to value ratio, the value of the loan divided by the value of the collateral, used in mortgage funding.
LVSS	The RBA's Low Value Settlement Service.
M1	A measurement of money in the economy: currency plus all the private balances in ADIs.
M2	A measurement of money in the economy: M1, plus deposits that are less liquid, plus credit union and building society deposits.
M3	A measurement of money in the economy: includes M2 and deposits with all financial institutions.
magnetic stripe	An embedded piece of magnetic tape, generally on the back of a card, used to allow machines to read it.

magstripe	see Magnetic stripe
malware	Software that has a hidden purpose (normally sinister), different to what the consumer was expecting.
MAMBO	Me At My Bank Online: defunct private bank proposal for real-time payments, eventually replaced with NPP.
margin lending	The lending of money, generally on a tradable or liquid asset such as shares, FX, commodities or funds, using the asset as collateral for the purpose of gearing the investment.
merchant	Generally the payee in a transaction, the party providing goods or services to a consumer.
merchant bank	Another name for a business or institutional bank.
merchant service fee	The fee a merchant acquirer charges a merchant, generally for accepting a card.
merchant surcharge	The fee a merchant may charge a consumer, generally for accepting a card.
middleware	Software in between the data and the user interfaces.
MII	Major Industry Identification Number, the first digit of a BIN/IIN, PAN, or ISO/IEC 7812 number, identifying the industry of the card issuer. MII numbers 4 and 5 are used for financial institutions.
monetary policy	The use of the supply of money, generally through interest rate control, by central banks to achieve high employment, currency stability and economic prosperity.
money	A medium of exchange in commerce, a unit of account (measuring the value of goods or services) and a store of value.
money base	A measurement of money in the economy: currency on issue and debts of the Reserve Bank in private hands.
money laundering	The criminal movement of money (washing through the system) to avoid detection by authorities. The money could be the proceeds of crime, or a transfer to avoid tax reporting and taxation.
money service business	A financial service company that transfers money, especially overseas.
Moore's Law	That the number of transistors on an integrated circuit would double every two years.
MSF	Merchant service fee
MT	SWIFT ISO 15022 messages, message types

mule account	A criminal operation's use of a small investor's bank account to knowingly or unknowingly launder money, sometimes through the use of identity theft or account takeover.
mutual	An organisation owned by its members or depositors. Generally, the original structure of credit unions and building societies. Normally a not-for-profit organisation.
mutual bank	A bank that is mutually owned by members or depositors, usually previously a mutual financial institution, like a credit union.
MX	The new SWIFT messages, based on ISO 20022.
MyGov	A federal government initiative that provides online digital identity and a government services access portal to Australian residents.
NAB	National Australia Bank
narrow-based tax	A tax, such as a sales tax or excise targeting a specific product family or industry.
NDEF	The NFC Forum's protocol for wireless communication: NFC Data Exchange Format.
Neo banks	A family of new, generally private banks, that were granted licenses on or after 2018.
.NET	Dot NET — a modern programming platform from Microsoft.
net off	The cancelling of individual debts and consolidation into one or fewer net transactions to efficiently facilitate settlement.
net present value	The value of an investment in today's dollars, normally looking at a three or five-year horizon.
net stable funding ratio	The funds of a bank (available stable funding) divided by (through shareholder equity and deposit book) the weighted assets (money lent out or required stable funding).
NFC	Near-field communication, used in tracking and for card or mobile-based payments.
NFC Forum	A group standardising the use of NFC for electronic device communication.
Nostro	Our money with you. A reconciliation account used by banks to track their money held in other institutions.
note	A paper (or plastic) note issued by the Reserve Bank as legal tender.

NPP	New Payments Platform, a domestic real-time payment system initiated by the RBA.
NPPA	New Payments Platform Australia Limited — a company owned by banks that runs NPP.
OECD	Organisation for Economic Co-operation and Development, a group of 37 wealthier countries, includes Australia.
off-system BSB	A BSB that is not directly on a bank ledger, used to funnel money and auto-reconcile Direct Entry payments for corporations. A form of sub accountin, with each account number corresponding to a different customer or sub account.
off us	An acquirer who is also an issuer, when a customer of another bank presents (usually a card) at this bank's acquiring device, normally either point of sale or at an ATM. The bank needs to switch the transaction to the other bank.
onboard	The process of bringing on a customer or vendor, and completion of due diligence (including KYC) to facilitate the commencement of business.
on us	An acquirer who is also an issuer, when a customer of the bank presents (usually a card) at the same bank's acquiring device, normally either point of sale or at an ATM. The bank is able to switch the transaction internally and save costs.
open banking	The general ability to access banking records in a secure way through APIs.
open data	The ability to access information from private or public organisations, generally through APIs.
open loop loyalty	An open loop program allowing points earned at one merchant to be redeemable at another.
open loop payment	A payment system that is open to multiple banks, especially where the payer and payee banks are different.
open source	Code is available for people to see, often accompanied with a license to use it without cost.
OSBSB	see Off-System BSB
Osko	A marketing brand of NPP, run by the BPAY organisation.
P2P	Peer-to-peer or person-to-person, an interaction between any two parties, accessible by the mass market.
PAN	On cards, the primary account number, the full number of an account.

party	A legal entity such as an individual, partnership or company.
PayID	The payment address of a payee in NPP, either email, mobile number, ABN or corporate name. Uses the NPP addressing service. Compare with Osko.
passbook	A private version of a bank ledger that records debits and credits to an account. No longer in wide use.
payment	Exchange of value (and information) between a payer and a payee.
payment gateway	A solution, generally on the Internet, to process a payment on behalf of a merchant.
payment handshake	The exchange of payment addressing credentials between a payer and payee to allow a payment to be made.
payment rail	The underlying clearing system of a payment. Like railway tracks with different widths (gauges), different payment types flow down different wires and systems, often called rails.
PCI	Short form of PCI SSC
PCI DSS	Payment Card Industry Data Security Standard, designed to protect data associated with the issue and use of cards.
PCI PA-DSS	Payment Card Industry Payment Application Data Security Standard
PCI PTS	Payment Card Industry PIN Transaction Security
PCI SSC	Payment Card Industry Security Standards Council, formed by American Express, Discover, JCB, Mastercard and Visa to oversee the PCI DSS, PCI PA-DSS and PCI PTS standards.
PED	PIN entry device, also known as PIN pad, EFTPOS or merchant terminal.
performing loans	A loan that is being actively repaid.
PEXA	Property Exchange Australia
phishing	An illegal attempt to get private information, such as login details, by pretending to be a legitimate party, usually over email or SMS.
PIN	Personal identification number, today usually a numeric passcode used to access funds in banking.
PIN pad	see PED

PKI	Public key infrastructure, the infrastructure of asymmetric encryption that was a breakthrough in cryptography. Anyone could now encrypt, but only the holder of the private key could decrypt.
port (bank account)	The moving of a bank account from one institution to another by facilitating the transfer of payment addressing details such as PayID.
POTS	Plain old telephone service
private bank	A division within a bank that offers services to high net worth individuals and medium-sized businesses through relationship managers.
private key	Part of the encryption key. This key has the power to decrypt a message and is not externally shared.
promissory note	A promise to pay with terms and conditions specified.
proof of work	In blockchain, a method of ensuring that a transaction is genuine, by giving the participants with the most processing power the authority to allow a transaction.
PSP	Payment service provider
public key	Part of the encryption key. This key can encrypt the message, but is irreversible without the private key.
pull payment	A method of payment where the payment is pulled from the payer's account by the payee.
push payment	A method of payment where the payment is pushed from the payer's account to the payee.
quantitative easing	In monetary policy, the action of a central bank to inject more money into a distressed economy.
quantum computing	A new (mostly theorised) form of computing that uses probabilistic quantum states rather than fixed digital states to power computing.
quid	Originally a gold sovereign, one pound sterling.
rail	see Payment rail
rationalisations	The taking over or merging of capabilities or organisations.
RBA	Reserve Bank of Australia, Australia's central bank.
regtech	A regulatory services related technology company.

relational database management system	A system that stores data, where data elements are often related to other elements. Examples are Microsoft SQL, Oracle and MySQL.
relative terms or relative value	With inflation, the value of a transaction in today's money.
replicate	Copying infrastructure, especially a database, in the event that if one fails, the other should survive.
RFID	Radiofrequency identification
retail bank	The more well-known type of bank that offers services to the bulk of the population and to small businesses.
retail margin	The retail profit or margin on foreign exchange.
revolving line of credit	Credit accounts that, once paid off, can be reused on similar terms.
rich information	Additional information, generally associated with a payment transaction, such as payment advice or invoice.
risk-weighted asset	The value of a debt instrument to the bank, expressed as a percentage, to be valued by multiplying it by the asset (where the bank lends money to another party). Low values are low risk, high values are high risk.
RITS	RBA Information and Transfer System, the main money moving and account keeping system of the RBA.
RTGS	Real-time gross settlement
RWA	Risk-weighted asset
sanctions	Generally refers to sanctions imposed by the United Nations Security Council. These may include preventing payments to individuals, organisations or states.
sandbox	An area or website where APIs can be trialled and tested before a subscriber implements their production software.
savings bank	An archaic term for what is now called a retail bank.
SCCI	Specialist credit card institution (non-banks), previously required an ADI license, now an ASIC credit license.
schemes	A commercial brand and system of payment, normally Mastercard and Visa card solutions, but also American Express, eftpos and others.

securities clearing	The clearing or movement of a financial security from one owner to another.
securities event	An event associated with a security, such as a news event, a dividend payment or a share split.
Security Council	see UN Security Council
seignor/seigneur	Lord, who minted coins (old French).
seigniorage	Profit from minting coins (or notes).
series payment	A payment generally using SWIFT, where the customer payment message and the bank-to-bank transfer follows the chain. As the message moves so does the money. Compare with cover payment.
settlement	Usually the financial settlement of a payment, when actual money is taken, though can be in several stages: merchant settlement, scheme settlement, customer settlement and financial settlement. Normally occurs after payment clearing.
SIM	Subscriber identity module, a miniaturised smart card used in mobile phones to access the mobile network, providing a unique identity.
single message system	In card processing, one message is both the authorisation and scheme settlement.
Six Pillars	A precursor to the Four Pillars policy that restricted takeovers of and mergers between the Big Four banks, National Mutual and AMP from 1990 to 1996.
skimming	A generally illegal act of reading the magnetic stripe of a car, in order to commit credit card fraud.
SMR	see Suspicious matter report
SMS (card payments)	see Single message system
SMS (telecommunications)	Short message service or text message sent to a mobile number.
SOC	System and Organisation Controls, a standard for controls, especially in IT.
sovereign, gold	The British gold standard coin, roughly a quarter of a troy ounce, eventually the pound sterling though, these days, worth much more.
spread	The buy-sell difference, especially in FX and commodities.

SQL	see Structured query language
stand-in	A final backup capability in the event of a total system failure
startup	A newly-formed company that seeks to achieve significant early growth.
step-up	In the context of security, the notion that access to more restricted functionality requires more sophisticated authentication, such as through a second factor of authentication.
STP	see Straight-through processing
straight-through processing	The ability to automate the processing of data without human intervention (or re-keying).
structured query language	A type of computer code to retrieve data in a systematic way from most relational database management systems.
Supply Nation	An Australian indigenous organisation that facilitates and supports indigenous supply to corporate Australia.
surface mail	Conventional paper-based mail sent over land or sea. Generally slower than air mail and much slower than electronic mail.
suspicious matter report	A report given to AUSTRAC of a customer transaction or activity at a financial institution that is deemed to be suspicious.
sweep	The movement of money from one account to another account as a bank process.
SWIFT	Society for Worldwide Interbank Financial Telecommunication, an international payment system.
SWIFT BIC	see BIC
SWIFT FIN	The popular legacy SWIFT financial messages, MT.
SWIFT gpi	SWIFT global payments initiative, allows corporate access or smaller bank access to SWIFT through SWIFT APIs.
synchronised pricing behaviour	When two organisations change their price simultaneously, may or may not be collusion.
tag name	In XML, the name of the data field.
tax payer	An entity liable for tax in the given jurisdiction.
tax loss	A negative tax event.
TFN	Tax file number, a unique identification number issued to taxpayers by the ATO.

threshold transaction report	A report given to AUSTRAC of a series of customer transactions made at around the same time through the same facility, involving cash of $10 000 or more.
trading bank	An archaic term which can refer to what is now called a business bank or institutional bank, or to the treasury unit within a bank.
transaction	A payment often associated with the exchange of goods or services.
transactional	A dealing that is completed in one short sitting where, generally, both sides of the ledger are fulfilled, e.g., the payment and the exchange of goods, or a barter exchange.
transport layer security	Used on the Web to encrypt almost all traffic.
travellers cheque	A negotiable instrument that can be used to redeem cash, normally used overseas by travellers. Not as common in recent times with the rise of cards and widespread retail foreign exchange dealers.
TT	Telegraphic transfer
TTR	see Threshold transaction report
UN	United Nations
unencrypted	Unencrypted data is also called clear text or data sent in the clear. It is data that can be directly read.
unicorn	A privately held startup worth more than $1 billion.
unique value proposition	A value proposition from a product or company that is unique in the market.
Unix	An operating system developed by Sun, now Oracle.
UNSC	see UN Security Council
UN Security Council	The Security Council of the United Nations, applies sanctions against individuals, organisations and states, freezes assets and blocks payments among other sanctions, bans and blockades.
US SEC	United States Security and Exchange Commission (equivalent of Australia's ASIC).
USD	United States dollar

USSD	Unstructured Supplementary Service Data, a mobile communication protocol similar to SMS, Used in some countries to transfer money through simple mobile phones without a smartphone.
value	The human desirability of a thing sometimes measured in money.
virtual account	An account that does not exist as a traditional and separate bank account but uses account numbers etc. to effect payments on aggregated funds, controlled by a third party.
Vostro	Your money with us — basically an institutional transaction account in a bank.
voting block	A group of stakeholders that can aggregate their interest as one large voter.
wallet	A payment solution that retains money or information about the customer over a period of time across multiple purchases.
white-labelled	An offering produced by one supplier and branded differently by multiple retailers.
Wi-Fi	Wireless fidelity, a high bandwidth radiofrequency protocol, used at home.
Windows	Microsoft's operating system for computers.
X.25	A type of network link, common in early banking networks, from the late 1970s to about 2010, to allow telecommunications lines to provide a wide area network.
XML	eXtensible Markup Language, inspired by HTML, a modern way to exchange data in APIs.
Y2K bug	A defect in programs that were not designed to last as long as they did, where the year "2000" would be treated as "1900" and result in system failure.
yuan	Chinese unit of currency

BIBLIOGRAPHY

AAT 2020; Seribu Pty Ltd and Commissioner of Taxation (Taxation) [2020] AATA 1840 (16 June 2020); Administrative Appeals Tribunal

ABS 2016; Census of Population and Housing: Characteristics of Aboriginal and Torres Strait Islander Australians; ABS

ABS 2020; Overview of Labour Statistics; ABS

ACCC 2018; Residential Mortgage Price Inquiry — Final report; ACCC

ACCC 2019; Foreign Currency Conversion Services Inquiry — Final report; ACCC

ACCC 2020; Home Loan Pricing Inquiry — Final report; ACCC

Ahmed, Ahmed Elsheikh M. 2011; The Long-Run Relationship between Money Supply, Real GDP, and Price Level: Empirical Evidence from Sudan

Alberici, Emma 2020; Coronavirus Stimulus Measures Like JobKeeper are Keeping Zombie Businesses Alive, Warn Insolvency Practitioners; ABC; 24 July 2020

Anderlini, Jamil 2009; China Calls for New Reserve Currency; Financial Times; 24 March 2009

APRA 2018; Outsourcing Involving Cloud Computing Services; 24 September 2018

Aschhoff, Gunther 1982; The Banking Principles of Hermann Schulze-Delitzsch and Friedrich Wilhelm Raiffeisen; German Yearbook on Business History 1982

ASIC 2016; ePayments Code; ASIC

Atkin, Tim and Cheung, Belinda 2017; How Have Australian Banks Responded to Tighter Capital and Liquidity Requirements? Bulletin — June Quarter 2017; RBA

AUSTRAC 2019; Press release: AUSTRAC Applies for Civil Penalty Orders against Westpac; 20 November 2019

Baird, Bruce et al. 2007; Final Report on Inquiry into Home Loan Lending Practices and the Processes Used to Deal with People in Financial Difficulty; House of Representatives Standing Committee on Economics, Finance and Public Administration; Parliament of the Commonwealth of Australia

Balme, J., and Morse, K. 2006; Shell beads and social behaviour in Pleistocene Australia. Antiquity, 80(310), 799-811

Balmuth, M. S. 1975; The critical moment: The transition from currency to coinage in the eastern Mediterranean. World Archaeology, 6(3), 293-8

Banks, Gary et al. 1991; Availability of Capital; Industry Commission Report No. 18 (now Productivity Commission)

Barnish, S. 1985; The Wealth of Iulianus Argentarius: Late Antique Banking and the Mediterranean Economy

Beeby, George 1933; Aspects of the Financial and Banking Problem: "Credit" Theories Examined; The Age; 22 July 1933, 6

BIS 2017; Basel III leverage ratio framework — Executive Summary; Bank for International Settlements

Black, Susan et al. 2012; A History of Australian Corporate Bonds; Research Discussion Paper; RBA; 2012-09

Bolt, Wilko et al. 2010; Incentives at the Counter: An Empirical Analysis of Surcharging Card Payments and Payment Behaviour in the Netherlands; https://doi.org/10.1016/j.jbankfin.2009.09.008

Booker, John and Craig, Russell 2002; Balancing debt in the absence of money: Documentary credit in New South Wales, 1817-20. Business History, 44(1), 1-20; https://doi.org/10.10.1080/713999258

Burns, Ken and Novic, Lynn 2007; The War: At Home: War Production; PBS

Butlin, S 1968; Foundations of the Australian monetary system; 1788–1851; Sydney University Press

Byrnes, Wayne 2017; Individual Challenges and Mutual Opportunities; Wayne Byrnes, Chairman — Keynote address at Customer Owned Banking Convention, Brisbane; 23 Oct 2017; APRA

Carment, David 1980; The wills massacre of 1861: Aboriginal-European conflict on the colonial Australian frontier. Journal of Australian Studies, 4(6) 49-55; https://doi.org/10.1080/14443058009386807

Cobbett, William 1846; Paper against gold, or, the mystery of the Bank of England: Of the debt, of the stocks, of the sinking fund, and of all the other tricks and contrivances, carried on by the means of paper money; John Doyle

Coleman, David et al. 2016; Review of the Four Major Banks: First Report; House of Representatives Standing Committee on Economics; Parliament of the Commonwealth of Australia

Coleman, David et al. 2017a; Review of the Four Major Banks: Second Report; House of Representatives Standing Committee on Economics; Parliament of the Commonwealth of Australia

Coleman, David et al. 2017b; Review of the Four Major Banks: Third Report; House of Representatives Standing Committee on Economics; Parliament of the Commonwealth of Australia

Connell, J. 1977; The Bougainville connection: Changes in the economic context of shell money production in Malaita. Oceania, 48(2), 81-101

CoreLogic 2018; Housing Affordability Report; June Quarter 2018; CoreLogic

Crook, Penny et al. 2003; Assessment of Historical and Archaeological Resources of the Paddy's Market Site, Darling Harbour, Sydney; Volume 1 of the Archaeology of the Modern City Series A; Historic Houses Trust of New South Wales

Dadabhoy, Bakhtiar 2013; Barons of banking; Random House

Dastyari, Sam et al. 2015; Final Report on Digital Currency — Game Changer or Bit Player; Senate Economics Reference Committee; Parliament of the Commonwealth of Australia

Delaney, Luc et al. 2020; Cash Use in Australia: Results from the 2019 Consumer Payments Survey; RBA Bulletin — June 2020

Department of Industry, Science, Energy and Resources 2020; The National Blockchain Roadmap: Progressing towards a Blockchain-empowered Future

Dhavalikar, M. K. 1975; The beginning of coinage in India. World Archaeology, 6(3), 330-338

Doherty, Emma et al. 2018; Money in the Australian Economy; Reserve Bank of Australia — Bulletin

Eggleston, Alan et al. 2009; Report on Bank Mergers; Senate Economics Reference Committee; Parliament of the Commonwealth of Australia

Eggleston, Alan et al. 2011; Final Report on Inquiry into Competition within the Australian Banking Sector; Senate Economics Reference Committee; Parliament of the Commonwealth of Australia

Eidem, Jesper 2008; Old Assyrian Trade in Northern Syria: The Evidence from Tell Leilan

Ershad, Hussain Mohammed and Mahfuzul, Haque A. B. M. 2017; Empirical Analysis of the Relationship between Money Supply and Per Capita GDP Growth Rate in Bangladesh

FATF 2012; International Standards on Combating Money Laundering and the Financing of Terrorism & Proliferation 2012; FATF

FCA 2003; Visa International Service Association v Reserve Bank of Australia; Federal Court of Australia; [2003] FCA 977

Feldstein, Martin and Stock, James H. 1993; The Use of a Monetary Aggregate to Target Nominal GDP; Monetary Policy; The University of Chicago Press

Ferguson, Roger W. Jr 2003; September 11, The Federal Reserve and the Financial System; Speech at Vanderbilt University, Nashville, Tennessee; https://www.bis.org/review/r030207d.pdf

First Data 2010; Asia Pacific Fact Sheet https://www.firstdata.com/downloads/communications/apac-factsheet.6.11.10.pdf

Fisher, Irving 1933; Stamp script; New York; Adelphi Company

Fitzgerald, Shirley and Golder, Hilary 1994; Pyrmont and Ultimo under siege, Hale & Iremonger, Sydney

Fox, Ryan and Finlay, Richard 2012; Dwelling Prices and Household Income; RBA; Bulletin December Quarter 2012

Gardner, Dana 2012; Enterprise Architecture and Transformation at the Crossroads; eCommerce Times, Enterprise IT; 12 March 2012

Gavel, Tim 2000; Transcript: Walker Disqualified Metres from Gold; ABC; https://www.abc.net.au/worldtoday/stories/s190230.htm

Gilbert + Tobin 2016; Form A; Commonwealth of Australia; Competition and Consumer Act 2010 — subsections 88 (1A) and (1); Exclusionary Provisions and Associated Cartel Provisions: Application for Authorisation; Bendigo and Adelaide Bank and others re Apple Pay; https://www.accc.gov.au/system/files/public-registers/documents/D16%2B98591.pdf

Graeber, David 2011; Debt: The first 5,000 years; Melville House

Guardian, The 2018; A Recent History of Australia's Banking Scandals; https://www.theguardian.com/australia-news/ng-interactive/2018/apr/19/a-recent-history-of-australias-banking-scandals

Harris, Peter et al. 2018; Competition in the Australian Financial System; Productivity Commission

Hasluck, Paul 1997; The chance of politics; Melbourne; Text Publishing

Hayne, Kenneth Madison 2019; Final Report of the Royal Commission into Misconduct in the Banking, Superannuation and Financial Services Industry; Commonwealth of Australia

Heydarian, R. J. 2015; Asia's New Battlefield: The USA, China and the struggle for the Western Pacific; Zed Books

Hondroyiannis, G. and Papaoikonomou D. 2017; The effect of card payments on VAT revenue: New evidence from Greece. Economic Letters; August 2017

Hook, Fiona 2009; Archaeology in Oceania, 2009; Wiley Online Library; Volume 44, Issue S1

Hume, David 1752; Of the balance of trade

Jefferson, Thomas et al. 1776; Declaration of Independence; United States of America

Jevons, William Stanley 1875; Money and the mechanism of exchange

Judy (Judge) 2015; Judge Judy; Online Scammer?!/Music Blaring Recklessness?!/Baby Daddy Drama!; S20, Ep54; 12 Nov. 2015

Kagan, D. 1982; The dates of the earliest coins. American Journal of Archaeology, 86(3), 343-360

Keister, Orville R. 1963; Commercial Record Keeping in Ancient Mesopotamia; The Accounting Review

Kerwin, Dale Wayne 2006; Aboriginal Dreaming Tracks or Trading Paths: The Common Ways; Thesis (PhD Doctorate); Griffith University

Keynes, Maynard 1930; Economic Possibilities for our Grandchildren — Essays in Persuasion, New York, NY: W.W. Norton & Co., 1963, 358-373

Keynes, Maynard 1936; The general theory of employment, interest and money; Palgrave Macmillan

Khanna, Vikramaditya S. 2005; The Economic History of the Corporate Form in Ancient India; University of Michigan

King, Rachael 2017; New United States Dollar Bills will not be Polymer — Fed official; Central Banking; centralbanking.com

Kohler, Marion and van der Merwe, Michelle 2015; Long-run Trends in Housing Price Growth; RBA; September Quarter 2015

Kruszelnicki, Karl S. 2010; Frog Fable Brought to Boil; Dr Karl's Great Moments in Science; Australian Broadcasting Corporation

Laker, John et al. 2018; APRA Prudential Inquiry into the Commonwealth Bank of Australia; APRA

Lenihan, Denis 2014; Chifley and the Banks 1947: Will We Ever Know What Really Happened?

Liu, Qiu-gen and Chai, Ying-kun 2010; Chinese Private Banks and Banking Houses in Ming and Qing Dynasties

Manville, H. E. 2000; The Bank of England countermarked dollars, 1797-1804. British Numismatic Journal, 70, 103-17

Marks, Lucy 2018; Did Aboriginal and Asian People Trade before European Settlement in Darwin? Curious Darwin; Australian Broadcasting Commission

Markwell, Donald J. 2000; Keynes and Australia, Reserve Bank of Australia

Martin, Stephen et al. 1991; A Pocket Full of Change: Report on the Inquiry into Banking and Deregulation; The House of Representatives Standing Committee on Finance and Public Administration; Parliament of the Commonwealth of Australia

ME Bank 2018; Household Financial Comfort Report; ME Bank. Fourteenth survey; Insights from National Research into the Financial Psychology of Australian Households

Merrett, D. 2013; The Australian bank crashes of the 1890s revisited. Business History Review, 87(3), 407-429. https://doi.org/10.1017/S0007680513000706

Mihm, Stephen 2006; No Ordinary Counterfeit; New York Times; 23 July 2016

Monaghan, J. 1966; Australians and the Gold Rush: California and Down Under, 1849-1854; University of California Press

Moore, Geoffrey A. 1998; Crossing the Chasm, Marketing and Selling Products to Mainstream Customer; Capstone

Morgan, E. S. and Morgan, H. M. 1962; Stamp Act Crisis: Prologue to Revolution; University of North Carolina Press

Murphy, Niall c. 2020; In Conversation (with Ben Treynor Sloss); Google; https://landing.google.com/sre/interview/ben-treynor-sloss/

Murray, David et al. 2014; Financial System Inquiry Final Report, Australian Government — The Treasury

Murray, R. 1996; What really happened to the Kooris? Quadrant Magazine, 40(11), 10

Nakamoto, Satoshi 2008; Bitcoin: A Peer-to-Peer Electronic Cash System; bitcoin.org

Napier, Mellis 1936; Report of the Royal Commission Appointed to Inquire into the Monetary and Banking Systems at Present in Operation in Australia; Commonwealth of Australia

Nelson, C. M. 1993; Evidence for Early Trade between the Coast and Interior of East Africa; WAC Mombassa Intercongress Conference Volume

Northfield, Rebecca 2018; The debt science owes to alchemy; Engineering and Technology, 15 March 2018

Obama, Barak 2020; Former President Obama Holds Town Hall on Racial Justice & Police Reform; https://www.c-span.org/video/?472749-1/town-hall-president-obama-racial-justice-police-reform

Owen, Mike 2014; Unravelling the mystery of Arnhem Land's ancient African coins; Australian Geographic

Patty, Anna 2020; "The worst 12 months of my life": Fogo Brazilia franchisees seek compensation; SMH; 26 July 2020

Pal, Rajat K. 2018; Are Indus Valley Seals Proto-Coins? https://www.boloji.com/articles/50203/are-indus-valley-seals-proto-coins

Phillips, Bronwyn and Hock, Peter 2011; 100 Years Together; Commonwealth Bank of Australia

Pollari, Ian and Raisbeck, Murray 2017; Forging the Future: How Financial Institutions are Embracing Fintech to Evolve and Grow; KPMG

Prelec, D. and Simester, D. 2001; Always leave home without it: A further investigation of the credit-card effect on willingness to pay. Marketing Letters 12, 5-12 https://doi.org/10.1023/A:1008196717017

Productivity Commission 2017; Inquiry Report — Data Availability and Use; Productivity Commission

Productivity Commission 2018; Inquiry Report — Competition in the Australian Financial System; Productivity Commission

Puffers, Ken et al 2007; A design science research methodology for information systems research, Journal of Management Information Systems; 24:3, 45-77, DOI: 10.2753/MIS0742-1222240302

RBA 2020; Retail Payments data May 2020; issued 7 July 2020; Reserve Bank of Australia

Relethford, J. H. 2008; Genetic evidence and the modern human origins debate. Heredity 100, 555-563

Reserve Bank of Australia c2020; Unemployment, its Measurement and Types; Reserve Bank of Australia Education

Ripoll, Bernie et al. 2009; Final Report on Inquiry into Financial Products and Services in Australia; Parliamentary Joint Committee on Corporations and Financial Services; Parliament of the Commonwealth of Australia

Roosevelt, Franklin D. et al. 1944; Final Act and Related Documents of the United Nations Monetary and Financial Conference; United States of America — Department of State

Roy, Deepankar 2011; Management of Payment and Settlement Systems in India: Critical Review and Challenges

Sacca, Chris 2016; Shark Tank — United States episode; ABC(US); aired on 15 January 2016

Scheidel, W. 2010; Coin quality, coin quantity, and coin value in early China and the Roman world. American Journal of Numismatics, 22, 93-118

Schuh, Scott et al. 2010; Who Gains and Who Loses from Credit Card Payments? Theory and Calibrations; Federal Reserve Bank of Boston; Public Policy Discussion Papers No. 10-03

Scott, Susan and Zachariadis, Markos 2013; The Society for Worldwide Interbank Financial Telecommunication (SWIFT): Co-operative Governance for Network Innovation, Standards, and Community; Routledge

Scripture, Edward Wheeler 1897; The new psychology; Harvard University

Simon, H. 1969; The sciences of the artificial. Cambridge, MA: MIT Press

Smith, Adam 1776; An inquiry into the nature and causes of the wealth of nations

Sterba, Richard L. A. 1976; The organization and management of the temple corporations in Ancient Mesopotamia. Academy of Management Review, 1(3), 16-26

Sturm, Jan-Egbert and Williams, Barry 2002; Deregulation, Entry of Foreign Banks and Bank Efficiency in Australia. CESifo Working Paper Series No. 816; https://ssrn.com/abstract=367160

Sykes, Trevor 1998; Two centuries of panic: A history of corporate collapses in Australia; Allen & Unwin

Taylor, Beth 2016; Making Sense of Dollars and Cents... Fifty Years On; National Film and Sound Archive of Australia https://www.nfsa.gov.au/latest/making-sense-dollars-and-cents-50-years#:~:text=Arguably%20the%20most%20well%2Dloved,'Click%20go%20the%20shears'

Thomson, Craig et al. 2008; Final Report on Competition in the Banking and Non-banking Sectors; House of Representatives Standing Committee on Economics; Parliament of the Commonwealth of Australia

Turnbull, Shann 2018; Submission in response to Productivity Commission Draft Report of January 2018 on "Competition in the Australian Financial System;" International Institute for Self-governance

Wakefield, Max et al. 2019; A Cost-benefit Analysis of Polymer Banknotes, Reserve Bank of Australia

Wallis, Stan et al. 1997; Financial System Inquiry (1996) Final Report, Australian Government — The Treasury

Webb, Stephen 1995; Palaeopathology of Aboriginal Australians: Health and Disease Across a Hunter-Gatherer Continent; Cambridge University Press

Weier, M., Dolan, K., Powell, A., Muir, K., and Young, A. 2019; Money Stories: Financial Resilience among Aboriginal and Torres Strait Islander Australians 2019; First Nations Foundation Centre for Social Impact (CSI) – UNSW Sydney, for National Australia Bank

Wilson, Tim et al. 2019; Review of the Four Major Banks: Fourth Report; House of Representatives Standing Committee on Economics; Parliament of the Commonwealth of Australia

Wilson, Tim et al. 2020; Review of the Four Major Banks: Fifth Report; House of Representatives Standing Committee on Economics; Parliament of the Commonwealth of Australia

Zwalve, Willem J 2001; Callistus's Case: Some Legal Aspects of Roman Business Activities; The Transformation of Economic Life under the Roman Empire; Proceedings of the Second Workshop of the International Network Impact of Empire (Roman Empire, c. 200 B.C. — A.D. 476), Nottingham, 4-7 July 2001

Various archived news articles from:

1. ABC
2. The Age, Fairfax
3. The Australian Financial Review, Fairfax
4. The Australian, News Corp
5. The Guardian, Guardian Media Group
6. The Sydney Morning Herald, Fairfax
7. Other newspapers digitised by Newspapers.com
8. Other newspapers digitised by the National Library of Australia

Various corporate websites of the named organisations, accessed directly or through the Internet Archive project.

Various legal instruments of the Commonwealth of Australia:

1. Anti-Money Laundering and Counter-Terrorism Financing Act 2006
2. Australian Information Commissioner Act 2010
3. Australian Note Act 1910
4. Bank Account Debits Tax Act 1982
5. Banking Act 1945-1959
6. Banking (Transitional Provisions) Act 1959
7. Bills of Exchange Act 1909
8. Cash Transaction Reports Act 1988
9. Cheques and Payment Orders Act or Cheques Act 1986
10. Coinage Act 1909
11. Commonwealth Bank Act 1911-1953; Commonwealth Banks Act 1959-1974; Commonwealth Banks Restructuring Act 1990; Commonwealth Bank Sale Act 1995
12. Commonwealth of Australia Constitution Act 1901
13. Competition and Consumer Act 2010
14. Corporations Act 1989-2011
15. Currency Act 1965
16. Currency (Restrictions on the Use of Cash) Bill 2019
17. Electronic Conveyancing National Law, as enacted by the States and Territories of Australia 2012-2020

18. Financial Corporations Act 1974
19. Financial Transaction Reports Act 1988
20. Freedom of Information Act 1982
21. Payment Systems and Netting Act 1998
22. Payments Systems (Regulation) Act 1998
23. Privacy Act 1988
24. Proceeds of Crime Act 2002
25. Reserve Bank Act 1959-1973

Various news releases, reports and publications, officially published by:

1. Australian Bureau of Statistics (ABS), incl. data collections
2. Australian Consumer and Competition Commission (ACCC)
3. Australian Financial Complaints Authority (AFCA), incl. AFCA Datacube
4. Australian Government — Administrative Appeals Tribunal
5. Australian Government — Productivity Commission
6. Australian Government — The Treasury
7. Australian Human Rights Commission
8. Australian Payments Council
9. Australian Payments Network (AusPayNet)
10. Australian Prudential Regulation Authority (APRA)
11. Australian Securities and Investments Commission (ASIC)
12. Australian Taxation Office (ATO)
13. Australian Transaction Reports and Analysis Centre (AUSTRAC)
14. Commonwealth of Australia Gazette, National Library of Australia
15. Federal Court of Australia
16. Financial Action Task Force (FATF), international body
17. High Court of Australia
18. International Monetary Fund (IMF), international body
19. Office of the Australian Information Commissioner (OIAC)
20. Organisation for Economic Co-operation and Development (OECD), international body, incl. data collections

21. Reserve Bank of Australia (RBA), incl. data collections
22. United Nations, international body, various organisations
23. United Nations Security Council (UNSC), international body
24. World Bank, international body

About the Editors

Audrey van Ryn is a trained teacher, and taught English and music in Auckland secondary schools for four years, followed by two years teaching English as a second language. She currently works as a copy editor, mostly via the online platform Freelancer. Since 2010, she has been the secretary of Civic Trust Auckland, a community heritage and environmental group, and she is also the secretary of a new group in Auckland called Community Groups Feeding the Homeless.

Kym Dunbar is a former journalist and newspaper sub editor. She went on to work as a technical writer and editor for the Australian Defence Force and its subcontractors. For the past decade, she has successfully freelanced as a writer and editor through Freelancer. Kym is passionate about her dogs, White Swiss Shepherds, and her imported boy, Iron, is from Slovakia. She is proud of his success as an Australian champion and his contribution to the breed in Australia. She also participates in dog shows and dog sports.

About the Layout Designer

Petya Tsankova is a London-based graphic designer with an educational background in Fine Art and more than 18 years of experience across diverse visual communication disciplines. For the last five years, she has focused her industry expertise on Book Cover and Layout Design services.

About the Cover Designer

S M Shamim-Ur- Rashid is a highly experienced graphic designer with a successful track record in designing eBook covers, book covers, flyers, brochures, album arts, podcast covers, PDF materials and so on. Having more than eight years of experience in the traditional graphics field, he is now learning to draw free-hand cartoons and comics. He has excellent expertise in Adobe Photoshop and Illustrator software. Being an individual with a result-driven approach and relentless in pursuit of excellence, he strives to ensure that every penny you pay is worth paying. He is currently a Master's student at Flinders University, Adelaide. He works exclusively at fiverr. He can be reached at fiverr.com/shamimrashid

INDEX

Symbols

2Checkout: 230

7-Eleven: 234

9/11: 51, 53, 277, 278, 279, 396, 397, 403, 405

48 Martin Place: 23

86 400 (bank): 85, 95

100 message: 215, 240

120 Pitt Street: 23

200 message: 215, 240

401(k): 353, 385

1984 (George Orwell novel): 397

A

ABA file: 263, 392

Abbott, Tony: 414

ABN: 310, 312

ABN Amro Bank: 93

ACCC: 39, 49, 64, 68, 70, 114, 160, 203, 237, 246, 249, 292, 326, 344, 376 410, 414

Accenture: 154

Access Card: 203

accommodative and synchronised pricing behaviour: 39, 68

account aggregation: 340

account number: 25, 258, 267, 280, 312, 412

account takeover: 166

Account Types: 103

account unification: 391

ACDES: 125, 175, 178, 321

ACH, automated clearing house (US): 285

ACI: 152, 336

acquirer: 97, 195, 337, 374, 388

ADB: See Asia Development Bank

Additional Tier 1: 59

Adelaide: 101

Adelaide Bank: 84

Adelaide Hills: 19

ADI: 46, 50, 52, 57

Administrative Appeals Tribunal: 76

AFCA: See Australian Financial Complaints Authority

AFI: 128

Africa: 324

Afterpay: 336, 337, 342

AGC: 342

AGC CreditLine: 204

agency banking: 96

Agile: 137, 414

Agricultural Bank of China: 93

AI/ML: 153, 158, 330, 365, 398, 399, 415

Airbnb: 343, 348

Airbus A380: 291

Air New Zealand: 338

Airtasker: 365, 415

Albert: 136, 225, 226, 229, 337, 382

Aldi: 392

Alibaba: 296, 331, 348, 393, 402

Aliexpress: 348, 393, 399

Alipay: 331, 332, 396

Alliance Bank: 84

Allied Wallet: 230

alluvial gold: 19

Alphabet Inc: 330

Al-Qaeda: 52

alternative payment method: 332

Amazon: 135, 330, 393, 396, 399

Amazon Alexa: 158

Amazon Pay: 330

Amazon Web Services: 135

American Express: 84, 186, 196, 199, 205, 209, 219, 220, 222, 225, 227, 239, 241, 246, 247, 248, 251, 297, 348, 410

American Revolution: 11, 181

Americas Cup: 71
Amex. See American Express
AML/CTF: 49, 51, 53, 54, 96, 152, 277, 295, 296, 297, 298, 299, 343, 357, 358, 392, 398
AML/CTF Act: 232
AML/CTF program: 54
Amman: 92
amortised: 114
AMP: 49
AMP Bank: 84
Andreessen Horowitz: 329
Android: 226, 227, 235, 237, 330, 348, 378
Android Pay: 235
Angus & Robertson: 213
Animal Farm: 420
Annual Review into the Four Major Banks: 49, 68
Ansett: 338
Ant Financial: 297, 331
anti-competitive: 203, 237, 326, 410
ANZ: 19, 39, 60, 63, 81, 82, 83, 92, 96, 98, 160, 189, 198, 203, 204, 207, 210, 234, 236, 244, 258, 270, 289, 306, 307, 308, 361, 375
ANZAC: 24
ANZ Blade Pay: 230
ANZ GoMoney: 136, 306, 376
ANZi: 329
ANZ MoneyManager: 340, 376
ANZ New Zealand: 98
ANZ Secure Gateway: 230
Apache: 157
APCA: 175, 188, 259, 302, 306. See AusPayNet
APCA ID: 260
APCS: 125, 188, 321
API: 141, 160, 286, 309, 311, 315, 316, 392, 406, 409
APIGEE: 141
APM. See alternative payment method
app: 126, 167, 234, 235, 237, 238, 308, 343, 344, 365
Apple: 134, 212, 228, 234, 235, 237, 330, 334, 376, 415, 418
Apple App Store: 103
Apple iPhone: 136
Apple Pay: 227, 236, 237, 246, 340, 343, 376, 406, 414
Apple Siri: 158
application service provider: 135, 392
APRA: 41, 47, 51, 52, 57, 66, 68, 70, 83, 85, 89, 90, 92, 95, 97, 117, 123, 153, 156, 168, 250, 363, 373, 406, 416
APRA Prudential Inquiry into CBA: 63
Arab Bank Australia: 92
Arabia: 9
Archimedes: 381
architecture: 135
Ariba: 402
Armaguard: 177, 203
Army Defence Credit Union: 86
artificial intelligence: See AI/ML
AS 2805: 215, 216, 307, 378
ASF: See available stable funding
Asia Development Bank: 41, 384
Asian Infrastructure Investment Bank: 41, 384
ASIC: 40, 47, 64, 67, 122, 123, 214, 298, 357, 387, 406, 411
ASIC chip: 351, 355, 356
ASL: 94, 104, 210, 308, 387
ASP: See application service provider
Assembly Payments: 230
asset finance: 342
assisted channels: 141
ASX: 28, 84, 321, 322, 344, 357, 361
asymmetric encryption: 163, 385
Atkins, Richard: 15
ATM: 95, 106, 126, 141, 152, 176, 178, 195, 257, 286, 289
ATM direct charging: 253
ATO: 64, 71, 76, 119, 121, 160, 228, 285, 315, 357, 359, 364, 397, 398, 403
Attorney General: 364, 403, 406
Auckland Savings Bank: 98
Auguste Comte: 414
Auroracoin: 357
AusPayNet: 56, 125, 175, 188, 208, 209, 216, 217, 225, 227, 242, 261, 262, 392
Aussie Red: 401
Austnet: 199, 203, 210, 211, 336
AUSTRAC: 49, 53, 63, 64, 66, 153, 212, 228, 277, 289, 298, 299, 313, 354, 357, 364, 398
Austraclear: 321
Australia and New Zealand Banking Group: See ANZ
Australia Card: 71, 364, 403
Australian Bank: 204, 211, 314
Australian Bank Employees Union: 99
Australian Banking Association: 73, 124, 226, 263, 392
Australian Bank Officers Association: 34, 99
Australian Bureau of Statistics: 38
Australian Capital Territory: 101, 347
Australian Cash Distribution And Exchange System: See ACDES
Australian Central Credit Union: 90
Australian Consumer and Competition Commission: See ACCC
Australian dollar: 37
Australian Financial Complaints Authority: 69, 76, 418
Australian Financial Institutions Commission: 57
Australian Information Commissioner Act: 159
Australian Insurance Employees Union: 99
Australian Insurance Staffs Federation: 99

Australian Military Bank: 86, 219
Australian Mutual Bank: 86
Australian National University: 157
Australian Notes Act: 21, 25
Australian Overland Telegraph Line: 24
Australian Payments Council: 56, 125, 160
Australian Payments Network: See AusPayNet
Australian Payments Systems Council: 45, 47, 56, 125
Australian Privacy Principles: 362
Australian Restructuring Insolvency and Turnaround Association: 122
Australian Securities and Investment Commission: See ASIC
Australian Settlements Limited: See ASL
Australian Unity Bank: 86
Australia Post: 96, 214, 269, 336, 341, 365, 376, 406
Auswide Bank: 86
authentication: 141, 166, 167, 221, 271, 362, 365, 396, 403, 406
authorisation: 141, 202, 215, 216, 240, 241, 250, 260, 286, 343, 348, 365
Authorised Deposit-taking Institution: See ADI
Authorize.net: 230
automated fuel dispenser: 215, 216, 347
automatic teller machine: See ATM
availability of capital: 70
available stable funding: 62
Azupay: 337
Azure: 135

B

B2B: 284, 299, 359, 402, 408
B2B lending: 120
B2C: 373
Bain Capital: 85
balance of payments: 36, 41
balance transfer: 124
Ballarat Banking Company: 32
Bambora: 225, 230, 271, 336
banana smoothie: 39, 375
Bancor: 36, 383, 384, 423
Bangladesh Bank: 279
bank: 4, 17, 20, 31, 81
bank account: 103
BankAmericard: 382
Bank Australia: 86
bank-bashing: 83, 385
bank bills: 39, 321
Bankcard: 203, 344, 374, 376
bank cheque: 185, 323
Bankers Trust: 412
Bank First: 88
Bank for International Settlements: 41, 50, 58
bank guarantee: 186
Bank Holiday: 101
bank identification code: See BIC
Banking Act: 33, 34, 85
Banking Crisis of 1893: 20
Banking Industry Architecture Network: See BIAN
bank levy: 73
bankmecu: 86
Bank of Adelaide: 32
Bank of America: 93
Bank of Australasia: 19, 32, 376
Bank of Australia: 18
Bank of Baroda: 93
Bank of China: 92, 298
Bank of Communications co: 93
Bank of Cyprus: 84
Bank of England: 12, 26
Bank of New South Wales: 17, 32, 34, 81, 412
Bank of New York Mellon: 93
Bank of New Zealand: 32, 98
Bank of Nova Scotia: 93
Bank of Queensland: 84, 96, 210
Bank of Sydney: 92
Bank of Taiwan: 93
Bank of Tokyo: 32
Bank of US: 86
Bank@Post: 96, 214, 270, 376
Bankstown City Unity Bank: 88
Banksys: 230
BankVic: 88
Bankwest: 48, 219
barcode: 313, 338
barter: 10
Bartercard: 359
base erosion profit shifting: 75, 390
BASE I: 215
BASE II: 215, 241
Basel: 41, 50, 58, 61, 66, 378, 381, 390, 404
batch settlement: 27
Bathurst: 19
BBAN: 280
BBC Hardware: 207
BBPOS Wisepad: 230
BCP: See business continuity planning
BCU: 88
B&E: 86
Beat the Q: 343, 402
BECS: See Direct Entry
Beeby, George Stephenson: 421
Beem It: 213, 307, 312, 313, 316, 374, 376, 409
Bendigo and Adelaide Bank: 84, 210, 237
Bendigo Bank: 84, 199, 204, 211, 308
BEPS: See base erosion profit shifting
Beyond Bank Australia: 86
Beyond Payment Systems: 337

BIAN: 285
BIC: 280, 309
big data: 153, 157, 160, 161
Big Four: 46, 48, 57, 60, 62, 64, 69, 70, 73, 81, 83, 98, 106, 116, 119, 124, 176, 257, 270, 276, 298, 306, 308, 324, 374, 375, 376, 387, 403, 416, 418
big tech: 330, 396, 407, 418
bilateral settlement: 27
biller code: 267
bill of lading: 296
Bills of Exchange Act: 25, 182
BIN: 205, 209
BIN sponsor: 214, 337
biometrics: 54, 364, 396, 403, 407, 423
birth certificate: 364, 405
BIS: See Bank for International Settlements
Bitcoin: 95, 349, 383, 384, 394, 395
Bitpay: 359
BitRocket: 358
Bitstamp: 358
Bit Trade: 358
Blackberry: 235
Black Card: 102
Black Lives Matter: 173
blackmail: 55
black market: 14
black swan event: 66
Black Tuesday: 124
Blair, Andrew: 284
Bletchley Park: 158
Bligh, William: 14
blockchain: 350, 359, 369, 378, 394
Bluetooth: 226, 230, 237, 390, 407
BNK Banking Corporation: 86
BNP: 32
BNP Paribas: 93
Bolt: 227, 337
bond market: 40
bonds: 39, 321
bonus: 100
BoP: See balance of payments
Border Bank: 88
Borders (bookstore): 213
Boston Tea Party: 12
Bounty, HMS: 14
BP: 207, 347
BPAY: 57, 68, 106, 124, 125, 126, 267, 271, 288, 298, 305, 306, 312, 316, 321, 332, 341, 374, 408, 409, 412
BPAY View: 268, 269, 271, 315, 336
BPoint: 230
Bragg, Andrew: 49
Braintree: 230, 337
branch: 25
breakage: 212
breaking up: 375
Bretton Woods: 35, 41, 43, 377, 383, 419, 420
bribe: 155, 173
Brisbane: 101, 346
Brisbane Permanent Building and Banking Company: 32
British-Australia Telegraph Company: 24
broad-based tax: 73
broad money: 128, 322, 348, 358, 369, 371, 374, 383, 411
brochureware: 333
Broken Hill Community Credit Union: 91
BS 11 (NZ banking standard): 98
BSB: 187, 258, 261, 267, 280, 309, 312, 408, 412
BT Australia: 83
BTC Markets: 358
bubonic plague: 9
build: 136
building society: 89
bullion: 12, 19, 21, 60
Bundll: 342
Bureau of Meteorology: 362
Burnett Permanent Building Society: 86
Burroughs: 225
business bank: 97, 99
business case: 135
business continuity planning: 167
business loan: 120
business operations: 142, 145
business requirements: 135
business units: 99
buy now, pay later: 204, 253, 332, 342, 363, 378, 388, 410

C

Cabcharge: 315, 344
cablewire: 24
Cadmus: 336
cain (ISO 20022): 216, 286
Cairns Penny Savings & Loans: 86
Calcutta: 15, 404
California: 19
Caltex: 207, 347
Campbell Committee: 45, 249
Campbell Inquiry: 46
Campbell, Keith: 45
camt (ISO 20022): 286
Canada: 41, 234
Canadian Imperial Bank of Commerce: 93
capital adequacy: 58, 70, 127, 130
capital markets: 40
capital notes: 41
card: 101, 195, 314, 330
Card: 305
Card Access Services: 336
card economics: 241
Cardlink: 202, 203, 269, 306
card-not-present: 218, 220, 224, 228, 229
card-present: 218, 221
card switch: 134, 210
cash: 101, 171

cash advance: 111, 214, 267
Cashcard: 203, 210, 211, 336
cash cheque: 184
cashierless payments: 330
Cashless Debit Card: 102
cash management trust: 123
Cash Transaction Reports Act: 53
casino: 339
Castles: 227
Catch Me if You Can: 185
CBA: 22, 23, 31, 34, 48, 49, 60, 63, 64, 65, 68, 70, 76, 82, 96, 98, 100, 102, 103, 107, 109, 119, 124, 125, 134, 152, 153, 155, 178, 189, 199, 203, 204, 207, 210, 217, 225, 229, 230, 234, 235, 237, 238, 253, 262, 270, 278, 291, 306, 308, 313, 316, 325, 329, 332, 337, 342, 354, 361, 365, 372, 374, 375, 382, 385, 390, 396, 397, 412
CBA Innovation Lab: 103
CBA Staff Co-operative: 87
CbC or CbCR: See Country by Country Reporting
CBM: 55
CCL Secure: 173
CDBC: See central bank digital currency
CECS: 125, 209, 216, 253, 321: See also EFTPOS, eftpos, eftpos Hub, Clearing System 3 or IAC
Central African Republic: 52
central bank: 17, 22, 23, 27, 31, 34, 36, 39, 40, 44, 60, 82, 97, 284, 291, 300, 301, 302, 352, 355, 358, 383, 384, 404, 419
central bank digital currency: 358
Central Bank of India: 404
centralised banking: 406
central ledger: 28
Central Murray Credit Union: 90
Central West Credit Union: 90
Centrelink: 405
CEO: 22, 33, 45, 48, 49, 98, 100, 134, 376, 386, 422
certificate: 165
CGM (remittance provider): 298
chain of custody: 402
Chaos Monkey: 167
charge card: 196
Charge Card Services: 124, 196, 199, 203, 204, 271
chasm: 335, 377, 381, 408
check digit: 205, 262, 267, 268
Checkout: 230
Chennai: 16
cheque: 9, 25, 27, 101, 181, 182, 283, 376
cheque account: 109
cheque book: 182
Cheques and Payment Orders Act: 182
cheque, savings or credit: 208
cheque-stop: 182, 183, 189
CHESS: 321, 322, 361
Chicago Mercantile Exchange: 321
chief financial officer: 98, 100, 143, 212, 375
chief information officer: 98
chief legal counsel: 99
chief operating officer: 99
chief risk officer: 99
Chifley, Ben: 31, 33, 34, 44, 64, 405
China: 9, 214, 220, 354
China Construction Bank Co: 93
China Everbright Bank Co: 93
China Merchants Bank Co: 93
China UnionPay: 92, 214, 220, 241, 252, 298, 408
chip and pin: 222, 377, 407
CHOICE: 68, 107, 219
CISCO: 95, 337
Citibank: 92, 96, 166, 205, 210, 298, 308, 342, 374
Claytons: 316
Clear2Pay: 152, 336
clearing: 27, 178, 185, 188, 190, 215, 216, 257, 258, 259, 263, 280, 285, 286, 287, 290, 298, 299, 302, 306, 310, 321, 325, 351, 353
Clearing System 1: 188
Clearing System 2: 259
Clearing System 3: 216
Clearing System 4: 302
Clearing System 5: 175
click clacks: 201
click to pay: 232
Clipp: 344
closed loop: 198, 211, 212, 344, 347, 359
cloud: 135, 392, 423
CLS Bank: 300, 302, 321, 408
CMC Markets: 83, 293
Coastline Credit Union: 91
COBOL: 133
CoffeeClub: 338
COIN: 125, 188, 216, 258, 356, 376
Coinage Act: 24
Coinbase: 358
CoinJar: 358
coins: 11, 12, 16, 21, 26, 41, 60, 125, 128
CoinSpot: 358
Coles: 57, 205, 210, 235, 338, 392
Coles Myer: 338
collective investment vehicles: 284
Colonial First State: 82
colonisation: 11
Commerce: 3
Commercial Banking Company of Sydney: 32
Commercial Bank of Australia: 32
commercial, off the shelf software: See COTS
commissariat: 14
commodities: 142, 372

Commodore: 134
Common Equity Tier 1: 59
Common Reporting Standard: 75, 104, 378, 390, 397, 407
Commonwealth Bank Act: 23
Commonwealth Bank of Australia: See CBA
Commonwealth Bank Officers Association: 99
Commonwealth Employment Services: 38
Commonwealth of Australia: 21
Commonwealth Public Servants Credit Union: 86
Commsec: 83
communism: 420
Community Bank: 84
companion cards: 251
Competition and Consumer Act: 159
Competition in the Australian Financial System (inquiry): 70, 82, 227, 375, 408
compliance training: 100
Comptoir National d'Escompte de Paris: 32
computerised ledger: 28
computers: 28
concept: 135
confidential: 394
configuration: 138
Connex: 238
Conrad Jupiters: 339
constitution: 32, 38
Consumer Data Right: 47, 70, 71, 160, 363, 386, 394
Consumer Data Right Bill: 159
consumerism: 196, 377, 389
Consumer Price Index: See CPI
contactless payment: 209, 227, 233, 234, 235, 236, 238, 347, 377, 418
continuous development: 137
Continuous Linked Settlement: See CLS Bank
contract: 154
contracts for difference: 293
conveyancer: 112, 323
convicts: 12
Conways Law: 126, 139, 143, 288, 289
copper: 9, 11, 13, 42, 43
copyright: 394
Corda: 361, 365
core banking: 76, 103, 109, 142, 262, 300, 378, 404
corporate accounts: 103
Corporations Act: 67
correspondent banking: 105, 276, 278, 281, 296
Costello, Peter: 47, 72, 82
COTS: 223, 227
Council of Australian Governments: 323
countercyclical capital buffer: 59
counterfeit: 11, 172, 173, 176, 248
Country by Country Reporting: 75, 390
coup: 15
cover payment: 277
COVID-19: 26, 35, 46, 49, 52, 65, 85, 108, 118, 120, 122, 127, 159, 161, 174, 234, 246, 248, 253, 337, 338, 343, 371, 375, 389, 390, 396, 402, 403, 404, 405
COVIDSafe: 396, 397
cowry shells: 9
CPI: 370
CPS 231 (APRA standard): 98
Creative Commons: 394, 399
credit card: 111, 267, 377, 410
credit check: 183, 197, 202, 252, 364, 389, 410
CreditMe2U: 233
credit score: 363, 388, 406, 410
Credit Suisse: 93
credit transfer: 182
Credit Union Australia: 90
credit unions: 90
Credit Union SA: 90
CRM: 145
CRN (BPAY): 267
crossing a cheque: 184
cross-sell: 83, 347, 412
crowdfunding: 67, 341, 357
Crown Casino: 339
CRS: See Common Reporting Standard
crude oil: 402
cryptocurrency: 5, 49, 54, 73, 74, 76, 219, 228, 332, 340, 349, 355, 359, 369, 378, 384, 394, 395, 406
cryptocurrency exchanges: 55, 357, 358
cryptocurrency wallet: 358, 372
CS1: See paper instruments
CS2: See Direct Entry
CS3: See CECS
CS4: See HVCS
CS5: See cash
CSIRO: 28, 160, 172
CSIRO Co-op Credit Society: 86
CTF: See AML/CTF
Cubic Corporation: 348
CueCard: 203
currency: 4, 10, 128
currency: See also cash
Currency Act: 178
Curtin, John: 32, 37
Cuscal: 57, 84, 85, 86, 88, 89, 90, 95, 104, 177, 210, 211, 213, 308, 311, 387
custodians: 353
customer information repository: 142
customer reference number (BPAY): See CRN (BPAY)
customer relationship management (software): See CRM
customisation: 138
CVV: 220
CyberSource: 217, 230
cyclical development: 136

D

D2000: 292
darknet: 354
Data 61: 160
Data Availability and Use (inquiry): 70
Databank: 136
data centres: 134
data lake: 143
data matching: 74
DataMesh: 337
data normalisation: 143
data sovereignty: 363
data warehouse: 143, 156
David Jones: 205, 212
DBS Bank: 93
DCE: See cryptocurrency exchanges
D-Day landing: 36
DE. See Direct Entry
dealing room: 292
de-bank: 69, 297, 311, 354
debentures: 321
debit card: 202
debit mandate: 260, 314, 408
Debit Mastercard: 211, 251
debt to income: 111, 114
Decentralized Identity Foundation: 365
decimalisation: 42, 172, 187
Decimalisation: 15
decommoditisation: 402
deed of company arrangement: 121
default: 21, 52, 58, 60, 186, 342, 364
Defence Bank: 86
Defence Force Credit Union: 86
deferred net settlement: 27, 188, 190, 217, 263, 271, 301, 322, 424
DEFT: 271
Deliveroo: 343
delivery conditions: 294
delivery versus payment: 185, 293, 302, 321, 322, 323, 324, 325
Delphi Bank: 84
Democratic Republic of the Congo: 52
demurrage: 293
demutualise: 84, 85, 89
Department of Foreign Affairs and Trade: 53
Department of Human Services: 102
departure tax: 345
deployment: 136
depreciation: 116
depression: 24, 26, 31, 35, 38, 52, 174, 405, 421
deregulation: 40, 45, 46, 47, 50, 85, 92, 128, 130, 182, 229
derivatives: 61, 62, 123, 283, 402
designated payment system: 250, 251
designated service: 54
design thinking: 138
detailed design: 136
Deutsche Bank: 93, 205, 291, 374
DevOps: 138
dial-up: 225
diamond: 390
Dick Smith: 213
Diebold Nixdorf: 226
differential value: 370
Digital Asset Holdings: 361
digital bank: 82, 84, 85, 405
digital currency: 49, 54, 340, 348, 355, 358, 395, 422
digital currency exchange. See cryptocurrency exchanges
Digital Currency: Game Changer or Bit Player: 49, 54, 73
digital identity: 362, 364
digital signature: 164
digital wallet: 231, 235, 314
Diners Club: 196, 201, 239, 241, 248, 250
Direct 365: 293
direct debit: 260
Direct Entry: 67, 101, 106, 109, 125, 141, 231, 241, 257, 267, 289, 300, 305, 310, 311, 316, 321, 325, 360, 374, 376, 408
DirectOne: 336
disaster recovery: 167
Discover Card: 201
dishonour: 183, 188, 191
Disruption: 381
Distra: 336
distributed ledger: 3, 348, 355, 361
district court: 77
diversity: 416
DMS: See dual message system
Dnister Ukrainian Credit Co-operative: 91
Document Verification Service: See DVS
Dodo: 392
Dollarmites: 68, 107
domain architectures: 140
DoorDash: 343
dormant account: 122
dot com: 218, 238, 297, 331, 335, 336, 337, 340, 343
double-entry: 424
double-sided transactions: 39
DR. See disaster recovery
drivers licence: 102, 364, 365, 405
DTI. See debt to income
dual message system: 215, 241
ducat (Dutch coin): 13
DvP: See delivery versus payment
DVS: 364, 403, 406
DXC: 154

E

Earthport: 299
East India Company: 11, 12, 119

Eastlink: 346
eBay: 95, 231, 294, 296, 330, 331, 336, 343, 348, 393, 399
ECHELON: 363
economies: 3
e-conveyancing: 323, 406
Edison, Thomas: 334
EDS: 204
EFTech: 225, 229
EFTEL: 210: See Electronic Funds Transfer Services
EFTPOB: 214, 270
eftpos: 57, 92, 125, 126, 210, 217, 238, 298, 307, 316, 321, 358, 407, 409, 410
EFTPOS: 47, 125, 195, 207, 215, 216, 225, 257, 263, 286, 345, 374
eftpos Hub: 125, 209, 210, 217, 252
eGate: 230
Einstein, Albert: 226, 377
eInvoicing: 315, 409
Elders Rural Bank: 84
Electricity Commission Employees Credit Union Co-operative: 88
Electronic Funds Transfer Services: 199, 210
electronic mail. See email
electronic money: 348, 349, 355, 377
electronic signature: 164
email: 166, 260, 263, 269, 283, 306, 310, 312, 316, 333, 338, 339, 364, 394
email address: 269, 312
embedded payments: 330, 340, 343
emFund: 161
emojis: 312
employment: 11, 35, 36, 37, 38, 115, 391
EMV: 217, 221, 233, 242, 244, 313, 348, 390, 395
EMVCo: 220
encryption: 163, 164, 217, 218, 221, 223, 231, 360, 395
Endeavour Mutual Bank: 86
English, Scottish and Australian Bank: 32
English shilling: 13
Enigma: 158
enterprise architecture: 139
enterprise resource planning: 332
enumeration attack: 311
Envestnet: 340
EPAL. See eftpos
ePath: 230, 336
ePayments Code: 67, 70, 219, 245, 249, 321, 343
equal opportunity: 100
Equifax: 197, 364
equities: 142, 284, 372, 411
equity trading: 123
eReceipts: 409
Ericsson: 225
ERP: 271: See enterprise resource planning
ESA: 62, 104, 127, 130, 168, 190, 240, 300, 309, 325, 356, 383, 387, 412
Escrow: 296
Escrow.com: 296
eSec Payments: 336
E.SUN Commercial Bank: 93
e-TAG: 346
eTeam: 340
Ethereum: 355, 360, 361, 362
E-Toll: 346
ETrade: 83
Eureka: 381
Euro Alliance of Payment Schemes: 408
Eurobonds: 40
Eurocard: 220
Europay: 220
Europe: 36, 50, 92, 98, 160, 190, 220, 246, 276, 280, 291, 298, 301, 309, 384, 408
European Union: 161
eWay: 218, 230, 336
E-Way: 346
eWise: 340
exchange of value: 10
Experian: 197, 348
expert: 414

F

Facebook: 330, 365, 403, 422
Face Verification Service: 364
fair go: 420
Fair Work: 399
Fair Work Commission: 99
Falcon: 244
Family First Credit Union: 91
fapiao: 409
Faraday, Michael: 233
Farrow Group: 89
FASTCARD: 344
Fast Settlement Service: 310, 404
FATCA: 74, 104, 407
FATF: 51, 53, 54, 55, 66, 277, 278, 280, 378, 390, 395, 407
Fat Zebra: 230, 336
FBI: 354
FDX: 285
Federal Bank of New York: 279
Federal Court: 77
federation: 21
Fedwire: 281
fee: 182
fiat currency: 25, 44, 171, 423
file transfer: 289
Finance Sector Union: 99
Financial Claims Scheme: 48, 51, 57, 66, 90, 93, 106, 168, 316, 404, 411
Financial Data Exchange: See FDX
Financial Information eXchange: See FIX
financial literacy: 102
financial message: 282, 286
Financial Services Council: 284
Financial Services Guide: 67, 298, 372, 413

financial settlement: 28
Financial Stability Standards: 321
financial switch or financial switching network: See card switch
Financial System Inquiry (1996-1997): See Wallis Report
Financial Systems Inquiry (2014): See Murray Report
Financial Transaction Reports Act: 53
Finastra: 152
FinCEN: 278
fines: 54, 65, 178, 212, 223, 277, 295, 297, 299, 314, 364, 385, 397, 398
Finland: 190
fintech: 49, 70, 103, 331, 336, 377, 387, 407, 414
firearms: 24
Firefighters & Affiliates Credit Co-operative: 90
Firefighters Mutual Bank: 88
Fire Service Credit Union: 90
First Choice Credit Union: 90
First Commercial Bank: 93
First Data: 183, 203, 210, 211, 229, 230, 297, 336
First Option Bank: 87
FIS: 152, 183, 230, 336
fiscal policy: 74, 126, 352
Fiserv: 135, 183, 189, 229, 306, 310
Fisher, Fisher: 22
Fisher, Irving: 421
Fitbit: 235
Five Eyes: 363
FIX: 284, 285
fixed rate: 116
FlexiCard: 203
flexigroup: 270, 336, 342
float: 37, 43, 50, 59, 70, 126, 248, 291, 385, 412, 419
float revenue: 183, 185, 263
Floyd, George: 173
Flybuys: 338
Fogo Brazilia: 122
Foodplus: 207
Ford Co-operative Credit Society: 87
foreign bank: 92
foreign currency: 13, 40, 43, 76, 127, 198, 213, 296, 358, 372, 377, 383, 392
Foreign Currency Conversion Services Inquiry: 69, 292
Foreign Currency Pricing Inquiry: 298
foreign exchange: 13, 69, 97, 213, 283, 291, 295, 297, 298, 325, 341
foreign exchange accounts: 128
foreign exchange cards: 213
Forex: See foreign exchange
forgery: 182
FORTRAN: 133
Forty-Niners: 19
Four Pillars: 46, 48, 81, 82, 83, 373, 375, 376, 403
franchise: 84, 122
Frankie Financial: 337
Fraser, Malcolm: 38, 45
fraud: 54, 55, 67, 96, 122, 144, 156, 166, 167, 183, 185, 187, 195, 212, 218, 222, 240, 242, 250, 278, 280, 292, 293, 295, 299, 313, 324, 337, 353, 354, 358, 398
fraud risk: 244
Freedom of Information Act: 159
Freelancer: 415
Freeman, Cathy: 417
free trade: 11
frequent flyer: 111, 219, 338
FSG: See Financial Services Guide
FSS: See Fast Settlement Service or Financial Stability Standards
fuel station: 195, 207, 214, 247, 314, 346, 347
full employment: 36, 37, 38, 40, 102, 377, 420
fungible: 372, 401
future of financial advice: 48, 67, 388, 413
fuzzy match: 278
FX. See foreign exchange
FX spot: 28, 292
FX swap: 40

G

G7: 53
G20: 75, 378
gambling: 219
gambling tokens: 339
Garmin: 235
Gartner: 333
Gateway Bank: 87
GBG (identity verifier): 364
G&C Mutual Bank: 87
GDP: 128, 130, 340, 369
GDPR: See General Data Protection Regulation
gearing: 58, 106, 116
GE Capital: 96, 205, 342
Geelong Bank: 87
GE Money: 205
General Data Protection Regulation: 363
General Electric: 190, 205
general insurance: 123
general ledger: 143, 332
Genpact: 135, 190
GFC: 39, 46, 47, 48, 51, 58, 61, 64, 75, 92, 98, 116, 124, 128, 168, 178, 349, 383, 384, 404, 405
Giesecke+Devrient: 222
gift cards: 102, 203, 212, 219, 338
GiroPOST: 214
GitHub: 133, 161
GL: See general ledger
Global Financial Crisis: See GFC
global markets: 97, 99, 123, 277, 292
Global Payments Network: 218

GNU General Public License: 394
Go Card: 347
GoCatch: 344
gold: 12, 19, 21, 23, 24, 25, 26, 36, 37, 44, 60, 72, 127, 171, 177, 228, 291, 349, 376, 384, 419, 422, 423
Gold Bullion Act: 19
Goldfields Credit Union: 86
Goldfields Money: 86
gold mohur (Indian coin): 13
gold rush: 19, 20, 376
gold sovereign: 20
Google: 135, 226, 234, 235, 236, 237, 330, 334, 365, 415, 418
Google Assistant: 158
Google BigQuery: 157
Google Cloud: 135
Google Pay: 232, 235, 246, 340, 406
Google Play: 103
Google Ventures: 329
Google Wallet: 226, 234, 235
Goulburn Murray Credit Union Co-operative: 91
Government Direct Entry System: 262
government gazette: 21
Government Savings Bank of NSW: 23
governor general: 38
GPayments: 218, 336
GPL: 399. *See* GNU General Public License
GPS dot: 390
Great Britain: 12, 13, 17, 26
Great Depression: 50
Greater Bank: 87
Greater Newcastle: 87
Great Recoinage: 17, 20
Green Card: 347
GreenID: 364
gross domestic product: See GDP
Groupon: 339
groupthink: 416
GroupTogether: 330
GSICEPS: 407
GST: 49, 72, 73, 184, 200, 248, 249, 315, 357, 359, 409
guilder (Dutch coin): 13
Guinea-Bissau: 52
guinea (British coin): 13, 20
gun cabinets: 24

H

HA. See high availability
hack-a-thons: 387
hackers: 231, 279, 358, 393
Hadoop: 157
Handycard: 203
hard currency: 23, 423
hardware security module: 165, 221
hash: 164, 217, 350, 360
Hawke, Bob: 45, 71, 99, 414
HCD: See human-centred design
HCL: 154
headless banking: 392
headline interest rates: 68
health insurance: 123
Health Professionals Bank: 88
HECS: 420
Henry Ford: 138
Heritage Bank: 87, 213
Hewson, John: 72
hexadecimal: 164
Hey You: 343
hierarchy: 98, 386
high availability: 157, 167, 197
High Court: 33, 34, 77
high-quality liquid assets: See HQLA
High Value Clearing System: See HVCS
history of money: 9
Hobart Savings Bank: 33
Hockey, Joe: 48
holey dollar: 16
Holstein: 401
home loan: 113
Home Loan Pricing Inquiry: 69, 403
Hong Kong: 98, 347
Horizon Bank: 87
Horizon Credit Union: 87
Hornsby Teachers Association Credit: 88
hospitality: 343
host card emulation: 235
hosted payment page: 224, 230
Hottelings Law: 198
Howard, John: 45, 72
HQLA: 62, 130, 373
HSBC: 92, 298, 308, 374
HSM: See hardware security module
Hua Nan Commercial Bank: 93
Huawei: 235
human-centred design: 138
human resources: 143
humbugging: 102
Hume Bank: 87
Hume, David: 11
Humm: 342
Hunter, John: 13
Hunter United Employees' Credit Union: 91
HVCS: 47, 101, 125, 302, 321
Hyde Park Barracks: 339
hype cycle: 333, 381
Hypercom: 229, 336
hyperinflation: 25, 26, 126, 419
Hyperledger: 361, 376

I

IaaS: See*e* infrastructure as a service
IAC: 125, 209, 217, 321
IBAN: 280
IBM: 133, 134, 154, 204, 285, 335, 361, 404
IBM Information FrameWork: See IFW

IBM Verify Credentials: 365
Iceland: 354, 357
ICO: 357, 394
iCRN: 271
identity: 362
identity theft: 71, 166
Ideo: 226
IDM: 63, 65, 152, 178, 190, 278, 337, 372
IDMatrix: 364
iframe: 224, 230
IFTI: 55, 277, 278, 295, 299, 313, 357, 372, 395, 397, 398, 409
IFW: 285
IFX: 285
Illawarra Credit Union: 91
Illion: 197
IMB Bank: 87
immigration visa: 364, 403, 405
imprinters: 201
IMT: See International Money Transfer
in1bank: 85
Independent Reserve: 358
India: 13
Indian Financial System Code: 281
Indiegogo: 341
Indigenous: 101
Indigenous Australians: 9
Indigenous Consumer Assistance Network: 102
indigenous-owned credit union: 91
Indonesia: 10
Indue: 95, 102, 104, 210, 308, 387
Industrial and Commercial Bank of China: 93
Industrial Awards: 99, 401
inflation: 10, 25, 35, 38, 50, 126, 130, 345, 370, 371, 383, 411, 419
information technology: 133
Infosys: 154
InfoTrac: 326
infrastructure: 144
infrastructure as a service: 135
ING Australia: 83, 92
ING Bank: 92, 308
Ingenico: 225, 227, 230, 271, 336
Ingogo: 344
ingots: 19
ING Ventures: 329
initial coin offering: See ICO
initial public offering: See IPO
innovation: 103
InPayTech: 261
Inquiry into Competition within the Australian Banking Sector: 48, 64
Inquiry into School Banking: 68
Inquiry into the Australian Financial System (1979-1981): See Campbell Committee
InstaRem: 298
institutional bank: 31, 93, 97, 98, 99
insufficient funds: 182
insurance: 296
insurance claim: 49, 63, 398
integration architecture: 141
Intel: 361
Intel Capital: 329
Intellect Design Arena: 152
Intellect Holdings: 336
intelligent deposit machine: See IDM
interchange: 70, 72, 111, 200, 219, 236, 238, 241, 242, 246, 250, 341, 388, 403
interchange plus: 229
intermediary bank: 276
internal ratings-based: 60, 62
International Bank for Reconstruction and Development: 36
international banking: 99
international clearing union: 36
international funds transfer instruction: See IFTI
International Monetary Fund: 36, 41
International Money Transfer: 275
international payment: 275
Internet: 217, 349, 423
Internet banking: 126, 141, 166, 215, 268, 269, 271, 283, 396
Internet of things: 390, 402
Internet payment: 217, 349
Internet Protocol: 281
Internet Society: 394
Intuit: 271, 332, 340
Investec Bank: 93
investment bank: 97
Investment Bank: 41, 384
investment product distribution: 412
invoice: 120
IoT: See Internet of things
IOU: 238, 277, 279, 283, 356, 383, 384, 406
I owe you: See IOU
IP: 316, 382, 393, 394, 424
iPhone: 237, 330, 415
IPO: 82, 199, 325, 357, 412
IP Payments: 230, 271, 336
Iran: 52
Iraq: 52
IRB: See internal ratings-based
ISIL: 52
ISO 3166: 280
ISO 8583: 215, 216, 236, 240, 283, 307, 378
ISO 9362: 280
ISO 9564: 224
ISO 13616: 280
ISO 15022: 283, 284
ISO 18092: 233
ISO 20022: 57, 152, 162, 216, 242, 283, 289, 306, 307, 309, 310, 378, 390, 392, 398
ISO 27001: 156
ISO/IEC 7810: 205
ISO/IEC 7811: 205
ISO/IEC 7812: 205

ISO/IEC 7813: 206
ISO/IEC 14443: 233, 234
ISO/IEC 18004: 313
issuer bank: 97, 195, 241, 244
iterative development: 137
IT operations: 144
iTunes: 212, 228
IWL: 83

J

Japan: 336
jaws: 375, 403
JCB: 214, 220, 241
JD Edwards: 332
Jefferson, Thomas: 386
Jersey: 401
JobKeeper: 35, 52
JobSeeker: 420
Johanna (Portuguese coin): 13
Jordan: 92
JPMorgan Chase Bank: 94
JSON: 286
Judge Judy: 355
Judo Bank: 85
junket: 138
Just Walk Out: 330, 396

K

Kaching: 136, 234, 330
Kama Sutra: 163
kanban: 137
Kangaroo Bonds: 40
Keating, Paul: 45, 46, 47, 50, 56, 70, 71, 82, 414
KEB HANA Bank: 94
Kennedy, John F.: 137
Keycard: 203
KeyCorp: 136, 225, 229, 336
Keynes, John Maynard: 35, 36, 383, 415, 421
Keypass: 365
King, Philip Gidley: 13
Kiwibank: 98
KKR: 205
Klarna: 342
know your customer. See KYC
Kodak: 335, 382
Kogan: 392
KPMG: 103, 306, 332
Kraken: 358
Kuhn, Thomas: 377
KYC: 54, 104, 213, 277, 278, 296, 298, 337, 362, 365, 395, 397, 398, 403

L

Laboratories Credit Union: 91
Landlords and Tenants Act: 342
lastminute.com: 343
Latitude: 93, 96, 205, 342
Launceston: 376
Launceston Bank for Savings: 33
Launceston Equitable Building & Investment Society: 86
LayBuy: 342
lay-by system: 342, 378
LCR: See liquidity coverage ratio
lean: 137
least cost routing: 49, 209, 252
Lebanon Bombing: 52
ledger: 10, 25, 101, 105, 107
legal tender: 21, 25, 128, 176, 177, 383
Lendlease: 204
letter of credit: 26, 186, 283, 295
leverage ratio: 61
Lexcen, Ben: 71
LEXTECH: 326
LGBTI: 416
Libra: 330, 422
Libya: 52
life insurance: 123
Link: 325
Linkly: 230, 336, 337
Linkt: 346
Linux: 134, 361
liquidation: 120
liquidity: 39, 40, 51, 62, 105, 291, 298, 302, 356, 412
liquidity coverage ratio: 62, 130
liquidity operations: 130
Liquorland: 207
Litecoin: 356
Lithuanian Co-operative Credit Society Talka: 91
LLL Australia: 85
loan sharks: 102
Loan to income: See debt to income
loan to value ratio: 60, 114
local court: 77
London: 12, 16, 19, 20, 34, 41, 98, 291, 376
long-term incentives: 100
LoRaWAN: 390, 407
Low Value Clearing Service: 258, 263, 376
Low Value Settlement Service: 190, 259, 263, 310
loyalty: 111, 124, 200, 219, 242, 251, 292
Loyalty App: 338
loyalty card: 203, 237, 338
loyalty points: 219
LTI: See debt to income
LVCS: See Low Value Clearing Service
LVR: See loan to value ratio
LVS: See Low Value Settlement Service
Lyons, Joseph: 31
Lysaght Credit Union: 91

M

M1, M2 and M3: 128
Macarthur Credit Union: 91
Macarthur, John: 15
machine learning: See AI/ML

Macquarie Bank: 23, 57, 62, 84, 205, 271, 308, 375, 412
Macquarie Capital: 324, 329
Macquarie Credit Union: 91
Macquarie, Lachlan: 16, 17
Macquarie River: 19
Madras: 16
magnetic stripe: 206, 221, 226, 245, 330, 339, 345
Mahindra Tech: 154
mainframe: 28, 133
Maitland Mutual: 87
Ma, Jack: 331, 378
Makassar: 10
Maleny Credit Union: 91
Mali: 52
malware: 167, 279
MAMBO: 48, 152, 269, 285, 288, 306, 307, 312, 316, 376
managed funds: 123
managed service: 135
managed services: 144
manager of managers: 98, 386
Manchester Unity: 86
mandatory leave: 101
margin lending: 116, 293, 341
margin loan: 63, 123
Martin Committee: 46, 50, 417
Martin Review: 45, 56, 182, 208
Marx, Karl: 420
Mary, Queen of Scots: 163
mass adoption: 241, 335, 377, 395, 399, 412
Mastercard: 67, 108, 125, 196, 198, 199, 211, 270, 286, 298, 348, 374, 378, 382, 392, 410
Mastercard Digital Enablement Service: 227, 235
Mastercard PayPass: 234
Mastercard SecureCode: 222
master services agreement: 154, 155, 401
mateship: 420
Mayborough Permanent Building Society: 86
MBF: 96
McDonalds: 234
MDES: See Mastercard Digital Enablement Service
Me 2 U: 233
ME Bank: 387
Medicare: 307, 405, 420
Mediclaims: 307
Mega International Commercial Bank Co: 94
Melbourne: 20, 101, 346
Melbourne Royal Mint: 20, 21, 42
Members Banking Group: 87
Members Equity Bank: 88
Menulog: 343
Menzies, Robert: 24, 34, 42
merchant: 228
merchant bank: 97, 412
merchant service fee: See MSF
merchant settlement: 27
Merchant Suite: 230
merchant surcharge: 48, 200, 247, 249, 250, 337, 344
Merino: 15, 401
Mesopotamia: 119
message system: 240
metroCARD: 348
MFundEC: 284
MICR: 187
microdot: 390
Microsoft: 134, 135, 237, 332, 335
Microsoft Azure: 135
Microsoft Cortana: 158
Microsoft Dynamics: 332
Microsoft Money: 332
Microsoft Passport: 231, 238
Microsoft Wallet: 231
Microsoft Windows: 134, 136, 236
middleware: 141, 291
MIGS: 217
Minority Report: 396
Mint: 160, 340
MIT: 139
Mizuho Bank: 94
MLC: 82
MNGS: 217
Mobil: 207, 347
mobile phone: 173, 216, 222, 227, 228, 229, 232, 234, 235, 268, 306, 330, 339, 347, 407, 421
mobile phone number: 310, 312
mobile virtual network operator: 392
Mondex: 348, 349, 383
monetary policy: 11, 16, 35, 38, 40, 50, 97, 113, 126, 178, 241, 249, 358, 369, 371, 383, 384, 419
money: 3, 10, 128, 348, 369, 419
money base: 40, 127, 128, 369, 383
Moneygram: 280, 297
money laundering: 53, 122, 268, 277, 278, 279, 339, 341, 349, 354, 358, 378
money markets: 39, 98, 123, 128, 374
MoneyMe: 342
money service business: 54, 278, 297, 406
MongoDB: 157
Moodys: 40
Moore, Geoffrey: 335
Moores Law: 404
Morgan Stanley: 325
mortgage: 113
mortgage broking: 117
MOTO: 218
MOVE Bank: 88
M-PESA: 233
MPGS: 217
MSB: See money service business
MSF: 70, 72, 195, 227, 229, 246, 247, 337, 389
Mt. Gox: 358
MT (SWIFT message protocol): 283

MUFG Bank: 94
mule accounts: 54
Mulesoft: 141
Murray, David: 48, 134
Murray Report: 48, 60, 62, 64
mutual bank: 81, 86, 87, 90, 97, 387
mutual TLS: 166
mx51: 136, 337
MX (SWIFT message protocol): 284
Myer: 85, 205
MyerOne: 338
MyGov: 71, 365, 406, 422
myki: 347
MYOB: 271, 332
MyState Bank: 84
MyWay: 347

N

NAB: 49, 60, 63, 81, 96, 98, 189, 203, 204, 207, 210, 229, 237, 270, 278, 306, 337, 361, 375, 397
NAB Labs: 103
NABTrade: 83
NAB Transact: 230
NAB Ventures: 329
Nacha: 285
Nakamoto, Satoshi: 349, 351, 394
narrow-based tax: 73
NASDAQ: 335
National Australia Bank: See NAB
National Bank of Australasia: 32
National Clearing Code: 281
National Consumer Credit Protection Act: 67
National Deposit Insurance Corporation: 89
National Electronic Conveyancing System: 323
National Mutual: 376
Nayax: 229
NBFI: See non-banking financial institution
NBN: 372
NCR: 225
NDA: See non-disclosure agreement
NDEF: 233, 234, 235
NECDL: 324
negative gearing: 40, 48, 115
neo bank: 85, 343, 365, 387
Netflix: 167
Netherlands: 13, 282
net off: 27, 298, 301
net present value: 107
net settlement: 27
net stable funding: 62
neurodiversity: 416
Newcastle: 331
Newcastle and Hunter River Public Service Starr-Bowkett Building Co-operative Society: 87
Newcastle Permanent Building Society: 89
News Corp: 218
New South Wales: 12, 19, 100, 101, 119, 183, 197, 229, 261, 280, 326, 331, 346, 348, 360
Newton, Isaac: 385, 386
New York: 98
New Zealand: 276, 286, 336
New Zealand Post: 98
NFC: 233, 234, 235, 236, 237, 344, 348, 407
NFC Forum: 233
NICTA: 157, 160
nigerian letter scam: 280
non-banking financial institution: 341
non-disclosure agreement: 154, 393, 394
non-functional requirements: 135
non-repudiation: 164
Norris, Ralph: 134
Northern Inland Credit Union: 91
Northern Territory: 101, 102, 348
Northern Trust Company: 94
North Korea: 52, 173
Norton Ofax: 229
NoSQL: 157
Nostro: 105, 275, 279
note: 23
Note Printing Australia: 173
notes: 12, 17, 21, 24, 25, 26, 60, 73, 125, 127, 128, 171
not negotiable: 184
NPP: 68, 70, 106, 152, 161, 162, 213, 271, 285, 288, 306, 323, 332, 341, 374, 376, 398, 407, 408, 409, 412
NPPA: 57, 68, 125, 126, 308, 392, 408
NPV: See net present value
NRMA: 385
NSA: See United States National Security Agency
NSFR. See net stable funding
NSW Corps: 15
NXP MIFARE: 347

O

OAuth: 365
Octopus: 347
OECD: 75, 130, 378
OECD Price Level Index: 399
OFAC: 278
office of the australian information commissioner: 71, 363
offset account: 118
off-system bsb: 392
off-system BSB: 263, 271, 299
off us: 239
OFX: 285
oil crisis: 50
onboarding: 143, 228, 230
Once: 270
online identity: 364
on us: 239

Opal: 348
open API: 316, 392, 394
open banking: 70, 159, 161, 162, 286, 341, 363, 392, 406
open data: 49, 70, 386, 395
open ledger: 359, 361, 394, 410, 423
open loop: 211, 212, 338
Openpay: 337, 342, 402
open ratings: 393
open source: 393, 394
opstech: 399
Optus: 57, 100, 233, 392
Oracle: 332
oracle (smart contract participant): 362
Orange Credit Union: 91
OrbitRemit: 298
Ordermentum: 402
Orwell, George: 397, 420
OSBSB. See off-system BSB
Osko: 124, 271, 312, 316, 408
Otto Niemeyer: 26
Outsourcing: 153
overdraft facility: 109
overlay services: 312
overnight box: 101
Oversea-Chinese Banking Corporation: 94
overseas bank draft: 185
overseas banks: 92
Oyster: 347
Oz Forex: 298

P

P2P: 95, 213, 232, 233, 305, 306, 308, 341, 401
P2P lending: 341, 373, 411
PaaS: See platform as a service
Pacific Islands: 276
pacs (ISO 20022): 287, 310
Paddys Markets: 9
pagoda (Indian coin): 13
pain (ISO 20022): 287, 310
PAN: 205, 222, 223, 224, 234, 235, 262
paper instruments: 181
paradigm shift: 377
Paris: 53
parking payments: 346
Parliamentary Joint Committee on Corporations and Financial Services (inquiry): 413
party to an account: 103
passbook: 107
Passenger Movement Charge: 345
passport: 102, 364, 403, 405
patent: 313, 360, 394
PAX: 227
payables: 259
payday lenders: 183
PayID: 312, 337
Paymark: 408
Paymate: 336
payment: 3, 141
Payment Adviser: 261
payment gateway: 144, 217, 218, 229, 270, 336, 337, 340, 392
payment handshake: 407
payment notification: 315
payment rail: 296, 307, 347, 407, 408, 409
Payment Service Directive: 160
payment service provider. See PSP
payments on behalf of: 343
Payments Service Directive: 161
Payments System Board: 46, 56, 250, 270, 306, 312
Payment System Board: 47
Payment Systems (Regulation) Act: 250
payment unification: 390
payment versus payment: 300, 321
PayPal: 57, 68, 95, 228, 229, 230, 231, 232, 238, 271, 330, 331, 332, 336, 343, 392, 393, 406
PayPal Check-in: 343
PayPal fees: 231
PayPass Digital Checkout: 232
payslip: 315
PC-EFTPOS: 230, 336, 337
PCI: 156, 217, 222, 226, 227, 244, 390
PCI DSS: 230
PDS: See Product Disclosure Statement
PED: 109, 141, 206, 217, 224, 225, 227, 229, 230, 336, 337, 344, 347, 378, 382
Peel Cunningham County Council Employees Credit Union: 88
pegged foreign exchange: 13, 24
pence: 12
penny test: 262
Peoples Bank of China: 384
People's Choice Credit Union: 90
Peoplesoft: 332
PEP: See politically exposed persons
Pepperstone: 293
performance, feedback and review: 100
performing loan: 63
permissioned ledger: 361
personal computers: 134
personal financial management: 340, 376
personal loan: 113
Perth Mint: 21
PEXA: 113, 125, 316, 321, 324, 325, 326, 373, 374
Philippines: 279
Philips: 335
phishing attacks: 166, 396
Pi: 226, 382
pilot: 155
PIN: 164, 198, 207, 221, 222, 224, 225, 347, 362, 407

Pizza Hut: 218
PizzaNet: 218
PKI: 163, 164, 165, 221, 349
P&L. See profit and loss
plastic note. See polymer note
platform as a service: 135
platinum: 44, 72
P&N Bank: 88
POBO. See payments on behalf of
point-of-sale: 336
Poland: 190
Police Bank: 88
Police Credit Union: 91
Police Financial Services: 88
Police & Nurses: 88
POLi Payments: 298, 332, 340, 408
politically exposed persons: 55
polymer note: 172, 173, 377
portability: 47, 312, 314, 408
Portugal: 13
postal money order: 186
Post Billpay: 270
POTS: 225, 234
pounds: 12
PPF. See purchase payment facility
pre-authorisation: 215, 216, 241
premier: 100
Premier Payments: 230
Premier Technologies: 336
premium cards: 229, 243, 244, 251
prepaid cards: 212
Presto: 136, 230, 337
PrimeID: 364
Privacy Act: 159, 362
privacy policy: 362
private bank: 31, 33, 34, 35, 81, 97, 99, 127, 316, 405, 412
private equity: 329
private key: 163, 164, 165, 166, 221, 351, 358, 359, 396
Privy Council: 34, 77, 375
Proceeds of Crime Act: 178
proclamation of coins: 13, 24
procurement: 154
Product Disclosure Statement: 67, 298, 372, 398, 413
production support: 136
Productivity Commission: 69, 375
profit and loss: 33, 98
programmer: 415
project planning and management: 135
promissory note: 14, 17, 23, 39, 182
proof of age card: 364, 405
proof of stake: 352, 356
proof of work: 350, 352, 356
proofs of concept: 155
property: 20, 40, 60, 72, 89, 115, 117, 125, 181, 185, 271, 321, 323, 370, 388, 405, 411
property settlement: 323, 326
proprietary card: 203
Prospa: 342
prosperity: 11, 102
proto-coins: 11
Provenco: 336
PSD2. See Payment Service Directive
PSP: 230, 336
public holiday: 101
public key: 164, 165, 359, 395
public key encryption: 163
public works credit unions: 87
pull payment: 190, 239, 260, 314
Pulse Credit Union: 91
purchase payment facility: 95, 387
push payment: 235, 260, 314, 407

Q

Qantas: 88, 205, 213, 312, 338
QBANK: 88
QPCU: 88
QR code: 232, 235, 271, 308, 313, 337, 338, 407
QSI Payments: 218, 336
quantitative easing: 40, 178, 349, 383, 419
quantum computing: 385, 395
quantum physics: 377, 381
Qudos Mutual/Qudos Bank: 88
Queensland: 101, 197, 347
Queensland Country Bank: 88
Queensland National Bank: 32
Quest: 229, 336
Quickbooks: 271, 332
Qvalent: 230

R

R3CEV: 361, 365, 376
Rabobank: 92
rails. See payment rail
Railways Credit Union: 88
RAMAC: 404
RapidID: 364
RBA: 34, 38, 39, 41, 46, 47, 50, 51, 57, 64, 70, 90, 92, 95, 96, 104, 106, 123, 125, 127, 128, 129, 130, 156, 162, 171, 172, 174, 175, 191, 237, 248, 249, 258, 268, 271, 288, 300, 307, 308, 310, 321, 326, 337, 344, 345, 373, 374, 376, 387, 406
RDBMS. See relational database management system
real-time banking: 152
real-time payment: 300, 305
real-time settlement: 27
receivership: 120
recession: 25, 26, 50, 52, 196
recession Australia had to have: 50, 225

reconciliation: 105, 145, 268, 271, 408
Reconciliation Action Plan (Indigenous): 102
RediATM: 203
RediCard: 203, 211
RediTeller: 203
redraw account: 118
Regional Australia Bank: 88
registered liquidator: 121
regtech: 49, 153, 336, 337, 398, 399
regulation: 373
regulations: 31
regulators: 31, 144, 249, 397, 399
Reinventure: 329, 337, 343
relational database management system: 156
Reliance Bank: 88
Remitly: 298
replicate: 395
repos: 39
repossession: 117
repurchase agreements: 39
request for comments: 394
request for information: 155
request for proposal: 155
request for quotation: 402
request to pay: 315
required stable funding: 63
research and development: 329
Reserve Bank Act: 34, 56, 178
Reserve Bank of Australia: See RBA
Reserve Bank of New Zealand: 98
resident: 75
Residential Mortgage Price Inquiry: 403
retail bank: 46, 82, 83, 97, 99, 292, 293
retail banking: 84
retail margin: 292, 296, 298
retirement savings account: 119
Reuters: 291
Rêv: 213
revolving line of credit: 110, 196, 197, 342, 410
Rewardle: 338
rewards: 219
RFID: 165, 233, 346
rich information: 162, 200, 270, 305, 307, 312, 314, 315, 325
rideshare: 344
RIM: 235, 236
Ripple: 356, 361
risk: 57, 167, 293, 321, 324
risk-based approach: 54, 66
risk management plan: 135
risk weight: 48, 60, 113
risk-weighted asset: 59, 66, 70, 104, 127, 130, 388, 405
RITS: 175, 190, 240, 259, 268, 271, 300, 309, 310, 321, 325
road tolls: 346
robbery: 18
Roman: 119
Ross, Jeanne: 139
Royal Bank of Canada: 94
royal commission: 33, 45, 50, 65, 83, 100, 103, 117, 153, 204, 253, 270, 372, 376, 385, 413, 414, 417
Royal Commission: 31, 49, 50, 107
Royal Mint: 19, 20
RSA: 163
RTGS: 47, 125, 241, 286, 300, 301, 302, 305, 309, 321, 322, 325, 408
rum: 12, 16
Rum Rebellion: 15
RuPay: 408
rupee (Indian coin): 13
Rural and Industries Bank of Western Australia: 32
Rural Bank: 84
Rural Bank of New South Wales: 32
RWA: See risk-weighted asset

S

SaaS: See software as a service
Safeway: 207
Sage: 332
salary review: 100
Salesforce: 135
Samsung: 235, 236, 237
Samsung Pay: 246, 406
Sanctions: 52
sandbox: 316
San Francisco: 19
SAP: 152, 285, 332
SAP Ariba: 143, 155, 332, 348, 361
Sapphire Ventures: 329, 332
SAP Ventures: 329, 332
SARS: 331
Satoshis: 356
Saville, Jane: 417
savings bank: 18, 22, 82, 97, 106, 270
Savings Bank of South Australia: 32
savings passbook: 25
SCCI: 67, 95, 96, 105, 214, 250, 337, 387, 392
scheme: 27, 57, 69, 77, 195, 198, 270, 275, 277, 296, 297, 316, 321, 331, 332, 336, 338, 345, 348, 356, 359, 388, 390, 407, 408, 409, 410
scheme settlement: 27
School Banking: 107
Schrödinger, Erwin: 377
Schulze-Delitzsch, Hermann: 90, 389
screen-scraping: 340, 376
scrum: 137
SCTR: See Significant Cash Transaction Reports
Scullin, John: 26
Seattle: 401
Second Life: 339
Securency: 173

SecurePay: 336, 341
Secure Remote Commerce: 232
securitise: 58, 372, 391
Security: 144, 395
Security Council: See UNSC
seignior: 11, 177
seigniorage: 172, 177
self-managed superannuation funds: 123, 411
SendFX: 298
Seribu: 76
series payment: 277
service design: 139
settlement: 27, 36, 62, 142, 151, 175, 182, 188, 190, 195, 201, 215, 263, 271, 277, 283, 286, 292, 298, 300, 302, 309, 310, 321, 322, 323, 351, 353, 356, 383, 384, 389, 405
Settlement: 287
settlement before interchange (SBI): 286
Seven-Eleven: 347
SHA-256: 164, 350
shared economy: 348
shared ledger: 350, 359, 393, 394, 395
shareholder: 40, 73, 98, 103, 120, 199, 329, 353, 381, 385, 414
shareholder equity: 59
Share Trading: 83
Shell: 207
shells: 9
shilling: 12, 13
Shinhan Bank Co: 94
short-term debt instruments: 39
short-term incentive: 100
SIBOS: 276
Sienna Technologies: 336
Significant Cash Transaction Reports: 55
Significant Global Entities: 75
silver: 11, 12, 17, 21, 24, 42, 44, 72, 177, 212
SIM: 165, 222, 233, 235, 396, 421
Simmons, Michelle: 396
SimplePay: 337
Simpli: 326
Singapore: 98, 337
single message system: 215, 216, 240, 241, 286
single person dependencies: 101
Six Pillars: 82, 376
skimming: 221
Skye: 270
Slyp: 337
Small Business Superannuation Clearing House: 285
smart contracts: 362, 394
SmartPay: 336
Smart Rider: 347
SME: 85, 99, 119, 120, 331, 332, 404
SMR: 55, 277, 278, 397, 398
SMS (card messaging): See single message system
SMSF: See self-managed superannuation funds
SMS (text message): 167, 222, 233, 236, 364
SOC: 156
social enterprises: 90
social media: 330
Société Général: 94
Society One: 373
SoftBank: 331
software as a service: 135
software development life cycle: 135
solicitor: 54, 55, 112, 323
solution architectures: 140
Somalia: 52
songlines: 9
sort code: 187, 281
Soul Pharmacy: 96
source code: 394
South Africa: 276
South Australia: 89, 101, 348
South Australian Government: 19
Southern Cross Credit Union: 90
South Sudan: 52
South-West Credit Union Co-operative: 91
South West Slopes Credit Union: 91
Soviet Union: 36
Sovrin: 365
spanish dollar: 17
Spanish dollar: 13, 16
Special Account: 32, 33
specie payment: 23
spouse maintenance: 71, 248
spread: 292, 293, 297
sprint: 137
SQL: 156
Square: 226, 228, 229, 230, 271, 337, 406
SSL: 166
Stack Overflow: 133
staff: 100
Stamp Act: 11, 181, 397
stamp duty: 25, 74, 117, 181, 182, 183, 323
Stampii: 338
stamp script: 421
Standard Chartered Bank: 94, 337
Standard & Poors: 40
stand-in: 216, 241
Starbucks: 330
Starr-Bowkett: 87
Star Trek: 419
startup: 120, 329, 332, 336, 339, 340, 342, 354, 361, 377, 389, 397, 414
State Bank of India: 94, 298
State Bank of South Australia: 32
State Bank of Victoria: 204
statement of work: 154
State Savings Bank of Victoria: 32

State Street Bank and Trust Company: 94
STEM: 414
Stephen Martin: 46
step-up: 222
St George Bank: 48, 166
St George Building Society: 28
stock market: 40
stolen wages: 102
store credit: 195, 204, 231
store credit card: 197, 203, 205, 270
stored value cards: 212, 213, 228
store of value: 11
store tokens: 9
Storm Financial: 63, 65
STP: 409: See straight-through processing
straight-through processing: 281
Stripe: 228, 230, 271, 337, 393, 406
structured query language: See SQL
sub accounts: 263
Sudan: 52
Sumitomo Mitsui Banking Corporation: 94
Summerland Credit Union: 91, 219
Suncorp: 344
Suncorp Bank: 84, 210
superannuation: 123, 315
SuperEC: 284
supernotes: 173
SuperStream: 119, 285
Supply Nation: 102, 155
supreme court: 77
suptech: 399
surface mail: 279, 333
suspicious matter report: See SMR
Swagger: 161, 393
SwapClear: 321
SWIFT: 68, 105, 125, 162, 258, 261, 275, 305, 306, 313, 356, 374, 392, 408
SWIFT Access Lite: 291
SWIFT Alliance Access: 290
SWIFT Alliance Entry: 290
SWIFT Alliance Gateway: 309
SWIFT Alliance Integrator: 291
SWIFT Alliance Messaging Hub: 290
SWIFT BIC. See BIC
SWIFT FileAct: 258
SWIFT FIN: 282
SWIFT gpi: 282
SWIFT InterAct: 283
SWIFTNet: 282
SWIFTNet Link: 291
SwimEC: 284
switch to issuer: 252
Switzerland: 58, 282
Sydney: 346
Sydney Credit Union: 86
Sydney Harbour Bridge: 346
Sydney Hospital: 16
Sydney Mutual Bank: 86
Sydney Olympics: 347, 417
Sydney Royal Mint: 20, 21
symmetric encryption: 163, 396
systemically important bank: 60

T

T+1: 28
T+2: 28, 292, 322
TAB: 278, 397
TAB Employees Credit Union: 87
Tafmo: 336
Taishin International Bank Co: 94
Taiwan Business Bank: 94
Taiwan Co-operative Bank: 94
Taliban: 52
Talk to MLC: 136
Tandem NonStop: 133
Tandy Radio Shack: 134
Taobao: 331
tap and go: 233
tap and ride: 348
Tasmania: 101, 339, 347
tax avoidance: 398
tax evasion: 278, 398
tax file number: 71, 364, 405
taxi: 200, 213, 226, 344, 347, 409
taxpayer: 72, 74, 75, 76, 121, 325, 364
T-Card: 347
TCS: 154
TCS BaNCS: 152, 378
Tea Act: 12
Teachers Mutual Bank: 88
Teachers Mutual Bank and UniBank: 88
technological unemployment: 415
TeleCheck: 183
telegram: 26
telegraph: 24, 275, 283, 291, 297
telegraphic transfer: 275, 279, 288, 296
Teleware: 332
telex: 275, 283
Telling: 28
Telstra: 204, 225, 232, 233, 257, 258, 270, 392, 396, 412
Telstra Ventures: 329
Tencent: 332
term deposits: 110
terminals: 28
terms and conditions: 376, 398
terrorism financing: 53, 277, 278, 358, 378
terrorist organisations: 52
testing: 136, 137
TFN: See tax file number

The Australian Financial System Review Group (1983-1984): See Martin Review
The Capricornian: 91
The Dismissal: 38
theft: 12, 18, 171, 177, 198, 206, 221, 224, 236, 244, 358
THE MAC: 91
The Payment App: 337, 344
The Residential Mortgage Price Inquiry: 68
Thomas Cook: 297
threshold transaction report: See TTR
Thumbzup: 230
Tier 1 capital: 61, 373
Tier 2 capital: 59
time payments: 341
tiny URL: 261
TLS: 166, 395
tools: 9, 10
Total Capital: 59
Touchcorp: 336
TPG: 392
trade: 293
trademark: 313, 394
trading bank: 18, 31, 33, 97, 280, 291
trading platforms: 142
Traditional Credit Union: 91
training: 100
transaction: 4
transaction account: 108
transactional: 10, 195, 342
Transax: 183
TransferWise: 298, 392
transportation: 12
Transport Credit Union: 86
transport layer security: See TLS
Transport Mutual Credit Union: 91
Transurban: 346
Travelex: 297
travel insurance: 244
travellers cheques: 186, 199, 283, 292, 297
travel payments: 344
Traxpay: 332
treasury: 21, 69
treasury bills: 25
treasury notes: 39
trough of disillusionment: 333, 335, 377, 408
troy ounce: 13
trust account: 112
TT: See telegraphic transfer
TTR: 55, 63, 153, 277, 278, 397, 398
Turing, Alan: 158
Turing Test: 158, 159
Turnbull, Malcolm: 414
Turnbull, Shann: 421
two factors of authentication: 167
two-up: 339
Tyro: 95, 96, 229, 230, 337

U

UBank: 103
Uber: 348, 415
Uber Eats: 343
UBS AG: 94
Udax: 336
UN: 295: See United Nations
unassisted channels: 141
unclaimed money: 122
underemployed: 38
unemployment: 35, 38, 50, 415
unicorn: 329
UNIFI: 284
Union Bank of Australia: 32
Union Bank of India: 94
Unions: 99
United Kingdom: 18, 24, 36, 42, 92, 98, 116, 160, 161, 162, 163, 173, 187, 190, 276, 286, 307, 347, 363, 405, 406
United Nations: 52, 289
United Nations Convention: 53
United Nations Monetary and Financial Conference: 36
United Overseas Bank: 94
United States: 12, 173, 298
United States Declaration of Independence: 386
United States dollar: 24, 37, 213
United States Government: 331
United States independence: 12
United States National Security Agency: 363
United States Securities and Exchange Commission: 341
unit of account: 10
Unity Bank: 88
University Admission Centre: 360
University of New South Wales: 157, 396
Unix: 134
UNSC: 52, 53, 407
UNSC sanctioned entities: 53, 54, 55, 277, 278, 279, 295, 296, 354
UN Security Council: 53
Up: 84
Upwork: 415
US: 12, 19, 36, 51, 98, 173, 178, 190, 196, 226, 246, 276, 282, 284, 285, 309, 383, 408
USD: 276, 291, 300
US dollar: 36, 43, 173, 300, 349, 384
USSD: 233, 421
US SEC: See United States Securities and Exchange Commission
UX design: 139

V

Vapourware: 333
Värde: 96, 205
variable rate: 116
Veda: 197
vending machine: 340
venture capital: 329

Venture Studio: 329
Verifact: 225
Verifi: 364
Verified by Visa: 222
Verifone: 227, 229, 230, 336
Versailles: 35
Vic Martin: 45
Victoria: 20, 34, 101, 183, 280, 347
Victorian Teachers Credit Union: 88
Victoria Teachers: 88
Virgin: 205, 338
virtual account: 106, 263
virtual currency: 340
Visa: 67, 196, 198, 199, 211, 298, 299, 348, 374, 376, 378, 382, 392, 410
Visa B2B Connect: 410
Visa Cash: 348
Visa Debit: 84, 125, 211
Visa Direct: 410
VisaNet: 217
Visa payWave: 234
Visa Plaid: 410
Visa Token Service: 227, 235
ViVOTech: 234
VixVerify: 364
Vodafone: 233, 392
Volt Bank: 85
voluntary administration: 120
Vostro: 105, 275, 276, 277, 279
VPN: 258

W

Wages Accord: 99
wallet: 95, 141, 172, 207, 231, 237, 238, 307, 330, 332, 340, 351, 354, 355, 357, 358, 359, 381, 395, 401, 407, 408
Wallis Report: 47, 56, 82, 96, 250
Wallis, Stan: 47
Warwick Credit Union: 91
Waterfall: 135
WAW Credit Union Co-operative: 91
wealth management: 82, 99
WeChat: 332
Weekly Cairns Co-op Penny Savings and Loans Bank: 86
Wells Fargo: 297
Wesfarmers: 338
Western Australia: 21, 101, 347
Western Union: 280, 297
Westpac: 17, 39, 48, 49, 61, 81, 96, 100, 103, 108, 136, 160, 166, 189, 199, 203, 204, 207, 210, 229, 230, 234, 237, 251, 263, 270, 278, 289, 299, 306, 311, 314, 329, 337, 339, 341, 342, 343, 353, 361, 372, 375, 396, 397
Westpac Live: 340
Westpac New Zealand: 98
WestpacTrade: 83
West Texas Intermediate: 401
WhatsApp: 330
White, Harry Dexter: 36
white-label: 219, 392
Whitlam, Gough: 38
Wi-Fi: 226, 237, 390, 407
Wiise: 332
Wincor Nixdorf: 226, 229
Wintel: 134
Wish: 399
women: 100
wool: 15
Woolworths: 205, 207, 210, 338, 392
Woolworths Employees Credit Union: 89
Woolworths Team Bank: 89
Woori Bank: 94
workflow: 142
working hours: 101
World Bank: 36, 41
WorldFirst: 298
Worldline: 230
WorldPay: 230
World Remit: 298
World Trade Organisation: 401
World War I: 35, 99
World War II: 11, 25, 32, 35, 36, 39, 42, 92, 158, 309, 342, 383
World Wide Web: 331
Wotif.com: 343
wrap accounts: 123
Wright brothers: 334
WSO2: 141

X

X15: 329
X.25: 28, 216, 225, 257, 258, 281
x86: 134
XAC: 230
XE (remittance provider): 298
Xero: 271, 332
Xerox: 335
Xinja Bank: 85
XML: 75, 216, 284, 286, 314, 315
XPay: 313
XPOS: 136, 229
Xref: 364
XRP: 356

Y

Yahoo: 331
Yemen: 52
Yodlee: 160, 340, 376
Yokohama Specie Bank: 32
Youthsaver: 107
yuan: 384, 409

Z

Ziaochuan, Zhou: 384
Zimbabwe: 383
Zip Money: 337
Zip Pay: 337, 342
Zomato: 343
zombie companies: 122

www.ingramcontent.com/pod-product-compliance
Lightning Source LLC
Chambersburg PA
CBHW060640060326
40690CB00020B/4466

* 9 7 8 0 6 4 8 8 8 2 4 4 2 *